PREFACE FROM USGBC

The built environment has a profound impact on our natural environment, economy, health, and productivity. Breakthroughs in building science, technology, and operations are now available to designers, builders, operators, and owners who want to build green and maximize both economic and environmental performance.

Through the LEED® green building certification program, the U.S. Green Building Council (USGBC) is transforming the built environment. The green building movement offers an unprecedented opportunity to respond to the most important challenges of our time, including global climate change, dependence on non sustainable and expensive sources of energy, and threats to human health. The work of innovative building professionals is a fundamental driving force in the green building moment. Such leadership is a critical component to achieving USGBC's mission of a sustainable built environment for all within a generation.

USGBC MEMBERSHIP

USGBC's greatest strength is the diversity of our membership. USGBC is a balanced, consensus-based nonprofit with more than 18,000 member companies and organizations representing the entire building industry. Since its inception in 1993, USGBC has played a vital role in providing a leadership forum and a unique, integrating force for the building industry. USGBC's programs have three distinguishing characteristics:

Committee-based

The heart of this effective coalition is our committee structure, in which volunteer members design strategies that are implemented by staff and expert consultants. Our committees provide a forum for members to resolve differences, build alliances, and forge cooperative solutions for influencing change in all sectors of the building industry.

Member-driven

Membership is open and balanced and provides a comprehensive platform for carrying out important programs and activities. We target the issues identified by our members as the highest priority. We conduct an annual review of achievements that allows us to set policy, revise strategies, and devise work plans based on members' needs.

Consensus-focused

We work together to promote green buildings, and in doing so, we help foster greater economic vitality and environmental health at lower costs. We work to bridge ideological gaps between industry segments and develop balanced policies that benefit the entire industry.

Contact the U.S. Green Building Council
2101 L Street, NW
Suite 500
Washington, DC 20037
(800) 795-1747 Office
(202) 828-5110 Fax
www.usgbc.org

COPYRIGHT

DISCLAIMER

U.S. Green Building Council
2101 L Street, NW
Suite 500
Washington, DC 20037

TRADEMARK

LEED® is a registered trademark of the U.S. Green Building Council.
LEED Reference Guide for Green Building Design and Construction
For the Design, Construction and Major Renovations of Commercial and Institutional Buildings
Including Core & Shell and K–12 School Projects
2009 Edition
ISBN # 978-1-932444-14-8

ACKNOWLEDGMENTS

The LEED Reference Guide for Green Building Design and Construction, 2009 Edition, has been made possible only through the efforts of many dedicated volunteers, staff members, and others in the USGBC community. The Reference Guide drafting was managed and implemented by USGBC staff and consultants and included review and suggestions by many Technical Advisory Group (TAG) members. We especially extend our deepest gratitude to all of our LEED committee members who participated in the development of this guide, for their tireless volunteer efforts and constant support of USGBC's mission:

LEED Steering Committee

Scot Horst, Chair, LSC	Horst, Inc
Joel Ann Todd, Vice-Chair, LSC	Joel Ann Todd
Muscoe Martin	M2 Architecture
Stuart Carron	JohnsonDiversey, Inc.
Holley Henderson	H2 Ecodesign, LLC
Christine Magar	Greenform
Kristin Shewfelt	Architectural Energy Corporation
Jessica Millman	Agora DC
Bryna Dunn	Moseley Architects
Neal Billetdeaux	JJR
Greg Kats	Managing Good Energies
Mark Webster	Simpson Gumpertz & Heger
Bob Thompson	EPA Indoor Environment Management Branch
Malcolm Lewis	Constructive Technologies Group, Inc.
John Boecker	7Group
Sara O'Mara	Choate Construction Company
Alex Zimmerman	Rep Canada Green Building Council
Ian Theaker	Rep Canada Green Building Council

Sustainable Sites TAG

Bryna Dunn, Chair	Moseley Architects
Stewart Comstock, Vice-Chair	Maryland Department of the Environment
Michele Adams	Cahill Associates
Gina Baker	Burt Hill
Ted Bardacke	Global Green USA
Stephen Benz	Sasaki
Mark Brumbaugh	Brumbaugh & Associates
Laura Case	Emory University Campus Services
Zach Christeson	the HOK Planning Group
Jay Enck	Commissioning & Green Building Services

Ron Hand   E/FECT. Sustainable Design Solutions
Richard Heinisch   Acuity Lighting Group
Michael Lane   Lighting Design Lab
Marita Roos   HNTB
Zolna Russell   Hord Coplan Macht, Inc.
Alfred Vick   Ecos Environmental Design, Inc.

Water Efficiency TAG

Neal Billetdeaux, Chair   JJR
John Koeller, Vice-Chair   Alliance for Water Efficiency
David Carlson   Columbia University
Bill Hoffman   H.W. Hoffman and Associates, LLC
Geoff Nara   Civil & Environmental Consultants
Stephanie Tanner   U.S. Environmental Protection Agency
Daniel Yeh   University of South Florida
David Bracciano   Tampa Bay Water
Robert Rubin   NCSU-BAE and McKim & Creed
Winston Huff   SSR Engineers
Robert Benazzi   Jaros Baum & Bolles
Gunnar Baldwin   TOTO USA, INC
Heather Kinkade   Forgotten Rain, LLC
Shabbir Rawalpindiwala   Kohler Company
Bill Wall   Clivus New England, Inc.

Energy and Atmosphere TAG

Greg Kats, Chair   GoodEnergies
Marcus Sheffer, Vice-Chair   7group
Drury Crawley   US Department of Energy
Jay Enck   Commissioning & Green Building Solutions, Inc.
Ellen Franconi   IPMVP and AEC
Mark Frankel   New Buildings Institute
Nathan Gauthier   Harvard Green Campus Initiative
Rusty Hodapp   Dallas/Fort Worth, Energy & Transportation Management
John Hogan   City of Seattle Department of Planning & Development
Bion Howard   Building Environmental Science and Technology
Dan Katzenberger   Engineering, Energy, and the Environment
Bob Maddox   Sterling Planet
Brenda Morawa   BVM Engineering, Inc.
Erik Ring   LPA, Inc.
Michael Rosenberg   Oregon Department of Energy
Mick Schwedler   Trane
Gord Shymko   IPMVP and G.F. Shymko & Associates
Gail Stranske   CTG Energetics
Michael Zimmer   Thompson Hine LLP

Materials and Resources TAG

Mark Webster, Chair   Simpson Gumpertz & Heger Inc.
Steven Baer, Vice-chair   Five Winds International
Paul Bertram   NAIMA
Chris Dixon   NBBJ

Ann Edminster	Design AVEnues
Lee Gros	Lee Gros Architect and Artisan, Inc
Theresa Hogerheide-Reusch	Reusch Design Services
Nadav Malin	BuildingGreen, LLC.
Nancy Malone	Siegel & Strain Architects
Kirsten Ritchie	Gensler
Wayne Trusty	Athena Sustainable Materials Institute
Denise Van Valkenburg	MASCO Retail Cabinet Group
Gabe Wing	Herman Miller, Inc.

Indoor Environmental Quality TAG

Bob Thompson, Chair	EPA Indoor Environment Management Branch
Steve Taylor, Vice-Chair	Taylor Engineering
Nancy Clanton	Clanton and Associates
Alexis Kurtz	Ove Arup &Partners
George Loisos	Loisos+ Ubelohde
Prasad Vaidya	The Weidt Group
Daniel Bruck	BRC Acoustics & Tech.
David Lubman	David Lubman & Associates
Charles Salter	Salter Associates
Ozgem Ornektekin	DMJM Harris
Jude Anders	Shoreline Concepts, LLC
Brian Cloward	Mithun Architects+Designers+Planners
Larry Dykhuis	Herman Miller, Inc
Francis (Bud) Offerman	Indoor Environmental Engineering
Christopher Schaffner	The Green Engineer
Dennis Stanke	Trane Company

This edition of the reference guide builds on the work of those who helped create previous versions:

LEED for New Construction Version 2.2 Core Committee

James H. Goldman, Chair	Turner Construction
Tom Scarola, Vice-Chair	Tishman Speyer Properties
Lee Burgett	Trane Company
Craig Kneeland	New York State Energy Research & Development Authority
Joe Higgins	Fidelity Real Estate Company
Harry Gordon	Burt Hill Kosar Rittelmann Associates
Muscoe Martin	Wallace Roberts & Todd, LLC
Chris Dixon	Mithun
Bill Odell	HOK Architects
Chris Schaffner	The Green Engineer
Wayne Trusty	Athena Sustainable Materials Institute
Jerry Yudelson	Greenway Consulting Group, LLC
Charlotte Matthews	Bovis Lend Lease
John McFarland	WorkingBuildings LLC
Prasad Vaidy	The Weidt Group
Aalok Deshmuk	The Rocky Mountain Institute

LEED for Core & Shell Version 2.0 Core Committee

Jerry Lea, Chair	Hines Corporation
Christine Magar, Vice-Chair	Greenform
Peter Bartels	Power Construction Company, LLC
Clark Bisel	Flack + Kurtz
Gary Gardner	Davis Gardner Gannon Pope Architecture
Art Gensler	Gensler
Russell Perry	SmithGroup
Joe Van Belleghem	BuildGreen Developments, Inc.
Ken Wilson	Envision Design
Sally Wilson	CB Richard Ellis
Jerry Yudelson	Greenway Consulting Group, LLC

LEED for Schools Core Committee

Robert Kobet, Chair	Sustainaissance International
Jyoti Sharma, Vice-Chair	Wake County Public Schools
Anja Caldwell	Montgomery County Public Schools
Gregory Churchill	Oregon State Energy Office
Charles Eley	Architectural Energy Corporation
Deane Evans, NJIT	Center for Architecture and Building Science Research
William Orr	California Integrated Waste Management Board
Larry Schoff	Energy Efficient Solutions
Katrina Shum-Miller	Green Building Services
Timothy Sisson	York International
Brenda Stokes	Bibb County Public Schools

A special thanks to USGBC staff for their invaluable efforts in developing this LEED Reference Guide especially Sonia Punjabi for her technical expertise and extraordinary commitment, Lauren Riggs for her dedication and hard work, and Brendan Owens and Peter Templeton for their vision and guidance.

TABLE OF CONTENTS

*Credit not applicable to all Rating Systems, please refer to the credit for more details.

*Credit not applicable to all Rating Systems, please refer to the credit for more details.

LEED 2009 for New Construction, Core & Shell, and Schools

100 base points; 6 possible Innovation in Design and 4 Regional Priority points

Certified   40–49 points
Silver   50–59 points
Gold   60–79 points
Platinum   80 points and above

*Credit not applicable to all Rating Systems, please refer to the credit for more details.

INTRODUCTION

I. WHY MAKE YOUR BUILDING GREEN?

The environmental impact of the building design, construction, and operations industry is enormous. Buildings annually consume more than 30% of the total energy and more than 60% of the electricity used in the United States. In 2006, the commercial building sector produced more than 1 billion metric tons of carbon dioxide, an increase of more than 30% over 1990 levels.[1] Each day 5 billion gallons of potable water are used solely to flush toilets. A typical North American commercial building generates about 1.6 pounds of solid waste per employee per day[2]; in a building with 1,500 employees, that can amount to 300 tons of waste per year. Development alters land from natural, biologically diverse habitats to hardscape that is impervious and devoid of biodiversity. The far-reaching influence of the built environment necessitates action to reduce its impact.

Green building practices can substantially reduce or eliminate negative environmental impacts through high-performance, market-leading design, construction, and operations practices. As an added benefit, green operations and management reduce operating costs, enhance building marketability, increase workers' productivity, and reduce potential liability resulting from indoor air quality problems.

Examples abound. Energy efficiency measures have reduced operating expenses of the Denver Dry Goods building by approximately $75,000 per year. Students in day-lit schools in North Carolina consistently score higher on tests than students in schools using conventional lighting fixtures. Studies of workers in green buildings reported productivity gains of up to 16%, including less absenteeism and higher work quality, based on "people-friendly" green design. Karges Faulconbridge, Inc., renovated a former grocery store for its new headquarters and diverted 88% of the construction waste from landfills through reuse or recycling. The largest high-rise real estate project in Sacramento, the Joe Serna Jr. Environmental Protection Agency Headquarters Building (Cal/EPA), was able to save $610,000 a year by implementing energy efficiency measures, making it 34% more energy efficient than required by California's 1998 energy code. In short, green design, construction, and operations have environmental, economic, and social elements that benefit all building stakeholders, including owners, occupants, and the general public.

II. LEED® GREEN BUILDING RATING SYSTEM

Background on LEED®

Following the formation of the U.S. Green Building Council (USGBC) in 1993, the organization's members quickly realized that the sustainable building industry needed a system to define and measure "green buildings." USGBC began to research existing green building metrics and rating systems. Less than a year after formation, the members acted on the initial findings by establishing a committee to focus solely on this topic. The composition of the committee was diverse; it included architects, real estate agents, a building owner, a lawyer, an environmentalist, and industry representatives. This cross section of people and professions added a richness and depth both to the process and to the ultimate product.

The first LEED Pilot Project Program, also referred to as LEED Version 1.0, was launched at the USGBC Membership Summit in August 1998. After extensive modifications, LEED Green Building

Rating System Version 2.0 was released in March 2000, with LEED Version 2.1 following in 2002 and LEED Version 2.2 following in 2005.

As LEED has evolved and matured, the program has undertaken new initiatives. In addition to a rating system specifically devoted to building operational and maintenance issues (LEED for Existing Buildings: Operations & Maintenance), LEED addresses the different project development and delivery processes that exist in the U.S. building design and construction market, through rating systems for specific building typologies, sectors, and project scopes: LEED for Core & Shell, LEED for New Construction, LEED for Schools, LEED for Neighborhood Development, LEED for Retail, LEED for Healthcare, LEED for Homes, and LEED for Commercial Interiors.

Project teams interact with the Green Building Certification Institute (GBCI) for project registration and certification. GBCI was established in 2008 as a separately incorporated entity with the support of the U.S. Green Building Council. GBCI administers credentialing and certification programs related to green building practice. These programs support the application of proven strategies for increasing and measuring the performance of buildings and communities as defined by industry systems such as LEED.

The green building field is growing and changing daily. New technologies and products are being introduced into the marketplace, and innovative designs and practices are proving their effectiveness. The LEED rating systems and reference guides will evolve as well. Project teams must comply with the version of the rating system that is current at the time of their registration.

USGBC will highlight new developments on its website on a continual basis at www.usgbc.org.

Features of LEED®

The LEED Green Building Rating Systems are voluntary, consensus-based, and market-driven. Based on existing and proven technology, they evaluate environmental performance from a whole-building perspective over a building's life cycle, providing a definitive standard for what constitutes a green building in design, construction, and operation.

The LEED rating systems are designed for rating new and existing commercial, institutional, and residential buildings. They are based on accepted energy and environmental principles and strike a balance between known, established practices and emerging concepts. Each rating system is organized into 5 environmental categories: Sustainable Sites, Water Efficiency, Energy and Atmosphere, Materials and Resources, and Indoor Environmental Quality. An additional category, Innovation in Design, addresses sustainable building expertise as well as design measures not covered under the 5 environmental categories. Regional bonus points are another feature of LEED and acknowledge the importance of local conditions in determining best environmental design and construction practices.

The LEED Credit Weightings

In LEED 2009, the allocation of points between credits is based on the potential environmental impacts and human benefits of each credit with respect to a set of impact categories. The impacts are defined as the environmental or human effect of the design, construction, operation, and maintenance of the building, such as greenhouse gas emissions, fossil fuel use, toxins and carcinogens, air and water pollutants, indoor environmental conditions. A combination of approaches, including energy modeling, life-cycle assessment, and transportation analysis, is used to quantify each type of impact. The resulting allocation of points among credits is called credit weighting.

LEED 2009 uses the U.S. Environmental Protection Agency's TRACI[3] environmental impact categories as the basis for weighting each credit. TRACI was developed to assist with impact evaluation for life-cycle assessment, industrial ecology, process design, and pollution prevention.

LEED 2009 also takes into consideration the weightings developed by the National Institute of Standards and Technology (NIST); these compare impact categories with one another and assign a relative weight to each. Together, the 2 approaches provide a solid foundation for determining the point value of each credit in LEED 2009.

The LEED 2009 credit weightings process is based on the following parameters, which maintain consistency and usability across rating systems:

- All LEED credits are worth a minimum of 1 point.

- All LEED credits are positive, whole numbers; there are no fractions or negative values.

- All LEED credits receive a single, static weight in each rating system; there are no individualized scorecards based on project location.

- All LEED rating systems have 100 base points; Innovation in Design (or Operations) and Regional Priority credits provide opportunities for up to 10 bonus points.

Given the above criteria, the LEED 2009 credit weightings process involves 3 steps:

1. A reference building is used to estimate the environmental impacts in 13 categories associated with a typical building pursuing LEED certification.

2. The relative importance of building impacts in each category are set to reflect values based on the NIST weightings.[4]

3. Data that quantify building impacts on environmental and human health are used to assign points to individual credits.

Each credit is allocated points based on the relative importance of the building-related impacts that it addresses. The result is a weighted average that combines building impacts and the relative value of the impact categories. Credits that most directly address the most important impacts are given the greatest weight, subject to the system design parameters described above. Credit weights also reflect a decision by LEED to recognize the market implications of point allocation. The result is a significant change in allocation of points compared with previous LEED rating systems. Overall, the changes increase the relative emphasis on the reduction of energy consumption and greenhouse gas emissions associated with building systems, transportation, the embodied energy of water, the embodied energy of materials, and where applicable, solid waste.

The details of the weightings process vary slightly among individual rating systems. For example, LEED for Existing Buildings: Operations & Maintenance includes credits related to solid waste management but LEED for New Construction does not. This results in a difference in the portion of the environmental footprint addressed by each rating system and the relative allocation of points. The weightings process for each rating system is fully documented in a weightings workbook.

The credit weightings process will be reevaluated over time to incorporate changes in values ascribed to different building impacts and building types, based on both market reality and evolving scientific knowledge related to buildings. A complete explanation of the LEED credit weightings system is available on the USGBC website, at www.usgbc.org.

III. OVERVIEW AND PROCESS

The LEED Green Building Rating Systems for New Construction, Core & Shell, and Schools are a set of performance standards for certifying the design and construction of commercial or institutional buildings and high-rise residential buildings of all sizes, both public and private. The intent is to promote healthful, durable, affordable, and environmentally sound practices in building design and construction.

Prerequisites and credits in the LEED Green Building Rating Systems address 7 topics:

- Sustainable Sites (SS)
- Water Efficiency (WE)
- Energy and Atmosphere (EA)
- Materials and Resources (MR)
- Indoor Environmental Quality (IEQ)
- Innovation in Design (ID)
- Regional Priority (RP)

LEED prerequisites and credits have identical structures; see Section XI of this Introduction.

Minimum Program Requirements

A project must adhere to LEED's Minimum Program Requirements (MPRs), or possess minimum characteristics in order to be eligible for certification under LEED 2009. These requirements define the categories of buildings that the LEED rating systems were designed to evaluate, and taken together serve three goals: (1) give clear guidance to customers, (2) protect the integrity of the LEED program, and (3) reduce challenges that occur during the LEED certification process. The MPRs will evolve over time in tandem with the LEED rating systems. In order to be eligible for certification under any LEED 2009 Rating System, projects must comply with each associated MPR. The MPRs can be found in the LEED 2009 Rating Systems. In addition, definitions and more extensive guidance on certain issues are provided in a separate document, titled Supplemental Guidance, available on the USGBC website.

The Green Building Certification Institute (GBCI) reserves the right to revoke LEED certification from any LEED 2009 project upon gaining knowledge of non-compliance with any applicable MPRs. If such a circumstance occurs, no registration or certification fees paid to GBCI will be refunded.

When to Use LEED for New Construction

LEED for New Construction was designed primarily for new commercial office buildings, but it has been applied to many other building types by LEED practitioners. All commercial buildings, as defined by standard building codes, are eligible for certification as LEED for New Construction buildings. Examples of commercial occupancies include offices, institutional buildings (libraries, museums, churches, etc.), hotels, and residential buildings of 4 or more habitable stories.

LEED for New Construction addresses design and construction activities for both new buildings and major renovations of existing buildings. A major renovation involves major HVAC renovation, significant envelope modifications, and major interior rehabilitation. For a major renovation of an existing building, LEED for New Construction is the appropriate rating system. If the project scope does not involve significant design and construction activities and focuses more on operations and maintenance activities, LEED for Existing Buildings: Operations & Maintenance is more appropriate because it addresses operational and maintenance issues of working buildings.

Some projects are designed and constructed to be partially occupied by the owner or developer, and partially occupied by other tenants. In such projects, the owner or developer has direct influence over the portion of the work that they occupy. For such a project to pursue LEED for New Construction certification, the owner or tenant must occupy more than 50% of the building's leasable square footage. Projects in which 50% or less of the building's leasable square footage is occupied by an owner should pursue LEED for Core & Shell certification.

When to Use LEED for Core & Shell

The LEED for Core & Shell Rating System is a market-specific application that recognizes the unique nature of core and shell development. The LEED for Core & Shell Rating System acknowledges the limited level of influence a developer can exert in a speculatively developed building.

LEED for Core & Shell was developed to serve the speculative development market, in which project teams do not control all scopes of a whole building's design and construction. Depending on how the project is structured, this scope can vary significantly from project to project. The LEED for Core & Shell Rating System addresses a variety of project types and a broad project range.

LEED for Core & Shell can be used for projects in which the developer controls the design and construction of the entire core and shell base building (e.g., mechanical, electrical, plumbing, and fire protection systems) but has no control over the design and construction of the tenant fit-out. Examples of this type of project can be a commercial office building, medical office building, retail center, warehouse, and lab facility.

If a project is designed and constructed to be partially occupied by the owner or developer, then the owner or developer has direct influence over that portion of the interior build-out work. For these projects to pursue LEED for Core & Shell certification, the owner must occupy 50% or less of the building's leasable square footage. Projects in which more than 50% of the building's tenant space is occupied by a owner should pursue LEED for New Construction certification.

Because of the nature of the core and shell project type and scope, LEED for Core & Shell certification has some unique aspects. Further guidance on these can be found in the appendixes to the Reference Guide. Project teams should review these appendixes for guidance.

Core & Shell Appendix 1 – Default Occupancy Counts

- Guidance is provided for Core & Shell projects, which typically do not know what the actual building occupancy, for how for determining FTE and transient occupants.

Core & Shell Appendix 2 – Core & Shell Energy Modeling Guidelines

- Guidance is provided on how to model building systems that are beyond the developer's scope of work.

Core & Shell Appendix 3 – Core & Shell Project Scope

- This checklist is to be provided to GBCI for certification and precertification, and is intended to show what portions of the work is within the developer's control.

Core & Shell Appendix 4 – Tenant Lease or Sales Agreement

- The LEED for Core & Shell Rating System allows developers to achieve compliance with the requirements for certain credits through a binding tenant lease or sales agreement.

Core & Shell Appendix 5 – LEED for Core & Shell Precertification Guidance

- Precertification, signifying the developer's commitment to achieving full certification upon completion of construction, enables a Core & Shell project to market the advantages of a green building to potential tenants.

For more information about the Core & Shell appendixes, see Section IX of this Introduction.

When to Use LEED for Schools

LEED for Schools addresses design and construction activities for both new school buildings and major renovations of existing school buildings.

LEED for Schools must be used for the construction or major renovation of an academic building on K–12 school grounds. Other projects on a school campus may qualify under 2 or more LEED rating system project scopes; for example, nonacademic buildings on a school campus, such as administrative offices, maintenance facilities, or dormitories, are eligible for either LEED for New Construction and LEED for Schools. Projects involving postsecondary academic buildings or prekindergarten buildings may also choose to use either LEED for New Construction or LEED for Schools.

If the project scope does not involve significant design and construction activities and focuses more on operations and maintenance activities, LEED for Existing Buildings: O&M is the appropriate rating system.

Many projects neatly fit the defined scope of only 1 LEED rating system; others may be eligible for 2 or more. The project is a viable candidate for LEED certification if it can meet all prerequisites and achieve the minimum points required in a given rating system. If more than 1 rating system applies, the project team can decide which to pursue. For assistance in choosing the most appropriate LEED rating system, please e-mail leedinfo@usgbc.org.

Registration

Project teams interested in earning LEED certification for their buildings must first register the project with GBCI. Projects can be registered on the GBCI website (www.gbci.org). The website also has information on registration costs for USGBC national members as well as nonmembers. Registration is an important step that establishes contact with GBCI and provides access to software tools, errata, critical communications, and other essential information.

LEED-Online

LEED-Online is the primary resource for managing the LEED documentation process. From LEED-Online, project teams can manage project details, complete documentation requirements for LEED credits and prerequisites, upload supporting files, submit applications for review, receive reviewer feedback, and ultimately earn LEED certification. LEED-Online provides a common space where members of a project team can work together to document compliance with the LEED rating system. All project teams pursuing LEED certification are required to use LEED-Online and its submittal documentation paths. LEED submittals are instrumental in demonstrating credit compliance because they contain all the documentation requirements for any given LEED credit. Additionally, LEED-Online contains embedded calculators and tables to ensure that the submittal package delivered to GBCI is complete and accurate.

LEED-Online also features several support capabilities. It enables team members to view and submit credit interpretation requests, contact customer service, generate project-specific reports, and consult supplementary LEED resources, such as FAQs, tutorials, offline calculators, and sample documentation. Applicants with multiple projects will have access to reporting tools that use data from projects across their entire LEED portfolio. LEED certificates for successful projects are also issued through LEED-Online.

Credit Interpretation Requests and Rulings

In some cases, a LEED project team may encounter challenges when interpreting the requirements of a prerequisite or credit for their project, perhaps because the reference guide does not sufficiently address a specific issue or a conflict requires resolution. To address such issues, a credit interpretation ruling process has been established for each LEED rating system. See the GBCI website for more information, at www.gbci.org.

Credit interpretation requests must be submitted online. Provide a brief but clear description of the challenge encountered, refer to the prerequisite or credit information found in the rating system and reference guide, and emphasize the intent of the prerequisite or credit. If possible, the project team should offer potential solutions to the problem or a proposed interpretation. Follow the detailed instructions in LEED-Online.

Communications related to credit interpretation requests will be in electronic format.

Review and Certification

To earn LEED certification, the applicant project must satisfy all the prerequisites and credits worth the minimum number of points to warrant the desired project rating under LEED for New Construction, Core & Shell, or Schools. Projects must comply with the version of the rating system that is current in LEED-Online at the time of project registration.

Appeals

Appeals may be filed after the design phase review, the construction phase review, or the full application review. Please see the GBCI website for more information on appeals.

Fees

Information on certification fees can be found on the GBCI website. GBCI will acknowledge receipt of the application and proceed with application review when all project documentation and payments have been received and processed. Registration fees, appeal review fees, and any additional fees required to expedite LEED certification are not refundable.

Updates and Addenda

This is the first edition of the LEED Reference Guide for Green Building Design and Construction, 2009. As building science and technology continue to improve and evolve, updates and addenda will be made available. USGBC cannot be held liable for any criteria set forth herein that may not be applicable to later versions of LEED rating systems, and GBCI reserves the right to modify its policies from time to time. Updates and addenda will be accumulated between revisions and will be formally incorporated in major revisions. In the interim, between major revisions, USGBC may issue updates or addenda to clarify criteria.

The prerequisites, credits, amendments and addenda current at the time of project registration will continue to guide the project throughout its certification process

Information Privacy & Policy Guidelines

For more information on the privacy policy of the U.S. Green Building Counil, Inc. (USGBC), refer to the Policies and Guidelines section of the USGBC website, at www.usgbc.org. With the support of its members, volunteers, and other stakeholders, USGBC is the developer of the LEED rating systems.

Green Building Certification Institute, Inc. (GBCI) implements the LEED rating systems and carries out credentialing programs relating to LEED. For more information on the privacy policy of GBCI including the privacy policy on documentation submitted through LEED-Online, refer to the Policies and Guidelines section of the GBCI website, at www.gbci.org. Projects whose information should be treated as confidential may select this option during registration; project confidentiality status may be changed at any time through LEED-Online. Please review the GBCI privacy policy for further details.

IV. LEED-ONLINE DOCUMENTATION REQUIREMENTS

All LEED for New Construction, Core & Shell, and Schools certification applications must include the required LEED-Online documentation: general documentation requirements, documentation requirements for all prerequisites, and documentation requirements for all pursued credits.

General Requirements

LEED certification application requires the submission of an overall project narrative with the completed LEED-Online documentation requirements. The project narrative describes the applicant's organization, building, site, and team. This narrative helps the LEED review team understand the major elements of the project and building performance, and it also aids in highlighting projects in future communications efforts. General documentation also requires the basic details pertaining to project site conditions, construction scope and timeline, occupant and usage data, and project team identification. Project teams must address all the elements in the general documentation requirements, providing details and clarifications where appropriate, and they may include any optional elements that are helpful in describing the project.

Credit Substitution

The LEED 2009 rating systems do not allow credit substitution using another version. Currently registered LEED projects that want to use LEED 2009 credits need to switch to the new version in entirety. USGBC expects that most projects will find this switch feasible and advantageous.

V. CERTIFICATION APPLICATION

LEED for Core & Shell Precertification Application

Precertification is formal recognition by GBCI that the owner or developer has established LEED for Core & Shell certification as a goal. Precertification is unique to LEED for Core & Shell, and projects may pursue it, or not, at their discretion. It gives core and shell building owners and developers a marketing tool to attract potential tenants and financiers who recognize the benefits of a LEED-certified building. Precertification generally occurs early in the design process and is based on declared goals and the intent to use green strategies, systems, and/or features, not actual achievement of these features.

Once a project is registered as a LEED Core & Shell project with GBCI, a project team that chooses to seek precertification may complete the LEED Core & Shell precertification documentation requirements and submit the project for review. Because much of the value of precertification occurs early in a project's development, the project team's documentation and GBCI's review is necessarily less rigorous and comprehensive than the LEED Core & Shell certification application. Project teams must confirm that the project intends to meet the requirements of a credit. For detailed information on Core & Shell precertification, refer to Appendix 5.

Precertificaiton is not required for a documented and completed building, nor is it confirmation of, or a commitment to achieve, LEED for Core & Shell certification. Precertification is not LEED Certification. Please see Appendix 5 for further information on LEED for Core & Shell precertification.

LEED for New Construction, Core & Shell, and Schools Certification Application

To earn LEED certification, the applicant project must satisfy all the prerequisites and qualify for a minimum number of points to attain the established project ratings as listed below. Having satisfied the basic prerequisites of the program, applicant projects are then rated according to their degree of compliance within the rating system.

After registration, the project design team should begin to collect information and perform calculations to satisfy the prerequisite and credit documentation requirements. Because documentation should be gathered throughout design and construction, it is helpful to designate a LEED team leader who will be responsible for managing its compilation.

LEED for New Construction, Core & Shell, and Schools provides the option of splitting a certification application into two phases: design and construction. Documentation for design phase credits, identified in LEED-Online, can be submitted for review at the end of the design phase; the submittals for these credits can be fully evaluated based on documentation available during this phase of the project. For example, if a project site meets the requirements of LEED for New Construction SS Credit 3, Brownfield Redevelopment, the likelihood of credit achievement can be assessed before construction is complete. The LEED credit itself, however, is not awarded at the design review stage.

Design Phase Review

Each project is allotted a design phase review that consists of a preliminary design phase review and a final design phase review. GBCI formally rules on the design phase application by designating each attempted credit as either anticipated or denied. Participating in a design phase review does not guarantee award of any credit and will not result in LEED certification. This process enables project teams to assess the likelihood of credit achievement and requires follow-through to ensure the design is executed in the construction phase according to design specifications.

Construction Phase Review

At the completion of construction, the project team submits all attempted credits for review, including any newly attempted design credits. If the project team has had a design phase review and any of the design phase anticipated credits have since changed, additional documentation must be submitted to substantiate continued compliance with credit requirements. Upon receipt of the full certification application and fee, a final review will be conducted. All applicant-verified design phase credits that were designated as anticipated and have not changed since the design phase review will be declared as awarded. All other credits will be designated as either awarded or denied.

Project teams should refer to LEED-Online and the rating system scorecards to get information on credits that can be submitted for design phase review and credits that must be submitted for construction phase review.

LEED for New Construction, Core & Shell, and Schools certifications are awarded according to the following scale:

Certified   40–49 points
Silver   50–59 points
Gold   60–79 points
Platinum   80 points and above

GBCI recognizes buildings that achieve 1 of these rating levels with a formal letter of certification.

VI. CERTIFICATION STRATEGY

Timeline and Project Design Phases

Project teams should study the principles and objectives of LEED as early in the site selection and design process as possible. The project design phases mentioned throughout this reference guide correspond to the architectural design and planning steps commonly used in the construction industry:

1. **Predesign** entails gathering information, recognizing stakeholder needs, and establishing project goals.

2. **Schematic design** explores several design options and alternatives, with the intent to establish an agreed-upon project layout and scope of work.

3. **Design development** begins the process of spatial refinement and usually involves the first design of a project's energy systems.

4. **Construction documents** carry the design into the level of details for all spaces and systems and materials so that construction can take place.

5. **Construction**.

6. **Substantial completion** is a contractual benchmark that usually corresponds to the point at which a client could occupy a nearly completed space.

7. **Final completion**.

8. **Certificate of occupancy** is the official recognition by a local building department that a building conforms to applicable building and safety codes.

Related Credits

When pursuing LEED certification, it is important to consider how credits are interconnected and how their synergies and trade-offs will ultimately affect both the project and the other credits the team may consider pursuing. Consult the Related Credits section of each prerequisite and credit to help inform design and construction decisions leading to certification.

Consistent Documentation across Credits

Several kinds of project information are required for consistent LEED documentation across various credits. Pay special attention to overlapping project data; doing so will help the application and review process go smoothly.

Operations and Maintenance in LEED for New Construction, Core & Shell, and Schools Certified Buildings

The LEED Reference Guide for Green Building Design and Construction contains information on operations and maintenance to help project teams streamline green O&M practices once the LEED design and construction project has been completed. Although not required as part of the LEED certification process, upfront planning for green operations and maintenance can help building owners, operators, and maintenance staff ensure that the building continues to operate in a sustainable manner.

VII. EXEMPLARY PERFORMANCE STRATEGIES

Exemplary performance strategies result in performance that greatly exceeds the performance level or expands the scope required by an existing LEED for New Construction, Core & Shell, or Schools credit. To earn exemplary performance credits, teams must meet the performance level defined by the next step in the threshold progression. For credits with more than 1 compliance path, an Innovation in Design point can be earned by satisfying more than 1 compliance path if their benefits are additive. See the Innovation in Design credit section for further details.

The credits for which exemplary performance points are available through expanded performance are noted throughout this reference guide and in LEED-Online by the logo shown below.

The list for exemplary performance points available is as follows:

Sustainable Sites

SS Credit 2	Development Density and Community Connectivity
SS Credit 4	Alternative Transportation
SS Credit 5	Site Development
SS Credit 6	Stormwater Design
SS Credit 7	Heat Island Effect
SS Credit 10	Joint Use of Facilities (Schools only)

Water Efficiency

WE Credit 2	Innovative Wastewater Technologies
WE Credit 3	Water Use Reduction
WE Credit 4	Process Water Use Reduction (Schools only)

Energy and Atmosphere

EA Credit 1	Optimize Energy Performance
EA Credit 2	On-site Renewable Energy
EA Credit 3	Enhanced Commissioning
EA Credit 6	Green Power

Materials and Resources

MR Credit 1	Building Reuse: Maintain Existing Walls, Floors, and Roof (Core & Shell only)
MR Credit 2	Construction Waste Management
MR Credit 3	Materials Reuse
MR Credit 4	Recycled Content
MR Credit 5	Regional Materials
MR Credit 6	Rapidly Renewable Materials (New Construction and Schools only)
MR Credit 7	Certified Wood (Core & Shell, MR Credit 6)

Indoor Environmental Quality

IEQ Credit 3	Construction Indoor Air Quality Management Plan (Core & Shell only)
IEQ Credit 8	Daylight and Views
IEQ Credit 9	Enhanced Acoustical Performance (Schools only)
IEQ Credit 10	Mold Prevention (Schools only)

VIII. REGIONAL PRIORITY

To provide incentive to address geographically specific environmental issues, USGBC regional councils and chapters have identified 6 credits per rating system that are of particular importance to specific areas. Each Regional Priority credit is worth an additional 1 point, and a total of 4 additional points may be earned by achieving Regional Priority credits, with 1 point earned per credit. Upon project registration, LEED-Online automatically determines a project's Regional Priority credits based on its zip code. If the project achieves more than 4 Regional Priority credits, the team can choose the credits for which these points will apply. The USGBC website also contains a searchable database of Regional Priority credits.

IX. CORE & SHELL APPENDIXES

Appendix 1

Default Occupancy Counts: presents default occupancy counts for Core & Shell projects. Because of the nature of core and shell development, the project team may not know the tenant makeup and occupancy during the building's design phase. For some credits, the team will need to refer to the default occupancy count table to determine credit compliance. The occupancy counts must be consistent across all credits.

Appendix 2

Core & Shell Energy Modeling Guidelines: gives guidelines for Core & Shell energy modeling. These guidelines are intended to ensure that projects in different markets approach the energy modeling requirements in a similar manner and to establish a minimum benchmark for energy optimization. Consult this appendix when modeling both the designed core and shell spaces and the tenant spaces that are not part of the project design and construction scope.

Appendix 3

Core & Shell Project Scope Checklist: contains a checklist for tenant interiors to help Core & Shell teams define the owner-tenant division in the project design and certification and precertification review process.

Appendix 4

Tenant Lease or Sales Agreement: offers a way for Core & Shell projects to earn points by making credit requirements part of a binding sales agreement or tenant lease. This expands the area of project owner and design team "control" from design and construction to tenant sales and lease agreement negotiation, and is designed to give Core & Shell projects with a limited scope of work the ability to achieve credits that would otherwise be beyond their control, by committing the tenant(s) to green building practices in the tenant's scope of work.

Appendix 5

LEED for Core & Shell Precertification Guidance: explains how Core & Shell project teams can earn precertification by making a commitment to comply with the requirements for full certification. Precertification can help attract financing and enhance a building's appeal to potential tenant.

X. TOOLS FOR REGISTERED PROJECTS

LEED offers additional resources for LEED project teams on the USGBC website, at www.usgbc. org/projecttools. The Registered Projects Tools website provides resources for starting the project, including rating system errata, documentation requirements, and referenced industry standards. Also consult the website for the following:

Declarant definitions and other definitions. This resource describes the team members who are required to sign off on certain documentation requirements and indicates the prerequisites and credits for which each team member is responsible. The required declarant is noted in the corresponding credit documentation section of LEED-Online.

Licensed Professional Exemption Form. The Licensed Professional Exemption Form can be used by a project team's registered professional engineer, registered architect, or registered landscape architect as a streamlined path to certain credits, bypassing otherwise-required submittals. This form is used in conjunction with the declarations in LEED-Online to document any exemptions. The form is required for any eligible submittal requirements the project team wishes to waive; the exemption is invalid without a properly executed Licensed Professional Exemption Form. Licensed Professional Exemptions are noted in the corresponding credit documentation section of LEED-Online.

XI. HOW TO USE THIS REFERENCE GUIDE

The LEED for Green Building Design and Construction Reference Guide is a supporting document to the LEED for New Construction, Core & Shell, and Schools rating systems. The guide helps project teams understand the criteria, the reasons behind them, strategies for implementation, and documentation requirements. It includes examples of strategies that can be used in each category, case studies of buildings that have implemented these strategies successfully, and additional resources. It does not provide an exhaustive list of strategies for meeting the criteria or all the information that a project team needs to determine the applicability of a credit to the project.

Rating System Pages

The rating system, published in its entirety on the USGBC website, is imbedded in this reference guide. Each prerequisite and credit discussion begins with a gray page that mirrors the rating systems' Intent and Requirements. This Reference guide addresses the Intents and Requirements for the following Rating Systems: LEED 2009 for New Construction, LEED 2009 for Core & Shell and LEED 2009 for Schools.

In instances where a particular Rating system has a unique intent and/or requirements, the layout of the rating system pages will highlight the intent or requirements. The following is an example of where certain New Construction and Schools requirements are identical (i.e., NC & Schools), but where there are additional New Construction-specific requirements (i.e., NC: Additional Requirement):

NC & SCHOOLS

Achieve IEQ Credit 7.1: Thermal Comfort—Design

Agree to conduct a thermal comfort survey of building occupants (adults and students of grades 6 and above) within 6 to 18 months after occupancy. This survey should collect anonymous responses about thermal comfort in the building, including an assessment of overall satisfaction with thermal performance and identification of thermal comfort problems. Agree to develop a plan for corrective action if the survey results indicate that more than 20% of occupants are dissatisfied with thermal comfort in the building. This plan should include measurement of relevant environmental variables in problem areas in accordance with ASHRAE Standard 55-2004 (with errata but without addenda).

New Construction and Schools requirements

NC Additional Requirement

Provide a permanent monitoring system to ensure that building performance meets the desired comfort criteria as determined by IEQ Credit 7.1: Thermal Comfort—Design. Residential projects are not eligible for this credit.

The additional New Construction-specific requirements

Prerequisite and Credit Format

Each prerequisite or credit is organized in a standardized format for simplicity and quick reference. The first section summarizes the main points regarding the green measure and includes the intent, requirements, required submittals for certification, and a summary of any referenced industry standard. Subsequent sections provide supporting information to help interpret the measure and offer links to resources and examples. The sections for each credit are described in the following paragraphs.

Intent identifies the main sustainability goal or benefit of the prerequisite or credit.

Requirements specifies the criteria that satisfy the prerequisite or credit and the number of points available. The prerequisites must be achieved; the credits are optional, but each contributes to the overall project score. Some credits have 2 or more paths with cumulative points. Other credits have several options from which the project team must choose. For example, Energy & Atmosphere Credit 1, Optimize Energy Efficiency Performance, has 3 options, but a project can apply for only 1, depending on the type of building.

Benefits and Issues to Consider addresses the environmental benefits of the activity encouraged by the prerequisite or credit, and economic considerations related to first costs, life-cycle costs, and estimated savings.

Related Credits acknowledges the trade-offs and synergies within the LEED rating system credit categories. Achieving a particular credit may make it worthwhile and comparatively easy to pursue related credits; the converse is also possible.

The **Summary of Referenced Standards**, where applicable, introduces the required standards used to measure achievement of the credit intent. Teams are strongly encouraged to review the full standard and not rely on the summary.

Implementation discusses specific methods or assemblies that facilitate achievement of the requirements.

Timeline and Team guides the project team by identifying who should lead an effort and when the tasks should begin.

Calculations offers sample formulas or computations that determine achievement of a particular prerequisite or credit. Most calculations are facilitated in LEED-Online.

The **Documentation Guidance** section provides the first steps in preparing to complete the LEED-Online documentation requirements.

Examples illustrates strategies for credit achievement.

Exemplary Performance, if applicable, details the level of performance needed for the award of points in addition to those for credit achievement.

Regional Variations outlines concerns specific to the geographic location of the building.

Resources offers suggestions for further research and provide examples or illustrations, detailed technical information, or other information relevant to the prerequisite or credit. The resources include websites, online materials, and printed books and articles that can be obtained directly from the organizations listed.

Definitions clarifies the meaning of certain terms relevant to the prerequisite or credit. These may be general terms or terms specific to LEED for New Construction, Core & Shell, and Schools. A complete glossary is found at the end of this reference guide.

Throughout these sections, the rating system specific information is called out by enclosing the information in a gray box; the relevant rating systems are identified by NC (New Construction), CS

(Core & Shell) or Schools as printed in the top left corner of the gray box. Similarly, rating system specific intents and requirements are identified in the Rating System Pages. This method provides clarity to the credit discussions and provides the relevant information needed for different project types where necessary.

Endnotes

[1] Energy Information Administration. "Emissions of Greenhouse Gas Report." Report DOE/EIA-0573(2006). Released 28 November 2007. http://www.eia.doe.gov/oiaf/1605/ggrpt/carbon.html#commercial

[2] Office of the Federal Environmental Executive. <http://ofee.gov/wpr/wastestream.asp> Last modified 24 April 2008.

[3] Tools for the Reduction and Assessment of Chemical and Other Environmental Impacts (TRACI). U.S. Environmental Protection Agency, Office of Research and Development. http://www.epa.gov/nrmrl/std/sab/traci/.

[4] Relative impact category weights based on an exercise undertaken by NIST (National Institute of Standards and Technology) for the BEES program. http://www.bfrl.nist.gov/oae/software/bees/.

Overview

The selection and development of a building's site are fundamental components of sustainable building practices. Environmental damage caused by construction may take years of work to remedy.

The Sustainable Sites credit section addresses environmental concerns related to building landscape, hardscape, and exterior building issues. The LEED Sustainable Sites credits for New Construction, Core & Shell, and Schools promote the following measures:

Selecting and Developing the Site Wisely

Buildings affect ecosystems in a variety of ways. Development of a greenfield, or previously undeveloped site, consumes land. Development projects may also encroach on agricultural lands and wetlands or water bodies and compromise existing wildlife habitats. Choosing a previously developed site or even a damaged site that can be remediated reduces pressure on undeveloped land. Developing a master plan for the project site helps engrain environmental considerations as adaptations or expansions of site facilities occur over time. Planning for joint use of facilities integrates the project into the surrounding community and conserves material and land resources though optimized use of infrastructure.

Reducing Emissions Associated with Transportation

Environmental concerns related to buildings include vehicle emissions and the need for vehicle infrastructure as building occupants travel to and from the site. Emissions contribute to climate change, smog, acid rain, and other air quality problems. Parking areas, roadways, and building surfaces increase stormwater runoff and contribute to the urban heat island effect. In 2006, 76% of commuters in America ages 16 and older drove to work alone. Of the remaining 24% who used alternative means of transportation (including working from home), only 5% used public transportation and 11% carpooled.[1] Locating the project near residential areas, providing occupants with cycle racks, changing facilities, preferred parking, and access to mass transit and alternative-fuel fueling stations can encourage use of alternative forms of transportation. Promoting mass transit reduces the energy required for transportation as well as the space needed for parking lots, which encroach on green space.

Planting Sustainable Landscapes

Conventional plant designs and landscape maintenance practices often require irrigation and chemicals. Sustainable practices minimize the use of irrigation, fertilizers, and pesticides and can prevent soil erosion and sedimentation. Erosion from precipitation and wind causes degradation of property as well as sedimentation of local water bodies—and building sites can be major sources of sediment. Loss of nutrients, soil compaction, and decreased biodiversity of soil organisms can severely limit the vitality of landscaping. Sedimentation caused by erosion increases turbidity levels, which degrades aquatic habitats, and the buildup of sediments in stream channels can lessen flow capacity, increasing the possibility of flooding. Sustainable landscaping involves using or restoring native and adapted plants, which require less maintenance and irrigation and fewer or no applications of chemical fertilizers and pesticides compared with most introduced species. Sustainable landscaping thus reduces maintenance costs over the life of the building.

Protecting Surrounding Habitats

Development of building sites can encroach on agricultural lands and adversely affect wildlife habitat. As animals are displaced by development, they become crowded into increasingly smaller spaces, and eventually the population exceeds the carrying capacity of the area. Overall biodiversity, as well as individual plant and animal species, may be threatened. Preserving and restoring native and adapted vegetation and other ecological features on the site provide wildlife habitat.

Managing Stormwater Runoff

As areas are developed and urbanized, surface permeability is reduced, which in turn increases the runoff transported via pipes and sewers to streams, rivers, lakes, bays, and oceans. Impervious surfaces on the site may cause stormwater runoff that harms water quality, aquatic life, and recreation opportunities in receiving waters. For instance, parking areas contribute to stormwater runoff that is contaminated with oil, fuel, lubricants, combustion by-products, material from tire wear, and deicing salts. Runoff accelerates the flow rate of waterways, increasing erosion, altering aquatic habitat, and causing erosion downstream. Effective strategies exist to control, reduce, and treat stormwater runoff before it leaves the project site.

Reducing the Heat Island Effect

The use of dark, nonreflective surfaces for parking areas, roofs, walkways, and other surfaces contributes to the heat island effect. These surfaces absorb incoming solar radiation and radiate that heat to the surrounding areas, increasing the ambient temperature. In addition to being detrimental to site habitat, this increase raises the building's external and internal temperature, requiring more energy for cooling. The Lawrence Berkeley National Laboratory estimates that 1/6 of the electricity consumed in the United States is used to cool buildings. By installing reflective surfaces and vegetation, the nation's homes and businesses could save $4 billion a year in reduced cooling energy demand by 2015.[2]

Eliminating Light Pollution

Poorly designed exterior lighting may add to nighttime light pollution, which can interfere with nocturnal ecology, reduce observation of night skies, cause roadway glare, and hurt relationships with neighbors by causing light trespass. Reducing light pollution encourages nocturnal wildlife to inhabit the building site and causes less disruption to birds' migratory patterns. Thoughtful exterior lighting strategies may also reduce infrastructure costs and energy use over the life of the building.

Summary

The LEED Sustainable Sites credits for New Construction, Core & Shell, and Schools promote responsible, innovative, and practical site design strategies that are sensitive to plants, wildlife, and water and air quality. These credits also mitigate some of the negative effects buildings have on the local and regional environment. Project teams undertaking building projects should be cognizant of the inherent impacts of development on land consumption, ecosystems, natural resources, and energy use. Preference should be given to buildings with high-performance attributes in locations that enhance existing neighborhoods, transportation networks, and urban infrastructures. During initial project scoping, give preference to sites and land-use plans that preserve natural ecosystem functions and enhance the health of the surrounding community.

LEED Project Boundary

For single-building developments, the LEED submittal typically covers the entire project scope and is generally limited to the site boundary. However, in some cases a project is a portion of a larger multiple-building development. In these situations, the project team may determine the limits of the project submitted for LEED certification differently from the overall site boundaries. This LEED project boundary is the portion of the project site that is submitted for LEED certification and must be used consistently across all Sustainable Sites prerequisites and credits.

CREDIT	TITLE	NC	SCHOOLS	CS
SS Prerequisite 1	Construction Activity Pollution Prevention	Required	Required	Required
SS Prerequisite 2	Environmental Site Assessment	NA	Required	NA
SS Credit 1	Site Selection	1 point	1 point	1 point
SS Credit 2	Development Density and Community Connectivity	5 points	4 points	5 points
SS Credit 3	Brownfield Redevelopment	1 point	1 point	1 point
SS Credit 4.1	Alternative Transportation—Public Transportation Access	6 points	4 points	6 points
SS Credit 4.2	Alternative Transportation—Bicycle Storage and Changing Rooms	1 point	1 point	2 points
SS Credit 4.3	Alternative Transportation—Low-Emitting and Fuel-Efficient Vehicles	3 points	2 points	3 points
SS Credit 4.4	Alternative Transportation—Parking Capacity	2 points	2 points	2 points
SS Credit 5.1	Site Development—Protect or Restore Habitat	1 point	1 point	1 point
SS Credit 5.2	Site Development—Maximize Open Space	1 point	1 point	1 point
SS Credit 6.1	Stormwater Design—Quantity Control	1 point	1 point	1 point
SS Credit 6.2	Stormwater Design—Quality Control	1 point	1 point	1 point
SS Credit 7.1	Heat Island Effect—Nonroof	1 point	1 point	1 point
SS Credit 7.2	Heat Island Effect—Roof	1 point	1 point	1 point
SS Credit 8	Light Pollution Reduction	1 point	1 point	1 point
SS Credit 9	Tenant Design and Construction Guidelines	NA	NA	1 point
SS Credit 9	Site Master Plan	NA	1 point	NA
SS Credit 10	Joint Use of Facilities	NA	1 point	NA

CONSTRUCTION ACTIVITY POLLUTION PREVENTION

	NC	SCHOOLS	CS
Prerequisite	SS Prerequisite 1	SS Prerequisite 1	SS Prerequisite 1
Points	Required	Required	Required

Intent

To reduce pollution from construction activities by controlling soil erosion, waterway sedimentation and airborne dust generation.

Requirements

NC, SCHOOLS & CS

Create and implement an erosion and sedimentation control plan for all construction activities associated with the project. The plan must conform to the erosion and sedimentation requirements of the 2003 EPA Construction General Permit OR local standards and codes, whichever is more stringent. The plan must describe the measures implemented to accomplish the following objectives:

- To prevent loss of soil during construction by stormwater runoff and/or wind erosion, including protecting topsoil by stockpiling for reuse.

- To prevent sedimentation of storm sewers or receiving streams.

- To prevent pollution of the air with dust and particulate matter.

The EPA's construction general permit outlines the provisions necessary to comply with Phase I and Phase II of the National Pollutant Discharge Elimination System (NPDES) program. While the permit only applies to construction sites greater than 1 acre, the requirements are applied to all projects for the purposes of this prerequisite. Information on the EPA construction general permit is available at http://cfpub.epa.gov/npdes/stormwater/cgp.cfm.

	SS
NC	Prerequisite 1
SCHOOLS	Prerequisite 1
CS	Prerequisite 1

1. Benefits and Issues to Consider

Environmental Issues

The loss of topsoil is the most significant on-site consequence of erosion. Topsoil is biologically active and contains organic matter and plant nutrients. Loss of topsoil greatly reduces the soil's ability to support plant life, regulate water flow, and maintain the biodiversity of soil microbes and insects that control disease and pest outbreaks. Loss of nutrients, soil compaction, and decreased biodiversity can severely limit the vitality of landscaping. This can lead to additional site management and environmental concerns, such as increased use of fertilizers, irrigation, and pesticides, as well as increased stormwater runoff that adds to the pollution of nearby lakes and streams.

The off-site consequences of erosion from developed sites include a variety of water quality issues. Runoff from developed sites carries pollutants, sediments, and excess nutrients that disrupt aquatic habitats in the receiving waters. Nitrogen and phosphorus from runoff hasten eutrophication by causing unwanted plant growth in aquatic systems, including algal blooms that alter water quality and habitat conditions. Such growth can also decrease recreation potential and diminish the population diversity of indigenous fish, plants, and animals.

Sedimentation also contributes to the degradation of water bodies and aquatic habitats. The buildup of sediments in stream channels can lessen flow capacity as well as increase flooding and turbidity levels. Turbidity reduces sunlight penetration into water and leads to reduced photosynthesis in aquatic vegetation, causing lower oxygen levels that cannot support diverse communities of aquatic life.

Airborne dust from construction activity can have both environmental and human health impacts. Fine dust particles enter airways and lungs with ease and have been linked to numerous health problems including asthma, decreased lung function, and breathing difficulties. In addition, dust particles can travel long distances before settling in water bodies, increasing the acidity of lakes and streams and changing nutrient balances.

Economic Issues

Erosion and sedimentation control measures are required by local building codes in most areas to minimize difficult and expensive mitigation measures in receiving waters. The cost will include some minimal expense associated with installing and inspecting the control measures, particularly before and after storm events, and will vary depending on the type, location, topography, and soil conditions of the project.

2. Related Credits

Minimizing site disturbance during construction and carrying out site restoration efforts to prevent erosion and sedimentation will also contribute to achievement of the following credits:

- SS Credit 5.1: Site Development—Protect or Restore Habitat
- SS Credit 5.2: Site Development—Maximize Open Space

Limiting the disruption of a site's natural hydrology and adopting a low-impact development strategy will assist projects in achieving the following credits:

- SS Credit 6.1: Stormwater Design—Quantity Control
- SS Credit 6.2: Stormwater Design—Quality Control

3. Summary of Referenced Standard

2003 EPA Construction General Permit
U.S. Environmental Protection Agency (EPA) Office of Water

The construction general permit outlines a set of provisions construction operators must follow to comply with NPDES stormwater regulations. The permit covers any site 1 acre or larger as well as smaller sites that belong to a larger common plan of development or sale. It replaces and updates previous EPA permits.

	SS
NC	Prerequisite 1
SCHOOLS	Prerequisite 1
CS	Prerequisite 1

4. Implementation

Erosion typically occurs when foot traffic, runoff, or vehicle traffic damages vegetation that would otherwise hold the soil. Identifying and eliminating these and other causes will minimize soil loss and preserve receiving water quality.

This prerequisite effectively extends the National Pollutant Discharge Elimination System (NPDES) requirements for construction activities (which currently apply only to projects of 1 acre or larger) to all projects pursuing LEED Certification. Typically, the civil engineer or landscape architect identifies erosion-prone areas and outlines soil stabilization measures. The contractor then adopts a plan to implement those measures and responds to rain and other erosion-causing events accordingly. The erosion and sedimentation control plan should be incorporated into the construction drawings and specifications, with clear instructions regarding responsibilities, scheduling, and inspections.

If a stormwater pollution prevention plan is required for the project by NPDES or local regulations, an erosion and sedimentation control plan may already exist. In that case, to meet this prerequisite, confirm that the plan meets the prerequisite's requirements and is implemented. If an erosion and sedimentation control plan is not required for purposes other than LEED, use the referenced standard listed above as a guideline on how to compose the plan. Table 1 shows common strategies for controlling erosion and sedimentation on construction sites.

Table 1. Strategies for Controlling Erosion and Sedimentation

Control Technology	Description
Stabilization	
Temporary Seeding	Plant fast-growing grasses to temporarily stabilize soils
Permanent Seeding	Plant grass, trees, and shrubs to permanently stabilize soil
Mulching	Place hay, grass, woodchips, straw, or gravel on the soil surface to cover and hold soils
Structural Control	
Earth Dike	Construct a mound of stabilized soil to divert surface runoff volumes from distributed areas or into sediment basins or sediment traps
Silt Fence	Construct posts with a filter fabric media to remove sediment from stormwater volumes flowing through the fence
Sediment Trap	Excavate a pond area or construct earthen embankments to allow for settling of sediment from stormwater volumes
Sediment Basin	Construct a pond with a controlled water release structure to allow for settling of sediment from stormwater volumes

5. Timeline and Team

During the design phase, the civil engineer or landscape architect should compare local codes with the requirements of this prerequisite and create an erosion and sedimentation control plan. The general contractor should work with the project team's civil engineer or landscape architect to implement the plan during the construction phase and throughout project completion. The general contractor should photograph and maintain erosion and sedimentation control measures on-site during the various stages of construction. Once the site is stabilized, the general contractor should remove any temporary erosion and sedimentation control measures.

6. Calculations

There are no calculations required for this prerequisite.

7. Documentation Guidance

As a first step in preparing to complete the LEED-Online documentation requirements, work through the following measures. Refer to LEED-Online for the complete descriptions of all required documentation.

- Develop an erosion and sedimentation control drawing and/or a written erosion and sedimentation control plan with specifications that detail the erosion and control best management practices used on the project site and the responsible parties for implementation.

- Over the course of site work activities, document implementation of the erosion and sedimentation control plan through date-stamped photos, inspection logs or reports, descriptions of corrective action in response to problems, etc.

8. Examples

Background

The project is major renovation of a 50,000-square-foot residence hall on a large campus. As a part of the scope of work, the project team intends to remove soil, change contours, and alter the site drainage. To meet the credit requirements, the team will incorporate silt fencing, catch basin sediment traps, and silt sack sediment traps. The following table outlines the controls in place during construction.

Control Strategy	Description
Vehicle tracking	Approximately 8,800 square feet of lawn and topsoil will be removed and replaced by a free-draining gravel material to allow truck access with minimal soil displacement.
Silt fencing	Silt fencing with straw bale barrier will be installed along the north, east, and west elevations. The south elevation will have a silt fence barrier without straw bales.
Sediment basin	The site has 2 existing catch basins, 1 on the west and 1 on the north, plus 9 smaller catch basins on the south elevation. Each catch basin will have sediment traps. One existing catch basin, located within the site perimeter fence, will have a sediment trap with a straw bale barrier.
Inspections	Silt fencing and sediment traps will be inspected and maintained on a weekly basis by the general contractor. In the event of significant rainfall, controls will be inspected at the end of the workday or the following morning.
Permanent seeding and planting	Undisturbed site areas containing existing landscaping and trees will be protected from truck and vehicle traffic. Upon completion, disturbed areas of the site will be immediately seeded and planted with permanent vegetation.

9. Exemplary Performance

This prerequisite is not eligible for exemplary performance under the Innovation in Design section.

10. Regional Variations

Project teams should adhere to either local erosion and sedimentation control standards and codes, or the requirements of the 2003 EPA construction general permit, whichever is more stringent. This requirement also applies to projects seeking certification outside the United States.

11. Operations and Maintenance Considerations

The project team and groundskeeper should create an ongoing maintenance plan for permanent erosion control measures to prevent future or recurring erosion of site areas caused by damaging storms and traffic. At a minimum, the maintenance plan should include periodic visual inspections to identify any areas that are either eroding or susceptible to erosion and include recommendations for typical corrective actions. For example, identifying and promptly replacing dead or dying vegetation can prevent potential washouts during high-intensity storms. Additionally, it is helpful to construct direct paths for foot and vehicle traffic to avoid degrading the site.

	SS
NC	Prerequisite 1
SCHOOLS	Prerequisite 1
CS	Prerequisite 1

12. Resources

Please see USGBC's LEED Registered Project Tools (http://www.usgbc.org/projecttools) for additional resources and technical information.

In addition to the resources below, check with state and local organizations for information on erosion and sedimentation control in your project region.

Websites

CPESC, Inc.

http://www.cpesc.net

The searchable directory on this website identifies certified erosion and sedimentation control professionals by state.

Environment Canada, Freshwater, Sediment

http://www.ec.gc.ca/water/en/nature/sedim/e_sedim.htm

This site includes information on the environmental effects of sedimentation.

Erosion Control Technology Council

http://www.ectc.org

This nonprofit organization develops performance standards, testing procedures, and guidance on the application and installation of rolled erosion control products.

International Erosion Control Association

http://www.ieca.org

This organization's mission is to connect, educate, and develop the worldwide erosion and sediment control community.

Soil Erosion and Sedimentation in the Great Lakes Region

http://www.great-lakes.net/envt/pollution/erosion.html

This resource from the Great Lakes Information Network provides links to education and training opportunities, materials, manuals, maps, and other resources related to soil erosion, sedimentation, and watershed management.

U.S. EPA, Erosion and Sediment Control Model Ordinances

http://www.epa.gov/owow/nps/ordinance/erosion.htm

This resource is geared to helping municipalities draft ordinances for erosion and sedimentation control and could help companies develop policies to meet this LEED for New Construction prerequisite.

13. Definitions

Erosion is a combination of processes or events by which materials of the earth's surface are loosened, dissolved, or worn away and transported by natural agents (e.g., water, wind, or gravity).

Eutrophication is the increase in chemical nutrients, such as the nitrogen and phosphorus often found in fertilizers, in an ecosystem. The added nutrients stimulate excessive plant growth, promoting algal blooms or weeds. The enhanced plant growth reduces oxygen in the land and water, reducing water quality and fish and other animal populations.

The **National Pollutant Discharge Elimination System (NPDES)** is a permit program that controls water pollution by regulating point sources that discharge pollutants into waters of the United States. Industrial, municipal, and other facilities must obtain permits if their discharges go directly to surface waters.

Sedimentation is the addition of soil particles to water bodies by natural and human-related activities. Sedimentation often decreases water quality and can accelerate the aging process of lakes, rivers, and streams.

A **stormwater pollution prevention plan** describes all measures to prevent stormwater contamination, control sedimentation and erosion during construction, and comply with the requirements of the Clean Water Act.

Stormwater runoff consists of water from precipitation that flows over surfaces into sewer systems or receiving water bodies. All precipitation that leaves project site boundaries on the surface is considered stormwater runoff.

ENVIRONMENTAL SITE ASSESSMENT

	NC	SCHOOLS	CS
Prerequisite	NA	SS Prerequisite 2	NA
Points	NA	Required	NA

Intent

To ensure that the site is assessed for environmental contamination and if contaminated, that the environmental contamination has been remediated to protect children's health.

Requirements

SCHOOLS

Conduct a Phase I Environmental Site Assessment (as described in ASTM E1527-05) to determine whether environmental contamination exists at the site. If contamination is suspected conduct a Phase II Environmental Site Assessment (as described in ASTM E1903-97, 2002).

Schools sites that are contaminated by past use as a landfill are ineligible for LEED certification. If a site is otherwise contaminated, it must be remediated to meet local, state, or federal EPA region residential (unrestricted) standards, whichever is most stringent. Documentation from the authority (such as EPA's "Ready for Reuse" document) must be provided to prove that safe levels of contamination have been achieved. Because the remediation process leads to significant environmental benefit, 1 point in SS Credit 3: Brownfield Redevelopment can be achieved for successful documented remediation of the site.

	SS
NC	NA
SCHOOLS	Prerequisite 2
CS	NA

1. Benefits and Issues to Consider

Environmental Issues

Daily school activities create numerous opportunities for students to come into direct contact with soil. On school playgrounds, younger children may sit, crawl, or play on the ground or put things in their mouths that have touched soil. Students of all ages are exposed to soil during regular use of playing fields.

Exposure to harmful substances can have a significant impact on children's health and well-being. Children are at greater risk than adults for exposure to and possible illness from environmental hazards because of their decreased ability to detoxify substances and greater sensitivity during development and growth. Cumulative exposure to environmental pollutants may lead to the development of serious health problems, both in the short term and later in life. Children are at risk of developing learning disabilities, chronic and acute respiratory diseases, cancer, and other illnesses caused by damage to the nervous system from hazardous substances. The incidence of chronic childhood diseases such as asthma and bronchitis is increasing. Additionally, cancer rates are increasing, especially childhood cancers such as leukemia.

Many potential building sites in urban locations have been abandoned because of actual or possible contamination from previous industrial or municipal activities. Although contaminated sites may be unavoidable in certain urban neighborhoods, identifying contaminants and remediating these sites can help ensure that schools are safe environments for all occupants.

Economic Issues

Phase I environmental site assessments are often required by lending agencies or local building codes. The cost of conducting the assessment is relatively inexpensive compared with the overall construction costs of a project. If there is potential for contamination, the cost of a Phase II environmental site assessment can be somewhat greater. Remediation of brownfield sites can be costly and time-intensive if extensive effort is required to characterize the contamination, evaluate cleanup options, and perform cleanup activities. However, substantially lower property costs can offset remediation costs and time delays. The cost of remediation strategies varies by site and region.

2. Related Credits

Projects that both conduct Phase I and Phase II environmental site assessments and implement site remediation efforts as described in this prerequisite are eligible to achieve the following credit:

- SS Credit 3: Brownfield Redevelopment

3. Summary of Referenced Standards

ASTM E1527-05, Phase I Environmental Site Assessment
ASTM International
http://www.astm.org

A Phase I environmental site assessment is a report prepared for a real estate holding that identifies potential or existing environmental contamination liabilities. The analysis typically addresses both the underlying land as well as physical improvements to the property; however, a Phase I assessment does not involve actual collection of physical samples or chemical analyses of any kind. It includes consideration of potential soil contamination, groundwater quality, and surface water quality and sometimes considers issues related to hazardous substance uptake by biota. The examination of a site may include these actions: definition of any chemical residues within structures; identification of possible asbestos in building materials; inventory of hazardous substances stored or used on site; assessment of mold and mildew; and evaluation of other indoor air quality parameters.

ASTM E1903-97, Phase II Environmental Site Assessment, effective 2002
ASTM International
http://www.astm.org

	SS
NC	NA
SCHOOLS	Prerequisite 2
CS	NA

A Phase II environmental site assessment is an investigation that collects original samples of soil, groundwater, or building materials to analyze for quantitative values of various contaminants. This investigation is normally undertaken when a Phase I assessment has determined a potential for site contamination. The substances most frequently tested are petroleum hydrocarbons, heavy metals, pesticides, solvents, asbestos, and mold.

4. Implementation

Conduct a Phase I environmental site assessment with the assistance of remediation experts. There are many ways to determine whether a site may be contaminated. No physical testing of soil, water, or air is performed in this phase, and it usually takes only a few weeks to determine the results. The assessment should be performed by a professional and must include the following:

1. A review of historical records related to the site. This should include local, state, and federal databases; site plans, permits, and deeds; aerial photographs and topographic maps; previous environmental reports, and so on.

2. A visit to the site to identify potential features or elements that may indicate the presence of hazardous substances. During the visit, the environmental professional will note factors such as stains, corrosion, odors, areas of stagnant water, and the presence of storage containers, drums, or piping. Possible migration pathways, sewage and wastewater systems, and adjacent properties may also be assessed.

3. Interviews with people who know the site's history and use, such as owners or managers of the site, government officials, or neighbors.

4. A report documenting the results of the analysis, assessing the potential for the existence of contamination, and identifying whether additional investigation is needed.

If there are no signs of suspected contamination from the Phase I assessment, no additional testing is required for compliance with SS Prerequisite 2.

If the Phase I assessment finds reasons to suspect contamination of the site and recommends further testing, a Phase II assessment must be performed to determine what corrections, if any, are necessary. This assessment consists of collecting samples from the site to be analyzed for suspected contaminants, such as petroleum hydrocarbons, heavy metals, solvents, pesticides, asbestos, or mold. If critical levels of contaminants are found during the Phase II assessment, the site must be remediated to residential (unrestricted) use standards to meet this prerequisite. However, former landfill sites cannot be remediated to meet the prerequisite requirements and should not be selected as building sites for schools.

Remediation actions depend on the nature of the contamination. Common strategies include pump-and-treat activities, bioreactors, land farming, and in situ remediation. It is strongly recommended that projects use standards equivalent or more stringent than EPA Region 9 cleanup standards in developing the remediation plan, since these are set at the most appropriate level for protecting children's health and safety.

5. Timeline and Team

During the site selection process, developers should contract with environmental professionals to conduct site assessments and, if necessary, determine a schedule for cleanup based on the remediation methods selected. If a site is determined to be contaminated, contact state and local regulators to identify the rules governing the site and explore financial assistance programs. It may also be helpful to contact the regional EPA Office of Solid Waste and Emergency Response, which may provide site characterization and remediation support. General contractors need to incorporate remediation activities into the construction schedule.

6. Calculations

There are no calculations associated with this credit.

7. Documentation Guidance

As a first step in preparing to complete the LEED-Online documentation requirements, work through the following measures. Refer to LEED-Online for the complete descriptions of all required documentation.

- Retain copies of the executive summaries from all ASTM site assessments performed.

- If remediation efforts were necessary, prepare a description of the efforts.

- Acquire documentation from the governing authority (local, state, or federal EPA region) that shows remediation to standards for residential (unrestricted) use has been completed.

8. Examples

There are no examples for this credit.

9. Exemplary Performance

This prerequisite is not eligible for exemplary performance under the Innovation in Design section.

10. Regional Variations

Preliminary screening levels or remediation criteria may differ by region. Be aware of the stringency of local and regional criteria relative to EPA standards.

11. Operations and Maintenance Considerations

For project sites that complete the Phase I and II assessment process and require ongoing remediation, the project team and owner should keep careful records of remediation activities and develop a plan for ongoing compliance with the monitoring and reporting requirements of the relevant federal, state, or local regulatory agency.

12. Resources

Please see USGBC's LEED Registered Project Tools (http://www.usgbc.org/projecttools) for additional resources and technical information. For resources related to site remediation, please see SS Credit 3: Brownfield Redevelopment.

California Department of Toxic Substance Control
http://www.dtsc.ca.gov/Schools/index.cfm
The mission of this department is to "assist school districts in the assessment of school properties by ensuring that environmental conditions are expeditiously investigated, evaluated, and if necessary, remediated to protect public health and the environment."

Preliminary Remediation Goals for EPA Region 9
http://www.epa.gov/region09/waste/sfund/prg/files/04prgtable.pdf
Preliminary remediation goals are tools for evaluating and cleaning up contaminated sites. They are intended to help risk assessors and others perform initial screening-level evaluations of environmental measurement results. The remediation goals for Region 9 are generic; they are calculated without site specific information. However, they may be recalculated using site-specific data.

13. Definitions

A **brownfield** is real property whose use may be complicated by the presence or possible presence of a hazardous substance, pollutant, or contaminant.

In situ remediation involves treating contaminants in place using injection wells, reactive trenches, or other technologies that take advantage of the natural hydraulic gradient of groundwater; they usually minimize disturbance of the site.

Remediation is the process of cleaning up a contaminated site by physical, chemical, or biological means. Remediation processes are typically applied to contaminated soil and groundwater.

A **site assessment** is an evaluation of a site's aboveground and subsurface characteristics, including its structures, geology, and hydrology. Site assessments are typically used to determine whether contamination has occurred, as well as the extent and concentration of any release of pollutants. Information generated during a site assessment is used to make remedial action decisions.

	SS
NC	NA
SCHOOLS	Prerequisite 2
CS	NA

	NC	SCHOOLS	CS
Credit	SS Credit 1	SS Credit 1	SS Credit 1
Points	1 point	1 point	1 point

Intent

To avoid the development of inappropriate sites and reduce the environmental impact from the location of a building on a site.

Requirements

NC, SCHOOLS & CS

Do not develop buildings, hardscape, roads or parking areas on portions of sites that meet any of the following criteria:

- Prime farmland as defined by the U.S. Department of Agriculture in the United States Code of Federal Regulations, Title 7, Volume 6, Parts 400 to 699, Section 657.5 (citation 7CFR657.5).

- Previously undeveloped land whose elevation is lower than 5 feet above the elevation of the 100-year flood as defined by the Federal Emergency Management Agency (FEMA).

- Land specifically identified as habitat for any species on federal or state threatened or endangered lists.

- Land within 100 feet of any wetlands as defined by the U.S. Code of Federal Regulations 40 CFR, Parts 230-233 and Part 22, and isolated wetlands or areas of special concern identified by state or local rule, OR within setback distances from wetlands prescribed in state or local regulations, as defined by local or state rule or law, whichever is more stringent.

- Previously undeveloped land that is within 50 feet of a water body, defined as seas, lakes, rivers, streams and tributaries that support or could support fish, recreation or industrial use, consistent with the terminology of the Clean Water Act.

- Land that prior to acquisition for the project was public parkland, unless land of equal or greater value as parkland is accepted in trade by the public landowner (park authority projects are exempt).

	SS
NC	Credit 1
SCHOOLS	Credit 1
CS	Credit 1

1. Benefits and Issues to Consider

Environmental Issues

As nonurban development increases, the importance of prudent site selection increases as well. Prevention of habitat encroachment is an essential element of sustainable site selection. The best strategy for selecting a building site is to choose a previously developed site. Because these sites have already been disturbed, further damage to the environment is limited and sensitive land areas can be preserved. This prevents the need for expanded transportation and utility infrastructure and likely affords building occupants more access to alternative transportation, further limiting the overall environmental impact of the development project.

The site surrounding a building defines its character and provides the first impression for its occupants and visitors. Creative and careful site designs can integrate natural surroundings with a building, providing a strong connection between the built and natural environments and minimizing adverse impacts on the undisturbed portions of a site. For school projects, this connection with the natural world can help students see how a school building and its occupants exist within a larger ecosystem.

Habitat preservation is the most effective means to meet the requirements of the Endangered Species Act and to minimize developmental impacts on indigenous wildlife. Not building on inappropriate sites preserves these areas for wildlife, recreation, and ecological balance.

Economic Issues

Site selection can play an important role in the way that the public responds to and gets involved with a proposed development. Channeling development away from sensitive ecological areas in favor of previously disturbed sites can encourage public support for a project and speed public review periods, thus minimizing or preventing obstacles traditionally encountered during project scoping. Economically, this can also save on mitigation costs that a developer would incur if the proposed development were approved within a sensitive area.

Appropriate site selection can reduce the risk of property damage due to natural events such as landslides, floods, sinkholes, and soil erosion. Although site survey and selection activities may entail initial costs, increased property values can offset these costs in the future.

2. Related Credits

Previously developed sites are more likely to have access to established public transportation systems and community services and may also present an opportunity to remediate a contaminated site. Protecting sensitive areas of the site by limiting development to a smaller footprint can increase open space and protect habitat. For these reasons, this credit is related to the following:

- SS Credit 2: Development Density and Community Connectivity
- SS Credit 3: Brownfield Redevelopment
- SS Credit 4.1: Alternative Transportation—Public Transportation Access
- SS Credit 5.1; Site Development—Protect or Restore Habitat
- SS Credit 5.2: Site Development—Maximize Open Space
- SS Credit 6.1: Stormwater Design—Quantity Control
- SS Credit 6.2: Stormwater Design—Quality Control

3. Summary of Referenced Standards

U.S. Department of Agriculture, United States Code of Federal Regulations Title 7, Volume 6, Parts 400 to 699, Section 657.5 (citation 7CFR657.5), Definition of Prime Agricultural Land

http://www.gpoaccess.gov/cfr/index.html

Go to "Browse and/or search the CFR." See also "Identification of Important Farmlands."

ftp://ftp-fc.sc.egov.usda.gov/CT/soils/2007_prime-important.pdf

This standard states, "Prime farmland is land that has the best combination of physical and chemical characteristics for producing food, feed, forage, fiber, and oilseed crops and is also available for these uses (the land could be cropland, pastureland, rangeland, forest land, or other land, but not urban built-up land or water). It has the soil quality, growing season, and moisture supply needed to economically produce sustained high yields of crops when treated and managed, including water management, according to acceptable farming methods. In general, prime farmlands have an adequate and dependable water supply from precipitation or irrigation, a favorable temperature and growing season, acceptable acidity or alkalinity, acceptable salt and sodium content, and few or no rocks. They are permeable to water and air. Prime farmlands are not excessively erodible or saturated with water for a long period of time, and they either do not flood frequently or are protected from flooding. Examples of soils that qualify as prime farmland are Palouse silt loam, 0% to 7% slopes; Brookston silty clay loam, drained; and Tama silty clay loam, 0% to 5% slopes."

Federal Emergency Management Agency, Definition of 100-Year Flood

Federal Emergency Management Agency

www.fema.gov

This referenced standard addresses flood elevations. FEMA defines a 100-year flood as the flood elevation that has a 1% chance of being reached or exceeded each year. It is not the most significant flood in a 100-year period. Instead, 100-year floods can occur many times within a 100-year period. See the FEMA website for comprehensive information on floods.

Endangered Species Lists

U.S. Fish and Wildlife Service, List of Threatened and Endangered Species

http://www.fws.gov/endangered/

This referenced standard addresses threatened and endangered wildlife and plants. The service also maintains a list of the country's native plants and animals that are candidates for addition to the federal list.

National Marine Fisheries Service, List of Endangered Marine Species

http://www.nmfs.noaa.gov/pr/species/esa_species.htm

In addition to this federal list, state agencies provide state-specific lists of endangered or threatened wildlife and plant species.

United States Code of Federal Regulations, 40 CFR, Parts 230-233, and Part 22, Definition of Wetlands

http://www.gpoaccess.gov/cfr/index.html

This referenced standard addresses wetlands and discharges of dredged or filled material into waters regulated by states. The definition of wetland areas pertaining to this credit, found in Part 230, is as follows: "Wetlands consist of areas that are inundated or saturated by surface or ground water at a frequency and duration sufficient to support, and that under normal circumstances do support, a prevalence of vegetation typically adapted for life in saturated soil conditions."

4. Implementation

Before selecting a site, evaluate the potential environmental disturbance that will occur as a result of construction, and avoid developing sites that exhibit any of the characteristics listed in the restricted criteria. After considering the proposed use of the building, compile a list of sites that have already

	SS
NC	Credit 1
SCHOOLS	Credit 1
CS	Credit 1

been developed that fit the needs for the building's use. Inventorying the important environmental characteristics of a site will help the project team protect resources and ecological services.

Restricted areas include previously undeveloped land that is within 50 feet of a water body. As defined in the Clean Water Act, small man-made ponds such as those used in stormwater retention, fire suppression, and recreation, are exempt from this requirement. Man-made wetlands and other water bodies created to restore natural habitats and ecological systems are not exempt and must meet the 50-foot setback criteria to comply with the requirements of this credit.

Once a site has been selected, consider taking measures to preserve the site's natural features, and use design features that complement these natural features. Building in dense blocks can minimize the development footprint and site disturbance and help preserve the site's ecologically significant areas. It may be appropriate to incorporate some of the site's existing natural features into the design, such as natural shelter from trees or terrain, natural areas for outdoor activities, and water features for thermal, acoustic, and aesthetic benefit. Building designers should also take into account wildlife that lives on the site. For example, glazing on buildings sited near open space, wetlands, and water bodies that naturally attract birds can increase the potential for bird collisions. Site buildings on the property to minimize the reflection of existing vegetation. Buildings facing open space, wetlands, and water bodies may require measures to reduce the potential for bird collisions. (See bird-safe strategies and references under SS Credits 5.1 and 5.2.)

5. Timeline and Team

During the site selection process, the project team should include landscape architects, ecologists, environmental engineers, and civil engineers, as well as local professionals who can provide site-specific expertise. A government official, ecologist, or other qualified professional should survey the site and inventory the important environmental characteristics, including wetlands, sloped areas, important habitat areas, and forested areas. Community coordination and consideration of public comments can help preempt negative community reaction.

6. Calculations

There are no calculations required for this credit.

7. Documentation Guidance

As a first step in preparing to complete the LEED-Online documentation requirements, work through the following measures. Refer to LEED-Online for the complete descriptions of all required documentation.

- Record any special circumstances regarding compliance with the site selection criteria.

8. Examples

There are no examples for this credit.

9. Exemplary Performance

This credit is not eligible for exemplary performance under the Innovation in Design section.

10. Regional Variations

There are no regional variations associated with this credit.

11. Operations and Maintenance Considerations

Environmentally sensitive portions of the site should be protected during both initial construction and later facility alterations and additions. For sites that contain environmentally sensitive areas, clearly demarcate on the site plans the sections that should be protected and remain undeveloped during future alterations and additions. Include labels that describe the nature of the sensitive area and ensure that these documents are transferred to the building owners and the facility manager and staff.

12. Resources

Please see USGBC's LEED Registered Project Tools (http://www.usgbc.org/projecttools) for additional resources and technical information.

Websites

ESRI

http://www.esri.com/

This software company creates tools for geographic information systems (GIS) mapping. Its website includes an option to make a map of all flood areas within a user-defined location.

Natural Resources Defense Council

http://www.nrdc.org

NRDC uses law, science, and advocacy to protect wildlife and wild places and to ensure a safe and healthy environment.

Print Media

Constructed Wetlands in the Sustainable Landscape, by Craig Campbell and Michael Ogden (John Wiley & Sons, 1999).

Holding Our Ground: Protecting America's Farms and Farmland, by Tom Daniels and Deborah Bowers (Island Press, 1997).

Saved By Development: Preserving Environmental Areas, Farmland, by Rick Pruetz (Arje Press, 1997).

Wetland Indicators: A Guide to Wetland Identification, Delineation, Classification, and Mapping, by Ralph W. Tiner (Lewis Publishers, 1999).

13. Definitions

The **development footprint** is the area affected by development or by project site activity. Hardscape, access roads, parking lots, nonbuilding facilities, and the building itself are all included in the development footprint.

An **ecosystem** is a basic unit of nature that includes a community of organisms and their nonliving environment linked by biological, chemical, and physical processes.

An **endangered species** is threatened with extinction because of harmful human activities or environmental factors.

Previously developed sites once had buildings, roadways, parking lots, or were graded or otherwise altered by direct human activities.

LEED REFERENCE GUIDE FOR GREEN BUILDING DESIGN AND CONSTRUCTION

	NC	SCHOOLS	CS
Credit	SS Credit 2	SS Credit 2	SS Credit 2
Points	5 points	4 points	5 points

Intent

To channel development to urban areas with existing infrastructure, protect greenfields and preserve habitat and natural resources.

Requirements

NC, SCHOOLS & CS

OPTION 1. Development Density

Construct or renovate a building on a previously developed site AND in a community with a minimum density of 60,000 square feet per acre net. The density calculation is based on a typical two-story downtown development and must include the area of the project being built.

SCHOOLS Additional Requirement

For the purposes of this option, physical education spaces that are part of the project site, such as playing fields and associated buildings used during sporting events only (e.g., concession stands) and playgrounds with play equipment, are excluded from the development density calculations.

OR

OPTION 2. Community Connectivity

Construct or renovate a building on a site that meets the following criteria:

- Is located on a previously developed site
- Is within 1/2 mile of a residential area or neighborhood with an average density of 10 units per acre net
- Is within 1/2 mile of at least 10 basic services
- Has pedestrian access between the building and the services

For mixed-use projects, no more than 1 service within the project boundary may be counted as 1 of the 10 basic services, provided it is open to the public. No more than 2 of the 10 services required may be anticipated (i.e. at least 8 must be existing and operational). In addition, the anticipated services must demonstrate that they will be operational in the locations indicated within 1 year of occupation of the applicant project. Examples of basic services include the following:

NC, SCHOOLS & CS (continued)

- Bank
- Place of Worship
- Convenience Grocery
- Day Care Center
- Cleaners
- Fire Station
- Beauty Salon
- Hardware

- Laundry
- Library
- Medical or Dental Office
- Senior Care Facility
- Park
- Pharmacy
- Post Office
- Restaurant

- School
- Supermarket
- Theater
- Community Center
- Fitness Center
- Museum

NC & CS Additional Requirement

Proximity is determined by drawing a 1/2-mile radius around a main building entrance on a site map and counting the services within that radius.

SCHOOLS Additional Requirement

Proximity is determined by drawing a 1/2-mile radius around any building entrance on a site map and counting the services within that radius.

1. Benefits and Issues to Consider

Urban sprawl affects quality of life because commuters spend increasing amounts of time in automobiles. In addition, families often require more vehicles to accommodate their needs, resulting in higher costs of living. The redevelopment of urban areas helps restore, invigorate, and sustain established urban living patterns, creating a more stable and interactive community.

	SS
NC	Credit 2
SCHOOLS	Credit 2
CS	Credit 2

Environmental Issues

Consider proximity to transportation and community services. Developments located within walking distance of existing or planned basic services limit urban sprawl and reduce transportation impacts, such as air pollution and greenhouse gas emissions. Facilitating walkable access to basic services may improve productivity of building occupants by reducing the time spent driving and finding parking space. In addition, increased levels of physical activity can improve occupants' health.

Urban redevelopment affects all areas of site design, including site selection, transportation planning, building density, and stormwater management. Many cities have existing buildings that could be rehabilitated, an approach that reduces the demand for new materials. The potential trade-offs for sites in dense areas include limited open space and factors that could harm indoor environmental quality, such as contaminated soils, undesirable air quality, or limited daylighting opportunities.

Economic Issues

A significant economic benefit of infill development is that it may make new infrastructure, including roads, utility services, and other amenities, unnecessary. If public transportation serves an urban site, a project's parking capacity can be downsized, with significant cost reductions. Urban infill development sometimes requires significant additional costs compared with suburban development because of site constraints, contaminated soils, and other issues. However, municipal and county incentives for urban infill projects may be available.

SCHOOLS Students who can easily and safely walk or bike to after-school activities learn to become self-sufficient without depending on cars, establishing a healthy precedent for their future lifestyle choices.

Locating a school close to community resources provides enhanced educational opportunities both during and after school hours. Community-oriented activities can be integrated into the curriculum, encouraging students to become actively engaged in hands-on learning. Facilities such as parks, libraries, community centers, and other nearby schools can help expand a school's resources for academic and recreational instruction. Having a variety of establishments close to a school provides students with easy access to extracurricular activities and after-school jobs.

Building a school in a dense urban environment not only affords students, faculty, and staff greater access to community amenities, but also creates numerous opportunities for joint-use spaces that both the school and community can enjoy. On the other hand, security concerns may be heightened in a dense urban environment and are particularly important to address in shared spaces.

	SS
NC	Credit 2
SCHOOLS	Credit 2
CS	Credit 2

2. Related Credits

Channeling development toward urban areas increases the likelihood of locating the project on a previously developed area and near public transportation, thus assisting project teams with earning the following credits:

- SS Credit 1: Site Selection
- SS Credit 4.1: Alternative Transportation—Public Transportation Access

3. Summary of Referenced Standards

There are no standards referenced for this credit.

4. Implementation

To achieve this credit, the best approach is to give preference to sites in an urban area. Work with local jurisdictions to follow the area's urban development plan, and meet or exceed density goals. Consider using community resources and sharing the project building's resources with neighbors. Choose sites based on infrastructure, transportation, and quality-of-life considerations. Consider renovating an existing building in an area where community revitalization is already underway and the required development density will be met by the time the project is completed.

OPTION 1. Development Density

To determine the development density, assess the density of the LEED project site, as well as the densities of surrounding developments. Determine the total area of the project site and the total square footage of the building. For projects that are part of a larger property (such as a campus), define the project area (outlined in the LEED project's scope). The project area must be defined consistently throughout LEED documentation.

Calculate the density of the project site and the density radius using the equations below. Overlay the density radius on a site map that includes the project site and surrounding areas, originating from the center of the LEED project site. This is the density boundary. For each property within the density boundary, including the LEED project site and any properties that intersect the density boundary, create a table with the building square footage and site area of each property. Include all properties except for undeveloped public areas, such as parks and water bodies. Do not include public roads and right-of-way areas. Information on neighboring properties can be obtained from your city or county zoning department.

SCHOOLS For the purposes of this option, physical education spaces that have beenincluded as part of the project site—such as playing fields, buildings used during sporting events only (e.g., concession stands), and playgrounds with play equipment—are excluded from the development density calculations.

OPTION 2. Community Connectivity

Consider both residential and commercial neighbors when determining the community connectivity of a project. Prepare a site map (Figure 1) and draw a 1/2-mile radius around the main building entrance. Radii may be drawn around multiple entrances for projects with multiple buildings or more than 1 main entrance. The combination of the area in these radii would then be considered the project radius.

Figure 1. Sample Map for Community Connectivity

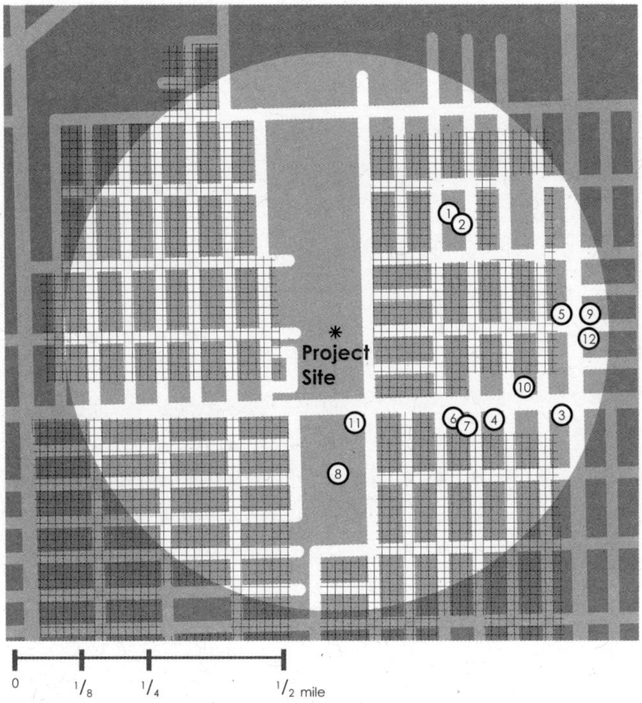

	SS
NC	Credit 2
SCHOOLS	Credit 2
CS	Credit 2

Legend:

① Mercantile National Bank, **Bank**
② Chicago Ghanaian Sda Church, **Place of Worship**
③ St. Gall Preschool, **Day Care**
④ Francia Unisex, **Beauty**
⑤ Ace Hardware, **Hardware**
⑥ Sevan Dal Medical Clinic, **Medical**
⑦ Lourdes E. Balquierda DDS, **Dental**
⑧ Senka Park, **Park**
⑨ Walgreens, **Pharmacy**
⑩ Pizza Castle, **Restaurant**
⑪ Sandoval Elementary, **School**
⑫ La Primera Grocery, **Supermarket**
▦ Residential Area with 10 units per Acre or more

Mark all residential developments within the radius. For the project to earn this credit, a residential area with a minimum density of 10 units per acre must be present within the radius.

Mark all commercial buildings within the radius. At least 10 basic services must be present within the radius for the project to earn this credit. Services other than those listed in the credit requirements will be considered on a project-by-project basis.

List each of the identified services, the business name, and the service type to confirm compliance. Table 1 illustrates an example.

	SS
NC	Credit 2
SCHOOLS	Credit 2
CS	Credit 2

Table 1. Sample Community Connectivity Tabulation

Service Identification (Corresponds to uploaded Vicinity Plan)	Business Name	Service Type
1	Restaurant 1	Restaurant
2	Grocery 1	Convenience Grocery
3	Urgent Care 1	Medical
4	Pharmacy 1	Pharmacy
5	Gym 1	Fitness
6	Hair Care 1	Beauty
7	Bank 1	Bank
8	Restaurant 2	Restaurant
9	Cleaners 1	Cleaners
10	Post Office 1	Post Office

With the exception of restaurants, no service may be counted more than once in the calculation. Up to 2 restaurants may be counted toward achievement of this credit. Count only those services that can be accessed by pedestrians from the project; that is, pedestrians must be able to walk to the services without being blocked by walls, highways, or other barriers.

The project building itself cannot be considered 1 of the 10 basic services; however, in a mixed-use building, a maximum of 1 service within the building may be counted as 1 of the 10. A service in a mixed-use project must be open to the public.

Up to 2 services that are anticipated to be built in the near future can count toward this credit; at least 8 services must be existing and operational. Any anticipated services must be documented by lease agreements or other appropriate documentation (e.g., a letter from the owner or other appropriate party) to demonstrate that they will be operational in the locations indicated within a year of occupation of the project building.

5. Timeline and Team

During the site selection process, the building owner and developer, along with the entire team, should assess various options for locating the building based on density and proximity to existing infrastructure to meet the requirements of this credit

6. Calculations

OPTION 1. Development Density

STEP 1

Calculate the development density for the project by dividing the total square footage of the building by the total site area in acres. The development density must be 60,000 square feet or more per acre (Equation 1).

Equation 1

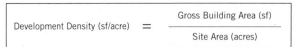

$$\text{Development Density (sf/acre)} = \frac{\text{Gross Building Area (sf)}}{\text{Site Area (acres)}}$$

STEP 2

Convert the total site area from acres to square feet and calculate the square root of this number. Then multiply the square root by 3 to determine the appropriate density radius (Equation 2). The square root function normalizes the calculation by removing effects of site shape.

Equation 2

$$\text{Density Radius (lf)} \quad = \quad 3 \quad X \quad \sqrt{\left[\text{Site Area (acres)} \quad X \quad 43,560 \text{ (sf/acre)} \right]}$$

STEP 3

Calculate the average property density within the density boundary by adding up the square footage values and site areas of each property and dividing the total square footage by the total site area. The average property density of the properties within the density boundary must be 60,000 square feet or more per acre. If this requirement is met, LEED for New Construction and LEED for Core & Shell projects earn 5 points under this credit; LEED for Schools projects earn 4 points.

Equation 3

$$\frac{\text{Average Property Density}}{\text{within Density Boundary}} \quad = \quad \frac{\Sigma \text{ Square Footage}}{\Sigma \text{ Site Area}}$$

OPTION 2. Community Connectivity

There are no calculations required for this option.

7. Documentation Guidance

As a first step in preparing to complete the LEED-Online documentation requirements, work through the following measures. Refer to LEED-Online for the complete descriptions of all required documentation.

- For development density, keep records of the project site and building development area and prepare a project site vicinity plan that highlights the development density radius.

- For community connectivity projects, create a site vicinity plan that highlights the half-mile radius, locations and types of qualifying services, and location of residential areas.

8. Examples

EXAMPLE 1. Development Density

A 30,000-square-foot office building is located on a 0.44-acre urban site. The building density, calculated by dividing the square footage of the building space by the site area in acres, is 68,182 square feet per acre (Table 2). The density thus exceeds the 60,000 minimum required by the credit.

Table 2. Building Density Calculation

Project Building	Building Space (sf)	Site Area (acres)
Project	30,000	0.44
Density (sf/acre)		68,182

Next, the density radius is calculated using the following equation.

Equation 2

$$\text{Density Radius (lf)} \quad = \quad 3 \quad X \quad \sqrt{\left[.0.44 \text{ (acres)} \quad X \quad 43,560 \text{ (sf/acre)} \right]} \quad = \quad 415 \text{ (feet)}$$

The density radius of 415 feet is applied to an area plan of the project site and surrounding area.

	SS
NC	Credit 2
SCHOOLS	Credit 2
CS	Credit 2

The plan identifies all properties that are within or are intersected by the density radius. The plan includes a scale and a north indicator (Figure 2).

Figure 2. Sample Area Plan

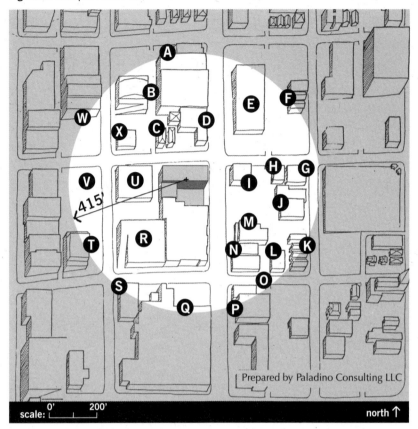

Prepared by Paladino Consulting LLC

scale: 0' 200'   north ↑

For each property located within the density radius, the project team determined the building space and site area (Table 3). These values are summed and the average density is calculated by dividing the total building square footage by the total site area.

Table 3. Sample Area Properties

Properties within Density Radius	Building Space (sf)	Site Area (acres)		Properties within Density Radius	Building Space (sf)	Site Area (acres)
Project Site	30,000	0.44		M	24,080	0.64
A	33,425	0.39		N	28,740	0.3
B	87,500	1.58		O	6,690	0.15
C	6,350	0.26		P	39,000	0.39
D	27,560	0.32		Q	348,820	2.54
E	66,440	1.17		R	91,250	1.85
F	14,420	1.36		S	22,425	0.27
G	12,560	0.2		T	33,650	0.51
H	6,240	0.14		U	42,400	0.52
I	14,330	0.22		V	—	0.76
J	29,570	0.41		W	19,200	0.64
K	17,890	0.31		X	6,125	0.26
L	9,700	0.31				
Total Building Space (sf)					1,018,36	
Total Site Area (acres)					5	15.94
Average Density (sf/acre)						63,887

	SS
NC	Credit 2
SCHOOLS	Credit 2
CS	Credit 2

For this example, the average building density of the surrounding area is greater than 60,000 square feet per acre; thus, the example qualifies for 5 points under LEED for New Construction or LEED for Core & Shell.

EXAMPLE 2. Community Connectivity

A LEED for Schools project is located in a suburban neighborhood. To determine the connectivity of the project, both residential and commercial adjacencies must be considered.

A site map is prepared (See Figure 1, above) and a 1/2-mile radius is drawn around the school building's main entrance. Residential developments within the radius are identified. A residential area with a minimum density of 10 units per acre is identified within the radius and labeled on the site map.

Ten basic services are located within the 1/2-mile radius and within pedestrian access. Table 4 illustrates this example.

Table 4. Sample Community Connectivity Tabulation

Service Identification (Corresponds to uploaded Vicinity Plan)	Business Name	Service Type
1	Bush's Garden of Eating	Restaurant
2	Goodwells Natural Foods	Convenience Grocery
3	Detroit Medical Center	Medical
4	Knight's Drugs	Pharmacy
5	Cass United Methodist	Place of Worship
6	3rd Avenue Hardware Co.	Hardware
7	National City Bank	Bank
8	Deli Unique	Restaurant
9	University Cleaners	Cleaners
10	Burton International	School

In this example, the LEED for Schools project earns 4 points for demonstrating community connectivity.

9. Exemplary Performance

Based on evidence that higher-density locations can achieve substantially and quantifiably higher environmental benefits, the following threshold requirements can be used to qualify a LEED for New Construction, a LEED for Core & Shell, and a LEED for Schools project for exemplary performance under the Innovation in Design section. Projects must first meet the requirements of Option 1 under SS Credit 2, Development Density and Community Connectivity. Additionally, the project must meet 1 of the 2 following requirements:

- The project itself must have a density at least double that of the average density within the calculated area (see Equations 1 and 3).

OR

- The average density within an area twice as large as that for the base credit achievement must be at least 120,000 square feet per acre. To double the area, use Equation 2 but double the project site area first.

10. Regional Variations

There are no regional variations associated with this credit.

11. Operations and Maintenance Considerations

Buildings in dense urban centers, particularly in zero lot-line situations, can present challenges for sustainable operations practices that require space. For example, designating adequate space for recycling storage is more difficult than for projects on expansive lots. During design, the project team should consider the critical aspects of sustainable operations and ensure that the building's layout supports these functions.

Densely developed communities may have air quality problems, making it difficult for building occupants and facility operators to address health and comfort issues. Consider optimizing the building's design for air quality protection by positioning air intakes away from pollutant sources, using superior filtration media, and selecting materials that do not contribute to indoor air quality issues. Encourage building operations staff to actively manage for high indoor air quality through the use of EPA's Indoor Air Quality Building Education and Assessment Model, known as I-BEAM) or other strategies.

	SS
NC	Credit 2
SCHOOLS	Credit 2
CS	Credit 2

12. Resources

Please see USGBC's LEED Registered Project Tools (http://www.usgbc.org/projecttools) for additional resources and technical information.

Websites

Congress for New Urbanism

http://www.cnu.org

The Congress for New Urbanism promotes the efficient use of infrastructure and the preservation of habitats and farmland.

International Union for the Scientific Study of Population

http://www.iussp.org

IUSSP promotes scientific studies of demography and population-related issues.

Urban Land Institute

ULI Washington

http://www.washington.uli.org

The Urban Land Institute is a nonprofit organization based in Washington, D.C., that promotes the responsible use of land to enhance the total environment.

Print Media

Changing Places: Rebuilding Community in the Age of Sprawl, by Richard Moe and Carter Wilkie (Henry Holt & Company, 1999).

Density by Design: New Directions in Residential Development, by Steven Fader (Urban Land Institute, 2000).

Green Development: Integrating Ecology and Real Estate, by Alex Wilson, et al. (John Wiley & Sons, 1998).

Once There Were Greenfields: How Urban Sprawl Is Undermining America's Environment, Economy, and Social Fabric, by F. Kaid Benfield, et al. (Natural Resources Defense Council, 1999).

Suburban Nation: The Rise of Sprawl and the Decline of the American Dream, by Andres Duany, et al. (North Point Press, 2000).

13. Definitions

Building density is the floor area of the building divided by the total area of the site (square feet per acre).

Greenfields are sites not previously developed or graded that could support open space, habitat, or agriculture.

A **mixed-use** project involves a combination of residential and commercial or retail components.

Neighborhood is synonymous with **residential area**.

Pedestrian access allows people to walk to services without being blocked by walls, freeways, or other barriers.

Previously developed sites once had buildings, roadways, parking lots, or were graded or otherwise altered by direct human activities.

Property area is the total area within the legal property boundaries of a site; it encompasses all areas of the site, including constructed and nonconstructed areas.

	SS
NC	Credit 2
SCHOOLS	Credit 2
CS	Credit 2

Public transportation consists of bus, rail, or other transit services for the general public that operate on a regular, continual basis.

A **residential area** is land zoned primarily for housing at a density of 10 units per acre or greater. These areas may have single-family and multifamily housing and include building types such as townhomes, apartments, duplexes, condominiums, or mobile homes.

Site area is synonymous with property area.

BROWNFIELD REDEVELOPMENT

	NC	SCHOOLS	CS
Credit	SS Credit 3	SS Credit 3	SS Credit 3
Points	1 point	1 point	1 point

Intent

To rehabilitate damaged sites where development is complicated by environmental contamination and to reduce pressure on undeveloped land.

Requirements

NC & CS

OPTION 1

Develop on a site documented as contaminated (by means of an ASTM E1903-97 Phase II Environmental Site Assessment or a local voluntary cleanup program).

OR

OPTION 2

Develop on a site defined as a brownfield by a local, state, or federal government agency.

SCHOOLS

Projects can achieve this point only via SS Prerequisite 2: Environmental Site Assessment and remediating site contamination.

	SS
NC	Credit 3
SCHOOLS	Credit 3
CS	Credit 3

1. Benefits and Issues to Consider

Environmental Issues

Many potential building sites in urban locations have been abandoned because of actual or possible contamination from previous industrial or municipal activities. EPA estimates that there are more than 450,000 brownfields in the United States.[3] These sites can be remediated and redeveloped for reuse. Remediation efforts remove hazardous materials from a site's soil and groundwater, reducing the exposure of humans and wildlife to health risks as a result of environmental pollution. Redevelopment of brownfield sites provides an alternative to developing on greenfield sites, preserving undeveloped areas for future generations and decreasing the overall environmental impact of development. Brownfields often have existing infrastructure improvements that make the construction of new utilities and roads unnecessary, avoiding further environmental impacts. In some instances, rather than remediate the contamination, it may be more sensible to leave contaminants in place and instead stabilize and isolate the contaminants to prevent human exposure.

Economic Issues

Remediation of brownfield sites can be costly and time-intensive if extensive effort is required to characterize the contamination, evaluate cleanup options, and perform cleanup activities. However, substantially lower property costs can offset remediation costs and time delays. The cost of remediation strategies varies by site and region.

Weigh the value of a remediated property against cleanup costs to determine whether the site is economically viable for redevelopment. In the past, developers have been reluctant to redevelop brownfield sites because of potential liability associated with previous owners' contamination. In recent years, EPA and many state and local government agencies have begun to provide incentives for brownfield redevelopment by revising regulations to reduce the liability of developers who choose to remediate contaminated sites.

Perception of a building site by the building owner and future building occupants must also be weighed. Building owners may be wary of cleanup requirements and the potential for liability should contaminants migrate and affect neighbors. Building occupants may worry about health risks from breathing contaminated air or coming into contact with contaminated soil.

Brownfields can be in attractive locations and are often less expensive than similar uncontaminated properties. Additionally, remediation and reclamation of contaminated sites can increase local tax bases[4] and contribute to social and economic revitalization of depressed or disadvantaged neighborhoods.

2. Related Credits

Projects that are developed on brownfield sites will likely qualify for this credit as well:

- SS Credit 1: Site Selection

SCHOOLS   This credit is achieved by projects that conduct Phase I and Phase II environmental site assessments and document site remediation efforts. Refer to the following prerequisite:

- SS Prerequisite 2: Environmental Site Assessment

3. Summary of Referenced Standards

	SS
NC	Credit 3
SCHOOLS	Credit 3
CS	Credit 3

U.S. EPA, Definition of Brownfields

EPA Sustainable Redevelopment of Brownfields Program

www.epa.gov/brownfields

With certain legal exclusions and additions, "brownfield site" means real property, the expansion, redevelopment, or reuse of which may be complicated by the presence or potential presence of a hazardous substance, pollutant, or contaminant (Public Law 107-118, H.R. 2869, Small Business Liability Relief and Brownfields Revitalization Act). See the website for additional information and resources.

ASTM E1527-05, Phase I Environmental Site Assessment

ASTM International

http://www.astm.org

A Phase I environmental site assessment is a report prepared for a real estate holding that identifies potential or existing environmental contamination liabilities. The analysis typically addresses both the underlying land as well as physical improvements to the property; however, techniques applied in a Phase I assessment never include actual collection of physical samples or chemical analyses of any kind. It includes consideration of potential soil contamination, groundwater quality, surface water quality and sometimes considers issues related to hazardous substance uptake by biota. The examination of a site may include these actions: definition of any chemical residues within structures; identification of possible asbestos in building materials; inventory of hazardous substances stored or used on site; assessment of mold and mildew; and evaluation of other indoor air quality parameters.

ASTM E1903-97, Phase II Environmental Site Assessment, effective 2002

ASTM International

http://www.astm.org

Phase II environmental site assessment is an investigation that collects original samples of soil, groundwater, or building materials to analyze for quantitative values of various contaminants. This investigation is normally undertaken when a Phase I assessment has determined a potential for site contamination. The most frequent substances tested are petroleum hydrocarbons, heavy metals, pesticides, solvents, asbestos, and mold.

4. Implementation

If contamination is suspected, conduct a Phase II environmental site assessment to determine whether remediation of the site is necessary. The Phase II assessment requires that an environmental professional test the soil, air, and water to identify what kinds of contaminants exist and at what levels. The type of tests conducted varies, but typically the easiest and least expensive methods are used initially and involve taking samples, which are then sent to a laboratory for analysis. This initial sampling screens for broad categories of contaminants. If sufficient contamination is found or further investigation is needed, more sophisticated tests must be performed. Contaminant-specific testing involves more time and additional cost but is needed to identify specific contaminants and determine effective remediation strategies, if required.

Use remediation experts to develop a master plan for any site cleanup. Prioritize remediation activities according to available funds and specific site considerations, and establish time frames for completing each activity.

The site should be cleaned using proven technologies that will not damage aboveground or underground natural features. The appropriate technology for a specific site depends on the contaminants present, hydrogeologic conditions, and other factors. Traditional remediation efforts for contaminated groundwater are termed "pump-and-treat"; they involve pumping contaminated

SS	
NC	Credit 3
SCHOOLS	Credit 3
CS	Credit 3

groundwater to the surface and treating it with physical or chemical processes. Contaminated soils can be remediated in a variety of ways. Consider in situ remediation schemes that treat contaminants in place instead of off-site. Advanced technologies such as bioreactors and in situ applications are sometimes more cost-effective than hauling large quantities of contaminated soil to an approved disposal facility. Innovative remediation efforts (such as solar detoxification technologies) are currently being developed and are expected to reduce remediation costs in the future. Evaluate the environmental implications of each strategy to make sure that it will not cause problems elsewhere.

Finally, identify and implement the most cost-effective strategy, and once remediation is complete, continue to monitor the site for the identified contaminants to ensure that contamination problems do not return.

5. Timeline and Team

During the site selection process, developers should contract with an environmental consultant to conduct site assessments, identify contaminants, and determine a schedule for cleanup based on the remediation methods selected. Contact state and local regulators to identify the rules governing the site and find financial assistance programs. It may also be helpful to contact the regional EPA Office of Solid Waste and Emergency Response, which may provide site characterization and remediation support. General contractors need to incorporate remediation activities into the construction schedule.

6. Calculations

There are no calculations required for this credit.

7. Documentation Guidance

As a first step in preparing to complete the LEED-Online documentation requirements, work through the following measures. Refer to LEED-Online for the complete descriptions of all required documentation.

- For new construction and Core & Shell projects, prepare descriptions of site contamination and remediation efforts undertaken by the project.
- For schools projects, retain the executive summary from ASTM site assessments performed.

8. Examples

There are no examples for this credit.

9. Exemplary Performance

This credit is not eligible for exemplary performance under the Innovation in Design section.

10. Regional Variations

Preliminary screening levels or remediation criteria may differ by region.

11. Operations and Maintenance Considerations

Some remediation efforts may require ongoing activities. The project team and owner should keep careful records of remediation activities and develop a plan for ongoing compliance with the monitoring and reporting requirements of the relevant federal, state, or local regulatory agency.

12. Resources

Please see USGBC's LEED Registered Project Tools (www.usgbc.org/projecttools) for additional resources and technical information.

Brownfields Technology Support Center

http://www.brownfieldstsc.org

This public center provides technical support to federal, state, and local officials on issues related to site investigation and cleanup.

Environmental Law Institute, Brownfields Center

http://www.brownfieldscenter.org/big/about.shtml

The Environmental Law Institute's Brownfields Center provides information on brownfields cleanup and redevelopment with a focus on the concerns and needs of community groups across the country.

National Institutes of Health, National Institutes of Environmental Health Sciences, Superfund Basic Research Program

http://www.niehs.nih.gov/research/supported/sbrp/

The primary mission of SBRP is to support research and outreach activities that address the broad, complex health and environmental issues raised by hazardous waste sites.

New York State Department of Health, Guidance for Evaluating Vapor Intrusion

http://www.health.state.ny.us/environmental/investigations/soil_gas/svi_guidance/index.htm

This document provides guidance on identifying and addressing actual and potential human exposure to subsurface vapors associated with known or suspected volatile chemical contaminants.

Preliminary Remediation Goals for EPA Region 9

http://www.epa.gov/region09/waste/sfund/prg/files/04prgtable.pdf

Preliminary remediation goals are tools for evaluating and cleaning up contaminated sites. They are intended to help risk assessors and others perform initial screening-level evaluations of environmental measurement results. The remediation goals for Region 9 are generic; they are calculated without site specific information. However, they may be recalculated using site-specific data.

U.S. EPA, Office of Research and Development, Technical Approaches to Characterizing and Cleaning Up Brownfield Sites

http://www.epa.gov/ORD/NRMRL/pubs/625r00009/625r00009.htm

This document assists communities, decision makers, states, municipalities, researchers, and the private sector in addressing issues related to brownfield site redevelopment. The document helps users understand the problems associated with the redevelopment of these sites, the sources of information that could help to assess the sites, and the regulatory groups that should be involved in the process. The guidance has appendices of relevant terms, references, and applicable technologies.

U.S. EPA, Sustainable Redevelopment of Brownfields Program

http://www.epa.gov/brownfields

This is a comprehensive website on brownfields that includes projects, initiatives, tools, tax incentives and other resources to address brownfield remediation and redevelopment. For information by phone, contact your regional EPA office.

Print Media

ASTM Standard Practice E1739-95: Risk-Based Corrective Action Applied at Petroleum Release Sites, ASTM International

http://www.astm.org

This document is a guide for risk-based corrective action (RBCA), a decision-making process that is specific to cleaning up petroleum releases at contaminated sites. It presents a tiered approach to site assessment and remedial actions. It also includes a comprehensive appendix with risk calculations and sample applications.

SS	
NC	Credit 3
SCHOOLS	Credit 3
CS	Credit 3

EPA OSWER Directive 9610.17: Use of Risk-Based Decision-Making in UST Correction Action Programs, U.S. Environmental Protection Agency, Office of Underground Storage Tanks
http://www.epa.gov/swerust1/directiv/od961017.htm

This document addresses the application of risk-based decision-making techniques to properties where leaking underground storage tanks (USTs) pose risks to human health and the environment. The guidelines included can assist in making decisions in a manner consistent with federal law, specifically CERCLA and RCRA programs. Risk-based decision making uses risk and exposure assessment methodology to determine the extent and urgency of cleanup actions. The goal is to protect human health and the environment. This standard includes several examples of state programs that use risk-based decision making in legislation regarding leaking USTs.

13. Definitions

A **brownfield** is real property whose use may be complicated by the presence or possible presence of a hazardous substance, pollutant, or contaminant.

The **Comprehensive Environmental Response, Compensation, and Liability Act**, or CERCLA, is more commonly known as Superfund. Enacted in 1980, CERCLA addresses abandoned or historical waste sites and contamination by taxing the chemical and petroleum industries and providing federal authority to respond to releases of hazardous substances.

In situ remediation involves treating contaminants in place using injection wells, reactive trenches, or other technologies that take advantage of the natural hydraulic gradient of groundwater; they usually minimize disturbance of the site.

The **Resource Conservation and Recovery Act** (**RCRA**) addresses active and future facilities and was enacted in 1976 to give EPA authority to control hazardous wastes from cradle to grave, including generation, transportation, treatment, storage, and disposal. Some nonhazardous wastes are also covered under RCRA.

Remediation is the process of cleaning up a contaminated site by physical, chemical, or biological means. Remediation processes are typically applied to contaminated soil and groundwater.

A **site assessment** is an evaluation of a site's aboveground and subsurface characteristics, including its structures, geology, and hydrology. Site assessments are typically used to determine whether contamination has occurred, as well as the extent and concentration of any release of pollutants. Information generated during a site assessment is used to make remedial action decisions.

ALTERNATIVE TRANSPORTATION—PUBLIC TRANSPORTATION ACCESS

	NC	SCHOOLS	CS
Credit	SS Credit 4.1	SS Credit 4.1	SS Credit 4.1
Points	6 points	4 points	6 points

Intent

To reduce pollution and land development impacts from automobile use.

Requirements

NC, SCHOOLS & CS

OPTION 1. Rail Station Proximity

Locate the project within 1/2-mile walking distance (measured from a main building entrance) of an existing or planned and funded commuter rail, light rail or subway station.

OR

OPTION 2. Bus Stop Proximity

Locate the project within 1/4-mile walking distance (measured from a main building entrance) of 1 or more stops for 2 or more public, campus, or private bus lines usable by building occupants.

SCHOOLS Additional Requirement

A school bus system may count as 1 of these lines.

OR

SCHOOLS

OPTION 3. Pedestrian Access

Show that the project school has an attendance boundary such that at least 80% of students live within no more than 3/4-mile walking distance for grades 8 and below, and 1 1/2-mile walking distance for grades 9 and above. In addition, locate the project on a site that allows pedestrian access to the site from all residential neighborhoods that house the planned student population.

ALL OPTIONS

For all options (Options 1, 2, and 3 for Schools), provide dedicated walking or biking lanes to the transit lines that extend from the school building at least to the end of the school property in 2 or more directions without any barriers (e.g., fences) on school property.

1. Benefits and Issues to Consider

Environmental Issues

The extensive use of single-occupancy vehicles and their heavy reliance on petroleum contribute to environmental problems. Fortunately, alternatives to conventional transportation methods exist. Many people are willing to use other options, if they are convenient. The use of mass transit helps reduce energy demand for transportation and associated greenhouse gas emissions, as well as the space needed for parking lots that encroach on the green space of a building site. Minimizing parking lots reduces a building's footprint and sets aside more space for natural areas or greater development densities.

Reductions in single-occupancy vehicle use directly affect fuel consumption and air and water pollution from vehicle exhaust. On the basis of passenger miles traveled, public transportation is twice as fuel efficient as private vehicles and annually saves 45 million barrels of oil.[5] Another benefit of public transportation is the associated reduction in the need for infrastructure. Parking facilities and roadways for automobiles affect the environment because impervious surfaces, such as asphalt, increase stormwater runoff while contributing to urban heat island effects.

Economic Issues

Many occupants, school employees, students, and parents view proximity to mass transit as a benefit, and this can increase the value and marketability of a building. For building occupants, costs associated with traveling to and from the workplace can be significantly reduced by access to public transportation. Not only is this an economic benefit for building occupants, it helps business owners attract and retain employees.

Reducing the size of parking areas based on anticipated use of public transportation by building occupants may alter operating costs associated with parking lot maintenance. If local utilities charge for stormwater based on impervious surface area, minimizing these areas can result in lower stormwater fees.

2. Related Credits

Sites close to existing public transportation infrastructure tend to be in more densely developed areas, including previously developed areas. The following credits may be more likely achievable for projects in such locations:

- SS Credit 1: Site Selection
- SS Credit 2: Development Density and Community Connectivity

3. Summary of Referenced Standards

There are no standards referenced for this credit.

4. Implementation

Select a site that has convenient access to existing transportation networks to minimize the need for new transportation lines. Local transit authorities can provide maps and directories that will be help identify the available transportation options.

Consider developing a transportation management plan that evaluates anticipated transportation use patterns and offers alternatives aimed at reducing commuting by single-occupancy vehicles. This management plan could be considered a comprehensive approach to addressing the 4 credits within SS Credit 4, Alternative Transportation. This is particularly useful for large buildings, buildings that are part of a master plan implementation, and developments with multiple buildings.

If possible, survey future building occupants about whether the available public transportation options meet their needs. Look for functional sidewalks, paths, and walkways that lead directly to existing mass transit stops.

If a light rail or subway station is sited, planned, and funded at the time the project is completed, it satisfies the intent of this credit. If private shuttle buses will be used to meet the requirements, they must connect to public transportation and operate during the most frequent commuting hours.

	SS
NC	Credit 4.1
SCHOOLS	Credit 4.1
CS	Credit 4.1

SCHOOLS If the attendance boundary compliance path is pursued, analyze the incoming student population to develop an attendance boundary showing the proportion of students living within walking distance. Work with the city planning department to identify any proposed development or change to infrastructure that might affect students' ability to walk safely to school on proposed routes.

Locate the school on a site that allows safe pedestrian access from all residential neighborhoods that house the planned student population. The team's design should provide dedicated walking or bike routes from the school building to the end of the school property in 2 or more directions. These routes should have adequate space and be appropriately separated from vehicular traffic for safety reasons. If possible, design separate paths for bicycles and pedestrians and provide signage identifying their designated uses. If a single path is used for walking and biking, it must be wide enough for both pedestrians and bicyclists. Walking routes and bike lanes on school property should not be obstructed by barriers that would prevent student access, but barriers that students can easily pass through, such as fences with gates, are acceptable.

5. Timeline and Team

Achieving this credit requires proximity to existing transit infrastructure. If the project is in the site selection phase, the architect, design team, and client should determine which options for the project site location will best meet the public transportation access requirements for this credit.

6. Calculations

OPTION 1 and OPTION 2

Use an area drawing, aerial photograph, or map to calculate the walking distance to the transit stops. If the building has multiple main or public entrances, project teams can measure walking distances from multiple building entrances. Software tools like Google™ Maps Pedometer (http://www.gmap-pedometer.com) may be useful for determining walking distance.

SCHOOLS

OPTION 3

Assess the percentage of the total incoming student population that falls within the specified walking distance radius.

7. Documentation Guidance

As a first step in preparing to complete the LEED-Online documentation requirements, work through the following measures. Refer to LEED-Online for the complete descriptions of all required documentation.

- Identify local rail stations or bus routes serving the project building.

- Develop a site vicinity plan, to scale, and label walking paths between the project building's main entrance and rail stations or bus stops.

SS	
NC	Credit 4.1
SCHOOLS	Credit 4.1
CS	Credit 4.1

- If the team anticipates rail development, obtain verification of funding for the rail project.
- For schools projects pursuing pedestrian access credit, create an attendance boundary map showing a 3/4-mile radius for grades K–8, or a 1 1/2-mile radius for grades 9 and above.
- In addition to the above, schools projects should dedicate bike and walking paths leading from the school building to the end of the school property in 2 or more directions.

8. Examples

EXAMPLE 1

A downtown office building is located within walking distance of public transportation. Figure 1 shows a rail station within 1/2-mile walking distance from the building's main entrance. The map includes a scale bar.

Figure 1. Sample Area Drawing: Distance to Rail

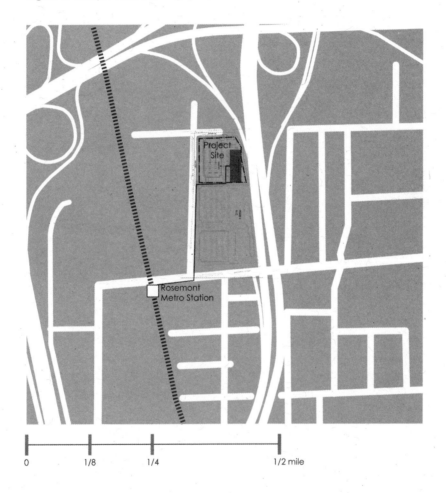

EXAMPLE 2

A school building is sited in a suburban commercial district. Figure 2 shows 2 bus lines within 1/4-mile walking distance of the building's main entrance. The map also shows 2 dedicated bike paths to the transit stops that extend from the school building in 2 directions.

Figure 2. Sample Area Drawing

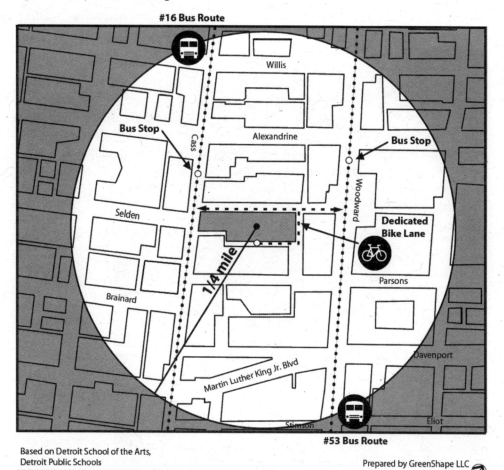

	SS
NC	Credit 4.1
SCHOOLS	Credit 4.1
CS	Credit 4.1

Based on Detroit School of the Arts,
Detroit Public Schools

Prepared by GreenShape LLC

9. Exemplary Performance

Project teams may earn an Innovation in Design credit for exemplary performance by complying with the requirements of 1 of the 2 options described below.

OPTION 1. Comprehensive Transportation Management Plan

Institute a comprehensive transportation management plan that demonstrates a quantifiable reduction in personal automobile use through any of multiple alternative options. Only 1 point is available for implementing such a plan under SS Credit 4—Alternative Transportation.

OPTION 2. Double Transit Ridership

Because projects in locations with good mass transit can achieve substantially and quantifiably higher environmental benefits, meeting the following threshold qualifies a project for exemplary performance. The Center for Clean Air Policy has found that average transit ridership increases by 0.5% for every 1.0% increase in growth of transit service levels, which leads to the conclusion that quadrupling transit service generally doubles transit ridership.

To achieve exemplary performance, meet the following minimum requirements:

- Locate the project within 1/2 mile of at least 2 existing commuter rail, light rail, or subway lines.

OR

- Locate the project within 1/4 mile of at least 2 or more stops for 4 or more public or campus bus lines usable by building occupants.

AND

- Frequency of service must be at least 200 transit rides per day, total, at these stops. A combination of rail and bus lines is allowable. This strategy is based on the assumption that the threshold of the base credit would provide, in most cases, at least 50 transit rides per day (half-hourly service 24 hours per day or more frequent service for less than 24 hours per day). If, on average, transit ridership increases by 0.5% for every 1.0% increase in transit service, then quadrupling the number of rides available would, on average, double the transit ridership: 4 x 50 rides = 200 rides. Include a transit schedule and map with the LEED certification submittal.

> **SCHOOLS** If a school bus system is being counted as 1 of the required bus lines to meet the requirements of Option 2, exemplary performance can be achieved by locating the project within 1/2 mile of at least 1 or more stops for 2 or more public bus lines. Frequency of service must be at least 100 transit rides per day, total, at these stops.
>
> For school projects not using a school bus system to partially satisfy the Option 2 requirements, the exemplary performance requirements above apply.

10. Regional Variations
There are no regional variations associated with this credit.

11. Operations and Maintenance Considerations
Transit infrastructure can be underutilized if building occupants are not informed about public transportation opportunities or encouraged to use these systems. Consider working with building owners and operators to develop ongoing programs to support transit use and infrastructure. Appropriate strategies will vary by building ownership and occupancy type. For example, a multitenant facility with third-party management is less likely to provide subsidized transit passes than an owner-occupied facility, but it could establish a program to inform occupants about transit opportunities.

Programming options to consider include the following examples:

- Providing financial incentives or subsidized passes for public transportation.

- Instituting a "free ride home" program for public transportation commuters who need to work unexpected hours.

- Promoting the use of mass transit by providing information on transportation options, routes, services, and incentives.

- Participating in local or regional transportation planning to ensure that building occupants' needs are considered.

- Establishing a method for tracking public transportation ridership.

12. Resources
Please see USGBC's LEED Registered Project Tools (http://www.usgbc.org/projecttools) for additional resources and technical information.

Websites

ESRI

http://www.esri.com

This software company creates tools for geographic information systems (GIS) mapping.

GIS in Community-Based School Planning: A Tool to Enhance Decision Making, Cooperation, and Democratization in the Planning Process

http://eric.ed.gov/ERICDocs/data/ericdocs2sql/content_storage_01/0000019b/80/17/02/cf.pdf

"This paper examines Blue Valley School District's (Overland Park, Kansas) use of geographic information systems (GIS) to help it manage and plan for rapid growth and development areas. The GIS program helps school districts realize several planning related benefits that include an increase in the cooperative planning activities among stakeholders in the school planning process, achievement of a democratization level utilizing GIS technologies, and improvement in the planning process for school district residents, the Planning and Facilities Committee, and the school district's administration."

U.S. Census Bureau

http://www.census.gov

The population statistics, maps, and downloadable boundary files available on the U.S. Census Bureau's website can be used in determining attendance boundaries.

U.S. Department of Education, Institute of Education Sciences, National Center for Education Statistics

http://nces.ed.gov/index.asp

The National Center for Education Statistics is the primary federal entity for collecting and analyzing data related to education in the United States and other nations.

U.S. EPA, Office of Transportation and Air Quality

U.S. Environmental Protection Agency

http://www.epa.gov/otaq

This U.S. EPA website provides information on the types and effects of air pollution associated with automobile use and links to resources for organizations interested in promoting commuter choice programs.

U.S. EPA and Department of Transportation, Best Workplaces for Commuters

http://www.bestworkplaces.org/index.htm

This program publicly recognizes employers who have exemplary commuter benefits programs. It provides tools, guidance, and promotions to help employers give commuter benefits, reap the financial gains, and achieve national recognition.

13. Definitions

The **attendance boundary** is used by school districts to determine which students attend what school based on where they live.

A **campus or private bus** is a bus or shuttle service that is privately operated and not available to the general public. In LEED, a campus or private bus line that falls within 1/4 mile of the project site and provides transportation service to the public can contribute to earning credits.

Mass transit is designed to transport large groups of persons in a single vehicle, such as a bus or train.

Public transportation consists of bus, rail, or other transit services for the general public that operate on a regular, continual basis.

Walking distance is the length of the walkable pathway between the building and public transportation.

ALTERNATIVE TRANSPORTATION—BICYCLE STORAGE AND CHANGING ROOMS

	NC	SCHOOLS	CS
Credit	SS Credit 4.2	SS Credit 4.2	SS Credit 4.2
Points	1 point	1 point	2 points

Intent

To reduce pollution and land development impacts from automobile use.

Requirements

 NC

CASE 1. Commercial or Institutional Projects

Provide secure bicycle racks and/or storage within 200 yards of a building entrance for 5% or more of all building users (measured at peak periods)

Provide shower and changing facilities in the building, or within 200 yards of a building entrance, for 0.5% of full-time equivalent (FTE) occupants.

CASE 2. Residential Projects

Provide covered storage facilities for securing bicycles for 15% or more of building occupants.

 CS

CASE 1. Commercial or Institutional Projects 300,000 Square Feet or Less

Provide secure bicycle racks and/or storage within 200 yards of a building entrance for 3% or more of all building users (calculated on average for the year)

Provide shower and changing facilities in the building, or within 200 yards of a building entrance, for 0.5% of full-time equivalent (FTE) occupants.

CASE 2. Commercial or Institutional Projects Larger Than 300,000 Square Feet

Provide secure bicycle storage for 3% of the occupants for up to 300,000 square feet, then an additional 0.5% for the occupants for the space over 300,000 square feet. Mixed-use buildings with a total gross square footage greater than 300,000 square feet must apply this calculation for each use of the building

Provide shower and changing facilities in the building, or within 200 yards of a building entrance, for 0.5% of FTE occupants.

CASE 3. Residential Projects

Provide covered storage facilities for securing bicycles for 15% or more of building occupants. Case 3 must be used by residential buildings or the residential portion of a mixed use building.

ALL CASES

See Appendix 1 — Default Occupancy Counts for occupancy count requirements and guidance.

	SS
NC	Credit 4.2
SCHOOLS	Credit 4.2
CS	Credit 4.2

SCHOOLS

Provide secure bicycle racks and/or storage within 200 yards of a building entrance for 5% or more of all building staff and students above grade 3 level (measured at peak periods).

Provide shower and changing facilities in the building, or within 200 yards of a building entrance, for 0.5% of full-time equivalent (FTE) staff.

Provide dedicated bike lanes that extend at least to the end of the school property in 2 or more directions without any no barriers (e.g., fences) on school property.

1. Benefits and Issues to Consider

	SS
NC	Credit 4.2
SCHOOLS	Credit 4.2
CS	Credit 4.2

Environmental Issues

The environmental effects of automobile use include vehicle emissions that contribute to smog and air pollution, as well as environmental impacts from oil extraction and petroleum refining. Bicycling as an alternative to personal vehicle use offers a number of environmental benefits. Bicycle commuting produces no emissions, has zero demand for petroleum-based fuels, relieves traffic congestion, reduces noise pollution, and requires far less infrastructure for roadways and parking lots. Roadways and parking lots, on the other hand, produce stormwater runoff, contribute to the urban heat island effect, and encroach on green space.

Bicycles are more likely to be used for relatively short commuting trips. Displacing vehicle miles with bicycling, even for short trips, carries a large environmental benefit because a large portion of vehicle emissions occur in the first few minutes of driving. Following a cold start, emissions control equipment is less effective because of cool operating temperatures.

SCHOOLS Providing the opportunity for students to use bicycles for transportation increases the likelihood that they will continue to use bicycles for transportation as adults, which is an important component of reducing cultural dependency on automobiles.

Economic Issues

The initial cost of building bike storage areas and changing facilities or showers is typically low relative to the overall project cost. When buildings accommodate bicycling infrastructure, occupants can realize health benefits through bicycle and walking commuting strategies. Bicycling and walking also expose people to the community, encouraging interaction among neighbors and allowing for enjoyment of the area in ways unavailable to automobile passengers.

2. Related Credits

The materials used for paving on-site bicycle lanes can affect the heat island and stormwater properties of the project. Refer to the following credits:

- SS Credit 6: Stormwater Design
- SS Credit 7.1: Heat Island Effect—Nonroof

3. Summary of Referenced Standards

There are no standards referenced for this credit.

4. Implementation

Select a site that provides convenient access to safe bicycle pathways and secure bicycle storage areas for cyclists. Shower and changing areas for cyclists should be easily accessible from the bicycle storage areas.

Look for functional and direct paths that can be used by bicycle commuters, and size and locate bike racks and showering facilities appropriately.

Secure bike storage systems vary in design and cost. A common approach is to install racks where users can individually park and lock their bikes. Spaces should be easily accessible by building occupants throughout the year, free of charge. For residential projects, bike storage must be covered to protect bicycles from weather and theft. Commercial office buildings should consider regional commuting patterns and provide appropriate amenities. Retail developments should consider bicycle usage for both employees and retail customers.

For projects on a campus or for multiple building developments, showering facilities can be shared between buildings as long as the facilities are within 200 yards' walking distance of the entrance to the project building. The facilities can be unit showers or group showers.

SCHOOLS Because most schools are situated near residential zones, projects may have good opportunities for bicycle commuting. In K–12 schools, safety considerations are of critical concern. Design considerations include the following:

- Clear separation between vehicular and bicycle traffic (including clearly marked bicycle lanes and sidewalks that extend throughout the entire school zone).
- Secure bicycle storage (e.g., exterior bicycle racks located near entryways and administrative offices, interior bicycle storage rooms with controlled access).
- Well-designed exterior lighting that provides clear visibility and appropriate security.
- Permitted barriers that students can easily pass through during peak traveling hours (e.g., gates within fences).
- Privacy for students and staff in changing and showering facilities.

In addition to the physical facilities, schools should have clear policies about appropriate bicycle use on school grounds.

To meet the credit requirement, showering facilities for school staff must be provided. School administrators should be aware of the issues that could arise if students and staff share showering and changing facilities; ensure that staff have access to separate facilities. If it is not possible to build separate facilities, administrators should use scheduling to provide privacy.

Bicycle racks are simple structures that can be made by students in art or vocational classes. Creative designs could even use found objects, reinforcing the message of environmental stewardship.

5. Timeline and Team

Bicycle storage and shower facilities should be incorporated into design concepts during schematic design and design development. By considering bicycling early on, the project team can implement a successful alternative transportation program. For example, during the site selection phase, the project team can include proximity to existing bicycle commuting infrastructure as a criterion. Coordination among the architect, plumbing engineer, civil engineer, and/or landscape architect may be required for locating and designing bicycle storage and shower facilities. The project team should also consider future expansion opportunities.

6. Calculations

NC To determine the number of secure bicycle storage spaces and changing and showering facilities required for the building, follow the steps below.

STEP 1

Identify the total number of building occupants for each of the following occupancy types:

a. Full-time staff.

b. Part-time staff.

c. Peak transients (students, volunteers, visitors, customers, etc.).

d. Residents.

In buildings with multiple shifts, use only the highest-volume shift in the calculation but consider shift overlap when determining peak building use. For projects that include residential spaces, estimate the number of residents based on the number and size of units. Generally, assume 2 residents per 1-bedroom unit, 3 residents per 2-bedroom unit, etc. If occupancy is not known, see Appendix 1, Default Occupancy Counts, for occupancy count requirements and guidance.

STEP 2

For full-time and part-time staff, calculate the full-time equivalent (FTE) occupants based on a standard 8-hour occupancy period. An 8-hour occupant has an FTE value of 1.0; a part-time occupant has a FTE value based on work hours per day divided by 8 (see Equation 1). FTE calculations for each shift must be used consistently for all LEED credits.

Equation 1. FTE Staff Occupants

$$\text{Total FTE Staff Occupants} = \frac{\text{Total Staff Occupant Hours}}{8}$$

STEP 3

Calculate the number of secure bicycle spaces required for each group of occupants, according to Equation 2.

Equation 2. Number of Secure Bike Spaces

a. $\text{Staff Occupant Spaces} = \text{FTE Staff Occupants} \times 0.05$

b. $\text{Transient Spaces} = \text{Peak Transients} \times 0.05$

c. $\text{Resident Spaces} = \text{Residents} \times 0.15$

Certain types of transient populations can be excluded from these calculations if they cannot reasonably be expected to arrive by bicycle and thus use on-site storage facilities. For example, air travelers arriving at an airport will not need bicycle storage. Project teams should be prepared to justify the exclusion of any transients from the calculations.

STEP 4

Calculate the number of showers required for staff using Equation 3.

Equation 3. Staff Showering Facilities

$$\text{Showering Facilities} = \text{FTE Staff} \times 0.005$$

Transient occupants and residents are not counted in the showering facility calculation.

CS For buildings smaller than 300,000 gross square feet

To determine the number of secure bicycle storage spaces and changing and showering facilities required, follow the steps below. The threshold for bicycle storage for this credit was reduced to 3% to tailor this credit to the LEED for Core & Shell market, in recognition of the relationship between developers and tenants. The achievement of higher percentages is encouraged and should be evaluated on a project basis.

STEP 1

Follow Steps 1 and 2 in the LEED for New Construction calculations.

STEP 2

Calculate the number of secure bicycle spaces required for each group of occupants according to Equation 4.

Equation 4. Number of Secure Bike Spaces

a. $\text{Staff Occupant Spaces} = \text{FTE Staff Occupants} \times 0.03$

b. $\text{Transient Spaces} = \text{Peak Transients} \times 0.03$

c. $\text{Resident Spaces} = \text{Residents} \times 0.15$

Certain types of transient populations can be excluded from these calculations if they cannot reasonably be expected to arrive by bicycle and thus use on-site storage facilities. For example, air travelers arriving at an airport will not need bicycle storage. Project teams should be prepared to justify the exclusion of certain types of transients from the calculations.

STEP 3

Calculate the number of showers required for staff using Equation 3 under LEED for New Construction calculations.

For buildings 300,000 gross square feet or larger

Many core and shell buildings, particularly in the commercial office market, are larger than 300,000 square feet. For buildings of this scale, the bicycle storage requirement is based on the average annual building users for the square footage up to 300,000 (per use), with a separate allowance for the square footage above 300,000 square feet. To determine the number of secure bicycle storage spaces and changing and showering facilities required for the building, follow the steps below.

STEP 1

Follow Steps 1 and 2 in the LEED for New Construction calculations and sum the staff and transient populations to determine the total nonresident building users.

Certain types of transient populations can be excluded from these calculations if they cannot reasonably be expected to arrive by bicycle and thus use on-site storage facilities. For example, air travelers arriving at an airport will not need bicycle storage. Project teams should be prepared to justify the exclusion of certain types of transients from the calculations.

STEP 2

Prorate the average annual nonresident building users for the building square footage up to 300,000 square feet (see Equation 5), and the building square footage greater than 300,000 square feet (see Equation 6).

Equation 5

$$\text{Average Annual Building Users} \left[\leq 300{,}000 \text{ (sf)} \right] = \text{Average Annual Building Users} \times \frac{300{,}000 \text{ (sf)}}{\text{Building Square Footage}}$$

Equation 6

$$\text{Average Annual Building Users} \left[> 300{,}000 \text{ (sf)} \right] = \text{Average Annual Building Users} \times \frac{\text{Building Square Footage} - 300{,}000 \text{ (sf)}}{\text{Building Square Footage}}$$

STEP 3

Calculate the number of secure bicycle spaces required for each group of occupants, according to Equation 7.

Equation 7. Number of Secure Bike Spaces

a.
$$\text{Nonresident Spaces} \left[\leq 300{,}000 \text{ (sf)} \right] = \text{Average Annual Building Users} \left[\leq 300{,}000 \text{ (sf)} \right] \times 0.03$$

b.
$$\text{Nonresident Spaces} \left[> 300{,}000 \text{ (sf)} \right] = \text{Average Annual Building Users} \left[> 300{,}000 \text{ (sf)} \right] \times 0.005$$

c.
$$\text{Resident Spaces} = \text{Residents} \times 0.15$$

STEP 4

Calculate the number of showers required for staff using Equation 3 under LEED for New Construction calculations.

SCHOOLS To determine the number of secure bicycle storage spaces and changing and showering facilities required for the building, follow the steps below.

STEP 1

Identify the total number of building occupants for each occupancy type. In buildings with multiple shifts, use only the highest-volume shift but consider shift overlap when determining peak building use:

a. Full-time staff

b. Part-time staff

c. Students above grade 3

d. Peak transients (volunteers, visitors, etc.)

STEP 2

For full-time and part-time staff, calculate the full-time equivalent (FTE) number of occupants by following the guidance and Equation 1 under LEED for New Construction calculations above.

STEP 3

Calculate the number of secure bicycle spaces required for each group of occupants, according to Equation 8.

Equation 8. Number of Secure Bike Spaces

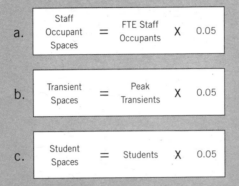

a. Staff Occupant Spaces = FTE Staff Occupants X 0.05

b. Transient Spaces = Peak Transients X 0.05

c. Student Spaces = Students X 0.05

Certain types of transient populations can be excluded from these calculations if they cannot reasonably be expected to arrive by bicycle and thus use on-site storage facilities. For example, air travelers arriving at an airport facility will not need bicycle storage. Project teams should be prepared to justify the exclusion of certain types of transients from the calculations.

STEP 4

Calculate the number of showers required for staff using Equation 3 under LEED for New Construction calculations based on FTE staff (excluding students and transient occupants).

7. Documentation Guidance

As a first step in preparing to complete the LEED-Online documentation requirements, work through the following measures. Refer to LEED-Online for the complete descriptions of all required documentation.

- Determine the number of occupants of each type and calculate the number of bicycle storage and showering facilities required.

- Develop a plan showing the location and quantity of bicycle storage and shower facilities and determine the distance between facilities and the building entry.

8. Examples

EXAMPLE 1. New Construction: College Classroom Building

Many college buildings house faculty, staff, and students, complicating the calculation of FTEs. In Table 1, the building occupants are separated into full-time and part-time users to simplify the calculation. The number of persons is multiplied by the number of hours they spend in the building each day and then divided by 8 to calculate the FTE value.

Table 1. Sample Occupancy Calculation for College Building

FTE Staff Occupant Calculations, Parrish Hall									
Occupants	**Persons**		**Person-Hours per Day**		**Total Person-Hours per Day**		**Hours per Day per FTE**		**FTEs**
Full-time staff									
Administrators	8	x	8	=	64	÷	8	=	8
Faculty	6	x	8	=	48	÷	8	=	6
Part-time staff									
Faculty	24	x	2	=	48	÷	8	=	6
Researchers	20	x	4	=	80	÷	8	=	10
Total FTE staff									30
Transient Occupant Calculation									
Occupants									Number at Peak Period
Students									310
Visitors									6
Total									316
Summary									
Total FTE staff									30
Transient occupants									316

In this example, the required number of secure bicycle storage space is 30 x 0.05 + 316 x 0.05 = 17.3, or 18 spaces.

The required number of changing and showering facilities is 30 x 0.005= 0.15, or 1.

EXAMPLE 2. Core & Shell: Commercial Office Building up to 300,000 sf

Many Core & Shell buildings are midsize, single-use commercial office buildings. These buildings are often programmed for single-shift occupancy. An example of the calculations for this type of building follows.

Building square footage: 125,000 sf

Gross square feet per employee (from Appendix 1 or tenant use as applicable): 250 sf/FTE

$$\text{FTE Occupants} = \frac{125,000}{250} = 500$$

$$\text{Secure Bicycle Spaces} = 500 \times 0.03 = 15 \text{ Bicycle Spaces}$$

$$\text{Shower and Changing Facilities} = 500 \times 0.005 = 2.5, \text{ or } 3$$

EXAMPLE 3. Schools: K–5 Elementary School

In the example in Table 2, the building occupants are separated into full-time staff, part-time staff, students above grade 3, and volunteers (transients). Figure 1 is a site map of the project showing the location of bike paths, bike storage, and showers.

Table 2. Sample Occupancy Calculation for Elementary School

FTE Staff Occupant Calculations								
Occupants	Persons		Person-Hours per Day		Total Person-Hours per Day		Hours per Day per FTE		FTEs
Full-time staff								
Administrators	6	x	8	=	48	÷	8	=	6
Faculty	54	x	8	=	432	÷	8	=	54
Part-time staff								
Faculty	6	x	4	=	24	÷	8	=	3
Maintenance	6	x	4	=	24	÷	8	=	3
Total FTE staff								66
Transient Occupant Calculation								
Occupants							Number at Peak Period	
Volunteers								8
Total transients								8
Student Occupant Calculation								
Grade 4								75
Grade 5								80
Total students above grade 3								155
Summary								
Total FTE staff								66
Total transient occupants								8
Total students above grade 3								155

In this example, the required number of secure bicycle storage spaces is 229 x 0.05 = 11.45, or 12.

The required number of changing and showering facilities is 66 x 0.005= 0.33, or 1.

Figure 1. Sample Site Map

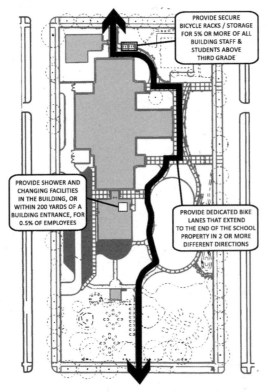

9. Exemplary Performance

Project teams may earn an Innovation in Design credit for exemplary performance by instituting a comprehensive transportation management plan that demonstrates a quantifiable reduction in personal automobile use. Only 1 point is available for implementing a comprehensive transportation management plan under SS Credit 4, Alternative Transportation. Projects that are awarded exemplary performance for SS Credit 4.1, Alternative Transportation—Public Transportation Access, Option 2, are not eligible for exemplary performance under this credit.

	SS
NC	Credit 4.2
SCHOOLS	Credit 4.2
CS	Credit 4.2

10. Regional Variations

This credit may have particular importance in areas that have good but unrealized potential for bicycle use or areas where bicycle use is not promoted by the municipality. Establishing bicycling facilities will help promote greater bicycle use.

Project teams in areas with poor air quality may also want to encourage bicycling as a way of reducing single-occupancy vehicle usage, a major contributor to air quality problems.

11. Operations and Maintenance Considerations

Consider working with building owners and operators to develop ongoing programs to support bicycle use. Appropriate strategies will vary by building ownership and occupancy type.

Program options include the following:

- Providing financial incentives for commuting via bicycle.
- Instituting a "free ride home" program for bicycle riders who need to work unexpected hours.
- Promoting bicycling to the community by providing information on safe bike routes, locations of secure bicycle parking, lockers, showers, etc.
- Providing discounts on bicycle accessories and maintenance at local bike shops.
- Participating in local or regional transportation planning to ensure that building occupants' needs are considered. Bike lanes along corridors leading to the project site can significantly influence ridership levels.
- Establishing a method for tracking bicycle ridership.

12. Resources

Please see USGBC's LEED Registered Project Tools (http://www.usgbc.org/projecttools) for additional resources and technical information.

Websites

Bicycle Coalition of Maine, Employer's Guide to Encouraging Bicycle Commuting
http://www.bikemaine.org/btwemployer.htm
This website from the Bicycle Coalition of Maine suggests ways to encourage and facilitate bike commuting.

Commuting Guide for Employers
http://www.self-propelled-city.com/index.php
This website outlines strategies employers can use to encourage employees to commute by bicycle.

Federal Highway Administration, Office of Human and Natural Environment, Bicycle and Pedestrian Program
http://www.fhwa.dot.gov/environment/bikeped/
The Federal Highway Administration's Office of Human and Natural Environment promotes access to and use and safety of bicycle and pedestrian transportation.

	SS
NC	Credit 4.2
SCHOOLS	Credit 4.2
CS	Credit 4.2

Pedestrian and Bicycle Information Center

http://www.bicyclinginfo.org

The Pedestrian and Bicycle Information Center provides information and resources for issues related to bicycle commuting, including health and safety, engineering, advocacy, education and facilities.

U.S. EPA, Transportation and Air Quality

http://www.epa.gov/otaq/

This website provides information on the types and effects of air pollution associated with automobile use and links to resources for organizations interested in promoting commuter choice programs.

U.S. EPA and U.S. Department of Transportation, Best Workplaces for Commuters

http://www.bestworkplaces.org/index.htm

This program publicly recognizes employers who have exemplary commuter benefits programs. It provides tools, guidance, and promotions to help employers give commuter benefits, reap the financial gains, and achieve national recognition.

13. Definitions

Bicycle racks, in LEED, include outdoor bicycle racks, bicycle lockers, and indoor bicycle storage rooms.

Full-time equivalent (FTE) represents a regular building occupant who spends 40 hours per week in the project building. Part-time or overtime occupants have FTE values based on their hours per week divided by 40. Multiple shifts are included or excluded depending on the intent and requirements of the credit.

Secure bicycle storage is an internal or external space that keeps bicycles safe from theft. It may include lockers and storage rooms.

Transient users are occupants who do not use a facility on a consistent, regular, daily basis. Examples include students in higher education settings, customers in retail settings, and visitors in institutional settings.

ALTERNATIVE TRANSPORTATION—LOW-EMITTING AND FUEL-EFFICIENT VEHICLES

	NC	SCHOOLS	CS
Credit	SS Credit 4.3	SS Credit 4.3	SS Credit 4.3
Points	3 points	2 points	3 points

Intent

To reduce pollution and land development impacts from automobile use.

Requirements

OPTION 1

NC & CS

Provide preferred parking[1] for low-emitting and fuel-efficient vehicles[2] for 5% of the total vehicle parking capacity of the site. Providing a discounted parking rate is an acceptable substitute for preferred parking for low-emitting/fuel-efficient vehicles. To establish a meaningful incentive in all potential markets, the parking rate must be discounted at least 20%. The discounted rate must be available to all customers (i.e., not limited to the number of customers equal to 5% of the vehicle parking capacity), publicly posted at the entrance of the parking area and available for a minimum of 2 years.

CS Additional Requirement
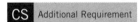

For project types that demonstrate market barriers to the definition of preferred parking closest to the main entrance, alternatives may be considered on a case-by-case basis.

SCHOOLS

Provide preferred parking[1] for low-emitting and fuel-efficient vehicles[2] for 5% of the total vehicle parking capacity of the site and at least 1 designated carpool drop-off area for low-emitting and fuel-efficient vehicles.

OR

OPTION 2

NC & CS

Install alternative-fuel fueling stations for 3% of the total vehicle parking capacity of the site. Liquid or gaseous fueling facilities must be separately ventilated or located outdoors.

SCHOOLS

Develop and implement a plan for the buses and maintenance vehicles serving the school to use 20% (by vehicles, fuel or both) natural gas, propane or biodiesel or to be low-emitting and fuel-efficient vehicles[2].

---

1 For the purposes of this credit "preferred parking" refers to the parking spots that are closest to the main entrance of the project (exclusive of spaces designated for handicapped persons) or parking passes provided at a discounted price.
2 For the purposes of this credit, low-emitting and fuel-efficient vehicles are defined as vehicles that are either classified as Zero Emission Vehicles (ZEV) by the California Air Resources Board or have achieved a minimum green score of 40 on the American Council for an Energy Efficient Economy (ACEEE) annual vehicle rating guide.

OR

OPTION 3

 NC

Provide low-emitting and fuel-efficient vehicles[1] for 3% of full-time equivalent (FTE) occupants.

Provide preferred parking[2] for these vehicles.

OR

OPTION 4

 NC

Provide building occupants access to a low-emitting or fuel-efficient vehicle-sharing program. The following requirements must be met:

- One low-emitting or fuel-efficient vehicle must be provided per 3% of FTE occupants, assuming that 1 shared vehicle can carry 8 persons (i.e., 1 vehicle per 267 FTE occupants). For buildings with fewer than 267 FTE occupants, at least 1 low emitting or fuel-efficient vehicle must be provided.

- A vehicle-sharing contract must be provided that has an agreement of at least 2 years.

- The estimated number of customers served per vehicle must be supported by documentation.

- A narrative explaining the vehicle-sharing program and its administration must be submitted.

- Parking for low-emitting and fuel-efficient vehicles must be located in the nearest available spaces in the nearest available parking area. Provide a site plan or area map clearly highlighting the walking path from the parking area to the project site and noting the distance.

1. Benefits and Issues to Consider

	SS
NC	Credit 4.3
SCHOOLS	Credit 4.3
CS	Credit 4.3

Environmental Issues

Vehicle operation significantly contributes to global climate change and air quality problems through the emission of greenhouse gases (GHGs) and pollutants generated from combustion engines and fuel evaporation. In the United States, the transportation sector has generated more carbon dioxide emissions than any other end-use sector since 1999, and in 2007 was responsible for nearly 30% of total GHG emissions.[6] Personal vehicles also generate large portions of the air pollutants responsible for smog and ground-level ozone, both of which have negative effects on human health.

Alternative-fuel and fuel-efficient vehicles offer the possibility of reducing air pollutants from vehicular travel as well as the negative environmental effects of producing gasoline. However, the extent to which alternative vehicles produce environmental benefits depends on the complete life-cycle of their fuels and the vehicle technology. For example, electric vehicles generate zero GHGs during operation, but the amount of GHGs emitted during the production of the electricity that these vehicles require varies greatly depending on the electricity source. Furthermore, the combustion of some alternative fuels releases less of certain pollutants but more of others. Because the environmental benefits of alternative fuels and alternative vehicles depend on complete fuel-cycle energy use and emissions, project teams should carefully consider available technologies and fuel sources before committing to purchasing vehicles or installing fuel stations.

Economic Issues

Initial costs for vehicles and buses using alternative fuel are higher than for conventional vehicles, and this may delay their purchase. Federal, state, and local government may offer tax incentives for purchasing alternative vehicles, which can help offset their higher initial costs. Different alternative-fuel vehicles need different fueling stations, and the costs vary. Hybrid vehicles are gaining traction in the marketplace, which should help drive down their cost. Providing preferred parking generally involves minimal extra cost. For fuel-efficient vehicles, reduced operating costs on a per-mile basis can offset higher initial purchase prices or higher fuel costs.

2. Related Credits

Ideally, overall parking capacity would not increase as a result of incorporating designated spaces for low-emitting or fuel-efficient vehicles. Projects that provide preferred parking without increasing overall capacity may be eligible for the following credit:

- SS Credit 4.4: Alternative Transportation—Parking Capacity

3. Summary of Referenced Standards

There are no standards referenced for this credit.

4. Implementation

NC & CS   If occupants of a project building use fleet vehicles (or if certain occupants are permitted to use a company vehicle), consider providing low-emitting and fuel-efficient vehicles. Assess the qualifying makes and models to determine the best way to meet the fleet needs for a project building.

Establishing alternative-fuel vehicle fueling stations requires the consideration of legal, technical, and safety issues that vary by fuel type. Project teams may want to start with the following actions:

- Poll future building occupants to determine which alternative fuel type is in highest demand.

- Compare the environmental and economic costs and benefits of alternative fuels to determine which type would be most beneficial.

- Research local codes and standards for fueling stations in the area.

- Compare fueling station equipment options and fuel availability. Price and complexity of installation vary with the type of fuel. Lack of availability may limit the feasibility of providing fueling stations for some types of fuels.

- Learn about the safety and maintenance issues associated with alternative fuels. Building personnel will need to be trained to operate and maintain the fueling stations.

Consider the building's use when establishing preferred parking for low-emitting and fuel-efficient vehicles. For commercial office buildings, the location of these designated spaces should be closest to the main entrance of the project. Offering discounted parking rates for low-emitting and fuel-efficient vehicles is another way to complying with this credit's requirements. Mixed-use projects should consider the traffic patterns related to each use. Because retail developments often require that employees not park near the main entrance, consider other kinds of incentives.

SCHOOLS   This credit can be achieved under Option 5 by specifying that 20% of all buses and maintenance vehicles will be low-emitting, or by using 20% alternative fuels. Schools should investigate the benefits and trade-offs of using alternative fuels when developing a plan for bus systems and maintenance vehicles.

When considering biodiesel, confirm warranty requirements with vehicle engine manufacturers. Ensure that storage tanks are thoroughly cleaned before transitioning to biodiesel, and make sure filters are changed frequently. Antigelling agents may be required in cold climates.

When pursuing Option 1 and providing preferred parking for fuel-efficient vehicles, schools may need to require stickers or other signifiers to enforce the policy. This option also requires the provision of at least 1 designated carpool drop-off area. The drop-off area should be situated to effectively manage the traffic patterns of carpool users, on-site parkers, and buses. Additionally, it should facilitate convenient carpooling for both students and staff.

5. Timeline and Team

The architect and design team, with the project owner, should choose the appropriate approach for the building's future users. Any fueling stations for alternative-fuel vehicles should be incorporated into design concepts during schematic design and design development. If such vehicles are purchased as part of the strategy, communicate requirements to procurement officials well in advance of the deadline for ordering the vehicles. Designating parking spaces is generally not as time sensitive as other strategies, but a plan should be developed early.

6. Calculations

OPTION 1

Designated Parking

To determine the number of preferred parking spaces for low-emitting and fuel-efficient vehicles required, multiply the total number of parking spaces in the project by 5%.

Discounted Parking

To determine the maximum rate to be offered to low-emitting and fuel-efficient vehicle users, multiply the regular rate by 80%.

	SS
NC	Credit 4.3
SCHOOLS	Credit 4.3
CS	Credit 4.3

NC & CS

OPTION 2

To determine the number of alternative-fuel vehicle fueling stations required, multiply the total number of parking spaces in the project by 3%.

NC

OPTION 3

To determine the number of low-emitting and fuel-efficient vehicles required, follow the steps below.

STEP 1

Identify the total number of full-time and part-time building occupants. In buildings with multiple shifts, use only the highest-volume shift in the FTE calculation but consider shift overlap when determining peak building use.

STEP 2

Calculate the number of FTE occupants based on a standard 8-hour occupancy period. An 8-hour occupant has an FTE value of 1.0; a part-time occupant has a FTE value based on work hours per day divided by 8 (see Equation 1). FTE calculations for each shift of the project must be used consistently for all LEED credits.

If occupancy is not known, see Appendix 1, Default Occupancy Counts, for occupancy count requirements and guidance.

Equation 1

$$\text{Total FTE Occupants} = \frac{\text{Total Occupant Hours}}{8}$$

STEP 3

Multiply the number of FTE occupants by 3% to determine the number of vehicles and preferred parking spaces to provide.

OPTION 4

To determine the number of low-emitting and fuel-efficient vehicles to be provided by a vehicle-sharing program, divide the project's FTE occupancy (see Equation 1) by 267 (1 vehicle must be provided for every 267 occupants; see Equation 2). If fewer than 267 FTEs occupy the building, provide a least 1 vehicle.

Equation 2

$$\text{Number of Low-Emitting and Fuel-Efficient Vehicles} = \frac{\text{FTE Occupancy}}{267}$$

SCHOOLS

OPTION 5

The 20% requirement can be met based on the percentage of vehicles that are classified as zero-emitting vehicles (ZEV) or compliant with American Council for an Energy-Efficient Economy (ACEEE) standards; the percentage of vehicles that use alternative fuel; or the percentage of total volume of fuel use that is met with alternative fuels.

Determine the total number of on-site buses and maintenance vehicles and multiply by 20% to determine the number that must either (a) be classified as ZEV or ACEEE compliant or (b) use alternative fuels. Combining strategies (e.g., 10% of vehicles are ZEV or ACEEE compliant and 10% use alternative fuels) is not allowed.

Alternatively, estimate the average fuel consumption of on-site buses and maintenance vehicles and multiply by 20% to determine the volume of alternative fuel that must be used.

7. Documentation Guidance

As a first step in preparing to complete the LEED-Online documentation requirements, work through the following measures. Refer to LEED-Online for the complete descriptions of all required documentation.

OPTION 1

- For designated spaces, record the number of on-site parking spaces, identify preferred spaces for low-emitting and fuel-efficient vehicles, and inform building occupants about the preferred spaces.

- For discounted parking, assemble information about the discount program and how it is communicated to occupants.

NC & CS

OPTION 2

- Prepare information about the number of fueling stations provided, the alternative fuel station type, manufacturer, model number, and the fueling capacity per station.

NC

OPTION 3

- Determine the FTE value and calculate the number of qualifying vehicles that must be provided.

- Record information about purchased vehicles, including make, model, and fuel type.

- Prepare a site plan showing the location of preferred parking spaces.

OPTION 4

- Prepare information about low-emitting and fuel-efficient shared vehicles, including quantity, make, model, and fuel type.

- Retain a copy of the contractual agreement with the vehicle sharing program.

- Assemble information about the vehicle sharing program, including estimates of the number of customers served per vehicle and descriptions of its administration.

- Develop a site plan or area map that highlights a pedestrian walkway from the parking area to the project site.

SCHOOLS

OPTION 5

- Perform calculations showing the percentage of vehicles or fuel consumption that meets the requirements.

- Assemble information about the alternative-fuel and/or low-emitting or high-efficiency vehicle program.

8. Examples

A LEED for New Construction project building provides designated parking for users of low-emitting or fuel-efficient vehicles. The project's total parking capacity is 335 spaces. Five percent of 335 is 16.75, so at least 17 preferred parking spaces near the building entrance must be provided. Figure 1 illustrates the location of preferred parking spaces.

Figure 1. Location of Preferred Parking

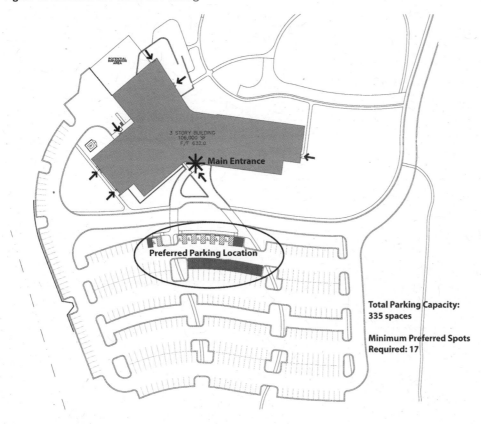

Total Parking Capacity:
335 spaces

Minimum Preferred Spots
Required: 17

9. Exemplary Performance

Projects may earn an Innovation in Design credit for exemplary performance by instituting a comprehensive transportation management plan that demonstrates a quantifiable reduction in personal automobile use using multiple alternative options. Only 1 exemplary performance credit is available for implementing a comprehensive transportation management plan under SS Credit 4, Alternative Transportation. Projects that are awarded exemplary performance for SS Credit 4.1, Alternative Transportation—Public Transportation Access, Option 2 are not eligible for exemplary performance under this credit.

10. Regional Variations

Certain regions have better-developed infrastructure for some types of alternative fuels than others. Consider the existing infrastructure when making decisions about which alternative fuel to offer at the project building.

11. Operations and Maintenance Considerations

Establish procedures for the use of preferred parking, communicate them to building occupants, and assign operations staff for their administration. The procedures might include providing a list of qualifying vehicles (make, model, year) based on the ACEEE Green Score, establishing a system for enforcing use of designated spaces (e.g, a permitting system), discounting paid parking, and tracking the use of preferred parking.

For project buildings with alternative-fuel fueling stations, special maintenance and safety procedures may be necessary. Ensure that building operators are given complete information about manufacture recommended maintenance and any applicable regulations and safety considerations for management of fuels.

12. Resources

Please see USGBC's LEED Registered Project Tools (http://www.usgbc.org/projecttools) for additional resources and technical information.

Websites

American Council for an Energy-Efficient Economy
http://www.greenercars.com
ACEEE is an online, searchable green car guide based on an evaluation of fuel efficiency and tailpipe emissions. It also offers hardcopies of Green Guide to Cars and Trucks, an annual publication of the American Council for an Energy-Efficient Economy.

California Air Resources Board, Certified Vehicles List
http://www.arb.ca.gov/msprog/ccvl/ccvl.htm
This site provides a list of all vehicles certified by CARB.

California Air Resources Board, Cleaner Car Guide
http://www.driveclean.ca.gov/en/gv/home/index.asp
CARB has developed a comprehensive, searchable buyer's guide to finding the cleanest cars on the market. The guide also lists advantages clean vehicles offer.

Center for Renewable Energy and Sustainable Technology
http://www.repp.org/hydrogen/index.html
This is the CREST's online page about fuel cells and hydrogen.

Clean Cities Vehicle Buyer's Guide For Fleets
http://www.nrel.gov/docs/fy04osti/34336.pdf
The Vehicle Buyer's Guide for Fleets is designed to educate fleet managers and policymakers about

alternative fuels and vehicles to help them determine whether the Energy Policy Act (EPAct) of 1992 affects them. Use the site to determine whether your fleet is covered under EPAct; obtain pricing and technical specifications for light and heavy-duty AFVs; find an alternative fueling station in your area; or research information about state AFV purchasing incentives and laws.

Electric Auto Association

http://www.eaaev.org

This nonprofit education organization promotes the advancement and widespread adoption of electric vehicles.

Electric Drive Transportation Association

http://www.electricdrive.org

Through policy, information, and market development initiatives, this industry association promotes the use of electric vehicles .

National Biodiesel Board

http://www.biodiesel.org

This trade association, representing the biodiesel industry, serves as the coordinating body for biodiesel research and development in the United States. The website provides information on the purchasing, handling, and use of biodiesel fuels.

Natural Gas Vehicle Coalition

http://www.ngvc.org/

The Natural Gas Vehicle Coalition consists of natural gas companies, vehicle and equipment manufacturers, service providers, environmental groups, and government organizations.

Rocky Mountain Institute Transportation Page

http://www.rmi.org/sitepages/pid191.php

This website offers information on the environmental impact of transportation and extensive information about Hypercar vehicles.

Union of Concerned Scientists, Clean Vehicle Program

http://www.ucsusa.org/clean_vehicles

This site provides information about the latest developments in alternative vehicles, the environmental impact of conventional vehicles, and documents such as the guide Buying a Greener Vehicle: Electric, Hybrids, and Fuel Cells.

U.S. Department of Energy, Fuel Economy

http://www.fueleconomy.gov/feg

This website offers comparisons of new and used cars and trucks based on gas mileage (mpg), greenhouse gas emissions, air pollution ratings, and safety information.

U.S. Department of Energy, Office of Transportation Technologies, Alternative Fuels Data Center

http://www.afdc.energy.gov

This center provides information on alternative fuels and alternatively fueled vehicles, a locator for alternative fueling stations, and more. Their Alternative Fuel Vehicles and Advanced Technology Vehicle Listing for 2007 can be found online at http://www.afdc.energy.gov/afdc/pdfs/my2007_afv_atv.pdf.

13. Definitions

Alternative-fuel vehicles use low-polluting, nongasoline fuels such as electricity, hydrogen, propane, compressed natural gas, liquid natural gas, methanol, and ethanol. In LEED, efficient gas-electric hybrid vehicles are included in this group.

	SS
NC	Credit 4.3
SCHOOLS	Credit 4.3
CS	Credit 4.3

Fuel-efficient vehicles have achieved a minimum green score of 40 according to the annual vehicle-rating guide of the American Council for an Energy Efficient Economy.

Full-time equivalent (**FTE**) represents a regular building occupant who spends 40 hours per week in the project building. Part-time or overtime occupants have FTE values based on their hours per week divided by 40. Multiple shifts are included or excluded depending on the intent and requirements of the credit.

Greenhouse gases are relatively transparent to the higher-energy sunlight but trap lower-energy infrared radiation (e.g., carbon dioxide, methane, and CFCs).

Hybrid vehicles use a gasoline engine to drive an electric generator and use the electric generator and/or storage batteries to power electric motors that drive the vehicle's wheels.

Low-emitting vehicles are classified as zero-emission vehicles (ZEVs) by the California Air Resources Board.

Preferred parking, available to particular users, includes designated spaces close to the building (aside from designated handicapped spots), designated covered spaces, discounted parking passes, and guaranteed passes in a lottery system.

ALTERNATIVE TRANSPORTATION—PARKING CAPACITY

	NC	SCHOOLS	CS
Credit	SS Credit 4.4	SS Credit 4.4	SS Credit 4.4
Points	2 points	2 points	2 points

Intent

To reduce pollution and land development impacts from automobile use.

Requirements

NC & CS

CASE 1. Non-Residential Projects

OPTION 1

Size parking capacity must meet but not exceed minimum local zoning requirements.

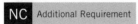 **NC** Additional Requirement

Provide preferred parking for carpools or vanpools for 5% of the total parking spaces.

OR

OPTION 2

For projects that provide parking for less than 5% (for New Construction) or 3% (for Core & Shell) of full-time equivalent (FTE) building occupants:

Provide preferred parking[1] for carpools or vanpools, marked as such, for 5% (for New Construction) or 3% (for Core & Shell) of total parking spaces. Providing a discounted parking rate is an acceptable substitute for preferred parking for carpool or vanpool vehicles. To establish a meaningful incentive in all potential markets, the parking rate must be discounted at least 20%. The discounted rate must be available to all customers (i.e. not limited to the number of customers equal to 5% of the vehicle parking capacity), publicly posted at the entrance of the parking area, and available for a minimum of 2 years.

OR

OPTION 3

Provide no new parking.

CASE 2. Residential Projects

OPTION 1

Size parking capacity to meet but not exceed minimum local zoning requirements

Provide infrastructure and support programs to facilitate shared vehicle use such as carpool drop-off areas, designated parking for vanpools, car-share services, ride boards and shuttle services to mass transit.

---

1 For the purposes of this credit "preferred parking" refers to the parking spots that are closest to the main entrance of the project (exclusive of spaces designated for handicapped persons) or parking passes provided at a discounted price.

NC & CS (continued)

OR

OPTION 2

Provide no new parking.

CASE 3. Mixed Use (Residential with Commercial/Retail) Projects

OPTION 1

Mixed-use buildings with less than 10% commercial area must be considered residential and adhere to the residential requirements in Case 2. For mixed-use buildings with more than 10% commercial area, the commercial space must adhere to non-residential requirements in Case 1 and the residential component must adhere to residential requirements in Case 2.

OR

OPTION 2

Provide no new parking.

ALL CASES

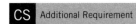 **CS** Additional Requirement

See Appendix 1 — Default Occupancy Counts for occupancy count requirements and guidance.

SCHOOLS

OPTION 1

Size parking capacity must meet but not exceed minimum local zoning requirements.

Provide preferred parking for carpools or vanpools for 5% of the total parking spaces.

OR

OPTION 2

Provide no new parking.

OR

OPTION 3

For projects that have no minimum local zoning requirements, provide 25% fewer parking spaces than the applicable standard listed in the 2003 Institute of Transportation Engineers (ITE) "Parking Generation" study at http://www.ite.org.

1. Benefits and Issues to Consider

Environmental Issues

Reducing private automobile use saves energy and avoids associated environmental problems, such as vehicle emissions that contribute to smog, air pollution, and greenhouse gas emissions, as well as environmental impacts associated with oil extraction and petroleum refining. The environmental benefits of carpooling are significant. For example, if 100 people carpooled (2 people per car) 10 miles to work and 10 miles home instead of driving separately, they would prevent emissions of about 970 pounds of carbon dioxide per day and would forgo 50 gallons of gas per day.[7]

Parking facilities also have negative impacts on the environment because asphalt surfaces increase stormwater runoff and contribute to urban heat island effects. By restricting the size of parking lots and promoting carpooling, project teams can reduce these effects and provide such benefits as more green space.

Economic Issues

Carpooling reduces the size of parking areas needed to support building occupants, allowing a building to accommodate more occupants without enlarging the parking area. Carpooling also helps reduce building costs, since less land is needed for parking and less infrastructure is needed to support vehicles. Smaller parking areas can decrease the amount of impervious surfaces on a site. This may result in reduced stormwater costs if the local utility bases its fees on impervious surface area. Moreover, because fewer cars on the road means less pollution, traffic congestion, and wear and tear to roadways, many municipalities and state governments offer tax incentives for carpooling programs.

2. Related Credits

Minimizing parking, particularly surface parking, by meeting but not exceeding zoning requirements can provide opportunities for enhancing open space, minimizing heat island effect, and minimizes stormwater runoff. See the following credits:

- SS Credit 5.1: Site Development—Protect and Restore Habitat
- SS Credit 5.2: Maximize Open Space
- SS Credit 6: Stormwater Management
- SS Credit 7.1: Heat Island Effect—Nonroof

3. Summary of Referenced Standards

Institute of Transportation Engineers, Parking Generation study, 2003
http://www.ite.org
Parking Generation, third edition, represents a significant change from the 1987 edition. Three times as much data are now available and 91 land uses are represented. In addition, this update incorporates parking demand data by hour of day. For the benefit of future analysis and research, this edition separates parking data records by various factors that may affect parking demand. The study links parking data to the hour of observation to provide a temporal understanding of parking demand and its peak hour. Additionally, this update separates out the influences of area type on parking demand, including (where data are available) information about sites that have priced parking.

	SS
NC	Credit 4.4
SCHOOLS	Credit 4.4
CS	Credit 4.4

4. Implementation

Limit the availability of parking to encourage the use of alternative forms of transportation to and from the site,. Choose a project site that is easily accessible from residential areas by bicycle or public transportation. Once the site is selected, determine how many cars are likely to drive to the site and compare this number with local zoning requirements. If parking demand is expected to be less than that required by local codes, consider seeking a variance with the appropriate authorities to provide less parking. However, any on-site parking reductions should be carefully balanced with community needs to avoid needlessly burdening surrounding neighborhoods with excessive street parking.

Where possible, develop transportation demand management strategies to reduce the number of parking spaces required to meet the needs of occupants. Transportation demand strategies may include publishing rosters with addresses to assist occupants, employees, and students in finding carpool partners, creating incentive programs for carpooling, providing a rideshare board, or setting parking fees at a level sufficient to encourage carpooling. When designing for schools, establish policies that will discourage or prohibit unnecessary student driving.

5. Timeline and Team

Discussions regarding reduction of parking capacity are most productive at the project concept phase. This may entail discussions with zoning and civic officials and could include community and neighborhood organizations. A traffic study can be a valuable tool for evaluating traffic patterns and expected commuting in single-occupancy vehicles. An additional team member may be engaged as part of the project team to develop this traffic study.

Because of their size or location or because of regulatory requirements, many projects may entail zoning negotiations over the parking requirements. Planned developments may have unique parking requirements that are valuable to consider and discuss as part of the overall alternative transportation strategies.

Design solutions to reduce parking capacity for the project site should be incorporated during schematic design and design development. The architect and design team, with the project owner, should choose the most appropriate approach for future occupants.

6. Calculations

Calculations are required for the options listed below; other approaches require no calculations.

NC

CASE 1, OPTION 1

Determine the number of parking spaces and multiply by 5% to determine the number of designated carpool or vanpool spaces required.

CASE 1, OPTION 2

Determine the number of FTE occupants (see below) and calculate the percentage for whom parking is provided. If parking is provided for less than 5% of FTEs, multiply the total number of parking spaces by 5% to determine the number of designated carpool or vanpool spaces required.

CS

CASE 1, OPTION 2

Determine the number of FTE occupants (see below) and calculate the percentage for whom parking is provided. If parking is provided for less than 3% of FTEs, multiply the total number of parking spaces by 3% to determine the number of designated carpool or vanpool spaces required.

SCHOOLS

OPTION 1

Determine the number of parking spaces and multiply by 5% to determine the number of designated carpool or vanpool spaces required.

OPTION 3

Determine the number of spaces recommended in the 2003 Institute of Transportation Engineers' Parking Generation study for average peak period demand and multiply by 75% to determine the maximum number of parking spaces allowable.

Full-Time Equivalent Occupants

To determine the number of full-time equivalent occupants, follow the steps below.

STEP 1

Identify the total number of full-time and part-time building occupants. In buildings with multiple shifts, use only the highest-volume shift in the FTE calculation but consider shift overlap when determining peak building use.

STEP 2

Calculate the full-time equivalent (FTE) number of occupants based on a standard 8-hour occupancy period. An 8-hour occupant has an FTE value of 1.0; a part-time occupant has a FTE value based on work hours per day divided by 8 (see Equation 1). FTE calculations for each shift of the project must be used consistently for all LEED credits.

If occupancy is not known, see Appendix 1, Default Occupancy Counts, for occupancy count requirements and guidance.

Equation 1: FTE Occupants

$$\text{Total FTE Occupants} = \frac{\text{Total Occupant Hours}}{8}$$

7. Documentation Guidance

As a first step in preparing to complete the LEED-Online documentation requirements, work through the following measure. Refer to LEED-Online for the complete descriptions of all required documentation.

- Prepare information about the amount and type of parking provided, and how carpooling or vanpooling is supported by infrastructure and/or programming. Depending on the option pursued, this might include information about parking capacity, number of preferred parking spaces, number of FTEs, zoning requirements, or copies of brochures that communicate carpooling and vanpooling support structures to occupants.

8. Examples

There are no examples for this credit.

9. Exemplary Performance

Projects may earn an Innovation in Design credit for point for exemplary performance by instituting a comprehensive transportation management plan that demonstrates a quantifiable reduction in personal automobile use. Only 1 exemplary performance credit is available for implementing a comprehensive transportation management plan under SS Credit 4, Alternative Transportation. Projects that are awarded exemplary performance for SS Credit 4.1, Alternative Transportation— Public Transportation Access, Option 2 are not eligible for exemplary performance under this credit.

10. Regional Variations

There are no regional variations associated with this credit.

11. Operations and Maintenance Considerations

For project buildings that include preferred parking, establish procedures for the use of this amenity, communicate them to building occupants, and assign operations staff for their administration. The procedures might include establishing a system for enforcing use of designated spaces (e.g, a permitting system), discounting paid parking, and tracking use of preferred parking.

12. Resources

Please see USGBC's LEED Registered Project Tools (http://www.usgbc.org/projecttools) for additional resources and technical information.

Websites
Commuting Guide for Employers
http://www.self-propelled-city.com/index.php
This website outlines strategies employers can use to encourage employees to commute by bicycle.

Smart Commute
http://www.smartcommute.org/
Smart Commute is a program of Research Triangle Park that has valuable information about telecommuting and carpool programs useful for any organization.

U.S. EPA and Department of Transportation, Best Workplaces for Commuters
http://www.bestworkplaces.org/index.htm
This program publicly recognizes employers who have exemplary commuter benefits programs. It provides tools, guidance, and promotions to help employers give commuter benefits, reap the financial gains, and achieve national recognition.

U.S. EPA, Transportation and Air Quality
http://www.epa.gov/otaq/
This site provides information on the types and effects of air pollution associated with automobile use and links to resources for organizations interested in promoting commuter choice programs.

13. Definitions

A **carpool** is an arrangement by which 2 or more people share a vehicle for transportation.

A **mixed-use** project involves a combination of residential and commercial or retail components.

Preferred parking, available to particular users, includes designated spaces close to the building (aside from designated handicapped spots), designated covered spaces, discounted parking passes, and guaranteed passes in a lottery system.

SITE DEVELOPMENT—PROTECT OR RESTORE HABITAT

	NC	SCHOOLS	CS
Credit	SS Credit 5.1	SS Credit 5.1	SS Credit 5.1
Points	1 point	1 point	1 point

Intent

To conserve existing natural areas and restore damaged areas to provide habitat and promote biodiversity.

Requirements

NC, SCHOOLS & CS

CASE 1. Greenfield Sites[1]

Limit all site disturbance to the following parameters:

- 40 feet beyond the building perimeter;

- 10 feet beyond surface walkways, patios, surface parking and utilities less than 12 inches in diameter;

- 15 feet beyond primary roadway curbs and main utility branch trenches;

- 25 feet beyond constructed areas with permeable surfaces (such as pervious paving areas, stormwater detention facilities and playing fields) that require additional staging areas to limit compaction in the constructed area.

CASE 2. Previously Developed[2] Areas or Graded Sites

Restore or protect a minimum of 50% of the site (excluding the building footprint) or 20% of the total site area (including building footprint), whichever is greater, with native or adapted vegetation[3]. Projects earning SS Credit 2: Development Density and Community Connectivity may include vegetated roof surface in this calculation if the plants are native or adapted, provide habitat, and promote biodiversity.

---

1. Greenfield sites are those that are not previously developed or graded and remain in a natural state.
2. Previously developed sites are those that previously contained buildings, roadways, parking lots or were graded or altered by direct human activities.
3. Native or adapted plants are plants indigenous to a locality or cultivars of native plants that are adapted to the local climate and are not considered invasive species or noxious weeds.

	SS
NC	Credit 5.1
SCHOOLS	Credit 5.1
CS	Credit 5.1

1. Benefits and Issues to Consider

Environmental Issues

Development on building sites often damages site ecology, indigenous plants, and regional animal populations. Natural areas provide important ecological services, including effective and natural management of stormwater volumes. Ecological site damage can be mitigated by restoring native and adapted vegetation and other ecologically appropriate features to a site, which in turn provide habitat for fauna. Other ecologically appropriate features are natural site elements beyond vegetation that maintain or restore the ecological integrity of a site. These may include water bodies, exposed rock, bare ground or other features that are part of the natural landscape within a region and provide habitat value. Establishing strict site boundaries and staging areas during construction reduces damage to the site and helps preserve wildlife habitats and migration corridors.

For school project teams, connecting a school building to its historical natural landscape can provide meaningful opportunities for student learning outside the classroom.

Economic Issues

Native or adapted plantings require less maintenance than nonnative plants and reduce costs over the building life cycle by minimizing the need for fertilizers, pesticides, and irrigation. In many cases, trees and other vegetation grown off-site are expensive and may not survive transplanting. Additional trees and other landscaping, as well as soil remediation and water features, will add to initial costs. To distribute costs over time, it may be advantageous to implement site restoration in phases. Strategic plantings can shade a building's and site's impervious areas, which can decrease cooling loads during warm months and reduce energy expenditures. If vegetated roofs are used to satisfy credit requirements, energy costs are generally lessened because of their insulating properties.

2. Related Credits

Protecting or restoring habitat provides open space, which minimizes the stormwater runoff and heat island problems that stem from impervious surfaces. Use of native vegetation on-site or as part of a vegetated roof may contribute to achieving the following credits:

- SS Credit 5.2: Site Development—Maximize Open Space
- SS Credit 6.1: Stormwater Design—Quantity Control
- SS Credit 6.2: Stormwater Design—Quality Control
- SS Credit 7.1: Heat Island Effect—Nonroof
- SS Credit 7.2: Heat Island Effect—Roof
- WE Credit 1: Water-Efficient Landscaping

3. Summary of Referenced Standards

There are no standards referenced for this credit.

4. Implementation

Preserve and enhance natural site elements, including existing water bodies, soil conditions, ecosystems, trees, and other vegetation. Identify opportunities for site improvements that would increase the area of native and adapted vegetation or other ecologically appropriate features. Monoculture plantings (e.g., turf) cannot contribute to the credit requirements even if they meet the definition of native or adapted vegetation. Restoration and maintenance activities might include removing unnecessary paved areas and replacing them with landscaped areas, or replacing large lawns with native or adapted plantings to promote biodiversity and provide habitat to native animals. If possible, connect protected or restored areas to habitat corridors adjacent to the project site.

For sites that contain both greenfield and previously developed areas, the project must comply with those site conditions' specific criteria. For example, if a 10-acre site contains 5 acres of greenfield and 5 acres of previously developed land, site disturbance must be limited in the greenfield area, and native and adapted vegetation must be protected or restored for at least 50% (excluding the building footprint) of the previously developed site area. In these situations, minimizing the development of the greenfield portion of the site is an environmentally sound choice.

During the construction process, establish clearly marked construction and disturbance boundaries and note the site protection requirements in construction documents. The contractor should delineate lay-down, recycling, and disposal areas and use paved areas for staging activities. Erecting construction fencing around the dripline of existing trees will protect them from damage and soil compaction by construction vehicles. Consider the costs and benefits of contractual penalties if protected areas outside the construction boundaries are destroyed. The contractor should coordinate infrastructure construction to minimize the disruption of the site and work with existing topography to limit cut-and-fill efforts for the project.

For urban projects with few landscape opportunities, consider installing a vegetated roof to help meet the credit requirements. A landscape architect can help select native, adapted, and noninvasive species; a structural engineer should confirm that the roof structure is designed to support the added weight of plant beds. Research the bird and insect species that are likely to use the roof and select plants that will provide food, forage, or nesting areas. Vegetated roofs that lack a diversity of habitat-providing species types and plant sizes do not meet the intent of the credit.

Assess the impact of building and site development on resident and migratory wildlife and determine the necessary measures to reduce the threat that building windows pose to birds. Building façades that reflect trees, vegetated open space, wetlands, and water bodies may require measures to reduce the potential for collisions (see guidance in SS Credit 5.2, Maximize Open Space). Teams should avoid planting trees and shrubs that attract wildlife in locations likely to be reflected in building glazing unless they also take measures to reduce bird collisions. Such plants should be placed either very close (3 feet or less) to windows or far enough away that the reflection will not be mistaken for actual vegetation.

5. Timeline and Team

Consult landscape architects, ecologists, environmental engineers, civil engineers, and local professionals who can provide site-specific expertise during the site design process can help in identifying opportunities to minimize the building footprint and impervious areas. Have an ecologist, a government official, or other qualified professional identify the site's important environmental characteristics, including wetlands, sloped areas, special habitat areas, and forested areas to be protected. In the construction documents, clearly identify construction entrances and site disturbance setbacks; verify their locations on the site before construction proceeds. During construction, the site superintendent or other responsible party should routinely inspect fences and boundaries to ensure that construction activities are not encroaching on the protected areas. If a vegetated roof is part of the strategy for achieving this credit, the roof designers should work with a structural engineer to address load issues.

SS	
NC	Credit 5.1
SCHOOLS	Credit 5.1
CS	Credit 5.1

6. Calculations

CASE 1. Greenfield Sites

There are no calculations required for this case.

CASE 2. Previously Developed Areas or Graded Sites

Compliance with the credit requirements is based on the project building's site area, the building footprint, and the size of site areas covered with native or adapted vegetation or other ecologically important site features. First subtract the building footprint from the total site area and multiply this area by 0.5 (Equation 1). Then multiply the total site area by 0.2. The larger of these 2 area calculations is equal to the area of restored or protected habitat required. Using scaled site drawings, determine the size of qualifying natural areas. These areas must contain polycultures of native or adapted plant species or otherwise meet the definition of an ecologically appropriate site feature.

Equation 1

$$\text{50\% of Site (excluding building footprint)} = \left(\text{Total Site Area} - \text{Building Footprint Area} \right) \times 0.5$$

Equation 2

$$\text{20\% of Total Site} = \text{Total Site Area} \times 0.2$$

The building footprint and site boundary used for SS Credit 5.1 must be applied consistently across other credits.

7. Documentation Guidance

As a first step in preparing to complete the LEED-Online documentation requirements, work through the following measures. Refer to LEED-Online for the complete descriptions of all required documentation.

- For greenfield sites, develop site plans that clearly demarcate disturbance boundaries.

- For previously developed or graded sites, prepare site plans that highlight the protected or restored site area and list native and adapted plant species.

8. Examples

CASE 1. Greenfield Sites

Figure 1 shows disturbance boundaries around the development footprint that protect the site's natural areas.

Figure 1. Example of Disturbance Boundaries

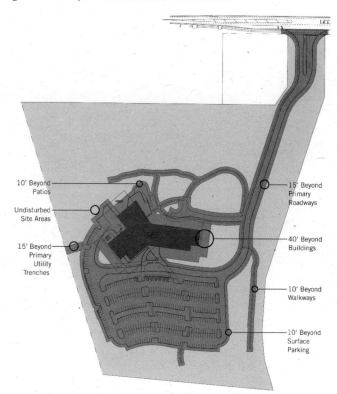

10' Beyond Patios

Undisturbed Site Areas

15' Beyond Primary Utility Trenches

15' Beyond Primary Roadways

40' Beyond Buildings

10' Beyond Walkways

10' Beyond Surface Parking

CASE 2. Previously Developed Areas or Graded Sites

Figure 2 shows the areas of a site used for calculating the percentage of site area qualifying as protected or restored.

Figure 2. Example of Site Drawing Showing Natural Areas

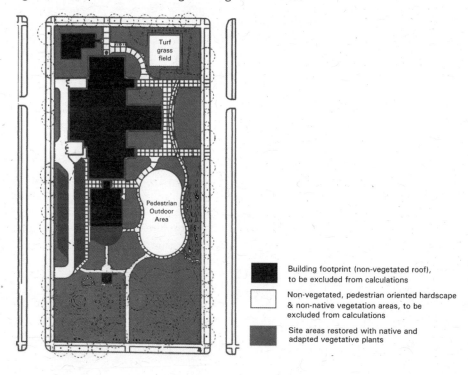

Turf grass field

Pedestrian Outdoor Area

Building footprint (non-vegetated roof), to be excluded from calculations

Non-vegetated, pedestrian oriented hardscape & non-native vegetation areas, to be excluded from calculations

Site areas restored with native and adapted vegetative plants

	SS
NC	Credit 5.1
SCHOOLS	Credit 5.1
CS	Credit 5.1

9. Exemplary Performance

Projects may earn an Innovation in Design credit for exemplary performance by restoring or protecting a minimum of 75% of the site (excluding the building footprint) or 30% of the total site (including building footprint), whichever is greater, with native or adapted vegetation.

10. Regional Variations

By definition, native and adapted plants vary with climate and region. Focus on protecting and restoring vegetation and ecological features that are appropriate to the local area.

11. Operations and Maintenance Considerations

Landscape design affects the type of maintenance needed to support the health of the plant species on site, as well as the frequency and methods for hardscape maintenance. Landscaping can also be a source of contaminants entering the building.

In vegetated areas near walkways, consider using plant species that will drop few leaves, petals, or berries to minimize hardscape maintenance requirements. Be aware that certain types of vegetation produce allergens that will affect building occupants. Avoid plantings that will harbor pest populations near the building shell.

Consider coordinating with building operators and landscape maintenance contractors or groundskeepers to establish a sustainable landscape management plan; the plan should include the following:

- A list of all plant species used in the site landscaping plan, with notations about which species meet the LEED definition of native or adapted species.

- Information about invasive species and pests that plantings may harbor.

- Best maintenance practices for the chosen plantings.

- Site maps that show boundaries around protected or restored habitat that should not be disturbed or developed during future projects.

For the first 2 to 3 years, watering and weeding may be necessary to establish new plantings. Once established, native and adapted plantings generally require minimal maintenance, so water and fertilizing applications shouldbe reduced or eliminated. Certain species may require occasional pruning or mowing to maintain. Fall mowing should not occur until after seeds have matured to ensure that annuals will return the next spring and to help perennials spread.[8]

12. Resources

Please see USGBC's LEED Registered Project Tools (http://www.usgbc.org/projecttools) for additional resources and technical information.

Websites

American Bird Conservancy

http://www.abcbirds.org

ABC is a national leader in reducing human effects on birds and wildlife. ABC's bird collision program supports national efforts to reduce bird mortality through education and advocacy.

American Society of Landscape Architects

http://www.asla.org

ASLA is the national professional association representing landscape architects. Its website provides information about products, services, publications, and events.

Birds and Buildings Forum

http://www.birdsandbuildings.org

This Chicago-based nonprofit organization supports bird-friendly design through education and advocacy. Its website maintains lists of organizations and resources.

Ecological Restoration

http://www.ecologicalrestoration.info

This quarterly print and online publication from the University of Wisconsin-Madison Arboretum provides a forum for people interested in all aspects of ecological restoration.

Lady Bird Johnson Wildlife Center

http://www.wildflower.org

The center, located in Austin, Texas, has the mission of educating people about the environmental necessity, economic value, and natural beauty of native plants. The website offers a number of resources, including a nationwide native plant information network and a national suppliers directory.

North American Native Plant Society

http://www.nanps.org

NANPS is a nonprofit association dedicated to the study, conservation, cultivation, and restoration of native plants. Its website contains links to state and local associations.

Plant Native

http://www.plantnative.org

This organization is dedicated to bringing native plants and nature-scaping into mainstream landscaping practices.

Society for Ecological Restoration International

http://www.ser.org

The mission of this nonprofit consortium of scientists, planners, administrators, ecological consultants, landscape architects, engineers, and others is to promote ecological restoration as a means of sustaining the diversity of life and to reestablish an ecologically healthy relationship between nature and culture.

Soil and Water Conservation Society

http://www.swcs.org

This organization focuses on fostering the science and art of sustainable soil, water, and related natural resource management.

The Nature Conservancy

http://www.nature.org

The Nature Conservancy is a conservation organization that works to protect ecologically important lands and water.

	SS
NC	Credit 5.1
SCHOOLS	Credit 5.1
CS	Credit 5.1

Print Media

Design for Human Ecosystems: Landscape, Land Use, and Natural Resources, by John Tillman Lyle (Island Press, 1999).
This text explores types of landscape design that function like natural ecosystems.

Landscape Restoration Handbook, by Donald Harker, Marc Evans, Gary Libby, Kay Harker, and Sherrie Evans (Lewis Publishers, 1999).
This resource is a comprehensive guide to natural landscaping and ecological restoration and provides information on 21 types of ecological restoration.

	SS
NC	Credit 5.1
SCHOOLS	Credit 5.1
CS	Credit 5.1

Bird-Safe Building Guidelines (New York City Audubon Society, Inc., May 2007). This publication provides useful information on minimizing bird collisions with buildings and offers case studies and design strategies for constructing new buildings and retrofitting existing buildings. The 38MB publication can be downloaded from http://www.nycaudubon.org/home/BirdSafeBuildingGuidelines.pdf

13. Definitions

Adapted (or introduced) plants reliably grow well in a given habitat with minimal winter protection, pest control, fertilization, or irrigation once their root systems are established. Adapted plants are considered low maintenance and not invasive.

Biodiversity is the variety of life in all forms, levels, and combinations, including ecosystem diversity, species diversity, and genetic diversity.

Building footprint is the area on a project site used by the building structure, defined by the perimeter of the building plan. Parking lots, landscapes, and other nonbuilding facilities are not included in the building footprint.

The **development footprint** is the area affected by development or by project site activity. Hardscape, access roads, parking lots, nonbuilding facilities, and the building itself are all included in the development footprint.

Greenfields are sites not previously developed or graded that could support open space, habitat, or agriculture.

Invasive plants are nonnative to the ecosystem and likely to cause harm once introduced. These species are characteristically adaptable and aggressive, have a high reproductive capacity, and tend to overrun the ecosystems they enter. Collectively, they are among the greatest threats to biodiversity and ecosystem stability.

Local zoning requirements are local government regulations imposed to promote orderly development of private lands and prevent land-use conflicts.

Native (or indigenous) plants are adapted to a given area during a defined time period and are not invasive. In North America, the term often refers to plants growing in a region prior to the time of settlement by people of European descent.

Open space area is usually defined by local zoning requirements. If local zoning requirements do not clearly define open space, it is defined for the purposes of LEED calculations as the property area minus the development footprint; it must be vegetated and pervious, with exceptions only as noted in the credit requirements section. Only ground areas are calculated as open space. For projects located in urban areas that earn a Development Density and Community Connectivity credit, open space also includes nonvehicular, pedestrian-oriented hardscape spaces.

Previously developed sites once had buildings, roadways, parking lots, or were graded or otherwise altered by direct human activities.

The LEED **project boundary** is the portion of the project site submitted for LEED certification. For single building developments, this is the entire project scope and is generally limited to the site boundary. For multiple building developments, the LEED project boundary may be a portion of the development as determined by the project team.

Retention ponds capture stormwater runoff and clear it of pollutants before its release. Some retention pond designs use gravity only; others use mechanical equipment, such as pipes and pumps, to facilitate transport. Some ponds are dry except during storm events; others permanently store water.

SITE DEVELOPMENT—MAXIMIZE OPEN SPACE

	NC	SCHOOLS	CS
Credit	SS Credit 5.2	SS Credit 5.2	SS Credit 5.2
Points	1 point	1 point	1 point

Intent

To promote biodiversity by providing a high ratio of open space to development footprint.

Requirements

NC, SCHOOLS & CS

CASE 1. Sites with Local Zoning Open Space Requirements

Reduce the development footprint[1] and/or provide vegetated open space within the project boundary such that the amount of open space exceeds local zoning requirements by 25%.

CASE 2. Sites with No Local Zoning Requirements (e.g. some university campuses, military bases)

Provide vegetated open space area adjacent to the building that is equal in area to the building footprint.

CASE 3. Sites with Zoning Ordinances but No Open Space Requirements

Provide vegetated open space equal to 20% of the project's site area.

ALL CASES

For projects in urban areas that earn SS Credit 2: Development Density and Community Connectivity, vegetated roof areas can contribute to credit compliance.

For projects in urban areas that earn SS Credit 2: Development Density and Community Connectivity, pedestrian-oriented hardscape areas can contribute to credit compliance. For such projects, a minimum of 25% of the open space counted must be vegetated.

Wetlands or naturally designed ponds may count as open space and the side slope gradients average 1:4 (vertical: horizontal) or less and are vegetated.

---

1   Development footprint is defined as the total area of the building footprint, hardscape, access roads and parking.

1. Benefits and Issues to Consider

Environmental Issues

Open space provides habitat for vegetation and wildlife. Even small open spaces in urban areas can provide refuges for wildlife populations that have become increasingly marginalized. Plants that support insects and other pollinators can help sustain populations higher up the food chain. Open space also reduces the urban heat island effect, increases stormwater infiltration, and provides human populations with a connection to the outdoors.

For school project teams, incorporating open space into the design of a school can facilitate a highly effective resource for teaching about natural systems, biodiversity, and other ecological and natural science subjects.

Economic Issues

Preserving topsoil, plants, and trees on a site can reduce landscaping costs. Even where rents are high and the incentive to build out to the property line is strong, well-designed open space can significantly increase property values. Reducing the footprint of a structure on a given site can have varying economic impacts. Building a vertical structure with the same square footage as a horizontal structure may add a small percentage to initial costs, depending on building size and use. However, a structure with a smaller footprint is generally more resource efficient, resulting in reduced material and energy costs. A more compact building with coordinated infrastructure can reduce initial project costs as well as operations and maintenance costs. Reduced earthwork, shorter utility lines, and reduced surface parking and paved areas all can decrease initial project costs. If vegetated roofs are used to satisfy credit requirements, energy costs are generally lessened because of their insulating properties.

2. Related Credits

Providing vegetated open space on the project site may contribute to stormwater mitigation goals and reduce the urban heat island effect, in turn helping project teams earn the following credits:

- SS Credit 6.1: Stormwater Design—Quantity Control

- SS Credit 6.2: Stormwater Design—Quality Control

- SS Credit 7.1: Heat Island Effect—Nonroof

- SS Credit 7.2 : Heat Island Effect—Roof

3. Summary of Referenced Standards

There are no standards referenced for this credit.

4. Implementation

Choose a development footprint and location that minimize disturbance of the existing ecosystem, taking into consideration building orientation, daylighting, heat island effect, stormwater generation, significant vegetation, existing green corridors, and other sustainable sites issues. Once the site and building location have been determined, work with a civil engineer to design and construct a compact parking, road, and building footprint layout to preserve open land and provide connections to adjacent ecosystems. The design team and the owner can reduce footprints by tightening program needs and stacking floor plans.

In a campus setting with no local zoning requirements, open space that is equal to the building footprint can be considered separate from the project site, as long as the open space is preserved for the life of the building.

When designing vegetated roofs, pay attention to support, waterproofing, and drainage issues. Vegetated roofs typically include a waterproof and root-repellent membrane, drainage system, filter cloth, lightweight growing medium, and plants. Modular systems are available, with all layers designed as movable interlocking grids, or individual layers can be installed separately.

	SS
NC	Credit 5.2
SCHOOLS	Credit 5.2
CS	Credit 5.2

Urban open space that includes hardscape surfaces should be accessible to pedestrians and provide recreation opportunities. Consider use of pervious paving for these surfaces to aid stormwater management. Examples of urban open space include pocket parks, accessible roof decks, plazas, and courtyards.

Naturally designed ponds provide ecosystem services, such as aquatic habitat, stormwater quality control, and nutrient recycling.

Assess the impact of building and site development on resident and migratory wildlife, and determine the necessary measures to alleviate the threat that building windows pose to birds. Site strategies to maximize vegetated open space may increase the number of bird collisions. Assess the problem and use bird-safe landscaping and façade treatments as appropriate. Specifically, plants that attract birds should be placed either very close to glazed façades (3 feet or less) or far enough away that they are not reflected in the windows. Bird-safe treatments for the building design and glazing include using exterior shading devices, introducing etched or frit patterns in the glass, and creating "visual markers" in sufficient locations. Visual markers are differentiated planes, materials, textures, colors, opacity, or other visually contrasting features that help fragment window reflections and reduce overall transparency and reflectivity.

For school projects, consider overlapping uses of site elements to reduce impervious surfaces and maximize open space. For example, bus drop-off space can be used for overflow parking, or playing fields can be constructed within specially designed retention basins. School project teams should also evaluate their long-term development plans to use resources efficiently and protect the environment in the process. To facilitate proper maintenance, demarcate greenfields, restored areas, and other outdoor areas such as playing fields.

5. Timeline and Team

Consult landscape architects, ecologists, environmental engineers, and civil engineers, as well as local professionals who can provide site-specific expertise during the site selection and design process to maximize open space. Have a government official, ecologist or other qualified professional identify important environmental characteristics, including wetlands, sloped areas, special habitat areas, and forested areas, to be protected, and facilitate collaboration between these professionals and the design team. If a vegetated roof is part of the strategy for achieving this credit, the roof designers should work with a structural engineer to address load issues.

6. Calculations

CASE 1

Determine the amount of open space required by local zoning requirements and multiply by 125% to determine the amount of open space necessary to meet the credit requirement.

CASE 3

Multiply the site area by 20% to determine the amount of open space necessary to meet the credit requirement.

ALL CASES

For projects in urban areas that can count pedestrian-oriented hardscape as open space, multiply the total open space by 25% to determine the portion that must be vegetated.

The building footprint and site boundary used for SS Credit 5.2 must be applied consistently across other credits.

7. Documentation Guidance

As a first step in preparing to complete the LEED-Online documentation requirements, work through the following measures. Refer to LEED-Online for the complete descriptions of all required documentation.

- Show that the qualifying open space meets or exceeds the amount required by the credit (see calculations).

- Prepare a site plan that highlights qualifying open space.

8. Examples

CASE 1. Sites With Local Zoning Open Space Requirements
Calculation for a high-rise commercial office building in an urban center

A 670,000-square-foot commercial office building has an overall site area of 116,700 square feet. The zoning requirement calls for making a minimum of 20% of the net lot area (23,340 square feet) public open space. The project is in an urban center, complies with SS Credit 2, Development Density and Community Connectivity, and has provided the following open space:

Pedestrian-oriented hardscape	15,000 (sf)
Vegetated open space on structure	17,500 (sf)
Vegetated open space on grade	500 (sf)
Total open space	33,000 (sf)
Percentage greater than zoning requirement	41.3%

The percentage of vegetated open space as a portion of the total open space provided is 54.5%. Because the project exceeds the zoning requirements by more than 25% and because more than 25% of the open space is vegetated, the credit requirements are met.

9. Exemplary Performance

Projects may earn an Innovation in Design credit for exemplary performance by demonstrating that they have doubled the amount of open space required for credit achievement. All designated open space must be within the LEED project boundary. For example, projects subject to local zoning requirements must increase the amount of open space provided by 50% instead of by 25%; projects not subject to local zoning requirements must provide open space equal to twice the building footprint; and urban projects where zero open space is required must provide open space equal to 40% of the site area.

10. Regional Variations

There are no regional variations associated with this credit.

11. Operations and Maintenance Considerations

For open spaces with native and adapted vegetation, refer to SS Credit 5.1, Site Development—Protect or Restore Habitat.

If open space consists of monoculture and/or nonnative plantings, optimize the landscape for sustainable operations by choosing species with relatively low water, fertilizer, and maintenance requirements.

Consider using plant species that will drop few leaves, petals, or berries, to minimize hardscape maintenance requirements. Be aware that certain types of vegetation produce allergens that will affect building occupants. Avoid plantings that will harbor pest populations near the building shell. Consider providing facilities within the landscape design for on-site composting of landscape waste.

Consider working with building operators and landscape maintenance contractors or groundskeepers to establish a sustainable landscape management plan. The plan should specify the following:

- Using organic fertilizers suited to installed species.

- Applying fertilizer only when nutrient deficiencies have been determined through soil testing, and selecting fertilizers based on the soil and plant characteristics.

- Using environmentally preferred maintenance equipment as defined in the LEED Reference Guide for Green Building Operations & Maintenance, SS Credit 2, Building Exterior and Hardscape Management Plan.

- Using integrated pest management techniques.

- Developing site maps that show boundaries around open space that should not be disturbed or developed during future projects.

	SS
NC	Credit 5.2
SCHOOLS	Credit 5.2
CS	Credit 5.2

12. Resources

Please see USGBC's LEED Registered Project Tools (http://www.usgbc.org/projecttools) for additional resources and technical information.

Websites
Green Roofs for Healthy Cities
http://www.greenroofs.org
This nonprofit industry association consists of individuals and public and private organizations committed to developing a market for green roof infrastructure products and services across North America.

Soil and Water Conservation Society
http://www.swcs.org
This organization focuses on fostering the science and art of sustainable soil, water, and related natural resource management.

The Nature Conservancy
http://www.nature.org
The Nature Conservancy is a conservation organization that works to protect ecologically important lands and water.

Print Media
Beyond Preservation: Restoring and Inventing Landscapes, by Dwight A. Baldwin, et al. (University of Minnesota Press, 1994).

Design for Human Ecosystems: Landscape, Land Use, and Natural Resources, by John Tillman Lyle and Joan Woodward (Milldale Press, 1999).

Landscape Restoration Handbook, by Donald Harker (Lewis Publishers, 1999).

13. Definitions

Adapted (or introduced) plants reliably grow well in a given habitat with minimal winter protection, pest control, fertilization, or irrigation once their root systems are established. Adapted plants are considered low maintenance and not invasive.

	SS
NC	Credit 5.2
SCHOOLS	Credit 5.2
CS	Credit 5.2

Biodiversity is the variety of life in all forms, levels, and combinations, including ecosystem diversity, species diversity, and genetic diversity.

Building footprint is the area on a project site used by the building structure, defined by the perimeter of the building plan. Parking lots, landscapes, and other nonbuilding facilities are not included in the building footprint.

The **development footprint** is the area affected by development or by project site activity. Hardscape, access roads, parking lots, nonbuilding facilities, and the building itself are all included in the development footprint.

Greenfields are sites not previously developed or graded that could support open space, habitat, or agriculture.

Invasive plants are nonnative to the ecosystem and likely to cause harm once introduced. These species are characteristically adaptable and aggressive, have a high reproductive capacity, and tend to overrun the ecosystems they enter. Collectively, they are among the greatest threats to biodiversity and ecosystem stability.

Local zoning requirements are local government regulations imposed to promote orderly development of private lands and prevent land-use conflicts.

Native (or indigenous) plants are adapted to a given area during a defined time period and are not invasive. In North America, the term often refers to plants growing in a region prior to the time of settlement by people of European descent.

Open space area is usually defined by local zoning requirements. If local zoning requirements do not clearly define open space, it is defined for the purposes of LEED calculations as the property area minus the development footprint; it must be vegetated and pervious, with exceptions only as noted in the credit requirements section. Only ground areas are calculated as open space. For projects located in urban areas that earn SS Credit 2, Development Density and Community Connectivity, open space also includes nonvehicular, pedestrian-oriented hardscape spaces.

The LEED **project boundary** is the portion of the project site submitted for LEED certification. For single building developments, this is the entire project scope and is generally limited to the site boundary. For multiple building developments, the LEED project boundary may be a portion of the development as determined by the project team.

	NC	SCHOOLS	CS
Credit	SS Credit 6.1	SS Credit 6.1	SS Credit 6.1
Points	1 point	1 point	1 point

Intent

To limit disruption of natural hydrology by reducing impervious cover, increasing on-site infiltration, reducing or eliminating pollution from stormwater runoff and eliminating contaminants.

Requirements

NC, SCHOOLS & CS

CASE 1. Sites with Existing Imperviousness 50% or Less

OPTION 1

Implement a stormwater management plan that prevents the postdevelopment peak discharge rate and quantity from exceeding the predevelopment peak discharge rate and quantity for the 1- and 2-year 24-hour design storms.

OR

OPTION 2

Implement a stormwater management plan that protects receiving stream channels from excessive erosion. The stormwater management plan must include a stream channel protection and quantity control strategies.

CASE 2. Sites with Existing Imperviousness is Greater Than 50%

Implement a stormwater management plan that results in a 25% decrease in the volume of stormwater runoff from the 2-year 24-hour design storm.

1. Benefits and Issues to Consider

Environmental Issues

Stormwater is a major source of pollution for all types of water bodies in the United States.[9] Soil compaction caused by site development and the expanse of impervious surfaces, such as roads and parking lots, produce stormwater runoff that contains sediment and other contaminants, including atmospheric deposition, pesticides, fertilizers, vehicle fluid leaks, and mechanical equipment waste. Increased stormwater runoff can overload pipes and sewers and damage water quality, affecting navigation and recreation. Furthermore, municipal systems that convey and treat runoff volumes require significant infrastructure and maintenance.

The health of streams is closely linked to stormwater runoff velocities and volumes. Increases in the frequency and magnitude of stormwater runoff due to development can increase bankfull events and erosion, widen channels, and cause downcutting in streams. Effective on-site management practices let stormwater infiltrate the ground, thereby reducing the volume and intensity of stormwater flows.[10] Additionally, reducing stormwater runoff helps maintain the natural aquifer recharge cycle and restore depleted stream base flows.

SCHOOLS For school project teams, including natural stormwater management systems that mimic a site's natural hydrology can function as a valuable learning tool. An outdoor classroom that allows students to observe the path and retention of stormwater can help students better understand the interrelationship of the built environment and natural systems.

Economic Issues

If natural drainage systems are designed and implemented at the beginning of site planning, they can be integrated economically into the overall development. Water retention features require investments for design, installation, and maintenance; these features can also add significant value as site amenities, and costs can be minimized if systems are planned early in the design. The use of pervious pavement as part of an infiltration strategy may reduce the need for expensive and space-consuming retention options as well as the infrastructure needed to support conveyance. Using stormwater for nonpotable purposes, such as flushing urinals and toilets, custodial applications, and building equipment uses, would lower costs for potable water. A water analysis can help determine the estimated volume of water available for reuse.

Even small stormwater collection and treatment systems lessen the burden on municipalities for maintenance and repair, resulting in a more affordable and stable tax base. Where public utilities provide stormwater collection and conveyance service, projects may be able to lower stormwater fees by implementing strategies for managing stormwater on-site. Check with the local stormwater utility for fee reduction programs.

2. Related Credits

Efforts to reduce the rate and quantity of stormwater runoff will result in increased on-site infiltration, reducing stormwater treatment needs. Such steps will help projects achieve the following credit:

- SS Credit 6.2: Stormwater Design—Quality Control

Efforts to decrease impervious surfaces on the project site through pervious pavements, vegetated roofing, and vegetated open space can help meet the requirements of the following credits:

- SS Credit 5.1: Site Development—Protect or Restore Habitat

- SS Credit 5.2: Site Development—Maximize Open Space

- SS Credit 7.1: Heat Island Reduction—Nonroof

- SS Credit 7.2: Heat Island Reduction—Roof

Harvested rainwater reduces stormwater runoff and can be reused inside the building in nonpotable applications or as landscape irrigation, assisting projects with earning these credits:

- WE Credit 1: Water-Efficient Landscaping

- WE Credit 3: Water Use Reduction

However, projects in dense urban areas that earn credit for development density and community connectivity may have difficulty finding space for stormwater mitigation features. See the requirements for the following:

- SS Credit 2: Development Density and Community Connectivity

	SS
NC	Credit 6.1
SCHOOLS	Credit 6.1
CS	Credit 6.1

3. Summary of Referenced Standards
There are no standards referenced for this credit.

4. Implementation
The best way to achieve this credit may depend on the condition of the site. For a largely undeveloped site, the goal is to preserve stormwater flows and design the project to preserve the natural soil conditions, habitat, and rainfall characteristics. For redevelopment of a previously developed site, the goal typically is to improve stormwater management to restore the natural functions of the site as much as possible and decrease the amount of stormwater runoff.

The best way to minimize stormwater runoff volume is to reduce the amount of impervious surface area. Reducing impervious area can minimize the need for stormwater infrastructure or even make it unnecessary. Stormwater runoff is also affected by site topography and site design. Strategies to minimize or mitigate stormwater runoff may include using pervious paving materials, harvesting stormwater for reuse in irrigation and indoor nonpotable water applications, designing infiltration swales and retention ponds, planting vegetated filter strips, installing vegetated roofs, and clustering development to reduce paved surfaces such as roads and sidewalks.

Ensure that site hardscape surfaces meet all loading and accessibility requirements.

Harvesting Stormwater
Stormwater harvested in cisterns or other kinds of tanks can be substituted for potable water in landscape irrigation, fire suppression, toilet and urinal flushing, and custodial uses.

Storage options range from small rain barrels to underground cisterns that hold large volumes of water. Designers of stormwater harvesting systems of any size should consider the following:

1. Water budget. How will the harvested water be used and when will it be needed? For example, if stormwater will be used to irrigate landscaping for 4 summer months, teams should estimate the amount of water needed and the amount and timing of precipitation expected.

2. Drawdown. The storage system design must provide for the use or release of water between storm events for the design storage volume to be available.

3. Drainage area. The size and permeability of the area draining to the storage system determines how much runoff will be available for harvesting. Vegetated roofs will reduce the volume of runoff collected from roof surfaces.

4. Conveyance system. Reused stormwater and graywater systems must not be connected to other domestic or commercial potable water systems. Pipes and storage units should be clearly marked (e.g., "Caution: Reclaimed water—do not drink").

5. Pretreatment. Screens or filters may be used to remove debris and sediment from runoff and to minimize pollutants.

6. Pressurization. Uses for harvested rainwater may require pressurization. For example, most irrigation systems require water pressure of at least 15 pounds per square inch (psi) to function properly. Stored water has a pressure of 0.43 psi per foot of water elevation, and the water pressure at the bottom of a 10-foot vault would be 4.3 psi (10 ft x 0.43 psi). Pressurization (pump, pressure tank, and filter) costs more but creates a more usable system.

State and local governments have different design requirements for capturing and reusing stormwater runoff. Regulations may specify locations where stormwater may be captured and reused, length of time stormwater can be held in a cistern, and type of water treatment required before reuse. Check with local authorities to determine best management practices that will affect collection and use of harvested stormwater.

Master Site Development Considerations

In urban settings with regional or master stormwater management systems, it may be possible (and in some cases required) to discharge site runoff into the master system. An off-site stormwater management system designed to manage runoff from the project site can contribute to achieving this credit, provided that the system meets the LEED requirements for all drainage areas that it serves.

5. Timeline and Team

The design of stormwater management systems will ideally take place during the earliest planning phases of the project. The most effective designs are integrated with the landscape and building plans to maximize pervious areas and take advantage of possible reuse opportunities.

During predesign, analyze the conceptual site plan and look for opportunities to decrease impervious area and thereby decrease runoff volumes. During design development, the civil engineer and landscape architect should design the stormwater management system and perform preliminary calculations to confirm compliance with this credit. During construction, the project team should confirm proper installation and operation of the stormwater management system by reviewing the contractor's as-built drawings.

6. Calculations

Various methods and computer-based software programs are available to estimate stormwater runoff rates and volumes. The rational method is widely accepted and used to determine peak site runoff rates. To determine total runoff quantities, however, the U.S. Natural Resources Conservation Service (NRCS) method is typically used. Several NRCS methods also exist for estimating the peak discharge rates. Which methods are used will depend on the available data and the preference of the civil engineer; however, the chosen method should be widely accepted and recognized.

Volume Captured via Collection Facilities

The amount of runoff reduced by a stormwater harvesting system is based on its storage volume, the rate at which the system is emptied, and the interval between storm events. Use Equation 1 to determine the amount of captured runoff and Equation 2 to assess the minimum drawdown rate necessary to empty the tank prior to the next rainfall event. If the actual drawdown rate is less than the minimum drawdown rate, the volume of runoff presumed to be captured by the system must be reduced accordingly.

Equation 1. Volume of Captured Runoff

$$V_r \text{ (cubic feet)} = \frac{(P)(Rv)(A)}{12"}$$

Where V_r = volume of captured runoff

P = average rainfall event (inches)

$R_v = 0.05 + (0.009)(I)$ where I = percentage impervious of collection surface

A = area of collection surface (sf)

Equation 2. Minimum Drawdown Rate

$$Q_r \text{ (cubic feet per second)} = \frac{\text{Tank Capacity (cubic feet)}}{\text{Rainfall Event Interval (seconds)}}$$

Where Q_r = minimum drawdown rate

CASE 1. Existing Imperviousness is 50% or Less (Largely Undeveloped Sites)

OPTION 1. Discharge Rate and Quantity

Determine the predevelopment discharge rate and quantity for the project. These values are typically calculated by the civil engineer using the surface characteristics of the site and data on storm event frequency, intensity, and duration. Calculate the rate and quantity for the 1-year and 2-year 24-hour design storms.

Determine the postdevelopment discharge rate and quantity for the project consistent with the predevelopment calculations. The postdevelopment rate and quantity must be equal to or less than the predevelopment values.

OPTION 2. Stream Channel Protection

Describe the project site conditions, measures taken, and controls implemented as part of the project scope that prevent excessive stream velocities and resulting erosion. Include numerical values for predevelopment and postdevelopment conditions to demonstrate that the rate and quantity of stormwater runoff in the postdevelopment condition are below critical values for the relevant receiving waterways.

CASE 2. Existing Imperviousness is Greater Than 50% (Largely Developed Sites)

Determine the predevelopment discharge rate and quantity for the project. These values are typically calculated by the civil engineer using the surface characteristics of the site and data on storm event frequency, intensity, and duration. Calculate the rate and quantity for the 2-year 24-hour design storm.

Determine the postdevelopment discharge rate and quantity for the project consistent with the predevelopment calculations. The postdevelopment rate and quantity must be at least 25% less than the predevelopment values.

7. Documentation Guidance

As a first step in preparing to complete the LEED-Online documentation requirements, work through the following measures. Refer to LEED-Online for the complete descriptions of all required documentation.

- Determine rates and quantities for pre- and postdevelopment conditions for the required storm events.

	SS
NC	Credit 6.1
SCHOOLS	Credit 6.1
CS	Credit 6.1

- Prepare a stormwater plan assessment. The assessment can be completed by the team during the design phase, taking local regulations into account, or prepared by a qualified civil engineer or other professional.

- List stormwater management strategies and record the percentage of rainfall that each is designed to handle.

8. Examples

EXAMPLE 1. Strategies for Stormwater Quantity Control

A commercial office project uses multiple strategies for stormwater quantity control. Figure 1 shows the project site plan documenting the stormwater strategies: a cistern for reusing harvested rainwater as irrigation, a constructed wetland and vegetated roof for on-site retention, and rain gardens, bioswales, and pervious paving to increase infiltration.

Figure 1. Sample Site Plan

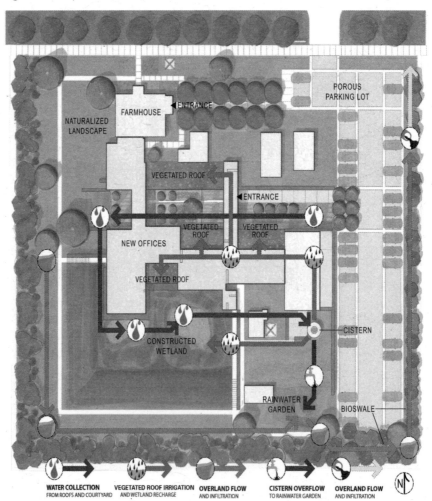

Diagram courtesy of Conservation Design Forum.

EXAMPLE 2. Volume of Captured Runoff

Rainwater is harvested from nonvegetated roof surfaces (10,000-sf roof area, 100% impervious). The system is designed to capture the runoff from 1 inch of rainfall (90% of the average rainfall event for humid watersheds). The volume of the proposed storage system is the amount of runoff captured (V_r):

$$V_r = \frac{(P)(R_v)(A)}{12"} = \frac{(1")(0.95)(10,000\ sf)}{12"} = 791.67\ cf\ (5,922\ gal)$$

Where:

$$R_v = 0.05 + (0.009)(I) = 0.05 + (0.009)(100) = 0.95$$

R_v = volumetric runoff coefficient

I = percentage imperviousness

The tank must be emptied after each storm. Using a tank that is 10-by-10-by-8 feet gives a total storage volume (V_s) of 800 cubic feet. Using a design storm interval of 3 days (72 hours), the drawdown rate (Q_r) is

$$Q_r = \frac{800\ (cf)}{259,200\ (sec)} = 0.003\ cf\ sor\ 1.37\ (gpm)$$

In this example, the captured rain must be drained within 3 days, or at a minimum rate of 1.4 gpm, for the tank to be emptied before the next storm. If the drainage rate is slower, full capacity cannot be assumed to be available during the 2-year 24-hour design storm.

Source: 2000 Maryland Stormwater Design Manual, Vols. I, II (MDE, 2000)

9. Exemplary Performance

No standardized exemplary performance option has been established for this credit. However, project teams may apply for exemplary performance by documenting a comprehensive approach to capture and treat stormwater runoff and demonstrating performance above and beyond the credit requirements. Only 1 exemplary performance credit may be achieved for SS Credit 6.1, Stormwater Design—Quantity Control, and SS Credit 6.2, Stormwater Design—Quality Control.

10. Regional Variations

The approach for achieving this credit varies dramatically across different regions and climate zones. The strategies employed in an urban environment where water is discharged to a municipal master system will be much different from the approach for a rural project that discharges to streams or lakes with high water quality standards. Regions that are generally dry and need to retain and reuse rain water but also have seasonally heavy rainfall can benefit greatly from collection and storage strategies.

11. Operations and Maintenance Considerations

The owner and site management team should adopt an ongoing inspection and maintenance plan to ensure the proper upkeep of the entire stormwater management system, including desired levels of vegetation and mulching, repair of washouts, and proper functioning of any controls. Preventing erosion will extend the life of installed stormwater management measures, since silting of infiltration trenches or dry retention wells may impair long-term performance. At a minimum, the maintenance plan should include periodic visual site inspections to identify unsatisfactory conditions and recommendations for typical corrective action. If stormwater harvesting systems are used, schedule periodic checks for leaks and blockages; occasional cleaning may be necessary to keep the system operating effectively.

	SS
NC	Credit 6.1
SCHOOLS	Credit 6.1
CS	Credit 6.1

12. Resources

Please see USGBC's LEED Registered Project Tools (http://www.usgbc.org/projecttools) for additional resources and technical information.

Websites

Center for Watershed Protection

http://www.cwp.org

A nonprofit dedicated to disseminating watershed protection information to community leaders and watershed managers, the center offers online resources, training seminars, and watershed protection techniques.

National Climate Data Center

http://www.ncdc.noaa.gov/oa/ncdc.html

This website provides historical rainfall data and isohyetal maps for various storm events.

Stormwater Manager's Resource Center

http://www.stormwatercenter.net

This site for practitioners and local government officials provides technical assistance on stormwater management issues.

U.S. Department of Agriculture, Natural Resources Conservation Service

http://www.nrcs.usda.gov

NRCS provides technical resources and financial assistance to land users, communities, and local governments for conserving soil, water, and natural resources.

U.S. EPA, Low-Impact Development

http://www.epa.gov/owow/nps/lid

This website provides valuable information on low-impact development through fact sheets, design guides, and cost estimates for low-impact development strategies that reduce stormwater runoff.

U.S. EPA, National Pollutant Discharge Elimination System

http://cfpub.epa.gov/npdes/stormwater/menuofbmps/index.cfm

This website offers help on managing stormwater, including fact sheets on the 6 minimum control measures for management best practices.

U.S. EPA, Office of Wetlands, Oceans, and Watersheds

http://www.epa.gov/owow

This website has information about watersheds, water resources, water conservation, landscaping practices, and water pollution.

Washington State Department of Natural Resources, Model Low-Impact Development Strategies for Big Box Retail Stores

http://dnr.metrokc.gov/wlr/stormwater/low-impact-development.htm

Prepared by King County, Washington, with EPA funding, this report focuses on stormwater best practices for retail development; the information is also relevant to other projects, such as schools and industrial park, that traditionally have large parking lots.

Print Media

Low-Impact Development Technical Reference Manual for Puget Sound (Puget Sound Action Team and Washington State University Pierce County Extension, 2005).

http://www.psp.wa.gov/downloads/LID/LID_manual2005.pdf.

This manual provides technical data, specifications, and performance data for low-impact development design strategies.

Stormwater Best Management Practice Design Guide (EPA/600/R-04/121A) (U.S. Environmental Protection Agency, September 2004).
http://www.epa.gov/nrmrl/pubs/600r04121/600r04121.htm.

Maryland Stormwater Design Manual (Maryland Department of the Environment, October 2000). http://www.mde.state.md.us/Programs/WaterPrograms/SedimentandStormwater/stormwater_design/index.asp.

	SS
NC	Credit 6.1
SCHOOLS	Credit 6.1
CS	Credit 6.1

13. Definitions

An **aquifer** is an underground water-bearing rock formation that supplies groundwater, wells, and springs.

Erosion is a combination of processes or events by which materials of the earth's surface are loosened, dissolved, or worn away and transported by natural agents (e.g., water, wind, or gravity).

Hydrology is the study of water occurrence, distribution, movement, and balances in an ecosystem.

Impervious surfaces have a perviousness of less than 50% and promote runoff of water instead of infiltration into the subsurface. Examples include parking lots, roads, sidewalks, and plazas.

Retention ponds capture stormwater runoff and clear it of pollutants before its release. Some retention pond designs use gravity only; others use mechanical equipment, such as pipes and pumps, to facilitate transport. Some ponds are dry except during storm events; others permanently store water.

Stormwater runoff consists of water from precipitation that flows over surfaces into sewer systems or receiving water bodies. All precipitation that leaves project site boundaries on the surface is considered stormwater runoff.

STORMWATER DESIGN—QUALITY CONTROL

	NC	SCHOOLS	CS
Credit	SS Credit 6.2	SS Credit 6.2	SS Credit 6.2
Points	1 point	1 point	1 point

Intent

To limit disruption and pollution of natural water flows by managing stormwater runoff.

Requirements

NC, SCHOOLS & CS

Implement a stormwater management plan that reduces impervious cover, promotes infiltration and captures and treats the stormwater runoff from 90% of the average annual rainfall[1] using acceptable best management practices (BMPs).

BMPs used to treat runoff must be capable of removing 80% of the average annual postdevelopment total suspended solids (TSS) load based on existing monitoring reports. BMPs are considered to meet these criteria if:

- They are designed in accordance with standards and specifications from a state or local program that has adopted these performance standards,

OR

- There exists infield performance monitoring data demonstrating compliance with the criteria. Data must conform to accepted protocol (e.g., Technology Acceptance Reciprocity Partnership [TARP], Washington State Department of Ecology) for BMP monitoring.

---

1   There are 3 distinct climates in the United States that influence the nature and amount of annual rainfall. Humid watersheds are defined as those that receive at least 40 inches of rainfall each year. Semiarid watersheds receive between 20 and 40 inches of rainfall per year, and arid watersheds receive less than 20 inches of rainfall per year. For this credit, 90% of the average annual rainfall is equivalent to treating the runoff from the following (based on climate):
- Humid Watersheds — 1 inch of rainfall
- Semiarid Watersheds — 0.75 inches of rainfall
- Arid Watersheds — 0.5 inches of rainfall

1. Benefits and Issues to Consider

Environmental Issues

As areas are developed and urbanized, surface permeability is reduced, resulting in increased stormwater runoff that is transported via urban gutters, pipes, and sewers to receiving waters. This stormwater contains sediment and other contaminants that have negative effects on water quality, navigation, and recreation. Furthermore, conveyance and treatment of stormwater require significant municipal infrastructure and maintenance.

Primary sources of stormwater pollution include atmospheric deposition, vehicle fluid leaks, and mechanical equipment wastes. During storm events, these pollutants are washed away and discharged to downstream waters, degrading aquatic habitats and decreasing the biological diversity of aquatic species.

Economic Issues

Planning early for natural drainage systems can help offset associated increased design and construction costs by integrating stormwater treatment strategies into the overall site plan. Although structural and nonstructural measures require upfront investments for design, installation, and maintenance, these features can also add significant value as site amenitiesÐsuch as vegetated infiltration swales that are part of the landscape designÐand reduce costs for landscape irrigation. Small-scale, on-site strategies also lessen the burden on municipal systems, resulting in a more affordable and stable tax base.

2. Related Credits

Using best management practices to capture and treat stormwater runoff assists project teams with reducing the overall volume of runoff. The following credit has related requirements:

- SS Credit 6.1: Stormwater Design—Quantity Control

Efforts to decrease impervious surfaces on the project site through pervious pavements, vegetated roofing, and vegetated open space can help meet the requirements of the following credits:

- SS Credit 5.1: Site Development—Protect or Restore Habitat

- SS Credit 5.2: Site Development—Maximize Open Space

- SS Credit 7.1: Heat Island Reduction—Nonroof

- SS Credit 7.2: Heat Island Reduction—Roof

Careful design of best management practices such as rain gardens, vegetated swales, and rainwater harvesting systems can reduce or eliminate the need for landscape irrigation, assisting project teams with earning the following credit:

- WE Credit 1: Water-Efficient Landscaping

3. Summary of Referenced Standards

There are no standards referenced for this credit.

4. Implementation

This credit can be achieved using either nonstructural or structural stormwater management measures (or both) to minimize or mitigate impervious area.

Nonstructural Measures

Nonstructural strategies, such as rain gardens, vegetated swales, disconnection of impervious areas, and pervious pavement, can be used to promote infiltration and capture and treat runoff. In these cases, stormwater is allowed to filter naturally into the soil. Most pollutants are then broken down by microorganisms.

Nonstructural measures are often preferred because they can be less expensive to construct and maintain and help recharge groundwater supplies.

Structural Measures

Structural measures, such as rainwater cisterns, manhole treatment devices, and ponds, can be used to remove the pollutants in runoff from impervious areas. In some cases, this water can be reused for irrigation or building flush fixtures.

Structural measures are preferred on urban or constrained sites and make it possible to effectively clean the runoff with minimal space allocation and land use. For existing sites with greater than 50% imperviousness, structural techniques may include restoring and repairing deteriorated storm sewers or separating combined sewers.

Stormwater Management Plan

The best way to minimize stormwater runoff volume and treatment requirements is to reduce the amount of impervious area and increase infiltration (Figure 1). Strategies to minimize or mitigate impervious surfaces and increase infiltration may include using pervious paving materials, harvesting stormwater for reuse in irrigation and indoor nonpotable water applications, designing infiltration swales and retention ponds, planting vegetated filter strips, installing vegetated roofs, and clustering development to reduce paved surfaces such as roads and sidewalks.

Figure 1. Strategies for Capturing and Treating Stormwater Runoff

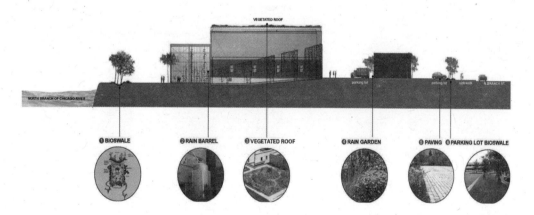

Drawing courtesy of City of Chicago, Department of General Services.

As part of the stormwater management plan process, describe the best management practices employed on the project site to capture and treat stormwater runoff. Describe how each measure contributes to reducing imperviousness and/or increasing infiltration. The plan must also document how BMPs are used to capture and treat stormwater runoff from 90% of the average annual rainfall. Annual rainfall is determined by the watershed where the project is located. Humid watersheds are defined as those that receive at least 40 inches of rainfall each year; semiarid watersheds receive between 20 and 40 inches of rainfall per year; and arid watersheds receive less than 20 inches of rainfall per year. For this credit, managing 90% of the average annual rainfall is equivalent to treating the runoff from the amounts listed in Table 1:

	SS
NC	Credit 6.2
SCHOOLS	Credit 6.2
CS	Credit 6.2

Table 1. Runoff Treatment Equivalents

Watershed	Rainfall per 24 Hours (ins)
Humid	1
Semiarid	0.75
Arid	0.5

To employ nonstructural controls, work with a civil engineer or landscape architect to determine the soil types and associated infiltration rates. Confirm that the soils can infiltrate water at a rate and quantity sufficient to absorb at least 90% of the annual rainfall volume.

If the project uses structural controls, confirm that the equipment can accommodate at least 90% of the annual rainfall volume.

If the project uses both structural and nonstructural measures, each of which is designed to handle less than 90% of the annual rainfall volume, describe how the measures work together to satisfy the requirements of this credit.

In addition, the BMPs used on the project must be capable of removing 80% of the average annual postdevelopment load of total suspended solids, based on existing monitoring reports. BMPs that qualify for this credit can be designed in accordance with standards and specifications from a state or local program (if that program has adopted the 80% standard), or by providing field performance monitoring data from an accepted protocol demonstrating compliance with the criterion. Table 2 provides sample documentation of TSS removal effectiveness for various BMPs.

Table 2. Management Practices for Removing Total Suspended Solids from Runoff

	Average TS Removal	Probable Rage of TSS Removal	Factors to Consider
Effectiveness of Managment Practices for Total Suspended Solids Removal from Runoff			
Infiltration Basin	75%	50 - 100%	soil percolation rates, trench surface area, stoarge volumes
Infiltration Trench	75%	50 - 100%	soil percolation rates, trench surface area, stoarge volumes
Vegetated Filter Stip	65%	40 - 90%	runoff volume, slope, soil infiltration rate
Grass Swale	60%	20 - 40%	runoff volume, slope, soil infiltration rates, vegetative cover, buffer length
Porous Pavement	90%	60 - 90%	percolation rates, storage volume
Open Grid Pavement	90%	60 - 90%	percolation rates
Sand Filter Infiltration Basin	80%	60 - 90%	treatment volume, filtration media
Water Quality Inlet	35%	10 - 35%	maintenance, sedimentation storage volume
Water Quality Inlet with Sand Filter	80%	70 - 90%	sedimentation storage volume, depth of filter media
Oil/Grit Separator	15%	10 - 25%	sedimentation storage volume, outlet configuration
Extended Dentention Dry Pond	45%	5 - 90%	storage volume, dentention time, pond shape
Wet Pond	60%	50 - 90%	pool volume, pond shape
Extended Dentention Wet Pond	80%	50 - 90%	pool volume, pond shape, detention time
Constructed Stormwater Wetlands	65%	50 - 90%	storage volume, detention time, pool shape, wetland's biota, seasonal variation

Source: Environmental Protection Agency's Guidance Specifying Management Measures for Sources of Non-Point Pollution in Coastal Waters. Table 4-7. January 1993.

5. Timeline and Team

During predesign, setting goals related to water, including stormwater management and water reuse, involves the owner, architect, and engineers. This is the appropriate time to analyze the local climate, codes, and applicable water laws and determine the process for obtaining permits and approval.

During schematic design, civil and mechanical engineers and landscape architects can help establish a comprehensive water budget for stormwater, irrigation water, and the building's water consumption. This water budget will consider available supply sources, such as rainwater and stormwater, municipally supplied nonpotable water, treated and untreated graywater, and treated blackwater, and provide the basis for making stormwater management decisions that complement the rest of the project. The civil engineer or landscape architect then identifies specific stormwater treatment measures appropriate for the project.

During design development, the civil engineer or landscape architect should design stormwater management systems, including water quality treatment, perform preliminary LEED calculations, and confirm or reassess stormwater management goals.

During construction documents, the civil engineer or landscape architect, in coordination with the architect and owner, should finalize the design of stormwater management systems and complete the required calculations and documentation.

6. Calculations

The calculation methods used will depend on the available data and the preference of the civil engineer; however, the chosen method should be widely accepted and recognized.

7. Documentation Guidance

As a first step in preparing to complete the LEED-Online documentation requirements, work through the following measures. Refer to LEED-Online for the complete descriptions of all required documentation.

- Develop a list of best management practices used to treat stormwater and a description of the contribution of each to stormwater filtration. Determine the percentage of annual rainfall treated by each practice.

- For structural controls, list and describe the pollutant removal performance of each measure; determine the percentage of annual rainfall treated by each.

8. Examples

A commercial office building is located on a 30,000-square-foot urban site with a high percentage of impervious area. The city is in a humid watershed, requiring treatment of stormwater runoff for 1 inch of rainfall. The site has just 3,000 square feet of vegetated area on the ground level yet can meet the credit requirements through a combination of strategies including a vegetated roof, pervious pavers, and flow-through planters.

The vegetated roof captures stormwater, which then evapotranspires from the otherwise impervious roof area. These systems mimic the hydrology of the site prior to development, reducing peak runoff rates and volume. The parking lot has pervious pavers whose high rate of permeability allows stormwater to infiltrate to the subgrade. Finally, flow-through planters collect and filter stormwater runoff, allowing pollutants to settle and filter out as the water percolates through the soil.

The BMPs employed on this project remove more than 80% of the total suspended solids from the stormwater and provide all the irrigation needed for the vegetated roof and other landscaped areas.

9. Exemplary Performance

No standardized exemplary performance option has been established for this credit. However, project teams may apply for exemplary performance by documenting a comprehensive approach to capture and treat stormwater runoff and demonstrate performance above and beyond the credit requirements. Only 1 exemplary performance credit may be achieved for SS Credit 6.1, Stormwater Design—Quantity Control, and SS Credit 6.2, Stormwater Design—Quality Control.

10. Regional Variations

The approach to this credit depends on the kind of watershed where the project is located and the annual rainfall on the project site. Humid watersheds are defined as those that receive at least 40 inches of rainfall each year; semiarid watersheds receive 20 to 40 inches of rainfall per year; arid watersheds receive less than 20 inches of rainfall per year.

Both structural and nonstructural BMPs used on the project must be specific to the site and appropriate for the region's climate to effectively capture and treat stormwater runoff.

11. Operations and Maintenance Considerations

The project should adopt an ongoing inspection and maintenance plan to ensure proper functioning of the installed stormwater controls. Silting of infiltration trenches or dry retention wells will reduce removal efficiency. At a minimum, the maintenance plan should include periodic visual site inspections to identify any areas of the site that are eroding or susceptible to erosion, as well as recommendations for typical corrective actions. Prevention of on-site erosion and entrainment of eroded materials into the stormwater runoff will extend the life of the BMPs.

Some pervious pavement systems require ongoing maintenance to remain effective. This might include quarterly vacuuming or washing. Limit application of deicing agents (sand or chemicals) to prevent clogging. Maintenance contracts and practices should reflect the requirements of the installed system.

Structural stormwater measures are likely to require more ongoing maintenance than nonstructural measures. Consider operating budgets when designing the stormwater management strategy.

12. Resources

Please see USGBC's LEED Registered Project Tools (http://www.usgbc.org/projecttools) for additional resources and technical information.

Websites
Pennsylvania Department of Environmental Protection, Technology Acceptance and Reciprocity Partnership
http://www.dep.state.pa.us/dep/deputate/pollprev/techservices/tarp/

U.S. EPA, Low-Impact Development
http://www.epa.gov/owow/nps/lid
This website provides valuable information on low-impact development through fact sheets, design guides, and cost estimates for low-impact development strategies that reduce stormwater runoff.

U.S. EPA, Office of Wetlands, Oceans, and Watersheds
http://www.epa.gov/owow
This website has information about watersheds, water resources, water conservation, landscaping practices, and water pollution.

Print Media

Guidance Specifying Management Measures for Sources of Non-Point Pollution in Coastal Waters (Document No. EPA 840B92002), (U.S. Environmental Protection Agency, January 1993).
http://www.epa.gov/owow/nps/MMGI
This document details a variety of management practices that can be incorporated to remove pollutants from stormwater volumes. Chapter 4, Part II, addresses urban runoff and suggests a strategies for treating and infiltrating stormwater volumes after construction is completed.

Low-Impact Development Technical Reference Manual for Puget Sound (Puget Sound Action Team and Washington State University Pierce County Extension, 2005).
http://www.psp.wa.gov/downloads/LID/LID_manual2005.pdf
This manual provides technical data, specifications, and performance data for low-impact development design strategies.

Maryland Stormwater Design Manual (Maryland Department of the Environment, October 2000)
http://www.mde.state.md.us/Programs/WaterPrograms/SedimentandStormwater/stormwater_design/index.asp

Stormwater Best Management Practice Design Guide (EPA/600/R-04/121A) (U.S. Environmental Protection Agency, September 2004)
http://www.epa.gov/nrmrl/pubs/600r04121/600r04121.htm

	SS
NC	Credit 6.2
SCHOOLS	Credit 6.2
CS	Credit 6.2

13. Definitions

Impervious surfaces have a perviousness of less than 50% and promote runoff of water instead of infiltration into the subsurface. Examples include parking lots, roads, sidewalks, and plazas.

Retention ponds capture stormwater runoff and clear it of pollutants before its release. Some retention pond designs use gravity only; others use mechanical equipment, such as pipes and pumps, to facilitate transport. Some ponds are dry except during storm events; others permanently store water.

Stormwater runoff consists of water from precipitation that flows over surfaces into sewer systems or receiving water bodies. All precipitation that leaves project site boundaries on the surface is considered stormwater runoff.

Total suspended solids (**TSS**) are particles that are too small or light to be removed from stormwater via gravity settling. Suspended solid concentrations are typically removed via filtration.

HEAT ISLAND EFFECT—NONROOF

	NC	SCHOOLS	CS
Credit	SS Credit 7.1	SS Credit 7.1	SS Credit 7.1
Points	1 point	1 point	1 point

Intent

To reduce heat islands[1] to minimize impacts on microclimates and human and wildlife habitats.

Requirements

NC, SCHOOLS & CS

OPTION 1

Use any combination of the following strategies for 50% of the site hardscape (including roads, sidewalks, courtyards and parking lots):

- Provide shade from the existing tree canopy or within 5 years of landscape installation. Landscaping (trees) must be in place at the time of occupancy.

- Provide shade from structures covered by solar panels that produce energy used to offset some nonrenewable resource use.

- Provide shade from architectural devices or structures that have a solar reflectance index [2] (SRI) of at least 29.

- Use hardscape materials with an SRI of at least 29.

- Use an open-grid pavement system (at least 50% pervious).

OR

OPTION 2

Place a minimum of 50% of parking spaces under cover[3]. Any roof used to shade or cover parking must have an SRI of at least 29, be a vegetated green roof or be covered by solar panels that produce energy used to offset some nonrenewable resource use.

---

1   Heat islands are defined as thermal gradient differences between developed and undeveloped areas.
2   The solar reflectance index (SRI) is a measure of the constructed surface's ability to reflect solar heat, as shown by a small temperature rise. It is defined so that a standard black surface (reflectance 0.05, emittance 0.90) is 0 and a standard white surface (reflectance 0.80, emittance 0.90) is 100. To calculate the SRI for a given material, obtain the reflectance value and emittance value for the material. SRI is calculated according to ASTM E 1980. Reflectance is measured according to ASTM E 903, ASTM E 1918, or ASTM C 1549. Emittance is measured according to ASTM E 408 or ASTM C 1371.
3   For the purposes of this credit, under cover parking is defined as parking underground, under deck, under roof, or under a building.

1. Benefits and Issues to Consider

Environmental Issues

The use of dark, nonreflective surfaces for parking, roofs, walkways, and other hardscapes contributes to the heat island effect by absorbing the sun's warmth, which then radiates into the surroundings. Because of heat island effect, ambient temperatures in urban areas are artificially elevated by 2° to 10°F compared with surrounding suburban and undeveloped areas.[11] The result is increased cooling loads in the summer, requiring larger heating, ventilating, and air-conditioning (HVAC) equipment and greater electricity consumption, both of which generate greenhouse gases and pollution. Heat islands are detrimental to site habitat, wildlife, and animal migration corridors. Plants and animals are also sensitive to large fluctuations in daytime and nighttime temperatures and may not thrive in areas affected by heat islands.

Economic Issues

The energy used to cool a building represents a substantial portion of the operating budget over its lifetime. Reducing heat islands can significantly lower cooling costs. According to the Department of Energy's Lawrence Berkeley National Laboratory, the annual energy savings potential of heat island reduction measures, studied in the metropolitan areas of Sacramento, Baton Rouge, and Salt Lake City, range from $4 million to $15 million.[12]

Efforts to reduce heat islands may translate into higher initial costs for additional landscaping, open-grid paving, or architectural shading devices. However, these items have an acceptable payback when integrated into a systems approach to maximizing energy savings. Some high-reflectance pavements, such as concrete made with white cement, may cost up to twice as much as those made with gray cement, but some blended cements (for example, slag) are very light in color and cost the same as or slightly less than Portland-only gray cement.[13] High-reflectance pavements also increase overall light levels and may enable a building to use fewer site lighting fixtures. Building owners should assess the cost of installing highly reflective pavements or coatings against possible energy savings from reduced site lighting.

2. Related Credits

Locating parking structures underground can help limit site disturbance and maximize open space, assisting with the following credit:

- SS Credit 5.2: Site Development—Maximize Open Space

Properly designed and installed open-grid pavements capture and treat stormwater runoff, helping project teams to earn points under the following credits:

- SS Credit 6.1: Stormwater Design—Quantity Control
- SS Credit 6.2: Stormwater Design—Quality Control

If vegetation is used to shade hardscapes, refer to the landscape irrigation requirements outlined in the following credit to reduce potable water use:

- WE Credit 1: Water-Efficient Landscaping

3. Summary of Referenced Standards

ASTM Intl. Standards

http://www.astm.org

ASTM E408–71(1996)e1, Standard Test Methods for Total Normal Emittance of Surfaces Using Inspection-Meter Techniques

This standard describes how to measure total normal emittance of surfaces using a portable inspection-meter instrument. The test methods are intended for large surfaces where nondestructive testing is required. See the standard for testing steps and a discussion of thermal emittance theory.

ASTM C1371–04a Standard Test Method for Determination of Emittance of Materials Near Room Temperature Using Portable Emissometers

This test method covers a technique for determination of the emittance of typical materials using a portable differential thermopile emissometer. The purpose of the test method is to provide a comparative means of quantifying the emittance of opaque, highly thermally conductive materials near room temperature as a parameter in evaluating temperatures, heat flows, and derived thermal resistances of materials.

ASTM E903–96, Standard Test Method for Solar Absorptance, Reflectance, and Transmittance of Materials Using Integrating Spheres

Referenced in the ENERGY STAR® roofing standard, this test method uses spectrophotometers and need only be applied for initial reflectance measurement. It specifies methods of computing solar-weighted properties using the measured spectral values. This test method is applicable to materials having both specular and diffuse optical properties. Except for transmitting sheet materials that are heterogeneous, patterned, or corrugated, this test method is preferred over Test Method E1084. The ENERGY STAR roofing standard also allows the use of reflectometers to measure roofing materials' solar reflectance. See the roofing standard for more details.

ASTM E1918–97, Standard Test Method for Measuring Solar Reflectance of Horizontal and Low-Sloped Surfaces in the Field

This test method covers the solar reflectance measurements, using a pyranometer, of various horizontal and low-sloped surfaces and materials. The test method is intended for use when the angle from a surface to the sun is less than 45 degrees.

ASTM C1549–04, Standard Test Method for Determination of Solar Reflectance Near Ambient Temperature Using a Portable Solar Reflectometer

This test method covers a technique for determining the solar reflectance of flat, opaque materials in a laboratory or in the field using a commercial, portable solar reflectometer. The purpose of the test method is to provide the solar reflectance data required to evaluate temperature and heat flows across surfaces exposed to solar radiation.

4. Implementation

Strategies for mitigating heat island effect include using materials with higher solar reflectance properties in the site design, providing shaded areas, and reducing hardscape surfaces.

Higher Solar Reflectance

Hardscape materials vary in their ability to reflect sunlight.

Table 1 provides the solar reflectance index (SRI) for standard paving materials. Dark paving materials generally have low reflectance and, consequently, low SRI values. Gray or white concrete has a higher reflectance and a higher SRI value. Both white and gray concrete will weather over time, and without proper maintenance their SRI value will decrease. Microsurfaces and coatings over asphalt pavement can be used to meet the required SRI value for this credit. Coatings and integral colorants can be used in cement or cast-in-place parking surfaces to improve solar reflectance. For projects with existing weathered gray concrete hardscapes, document that the weathered surfaces have been sufficiently cleaned and lightened to qualify for the default SRI values listed in Table 1.

Table 1. Solar Reflectance Index (SRI) for Standard Paving Materials

Material	Emissivity	Reflectance	SRI
Typical new gray concrete	0.9	0.35	35
Typical weathered* gray concrete	0.9	0.20	19
Typical new white concrete	0.9	0.7	86
Typical weathered* white concrete	0.9	0.4	45
New asphalt	0.9	.05	0
Weathered asphalt	0.9	.10	6

* Reflectance of surfaces can be maintained with cleaning. Typical pressure washing of cementitious materials can restore reflectance close to original value. Weathered values are based on no cleaning.

Project teams do not need to provide project-specific data measuring SRI values for new concrete. Documentation certifying that the concrete mix used for a project is equivalent to a previously used and tested mix is acceptable.

Because higher reflectance pavements increase overall light levels, lighting evaluations should include an assessment of the interreflected component and reflections off high-reflectance materials such as white concrete. High-reflectance materials can result in glare, which impairs vision and increases light pollution. Minimize the amount of light that is directed from site lighting fixtures directly onto reflective paving surfaces.

Shading

Vegetation can reduce heat islands by shading buildings and pavements from solar radiation and cooling the air through evapotranspiration. Provide shade using landscape features such as native trees, large shrubs, and non-invasive vines. Newly installed landscape features should provide the desired level of shading within 5 years of being planted. These must be in place at the time of building occupancy. Give trees and other vegetation adequate root space for reaching their anticipated size and shade coverage within 5 years. Trellises and other exterior structures can support vegetation to shade parking lots, walkways, and plazas. Deciduous trees allow solar heat gain during the winter months. Where tree planting is not possible, consider using architectural shading devices and structures to block direct sunlight. Solar energy system installations, including photovoltaics, can contribute to shading nonroof hardscapes.

Avoid placing trees and vegetation in locations likely to be reflected in building glazing unless specific measures are taken to reduce bird collisions. Such measures include using exterior shading devices, introducing etched or frit patterns in the glass, and creating "visual markers" in sufficient locations. Visual markers are differentiated planes, materials, textures, colors, opacity, or other visually contrasting features that help fragment window reflections and reduce overall transparency and reflectivity.

Reduce Hardscape

Limit the amount of impervious hardscape areas on the site to reduce heat island effect. For features such as parking lots, roads, and walkways, use open-grid pavement systems that are at least 50% pervious and accommodate vegetation within the open cells. Another way to reduce hardscape surfaces is to place at least 50% of parking under shading structures or under cover. This can include using multistory or underground parking structures. Any roof used to shade or cover surface parking must have an SRI of at least 29, be a vegetated roof, or be covered by solar panels. There is no SRI requirement for parking that is underground, under a deck, or under a building as long as any exposed parking surface area is 50% or less of the total parking surface area.

5. Timeline and Team

Early in design, the project team should involve the landscape architect, architect, and civil engineer in efforts to minimize hardscape surfaces on-site, assess whether open-grid paving can also assist with stormwater runoff mitigation, and evaluate the potential for locating parking underground or under cover. During the construction documents phase, designers should specify materials with a low emissivity that meet or exceed the SRI requirements on all nonroof surfaces. For projects that include cleaning of existing weathered gray concrete hardscapes, contractors must document that they have provided sufficient cleaning to achieve the required SRI values.

	SS
NC	Credit 7.1
SCHOOLS	Credit 7.1
CS	Credit 7.1

6. Calculations

OPTION 1

- Identify all nonroof hardscape surfaces on the project site and sum the total area (T), in square feet. Hardscapes must, at a minimum, include all roads, sidewalks, courtyards, and parking lots within the LEED project boundary.

- Identify all hardscape surfaces shaded by trees or other landscape features (at the time of building occupancy or within 5 years from the date of installation). Shade coverage must be calculated at 10 a.m., 12 noon, and 3 p.m. on the summer solstice. The arithmetic mean of these 3 values will be used as the effective shaded area. Calculated the effective shaded area (S).

- Identify all hardscape surfaces shaded by solar energy panels and sum the total area (E). The shaded area can be considered equivalent to the area covered by the panels on the site plan (from a direct overhead aerial perspective).

- Identify all hardscape surfaces shaded by architectural devices or structures that have an SRI of at least 29 and sum the total area (A). The shaded area can be considered equivalent to the area covered by the architectural devices or structures on the site plan (from a direct overhead aerial perspective).

- Identify all the hardscape surfaces that have an SRI of at least 29 and sum the total area (R). SRI can be calculated from emissivity and solar reflectance values. Emissivity is calculated according to ASTM E 408 or ASTM C 1371, and solar reflectance is calculated according to ASTM E 903, ASTM E 1918 or ASTM C 1549. Alternatively, use the SRI values for typical paving materials in Table 1 in lieu of obtaining specific emissivity and solar reflectance measurements for the listed materials.

- Identify all hardscape surfaces that have an open-grid paving system that is at least 50% pervious and sum the total area (O).

- Sum the area of all qualifying surfaces to determine the total qualifying area (Q), using Equation 1.

Each surface should be counted only once. For example, a 10-square-foot area that is 55% pervious, has an SRI of 30, and is shaded by a tree contributes 10 square feet to the total.

Equation 1

$$Q = (S + E + A + R + O)$$

- The total qualifying area must be 50% or more of the total hardscape area (T), as calculated in Equation 2.

	SS
NC	Credit 7.1
SCHOOLS	Credit 7.1
CS	Credit 7.1

Equation 2

$$Q > \frac{T}{2}$$

OPTION 2

- Determine the total number of parking spaces within the project boundary.

- Determine the number of parking spaces that are under cover (include underground, under deck, under roof, and under building). This number must be 50% or more of the total number of parking spaces.

The site and building footprint areas used in Option 1 calculations need to be consistent across the following credits:

- SS Credit 5.2: Site Development—Maximize Open Space
- SS Credit 6.1: Stormwater Design—Quantity Control
- SS Credit 6.2: Stormwater Design—Quality Control
- WE Credit 1: Water-Efficient Landscaping
- MR Credit 1: Building Reuse

Similarly, the number of parking spaces used to document compliance with Option 2 needs to be consistent with the requirements of this credit:

- SS Credit 4.4: Alternative Transportation—Parking Capacity

7. Documentation Guidance

As a first step in preparing to complete the LEED-Online documentation requirements, work through the following measures. Refer to LEED-Online for the complete descriptions of all required documentation.

- If surfaces are shaded, prepare a site plan that highlights all nonroof hardscape areas. Clearly label each portion of hardscape that counts toward credit achievement. List information about compliant surfaces (e.g., SRI values of reflective paving materials).

- If parking spaces are placed under cover, determine the total number of spaces and the portion covered. If applicable, assemble SRI values for the roofs that cover parking areas.

8. Examples

A building is located on a 25,000-square-foot site, of which 15,000 square feet is occupied by the building footprint and vegetated areas. The project team employs strategies to reduce heat island effect for nonroof surfaces, installing deciduous trees to shade parking and driveway areas and using light-colored concrete with an SRI of 35 for driving aisles and walkways (Figure 1). Areas that contain both light-colored hardscapes and are shaded by trees are counted only once. Table 2 lists the areas of qualifying surfaces.

Table 2. Sample Qualifying Surface Areas

Description	Area (sf)
Total nonroof hardscapes	10,000
Shaded areas	3,000
Areas of hardscapes with minimum SRI-29	4,000
Total qualifying surfaces	7,000

Figure 1. Shading and SRI for Credit Compliance

	SS
NC	Credit 7.1
SCHOOLS	Credit 7.1
CS	Credit 7.1

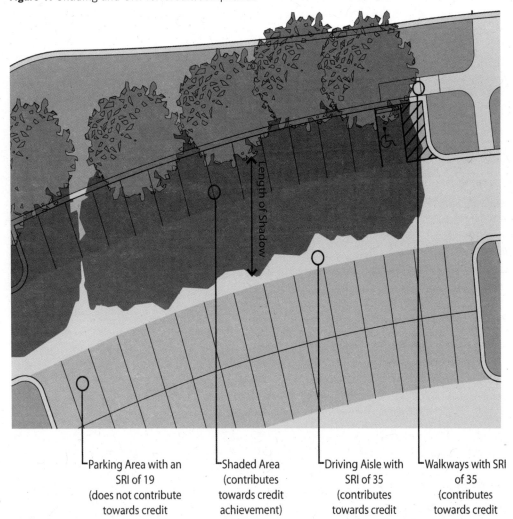

Length of Shadow

Parking Area with an SRI of 19 (does not contribute towards credit

Shaded Area (contributes towards credit achievement)

Driving Aisle with SRI of 35 (contributes towards credit

Walkways with SRI of 35 (contributes towards credit

Diagram courtesy of OWP/P

9. Exemplary Performance

Projects may earn an Innovation in Design credit for exemplary performance by demonstrating that either (1) 100% of nonroof impervious surfaces have been constructed with high-albedo or open-grid paving, or will be shaded within 5 years; or (2) 100% of the on-site parking spaces have been located under cover.

10. Regional Variations

Heat island intensities depend on weather and climate, proximity to water bodies, and topography.[14] Buildings in very cold climates or at high latitudes may not experience the same rise of surface and ambient temperatures. Buildings in urban areas and those in climate zones 1, 2, and 3 (as defined by ASHRAE 90.1–2007) are most affected by heat islands and are likely to benefit from measures to decrease cooling loads. In sunny climates, project teams should mitigate glare from reflective pavements into the building by providing shading devices. Consider hardscape surfaces and parking cover that is appropriate for the region's weather.

11. Operations and Maintenance Considerations

Surface materials with high reflectivity should be cleaned at least every 2 years to maintain good reflectance.

Some open-grid pavement systems require special maintenance to remain pervious. Request maintenance information from product manufacturers and/or installers and ensure that this information is given to the operations team.

Communicate proper care and maintenance of trees and other vegetation on the project site to landscaping and exterior maintenance crews to help ensure that the anticipated shading is achieved within 5 years.

12. Resources

Please see USGBC's LEED Registered Project Tools (http://www.usgbc.org/projecttools) for additional resources and technical information.

Websites

American Bird Conservancy

http://www.abcbirds.org

ABC is a national leader in reducing human effects on birds and wildlife. ABC's bird collision program supports national efforts to reduce bird mortality through education and advocacy.

American Concrete Pavement Association

http://www.pavement.com

This national association represents concrete pavement contractors, cement companies, equipment and material manufacturers, and suppliers. See Albedo: A Measure of Pavement Surface Reflectance, R&T Update (3.05) (June 2002): http://www.pavement.com/Downloads/RT/RT3.05.pdf

Birds and Buildings Forum

http://www.birdsandbuildings.org

This Chicago-based non-profit supports bird-friendly design through education and advocacy. Their website maintains lists of organizations and resources.

Lawrence Berkeley National Laboratory, Heat Island Group

http://eetd.lbl.gov/HeatIsland/

Lawrence Berkeley National Laboratory conducts heat island research to find, analyze, and implement solutions to minimize heat island effect. Current research efforts focus on the study and development of more reflective surfaces for roadways and buildings.

New York City Audubon

http://www.nycaudubon.org

This Audubon chapter takes a leadership role in reducing bird collisions with buildings. The chapter publishes Bird-Safe Building Guidelines, conducts monitoring, and through its Project Safe Flight, promotes bird-friendly design.

U.S. EPA, Heat Island Effect

http://www.epa.gov/heatisland

This site offers basic information about heat island effect, its social and environmental costs, and strategies to minimize its prevalence.

13. Definitions

Emissivity is the ratio of the radiation emitted by a surface to the radiation emitted by a black body at the same temperature.

Greenhouse gases are relatively transparent to the higher-energy sunlight but trap lower-energy infrared radiation (e.g., carbon dioxide, methane, and CFCs).

Hardscape consists of the inanimate elements of the building landscaping. Examples include pavement, roadways, stone walls, concrete paths and sidewalks, and concrete, brick, and tile patios.

Heat island effect refers to the absorption of heat by hardscapes, such as dark, nonreflective pavement and buildings, and its radiation to surrounding areas. Particularly in urban areas, other sources may include vehicle exhaust, air-conditioners, and street equipment; reduced airflow from tall buildings and narrow streets exacerbates the effect.

Impervious surfaces have a perviousness of less than 50% and promote runoff of water instead of infiltration into the subsurface. Examples include parking lots, roads, sidewalks, and plazas.

Infrared (or thermal) emittance is a parameter between 0 and 1 (or 0% and 100%) that indicates the ability of a material to shed infrared radiation (heat). The wavelength range for this radiant energy is roughly 5 to 40 micrometers. Most building materials (including glass) are opaque in this part of the spectrum and have an emittance of roughly 0.9. Materials such as clean, bare metals are the most important exceptions to the 0.9 rule. Thus clean, untarnished galvanized steel has low emittance, and aluminum roof coatings have intermediate emittance levels.

Open-grid pavement is less than 50% impervious and accommodates vegetation in the open cells.

Perviousness is the percentage of the surface area of a paving system that is open and allows moisture to soak into the ground below.

Solar reflectance, or **albedo,** is a measure of the ability of a surface material to reflect sunlight— visible, infrared, and ultraviolet wavelengths—on a scale of 0 to 1. Black paint has a solar reflectance of 0; white paint (titanium dioxide) has a solar reflectance of 1.

The **solar reflectance index (SRI)** is a measure of a material's ability to reject solar heat, as shown by a small temperature rise. Standard black (reflectance 0.05, emittance 0.90) is 0 and standard white (reflectance 0.80, emittance 0.90) is 100. For example, a standard black surface has a temperature rise of 90°F (50°C) in full sun, and a standard white surface has a temperature rise of 14.6°F (8.1°C). Once the maximum temperature rise of a given material has been computed, the SRI can be calculated by interpolating between the values for white and black. Materials with the highest SRI values are the coolest choices for paving. Because of the way SRI is defined, particularly hot materials can even take slightly negative values, and particularly cool materials can even exceed 100. (Lawrence Berkeley National Laboratory Cool Roofing Materials Database)

Undercover parking is underground or under a deck, roof, or building; its hardscape surfaces are shaded.

	SS
NC	Credit 7.1
SCHOOLS	Credit 7.1
CS	Credit 7.1

	NC	SCHOOLS	CS
Credit	SS Credit 7.2	SS Credit 7.2	SS Credit 7.2
Points	1 point	1 point	1 point

Intent

To reduce heat islands[1] to minimize impacts on microclimates and human and wildlife habitats.

Requirements

NC, SCHOOLS & CS

OPTION 1

Use roofing materials with a solar reflectance index[2] (SRI) equal to or greater than the values in the table below for a minimum of 75% of the roof surface.

Roofing materials having a lower SRI value than those listed below may be used if the weighted rooftop SRI average meets the following criteria:

$$\frac{\text{Area Roof Meeting Minimum SRI}}{\text{Total Roof Area}} \times \frac{\text{SRI of Installed Roof}}{\text{Required SRI}} \geq 75\%$$

Roof Type	Slope	SRI
Low-sloped roof	≤ 2:12	78
Steep-sloped roof	> 2:12	29

OR

OPTION 2

Install a vegetated roof that covers at least 50% of the roof area.

OPTION 3

Install high-albedo and vegetated roof surfaces that, in combination, meet the following criteria:

$$\frac{\text{Area Roof Meeting Minimum SRI}}{0.75} + \frac{\text{Area of Vegetated Roof}}{0.5} \geq \text{Total Roof Area}$$

Roof Type	Slope	SRI
Low-sloped roof	≤ 2:12	78
Steep-sloped roof	> 2:12	29

---

1   Heat islands are defined as thermal gradient differences between developed and undeveloped areas.
2   The Solar Reflectance Index (SRI) is a measure of the constructed surface's ability to reflect solar heat, as shown by a small temperature rise. It is defined so that a standard black (reflectance 0.05, emittance 0.90) is 0 and a standard white (reflectance 0.80, emittance 0.90) is 100. To calculate the SRI for a given material, obtain the reflectance value and emittance value for the material. SRI is calculated according to ASTM E 1980. Reflectance is measured according to ASTM E 903, ASTM E 1918, or ASTM C 1549. Emittance is measured according to ASTM E 408 or ASTM C 1371.

	SS
NC	Credit 7.2
SCHOOLS	Credit 7.2
CS	Credit 7.2

1. Benefits and Issues to Consider

Environmental Issues

The use of dark, nonreflective roofing surfaces contributes to the heat island effect by absorbing the sun's warmth, which then radiates into the surroundings. As a result, ambient temperatures in urban areas are artificially elevated, increasing cooling loads, electricity consumption, and emissions of greenhouse gases and pollution. Heat island effect is also detrimental to site habitat, wildlife, and animal migration corridors. Plants and animals are sensitive to large fluctuations in daytime and nighttime temperatures and may not thrive in areas affected by heat islands. Projects that earn SS Credit 7.2 by providing vegetated roofs contribute to increased habitat areas for birds, insects, and other wildlife.

Economic Issues

The energy used to cool a building represents a substantial portion of the operating budget over its lifetime. Vegetated roofs and roof surfaces with high SRIs can reduce costs associated with HVAC equipment. Vegetated roofs typically require additional investment; cool roofs that effectively reflect the sun's energy could cost the same as more conventional roofing systems. However, any upfront investment is likely to result in energy cost savings throughout the life cycle of the project. According to EPA researchers who monitored 10 buildings in California and Florida, cool roofs save residents and building owners 20% to 70% in annual cooling energy costs.[15] An increasing number of jurisdictions are beginning to require the use of cool roofs on new building projects.

SCHOOLS For schools, a vegetated roof can function as a living classroom, providing an added educational amenity.

2. Related Credits

Vegetated roofs help capture and treat stormwater while also providing habitat and open space, providing synergies with the following credits:

- SS Credit 5.1: Site Development—Protect or Restore Habitat
- SS Credit 5.2: Site Development—Maximize Open Space
- SS Credit 6.1: Stormwater Design—Quantity Control
- SS Credit 6.2: Stormwater Design—Quality Control

Vegetated roofs also reduce the availability of rainwater that may be harvested for nonpotable purposes, making it more challenging to achieve this water-efficiency credit:

- WE Credit 3: Water Use Reduction

Using highly reflective roofing materials and/or vegetated roofs can decrease cooling loads and help projects with earning this credit:

- EA Credit 1: Optimize Energy Performance

3. Summary of Referenced Standards

ASTM Standards

http://www.astm.org

ASTM E1980–01, Standard Practice for Calculating Solar Reflectance Index of Horizontal and Low-Sloped Opaque Surfaces

This standard describes how surface reflectivity and emissivity are combined to calculate a solar reflectance index (SRI) for a roofing material or other surface. The standard also describes a laboratory and field testing protocol that can be used to determine SRI.

ASTM E408–71(1996)e1, Standard Test Methods for Total Normal Emittance of Surfaces Using Inspection-Meter Techniques

This standard describes how to measure total normal emittance of surfaces using a portable inspection-meter instrument. The test methods are intended for large surfaces where nondestructive testing is required. See the standard for testing steps and a discussion of thermal emittance theory.

ASTM E903–96, Standard Test Method for Solar Absorptance, Reflectance, and Transmittance of Materials Using Integrating Spheres

Referenced in the ENERGY STAR roofing standard, this test method uses spectrophotometers and need only be applied for initial reflectance measurement. It specifies methods of computing solar-weighted properties using the measured spectral values. This test method is applicable to materials having both specular and diffuse optical properties. Except for transmitting sheet materials that are heterogeneous, patterned, or corrugated, this test method is preferred over Test Method E1084. The ENERGY STAR roofing standard also allows the use of reflectometers to measure roofing materials' solar reflectance. See the roofing standard for more details.

ASTM E1918–97, Standard Test Method for Measuring Solar Reflectance of Horizontal and Low-Sloped Surfaces in the Field

This test method covers the solar reflectance measurements, using a pyranometer, of various horizontal and low-sloped surfaces and materials. The test method is intended for use when the angle from a surface to the sun is less than 45 degrees.

ASTM C1371–04, Standard Test Method for Determination of Emittance of Materials Near Room Temperature Using Portable Emissometers

This test method covers a technique for determination of the emittance of typical materials using a portable differential thermopile emissometer. The purpose of the test method is to provide a comparative means of quantifying the emittance of opaque, highly thermally conductive materials near room temperature as a parameter in evaluating temperatures, heat flow, and derived thermal resistances of materials.

ASTM C1549–04, Standard Test Method for Determination of Solar Reflectance Near Ambient Temperature Using a Portable Solar Reflectometer

This test method covers a technique for determining the solar reflectance of flat, opaque materials in a laboratory or in the field using a commercial, portable solar reflectometer. The purpose of the test method is to provide the solar reflectance data required to evaluate temperature and heat flows across surfaces exposed to solar radiation.

4. Implementation

The choice of roofing can maximize energy savings and minimize the heat island effect. This credit can be achieved through high-reflectance surfaces, vegetated roofing, or a combination.

High-Reflectance Materials

The solar reflectance index (SRI) of a roofing material is calculated from emissivity and solar reflectance values. Multiple testing methods are available for measuring emissivity and solar reflectance; check the manufacturer's literature carefully to ensure the use of appropriate data. For example, some manufacturers measure visible reflectance, which differs from the solar reflectance measurement used in this credit. Visible reflectance correlates to solar reflectance, but the 2 quantities are not equal because solar gain covers a wider range of wavelengths than visible light. A material that exhibits a high visible reflectance usually has a lower solar reflectance. Typically, white roof products exhibit higher performance characteristics than nonwhite products. Performance varies by roofing materials, as well as brand. Check with roofing manufacturers and the Lawrence Berkeley National Laboratory's Cool Roofing Materials Database (see the Resources section) for specific information, including the **SRI value of a material**. **Table 1** provides examples of SRI values for typical roof surfaces. These values are for reference only, not for use as substitutes for actual manufacturer's data. Reflectance and emittance data for manufacturers are available from the Cool Roof Rating Council website (see the Resources section). Note that the infrared emittance of aggregates and cementitious materials is always 0.9.

Table 1. Solar Reflectance Index (SRI) for Typical Roofing Materials

SRI Values for Solar Infrared Temperatures	Solar Reflectance	Infrared Emittance	Temperature Rise	SRI
Gray EPDM	0.23	0.87	68°F	21
Gray asphalt shingle	0.22	0.91	67°F	22
Unpainted cement tile	0.25	0.9	65°F	25
White granular surface bitumen	0.26	0.92	63°F	28
Red clay tile	0.33	0.9	58°F	36
Light gravel on built-up roof	0.34	0.9	57°F	37
Aluminum coating	0.61	0.25	48°F	50
White-coated gravel on built-up roof	0.65	0.9	28°F	79
White coating on metal roof	0.67	0.85	28°F	82
White EPDM	0.69	0.87	25F	84
White cement tile	0.73	0.9	21F	90
White coating, 1 coat, 8 mils	0.8	0.91	14F	100
PVC white	0.83	0.92	11F	104
White coating, 2 coats, 20 mils	0.85	0.91	9F	107

Source: Lawrence Berkeley National Laboratory Cool Roofing Materials Database. These values are for reference only and are not for use as substitutes for actual manufacturer data.

Vegetated Roofs

A vegetated roof is a layered system that consists of vegetation, growing medium, filter fabric, drainage, and a waterproof membrane atop a conventional roof (Figure 1). A vegetated roof can be installed as a complete system or as a modular system consisting of interlocking trays. Potted plants do not usually count as a vegetated roof because they do not offer the same magnitude of environmental benefits, and so do not contribute to meeting the credit requirements.

Vegetated roofs can be very beneficial. They can reduce the heat island effect by replacing heat-absorbing surfaces with herbaceous plants, shrubs, and small trees to cool the air through evapotranspiration. They also retain stormwater, provide insulating benefits, are aesthetically appealing, have longer lifetimes than conventional roofs, and often require less maintenance than conventional roofs. Some vegetated roofs are actual gardens and require significant plant care; others have grasses and other plants that require no maintenance or irrigation. All types of vegetated roofs require semiannual inspection.

Occupants' use of roof gardens may be incompatible with high-reflectivity roofing materials. An area-weighted SRI equivalent may help allow for low-glare pavers where people congregate. The planted portions and unoccupied areas of the roof will offset a lower SRI.

Vegetated roofs may unwittingly cause bird collisions with adjacent structures, such as glazed buildings or penthouses. Measures to prevent or reduce bird collision include using exterior shading devices, introducing etched or frit patterns in the glass, and creating "visual markers" in sufficient locations. Visual markers are differentiated planes, materials, textures, colors, opacity, or other visually contrasting features that help fragment window reflections and reduce overall transparency and reflectivity. See strategies and references under SS Credits 5.1 and 5.2.

When designing green roofs, select native or adapted plant species to reduce or eliminate the need for irrigation. Where irrigation is required, consider using graywater or harvested stormwater to reduce potable water use.

Figure 1. Typical Vegetated Roof

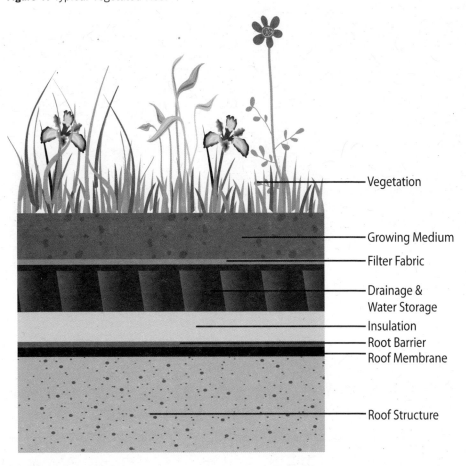

Vegetation

Growing Medium

Filter Fabric

Drainage & Water Storage

Insulation

Root Barrier

Roof Membrane

Roof Structure

5. Timeline and Team

Early in the design process, the project team should engage the architect, landscape architect, civil and mechanical engineers, and an ecologist in evaluating cool roof systems. Architects should specify roofing materials with a high SRI value in the construction documents, and the general contractor should work with vendors to procure manufacturers' data with compliant SRI values. When designing vegetated roofs, involve landscape architects and civil engineers to determine appropriate soil types, average rainfall, and regional plant species that provide wildlife habitat.

6. Calculations

Obtain the roofing material's SRI value from the manufacturer and complete the following steps.

STEP 1

Determine the total roof surface area of the project building (square feet).

STEP 2

Determine the area of the roof covered by mechanical equipment, solar energy panels, and appurtenances, and deduct these areas from the total roof surface area.

STEP 3

Determine whether the areas of qualifying reflective and vegetated roofing are adequate to meet the credit requirements, using Equation 1. If more than 1 type of low-slope or steep-slope material is used, determine the weighted rooftop SRI average and verify that 75% or more of the roof area complies with the credit requirements.

Equation 1

$$\left(\frac{\text{Area of Low — Slope SRI Material}}{78 \times \frac{0.75}{\text{SRI Value}}} + \frac{\text{Area of Steep — Slope SRI Material}}{29 \times \frac{0.75}{\text{SRI Value}}} + \frac{\text{Vegetated Roof Area}}{0.5} \right) \geq \left(\text{Total Roof Area} - \text{Deducted Area} \right)$$

7. Documentation Guidance

As a first step in preparing to complete the LEED-Online documentation requirements, work through the following measures. Refer to LEED-Online for the complete descriptions of all required documentation.

- Prepare roof drawings that show total roof area and the areas of reflective materials or vegetated roof systems.

- List the roofing products, and their emittance percentages, reflectance percentages, SRI values, and slopes. Retain product specifications that verify product characteristics.

8. Examples

A new office building has a 10,000-square-foot low-slope roof and is designed to have both highly reflective roofing materials and a vegetated roof system. The vegetated roof makes up 35% of the roof area. White EPDM roofing with a SRI of 85 covers 60% of the roof area, and the remaining 5% is covered by rooftop mechanical equipment. Table 2 summarizes the roofing types.

Table 2. Roofing Area Summary, by Type

Roofing Type	Area (sf)
Vegetated roof area	3,500
White EPDM roof area (SRI-85), low slope	6,000
Mechanical equipment	500
Total roof area	10,000

Using Equation 1,

$$\left(\frac{6,000}{78 \times \frac{0.75}{85}} + \frac{3,500}{0.5} \right) = 15,718 \text{ ffl} \left(10,000 - 500 \right)$$

In this example, the white EPDM roofing plus the vegetated roofing meets the requirements of this credit, so the project earns 1 point.

9. Exemplary Performance

Projects may earn an Innovation in Design credit for exemplary performance by demonstrating that 100% of the project's roof area (excluding any mechanical equipment, photovoltaic panels, and skylights) consists of a vegetated roof system.

10. Regional Variations

Heat island intensities depend on an area's weather and climate, proximity to water bodies, and topography. Buildings in very cold climates or at high latitudes may not experience the same rise of surface and ambient temperatures. Buildings in urban areas and those located in climate zones 1, 2, and 3 (as defined by ASHRAE 90.1–2007) are most affected by heat islands and are likely to benefit from measures to decrease cooling loads. Consider climate and rainfall at the site when determining the feasibility of a vegetated roof for the project building. In sunny climates, window shading devices will help mitigate glare from reflective roofing into the building.

11. Operations and Maintenance Considerations

Materials with high reflectivity must be periodically cleaned to maintain their heat island reduction properties. These surfaces should be cleaned at least every 2 years to maintain good reflectance.

Building operators should obtain the necessary information to maintain any vegetated roofing system. Extensive green roof systems with low-growing plants are generally easier to maintain than intensive systems with deeper soil and larger plants. The design team should select plantings that are easy to maintain and tolerant of extreme conditions, and avoid plants that produce airborne seeds that will litter the surroundings. The project team should establish an operations plan for inspecting the roof membrane and plantings, as well as maintaining drainage paths. Until plants are fully established, watering and fertilization might be necessary. Properly designed green roofs do not require mowing or cutting, but occasional weeding may be required.

In the roof design, consider including habitat for the animal and insect populations needed to pollinate the installed plantings, such as beehives and wild bee shelters. The project team should request maintenance information from product manufacturers and installers, and then make sure this information is given to the operations team.

12. Resources

Please see USGBC's LEED Registered Project Tools (http://www.usgbc.org/projecttools) for additional resources and technical information.

Websites

American Bird Conservancy

http://www.abcbirds.org

ABC is a national leader in reducing human effects on birds and wildlife. ABC's bird collision program supports national efforts to reduce bird mortality through education and advocacy.

Birds and Buildings Forum

http://www.birdsandbuildings.org

This Chicago-based non-profit supports bird-friendly design through education and advocacy. Their website maintains lists of organizations and resources.

Cool Roof Rating Council

http://www.coolroofs.org

This nonprofit organization is dedicated to implementing and communicating fair, accurate, and credible radiative energy performance rating systems for roof surfaces; supporting research into energy-related radiative properties of roofing surfaces, including durability; and providing education and objective support to parties interested in understanding and comparing roofing options.

U.S. EPA, ENERGY STAR Roofing Products

http://www.energystar.gov/index.cfm?c=roof_prods.pr_roof_products

This site provides solar reflectance levels required to meet ENERGY STAR requirements for qualified roof products.

Whole Building Design Guide, Extensive Green Roofs

http://www.wbdg.org/resources/greenroofs.php

This article by Charlie Miller, PE, details the features and benefits of constructing green roofs.

Fatal Light Awareness Program

http://www.flap.org

Initiated the Bird-Friendly Building Development Program for the City of Toronto, FLAP monitors and promotes bird-friendly design.

Green Roofs for Healthy Cities

http://www.greenroofs.com

This nonprofit industry association consists of individuals and public and private organizations committed to developing a market for green roof infrastructure products and services across North America.

Lawrence Berkeley National Laboratory, Heat Island Group, Cool Roofs

http://eetd.lbl.gov/HeatIsland/CoolRoofs/

This site offers a wealth of information about cool roof research and technology, including links to the cool roofing materials database.

New York City Audubon

http://www.nycaudubon.org

This Audubon chapter takes a leadership role in reducing bird collisions with buildings. The chapter publishes Bird-Safe Building Guidelines, conducts monitoring, and through its Project Safe Flight, promotes bird-friendly design.

Penn State University, Center for Green Roof Research

http://web.me.com/rdberghage/Centerforgreenroof/Home.html

The Center has the mission of demonstrating and promoting green roof research, education, and technology transfer in the Northeastern United States.

13. Definitions

An **area-weighted SRI is** a weighted average calculation that may be performed for buildings with multiple roof surfaces to demonstrate that the total roof area has an average solar reflectance index equal to or greater than that of a theoretical roof 75% of whose surfaces have an SRI of 78 and 25% have an SRI of 30.

Emissivity is the ratio of the radiation emitted by a surface to the radiation emitted by a black body at the same temperature.

Greenhouse gases are relatively transparent to the higher-energy sunlight but trap lower-energy infrared radiation (e.g., carbon dioxide, methane, and CFCs).

Hardscape consists of the inanimate elements of the building landscaping. Examples include pavement, roadways, stone walls, concrete paths and sidewalks, and concrete, brick, and tile patios.

Infrared emittance, or thermal emittance, is a parameter between 0 and 1 (or 0% and 100%) that indicates the ability of a material to shed infrared radiation (heat). The wavelength range for this radiant energy is roughly 4 to 40 micrometers. Most building materials (including glass) are opaque in this part of the spectrum, and have an emittance of roughly 0.9. Materials such as clean, bare metals are the most important exceptions to the 0.9 rule. Thus clean, untarnished galvanized steel has low emittance, and aluminum roof coatings have intermediate emittance levels.

Solar reflectance, or **albedo,** is a measure of the ability of a surface material to reflect sunlight—visible, infrared, and ultraviolet wavelengths—on a scale of 0 to 1. Black paint has a solar reflectance of 0; white paint (titanium dioxide) has a solar reflectance of 1.

The **solar reflectance index** (**SRI**) is a measure of a material's ability to reject solar heat, as shown by a small temperature rise. Standard black (reflectance 0.05, emittance 0.90) is 0 and standard white (reflectance 0.80, emittance 0.90) is 100. For example, a standard black surface has a temperature rise of 90°F (50°C) in full sun, and a standard white surface has a temperature rise of 14.6°F (8.1°C). Once the maximum temperature rise of a given material has been computed, the SRI can be calculated by interpolating between the values for white and black. Materials with the highest SRI values are the coolest choices for paving. Because of the way SRI is defined, particularly hot materials can even take slightly negative values, and particularly cool materials can even exceed 100. (Lawrence Berkeley National Laboratory Cool Roofing Materials Database)

SS	
NC	Credit 7.2
SCHOOLS	Credit 7.2
CS	Credit 7.2

LIGHT POLLUTION REDUCTION

	NC	SCHOOLS	CS
Credit	SS Credit 8	SS Credit 8	SS Credit 8
Points	1 point	1 point	1 point

Intent

To minimize light trespass from the building and site, reduce sky-glow to increase night sky access, improve nighttime visibility through glare reduction and reduce development impact from lighting on nocturnal environments.

Requirements

NC, SCHOOLS & CS

Project teams must comply with 1 of the 2 options for interior lighting AND the requirement for exterior lighting.

For Interior Lighting

OPTION 1

Reduce the input power (by automatic device of) all nonemergency interior luminaires with a direct line of sight to any openings in the envelope (translucent or transparent) by at least 50% between 11 p.m. and 5 a.m. After-hours override may be provided by a manual or occupant-sensing device provided the override lasts no more than 30 minutes.

OR

OPTION 2

All openings in the envelope (translucent or transparent) with a direct line of sight to any nonemergency luminaires must have shielding (controlled/closed by automatic device for a resultant transmittance of less than 10% between 11 p.m. and 5 a.m.).

For Exterior Lighting

Light areas only as required for safety and comfort. Lighting power densities must not exceed ANSI/ASHRAE/IESNA Standard 90.1-2007 (with errata but without addenda[1]) for the classified zone.

Classify the project under 1 of the following zones, as defined in IESNA RP-33, and follow all the requirements for that zone:

LZ1: Dark (developed areas within national parks, state parks forest land and rural areas)

Design exterior lighting so that all site and building-mounted luminaires produce a maximum initial illuminance value no greater than 0.01 horizontal and vertical footcandles at the site boundary and beyond. Document that 0% of the total initial designed fixture lumens (sum total of all fixtures on site) are emitted at an angle of 90 degrees or higher from nadir (straight down).

---

1   Project teams wishing to use ASHRAE approved addenda for the purposes of this prerequisite may do so at their discretion. Addenda must be applied consistently across all LEED credits.

NC, SCHOOLS & CS (continued)

LZ2: Low (primarily residential zones, neighborhood business districts, light industrial with limited nighttime use and residential mixed-use areas)

Design exterior lighting so that all site and building-mounted luminaires produce a maximum initial illuminance value no greater than 0.10 horizontal and vertical footcandles at the site boundary and no greater than 0.01 horizontal footcandles 10 feet beyond the site boundary. Document that no more than 2% of the total initial designed fixture lumens (sum total of all fixtures on site) are emitted at an angle of 90 degrees or higher from nadir (straight down).

LZ3: Medium (all other areas not included in LZ1, LZ2 or LZ4, such as commercial/industrial, and high-density residential)

Design exterior lighting so that all site and building-mounted luminaires produce a maximum initial illuminance value no greater than 0.20 horizontal and vertical footcandles at the site boundary and no greater than 0.01 horizontal footcandles 15 feet beyond the site. Document that no more than 5% of the total initial designed fixture lumens (sum total of all fixtures on site) are emitted at an angle of 90 degrees or higher from nadir (straight down).

LZ4: High[2] (high-activity commercial districts in major metropolitan areas)

Design exterior lighting so that all site and building-mounted luminaires produce a maximum initial illuminance value no greater than 0.60 horizontal and vertical footcandles at the site boundary and no greater than 0.01 horizontal footcandles 15 feet beyond the site. Document that no more than 10% of the total initial designed fixture lumens (sum total of all fixtures on site) are emitted at an angle of 90 degrees or higher from nadir (straight down).

LZ2, LZ3 and LZ4 - For site boundaries that abut public rights-of-way, light trespass requirements may be met relative to the curb line instead of the site boundary.

For All Zones

Illuminance generated from a single luminaire placed at the intersection of a private vehicular driveway and public roadway accessing the site is allowed to use the centerline of the public roadway as the site boundary for a length of 2 times the driveway width centered at the centerline of the driveway.

SCHOOLS Additional Requirement

Sports Field Lighting (Physical Education Spaces)

Physical education spaces (playing fields) do not need to comply with the lighting power density requirements of this credit, as per ANSI/ASHRAE/IESNA Standard 90.1-2007 section 9.4.5, exception E. Automatic Shutoff: All sports lighting must be automatically controlled to shut off no later than 11 p.m.. Manual override must be provided to avoid disruption of school sponsored sporting events.

---

2 To be LZ4, the area must be so designated by an organization with local jurisdiction, such as the local zoning authority.

Trespass Calculations

All trespass calculations must be submitted for 2 conditions: (1) with the sports lighting turned off and all other site lighting turned on, the light trespass requirements are as stated above, and (2) with just the sports lighting turned on, the light trespass requirements for horizontal and vertical footcandles (fc) may be increased to the following illuminance levels:

1. Benefits and Issues to Consider

Environmental Issues

Outdoor lighting is important for human safety. Illuminating connections between buildings and support facilities such as sidewalks, parking lots, roadways, and community gathering places is necessary for twilight and nighttime use. However, light trespass from poorly designed outdoor lighting systems can affect a site's nocturnal ecosystem, and light pollution limits night sky observations. Through thoughtful design and careful maintenance, outdoor lighting can address night sky visibility issues and site illumination requirements, while minimizing negative impacts on the environment.

Sensitively and creatively designed lighting systems promote a unique appreciation for a place at night. Yet even with the best of luminaries—those designed to reduce light pollution and requiring the lowest wattage—the added light will be reflected off surfaces and into the atmosphere. Using the minimum amount of lighting equipment, limiting or eliminating all landscape lighting, and avoiding light pollution through the careful selection of lighting equipment and controls enables nocturnal life to thrive while still providing for human nighttime activity.

Economic Issues

The initial cost and ongoing operational costs for exterior lighting can be greatly reduced by eliminating luminaries that do not enhance safety. Additionally, using the most efficacious light sources, luminaries, and controls will further reduce the energy costs of these systems. Long-life lamps can further increase operational savings by requiring a less frequent relamping cycle. However, the initial cost per luminaire may be somewhat higher because of increased costs associated with internal reflectors and shielding, more efficient lamp and ballast combinations, and controls.

2. Related Credits

This credit requires adherence to the lighting power densities of ASHRAE 90.1–2007. Any energy savings beyond this baseline, as well as savings stemming from integrated automatic controls, may contribute to achieving the following credit:

- EA Credit 1: Optimize Energy Performance

Automatic occupancy controls to shutoff interior perimeter lighting should be coordinated with occupant controllability objectives, as rewarded under this credit:

- IEQ Credit 6.1: Controllability of Systems—Lighting

3. Summary of Referenced Standard

ANSI/ASHRAE/IESNA Standard 90.1–2007, Energy Standard for Buildings Except Low-Rise Residential Lighting, Section 9 (without amendments)
American Society of Heating Refrigeration, and Air-Conditioning Engineers
http://www.ashrae.org
Standard 90.1–2007 was developed by the American Society of Heating, Refrigerating, and Air-Conditioning Engineers, Inc. (ASHRAE), under an American National Standards Institute (ANSI) consensus process. The Illuminating Engineering Society of North America (IESNA) is a joint sponsor of the standard. Standard 90.1 establishes minimum requirements for the energy-efficient design of buildings, except those that are low-rise residential. The provisions of this standard also do not apply to single-family houses; multifamily structures of 3 habitable stories or fewer above grade; mobile and modular homes; buildings without electricity or fossil fuel consumption; or equipment and portions of building systems that use energy primarily for industrial, manufacturing, or commercial processes. The standard provides criteria in the following general categories: building

envelope (Section 5); heating, ventilating, and air-conditioning (Section 6); service water heating (Section 7); power (Section 8); lighting (Section 9); and other equipment (Section 10). Within each section there are mandatory provisions as well as additional prescriptive requirements. Some sections also contain a performance alternate. The energy cost budget option (Section 11) allows the user to exceed some of the prescriptive requirements provided energy cost savings are made in other prescribed areas. However, in all cases, the mandatory provisions must still be met.

	SS
NC	Credit 8
SCHOOLS	Credit 8
CS	Credit 8

Section 9 of the standard provides requirements for the lighting of buildings. Only the exterior lighting requirements apply to this credit. **Table 3** lists the ASHRAE 90.1–2007 allowable building exterior lighting power densities.

Table 3. Lighting Power Densities for Building Exteriors

	Applications	Lighting Power Densities
Tradable Surfaces (Lighting power densities for uncovered parking areas, building grounds, building entrances and exits, canopies and overhangs and outdoor sales areas may be traded.)	**Uncovered Parking Areas**	
	Parking Lots and drives	0.15W/ft²
	Building Grounds	
	Walkways less than 10 feet wide	1.0W/linear foot
	Walkways 10 feet wide or greater Plaza areas Special Feature Areas	0.2W/ft²
	Stairways	1.0W/ft²
	Building Entrances and Exits	
	Main entries	30W/linear foot of door width
	Other doors	20W/linear foot of door width
	Canopies and Overhangs	
	Canopies (free standing and attached and overhangs)	1.25W/ft²
	Outdoor Sales	
	Open areas (including vehicle sales lots)	.5W/ft²
	Street frontage for vehicle sales lots in addition to "open area" allowance	20W/linear foot
Non-Tradable Surfaces (Lighting power density calculations for the following applications can be used only for the specific application and cannot be traded between surfaces or with other exterior lighting. The following allowances are in addition to any allowance otherwise permitted in the "Tradable Surfaces" section of this table.)	Building Facades	0.2W/ft² for each illuminated wall or surface or 5.0W/linear foot for each illuminated wall or surface length
	Automated teller machines and night depositories	270W per location plus 90W per additional ATM per location
	Entrances and gatehouse inspection stations at guarded facilities	1.25W/ft² of uncovered area (covered areas are included in the "Canopies and Overhangs" section of "Tradable Surfaces")
	Loading areas for law enforcement, fire, ambulance and other emergency service vehicles	0.5W/ft² of uncovered area (covered areas are included in the "Canopies and Overhangs" section of "Tradable Surfaces")
	Drive-up windows at fast food restaurants	400W per drive-through
	Parking near 24-hour retail entrances	800W per main entry

Source: Table 9.4.5, ANSI/ASHRAE/IESNA 90.1–2007.

4. Implementation

Interior Building Lighting

OPTION 1

All nonemergency interior lighting fixtures must be automatically controlled and programmed to turn off or have their input power reduced by at least 50% following regular business hours. Controls can be automatic sweep timers, occupancy sensors, or programmed master lighting control panels. The design can also include manual or occupancy based override capabilities that enable lights to be turned on after hours.

Twenty-four-hour operation projects are exempt from the after-hours override automatic shutoff, and thus must follow Option 2.

OPTION 2

All exterior openings, such as windows, must have shielding that can be automatically controlled and programmed to close from 11:00 p.m. to 5:00 a.m. Shielding options include automatic shades that have less than 10% transmittance.

An example is a timer-controlled automated rolling shade with the appropriate light transmittance.

> **CS** In core and shell buildings, these requirements are limited to the core and shell lighting. This typically includes lobby and core circulation spaces. If no light is provided to tenant spaces as part of the core and shell development, those spaces are exempt from these requirements. Core and shell projects that do not install any interior lighting as part of the project scope have met this requirement.

Exterior Lighting Power Density

Design the project's exterior lighting to meet lighting power densities that are equal to or less than the requirements set forth in SS Credit 8, Figure 1, ASHRAE 90.1–2007, Section 9, Table 9.4.5., Lighting for Exterior Areas.

Projects should light areas only as required for safety and comfort, provide only the light levels necessary to meet the design intent, and select efficient fixtures using efficacious sources to meet the lighting requirements of the site while minimizing light pollution.

Exterior Light Distribution

Design the project's exterior lighting to comply with the light pollution requirements for the project's zone. The lighting requirements address the site illumination level at and beyond the site boundary and the luminaire distribution relative to up-lighting. The exterior lighting must meet the light pollution requirements under both precurfew and postcurfew conditions. Curfew timers and controls can be effective parts of the overall lighting strategy, but controls cannot be used to make otherwise noncompliant exterior areas comply with the credit.

> **SCHOOLS** School projects must include curfew timers and controls in the design of sports field lighting, providing automatic shutoff no later than 11 p.m. The lighting designer should provide manual overrides to avoid disrupting evening sporting events that may run beyond the normal curfew.

Consider using low-intensity shielded fixtures and curfew controllers to turn off nonessential site lighting after 10:00 p.m. or immediately after closing (whichever is later) to further reduce the effects of light pollution. Minimize the lighting of architectural and landscape features. Where lighting is required for safety, security, egress, or identification, utilize down-lighting techniques rather than up-lighting.

	SS
NC	Credit 8
SCHOOLS	Credit 8
CS	Credit 8

For example, in environments that are primarily dark (LZ1), no landscape features should be illuminated and architectural lighting should be designed only when other strategies cannot provide the minimum amount of required lighting. In places with medium or high ambient brightness (LZ3 and LZ4), some low-level lighting of features, facades, or landscape areas may be appropriate in pedestrian areas, or for identifying and marking pedestrian paths in areas where light trespass is not likely to be an issue. However, even in areas of high ambient brightness, all nonessential lighting (including landscape and architectural lighting) should be minimized or turned off after hours. All adjustable luminaires should be properly aimed so that light from the luminaires does not cross project boundaries. Use controls wherever possible to turn off nonessential lighting after normal operating hours or after curfew.

At a minimum, consider the following strategies when designing the exterior lighted environment:

- Employ a lighting professional to assess the project's lighting needs and provide recommendations based specifically on lighting for a sustainable built environment.

- Carefully review and respond to any applicable lighting ordinances or bylaws that might affect the lighting design for the project site.

- Determine the environmental zone that the project falls under from Dark (LZ1) to High Ambient Brightness (LZ4). Understand the design implications of the environmental zone that is determined and study neighboring areas to identify potential light trespass problems.

- In most cases, it is better to have 2 luminaires with lower light output and good glare control than 1 higher-output luminaire.

- Select all lighting equipment carefully. Any type of luminaire, whether it is full cutoff, semi-cutoff or non-cutoff, can produce excessive brightness in the form of glare. For example, horizontal lamp positions in full cutoff luminaires tend to produce much less glare than vertical lamps.

- Design exterior lighting to produce minimal upward illumination from the luminaire and reflected light off of adjacent surfaces. Select luminaire locations carefully to control glare and contain light within the design area. Pay special attention to luminaires that are located near the property line to ensure that minimal measurable light from these luminaires crosses the LEED project boundary.

- Use the minimum amount of light necessary. Design and develop a control scheme to minimize or turn lighting off after hours or during post-curfew periods.

- Create a computer model of the proposed electric lighting design and simulate system performance. Use this model to calculate the specified illuminances demonstrating that illuminance values are as required at the project site boundary and at the required distance beyond the site boundary. Calculate the vertical light levels along and above the site boundary to a height of at least the highest luminaire on the site.

- After the lighting system is constructed, commission it to make sure that it is installed and operating properly. Perform maintenance on the system on a regular basis to make sure that it continues to operate properly and that light pollution is minimized.

5. Timeline and Team

Once the environmental zone is determined by the lighting designer, often in the schematic design phase, the design can move forward. Consider local light level requirements and the unique aspects of the site in relation to the light pollution thresholds of this credit.

As the exterior lighting is designed, a photometric analysis of the site should be performed at intervals to verify the project's continued compliance with the credit requirements. During the construction documents phase, the landscape architect, civil engineer, lighting designer, architect, electrical engineer, and others as appropriate should coordinate to verify the layout and compliance of the exterior fixtures.

6. Calculations

Interior Building Lighting

There are no calculations associated with this portion of the credit.

Exterior Lighting Power Density

Calculate the exterior lighting power density in accordance with ANSI/ASHRAE/IESNA 90.1–2007 Section 9 (see Table 1) and determine whether it is less than the allowable densities for the project site. Note that individual luminaire wattages must be input watts (not just lamp watts), including all ballast losses.

Exterior Sky Glow and Light Trespass

To measure compliance with the light trespass requirements, use lighting design software and develop a site illumination model (i.e., photometric site plan). The model should show the full extent of the site and all installed exterior lighting fixtures. Set up a horizontal calculation grid to measure the site illumination at the ground plane (the grid should extend to the property line and 10 feet beyond the site boundary for LZ2, and 15 feet beyond the site boundary for LZ3 and LZ4). Set a vertical calculation grid at the property boundary and at the extents of the LZ requirements (10 feet beyond the site boundary for LZ2, and 15 feet beyond the site boundary for LZ3 and LZ4) to measure vertical illumination. The calculation grid spacing should be a maximum of 10 feet x 10 feet and should exclude building interior areas.

Using manufacturers' fixture data, determine the initial lamp lumens for each luminaire. Additionally, from photometric data, determine the number of initial lamp lumens that are emitted at or above 90 degrees from nadir. Use these data to determine the percentage of lumens at or above 90 degrees.

Luminaires without photometric distribution data must be assumed to have 100% of their initial lamp lumens at or above 90 degrees. Luminaires with limited field adjustability must be assumed to have maximum tilt applied, and lumens at or above 90 degrees must be calculated from maximum tilted orientation. Luminaires with full range of field adjustability (those that can be aimed above 90 degrees from nadir) must be assumed to have 100% of the emitted fixture lumens at or above 90 degrees.

SCHOOLS For LEED for Schools projects with sports field lighting, perform this calculation with sports lighting turned off. The result must be less than or equal to the value referenced for the site's LZ.

For schools with sports field lighting, perform a second calculation with just the sports lighting turned on. Confirm that the light trespass requirements for horizontal and vertical footcandles do not exceed the following illuminance levels:

	SS
NC	Credit 8
SCHOOLS	Credit 8
CS	Credit 8

LZ1 = 0.10 fc at the site boundary, dropping to 0.01 fc within 10 feet of the boundary

LZ2 = 0.30 fc at the site boundary, dropping to 0.01 fc within 10 feet of the boundary

LZ3 = 0.80 fc at the site boundary, dropping to 0.01 fc within 15 feet of the boundary

LZ4 = 1.50 fc at the site boundary, dropping to 0.01 fc within 15 feet of the boundary

7. Documentation Guidance

As a first step in preparing to complete the LEED-Online documentation requirements, work through the following measures. Refer to LEED-Online for the complete descriptions of all required documentation.

Interior Lighting

- If automatic controls are used for interior lighting, prepare drawings showing their locations. Incorporate the sequence of operation for lighting into drawings and specifications or the building operation plan.

- If automatic shading devices are used to control interior lighting, prepare drawings of the devices, assembly specifications, or product data showing that they block at least 90% of the light, and incorporate the sequence of operation for automatic shading devices into drawings and specifications, or the building operation plan.

Exterior Lighting

- Determine the zone classification for a project site.

- Acquire manufacturer's data for lamps used on a project site.

- Prepare a description of the light trespass analysis procedure conducted to determine credit compliance.

- Develop a photometric site plan of parking areas that includes footcandle summary tables for light ratio.

SCHOOLS

- For sports field lighting on school grounds, develop a photometric site plan showing adherence to allowable light level limits, prepare drawings showing automatic controls for sports field lighting, and incorporate the sequence of operation for sports field lighting into drawings and specifications or the building operation plan.

8. Examples

EXAMPLE 1. Exterior Lighting Power Density and Trespass Assessment

Table 2 shows an example of how exterior lighting power density calculations are performed, and Table 15 demonstrates the data required to calculate the percentage of lumens emitted at or above 90 degrees from nadir.

Table 2. Sample Exterior Lighting Power Density Calculation

Site Lighting Power Density Calculation						
Site Lighting Fixture	Fixture Power (watts)	Total Fixtures (qty)	Total Fixture Power (watts)	Site Location	Site Area (sf)	LPD (w/sf)
Pole Fixture 1	250	14	3,500	Parking 1	32,000	0.11
Pole Fixture 1	250	8	2,000	Parking 2	18,000	0.11
Pole Fixture 2	115	1	115	Walkways 1	875	0.13
Bollard Fixture 1	40	4	160	Walkways 1	875	0.18
Bollard Fixture 1	40	6	240	Courtyard 1	1,500	0.16
Wall Washer 1	50	5	250	Building Façade N	2,500	0.10
Site Areas						
Identification	Area (sf)	ASHRAE 90.1.2004 Allowable LPD (w/sf)	Actual LPD (From Site Lighting Table)	Actual LPD Reduction (%)	Required LPD Reduction (%)	Complies (Yes/No)
Parking 1	32,000	0.25	0.11	27%	20%	YES
Parking 2	18,000	0.15	0.11	26%	20%	YES
Walkways 1 (10' wide)	875	0.2	0.16	21%	20%	YES
Courtyard 1	1,500	0.2	0.16	20%	20%	YES
Building Façade N	2,500	0.2	0.10	50%	50%	YES

Table 3. Lamp Lumen Calculation

Luminaire Type	Quantity of Installed Luminaires	Initial Fixture Lumens per Luminaire	Total Fixture Lumens (column 2 x column 3)	Initial Fixture Lumens from Luminaire above 90 Degrees (from nadir-straight down)	Total Fixture Lumens above 90 Degrees (column 2 x column 5)
A	10	4,600	46,000	100	1,000
B	20	11,900	238,000	0	0
C	5	2,000	10,000	2,000	10,000
Total			294,000		11,000

Figure 1 shows the photometric site plan generated by an illumination model. The example is in compliance with the credit requirements for a project located in LZ2: The light level at the property line does not exceed 0.1 footcandles, and the light level 10 feet beyond the property line does not exceed 0 footcandles.

Figure 1. Sample Illumination Model

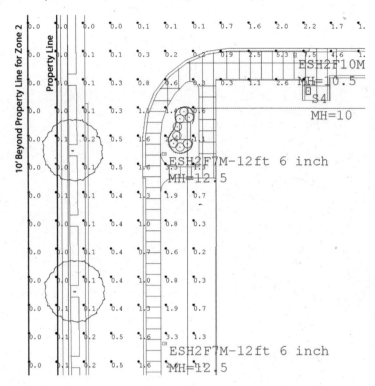

Figures 2–5 show how a shielded light can prevent light trespass and light pollution of the night sky.

Figure 2. Unshielded Floodlight

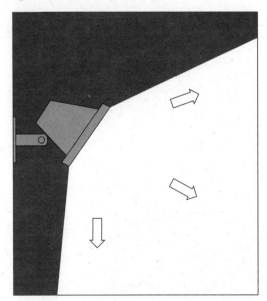

	SS
NC	Credit 8
SCHOOLS	Credit 8
CS	Credit 8

Figure 3. Task Area from Unshielded Floodlight

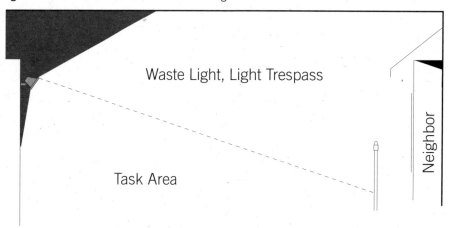

Figure 4. Shielded Floodlight

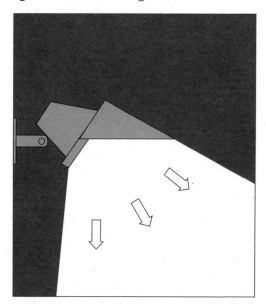

Figure 5. Task Area from Shielded Floodlight

9. Exemplary Performance

This credit is not eligible for exemplary performance under the Innovation in Design section.

	SS
NC	Credit 8
SCHOOLS	Credit 8
CS	Credit 8

10. Regional Variations

There are no regional variations associated with this credit.

11. Operations and Maintenance Considerations

Exterior luminaires must be periodically cleaned and relamped to maintain optimal light levels. Depending on the number of exterior luminaires, it may be beneficial to implement a schedule and policy for group relamping to help avoid lamp burnouts and to minimize the labor costs associated with spot relamping. Additionally, if group relamping is identified as an operational strategy during the design phase, the initial light levels can often be reduced while still maintaining the design illuminance. A rule of thumb to determine whether group relamping is likely to be economically feasible is if the labor cost to change a lamp exceeds the cost per lamp.

12. Resources

Please see USGBC's LEED Registered Project Tools (http://www.usgbc.org/projecttools) for additional resources and technical information.

Websites

American Society of Heating, Refrigeration, and Air-Conditioning Engineers
http://www.ashrae.org
ASHRAE advances the science of heating, ventilation, air conditioning, and refrigeration for the public's benefit through research, standards writing, continuing education, and publications. To purchase ASHRAE standards and guidelines, visit the bookstore on the ASHRAE website.

California Energy Commission (CEC)–2005, California Energy Efficiency Building Standards: Lighting Zones
http://www.energy.ca.gov/title24/2005standards/outdoor_lighting/2004-09-30_LIGHTING_ZONES.PDF
This site describes the outdoor lighting zones developed for use in the California Energy Efficiency Building Standards (Title 24), effective 2005.

Illuminating Engineering Society of North America
http://www.iesna.org
The mission of IESNA is to benefit society by promoting knowledge and disseminating information for the improvement of the lighted environment..

International Dark-Sky Association
http://www.darksky.org
This nonprofit agency is dedicated to educating about and providing solutions to light pollution.

Sky and Telescope
http://skytonight.com/resources/darksky
This site includes facts on light pollution and its impact on astronomy and information about purchasing light pollution-minimizing light fixtures.

Print Media

The IESNA Lighting Handbook, ninth edition, by Illuminating Engineering Society of North America (IESNA, 2000).

Lighting for Exterior Environments RP-33-99, by IESNA Outdoor Environment Lighting Committee (IESNA, 1999).

Concepts in Practice Lighting: Lighting Design in Architecture, by Torquil Barker (B.T. Batsford Ltd., 1997).

The Design of Lighting, by Peter Tregenza and David Loe (E & FN Spon, 1998).

ASNI/ASHRAE/IESNA Standard 90.1–2007 User's Manual, effective 2008.

13. Definitions

Curfew hours are locally determined times when lighting restrictions are imposed. When no local or regional restrictions are in place, 10:00 p.m. is regarded as a default curfew time.

A **footcandle** (**fc**) is a measure of light falling on a given surface. One footcandle is defined as the quantity of light falling on a 1-square-foot area from a 1 candela light source at a distance of 1 foot (which equals 1 lumen per square foot). Footcandles can be measured both horizontally and vertically by a footcandle meter or light meter.

A **full-cutoff luminaire** has zero candela intensity at an angle of 90 degrees above the vertical axis (nadir or straight down) and at all angles greater than 90 degrees from straight down. Additionally, the candela per 1,000 lamp lumens does not numerically exceed 100 (10%) at an angle of 80 degrees above nadir. This applies to all lateral angles around the luminaire.

Horizontal footcandles occur on a horizontal surface. They can be added together arithmetically when more than 1 source provides light to the same surface.

Light pollution is waste light from building sites that produces glare, is directed upward to the sky, or is directed off the site. Waste light does not increase nighttime safety, utility, or security and needlessly consumes energy.

Light trespass is obtrusive light that is unwanted because of quantitative, directional, or spectral attributes. Light trespass can cause annoyance, discomfort, distraction, or loss of visibility.

Safety and comfort light levels meet local code requirements and must be adequate to provide a safe path for egress without overlighting the area.

Shielding is a nontechnical term that describes devices or techniques that are used as part of a luminaire or lamp to limit glare, light trespass, or sky glow.

Sky glow is caused by stray light from unshielded light sources and light reflecting off surfaces that then enter the atmosphere and illuminate and reflect off dust, debris, and water vapor. Sky glow can substantially limit observation of the night sky, compromise astronomical research, and adversely affect nocturnal environments.

Vertical footcandles occur on a vertical surface. They can be added together arithmetically when more than 1 source provides light to the same surface.

	NC	SCHOOLS	CS
Credit	NA	NA	SS Credit 9
Points	NA	NA	1 point

Intent

To educate tenants about implementing sustainable design and construction features in their tenant improvement build-out.

Tenant design and construction guidelines benefit the Core & Shell certified project in 2 important ways: First, the guidelines will help tenants design and build sustainable interiors and adopt green building practices; second, the guidelines will help in coordinating LEED 2009 for Commercial Interiors and LEED 2009 for Core and Shell Development certifications.

Requirements

Publish an illustrated document that provides tenants with the following design and construction information:

- A description of the sustainable design and construction features incorporated in the core & shell project and the project's sustainability goals and objectives, including those for tenant spaces.

- Information on LEED for Commercial Interiors and how the core and shell building contributes to achieving these credits.

- Information that enables a tenant to coordinate space design and construction with the core and shell's building systems. Specific LEED 2009 for Commercial Interiors credits to be addressed when applicable include the following:

  - Water use reduction.
  - Optimize energy performance, lighting power.
  - Optimize energy performance, lighting controls.
  - Optimize energy performance, HVAC.
  - Energy use and metering.
  - Measurement and verification.
  - Ventilation and outdoor air delivery.
  - Construction indoor air quality management.
  - Indoor chemical and pollutant source control.
  - Controllability of systems.
  - Thermal comfort.
  - Daylighting and views.
  - Commissioning.
  - Elimination or control of environmental tobacco smoke.

- Recommendations, including examples, for sustainable strategies, products, materials, and services.

	SS
NC	NA
SCHOOLS	NA
CS	Credit 9

1. Benefits and Issues to Consider

Environmental Issues

Because of the speculative nature of the real estate market, a building's core and shell and interior tenant spaces are controlled by completely different entities. Responsibility for environmental impacts is therefore weighted differently for building owners, developers, and tenants. Tenants' potential to reduce energy use through efficient lighting design and daylighting strategies depends on the core and shell construction, and the base building mechanical system will directly influence tenants' ability to optimize occupants' indoor environmental quality.

LEED for Core & Shell buildings also offer ways for tenants to take advantage of the environmental benefits built into the project and can inspire tenants to take their own steps toward environmental stewardship. Core & Shell building efforts to reduce heat islands, plant native landscapes, and install low flow plumbing fixtures can significantly reduce tenants' energy and resource use, particularly where lease agreements require tenants to meter and pay for their own energy costs.

Economic Issues

Producing tenant design and construction guidelines will not have an economic impact on LEED for Core & Shell projects; however, the strategies and recommendations in the guidelines can require upfront investments on the part of building tenants. Tenants choosing to certify their build-out projects under the LEED for Commercial Interiors Rating System may incur additional costs for commissioning and certification. However, a carefully designed core and shell will provide base building elements that support cost-effective ways for tenants to earn credits under LEED for Commercial Interiors.

2. Related Credits

This credit is related to all LEED for Core & Shell credits the project team chooses to pursue within the scope of the LEED project. LEED for Core & Shell credits most likely to affect future building tenants are these:

- WE Credit 3: Water Use Reduction

- EA Credit 1: Optimize Energy Performance

- EA Credit 3: Enhanced Commissioning

- EA Credit 5: Measurement and Verification

- IEQ Prerequisite 2: Environmental Tobacco Smoke Control

- IEQ Credit 2: Increased Ventilation

- IEQ Credit 3: Construction Indoor Air Quality Management Plan

- IEQ Credit 5: Indoor Chemical and Pollutant Source Control

- IEQ Credit 6: Controllability of Systems

- IEQ Credit 7: Thermal Comfort

- IEQ Credit 8: Daylighting and Views

3. Summary of Referenced Standards

There are no standards referenced for this credit.

4. Implementation

The tenant design and construction guidelines are intended to educate future building tenants on the sustainability goals of the core and shell project, explain how tenants can incorporate green building strategies into the build-out of their own spaces, describe the synergies between LEED for Core & Shell and LEED for Commercial Interiors, and encourage tenants to pursue LEED for Commercial Interiors certification.

The recommendations in the tenant design and construction guidelines are meant to highlight building-specific best practices. The guidelines are not meant to be design requirements for the tenant. Some projects may adopt some or all of the guidelines as tenant requirements; however, that is not necessary to meet the requirements of this credit.

Tenant design and construction guidelines must include the following:

	SS
NC	NA
SCHOOLS	NA
CS	Credit 9

Core & Shell Sustainable Design and Construction Features

This portion of the tenant design and construction guidelines is meant to help the tenant design team understand and efficiently utilize the base building's systems and design features. Technical information, building features, and base building environmental policies should be clearly communicated. As appropriate for the project, the guidelines will include the following:

Reduced water use. Specify the building water use reduction goals; provide information about the it's water use fixtures and systems and how they assist in achieving these goals. Fixtures and systems recommendations should also be included. These can be presented in narrative form with product cut sheets.

Optimize energy performance. This section should outline the energy optimization features of the core and shell and provide information and recommendations about how tenants can further reduce energy use through design. Specific features to be highlighted:

Lighting power. The greatest opportunity for tenants to optimize energy consumption is in the area of lighting. LEED for Core & Shell building design can dramatically affect lighting power use by providing a base building design that allows for reduced lighting power without compromising light quality. So that tenants can optimize daylighting, a LEED for Core & Shell commercial office building design should consider floor-to-ceiling heights, the bay size, the type of glazing, and the depth of occupied spaces. Daylight shelves and glare control devices should also be considered. Skylights for top lighting should be considered for retail or manufacturing projects to further reduce lighting power.

Information on technical and design decisions about the base building should be included in the tenant design and construction guidelines to help the tenant understand and implement strategies to reduce lighting power. Recommendations regarding base building lighting fixtures installed may also be appropriate.

Lighting controls. Lighting power is integrally linked with tenant space lighting controls. Daylighting strategies that have been designed into the core and shell are best if coupled with tenant space layout and lighting controls. Base building design information, potential tenant space layouts, and technical recommendations should all be considered.

Heating, ventilation, and air-conditioning (HVAC). The HVAC system that the core and shell design team chooses will have a considerable effect on the tenant build-out. The information provided should include a description of the HVAC system, along with any energy efficiency features and suggestions as to how they can be best utilized. Building orientation and site issues, such as shading from surrounding buildings, may affect passive solar opportunities available for tenants.

Energy use and metering. Provide information on the building's expected energy use. Explain how the building's energy use is metered, provide instructions on how tenants can submeter their space, and describe how submetering can help foster tenant energy conservation.

	SS
NC	NA
SCHOOLS	NA
CS	Credit 9

Measurement and verification. Describe the building's measurement and verification plan, including what option is being used and how the core and shell measurement and verification plan will be carried out. Provide information about protocols that the tenants can use to create their own measurement and verification plans.

Ventilation and outdoor air delivery. Provide design and operational information for the ventilation system. This should describe how the air is provided to the space (e.g., underfloor, overhead, displacement, or natural ventilation). Include the amount of outside air that each system is capable of providing so that tenants can determine how much outside air is available to them. This document should describe the control system and identify opportunities for the tenant to adapt or fine-tune the control system by, for example, installing monitoring devices such as CO_2 sensors.

Construction indoor air quality management. The guidelines should highlight areas of the core and shell construction indoor air quality management plan that are applicable to the tenant build-out, particularly where tenant work may be sequenced at the same time.

Indoor chemical and pollutant source control. Illustrate the strategies used to achieve IEQ Credit 5. Because multiple tenants may share air return and supply systems, include information on the benefits of isolating hazardous gases or chemicals.

Controllability of systems. Describe the building's HVAC control systems. If the building incorporates natural ventilation, describe how it can be used and how it works with the building's other systems. For a completely mechanical system, provide details on how the tenants can use the control system to better regulate the thermal comfort in their spaces.

Thermal comfort. Explain how the building's HVAC system will help maintain thermal comfort in the building. Provide the design criteria of the system (including indoor and outdoor conditions) and document any other assumptions made for the thermal comfort calculations (including space internal loads, clothing, and metabolic rate of the people in the space).

Daylighting and views. Many of the issues related to daylighting are addressed in sections on energy optimization; however, views should also be considered. For commercial office buildings, consider supplying a tenant layout early in the project design so that potential tenants can consider the benefits of views within their space layouts.

Employees in retail or manufacturing projects can also benefit from views to the outdoors. Building siting and envelope design should be described.

Core and shell buildings that have been designed to optimize occupants' views to the outdoors should provide illustrations in the guidelines so that space layouts can take full advantage of this amenity. The benefits of views to tenants can be part of the building marketing and lease negotiation process.

Commissioning. Building commissioning can help ensure that a building is operating as intended. Provide details on the core and shell commissioning process. This may include the commissioning plan or report. Provide information on the building's design intent so that the tenant can evaluate whether the space is functioning as designed. Core and shell commissioning documents can also serve as a model for tenants to use for their own commissioning efforts.

Elimination or control of environmental tobacco smoke. If Option 1 of IEQ Prerequisite 2, Environmental Tobacco Smoke Control, is used, the smoking policy should be part of the tenant design and construction guidelines and clearly communicated during the lease negotiation. If Option 2 of this prerequisite is used, then separation, exhaust, and pressurization requirements will need to be clearly communicated so that they can be included in the tenant's scope of construction.

For mixed-use buildings that include a residential component, describe the methods used to achieve compliance with Option 3 of the prerequisite.

	SS
NC	NA
SCHOOLS	NA
CS	Credit 9

Recommendations for sustainable strategies, products, materials and service. This section of the tenant design and construction guidelines should describe recommended materials, products, and strategies to be employed in the tenant build-out. Descriptions of the sustainable strategies, products, materials, and services used in the core and shell building can be a resource when tenant design teams make selections for their space. For instance, if the base building has installed low-emitting materials (see IEQ Credit 4, Low-Emitting Materials), then the adhesives, sealants, paints, coatings, carpet systems, composite wood, and agrifiber products used should be listed in the guidelines. Sustainable material suppliers, manufactures, local salvaged material retailers, and construction waste recycling facilities may also be listed as resources in the guidelines.

Information Regarding the LEED for Commercial Interiors Rating System
This section of the tenant design and construction guidelines is meant to help the tenant pursue LEED for Commercial Interiors certification. General information about the LEED for Commercial Interiors rating system must be provided, with building-specific examples of the advantages of attaining LEED for Commercial Interiors certification. This section should outline the rating system, credit by credit, and describe specific methods that future tenants can use to achieve these credits. Pay particular attention to the synergies between the core and shell designs and how they assist with achieving credits under LEED for Commercial Interiors.

5. Timeline and Team
The tenant design and construction guidelines should evolve during the core and shell design process with input from the project architect, design team, and building owner. This document is part of the design submittal and should be finalized as project teams complete the design development stage and move into construction documents. The guidelines should be made available to tenants as part of the lease negotiations and must be provided prior to the start of any tenant design work.

6. Calculations
There are no calculations required for this credit.

7. Documentation Guidance
As a first step in preparing to complete the LEED-Online documentation requirements, work through the following measure. Refer to LEED-Online for the complete descriptions of all required documentation.

- Retain a copy of the tenant design and construction guidelines.

8. Examples
There are no examples for this credit.

9. Exemplary Performance
This credit is not eligible for exemplary performance under the Innovation in Design section.

10. Regional Variations
There are no regional variations associated with this credit.

11. Operations and Maintenance Considerations
In addition to informing the initial build-out of tenant spaces, tenant design and construction guidelines are useful for informing construction activities over the life of the building. particularly

	SS
NC	NA
SCHOOLS	NA
CS	Credit 9

in facilities with frequent tenant turnover, project teams should consider providing guidelines that can be updated. Investigate with the building owner ways to communicate this information to new tenants over the life of the building. Consider expanding the guidelines to cover LEED for Existing Buildings: Operations & Maintenance requirements for credits pertaining to facility alterations and additions.

Consider opportunities for optimizing operations at both the tenant scale and the building as a whole. For example, tenant-level metering and responsibility for utility bills provide a powerful incentive for tenants to conserve energy and are therefore rewarded under LEED for Commercial Interiors, but having access to whole-building utility data is critical for environmental benchmarking during the operations phase. Include building-level meters in the facility's design, or establish lease agreements that require tenants to disclose utility data to the facility owner or manager.

12. Resources

Please see USGBC's LEED Registered Project Tools (http://www.usgbc.org/projecttools) for additional resources and technical information.

13. Definitions

There are no definitions associated with this credit.

SITE MASTER PLAN

	NC	SCHOOLS	CS
Credit	NA	SS Credit 9	NA
Points	NA	1 point	NA

Intent

To ensure that the environmental site issues included in the initial development of the site and project are continued throughout future development caused by changes in programs or demography.

Requirements

SCHOOLS

The project must achieve at least 4 out of the following 7 credits using the associated calculation methods. This credit then requires that the achieved credits be recalculated using the data from the master plan. The 7 credits include:

- SS Credit 1: Site Selection
- SS Credit 5.1: Site Development—Protect or Restore Habitat
- SS Credit 5.2: Site Development—Maximize Open Space
- SS Credit 6.1: Stormwater Design—Quantity Control
- SS Credit 6.2: Stormwater Design—Quality Control
- SS Credit 7.1: Heat Island Effect—Nonroof
- SS Credit 8: Light Pollution Reduction

A site master plan for the school must be developed in collaboration with the school board or other decision-making body. Previous sustainable site design measures should be considered in all master-planning efforts, with intent to retain existing infrastructure whenever possible. The master plan, therefore, must include current construction activity plus future construction (within the building's lifespan) that affects the site. The master plan development footprint must also include parking, paving, and utilities.

	SS
NC	NA
SCHOOLS	Credit 9
CS	NA

1. Benefits and Issues to Consider

Environmental Issues

Schools continually adapt to shifting demographics, attendance boundaries, curricula, and sources of funding. Expansion of school facilities is often required to accommodate a school's changing needs. Schools whose buildings were designed for high performance and environmental stewardship will want to ensure that these goals remain priorities in future expansion projects. Developing a master plan helps preserve a systemic view of a project over time so that proposed changes can be evaluated within the framework of the original vision. Such a plan helps prevent the implementation of "quick fix" solutions that overlook long-term environmental concerns.

Economic Issues

A well-developed master plan could help secure future funding by establishing credibility with stakeholders who support the goals of the plan.

A master plan may propose that elements be built into the project in advance of their intended use. This may raise initial construction costs but will increase efficiency and reduce costs later on.

Project teams should also consider that school enrollment may decrease. A master plan should propose strategies to accommodate both increasing and decreasing enrollments.

2. Related Credits

The most closely related credits are 7 from Sustainable Sites; the achievement and recalculation of 4 of these 7 are needed for compliance:

- SS Credit 1: Site Selection
- SS Credit 5.1: Site Development—Protect or Restore Habitat
- SS Credit 5.2: Site Development—Maximize Open Space
- SS Credit 6.1: Stormwater Design—Quantity Control
- SS Credit 6.2: Stormwater Design—Quality Control
- SS Credit 7.1: Heat Island Effect—Nonroof
- SS Credit 8: Light Pollution Reduction

The project team should also be alert to possible community partnerships that could result from pursuit of this credit:

- SS Credit 10: Joint Use of Facilities

3. Summary of Referenced Standards

There are no standards referenced for this credit.

4. Implementation

Master plan discussions should include plans for community centers, fields, libraries, parks, wetlands, and other major projects so that the school can plan its campus with community needs in mind. There is potential overlap with SS Credit 10, Joint Use of Facilities.

In developing a master plan, work with decision makers to evaluate ways in which future expansion will provide the most benefit to both the school and the community. It is important to involve the local municipality and county in the earliest stages of developing a master plan. Geographic information systems data can provide detailed information about demographics, student enrollment, population, housing growth, and other factors that may affect future expansion needs. Schools and their governing boards should not feel restricted by a master plan if the future needs of the students and community are uncertain. Flexibility can be built into the master plan to accommodate a range of scenarios. Expansion is not always a necessity in the long-term evolution of a school. Sometimes, fluctuations in demographics and enrollment can result in reduced occupancy. Consider employing design strategies that allow components of the building to be modified as the school's needs change. As long as potential scenarios individually comply with the credit requirements, a variety of options can be included in the master plan. Future needs of the community should also be considered to help identify potential joint-use scenarios.

	SS
NC	NA
SCHOOLS	Credit 9
CS	NA

5. Timeline and Team

Discussions regarding a master planning exercise should take place well in advance of the predesign phase of the building development to allow for a comprehensive project strategy. In addition, the environmental and financial impacts should be projected and planned for well in advance. Discussions should include the project owner, architect, and design team. The entire project team should take advantage of design charrettes that allow public input for the school or building's development from surrounding residents, businesses, and other neighbors. This input will give schools a chance to be integrated into the community while helping planners determine how to minimize construction impacts to the area. The charrette process can reveal potential community alliances and partnerships, which teams can pursue under SS Credit 10, Joint Use of Facilities.

6. Calculations

Refer to the qualifying calculations for the following credits:

- SS Credit 1: Site Selection
- SS Credit 5.1: Site Development—Protect or Restore Habitat
- SS Credit 5.2: Site Development—Maximize Open Space
- SS Credit 6.1: Stormwater Design—Quantity Control
- SS Credit 6.2: Stormwater Design—Quality Control
- SS Credit 7.1: Heat Island Effect—Nonroof
- SS Credit 8: Light Pollution Reduction

The project team must recalculate for the entire master plan to demonstrate that the master plan achieves 4 or more of the 7 credits.

7. Documentation Guidance

As a first step in preparing to complete the LEED-Online documentation requirements, work through the following measures. Refer to LEED-Online for the complete descriptions of all required documentation.

- Prepare a description of the process by which a site's master plan was developed in collaboration with the school board or other decision-making body.
- Retain a copy of a site's master plan and written verification of its approval.

8. Examples

There are no examples for this credit.

9. Exemplary Performance

This credit is not eligible for exemplary performance under the Innovation in Design section.

10. Regional Variations

There are no regional variations associated with this credit.

11. Operations and Maintenance Considerations

The project's site master plan should be a required reference for future site alterations. To keep the plan relevant and help ensure its use, the project team should establish a regular schedule for reviewing and updating it; an updating cycle of 2 to 5 years is recommended. Accessibility by all stakeholders is also important; consider using a web-based system that allows for easy access by building operators, administrators, board members, and the larger community.

Designate the party responsible for overseeing the master plan's implementation. Because of the turnover typical of school boards, school administrators are likely the best option.

12. Resources

Please see USGBC's LEED Registered Project Tools (http://www.usgbc.org/projecttools) for additional resources and technical information.

Websites

National Clearinghouse for Educational Facilities, Master Planning Resources
http://www.edfacilities.org/rl/masterplan.cfm
This site includes examples of actual school master plans.

Print Media

Building a Vision for Chicago's Schools and Neighborhoods: A Framework for a Facilities Master Plan, by Andrea Lee (Neighborhood Capital Budget Group, 2005).
This report emphasizes the need for strategic planning to maximize limited funds for the maintenance, repair, and expansion of learning environments.

13. Definitions

In LEED, a master plan is an overall design or development concept for the school and associated buildings and site. This concept considers future use, growth, and contraction and includes ways for managing the facility and sustainable features. The master plan is typically illustrated with narrative descriptions, building plans, and site drawings of phases and planned development.

JOINT USE OF FACILITIES

	NC	SCHOOLS	CS
Credit	NA	SS Credit 10	NA
Points	NA	1 point	NA

Intent

To make the school a more integrated part of the community by enabling the building and its playing fields to be used for nonschool events and functions.

Requirements

`SCHOOLS`

OPTION 1

In collaboration with the school board or other decision-making body, ensure that at least 3 of the following spaces included in the school are accessible to and available for shared use by the general public: auditorium, gymnasium, cafeteria/cafetorium, 1 or more classrooms, playing fields, and/or joint parking.

Provide a separate entry to the spaces intended for joint use. The entry can be from a school lobby or corridor near an entrance convenient to public access, which can be secured from the rest of the school after normal school hours and has toilets available.

OR

OPTION 2

In collaboration with the school board or other decision-making body, engage in a contract with community or other organizations to provide at least 2 dedicated-use spaces in the building.

Dedicated-use spaces include, but are not limited to:

- Commercial office
- Health clinic
- Community service centers (provided by state, city, or county offices)
- Police offices
- Library or media center
- Parking lot
- One or more commercial sector businesses

Provide a separate entry to the spaces intended for joint use. The entry can be from a school lobby or corridor near an entrance convenient to public access, which can be secured from the rest of the school after normal school hours and which has toilets available.

SCHOOLS (continued)

OR

OPTION 3

In collaboration with the school district or other decision-making body, ensure that at least 2 of the following 6 spaces that are owned by other organizations/agencies are accessible to students:

- Auditorium
- Gymnasium
- Cafeteria
- One or more classrooms
- Swimming pool
- Playing field

Provide direct pedestrian access to these spaces from the school. In addition, provide signed agreements with the other organizations/ agencies that stipulate how they and the school district and organizations or agencies will share these spaces.

1. Benefits and Issues to Consider

Environmental Issues

Significant environmental benefits can be realized through joint-use agreements. Combining multiple functions into 1 site reduces the need to build on previously undeveloped land, minimizing the negative impacts of construction on local ecosystems. In addition, eliminating the need for a separate building to accommodate community functions reduces the amount of raw materials extraction, manufacturing, and transportation of goods required for construction. Other amenities like shared parking can reduce the amount of impervious paving, reducing stormwater runoff and minimizing the heat island effect.

Communities may gain new access or greater proximity to services that might be inaccessible under other circumstances. An example is the creation of a police substation on-site that gives both the school and the community greater access to law enforcement and security.

A joint-use agreement allows school spaces that would ordinarily be unused after school hours to provide the community with valuable program amenities.

Economic Issues

Many schools are overcrowded because of the scarcity of land and the cost of new construction. In joint-use situations, much of this cost can be divided among multiple organizations that use the space, reducing the individual costs for each. Savings can also be realized in ongoing operations and maintenance costs.

In addition to sharing costs of facilities and their operations, schools may be able to trade community access to space for in-kind services such as landscaping, snow removal, and garbage and recycling pickup services.

Schools may take advantage of amenities provided by certain types of shared facilities, such as parks, theaters, museums, libraries, playing fields, athletic facilities, computer labs, and health care services. Depending on the types of organizations that facilities are shared with, integration with the community may provide additional educational opportunities as well.

Schools may have to absorb the costs of ensuring that higher safety standards are met in shared facilities. Providing separate entryways, handicap accessibility, fire egress pathways, and additional signage may also increase initial costs. Separate metering for utilities may also be required. These costs may be shared and thus minimized by the organizations or agencies that will be occupying the joint-use or dedicated-use space.

	SS
NC	NA
SCHOOLS	Credit 10
CS	NA

2. Related Credits

Projects that accommodate joint use of facilities may be more likely to meet community connectivity criteria because of the proximity of the school to services and institutions within the neighborhood; these benefits are rewarded under the following credit:

- SS Credit 2: Development Density and Community Connectivity

3. Summary of Referenced Standards

There are no standards referenced for this credit.

4. Implementation

Joint-use agreements can be most effective when contact with the community is initiated early in the project. Sometimes a joint-use agreement can be developed before property has been purchased for the school. If joint-use opportunities are identified during the design phase, it might be possible for schools and other organizations to pool their resources to purchase property. The community might be able to fund more of the construction, while the school might contribute more over time in operation costs. Sharing costs can enable a community to build a larger gymnasium, theater, playing field, or library than would otherwise be affordable. The benefits of sharing spaces may increase over time, as both parties gain assets that could not be accrued separately.

The organizations and agencies that may benefit from joint-use agreements will vary by location but may include city managers, town or city planning commissions, town or city councils, and school boards. In some cases, local chapters of national organizations could be involved. In all cases, school administrators should use caution and make responsible decisions when determining appropriate organizations and services to engage in a joint-use plan.

The issue of security must be addressed, but added security measures may not necessarily add additional costs. Security can be treated as a design issue and achieved by careful planning and orientation of spaces. If joint use is planned from the beginning, public and school spaces can be separated by a door, or a shared gymnasium can be separated from the rest of the school during off-hours and from the public space during school hours. Restroom facilities should be made available to joint-use facilities, but additional restrooms might not be necessary. With careful planning, joint-use agreements can save money for both parties and still be cost-effective to build.

Many communities already use existing schools in some capacity for the sake of economy or convenience but might not be formally recognized for it. This credit acknowledges the environmental benefits of sharing spaces and resources.

5. Timeline and Team

In general, there are opportunities to achieve joint-use agreements throughout the planning, design, and subsequent operation of a school. If maximum cost savings are desired, project teams should look for these opportunities early in the stages of school design and planning and seek to establish joint-use agreements early. City managers, town authorities, school board members, PTA leaders, school principals, and community members are some of the people who should be involved in conversations about joint use, and design teams should be fully apprised of any decisions that could affect planning. Potential issues surrounding joint-use areas, such as access and separation, should be considered in the design process as soon as joint-use areas have been identified.

6. Calculations

There are no calculations required for this credit.

7. Documentation Guidance

As a first step in preparing to complete the LEED-Online documentation requirements, work through the following measures. Refer to LEED-Online for the complete descriptions of all required documentation.

- For schools with 3 shared public spaces, list the shared spaces, depict doors or security gates and accessible restroom facilities on project drawings, and retain evidence of communication used to notify the public of shared space availability.

- For schools with 2 dedicated-use spaces, list the shared spaces, depict doors or security gates and accessible restroom facilities on project drawings, retain a copy of the joint-use contract or agreement, and develop a drawing that shows pedestrian access to the community spaces.

8. Examples

Figure 1 shows how facility design can be optimized to promote shared use of facilities. In this example, the school has contracted with the community for a joint-use library, partially satisfying the requirements for Option 2. The library has been designed to be shared with the community and operate autonomously when the school is not in service. This was done by locating the library at the front of the campus, and locating stairs and restrooms adjacent to the space.

Figure 1. A sample plan demonstrating a joint use of facility

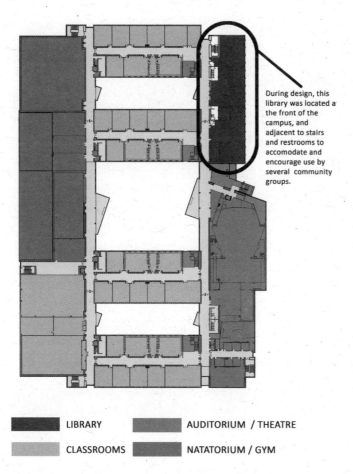

During design, this library was located at the front of the campus, and adjacent to stairs and restrooms to accomodate and encourage use by several community groups.

■ LIBRARY   ■ AUDITORIUM / THEATRE

■ CLASSROOMS   ■ NATATORIUM / GYM

9. Exemplary Performance

Projects may earn an Innovation in Design credit for exemplary performance by meeting the requirements of 2 of the 3 options listed above.

10. Regional Variations

There are no regional variations associated with this credit.

11. Operations and Maintenance Considerations

The joint use of facilities provides opportunities for shared costs and responsibilities associated with property maintenance and operations. These should be treated within joint-use agreements as explicitly as possible.

Updates to the master plan during operations to repurpose an existing structure could present opportunity to modify or expand upon any joint-use agreements.

12. Resources

Please see USGBC's LEED Registered Project Tools (http://www.usgbc.org/projecttools) for additional resources and technical information.

	SS
NC	NA
SCHOOLS	Credit 10
CS	NA

Websites

Abbott School Construction Program, Breaking Ground: Rebuilding New Jersey's Urban Schools

http://www.edlawcenter.org/ELCPublic/elcnews_040427_BreakingGround.pdf

This document describes the importance of community involvement in urban school revitalization.

American School and University, ASU Magazine, Shared Vision

http://asumag.com/mag/university_shared_vision

This article discusses community-school partnerships, joint use, and security, with particular reference to the Independence School District in Ohio.

Joint-Use Site Planning and Facility Design Committee Parking Study: Parking on Joint-Use School and Park Sites

http://www.edmonton.ca/CityGov/CommServices/JUAParkingReport.pdf

This study addresses the challenges of providing parking for users of multiple facilities on 1 site and provides case study information to illustrate how these challenges have been resolved in certain circumstances.

National Clearinghouse for Educational Facilities, A Citizen's Guide for Planning and Design

http://www.edfacilities.org/pubs/scc_publication.pdf

This document introduces a process for engaging all educational stakeholders in school planning that more adequately addresses the needs of the whole learning community.

National Trust for Historic Preservation, Model Policies for Preserving Historic Schools

http://www.preservationnation.org/resources/public-policy/center-for-state-local-policy/additional-resources/mpp-may-june_forum_schools_policy_insert.pdf

This document responds to the space limitations that existing schools face in comparison to more recently constructed facilities. The Trust proposes joint-use and joint-planning strategies for existing schools and their communities.

Seven Oaks School Division, Rental of School Facilities

http://www.7oaks.org/file/kg.pdf

This online document provides a model for creating guidelines for the rental of school spaces by outside parties.

13. Definitions

There are no definitions associated with this credit.

Endnotes

1 U.S. Census Bureau. "2006 American Community Survey: Selected Economic Characteristics." http://factfinder.census.gov/servlet/ADPTable?_bm=y&-qr_name=ACS_2006_EST_Goo_DP3&-geo_id=01000US&-context=adp&-ds_name=&-tree_id=305&-_lang=en&-redoLog=false&-format (accessed May 2008).

2 U.S. Environmental Protection Agency. "Heat Island Effect." http://www.epa.gov/heatisland/index.htm (accessed November 2008).

3 U.S. Environmental Protection Agency. "Brownfields and Land Revitalization: About Brownfields." http://www.epa.gov/brownfields/about.htm (accessed November 2008).

4 Ibid.

5   American Public Transportation Association. "Use of Public Transportation by One in Ten Americans Would Lead to Cleaner Air and Reduce U.S. Oil Dependency by 40 Percent." APTA News Release (July 17, 2002), http://www.apta.com/media/releases/energystudy.cfm (accessed November 2008).

6   *Emission of Greenhouse Gases in the United States 2007*. Energy Information Administration, U.S. Department of Energy, December 2008: ftp://ftp.eia.doe.gov/pub/oiaf/1605/cdrom/pdf/ggrpt/057307.pdf (accessed December 2008).

7   U.S. Environmental Protection Agency. *Emission Facts: Greenhouse Gas Emissions from a Typical Passenger Vehicle*. 2005. http://www.epa.gov/otaq/climate/420f05004.htm (accessed November 2008).

8   The Lady Bird Johnson Wildflower Center at the University of Texas at Austin. "How to Articles." http://www.wildflower.org/howto/show.php?id=4&frontpage=true (accessed November 2008).

9   U.S. Environmental Protection Agency. *Reducing Stormwater Costs through Low Impact Development (LID) Strategies and Practices*. 2007. www.epa.gov/owow/nps/lid/costs07/factsheet.html (accessed May 2008).

10   Ibid.

11   U.S. Environmental Protection Agency. "Heat Island Effect." http://www.epa.gov/heatisland/index.htm (accessed November 2008).

12   U.S. Environmental Protection Agency. "Heat Island Effect: Urban Heat Island Pilot Project (UHIPP)." www.epa.gov/hiri/pilot/index.html (accessed November 2008).

13   American Concrete Pavement Association. *Albedo: A Measure of Pavement Surface Reflectance*. 2002. www.pavement.com/Downloads/RT/RT3.05.pdf.

14   U.S. Environmental Protection Agency. "Heat Island Effect: Basic Information." http://www.epa.gov/hiri/about/index.html (accessed November 2008).

15   U.S. Environmental Protection Agency. "Heat Island Effect: Cool Roofs." www.epa.gov/heatisld/strategies/coolroofs.html (accessed May 2008).

Overview

Americans' consumption of the public water supply continues to increase. The U.S. Geological Survey estimates that between 1990 and 2000, this consumption increased 12%, to 43.3 billion gallons per day.[1] The public water supply is delivered to users for domestic, commercial, industrial, and other purposes and is the primary source of water for most buildings. In 2000, these uses represented about 11% of total withdrawals and slightly less than 40% of groundwater withdrawals, constituting the third-largest category of water use in the United States, behind thermoelectric power (48% of total withdrawals) and irrigation (34% of total withdrawals). This high demand for water is straining supplies, and in some parts of the United States, water levels in underground aquifers have dropped more than 150 feet since the 1940s.[2]

Only about 14% of withdrawn water is lost to evaporation or transpiration or incorporated into products or crops; the rest is used, treated, and discharged to the nation's water bodies.[3] Discharged water contaminates rivers, lakes, and potable water with bacteria, nitrogen, toxic metals, and other contaminants.[4] The U.S. Environmental Protection Agency (EPA) estimates that 1/3 of the nation's lakes, streams, and rivers are now unsafe for swimming and fishing.[5] Even so, water bodies in the United States are 50% cleaner[6] today than in the mid-1970s. And although consumption is rising, total U.S. withdrawals from the public water supply declined by nearly 9% between 1980 and 1985 and have varied by less than 3% for each 5-year interval since then.[7]

Those achievements can be largely attributed to the Clean Water Act and reductions in industrial, irrigation, and thermoelectric power withdrawals since 1980. Although the statistics show improvement, we are still far from sustainably using water. If total commercial building water consumption for all uses in the United States fell by just 10%, we could save more than 2 trillion gallons of water each year.[8]

Using large volumes of water increases maintenance and life-cycle costs for building operations and also increases consumers' costs for additional municipal supply and treatment facilities. Conversely, buildings that use water efficiently can reduce costs through lower fees, less sewage volume, reductions in energy and chemical use, and lower capacity charges and limits.

Efficiency measures can easily reduce water use in average commercial buildings by 30% or more.[9] In a typical 100,000-square-foot office building, low-flow plumbing fixtures coupled with sensors and automatic controls will save a minimum of 1 million gallons of water per year.[10] In addition, nonpotable water can be used for landscape irrigation, toilet and urinal flushing, custodial purposes, and building systems. Depending on local water costs, utility savings can be tens of thousands of dollars per year. Real estate firm Cushman and Wakefield, for example, implemented a comprehensive water management strategy at its Adobe headquarters in San Jose, California, in 2002 and achieved a 22% reduction in water use.[11]

The LEED for New Construction, LEED for Core & Shell, and LEED for Schools Water Efficiency (WE) prerequisites and credits encourage the use of strategies and technologies that reduce the amount of potable water consumed in buildings. Many water conservation strategies are no-cost; or provide a rapid payback. Other strategies, such as biological wastewater treatment systems and graywater plumbing systems, often require more substantial investment and are cost-effective only under certain building and site conditions.

The Water Efficiency (WE) prerequisites and credits address environmental concerns relating to building water use and disposal and promote the following measures:

Monitoring Water Consumption Performance

The first step to improving water efficiency is to understand current performance. Tracking water use alongside energy use can help organizations better understand how these resources relate to each other, make integrated management decisions that increase overall efficiency, and verify savings from improvement projects in both energy and water systems. Organizations that manage water and energy performance together can take advantage of this relationship to create greener, more sustainable buildings.

Reducing Indoor Potable Water Consumption

Reducing indoor potable water consumption may require using alternative water sources for nonpotable applications and installing building components, such as water-efficient fixtures, flow restrictors on existing fixtures, electronic controls, composting toilet systems, and waterless urinals. Lowering potable water use for toilets, showerheads, faucets, and other fixtures can reduce the total amount withdrawn from natural water bodies. A commercial building in Boston replaced 126 3.5-gallons-per-flush (gpf) toilets with low-flow, 1.6-gpf toilets and reduced total water use by 15%. With an initial cost of $32,000 and an estimated annual savings of $22,800, the payback for the renovation was 1.4 years. Another Boston building installed 30 faucet aerators and reduced annual indoor water consumption by 190,000 gallons. The cost of the materials and labor totaled $300, and the change is estimated to save $1,250 per year, with a simple payback of 2 months.[12]

Reducing Water Consumption to Save Energy and Improve Environmental Well-Being

In many buildings, the most significant savings associated with water efficiency result from reduced energy costs. Water efficiency cuts costs by reducing the amount of water that must be treated, heated, cooled, and distributed—all of which requires energy. Significant energy savings come through efficient use of hot water because water heating in commercial buildings accounts for nearly 15% of total building energy use.[13] For this reason, water conservation that reduces the use of hot water also conserves energy and reduces energy-related pollution. For example, U.S. government office buildings use an estimated 244 billion to 256 billion gallons of water each year. Approximately 138.3 billion Btus of energy is required to process this water annually, 98% of which is used to heat water. By implementing water-efficiency efforts, federal buildings could conserve approximately 40% of total water consumption and reduce related energy use by approximately 81.32 billion Btus per year.[14]

Practicing water conservation measures can also help improve both environmental and human well-being. A recent government survey showed that at least 36 states are anticipating local, regional or statewide water shortages by 2013.[15] Human health and environmental welfare are affected when reservoirs and groundwater aquifers are depleted because lower water levels can concentrate both natural contaminants, such as radon and arsenic, and human pollutants, such as agricultural and chemical wastes. Increasing water efficiency helps keep contaminants at safe levels.

Water efficiency also reduces energy consumption in the water supply and wastewater infrastructure. American public water supply and treatment facilities consume about 56 billion kilowatt-hours (kWh) each year[16]—enough electricity to power more than 5 million homes for an entire year.[17] Better water efficiency in commercial buildings will reduce the amount of energy consumed by water treatment facilities.

Practicing Water-Efficient Landscaping

Landscape irrigation practices in the U.S. consume large quantities of potable water. Outdoor uses, primarily landscaping, account for 30% of the 26 billion gallons of water consumed daily.[18] Improved landscaping practices can dramatically reduce and even eliminate irrigation needs. Maintaining or reestablishing native plants on building sites fosters a self-sustaining landscape that requires minimal supplemental water and provides other environmental benefits.

Native plants require less water for irrigation and attract native wildlife, thus creating a building site integrated with its natural surroundings. In addition, native plants tend to require less fertilizer and pesticides, avoiding water quality degradation and other negative environmental impacts.

In Schools, Use Water-Efficient Processes as a Teaching Tool

Many systems used for water efficiency provide a wealth of educational opportunities, including the study of biological systems, nutrient cycles, habitats, and the impact of human systems on local watersheds and natural resources. Students can calculate the effects of water conservation strategies on their own water use, simultaneously practicing math skills and environmental stewardship. Schools that have constructed wetlands or rain collection and distribution systems can consider making these technologies highly visible components of the school design.

CREDIT	TITLE	NC	SCHOOLS	CS
WE Prerequisite 1	Water Use Reduction	Required	Required	Required
WE Credit 1	Water Efficient Landscaping	2-4 points	2-4 points	2-4 points
WE Credit 2	Innovative Wastewater Technologies	2 points	2 points	2 points
WE Credit 3	Water Use Reduction	2-4 points	2-4 points	2-4 points
WE Credit 4	Process Water Use Reduction	NA	1 point	NA

WATER USE REDUCTION

	NC	SCHOOLS	CS
Prerequisite	WE Prerequisite 1	WE Prerequisite 1	WE Prerequisite 1
Points	Required	Required	Required

Intent

To increase water efficiency within buildings to reduce the burden on municipal water supply and wastewater systems.

Requirements

NC, SCHOOLS & CS

Employ strategies that in aggregate use 20% less water than the water use baseline calculated for the building (not including irrigation).

Calculate the baseline according to the commercial and/or residential baselines outlined below.[1] Calculations are based on estimated occupant usage and must include only the following fixtures and fixture fittings (as applicable to the project scope): water closets, urinals, lavatory faucets, showers, kitchen sink faucets and pre-rinse spray valves.

Commercial Fixtures, Fittings, and Appliances	Current Baseline
Commercial toilets	1.6 gallons per flush (gpf)* Except blow-out fixtures: 3.5 (gpf)
Commercial urinals	1.0 (gpf)
Commercial lavatory (restroom) faucets	2.2 gallons per minute (gpm) at 60 pounds per square inch (psi), private applications only (hotel or motel guest rooms, hospital patient rooms) 0.5 (gpm) at 60 (psi)** all others except private applications 0.25 gallons per cycle for metering faucets
Commercial prerinse spray valves (for food service applications)	Flow rate ≤ 1.6 (gpm) (no pressure specified; no performance requirement)

Residential Fixtures, Fittings, and Appliances	Current Baseline
Residential toilets	1.6 (gpf)***
Residential lavatory (bathroom) faucets	2.2 (gpm) at 60 psi
Residential kitchen faucet	
Residential showerheads	2.5 (gpm) at 80 (psi) per shower stall****

* EPAct 1992 standard for toilets applies to both commercial and residential models.

** In addition to EPAct requirements, the American Society of Mechanical Engineers standard for public lavatory faucets is 0.5 gpm at 60 psi (ASME A112.18.1-2005). This maximum has been incorporated into the national Uniform Plumbing Code and the International Plumbing Code.

*** EPAct 1992 standard for toilets applies to both commercial and residential models.

**** Residential shower compartment (stall) in dwelling units: The total allowable flow rate from all flowing showerheads at any given time, including rain systems, waterfalls, bodysprays, bodyspas and jets, must be limited to the allowable showerhead flow rate as specified above (2.5 gpm) per shower compartment, where the floor area of the shower compartment is less than 2,500 square inches. For each increment of 2,500 square inches of floor area thereafter or part thereof, an additional showerhead with total allowable flow rate from all flowing devices equal to or less than the allowable flow rate as specified above must be allowed. Exception: Showers that emit recirculated nonpotable water originating from within the shower compartment while operating are allowed to exceed the maximum as long as the total potable water flow does not exceed the flow rate as specified above.

1 Tables adapted from information developed and summarized by the U.S. Environmental Protection Agency (EPA) Office of Water based on requirements of the Energy Policy Act (EPAct) of 1992 and subsequent rulings by the Department of Energy, requirements of the EPAct of 2005, and the plumbing code requirements as stated in the 2006 editions of the Uniform Plumbing Code or International Plumbing Code pertaining to fixture performance.

NC, SCHOOLS & CS (continued)

The following fixtures, fittings and appliances are outside the scope of the water use reduction calculation:

- Commercial Steam Cookers
- Commercial Dishwashers
- Automatic Commercial Ice Makers
- Commercial (family-sized) Clothes Washers
- Residential Clothes Washers
- Standard and Compact Residential Dishwashers

1. Benefits and Issues to Consider

Environmental Issues

Reducing potable water use in buildings for urinals, toilets, showerheads, and faucets decreases the total amount withdrawn from rivers, streams, underground aquifers, and other water bodies. These strategies protect the natural water cycle and save water resources for future generations. In addition, water use reductions, in aggregate, allow municipalities to reduce or defer the capital investment needed for water supply and wastewater treatment infrastructure.

Conserving municipally supplied potable water also reduces chemical inputs at the water treatment works, as well as reduces energy use and the associated greenhouse gas emissions from treatment and distribution. The energy use and emissions generated to supply municipal water vary greatly across the United States and depend on the utility's water sources, the distances water is transported, and the type of water treatment applied. End-use water efficiency can greatly reduce negative environmental impacts. Comparing the environmental effects of off-site treatment and supply with those of on-site treatment is a worthwhile exercise. Because water heating in commercial buildings accounts for nearly 15% of building energy use, conservation measures will also reduce end-use energy and energy-related pollution.

Economic Issues

Reductions in water consumption decrease building operating costs and bring about wider economic benefits. Reduced water consumption allows municipalities to lessen or defer the capital investment needed for water supply and wastewater treatment infrastructure, thereby leading to more stable municipal taxes and water rates.

Many cost-effective systems and fixtures currently on the market support compliance with the requirement, but the cost of water efficiency measures varies widely. For example, installing tamper-proof faucet aerators on existing fixtures is a small expense compared with a rainwater-harvesting or graywater-recycling system. High-efficiency toilets and dry fixtures, such as nonwater toilet systems, often have higher initial costs than standard models.

Newer technologies may also have higher costs and limited availability because of production constraints, and they may entail different maintenance and repair expenses, such as special cartridge components and cleaning and sealing fluids. Teams should perform a full cost-benefit and life-cycle study before installing such products.

2. Related Credits

Efforts to increase rainwater harvesting, increase graywater use, and decrease the demand on local water aquifers may support the following credits:

- SS Credit 6.1: Stormwater Design—Quantity Control
- SS Credit 6.2: Stormwater Design—Quality Control
- WE Credit 1: Water-Efficient Landscaping
- WE Credit 2: Innovative Wastewater Technologies
- WE Credit 3: Water Use Reduction
- WE Credit 4: Process Water Use Reduction (Schools specific)

Additional energy use may be needed for certain reuse strategies. Active systems also require commissioning and should be considered in relation to the following credits:

- EA Prerequisite 1: Fundamental Commissioning of Building Energy Systems

	WE
NC	Prerequisite 1
SCHOOLS	Prerequisite 1
CS	Prerequisite 1

	WE
NC	Prerequisite 1
SCHOOLS	Prerequisite 1
CS	Prerequisite 1

- EA Credit 3: Enhanced Commissioning
- EA Credit 5: Measurement and Verification

3. Summary of Referenced Standards

The water efficiency baselines meeting these referenced standards are summarized in the Requirements section of WE Prerequisite 1, Water Use Reduction.

The Energy Policy Act (EPAct) of 1992 (and as amended)
This U.S. act addresses energy and water use in commercial, institutional, and residential facilities.

The Energy Policy Act (EPAct) of 2005
This statute became U.S. law in August 2005.

International Association of Plumbing and Mechanical Officials Publication IAPMO/ American National Standards Institute UPC 1–2006, Uniform Plumbing Code 2006, Section 402.0, Water-Conserving Fixtures and Fittings
http://www.iapmo.org
UPC defines water-conserving fixtures and fittings for water closets, urinals, and metered faucets. This ANSI-accredited code safeguards life, health, property, and public welfare by regulating and controlling the design, construction, installation, materials, location, operation, and maintenance or use of plumbing systems.

International Code Council, International Plumbing Code 2006, Section 604, Design of Building Water Distribution System
http://www.iccsafe.org
IPC defines maximum flow rates and consumption for plumbing fixtures and fittings, including public and private lavatories, showerheads, sink faucets, urinals, and water closets.

4. Implementation

Effective ways to reduce water use include installing flow restrictors and/or reduced flow aerators on lavatory, sink, and shower fixtures; installing and maintaining automatic faucet sensors and metering controls; installing low-consumption flush fixtures, such as high-efficiency water closets and urinals; installing nonwater fixtures; and collecting rainwater.

In certain cases, faucets with low-flow rates are not appropriate. For example, in kitchen sinks and janitors' closets, faucets are used to fill pots and buckets. Using a low-flow rate for tasks where the volume of water is predetermined does not save water and will likely cause frustration. Consider alternative strategies to reduce water use, such as installing special-use pot fillers and high-efficiency faucets or foot pedal–operated faucets.

WaterSense, a partnership program sponsored by EPA, helps consumers identify water-efficient products and programs. WaterSense-labeled products exceed the Uniform Plumbing Code and the International Plumbing Code standards for some high-efficiency fixtures or fittings. WaterSense products and other high-efficiency plumbing fixtures, fittings, and appliances can be installed in the same way as conventional EPAct plumbing fixtures, fittings, and appliances.

Although water-efficient dishwashers, laundry machines, and other water-consuming fixtures are not counted in the calculations for this credit, they may be included in exemplary performance calculations for WE Credit 3, Water Use Reduction.

To determine the most effective strategies for a particular condition, analyze the water conservation options available to the project based on location, code compliance (plumbing and safety), and overall project function. Determine where in the building the most water is used, evaluate potential alternative water-saving technologies, and examine the impacts of alternative fixtures and technologies. Compare the design case water use with the calculated EPAct baseline to determine the optimal water savings for plumbing fixtures and fittings. Once the design case water use has been determined, compare the volumes of water required for each end use with the volumes of alternative sources of water available on-site. Perform a detailed climate analysis to determine the availability of on-site resources and choose strategies that are appropriate and cost-effective.

	WE
NC	Prerequisite 1
SCHOOLS	Prerequisite 1
CS	Prerequisite 1

Table 1. UPC and IPC Standards for Plumbing Fixture Water Use

Fixture	UPC and IPC Standards	EPA WaterSense Standards
Water closets (gallons per flush, gpf)	1.60	1.28
Urinals (gpf)	1.00	0.5[a]
Showerheads (gallons per minute, gpm*)	2.50	1.5—2.0[b]
Public lavatory faucets and aerators (gpm**)	0.5	
Private lavatory faucets and aerators (gpm**)	2.2	1.5
Public metering lavatory faucets (gallons per metering cycle)	0.25	
Kitchen and janitor sink faucets	2.20	
Metering faucets (gallons per cycle)	0.25	

*When measured at a flowing water pressure of 80 pounds per square inch (psi).
**When measured at a flowing water pressure of 60 pounds per square inch (psi).
[a] On May 22, 2008, EPA issued a notification of intent to develop a specification for high-efficiency urinals. WaterSense anticipates establishing a maximum allowable flush volume of 0.5 gpf.
[b] On August 30, 2007, EPA issued a notification of intent to develop a specification for showerheads. WaterSense anticipates establishing a single maximum flow rate between 1.5 gpm and 2.0 gmp.

Some water-saving technologies affect on-site energy performance and require commissioning; this task should be addressed by a project's measurement and verification plan. Calibration is necessary for projects using automatic sensors or flow valves. See EA Prerequisite 1, Fundamental Commissioning of Building Energy Systems, and EA Credit 5, Measurement and Verification, for more information. Space constraints or characteristics of the plumbing fixtures and fittings in existing buildings may hinder water efficiency efforts.

5. Timeline and Team

During predesign, setting water goals and strategy involves the owner, architect, and engineers. Identify local water utilities and governing authorities and research codes and applicable water laws. Learn the process for obtaining permits and approval and set water goals and strategy.

During design development, the engineering team should develop and design water reuse and treatment systems, perform preliminary LEED calculations, and confirm or reassess water goals.

In construction documents, the architect, working with the owner, should specify efficient fixtures and appliances and complete LEED calculations and documentation.

During construction, the design team and owner should confirm proper selection, installation, and operation of water fixtures, fittings, and systems.

6. Calculations

The following section describes the calculation methodology for determining water savings. The calculated water use reduction for the project is the difference between the calculated design case and a baseline case. The percentage is determined by dividing the design case use by the baseline use. The methodology differs from traditional plumbing design, in which calculations are based on fixture counts; under this prerequisite, the water use calculation is based on fixture and fitting water consumption rates and estimated use by the occupants. Occupants' estimated use is determined by calculating full-time equivalent (FTE) and transient occupants and applying appropriate fixture use rates to each.

It may be advantageous to divide the facility into fixture usage groups, calculate water use for each, and sum the values to determine whole building performance.

Fixture Usage Groups

Fixture usage groups are subsets of washroom facilities used by different types of occupants. For each group, complete the template calculator. Indicate which fixtures are involved and which occupants they serve. If all occupants within the building have access to all fixtures, or if all fixtures are standard throughout the building, enter only a single fixture usage group. That is the simpler approach, but it may be more appropriate to define two or more groups to account for different fixtures in one area of the building or special usage patterns by a population within the building For example, if washrooms on the first floor are used primarily by transient retail customers and washrooms on the second floor are used by office workers, calculate each separately.

The following scenario illustrates the application of different fixture usage groups.

The Riggs Hotel is located in an urban center. The ground floor includes a restaurant open to the public, the hotel lobby, and administrative offices. The upper floors contain guest rooms. Restaurant, back-of-house, and guestroom restroom facilities each have different fixture and fitting models. The project team establishes 3 fixture usage groups to account for the distinct populations in the building and the specific restroom facilities they use: (1) restaurant (customers and restaurant staff), (2) administrative back-of-house (hotel administrators and operations staff), and (3) guest rooms (hotel guests).

NC & CS

Calculating Occupancy

Identify the number of building occupants by occupancy type. In buildings with multiple shifts, use the number of FTEs from all shifts. Include the following

a. Full-time staff

b. Part-time staff

c. Transients (students, visitors, retail customers)

d. Residents

For projects that include residential spaces, the number of residents should be estimated based on the number and size of units in the project. Generally, assume 2 residents per 1-bedroom unit, 3 residents per 2-bedroom unit, etc. If occupancy is not known (e.g., mixed-use and core and shell projects for which the tenants of the building are unknown during design), use Appendix 1, Default Occupancy Counts, for occupancy count requirements and guidance. If actual occupancy is known, project teams must use actual counts for calculating occupancy.

Calculate the FTE number of occupants based on a standard 8-hour daily occupancy period (40 hours per week). An 8-hour occupant has an FTE value of 1.0, and part-time occupants have an FTE value based on their hours per day divided by 8. FTE calculations for each shift of the project must be used consistently for all LEED credits.

Estimate the transient building occupants, such as students, visitors, and customers. Transient occupants can be reported as either daily totals or full-time equivalents. When using daily totals for transients, match the fixture uses for each occupancy type with the values shown in Table 2 (e.g., for the daily total of students, assume 0.5 lavatory faucet uses per daily student visitor). If transients are reported as a daily full-time equivalent value, fixture uses for FTEs must be assumed regardless of the transient population's identity (e.g., for students reported as FTEs, assume 3 lavatory faucet uses per student FTE). Use a transient occupancy number that is a representative daily average over the course of a year. If the number of transient visitors per day for retail facilities is unknown, refer to Appendix 1, Table 1, for default occupancy.

Table 2 provides default fixture use values for different occupancy types. These values should be used in the calculations for this credit unless special circumstances warrant modifications. Most buildings with students, visitors, and retail customers will also have FTE occupants. Half of all students and visitors are assumed to use a flush fixture and a lavatory faucet in the building and are not expected to use a shower or kitchen sink. A fifth of retail customers are assumed to use a flush and a flow fixture in the building and no shower or kitchen sink. The default for residential occupants is 5 uses per day of water closet and lavatory faucet, 1 shower, and 4 kitchen sink uses.

For consistency across LEED projects, the calculations require the use of a balanced, 1-to-1 gender ratio unless project conditions warrant an alternative. Provide a narrative description to explain any special circumstances.

Table 2. Default Fixture Uses, by Occupancy Type

Fixture Type	FTE	Student/Visitor	Retail Customer	Resident
	Uses/Day			
Water Closet				
— Female	3	0.5	0.2	5
— Male	1	0.1	0.1	5
Urinal				
— Female	0	0	0	n/a
— Male	2	0.4	0.1	n/a
Lavatory Faucet — duration 15 sec; 12 sec with autocontrol — residential, duration 60 sec	3	0.5	0.2	5
Shower — duration 300 sec — residential, duration 480 sec	0.1	0	0	1
Kitchen Sink, — duration 15 sec — residential, duration 60 sec	1 n/a	0 n/a	0 n/a	n/a 4

SCHOOLS

Calculating Occupancy

Identify the total number of building occupants for each occupancy type. In buildings with multiple shifts, use the number of full-time equivalents (FTEs) from all shifts.

  a. Full-time staff

  b. Part-time staff

  c. Students

  d. Transients (volunteers, visitors, etc.)

Calculate the FTE number of occupants based on a standard 8-hour occupancy period. An 8-hour occupant has an FTE value of 1.0, and part-time occupants have an FTE value based on their hours per day divided by 8. FTE calculations for each shift of the project must be used consistently for all LEED credits.

Estimate the transient building occupants, such as volunteers, visitors, and customers. Transient occupants can be reported as either daily totals or full-time equivalents. When using daily totals for transients, match the fixture uses for each occupancy type with the values shown in Table 3 (e.g., for the daily total of volunteers counted as transients, assume 0.5 lavatory faucet uses per transient volunteer). If transients are reported as a daily full-time equivalent value, fixture uses for FTEs must be assumed regardless of the transient population's identity (e.g., for volunteers reported as FTEs, assume 3 lavatory faucet uses per volunteer FTE). Use a transient occupancy number that is a representative daily average over the course of a year.

Transients include building visitors and other part-time or occasional building occupants. In deciding whether to count individuals as transients or FTE occupants, consider their plumbing fixture use patterns. For example, a volunteer who serves 4 hours each day in an elementary school will likely have the same plumbing usage patterns as FTE staff. This volunteer could therefore be considered to have a staff FTE value of 0.5. On the other hand, an individual who attends a high school basketball game may be expected to use the water closets and lavatory faucets in the school building only 50% of the time, and therefore should be reported as a visitor. Report transients as average daily totals.

Table 3. Default Fixture Uses, by Occupancy Type

Fixture Type	FTE	Student	Transient
Water Closet			
— Female	3	3	0.5
— Male	1	1	0.1
Urinal			
— Female	0	0	0
— Male	2	2	0.4
Lavatory faucet , duration 15 sec; 12 sec with autocontrol	3	3	0.5
Shower	0.1	0	0
Kitchen sink, nonresidential, duration 15 sec	1	0	0

Calculating Annual Occupancy for Schools with Multiple Sessions

If the school building is used for more than 1 session annually, calculate the session percentage for each session, based on the number of days in the session divided by the total number of days during which the school building operates annually, using Equation 1.

Equation 1. Session Percentage

$$\text{Session Percentage} = \frac{\text{Number of Days in Session}}{\text{Annual Days of Operation}}$$

Then calculate the annual occupants of each gender by multiplying the number of occupants in each session by the session percentage (from Equation 1) and adding the results of all sessions together, using Equation 2.

Equation 2. Annual Occupants by Gender

$$\left(\begin{array}{c} \text{Session A FTE} \\ \text{by Gender} \end{array} \times \begin{array}{c} \text{Session A} \\ \text{Percentage} \end{array} \right) + \left(\begin{array}{c} \text{Session B FTE} \\ \text{by Gender} \end{array} \times \begin{array}{c} \text{Session B} \\ \text{Percentage} \end{array} \right) = \begin{array}{c} \text{Annual} \\ \text{Occupants} \\ \text{by Gender} \end{array}$$

EXAMPLE 1

A school operates during a normal school year (175 days) in a co-ed session with 500 FTEs (50% male, 50% female). The school building is also used during the summer session (50 days) as a boys' soccer camp, with 200 male FTEs. Annual occupants by gender are calculated according to Equation 2. The project has an annual occupancy of 193 females and 259 males (rounded up). Table 4 provides default fixture use values for different occupancy types. Use these values in the calculations for this credit unless special circumstances warrant.

Plumbing Fixture Usage Patterns per Session

If plumbing fixture usage patterns change significantly between sessions, calculate the average daily uses per person for each fixture, using Equation 3.

EXAMPLE 2

During the normal school year (175 days), showers are used once every other day per person (0.5 times per day). During the summer session (50 days), which includes a soccer camp, showers are used more frequently—once per day per person . The average daily per person use of showers is calculated in Equation 3.

Equation 3

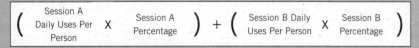

$$\left(\begin{array}{c} \text{Session A} \\ \text{Daily Uses Per} \\ \text{Person} \end{array} \times \begin{array}{c} \text{Session A} \\ \text{Percentage} \end{array} \right) + \left(\begin{array}{c} \text{Session B Daily} \\ \text{Uses Per Person} \end{array} \times \begin{array}{c} \text{Session B} \\ \text{Percentage} \end{array} \right)$$

For consistency across LEED projects, the calculations require the use of a balanced, 1-to-1 gender ratio unless specific project conditions warrant an alternative. Provide a narrative description to explain any special circumstances.

Design Case Water Consumption

The design case annual water use is determined by totaling the annual volume of each fixture type and subtracting any nonpotable water supply. The design case must use the rated flow rates and flush volumes for installed plumbing fixtures and fittings. Obtain water consumption data from the manufacturer's product literature.

Teams may add fixtures not listed in Table 4 that are regulated by the referenced standards.

Table 4. Sample Plumbing Fixtures and Fittings and Water Consumption

Flush Fixture	Flow Rate (gpf)	Flow Fixture	Flow Rate
Conventional water closet	1.6	Conventional private lavatory	2.2 gpm
High-efficiency toilet (HET), single-flush gravity	1.28	Conventional public lavatory	0.5 gpm or ≤ 0.25 gpc
HET, single-flush pressure assist	1.0	Conventional kitchen sink	2.2 gpm
HET, dual flush (full-flush)	1.6	Low-flow kitchen sink	1.8 gpm
HET, dual flush (low-flush)	1.1	Conventional shower	2.5 gpm
HET, foam flush	0.05	Low-flow shower	1.8 gpm
Nonwater toilet	0.0		
Conventional urinal	1.0		
High-efficiency urinal (HEU)	0.5		
Nonwater urinal	0.0		

Facilities in residences and apartments, private bathrooms in hotels and hospitals, and restrooms in commercial establishments where the fixtures are intended for the use of a family or an individual are considered private or private-use facilities. All other facilities are considered public or public use. If the classification for public or private use is unclear, default to public-use flow rates in performing the calculations associated with this credit.

Baseline Case Water Consumption

The baseline case annual water use is determined by setting the fixture and fitting water consumption to baseline rates listed in the requirements (as opposed to actual installed values in the design case).

Eligible Fixtures

This prerequisite is limited to savings generated by water using fixtures as shown in Table 1.

7. Documentation Guidance

As a first step in preparing to complete the LEED-Online documentation requirements, work through the following measures. Refer to LEED-Online for the complete descriptions of all required documentation.

- Determine the type and number of occupants.

- Retain manufacturers' data showing the water consumption rates, manufacturer, and model of each fixture and fitting.

- List plumbing fixtures by usage group, if applicable.

- Define any usage groups.

8. Examples

EXAMPLE 1

The results of various water-saving strategies for a 1.2-million-square-foot office building are shown in Figure 1. Savings are based on a water rate of $1.33 per 1,000 gallons.

Figure 1. Water Savings Assessment, by Strategy

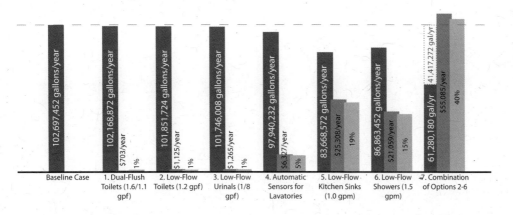

	WE
NC	Prerequisite 1
SCHOOLS	Prerequisite 1
CS	Prerequisite 1

Legend:
- Annual Water Consumption
- Annual Water Utility Savings
- Percent Savings over Baseline Case
- Annual Water Saved

9. Exemplary Performance

This prerequisite is not eligible for exemplary performance under the Innovation in Design section.

10. Regional Variations

Local building and health codes differ in their treatment of alternative plumbing fixtures, such as nonwater urinals, dual-flush water closets, and nonwater toilets. Confirm the legality of nontraditional approaches with code officials before selecting plumbing fixtures.

11. Operations and Maintenance Considerations

Consider installing submetering for water delivered to fixture and fittings to help operators manage water consumption and identify problems within the system. Integrating electronic data logging will facilitate consumption trend analysis.

Some water conservation technologies may require special cleaning or maintenance procedures. For example, nonwater urinals generally need to be cleaned according to manufacturer's specifications and their chemical traps appropriately maintained. Project teams should provide facility operators with appropriate maintenance information, manufacturers' contact information, and product specifications to facilitate proper operation.

A preventive maintenance program that includes plumbing fixture and fitting inspection and testing ensures that flow valves do not leak and that any sensors are calibrated correctly so that the fixtures flush and/or flow the appropriate amounts at the proper time.

For more information about water-saving opportunities through operations and maintenance, see the LEED Reference Guide for Green Building Operations & Maintenance, 2009 Edition

12. Resources

Websites

Please see USGBC's LEED Registered Project Tools (http://www.usgbc.org/projecttools) for additional resources and technical information.

	WE
NC	Prerequisite 1
SCHOOLS	Prerequisite 1
CS	Prerequisite 1

American Rainwater Catchment Systems Association

http://www.arcsa.org

ARCSA was founded to promote rainwater catchment systems in the United States. The ARCSA website provides regional resources, suppliers, and membership information, and publications such as the Texas Guide to Rainwater Harvesting.

American Water Works Association, Water Wiser: The Water Efficiency Clearinghouse

http://www.awwa.org/waterwiser

This web clearinghouse provides articles, reference materials, and papers on all forms of water efficiency.

Environmental Building News, Water: Doing More with Less

http://www.buildinggreen.com/auth/article.cfm/2008/2/3/Water-Doing-More-With-Less

This website features an article on building water efficiency.

Fine Homebuilding, Choosing a Toilet

http://www.taunton.com/finehomebuilding/pages/h00042.asp

This article includes several varieties of water-efficient toilets.

National Oceanic and Atmospheric Administration, National Climatic Data Center

http://www.ncdc.noaa.gov/cgi-bin/good-bye.pl?src=http://www.stateclimate.org The NCDC website is useful for researching local climate information such as data for rainwater harvesting calculations, and it also includes links to state climate offices.

North Carolina Division of Pollution Prevention and Environmental Assistance, Water Efficiency Manual for Commercial, Industrial, and Institutional Facilities

http://www.p2pays.org/ref/01/00692.pdf

This straightforward manual on water efficiency draws from a number of different North Carolina governmental departments.

Rocky Mountain Institute, Water

http://www.rmi.org/sitepages/pid128.php

This portion of RMI's website is devoted to water conservation and efficiency. The site contains information on watershed management and commercial, industrial, and institutional water use and articles on policy and implementation.

Terry Love's Consumer Toilet Reports

http://www.terrylove.com/crtoilet.htm

This website offers a plumber's perspective on many of the major toilets used in commercial and residential applications.

U.S. Department of the Interior, Water Measurement Manual: A Water Resources Technical Publication

http://www.usbr.gov/pmts/hydraulics_lab/pubs/wmm

This publication is a guide on effective water measurement practices.

U.S. EPA, How to Conserve Water and Use It Effectively

http://www.epa.gov/OWOW/nps/chap3.html

This document provides guidance for commercial, industrial, and residential water users on saving water and reducing sewage volumes.

U.S. EPA, Water Use Efficiency Program

http://www.epa.gov/owm/water-efficiency

This website provides an overview of EPA's Water Use Efficiency Program and information about using water more efficiently.

U.S. EPA, WaterSense

http://www.epa.gov/watersense

The WaterSense Program helps U.S. consumers save water and protect the environment. Look for the WaterSense label to help choose high-quality, water-efficient products. A variety of products are available, and they do not require a change in lifestyle.

Water Closet Performance Testing

http://www.ebmud.com/conserving_&_recycling/toilet_test_report/default.htm

This site provides 2 reports on independent test results for a variety of toilets' flush performance and reliability.

Print Media

Constructed Wetlands for Wastewater Treatment and Wildlife Habitat: 17 Case Studies, EPA 832/B-93-005 (U.S. EPA, 1993).

On-Site Wastewater Treatment Systems Manual (U.S. EPA, 2002). http://www.epa.gov/nrmrl/pubs/625r00008/html/625R00008.htm.

This document provides a focused, performance-based approach to on-site wastewater treatment and system management as well as valuable information on a variety of on-site sewage treatment options.

Water, Sanitary and Waste Services for Buildings, fourth edition, by A. Wise and J. Swaffield (Longman Scientific & Technical, 1995).

13. Definitions

An **aquifer** is an underground water-bearing rock formation or group of formations that supply groundwater, wells, or springs.

Automatic fixture sensors are motion detectors that automatically turn on and turn off lavatories, sinks, water closets, and urinals. Sensors can be hard wired or battery operated.

Blackwater definitions vary, but wastewater from toilets and urinals is always considered blackwater. Wastewater from kitchen sinks (perhaps differentiated by the use of a garbage disposal), showers, or bathtubs is considered blackwater under some state or local codes.

Metering controls limit the flow time of water. They are generally manual-on and automatic-off devices, most commonly installed on lavatory faucets and showers.

Nonpotable water. See **potable water.**

Nonwater (or composting) toilet systems are dry plumbing fixtures and fittings that contain and treat human waste via microbiological processes.

A **nonwater (or dry) urinal,** replaces a water flush with a trap containing a layer of buoyant liquid that floats above the urine, blocking sewer gas and odors.

On-site wastewater treatment is the transport, storage, treatment, and disposal of wastewater generated on the project site.

Potable water meets or exceeds EPA's drinking water quality standards and is approved for human consumption by the state or local authorities having jurisdiction; it may be supplied from wells or municipal water systems.

Process water is used for industrial processes and building systems such as cooling towers, boilers, and chillers. The term can also refer to water used in operational processes, such as dishwashing, clothes washing, and ice making.

	WE
NC	Prerequisite 1
SCHOOLS	Prerequisite 1
CS	Prerequisite 1

WATER EFFICIENT LANDSCAPING

	NC	SCHOOLS	CS
Credit	WE Credit 1	WE Credit 1	WE Credit 1
Points	2-4 points	2-4 points	2-4 points

Intent

To limit or eliminate the use of potable water or other natural surface or subsurface water resources available on or near the project site for landscape irrigation.

Requirements

NC, SCHOOLS & CS

OPTION 1. Reduce by 50% (2 points)

Reduce potable water consumption for irrigation by 50% from a calculated midsummer baseline case.

Reductions must be attributed to any combination of the following items:

- Plant species, density and microclimate factor
- Irrigation efficiency
- Use of captured rainwater
- Use of recycled wastewater
- Use of water treated and conveyed by a public agency specifically for nonpotable uses

Groundwater seepage that is pumped away from the immediate vicinity of building slabs and foundations may be used for landscape irrigation to meet the intent of this credit. However, the project team must demonstrate that doing so does not affect site stormwater management systems.

OR

OPTION 2. No Potable Water Use or Irrigation[1] (4 points)

Meet the requirements for Option 1.

AND

PATH 1

Use only captured rainwater, recycled wastewater, recycled graywater or water treated and conveyed by a public agency specifically for nonpotable uses for irrigation.

OR

PATH 2

Install landscaping that does not require permanent irrigation systems. Temporary irrigation systems used for plant establishment are allowed only if removed within 1 year of installation.

---

1   If the percent reduction of potable water is 100% AND the percent reduction of total water is equal to or greater than 50%, both Option 1 & Option 2 are earned.

1. Benefits and Issues to Consider

Environmental Issues

Landscape irrigation practices in the United States consume large quantities of potable water. Outdoor uses, primarily landscaping, account for 30% of the 26 billion gallons of water consumed daily in the United States.[20] Improved landscaping practices can dramatically reduce and even eliminate irrigation needs. Maintaining or reestablishing native or adapted plants on building sites fosters a self-sustaining landscape that requires minimal supplemental water and attracts native wildlife, creating a building site integrated with its natural surroundings. In addition, native or adapted plants tend to require less fertilizer and pesticides, minimizing water quality degradation and other negative environmental impacts.

Water-efficient landscaping helps conserve local and regional potable water resources. Maintaining natural aquifer conditions is important for providing reliable water sources for future generations. Consideration of water issues during planning can encourage development where resources can support it and prevent development that would exceed the resource capacity.

SCHOOLS For school projects, the use of native plantings can provide educational opportunities for students, allowing them to learn about the site's natural history. Students can observe plants' characteristics and seasonal changes to better understand the relationship between living organisms and the environment.

Economic Issues

Landscaping designed for the local climate and the site's microclimate is the most effective strategy to avoid escalating water costs for irrigation. The cost can be reduced or eliminated through thoughtful planning and careful plant selection and layout. Native or adapted plants further reduce operating costs because they require less fertilizer and maintenance than turf grass.

Although the additional design cost for a drip irrigation system may make it more expensive than a conventional system, a drip system usually costs less to install and has lower water use and maintenance requirements, generally resulting in a short payback period. Many municipalities offer rebates or incentives for water-efficient irrigation systems, dedicated water meters, and rain or moisture sensors.

Using graywater for irrigation also reduces the amount of wastewater delivered to water treatment facilities, which can provide cost savings while reducing both demand on the municipal infrastructure and the negative environmental impacts associated with large-scale treatment facilities. Irrigation system efficiency varies widely, and high-efficiency systems can also reduce potable water consumption. For example, high-efficiency drip irrigation systems can be 95% efficient, compared with 60% to 70% for sprinkler or spray irrigation systems.[21]

2. Related Credits

The use of native or adapted vegetation on the project site can assist project teams with earning the following credits:

- SS Credit 5.1: Site Development—Protect or Restore Habitat

- SS Credit 5.2: Maximize Open Space

- SS Credit 7.2: Heat Island Effect—Roof

In addition to reducing potable water consumption, rainwater capture systems can be used to manage stormwater runoff and can contribute to achieving the following credits:

	WE
NC	Credit 1
SCHOOLS	Credit 1
CS	Credit 1

- SS Credit 6.1: Stormwater Design—Quantity Control

- SS Credit 6.2: Stormwater Design—Quality Control

Landscape plantings can mitigate climate conditions and reduce building energy consumption by shading hardscape and south-facing windows and by aiding in passive solar design. These strategies can contribute to achieving the following:

- SS Credit 7.1: Heat Island Effect—Nonroof

- EA Prerequisite 2: Minimum Energy Performance

- EA Credit 1: Optimize Energy Performance

SCHOOLS For School projects, creating a diverse landscape that attracts wildlife can provide opportunities for students to learn about biodiversity in local ecosystems, helping to contribute to this credit:

- Schools Specific ID Credit 3: The School as a Teaching Tool

3. Summary of Referenced Standards
There are no standards referenced for this credit.

4. Implementation
Water-efficient landscaping varies with the site and region. Design landscaping with climate-tolerant plants that can survive on natural rainfall. Contour the land to direct rainwater runoff through the site and give vegetation an additional water supply. Minimize the area covered with conventional turf grass, and use techniques such as mulching and composting—practices that conserve water and help foster optimal soil conditions.

Recommended design principles include the following:

STEP 1. Planning and design
- Develop a site map showing existing or planned structures, topography, orientation, sun and wind exposure, use of space, and existing vegetation.

- Perform shadow profiles of landscape areas for each season based on middle-of-the-day conditions and illustrate the plant selections within the profiles.

- Reduce the heat island effect by providing adequate shade from trees and buildings; plant trees to increase shade canopy as necessary.

- Plan water use zones:

  - High—regular watering.

  - Moderate—occasional watering.

  - Low—natural rainfall.

STEP 2. Practical turf areas
- Plant turf grasses only for functional benefits such as recreational areas, pedestrian use, or specifically for soil conservation.

	WE
NC	Credit 1
SCHOOLS	Credit 1
CS	Credit 1

STEP 3. Soil analysis and preparation

- Analyze soil in each zone.

- Amend soil accordingly.

STEP 4. Appropriate use of plant materials

- Choose plants that will easily adapt to the site.

  - Consider the mature size and form when choosing plant material for the location and intended purpose.

  - Consider growth rate.

  - Do not plant monocultures (single species) or an excessive number of species.

  - Diversify species to discourage disease or insect infestations.

  - Select plant species that need little or no fertilization and, when necessary, specify organic and nonpetrochemical fertilizers.

  - Consider the role of plant selection in planning for integrated pest management.

STEP 5. Effective and efficient watering practices

- Regularly check irrigation systems for efficient and effective operation; verify watering schedules and duration on a monthly basis.

- Use drip, micromist, and subsurface irrigation systems where applicable; use smart irrigation controllers throughout. Provide computer-controlled monitoring and schedule modifications from a central location.

- Do not irrigate plants or turf between November and April.

- Do not irrigate shrubs between September and June.

- To prevent mold growth, make sure irrigation systems do not allow buildings to become saturated or water to be introduced into building air intakes. Systems should be designed to keep water away from buildings.

STEP 6. Mulch for trees, shrubs, and flower beds

- Keep landscape areas mulched to conserve moisture and prevent evaporative water loss from the soil surface to reduce the need for supplemental irrigation during dry periods.

Owners' preferences, use of the grounds, and maintenance expertise can also affect plant selection. However, the intent of this credit is to maximize the use of on-site natural resources to limit or eliminate the use of potable water for irrigation. This goal can be achieved by selecting native or adapted plants that require little or no irrigation, or by irrigating with high-efficiency equipment, captured rainwater, recycled graywater, or treated wastewater. Consider a combination of these strategies: First reduce potable water demand and then meet the irrigation demand in the most sustainable manner.

Planting native or adapted plants is an excellent approach because water conservation is built in and is not reliant on high-tech equipment and controls. In some climates, it is possible to eliminate or significantly cut the need for permanent irrigation with strategies like xeriscaping, which employs native plants.

For buildings without vegetation on the grounds, teams can earn points by reducing the use of potable water for watering any roof and courtyard garden space or outdoor planters, provided the planters and garden space cover at least 5% of the building site area (including building footprint, hardscape area, parking footprint, etc.). If the planters and garden space cover less than 5% of the building site area, the project is ineligible for this credit.

Hose bibs are not considered permanent irrigation and can be used for temporary irrigation during periods of drought. Additionally, temporary irrigation during the first year of building occupancy can help establish healthy plants that will need less water in the future. Project teams pursuing Option 2, No Potable Water Use or Irrigation, by eliminating permanent irrigation may install temporary irrigation for a period of 1 year depending on the needs of the site and the selected vegetation.

Reducing landscaped areas that require irrigation and installing alternative hardscaping materials that do not require irrigation are good ways to reduce landscape irrigation demands but should not be factored into the calculations for this credit.

Technologies

Using irrigation technology, rainwater capture, and advanced on-site wastewater treatment are all excellent ways of achieving this credit; they allow for a broader plant species palette while still conserving potable water supplies. High-efficiency irrigation strategies include the use of microirrigation systems, moisture sensors, rain shut-offs, and weather-based evapotranspiration controllers. Drip irrigation systems apply water slowly and directly to the roots of plants, using 30% to 50% less water than sprinklers.[22]

Efficient irrigation rotary heads can provide a greater radius of coverage and dispense water at a lower precipitation rate than more conventional systems. Properly pressurized spray heads and nozzles maximize efficiency by making sure that irrigation water droplets are properly sized and are not affected by wind and sun. For example, when pressure is too high, water droplets become finer and the spray patterns become distorted by wind, thereby decreasing efficiency. Upfront investments in pressure-regulating features like high-efficiency nozzles can save up to 30% on water use.[23]

Smart irrigation controls include soil moisture and evapotranspiration sensors that automatically adjust watering times to local conditions. Whereas conventional controllers turn irrigation on at the same time everyday for a set duration, these sensors conserve water by adjusting irrigation times based on daily weather. Rain sensors enhance water savings further by suspending the daily irrigation cycle based on precipitation levels.

Rainwater collection systems (e.g., cisterns, underground tanks, ponds) can significantly reduce or completely eliminate the amount of potable water used for irrigation. Rainwater can be collected from roofs, plazas, and paved areas and then filtered by a combination of graded screens and paper filters to prepare it for use in irrigation. Metal, clay, or concrete-based roofing materials are ideal for rainwater harvest; asphalt or lead-containing materials will contaminate the water. Rainwater with high mineral content or acidity may damage systems or plants, but pollutants can be filtered out by soil or mechanical systems before being applied to plants. Check local rainfall quantity and quality, since collection systems may be inappropriate in areas with rainfall of low quantity or poor quality. A project may achieve Option 2, No Potable Water Use or Irrigation, by demonstrating that the project's rainwater system's capacity meets all of the required thresholds on an average monthly and annual basis, ensuring maximum potable water savings.

Using groundwater that must be pumped away from the building's basement or foundation to irrigate the landscape is an innovative way to achieve credit this credit. However, installing a well specifically to collect groundwater for irrigation does not meet the intent of the credit to reduce potable water use for irrigation. Document the existence of nuisance groundwater and demonstrate the beneficial use of this resource. Additionally, Option 2, No Potable Water Use or Irrigation, can be met when landscape irrigation is provided by raw water that would otherwise be treated specifically for nonpotable uses.

Wastewater recovery can be accomplished either on-site or at the municipal level. On-site systems include graywater and wastewater treatment. In addition, many municipalities treat sewage to tertiary standards in central treatment plants, then redistribute that water regionally for irrigation use. Some water treatment facilities supply reclaimed water to off-site customers specifically for nonpotable uses such as landscape irrigation. If a public health situation warrants (e.g., irrigating near a swimming pool), as dictated by code, using potable water for irrigation is permissible and does not necessarily preclude achieving this credit.

SCHOOLS For school projects, including playgrounds and athletic fields in this credit is optional. However, if such areas are included, they must be included in all other applicable credit calculations.

5. Timeline and Team

Early in the design process, the landscape designer should determine the most appropriate use of native vegetation and the most efficient technology for the project site. Include the building owner, architect, civil engineer, and mechanical engineer in evaluating the feasibility of using nonpotable water for irrigation. Involve maintenance staff in the design meetings to communicate operations and maintenance needs and ensure that the design meets ongoing water-efficiency goals. After the initial landscape design team meeting, the landscape architect or architect should perform the baseline and design irrigation calculations to assess compliance with this credit.

6. Calculations

To calculate the percentage reduction in potable or natural water use for this credit, establish a baseline water use rate for the project and then calculate the as-designed water-use rate according to the steps listed below.

Standard Assumptions and Variables

- All calculations are based on irrigation during July.

- The landscape coefficient (K_L) indicates the volume of water lost via evapotranspiration and varies with the plant species, microclimate, and planting density. The formula for determining the landscape coefficient is given in Equation 3.

- The species factor (k_s) accounts for variation in water needs by different plant species, divided into 3 categories (high, average, and low water need). To determine the appropriate category for a plant species, use plant manuals and professional experience. This factor is somewhat subjective; however, landscape professionals know the general water needs of plant species. Landscapes can be maintained in acceptable condition at about 50% of the reference evapotranspiration (ET_o) value, and thus the average value of k_s is 0.5. If a species does not require irrigation once it is established, then the effective $k_s = 0$ and the resulting $K_L = 0$.

- The density factor (k_d) accounts for the number of plants and the total leaf area of a landscape. Sparsely planted areas will have less evapotranspiration than densely planted areas. An average k_d is applied to areas where shading from trees is 60% to 100%. This is equivalent to shrubs and groundcovers that shade 90% to 100% of the landscape area. Low k_d values are found where shading from trees is less than 60%, or where shrub and groundcover shading is less than 90%. For instance, a 25% ground shading from trees results in a k_d value of 0.5. In mixed plantings, where the tree canopy shades understory shrubs and groundcovers, evapotranspiration increases. This represents the highest level of landscape density; the k_d value is 1.0 to 1.3.

- The microclimate factor (k_{mc}) accounts for environmental conditions specific to the landscape, including temperature, wind and humidity. For instance, parking lots increase wind and temperature effects on adjacent landscapes. The average k_{mc} is 1.0; this refers to conditions where evapotranspiration is unaffected by buildings, pavements, reflective surfaces and slopes. High-k_{mc} conditions occur where evaporative potential is increased by heat-absorbing and reflective surfaces or exposure to high winds; examples include parking lots, west sides of buildings, west- and south-facing slopes, medians, and areas experiencing wind tunnel effects. Low-k_{mc} landscapes include shaded areas and areas protected from wind, such as north sides of buildings, courtyards, areas under wide building overhangs, and north-facing slopes.

STEP 1. Create the design case.

Determine the landscape area for the project. This number must represent the as-designed landscape area and must use the same project boundary used in all other LEED credits. Sort the total landscape area into the major vegetation types (trees, shrubs, groundcover, mixed, and turfgrass), listing the area for each.

Determine the following characteristics for each landscape area: species factor (k_s), density factor (k_d), and microclimate factor (k_{mc}). Recommended values for each are provided in Table 1. Select the low, average, or high value for each parameter as appropriate for the site. Project teams must be prepared to justify any variance from the recommended values..

Table 1. Landscape Factors

Vegetation type	Species Factor (k_s)			Density Factor (k_d)			Microclimate Factor (k_{mc})		
	Low	Average	High	Low	Average	High	Low	Average	High
Trees	0.2	0.5	0.9	0.5	1.0	1.3	0.5	1.0	1.4
Shrubs	0.2	0.5	0.7	0.5	1.0	1.1	0.5	1.0	1.3
Groundcover	0.2	0.5	0.7	0.5	1.0	1.1	0.5	1.0	1.2
Mixed trees, shrubs, groundcover	0.2	0.5	0.9	0.6	1.1	1.3	0.5	1.0	1.4
Turf grass	0.6	0.7	0.8	0.6	1.0	1.0	0.8	1.0	1.2

Calculate the landscape coefficient (K_L) by multiplying the 3 area characteristics, as shown in Equation 1.

Equation 1

$$K_L = k_s \times k_d \times k_{mc}$$

Determine the reference evapotranspiration rate (ET_0) for the region. This rate is a measurement of the total amount of water needed to grow a reference plant (such as grass or alfalfa), expressed in millimeters or inches. The values for ET_0 in various regions throughout the United States can be found in regional agricultural data (see Resources). The ET_0 for July is used in the LEED calculation because this is typically the month with the greatest evapotranspiration effects and, therefore, the greatest irrigation demands.

Calculate the project-specific evapotranspiration rate (ET_L) for each landscape area by multiplying the ET_0 by the K_L, as shown in Equation 2.

	WE
NC	Credit 1
SCHOOLS	Credit 1
CS	Credit 1

Equation 2

$$ET_L \text{ (in)} = ET_0 \times K_L$$

Determine the irrigation efficiency (IE) by listing the type of irrigation used for each landscape area and the corresponding efficiency. Table 2 lists irrigation efficiencies for different irrigation systems.

Table 2. Irrigation Types and Efficiencies

Type	Efficiency
Sprinkler	0.625
Drip	0.90

Determine, if applicable, the controller efficiency (CE), the percentage reduction in water use from any weather-based controllers or moisture sensor-based systems. This number must be supported by either manufacturer's documentation or detailed calculations by the landscape designer.

Determine, if applicable, the volume of reuse water (harvested rainwater, recycled graywater or treated wastewater) available in July. Reuse water volumes may depend on rainfall volume and frequency, building-generated graywater and wastewater, and on-site storage capacity. On-site reuse systems must be modeled to predict volumes generated on a monthly basis as well as optimal storage capacity. For harvested rainwater calculations, project teams may use either the collected rainwater total for July based on historical average precipitation, or historical data for each month to model collection and reuse throughout the year. The latter method allows the project team to determine what volume of water can be expected in the storage cistern at the beginning of July and add it to the expected rainwater volume collected during the month; it also allows the team to determine the optimal size of the rainwater cistern.

To calculate total water applied (TWA) and total potable water applied (TPWA) for each landscape area and the installed case, use Equations 3 and 4.

Equation 3

$$\text{Design Case TWA (gal)} = \left(\text{Area (sf)} \times \frac{ET_L \text{ (in)}}{IE} \right) \times CE \times 0.6233 \text{ (gal/sf/in)}$$

Equation 4

$$\text{Design Case TPWA (gal)} = \text{TWA (gal)} - \text{Reuse Water (gal)}$$

STEP 2. Create the baseline case.

In the baseline case, the k_s, k_d, and IE are set to average values representative of conventional equipment and design practices. The same k_{MC} and the reference ET_0 are used in both the design and the baseline cases. If the project substitutes low-water-using plants (such as shrubs) for high-water-using types (such as turf grass), the landscape areas can be reallocated in the baseline case, but the total landscape area must remain the same. The baseline cannot be 100% turf grass if typical landscaping practices in the region include trees, shrubs, and planting beds.

Calculate the TWA for the baseline case using Equation 5.

Equation 5

| Baseline Case TWA (gal) | = | Area (sf) | X | $\dfrac{ET_L \text{ (in)}}{IE}$ | X | 0.6233 (gal/sf/in) |

STEP 3

Calculate the percentage reduction in total irrigation water use (potable and reuse)

AND

the percentage reduction of potable water use for irrigation.

Calculate the percentage reduction of potable water use according to Equation 6.

Equation 6

$$\text{Percentage Reduction of Potable Water (\%)} = \left(1 - \frac{\text{Design (TPWA)}}{\text{Baseline (TWA)}} \right) \times 100$$

If the percentage reduction of potable water use for irrigation achieved is 50% or more, the requirements for Option 1 are met. If the percentage reduction of potable water use for irrigation achieved is 100% AND the percentage reduction of total water use for irrigation is 50% or more, Option 2 is achieved. If the percentage reduction of potable water use for irrigation is 100%, also calculate the percentage reduction of total water (potable plus reuse) according to Equation 7.

Equation 7

$$\text{Percentage Reduction of Total Water (\%)} = 1 - \frac{\text{Design (TWA)}}{\text{Baseline (TWA)}} \times 100$$

7. Documentation Guidance

As a first step in preparing to complete the LEED-Online documentation requirements, work through the following measures. Refer to LEED-Online for the complete descriptions of all required documentation.

- Perform calculations of the baseline and design case to show the percentage reduction in water demand, and report what portion of irrigation will come from each nonpotable source (if any).

- Prepare a landscape plan showing a planting schedule and irrigation system.

8. Examples

Figure 1. Rainwater Harvesting System

Water is collected from the building roof into a cistern, which feeds a drip irrigation system. Use of native plants reduces overall irrigation volumes, making it more likely that collected rainwater volumes will suffice for irrigation needs.

EXAMPLE 1

An office building in Austin, Texas, has a total site area of 6,000 square feet. The site comprises 3 landscape types: shrubs, mixed vegetation, and turf grass. All are irrigated with a combination of potable water and graywater harvested from the building. The reference ET0 for Austin in July, obtained from the local agricultural service, is 8.12. The high-efficiency irrigation case uses drip irrigation with an efficiency of 90% and consumes an estimated 4,200 gallons of graywater during July. Table 3 shows the calculations to determine total potable water use for the design case.

The baseline case uses the same reference ET0 and total site area. However, it uses sprinklers for irrigation (IE = 0.625), does not take advantage of graywater harvesting, and irrigates only shrubs and turf grass. Calculations to determine total water use for the baseline case are presented in Table 4.

The design case has an irrigation water demand of 14,632 gallons. Graywater reuse provides 4,200 gallons toward the demand, and this volume is treated as a credit in the water calculation. Thus, the total potable water use in July is 10,432 gallons. The baseline case has an irrigation demand of 38,967 gallons and uses no graywater. The project thus achieves a potable water savings of 73% and earns 2 points under WE Credit 1.

Table 3. Design Case (July)

Landscape Type	Area (sf)	Species Factor (k_s)	Density Factor (k_d)	Microclimate Factor (k_{mc})	K_L	ET_L	IE	TWA (gal)
Shrubs	1,200	Low 0.2	Avg 1.0	High 1.3	0.26	2.11	Drip	1,754.5
Mixed	3,900	Low 0.2	Avg 1.1	High 1.4	0.31	2.50	Drip	6,755
Turf grass	900	Avg 0.7	Avg 1.0	High 1.2	0.84	6.82	Sprinkler	6,122
Subtotal TWA (gal)								14,632
July rainwater and graywater harvest (gal)								(4,200)
TPWA (gal)								10,432

Table 4. Baseline Case (July)

Landscape Type	Area (sf)	Species Factor (k_s)	Density Factor (k_d)	Microclimate Factor (k_{mc})	K_L	ET_L	IE	TWA (gal)
Shrubs	1,200	Avg 0.5	Avg 1.0	High 1.3	0.65	5.28	Sprinkler	6,316.4
Turf grass	4,800	Avg 0.7	Avg 1.0	High 1.2	0.84	6.82	Sprinkler	32,650.8
Subtotal TWA (gal)								38,967

9. Exemplary Performance

This credit is not eligible for exemplary performance under the Innovation in Design section.

10. Regional Variations

Much of the United States is faced with increasing demands on existing water supplies, making it important to landscape sites appropriately for the climate. Appropriate landscaping should consider the site's climate and microclimate, sun exposure, soil type, drainage, and topography.

In hot, dry climates, emphasize drought-tolerant plants and xeriscape designs. Reducing or eliminating turf grass will lessen the demand on potable water; rocks and stone can be incorporated into the landscape instead. If turf grass is desired, select a species that can endure drought.

In hot, humid, and temperate climates, use native plants combined with rain or moisture sensors to avoid unnecessary watering in the wet seasons. The use of captured rainwater can help eliminate the use of potable water for irrigation.

In cold climates, install hardy, native hardy plants that will survive the winter months. Rain or moisture sensors will help prevent excessive watering.

	WE
NC	Credit 1
SCHOOLS	Credit 1
CS	Credit 1

11. Operations and Maintenance Considerations

Effective maintenance of the site landscape will require ongoing attention to the condition and effectiveness of any irrigation system and to the condition of the vegetation itself. To facilitate effective operation of the irrigation system, consider these strategies:

- Install submetering to help operators manage water consumption and identify problems within the system. Submetering may also present opportunities for operating cost savings, since many water utilities do not levy sewage charges on submetered water volumes that do not reach the sewage system. Consider integrating electronic data logging to facilitate consumption trend analysis.

- Consider developing a site landscape maintenance plan for facility operators that includes landscape and irrigation system design plans, species lists, and equipment specifications.

- Graywater systems may require special maintenance. Provide facility operators with appropriate systems manuals, manufacturers' contact information, and product specifications to facilitate proper operation.

- Provide specific guidance to building operators or landscape maintenance contractors about when and how temporary irrigation for plant establishment should be terminated, and metrics for ensuring the success of the establishment phase.

12. Resources

Please see USGBC's LEED Registered Project Tools (http://www.usgbc.org/projecttools) for additional resources and technical information.

Websites

America Rainwater Catchment Systems Association

http://www.arcsa.org/

ARCSA was founded to promote rainwater catchment systems in the United States. The ARCSA website provides regional resources, publications, suppliers, and membership information.

American Water Works Association, WaterWiser: The Water Efficiency Clearinghouse

http://www.awwa.org/waterwiser

The clearinghouse includes articles, reference materials, and papers on all forms of water efficiency.

Center for Irrigation Technology

http://www.cati.csufresno.edu/cit/

CIT is an independent research and testing facility that provides information to designers, manufacturers, and users of irrigation equipment.

Irrigation Association

http://www.irrigation.org

This nonprofit organization focuses on promoting products that efficiently use water in irrigation applications.

	WE
NC	Credit 1
SCHOOLS	Credit 1
CS	Credit 1

National Oceanic and Atmospheric Administration, National Climatic Data Center
http://www.ncdc.noaa.gov/oa/climateresearch.html
The NCDC site is useful for researching local climate information such as data for rainwater harvesting calculations, and it also includes links to state climate offices.

Rain Bird® ET Manager™ Scheduler
http://www.rainbird.com/landscape/products/controllers/etmanager.htm
This free software provides sufficient local evapotranspiration data for the United States and Canada. Access data from the closest or most climate-appropriate location.

Rocky Mountain Institute, Graywater Systems, Compost Toilets, and Rain Collection
http://www.rmi.org
This web resource from the Rocky Mountain Institute provides general information and links to resources on rain collection and graywater systems.

Texas Water Development Board website
http://www.twdb.state.tx.us
This website provides data from the state of Texas regarding water resources and services such as groundwater mapping and water availability modeling. The site also provides brochures on indoor and outdoor water efficiency strategies.

U.S. EPA, Water Efficient Landscaping: Preventing Pollution and Using Resources Wisely
http://www.epa.gov/watersense/docs/water-efficient_landscaping_508.pdf
This manual provides information about reducing water consumption through creative landscaping techniques.

Print Media

Landscape Irrigation: Design and Management, by Stephen W. Smith (John Wiley & Sons, 1996).
This text is a comprehensive guide to landscape irrigation strategies, techniques, and hardware.

Turf Irrigation Manual, fifth edition, by Richard B. Choate and Jim Watkins (Telsco Industries, 1994).
This manual covers all aspects of turf and landscape irrigation.

13. Definitions

Adapted (or introduced) plants reliably grow well in a given habitat with minimal winter protection, pest control, fertilization, or irrigation once their root systems are established. Adapted plants are considered low maintenance and not invasive.

An **aquifer** is an underground water-bearing rock formation or group of formations that supply groundwater, wells, or springs.

Conventional irrigation refers to the most common irrigation system used in the region where the building is located. A conventional irrigation system commonly uses pressure to deliver water and distributes it through sprinkler heads above the ground.

Drip irrigation delivers water at low pressure through buried mains and submains. From the submains, water is distributed to the soil from a network of perforated tubes or emitters. Drip irrigation is a high-efficiency type of microirrigation.

Evapotranspiration (ET) rate is the amount of water lost from a vegetated surface in units of water depth. It is expressed in millimeters per unit of time.

Graywater is defined by the Uniform Plumbing Code (UPC) in its Appendix G, Gray Water Systems for Single-Family Dwellings, as "untreated household waste water which has not come into contact with toilet waste. Greywater includes used water from bathtubs, showers, bathroom wash basins, and water from clothes-washer and laundry tubs. It must not include waste water from kitchen sinks or dishwashers." The International Plumbing Code (IPC) defines graywater in its Appendix C, Gray Water Recycling Systems, as "waste water discharged from lavatories, bathtubs, showers, clothes washers and laundry sinks." Some states and local authorities allow kitchen sink wastewater to be included in graywater. Other differences with the UPC and IPC definitions can likely be found in state and local codes. Project teams should comply with graywater definitions as established by the authority having jurisdiction in the project areas.

	WE
NC	Credit 1
SCHOOLS	Credit 1
CS	Credit 1

Integrated pest management (**IPM**) is the coordinated use of knowledge about pests, the environment, and pest prevention and control methods to minimize pest infestation and damage by the most economical means while minimizing hazards to people, property, and the environment.

The **landscape area** of the site is the total site area less the building footprint, paved surfaces, water bodies, and patios.

Microirrigation involves irrigation systems with small sprinklers and microjets or drippers designed to apply small volumes of water. The sprinklers and microjets are installed within a few centimeters of the ground; drippers are laid on or below grade.

Native (**or indigenous**) **plants** are adapted to a given area during a defined time period and are not invasive. In North America, the term often refers to plants growing in a region prior to the time of settlement by people of European descent.

Potable water meets or exceeds EPA's drinking water quality standards and is approved for human consumption by the state or local authorities having jurisdiction; it may be supplied from wells or municipal water systems.

Xeriscaping is a landscaping method that makes routine irrigation unnecessary. It uses drought-adaptable and low-water plants as well as soil amendments such as compost and mulches to reduce evaporation.

LEED REFERENCE GUIDE FOR GREEN BUILDING DESIGN AND CONSTRUCTION

INNOVATIVE WASTEWATER TECHNOLOGIES

	NC	SCHOOLS	CS
Credit	WE Credit 2	WE Credit 2	WE Credit 2
Points	2 points	2 points	2 points

Intent

To reduce wastewater generation and potable water demand while increasing the local aquifer recharge.

Requirements

NC, SCHOOLS & CS

OPTION 1

Reduce potable water use for building sewage conveyance by 50% through the use of water-conserving fixtures (e.g., water closets, urinals) or nonpotable water (e.g., captured rainwater, recycled graywater, on-site or municipally treated wastewater).

OR

OPTION 2

Treat 50% of wastewater on-site to tertiary standards. Treated water must be infiltrated or used on-site.

	WE
NC	Credit 2
SCHOOLS	Credit 2
CS	Credit 2

1. Benefits and Issues to Consider

Environmental Issues

Water closets and urinals do not require the same high level of water quality as faucets and showerheads. Reducing the amount of potable water needed for sewage conveyance reduces the total amount of water withdrawn from natural water bodies. Similarly, reducing or eliminating the volume of sewage that leaves the site reduces public infrastructure, chemical inputs, energy use, and emissions at municipal water treatment works. Water efficiency and reuse can greatly reduce negative environmental impacts.

Take into consideration the environmental impacts of off-site versus on-site treatment and supply. On-site wastewater treatment systems transform perceived "wastes" into resources that can be used on the building site and provide opportunities to enhance occupants' understanding of nutrient cycles. These resources include treated water volumes for potable and nonpotable use, as well as nutrients that can be applied to improve the site's soil conditions.

Economic Issues

Wastewater treatment systems and water recovery systems require initial capital investment in addition to regular maintenance over the building's lifetime. Project teams must balance these costs with the anticipated savings in water and sewer bills.

Facilities that generate large amounts of wastewater can realize considerable savings by recycling graywater. However, dual sanitary and graywater distribution piping doubles construction piping costs. In addition, local codes requiring filtration, disinfection treatment, overflow protection, and other measures add to the cost of construction, operation, and maintenance. In some systems, pumps are required for distribution, incurring additional energy costs for operation. If a graywater system is anticipated, project teams should install dual plumbing lines during the initial construction to avoid the substantial costs and difficulty of adding them later.

Collection and use of rainwater for nonpotable water applications has significantly fewer code requirements and associated costs. Collecting rainwater reduces the need for runoff devices and minimizes the need for municipal water, decreasing initial and operating costs. Water storage accounts for the highest cost in most rainwater systems.

If on-site water collection or treatment is being considered, compare the available on-site water supply with the amount of water demand projected for a typical year. This analysis can help determine storage capacity and, if treatment is necessary, the cost of water treatment systems. Conducting this type of analysis early in the design process can help identify synergies that reduce the cost of infrastructure, as well as the extent of site disturbance. For example, water storage can be located beneath a parking lot and may prove more economical if installed when the site is graded. Water storage may also be economically feasible if a cistern to collect rainwater is added to a stormwater detention system.

Water treatment can be incorporated into natural or constructed wetlands and add value as a site enhancement. Currently, packaged biological wastewater systems have an initial high cost, relative to the overall building cost, because of the novelty of the technology.

Some municipalities have developed infrastructure to provide a low-cost nonpotable water supply, commonly known as a purple pipe system. Reductions in the amount of potable water that a municipality must provide can lead to more stable water rates.

2. Related Credits

Efforts to harvest rainwater, reuse graywater, and decrease the demand on local water aquifers may support the following credits:

- SS Credit 6.1: Stormwater Design—Quantity Control

- SS Credit 6.2: Stormwater Design—Quality Control

- WE Prerequisite 1: Water Use Reduction

- WE Credit 1: Water-Efficient Landscaping

- WE Credit 3: Water Use Reduction

- WE Credit 4: Process Water Use Reduction (Schools specific)

	WE
NC	Credit 2
SCHOOLS	Credit 2
CS	Credit 2

Additional energy use may be needed for certain on-site wastewater treatment operations or for reuse strategies. These active systems also require commissioning and should be considered in relation to the following credits:

- EA Prerequisite 1: Fundamental Commissioning of Building Energy Systems

- EA Credit 3: Enhanced Commissioning

- EA Credit 5: Measurement and Verification

3. Summary of Referenced Standards

The water efficiency baselines meeting these referenced standards are summarized in the Requirements section of WE Prerequisite 1, Water Use Reduction.

The Energy Policy Act (EPAct) of 1992 (and as amended)
This act addresses energy and water use in commercial, institutional, and residential facilities.

The Energy Policy Act (EPAct) of 2005
This statute became U.S. law in August 2005.

International Association of Plumbing and Mechanical Officials, Publication IAPMO/ American National Standards Institute UPC 1–2006, Uniform Plumbing Code 2006, Section 402.0, Water-Conserving Fixtures and Fittings
http://www.iapmo.org
UPC defines water-conserving fixtures and fittings for water closets, urinals, and metered faucets. This ANSI-accredited code safeguards life, health, property, and public welfare by regulating and controlling the design, construction, installation, materials, location, operation, and maintenance or use of plumbing systems.

International Code Council, International Plumbing Code 2006, Section 604, Design of Building Water Distribution System
http://www.iccsafe.org
IPC defines maximum flow rates and consumption for plumbing fixtures and fittings, including public and private lavatories, showerheads, sink faucets, urinals, and water closets.

4. Implementation

This credit addresses water use in flush fixtures regulated by the Energy Policy Act of 1992 and subsequent rulings by the Department of Energy, the requirements of the Energy Policy Act of 2005, and the plumbing code requirements as stated in the 2006 editions of the Uniform Plumbing Code and International Plumbing Code.

Potable water is used for many functions that do not require high-quality water, including toilet and urinal flushing. Effective methods for reducing potable water use for sewage conveyance include installing high-efficiency and nonwater flush fixtures, collecting rainwater, and reusing graywater. Rainwater and graywater systems can significantly reduce potable water demand. Graywater systems reuse the wastewater collected from sinks, showers, and other sources for flushing toilets

	WE
NC	Credit 2
SCHOOLS	Credit 2
CS	Credit 2

and urinals and other functions that do not require potable water. Graywater treatment may be required prior to reuse according to specific end use and state jurisdiction.

The quality of rainwater is typically higher than collected graywater, so rainwater systems have significantly fewer code requirements and are often less expensive than graywater systems. Rainwater collected from impervious surfaces reduces stormwater runoff and control requirements. Stormwater retention or detention systems can be designed with cisterns to hold rainwater runoff for nonpotable use.

The feasibility of wastewater reuse and treatment strategies depends on the project's size and location. Some municipalities provide developments with a convenient and affordable nonpotable water supply, commonly known as a purple pipe system. Close proximity to a municipal or private treatment facility can also open the opportunity to reuse treated wastewater for projects that cannot develop their own wastewater treatment, graywater collection, or rainwater systems on-site.

Large projects or campus settings may have the necessary scale and land to support on-site wastewater treatment. In remote locations, it may be more cost-effective to use an on-site wastewater treatment system than to extend existing infrastructure. On-site wastewater treatment systems avoid the aquifer contamination problems of current septic system technology. Projects that plan to treat wastewater on-site can consider constructed wetlands, mechanical recirculating sand filters, and anaerobic biological treatment reactors.

Raw, untreated rainwater, stormwater, and graywater can be more corrosive than potable water because of microbiological levels and particulate buildup in tanks and lines. Using anticorrosive materials can prevent premature failure from such corrosion.

5. Timeline and Team

During predesign, setting water goals and strategy involves the owner, architect, and engineers. Study weather data to determine both average annual precipitation and seasonal precipitation patterns. Identify local water utilities and governing authorities and research codes and applicable water laws. Study the process for obtaining permits and set water goals and strategy.

During schematic design, mechanical and civil engineers can help establish a water budget with estimated volumes for end uses of nonpotable water (for flush fixtures, irrigation, process loads). Investigate rainwater, stormwater, municipally supplied nonpotable water, treated and untreated graywater, and treated blackwater as sources of supply.

A water budget enables comparison of trade-offs for water conservation strategies and evaluation of the impact of water infrastructure on other systems. In early design stages, architects and engineers can determine square footage areas required for rainwater or stormwater harvesting and on-site wastewater treatment to meet specific end-use demands. Estimate the feasibility and cost of different reuse and treatment strategies and compare environmental impacts of on-site versus off-site water supply. Water goals and strategy can then be confirmed or reassessed.

During design development, the engineering team should develop and design water reuse and treatment systems, perform preliminary LEED calculations, and confirm or reassess water goals.

In construction documents, the architect, working with the owner, should specify efficient fixtures and appliances and complete LEED calculations and documentation.

During construction, the design team and owner should confirm proper selection, installation, and operation of water fixtures, fittings, and systems.

6. Calculations

The following section describes the calculation methodology for determining reductions in potable water used for sewage conveyance and wastewater released into the municipal system. Wastewater calculations are based on the annual generation of blackwater volumes from flush fixtures. Flow fixtures are not included in calculations for this credit. The calculated water use reduction for the project is the difference between the calculated design case and a baseline case. The percentage is determined by dividing the design case use by the baseline use. The methodology differs from traditional plumbing design, in which calculations are based on fixture counts; under this credit, the water use calculation is based on fixture and fitting water consumption rates and estimated use by the occupants.

Refer to WE Prerequisite 1, Water Use Reduction, for information on calculating occupancy, defining fixture usage groups, and default values for fixture use by occupant type.

Design Case Water Consumption

The design case annual water use is determined by totaling the annual volume of each fixture type and subtracting any nonpotable water supply. The design case must use the rated flow rates and flush volumes for installed plumbing fixtures and fittings. Obtain water consumption data from the manufacturers' product literature.

Perform calculations for each type of blackwater-generating fixture (Table 4).

Table 4. Sample Blackwater-Generating Fixtures and Fittings and Water Consumption

Flush fixture	Flow rate (gpf)
Conventional water closet	1.6
High-efficiency toilet (HET), single-flush gravity	1.28
HET, single-flush pressure assist	1.0
HET, dual flush (full-flush)	1.6
HET, dual flush (low-flush)	1.1
HET, foam flush	0.05
Non-water toilet	0.0
Conventional urinal	1.0
High-efficiency urinal (HEU)	0.5
Nonwater urinal	0.0

If on-site collected rainwater or graywater is used for sewage conveyance, enter the estimated quantity in the calculation. The total annual quantity of nonpotable water is subtracted from the total annual design case water use. For graywater and rainwater volumes, calculations are required to demonstrate that these reuse volumes are sufficient to meet water closet demands.

Baseline Case Water Consumption

The baseline case annual water use is determined by setting the fixture and fitting water consumption to baseline rates listed in the requirements for WE Prerequisite 1 (as opposed to actual installed values in the design case).

7. Documentation Guidance

As a first step in preparing to complete the LEED-Online documentation requirements, work through the following measures. Refer to LEED-Online for the complete descriptions of all required documentation.

- Determine the type and number of occupants.

- Retain manufacturers' data showing the water consumption rates, manufacturer, and model of each fixture and fitting.

- Compile information about system schematics and capacity of any rainwater or graywater systems.

	WE
NC	Credit 2
SCHOOLS	Credit 2
CS	Credit 2

8. Examples

EXAMPLE 1. Wastewater Treatment System

On-site biological treatment transforms waste into resources that can be used on the building site. Figure 1 shows the steps for on-site treatment. As solids settle in the anaerobic septic tank, microbes begin to feed and break down the waste. The closed aerobic reactor is aerated by pumps to help remove aromatic compounds. The open aerobic reactors contain plants, algae, snails, and fish that further break down the organic waste. In the constructed wetland, aerobic and anaerobic reactions remove the remaining impurities and nitrates. This creates clean, nonpotable water that can be used in irrigation systems, water closets, or cooling towers.

Figure 1. On-site Biological Treatment of Wastewater

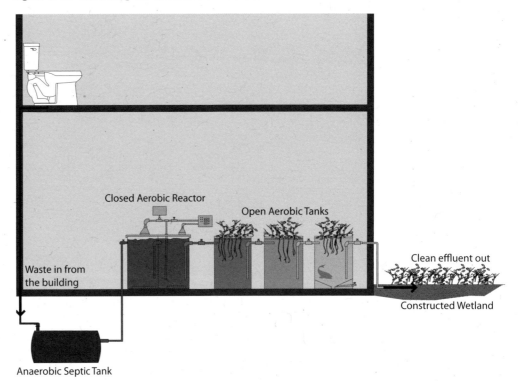

EXAMPLE 2. Calculating Design and Baseline Cases

Example 2 shows sample potable water calculations for sewage conveyance for a 2-story office building with 300 occupants. The calculations are based on a typical 8-hour workday. It is assumed that building occupants are 50% male and 50% female. Male occupants are assumed to use water closets once and urinals twice in a typical workday. Female occupants are assumed to use water closets 3 times.

First, the design case is considered to determine annual potable water use for sewage conveyance. The building uses either nonpotable rainwater or no water for sewage conveyance (i.e., fixtures are waterless urinals and composting toilets). **Table 6** summarizes the sewage generation rates; 92,700 gallons of potable water are used annually for sewage conveyance. In the example, 36,000 gallons of rainwater are harvested and directed to water closets for flushing.

Table 6. Design Case Calculations

	WE
NC	Credit 2
SCHOOLS	Credit 2
CS	Credit 2

Fixture Type	Daily Uses	Flowrate (gpf)	Occupants	Sewage Generation (gal)
Low-Flow Water Closet (Male)	0	1.1	150	0
Low-Flow Water Closet (Female)	3	1.1	150	495
Composting Toilet (Male)	1	0.0	150	0
Composting Toilet (Female)	0	0.0	150	0
Waterless Urinal (Male)	2	0.0	150	0
Waterless Urinal (Female)	0	0.0	150	0
Total Daily Volume (gal)				495
Annual Work Days				260
Annual Volume (gal)				128,700
Rainwater or Graywater Reuse Volume (gal)				(36,000)
Total Annual Volume (gal)				92,700

Table 7 summarizes baseline calculations. Sewage conveyance requires an estimated 327,600 gallons of potable water per year. Comparison of the baseline with the design case indicates that the building realizes a 72% reduction in potable water volumes used for sewage conveyance (1 – 92,700/327,600). Thus, this strategy earns 1 point. When developing the baseline, only the fixtures, sewage generation rates, and the water reuse credit are different from the design case; usage rates, occupancy, and number of workdays remain the same.

Table 7. Baseline Case Calculations

Fixture Type	Daily Uses	Flowrate (gpf)	Occupants	Sewage Generation (gal)
Water Closet (Male)	1	1.6	150	240
Water Closet (Female)	3	1.6	150	720
Urinal (Male)	2	1.0	150	300
Urinal (Female)	0	1.0	150	0
Total Daily Volume (gal)				1,260
Annual Work Days				260
Total Annual Volume (gal)				327,600

9. Exemplary Performance

Projects may be awarded an innovation credit for exemplary performance by demonstrating 100% reduction in potable water use for sewage conveyance, or by demonstrating on-site treatment and either re-use or infiltration of 100% of generated wastewater.

10. Regional Variations

Consider local climate and weather patterns when determining the feasibility of using rainwater to reduce potable water for plumbing fixture flushing. Depending on seasonal precipitation patterns, rainwater harvesting for on-site use may require a storage strategy. The cost of creating the necessary storage capacity may be justified if strategies for rainwater collection can be combined with the storage of graywater for reuse.

Climatic conditions also affect the viability of on-site treatment options. For example, biological treatment in hot, humid climates is more efficient and effective and requires less surface area than in a cold climate.

When considering an on-site rainwater, graywater, or blackwater system, first check with local government agencies for regulations and required permits. Each state has its own standards and

	WE
NC	Credit 2
SCHOOLS	Credit 2
CS	Credit 2

requirements for the installation and operation of such systems. Texas and California, for example, have standards that encourage the use of graywater systems, whereas other states have regulations that may limit or prohibit their use. Codes also may differ in how alternative plumbing fixtures, such as waterless urinals, dual-flush or low-flow water closets, and composting toilets systems, are handled. Confirm the legality of nontraditional approaches with code officials before committing to specific water-saving strategies.

11. Operations and Maintenance Considerations

Buildings designed to achieve low sewage conveyance volumes may have equipment or technologies that are unfamiliar to some facility owners and managers. Give them complete operating information, manufacturers' specifications and contact information, and tools for evaluating system effectiveness on an ongoing basis.

To ensure continued water savings and satisfaction for owners and occupants, maintenance staff must be trained in the operation and maintenance of any on-site wastewter treatment systems and specialized equipment. For example, waterless urinals generally need to be cleaned according to manufacturers' specifications and their chemical traps appropriately maintained, and 0.5-gallon and 0.2-gallon flushing urinals must also be maintained according to manufacturers' specifications.

12. Resources

Websites

Please see USGBC's LEED Registered Project Tools (http://www.usgbc.org/projecttools) for additional resources and technical information.

American Rainwater Catchment Systems Association
http://www.arcsa.org
ARCSA was founded to promote rainwater catchment systems in the United States. The ARCSA website provides regional resources, suppliers, and membership information, and publications **such as the** *Texas Guide to Rainwater Harvesting*.

Environmental Building News, Water: Doing More with Less
http://www.buildinggreen.com/auth/article.cfm/2008/2/3/Water-Doing-More-With-Less/
This website features an article on building water efficiency.

Fine Homebuilding, Choosing a Toilet
http://www.taunton.com/finehomebuilding/pages/h00042.asp
This article includes several varieties of water-efficient toilets.

National Oceanic and Atmospheric Administration, National Climatic Data Center
http://www.ncdc.noaa.gov/cgi-bin/good-bye.pl?src=http://www.stateclimate.org
The NCDC site is useful for researching local climate information such as data for rainwater harvesting calculations, and it also includes links to state climate offices.

Rocky Mountain Institute, Water
http://www.rmi.org/sitepages/pid128.php
This portion of RMI's website is devoted to water conservation and efficiency. The site contains information on watershed management and commercial, industrial, and institutional water use and articles on policy and implementation.

Terry Love's Consumer Toilet Reports
http://www.terrylove.com/crtoilet.htm
This website offers a plumber's perspective on many of the major toilets used in commercial and residential applications.

U.S. EPA Publication No. 832/B-93-005, Constructed Wetlands for Wastewater Treatment and Wildlife Habitat: 17 Case Studies, 1993

http://www.epa.gov/owow/wetlands/construc/

The case studies in this document provide brief descriptions of 17 wetland treatment systems that offer water quality benefits while also providing habitat. The projects described include constructed and natural wetlands; habitat creation and restoration; and the improvement of municipal effluent, urban stormwater, and river water quality.

U.S. EPA, WaterSense

http://www.epa.gov/watersense/

The WaterSense Program helps U.S. consumers save water and protect the environment. Look for the WaterSense label to help choose high-quality, water-efficient products. A variety of products are available, and they do not require a change in lifestyle.

Explore the link above to learn about how businesses and organizations can partner with WaterSense.

U.S. EPA, How to Conserve Water and Use It Effectively

http://www.epa.gov/OWOW/nps/chap3.html

This EPA document provides guidance for commercial, industrial, and residential water users on saving water and reducing sewage volumes.

U.S. EPA, On-site Wastewater Treatment Systems Manual

http://www.epa.gov/nrmrl/pubs/625r00008/html/625R00008.htm

This manual provides a focused and performance-based approach to on-site wastewater treatment and system management. It also includes information on a variety of on-site sewage treatment options.

Water Closet Performance Testing

http://www.ebmud.com/conserving_&_recycling/toilet_test_report/default.htm

This site provides 2 reports on independent test results for a variety of toilets' flush performance and reliability..

Print Media

Mechanical & Electrical Equipment for Buildings, eighth ddition, by Benjamin Stein and John Reynolds (John Wiley & Sons, 1992).

Sustainable Building Technical Manual (Public Technology, Inc., 1996): http://www.pti.org.

Water, Sanitary and Waste Services for Buildings, fourth edition, by A. Wise and J. Swaffield (Longman Scientific & Technical, 1995).

13. Definitions

An **aquifer** is an underground water-bearing rock formation or group of formations that supply groundwater, wells, or springs.

Automatic fixture sensors are motion detectors that automatically turn on and turn off lavatories, sinks, water closets, and urinals. Sensors can be hard wired or battery operated.

Blackwater definitions vary, but wastewater from toilets and urinals is always considered blackwater. Wastewater from kitchen sinks (perhaps differentiated by the use of a garbage disposal), showers, or bathtubs is considered blackwater under some state or local codes.

Composting toilet system. See **nonwater toilet system.**

WE	
NC	Credit 2
SCHOOLS	Credit 2
CS	Credit 2

Graywater is defined by the Uniform Plumbing Code (UPC) in its Appendix G, Gray Water Systems for Single-Family Dwellings, as "untreated household waste water which has not come into contact with toilet waste. Greywater includes used water from bathtubs, showers, bathroom wash basins, and water from clothes-washer and laundry tubs. It must not include waste water from kitchen sinks or dishwashers." The International Plumbing Code (IPC) defines graywater in its Appendix C, Gray Water Recycling Systems, as "waste water discharged from lavatories, bathtubs, showers, clothes washers and laundry sinks." Some states and local authorities allow kitchen sink wastewater to be included in graywater. Other differences with the UPC and IPC definitions can likely be found in state and local codes. Project teams should comply with graywater definitions as established by the authority having jurisdiction in the project areas.

Nonpotable water. See **potable water.**

Nonwater (or composting) toilet systems are dry plumbing fixtures and fittings that contain and treat human waste via microbiological processes.

A **nonwater (or dry) urinal,** replaces a water flush with a trap containing a layer of buoyant liquid that floats above the urine, blocking sewer gas and odors.

On-site wastewater treatment is the transport, storage, treatment, and disposal of wastewater generated on the project site.

Potable water meets or exceeds EPA's drinking water quality standards and is approved for human consumption by the state or local authorities having jurisdiction; it may be supplied from wells or municipal water systems.

Process water is used for industrial processes and building systems such as cooling towers, boilers, and chillers. The term can also refer to water used in operational processes, such as dishwashing, clothes washing, and ice making.

Tertiary treatment is the highest form of wastewater treatment and includes removal of organics, solids, and nutrients as well as biological or chemical polishing, generally to effluent limits of 10 mg/L biological oxygen demand (BOD) 5 and 10 mg/L total suspended solids (TSS).

	NC	SCHOOLS	CS
Credit	WE Credit 3	WE Credit 3	WE Credit 3
Points	2-4 points	2-4 points	2-4 points

Intent

To further increase water efficiency within buildings to reduce the burden on municipal water supply and wastewater systems.

Requirements

NC, SCHOOLS & CS

Employ strategies that in aggregate use less water than the water use baseline calculated for the building (not including irrigation).

The minimum water savings percentage for each point threshold is as follows:

Percentage Reduction	Points
30%	2
35%	3
40%	4

Calculate the baseline according to the commercial and/or residential baselines outlined below.[1] Calculations are based on estimated occupant usage and must include only the following fixtures and fixture fittings (as applicable to the project scope): water closets, urinals, lavatory faucets, showers, kitchen sink faucets and pre-rinse spray valves.

Commercial Fixtures, Fittings, and Appliances	Current Baseline
Commercial toilets	1.6 gallons per flush (gpf)* Except blow-out fixtures: 3.5 (gpf)
Commercial urinals	1.0 (gpf)
Commercial lavatory (restroom) faucets	2.2 gallons per minute (gpm) at 60 pounds per square inch (psi), private applications only (hotel or motel guest rooms, hospital patient rooms) 0.5 (gpm) at 60 (psi)** all others except private applications 0.25 gallons per cycle for metering faucets
Commercial prerinse spray valves (for food service applications)	Flow rate ≤ 1.6 (gpm) (no pressure specified; no performance requirement)

---

1   Table adapted from information developed and summarized by the U.S. Environmental Protection Agency (EPA) Office of Water based on requirements of the Energy Policy Act (EPAct) of 1992 and subsequent rulings by the Department of Energy, requirements of the EPAct of 2005, and the plumbing code requirements as stated in the 2006 editions of the Uniform Plumbing Code or International Plumbing Code pertaining to fixture performance.

NC, SCHOOLS & CS (continued)

Residential Fixtures, Fittings, and Appliances	Current Baseline
Residential toilets	1.6 (gpf)***
Residential lavatory (bathroom) faucets	2.2 (gpm) at 60 psi
Residential kitchen faucet	
Residential showerheads	2.5 (gpm) at 80 (psi) per shower stall****

*   EPAct 1992 standard for toilets applies to both commercial and residential models.

**   In addition to EPAct requirements, the American Society of Mechanical Engineers standard for public lavatory faucets is 0.5 gpm at 60 psi (ASME A112.18.1-2005). This maximum has been incorporated into the national Uniform Plumbing Code and the International Plumbing Code.

***   EPAct 1992 standard for toilets applies to both commercial and residential models.

**** Residential shower compartment (stall) in dwelling units: The total allowable flow rate from all flowing showerheads at any given time, including rain systems, waterfalls, bodysprays, bodyspas and jets, must be limited to the allowable showerhead flow rate as specified above (2.5 gpm) per shower compartment, where the floor area of the shower compartment is less than 2,500 square inches. For each increment of 2,500 square inches of floor area thereafter or part thereof, an additional showerhead with total allowable flow rate from all flowing devices equal to or less than the allowable flow rate as specified above must be allowed. Exception: Showers that emit recirculated nonpotable water originating from within the shower compartment while operating are allowed to exceed the maximum as long as the total potable water flow does not exceed the flow rate as specified above.

The following fixtures, fittings and appliances are outside the scope of the water use reduction calculation:

- Commercial Steam Cookers

- Commercial Dishwashers

- Automatic Commercial Ice Makers

- Commercial (family-sized) Clothes Washers

- Residential Clothes Washers

- Standard and Compact Residential Dishwashers

1. Benefits and Issues to Consider

See the Benefits and Issues section in WE Prerequisite 1.

2. Related Credits

See the Related Credits section in WE Prerequisite 1.

	WE
NC	Credit 3
SCHOOLS	Credit 3
CS	Credit 3

3. Summary of Referenced Standards

See the Referenced Standards section in WE Prerequisite 1

4. Implementation

See the Implementation section in WE Prerequisite 1.

5. Timeline and Team

See the Timeline and Team section in WE Prerequisite 1.

6. Calculations

See the Calculations section in WE Prerequisite 1.

7. Documentation Guidance

See the Documentation Guidance section in WE Prerequisite 1.

8. Examples

See the Examples section in WE Prerequisite 1

9. Exemplary Performance

Projects may earn an Innovation in Design credit for exemplary performance by demonstrating 45% reduction in projected potable water use.

10. Regional Variations

See the Regional Variations section in WE Prerequisite 1.

11. Operations and Maintenance Considerations

See the Operations and Maintenance section in WE Prerequisite 1.

12. Resources

See the Operations and Maintenance section in WE Prerequisite 1.

13. Definitions

See the Definitions in WE Prerequisite 1.

PROCESS WATER USE REDUCTION

	NC	SCHOOLS	CS
Credit	NA	WE Credit 4	NA
Points	NA	1 point	NA

Intent

To maximize water efficiency within buildings to reduce the burden on municipal water supply and wastewater systems.

Requirements

SCHOOLS

To receive this credit, buildings must have the following:

- No refrigeration equipment using once-through cooling with potable water

- No garbage disposals

- At least 4 process items where water use is at or below the levels shown in the table below. Inclusion of any equipment not listed in the table below must be supported by documentation showing a 20% reduction in water use from a benchmark or industry standard.

Equipment Type	Maximum Water Use	Other Requirements
Clothes washers*	7.5 gallons/ft³/cycle	
Dishwashers with racks	1.0 gallons/rack	
Ice machines**	lbs/day>175 20 gallons/100lbs	No water-cooled machines
	lbs/day<175 30 gallons/100/lbs	No water-cooled machines
Food steamers	2 gallons/hour	Boilerless steamers only
Prerinse spray valves	1.4 gallons per minute	

* Commercial CEE Tier 3a—Residential CEE Tier 1
** CEE Tier 3

	WE
NC	NA
SCHOOLS	Credit 4
CS	NA

1. Benefits and Issues to Consider

Environmental Issues

The reduction of potable water use in buildings for process water reduces the total amount withdrawn from rivers, streams, underground aquifers, and other water bodies. Another benefit of municipally supplied potable water conservation is reduced energy use and chemical inputs at municipal water treatment works, as well as reduced energy use and the associated greenhouse gas emissions from treatment and distribution. According to EPA, U.S. public water supply and treatment facilities consume about 56 billion kilowatt-hours (kWh) per year—enough electricity to power more than 5 million homes for an entire year.[24]

The use of garbage disposals introduces unprocessed food waste into the municipal water system, increasing the biochemical oxygen demand of the water and placing an unnecessary burden on sewage treatment facilities during processing. Eliminating garbage disposals preserves resources by enabling less process-intensive methods to be used in treating wastewater. Food waste can be composted instead and reintroduced into the nutrient cycle. Composting of kitchen waste can also be used in school vegetable gardens, providing opportunities for students to learn about plant biology and ecosystems.

Economic Issues

Reasonably priced, water-efficient appliances are becoming increasingly available as consumers and manufacturers recognize the economic and environmental benefits of water conservation. Substantial savings can be realized over the life of these products in both water and energy consumption. Water-efficient appliances may also reduce construction costs by minimizing the necessity for supply and wastewater plumbing. Reductions can also lead to more stable municipal taxes and water rates. By reducing water use and food disposal to the sewer, utility water treatment facilities can delay expansion and maintain stable water prices.

2. Related Credits

Some water-saving technologies affect energy performance and require commissioning; these should be addressed in the measurement and verification plan. For more information, see the requirements for the following:

- EA Prerequisite 1: Fundamental Commissioning of Building Energy Systems
- EA Credit 5: Measurement and Verification

3. Summary of Referenced Standards

There are no standards referenced for this credit.

4. Implementation

This credit addresses water use in dishwashers, clothes washers, ice machines, and other equipment not included in other WE credits or regulated by the Energy Policy Act of 1992 and subsequent rulings by the Department of Energy, the requirements of the Energy Policy Act of 2005, and the plumbing code requirements for fixture performance as stated in the 2006 editions of the Uniform Plumbing Code or International Plumbing Code. Assess all processes in the building that use water to identify opportunities for selecting high-efficiency equipment. Many types of equipment can be used to achieve compliance with this credit, provided they achieve a 20% reduction in water use over an acceptable benchmark or industry standard.

Garbage disposals and refrigeration equipment that uses once-through cooling with potable water are ineligible for this credit.

If the equipment that does not have an established baseline, the project team must cite other industry standards or benchmarks; the proposed baselines will be evaluated on a case-by-case basis.

5. Timeline and Team

During design development and while preparing construction documents, the architect should coordinate with the building owner to specify efficient fixtures and appliances and complete LEED calculations and documentation.

6. Calculations

No calculations are required for this credit if project teams are using equipment that has a baseline established in the credit requirements. Project teams that install equipment not listed in the credit requirements must establish a new baseline and demonstrate the equipment reduces process water use by at least 20%.

7. Documentation Guidance

As a first step in preparing to complete the LEED-Online documentation requirements, work through the following measures. Refer to LEED-Online for the complete descriptions of all required documentation.

- Retain documents showing the manufacturer, model, and water consumption rates of each appliance.

- Assemble information about the baseline water use based on industry standards or benchmarks for any equipment not listed in the credit requirements.

8. Examples

A closed-loop system in a cooling tower can reduce its need for potable water (Figure 1). The process fluid to be cooled is kept clean in a contaminant-free closed loop. This process reduces the potable water use of the system compared with a traditional once-through cooling system.

Figure 1. Water Reuse in Closed-Circuit Cooling Tower

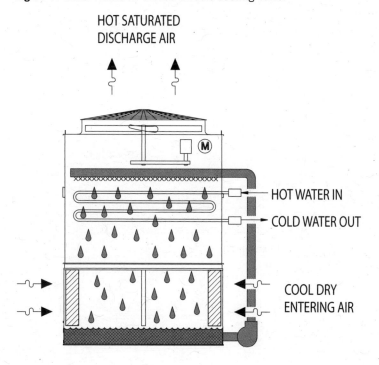

HOT SATURATED DISCHARGE AIR

HOT WATER IN

COLD WATER OUT

COOL DRY ENTERING AIR

9. Exemplary Performance

Projects may earn an innovation credit for exemplary performance by demonstrating a projected process water saving of 40%.

10. Regional Variations

There are no regional variations associated with this credit.

11. Operations and Maintenance Considerations

For water-using equipment, ensure that building operators receive design documents (in the case of refrigeration equipment) and manufacturers' specifications on installed equipment. If possible, submeter the water consumption of process uses, particularly for high-volume end uses, to help track water consumption and identify unexpected patterns (deviations from the manufacturer's specifications, for example) that may indicate product failures or occupant misuse.

To ensure continued water savings and satisfaction for owners and occupants, train maintenance staff in the operations and maintenance of any specialized equipment.

12. Resources

Please see USGBC's LEED Registered Project Tools (http://www.usgbc.org/projecttools) for additional resources and technical information.

Websites
American Water Works Association

http://www.awwa.org

AWWA is an international nonprofit scientific and educational society dedicated to the improvement of water quality and supply. Its website includes a resource guide to water industry products and services.

Consortium for Energy Efficiency

http://www.cee1.org

CEE is a North American nonprofit organization that works with its members to promote energy-efficient products, technologies, and services. CEE brings efficiency program administrators together, providing a forum for them to explore common interests, exchange information, and seek consensus with their colleagues as well as industry representatives and ENERGY STAR staff.

ENERGY STAR®

http://www.energystar.gov

ENERGY STAR is a joint program of U.S. EPA and the U.S. Department of Energy that promotes energy-efficient buildings, products, and practices.

Environmental Building News, Water: Doing More with Less

http://www.buildinggreen.com/auth/article.cfm/2008/2/3/Water-Doing-More-With-Less
This website features an article on building water efficiency.

National Oceanic and Atmospheric Administration, National Climatic Data Center

http://www.ncdc.noaa.gov

The NCDC website is useful for researching local climate information, such as data for rainwater harvesting calculations. It also includes links to state climate offices.

Rocky Mountain Institute

http://www.rmi.org/sitepages/pid128.php

This portion of RMI's website is devoted to water conservation and efficiency. The site contains information on commercial, industrial, and institutional water use, watershed management, and articles on policy and implementation.

U.S. Department of the Interior, Water Measurement Manual: A Water Resources Technical Publication

http://www.usbr.gov/pmts/hydraulics_lab/pubs/wmm

This publication is a guide to effective water measurement practices for better water management.

	WE
NC	NA
SCHOOLS	Credit 4
CS	NA

U.S. EPA, How to Conserve Water and Use It Effectively

http://www.epa.gov/OWOW/nps/chap3.html

An EPA document that provides guidance for commercial, industrial, and residential water users on saving water and reducing sewage volumes.

U.S. EPA, WaterSense

http://www.epa.gov/watersense/

WaterSense, a partnership program sponsored by the U.S. Environmental Protection Agency (EPA), makes it easy for Americans to save water and protect the environment. Look for the WaterSense label to choose quality, water-efficient products. Explore the link above to learn about WaterSense labeled products, saving water and how businesses and organizations can partner with WaterSense.

13. Definitions

An **aquifer** is an underground water-bearing rock formation or group of formations that supply groundwater, wells, or springs.

Biochemical oxygen demand is a measure of how fast biological organisms use up oxygen in a body of water. It is used in water quality management and assessment, ecology, and environmental science.

Potable water meets or exceeds EPA's drinking water quality standards and is approved for human consumption by the state or local authorities having jurisdiction; it may be supplied from wells or municipal water systems.

Process water is used for industrial processes and building systems such as cooling towers, boilers, and chillers. The term can also refer to water used in operational processes, such as dishwashing, clothes washing, and ice making.

Endnotes

[1] Hutson, Susan S., Nancy L. Barber, Joan F. Kenny, Kristin S. Linsey, Deborah S. Lumia, and Molly A. Maupin. Estimated Use of Water in the United States in 2000. U.S. Geological Survey, 2004. http://water.usgs.gov/pubs/circ/2004/circ1268/htdocs/text-trends.html (accessed May 2008).

[2] U.S. Geological Survey. "USGS Study Documents Water Level Changes in High Plains Aquifer." U.S. Geological Survey News Release, (February 9, 2004), http://www.usgs.gov/newsroom/article.asp?ID=121 (accessed May 2008).

[3] Solley, Wayne B., Robert R. Pierce, and Howard A. Perlman. Estimated Use of Water in the United States in 1995. U.S. Geological Survey, 1998. http://water.usgs.gov/watuse/pdf1995/html/ (accessed May 2008).

[4] U.S. Environmental Protection Agency, Office of Ground Water and Drinking Water. "List of Drinking Water Contaminants & MCLS." http://www.epa.gov/safewater/mcl.html (accessed May 2008).

[5] U.S. Environmental Protection Agency, Office of Wastewater Management. Water Permitting 101. 2002. http://www.epa.gov/npdes/pubs/101pape.pdf (accessed May 2008).

[6] Ibid.

[7] Hutson, Susan S., Nancy L. Barber, Joan F. Kenny, Kristin S. Linsey, Deborah S. Lumia, and Molly A. Maupin. Estimated Use of Water in the United States in 2000. U.S. Geological Survey, 2004. http://water.usgs.gov/pubs/circ/2004/circ1268/htdocs/text-trends.html (accessed May 2008).

8   U.S. Environmental Protection Agency, Office of Wastewater Management. Water Permitting 101. 2002. http://www.epa.gov/npdes/pubs/101pape.pdf (accessed May 2008).

9   U.S. Green Building Council. "LEED Certified Project List." http://www.usgbc.org/LEED/Project/CertifiedProjectList.aspx (accessed May 2008).

10 Based on 650 building occupants, each using an average of 20 gallons per day.

11 Knox III, Randy H. Case Study: Adobe's "Greenest Office in America" Sets the Bar for Corporate Environmentalism. U.S. Green Building Council. http://www.fmlink.com/ProfResources/Sustainability/Articles/article.cgi?USGBC:200707-16.html (accessed November, 2008).

12 Massachusetts Water Resources Authority. "Water Efficiency and Management for Commercial Buildings." http://www.mwra.state.ma.us/04water/html/bullet4.htm (accessed May 2008).

13 Energy Information Administration. "1999 Commercial Buildings Energy Consumption Survey." Commercial Buildings Energy Consumption Survey. http://www.eia.doe.gov/emeu/cbecs/background.html (accessed May 2008).

14 U.S. Department of Energy. "Water Efficiency: Water Efficiency Basics." http://www1.eere.energy.gov/femp/water/water_basics.html (accessed May 2008).

15 U.S. Environmental Protection Agency, WaterSense. "Why Water Efficiency?" http://www.epa.gov/owm/water-efficiency/water/why.htm (accessed May 2008).

16 U.S. Environmental Protection Agency, WaterSense. "WaterSense." http://www.epa.gov/watersense (accessed May 2008).

17 Ibid.

18 U.S. Environmental Protection Agency, Office of Water. Water-Efficient Landscaping. 2002. http://www.epa.gov/owm/water-efficiency/final_final.pdf (accessed January 2005).

19 Energy Information Administration, "1999 Commercial Buildings Energy Consumption Survey," Commercial Buildings Energy Consumption Survey. http://www.eia.doe.gov/emeu/cbecs/ (accessed May 2008).

20 Georgia Department of Natural Resources, Pollution Prevention Assistance Division. "The Sustainable Office Toolkit." http://www.p2ad.org/toolkit/modules_4_1.html (accessed May 2008).

21 Connellan, Goeff. Efficient Irrigation:A Reference Manual for Turf and Landscape. University of Melbourne, 2002.

22 Bilderback, T.E., and M.A. Powell. Efficient Irrigation. North Carolina Cooperative Extension Service Publication, 1996. http://www.bae.ncsu.edu/programs/extension/publicat/wqwm/ag508_6.html (accessed January 2005).

23 Riley-Chetwynd, Jennifer. "Irrigation for a Growing World." Presentation, Rainbird Corporation. (October 2008). http://www.watersmartinnovations.com/PDFs/Thursday/Sonoma%20B/1000-%20Jennifer%20Riley-Chetwynd-%20The%20Intelligent%20Use%20of%20Water-%20Irrigation%20for%20a%20Growing%20World.pdf (accessed November 2008).

24 U.S. Environmental Protection Agency. WaterSense. "Benefits of Water Efficiency" http://www.epa.gov/watersense/water/benefits.htm (accessed November 2008)

Overview

Buildings consume approximately 39% of the energy and 74% of the electricity produced annually in the United States, according to the U.S. Department of Energy.[1] Generating electricity from fossil fuels, such as oil, natural gas, and coal, negatively affects the environment at each step of production and use, beginning with extraction and transportation, followed by refining and distribution, and ending with consumption. For example, coal mining disrupts natural habitats and can devastate landscapes. Acidic mine drainage degrades regional ecosystems. Coal is rinsed with water, producing billions of gallons of sludge that must be stored in ponds. Mining itself is a dangerous occupation in which accidents and the long-term effects of breathing coal dust can shorten the lifespans of coal miners.

Electricity is most often generated by burning fossil fuels, whose combustion releases carbon dioxide and other greenhouse gases that contribute to climate change. Coal-fired plants accounted for more than half of U.S. electricity generation in 2006.[2] Burning coal releases harmful pollutants, such as carbon dioxide, sulfur dioxide, nitrogen oxides, small particulates, and mercury. Each megawatt of coal-generated electricity releases into the atmosphere an average of 2,249 pounds of carbon dioxide, 13 pounds of sulfur dioxide, and 6 pounds of nitrogen oxides.[3] More than 65% of the sulfur dioxide released into the air, or more than 13 million tons per year, comes from electricity generation, primarily coal-burning generators.[4] Mining, processing, and transporting coal to power plants create additional emissions, including methane vented from the coal during transport.

Natural gas, nuclear fission, and hydroelectric generators all have adverse environmental consequences as well. Natural gas is a major source of nitrogen oxide and greenhouse gas emissions. Nuclear power increases the potential for catastrophic accidents and raises significant waste transportation and disposal issues. Hydroelectric generating plants disrupt natural water flows and disturb aquatic habitats.

Green buildings address those issues in two ways. First, they reduce the amount of energy required for building operations, and second, they use more benign forms of energy. The better the energy performance of a building, the fewer greenhouse gases are emitted from energy production. Electricity generation using sources other than fossil fuels also reduces the environmental impacts from a building's energy use. Additionally, improved energy performance results in lower operating costs. As global competition for fuel accelerates, the rate of return on energy efficiency measures improves.

Energy Performance

The energy performance of a building depends on its design. Its massing and orientation, materials, construction methods, building envelope, and water efficiency as well as the heating, ventilating, and air-conditioning (HVAC) and lighting systems determine how efficiently the building uses energy. Therefore, the most effective way to optimize energy efficiency is to use an integrated, whole-building approach. Collaboration among all team members, beginning at project inception, is necessary in designing building systems.

Green schools provide a unique educational opportunity. Exploring the interdependence of building systems, design, and energy performance can foster ecological literacy. This study also helps students learn to think systemically about complex, real-world issues by seeing the relationships among buildings, human activities, resource consumption, and environmental impacts. If real-time monitoring is incorporated into the school's energy systems, students can see how the building responds to sunlight, moisture, temperature, and other environmental conditions, which can support the study of thermodynamics, earth sciences, and other subjects.

The Energy and Atmosphere (EA) section of the LEED Reference Guide for Green Building Design and Construction (LEED for New Construction, LEED for Schools, and LEED for Core & Shell) promotes three kinds of activities:

Tracking Building Energy Performance—Designing, Commissioning, Monitoring

Projects that achieve any level of LEED certification must at a minimum perform better than the average building. Specific levels of achievement beyond the minimum are awarded a proportional number of points. First, the building must be designed to operate at a high performance level. Next, it must be commissioned to ensure that what has been constructed meets the design intent. Third, a process for measurement and verification should be established to ensure the long-term performance of the building's energy systems.

The design of new facilities must be based on the designated mandatory and prescriptive requirements of ASHRAE 90.1-2007 or USGBC-approved local code, whichever is more stringent In addition, optimization of building energy performance beyond ASHRAE 90.1-2007 is required in EA Prerequisite 2, Minimum Energy Performance. This can be accomplished through building energy simulation modeling or prescriptive options.

Commissioning begins with the development of the owner's project requirements, followed at a minimum by additional steps that include creation of a formal commissioning plan, verification of equipment installation, and submission of a final report. Enhanced commissioning includes additional tasks, such as design and contractor submittal reviews, creation of a formal systems manual, verification of staff training, and a follow-up review before the warranty period ends.

Commissioning optimizes energy and water efficiency by ensuring that systems are operating as intended, thereby reducing the environmental impacts associated with energy and water usage. Additionally, commissioning can help ensure that indoor environmental quality is properly maintained. Properly executed commissioning can substantially reduce costs for maintenance, repairs, and resource consumption, and higher indoor environmental quality can enhance occupants' productivity.

Monitoring the performance of building systems begins with establishing a measurement and verification plan based on the best practices developed by the International Performance Measurement and Verification Protocol (IPMVP). The plan must cover at least one year of postconstruction occupancy. Monitoring involves using appropriate measuring instruments and can include the energy modeling.

Managing Refrigerants to Eliminate CFCs

The release of chlorofluorocarbons (CFCs) from refrigeration equipment destroys ozone molecules in the stratosphere through a catalytic process and harms Earth's natural shield from incoming ultraviolet radiation. CFCs in the stratosphere also absorb infrared radiation and create chlorine, a potent greenhouse gas. Banning the use of CFCs in refrigerants slows the depletion of the ozone layer and mitigates climate change.

The standard practice for new buildings is to install equipment that does not use CFC-based refrigerants. In LEED, points are awarded for systems that use refrigerants with a low potential for causing ozone depletion and climate change.

Using Renewable Energy

Teams have two opportunities to integrate renewable energy strategies into the LEED project: using on-site renewable energy systems and buying off-site green power. Projects can integrate systems that incorporate on-site electrical (photovoltaic, wind, hydro, wave, tidal, and biofuel-based), geothermal (deep-earth water or steam), or solar thermal (including collection and storage components) power. Credit for off-site renewable green power is achieved by contracting for a minimum purchase of green power.

Energy generation from renewable sources—such as solar, wind, and biomass—avoids air and water pollution and other environmental consequences associated with producing and consuming fossil and nuclear fuels. Although hydropower is considered renewable, it can have harmful environmental effects, such as degrading water quality, altering fish and bird habitats, and endangering species. Low-impact hydropower, if available, is recommended.

Renewable energy minimizes acid rain, smog, climate change, and human health problems resulting from air contaminants. In addition, using renewable resources avoids the consumption of fossil fuels, the production of nuclear waste, and the environmentally damaging operation of hydropower dams.

Renewable alternatives may be less expensive than traditional power in some areas. Utility and public benefit fund rebates may be available to reduce the initial cost of purchasing and installing renewable energy equipment. In some states, net metering can offset on-site renewable energy costs when excess electricity generated on site is sold back to the utility.

CREDIT	TITLE	NC	SCHOOLS	CS
EA Prerequisite 1	Fundamental Commissioning of Building Energy Systems	Required	Required	Required
EA Prerequisite 2	Minimum Energy Performance	Required	Required	Required
EA Prerequisite 3	Fundamental Refrigerant Management	Required	Required	Required
EA Credit 1	Optimize Energy Performance	1-19 points	1-19 points	3-21 points
EA Credit 2	On-site Renewable Energy	1-7 points	1-7 points	4 points
EA Credit 3	Enhanced Commissioning	2 points	2 points	2 points
EA Credit 4	Enhanced Refrigerant Management	2 points	1 point	2 points
EA Credit 5	Measurement and Verification	3 points	2 points	NA
EA Credit 5.1	Measurement and Verification—Base Building	NA	NA	3 points
EA Credit 5.2	Measurement and Verification—Tenant Submetering	NA	NA	3 points
EA Credit 6	Green Power	2 points	2 points	2 points

	NC	SCHOOLS	CS
Prerequisite	EA Prerequisite 1	EA Prerequisite 1	EA Prerequisite 1
Points	Required	Required	Required

Intent

To verify that the project's energy-related systems are installed, calibrated and perform according to the owner's project requirements, basis of design and construction documents.

Benefits of commissioning include reduced energy use, lower operating costs, reduced contractor callbacks, better building documentation, improved occupant productivity and verification that the systems perform in accordance with the owner's project requirements.

Requirements

NC, SCHOOLS & CS

The following commissioning process activities must be completed by the project team:

- Designate an individual as the commissioning authority (CxA) to lead, review and oversee the completion of the commissioning process activities.

  - The CxA must have documented commissioning authority experience in at least 2 building projects.

  - The individual serving as the CxA must be independent of the project's design and construction management, though the CxA may be an employee of any firms providing those services. The CxA may be a qualified employee or consultant of the owner.

  - The CxA must report results, findings and recommendations directly to the owner.

  - For projects smaller than 50,000 gross square feet, the CxA may be a qualified person on the design or construction teams who has the required experience.

- The owner must document the owner's project requirements. The design team must develop the basis of design. The CxA must review these documents for clarity and completeness. The owner and design team must be responsible for updates to their respective documents.

- Develop and incorporate commissioning requirements into the construction documents.

- Develop and implement a commissioning plan.

- Verify the installation and performance of the systems to be commissioned.

- Complete a summary commissioning report.

Commissioned Systems

Commissioning process activities must be completed for the following energy-related systems, at a minimum (if they are installed as part of the core and shell project):

- Heating, ventilating, air conditioning and refrigeration (HVAC&R) systems (mechanical and passive) and associated controls.
- Lighting and daylighting controls.
- Domestic hot water systems.
- Renewable energy systems (e.g. wind, solar).

	EA
NC	Prerequisite 1
SCHOOLS	Prerequisite 1
CS	Prerequisite 1

1. Benefits and Issues to Consider

Benefits of commissioning include reduced energy use, lower operating costs, fewer contractor callbacks, better building documentation, improved occupant productivity, and verification that the systems perform in accordance with the owner's project requirements.

Environmental Issues

Facilities that do not perform as intended may consume significantly more resources over their lifetimes than they should. Commissioning can minimize the negative impacts buildings have on the environment by helping verify that buildings are designed and constructed to operate as intended and in accordance with the owner's project requirements.

Economic Issues

If commissioning has not been previously included as part of the project delivery process, the costs associated with commissioning may be met with initial resistance. When the long-term benefits are taken into consideration, however, commissioning can be seen as a cost-effective way to ensure that the building is functioning as designed and that planned energy savings are realized in the operation of the building.

Improved occupant well-being and productivity are other potential benefits when building systems function as intended. Proper commissioning of building systems can reduce employee illness, tenant turnover and vacancy, and liability related to indoor air quality, and it can avoid premature equipment replacement.

2. Related Credits

The commissioning effort can affect many performance-based features encouraged in the LEED Rating System. Consider commissioning the energy-using systems addressed by the following credits:

- SS Credit 8: Light Pollution Reduction
- WE Credit 1: Water Efficient Landscaping
- WE Credit 2: Innovative Wastewater Technologies
- WE Credit 3: Water Use Reduction
- EA Credit 1: Optimize Energy Performance
- EA Credit 2: On-site Renewable Energy
- EA Credit 5: Measurement and Verification
- IEQ Prerequisite 1: Minimum Indoor Air Quality Performance
- IEQ Credit 1: Outdoor Air Delivery Monitoring
- IEQ Credit 2: Increased Ventilation
- IEQ Credit 5: Indoor Chemical and Pollutant Source Control
- IEQ Credit 6: Controllability of Systems
- IEQ Credit 7: Thermal Comfort

EA Prerequisite 1, Fundamental Commissioning, sets a minimum threshold for commissioning activities. Additional rigor and verification are awarded in this related credit:

- EA Credit 3: Enhanced Commissioning

3. Summary of Referenced Standards

There are no standards referenced for this prerequisite.

	EA
NC	Prerequisite 1
SCHOOLS	Prerequisite 1
CS	Prerequisite 1

4. Implementation

Relationship between Fundamental and Enhanced Commissioning

LEED for New Construction, LEED for Core & Shell, and LEED for Schools address building commissioning in 2 places, EA Prerequisite 1, Fundamental Commissioning of Building Energy Systems, and EA Credit 3, Enhanced Commissioning.

For LEED design and construction projects, the scope of services for the commissioning authority (CxA) and project team should be based on the owner's project requirements. The commissioning process activities must address the commissioned systems noted in the EA Prerequisite 1 requirements. Other systems, such as the building envelope, storm water management systems, water treatment systems, and information technology systems, may also be included in the commissioning process at the owner's discretion. EA Credit 3 requires that the CxA be involved early in the process to help facilitate a commissioning design review and a commissioning documentation review. As the project nears completion, enhanced commissioning requires oversight of staff training, a walk-through 10 months after completion, and the completion of a systems manual.

5. Timeline and Team

The commissioning process is a planned, systematic quality-control process that involves the owner, users, occupants, operations and maintenance staff, design professionals, and contractors. It is most effective when begun at project inception. All members of the project team are encouraged to participate in the commissioning activities as part of a larger commissioning team. The team approach to commissioning can speed the process and add a system of checks and balances.

The overall commissioning effort identified in both EA Prerequisite 1, Fundamental Commissioning of Building Energy Systems, and EA Credit 3, Enhanced Commissioning, is shown in Table 1 as divided into 12 basic steps. The steps are presented in sequential order; however, some tasks can begin at various points in the project or be completed at various points in the project. For example, the development of the commissioning plan may begin in the design phase, have multiple updates during the project, and be considered completed at some point during the construction phase.

Some of the steps are required for EA Prerequisite 1, Fundamental Commissioning of Building Energy Systems, and some are required for EA Credit 3, Enhanced Commissioning. Table 1 outlines the commissioning tasks, the team members primarily responsible for performing each project requirement, and the requirements common to EA Prerequisite 1 and EA Credit 3.

Table 1. Tasks and Responsibilities for EA Prerequisite 1 and EA Credit 3

Project Phases	Commissioning Tasks (Steps 1–12)	Rating System Tasks	Fundamental	Enhanced
Predesign, Design Phase				
Request for proposal Architect and engineer selection	1. Designate commissioning authority (CxA)	EA Prerequisite 1, Task 1 EA Credit 3, Task 1	Owner or project team	Owner or project team
Owners project requirements, basis of design	2. Document owner's project requirements; Develop basis of design	EA Prerequisite 1, Task 2	Owner or CxA* Design team	Owner or CxA* Design team
Schematic design	3. Review owner's project requirements and basis of design	EA Prerequisite 1, Task 2 EA Credit 3, Task 2	CxA**	CxA
Design development	4. Develop and implement commissioning plan	EA Prerequisite 1, Task 4	Project team or CxA*	Project team or CxA
Construction documents	5. Incorporate commissioning requirements into construction documents	EA Prerequisite 1, Task 3	Project team or CxA*	Project team or CxA
	6. Conduct commissioning design review prior to midconstruction documents	EA Credit 3, Task 2	N/A	CxA
Construction Phase				
Equipment procurement Equipment installation	7. Review contractor submittals applicable to systems being commissioned	EA Credit 3, Task 3	N/A	CxA
Functional testing Test and balance Performance testing acceptance	8. Verify installation and performance of commissioned systems	EA Prerequisite 1, Task 5	CxA	CxA
Operations and maintenance (O&M) manuals	9. Develop systems manual for commissioned systems	EA Credit 3, Task 4	N/A	Project team or CxA
O&M training	10. Verify that requirements for training are completed	EA Credit 3, Task 5	N/A	Project team or CxA
Substantial completion	11. Complete a summary commissioning report	EA Prerequisite 1, Task 6	CxA	CxA
Occupancy				
Systems monitoring	12. Review building operation within 10 months after substantial completion	EA Credit 3, Task 6	N/A	CxA

*Although EA Prerequisite 1 does not require the CxA to be on the project team until just before the equipment installation phase, if brought in earlier, he or she can also help the owner develop the project requirements and assist with other important commissioning tasks.

**Some commissioning tasks can be performed by the owner or other project team members. However, the review of the owner's project requirements and basis of design must be performed by the CxA. For EA Prerequisite 1, Fundamental Commissioning, this may be performed at any time before verification of equipment installation and acceptance.

STEP 1

Designate an individual as the commissioning authority (CxA) to lead, review, and oversee the completion of the commissioning process activities.

Ideally, the project team should designate an individual as the CxA as early as possible in the project timeline, preferably during predesign. The qualified individual designated as the CxA serves as an objective advocate for the owner and is responsible for the following:

- Directing the commissioning team and process in the completion of the commissioning requirements.

- Coordinating, overseeing, and/or performing the commissioning testing.
- Reviewing the results of the systems performance verification.

	EA
NC	Prerequisite 1
SCHOOLS	Prerequisite 1
CS	Prerequisite 1

For LEED projects, a qualified CxA should have experience with 2 other projects of similar managerial and technical complexity.

The owner may want to specify additional qualifications for the CxA, depending on the scope and nature of the commissioning. CxA certification programs are administered by various industry groups.

For projects larger than 50,000 square feet, the individual serving as the CxA on a LEED project must be independent of the project's design and construction teams.

The CxA may be a qualified staff member of the owner, an owner's consultant to the project, or an employee of a firm providing design and/or construction management services. The CxA may not, however, have responsibility for design (e.g., be the engineer of record) or for construction. The CxA must report results, findings, and recommendations directly to the owner.

For projects smaller than 50,000 square feet, the CxA may be a qualified staff member of the owner, an owner's consultant to the project, or an individual on the design or construction team (such as the engineer of record) and may have additional project responsibilities beyond leading the commissioning services.

For projects pursuing EA Credit 3, Enhanced Commissioning, the CxA may not be an employee of the design firm but may be contracted through this firm.

Table 2. Commissioning Authority Qualifications

Party Acting as Commissioning Authority (CxA)	Fundamental Commissioning Prerequisite[2, 4, 5]		Enhanced Commissioning Credit[3, 4, 5]
	< 50,000 (sf)	≥ 50,000 (sf)	
Employee or subcontractor of general contractor with construction responsibilities	Yes		
Employee or subcontractor, with construction responsibilities, of construction manager who holds constructor contracts	Yes		
Employee or subcontractor, with project design responsibilities, of the architect or engineer of record	Yes		
Disinterested employee or subcontractor of ceneral contractor or construction manager[1]	Yes	Yes	
Disinterested employee of architect or engineer[1]	Yes	Yes	
Disinterested subcontractor to architect or engineer[1]	Yes	Yes	Yes
Construction manager not holding constructor contracts	Yes	Yes	Yes
Independent consultant contracted to Owner	Yes	Yes	Yes
Owner employee or staff	Yes	Yes	Yes

[1] "Disinterested" means an employee or subcontractor who has no project responsibilities other than commissioning.
[2] EA Prerequisite 1 requirements (see Table 1 above).
[3] EA Credit 3 requirements (the CxA must review the owner's project requirements, basis of design, and design documents prior to midconstruction documents phase and perform a back-check).
[4] The same CxA overseeing the enhanced commissioning tasks must also oversee the fundamental commissioning tasks.
[5] Regardless of who employs the CxA, he or she "shall have documented commissioning authority experience in at least two building projects" and ideally meet the minimum qualifications of having "a high level of experience in energy systems design, installation and operation, commissioning planning and process management, hands-on field experience with energy systems performance, interaction, startup, balancing, testing, troubleshooting, operation, and maintenance procedures and energy systems automation control knowledge."
(From "Who Can Be the Commissioning Authority?" 01/03/06 LEED 2.2 Commissioning Subcommittee, posted under LEED Reference Documents, http://www.usgbc.org.)

	EA
NC	Prerequisite 1
SCHOOLS	Prerequisite 1
CS	Prerequisite 1

STEP 2

The owner must document the project requirements. The design team must develop the basis of design. The owner and design team are responsible for updates to their respective documents.

Clear and concise documentation of the owner's project requirements and the basis of design is a valuable part of any successful project delivery and commissioning process. These documents are used throughout the commissioning process to provide a baseline and focus for validating systems' energy and environmental performance.

Owner's Project Requirements

The owner's project requirements must be completed by the owner, CxA, and project team prior to the approval of contractor submittals of any commissioned equipment or systems. Updates during the design and construction process are the primary responsibility of the owner.

The owner's project requirements should detail the functional requirements of a project and the expectations of the building's use and operation as they relate to the systems to be commissioned. The owner's project requirements should address the following issues, as applicable to the project:

Owner and user requirements

Describe the primary purpose, program, and use of the proposed project (e.g., office building with data center, academic building addition and new gymnasium) and any pertinent project history. Provide any overarching goals relative to program needs, future expansion, flexibility, quality of materials, and construction and operational costs.

Environmental and sustainability goals

Describe any specific environmental or sustainability goals (e.g., LEED certification).

Energy efficiency goals

Describe overall project energy efficiency goals relative to the local energy code, ASHRAE standard, or LEED. Describe any goals or requirements for building orientation, landscaping, façade, fenestration, envelope and roof features that will affect energy use.

Indoor environmental quality requirements

For each program or area, describe the intended use, anticipated occupancy schedules, space environmental requirements (including lighting, temperature, humidity, acoustics, air quality, and ventilation), desired adjustability of system controls, and accommodations for after-hours use.

Equipment and system expectations

Describe the desired level of quality, reliability, type, automation, flexibility, and maintenance requirements for each of the systems to be commissioned. When known, provide specific efficiency targets, desired technologies, or preferred manufacturers for building systems.

Building occupant and O&M personnel requirements

Describe how the facility will be operated and by whom. Describe the desired level of training and orientation required for the building occupants to understand and use the building systems.

Basis of Design

The design team must document the basis of design for the systems to be commissioned prior to approval of contractor submittals of any commissioned equipment or systems. Updates during the design and construction process are the responsibility of the design team.

	EA
NC	Prerequisite 1
SCHOOLS	Prerequisite 1
CS	Prerequisite 1

The basis of design describes the systems to be commissioned and outlines any design assumptions that are not otherwise included in the design documents. This document should be updated with each subsequent design submission, with increasing specificity as applicable.

The basis of design should include the following, as applicable:

Primary design assumptions

Include space use, redundancy, diversity, climatic design conditions, space zoning, occupancy, operations, and space environmental requirements.

Standards

Include applicable codes, guidelines, regulations, and other references that will be put into practice.

Narrative descriptions

Include performance criteria for the HVAC&R systems, lighting systems, hot water systems, on-site power systems, and other systems to be commissioned.

STEP 3

The CxA must review the owner's project requirements and the basis of design for clarity and completeness. The owner and design team are responsible for updates to their respective documents.

The CxA must ensure that the basis of design reflects the owner's project requirements. Both documents must be reviewed by the CxA for completeness prior to the approval of contractor submittals of any commissioned equipment or systems.

STEP 4

Develop and implement a commissioning plan.

Unique to a particular project, the commissioning plan is the reference document that identifies the strategies, aspects, and responsibilities within the commissioning process for each phase of a project, for all project team members. This document outlines the overall process, schedule, organization, responsibilities, and documentation requirements of the commissioning process.

The commissioning plan is developed at the start of the commissioning process, preferably during design development, and is updated during the course of a project to reflect any changes in planning, schedule, or other aspects.

The following list outlines required components of the commissioning plan.

- Commissioning Program Overview
  - Goals and objectives.
  - General project information.
  - Systems to be commissioned.
- Commissioning Team
  - Team members, roles, and responsibilities.

EA	
NC	Prerequisite 1
SCHOOLS	Prerequisite 1
CS	Prerequisite 1

- Communication protocol, coordination, meetings, and management.
- Commissioning Process Activities
  - Documenting the owner's project requirements.
  - Preparing the basis of design.
  - Developing systems functional test procedures.
  - Verifying systems performance.
  - Reporting deficiencies and the resolution process.
  - Accepting the building systems.

Project teams pursuing the enhanced commissioning credit (EA Credit 3) may need to expand the commissioning plan to include the following commissioning process activities:

- Documenting the commissioning review process.
- Reviewing contractor submittals.
- Developing the systems manual.
- Verifying the training of operations personnel.
- Reviewing building operation after final acceptance.

Table 3. Required Commissioning Plan Components

Required Commissioning Plan Components
Brief overview of commissioning process.
List of all systems and assemblies included in commissioning authority's scope of work.
Identification of commissioning team and its responsibilities.
Description of management, communication, and reporting of commissioning process.
Overview of commissioning process activities for predesign, design, construction, and occupancy and operations phases, including development of owner's project requirements, review of basis of design, schematic design, construction documents and submittals, construction phase verification, functional performance test development and implementation, and 10-month warranty review.
List of expected work products.
List of commissioning process milestones.

STEP 5

Develop and incorporate commissioning requirements into the construction documents.

Typically, the project specifications are used to inform contractors of their responsibilities in the commissioning process. These specifications may describe the components listed in Table 4.

Often, all commissioning requirements are outlined in a section of the general conditions of the construction specifications. Placing all commissioning requirements in a single location gives responsibility for commissioning work to the general contractor, who can then assign responsibility to subcontractors. It is also valuable to refer to commissioning requirements on the drawings, in any bid forms, and in specification sections related to the systems to be commissioned.

Table 4. Commissioning Requirements for Construction Documents

	EA
NC	Prerequisite 1
SCHOOLS	Prerequisite 1
CS	Prerequisite 1

Commissioning team involvement.
Contractors' responsibilities.
Submittal review procedures for commissioned systems.
Operations and maintenance documentation, system manuals.
Meetings.
Construction verification procedures.
Startup plan development and implementation.
Functional performance testing.
Acceptance and closeout.
Training.
Warranty review site visit.

STEP 6

The CxA should conduct at least 1 commissioning design review of the owner's project requirements, basis of design, and design documents prior to midconstruction documents phase and back-check the review comments in the subsequent design submission.

This step is required by EA Credit 3, Enhanced Commissioning, but is not mandatory for achievement of EA Prerequisite 1, Fundamental Commissioning of Building Energy Systems.

The CxA should review the owner's project requirements, basis of design, and design documents to give the owner and design team an independent assessment of the state of the design for the commissioned systems. Typically, a design review performed by the CxA focuses on the following issues:

- Ensuring clarity, completeness, and adequacy of the owner's project requirements.

- Verifying that all issues discussed in the owner's project requirements are addressed adequately in the basis of design.

- Reviewing design documents for achieving the owner's project requirements and basis of design and coordination of commissioned systems.

Additional reviews by the CxA throughout the design and construction process may be advisable and appropriate depending on the project duration, phasing, and complexity.

STEP 7

The CxA should review contractor submittals applicable to the systems being commissioned for compliance with the owner's project requirements and basis of design. This review must be concurrent with the architect's or engineer's reviews and submitted to the design team and the owner.

This step is required by EA Credit 3, Enhanced Commissioning, but is not mandatory for achievement of EA Prerequisite 1, Fundamental Commissioning of Building Energy Systems.

The CxA should review the contractor submittals and identify any issues that might otherwise result in rework or change orders. The CxA should specifically evaluate the submittals for the following:

- Conformance with the owner's project requirements and basis of design.

- Fulfilling operation and maintenance requirements.

- Facilitating performance testing.

EA	
NC	Prerequisite 1
SCHOOLS	Prerequisite 1
CS	Prerequisite 1

The CxA review of contractor submittals does not typically replace or alter the scope or responsibility of the design team's role in approving submittals.

STEP 8

Verify the installation and performance of the systems to be commissioned.

Commissioning is conducted to verify the performance of commissioned systems as installed to meet the owner's project requirements, basis of design, and contract documents.

Verification of the installation and performance of commissioned systems typically includes 3 steps for each commissioned system: installation inspection, performance testing, and comparison of the results with the owner's project requirements and the basis of design.

- Installation inspections (sometimes called prefunctional inspections) are a systematic set of procedures intended to identify whether individual system components have been installed properly. Often this process occurs at startup of individual units of equipment and involves using "prefunctional checklists" or "startup and checkout forms" to ensure consistency in the inspections and document the process. Installation inspections may be performed by the CxA, the installing contractor, or others, depending on the procedures outlined in the commissioning plan. Installation inspections provide quality control to ensure that relatively minor issues (e.g., an improperly wired sensor, a control valve installed backward) are discovered and corrected prior to systems performance testing.

- Systems performance testing (sometimes called functional performance testing) occurs once all system components are installed, energized, programmed, balanced, and otherwise ready for operation under part- and full-load conditions. Testing should include each process in the sequence of operations under central and packaged equipment control, including startup, shutdown, capacity modulation, emergency and failure modes, alarms, and interlocks to other equipment.

Systems performance testing typically relies on testing procedures developed by the CxA specifically for the system to be tested. A wide variety of methods may be used to simulate and evaluate that the system being tested performs as expected (per the owner's project requirements, basis of design, and contract documents) in all modes of operation.

Systems performance testing may be performed by some combination of the CxA, the installing contractor, and others, depending on the procedures outlined in the commissioning specifications and the commissioning plan. It may reveal problems with the performance of the commissioned systems and may require significant follow-up and coordination among members of the project team.

- Evaluation of results is the final step. At each point in the process of installation inspections and systems performance testing, the CxA should evaluate whether the installed systems meet the criteria for the project as set forth by in the owner's project requirements and the basis of design documents.

Any discrepancies or deficiencies should be reported to the owner, and the team should work collaboratively to find an appropriate resolution.

STEP 9

Develop a systems manual that gives future operating staff the information needed to understand and optimally operate the commissioned systems.

This step is required by EA Credit 3, Enhanced Commissioning, but is not mandatory for achievement of EA Prerequisite 1, Fundamental Commissioning of Building Energy Systems.

Provide a systems manual in addition to the O&M manuals submitted by the contractor. The systems manual generally focuses on operating rather than maintaining the equipment, particularly the interactions.

	EA
NC	Prerequisite 1
SCHOOLS	Prerequisite 1
CS	Prerequisite 1

The systems manual should include the following for each commissioned system:

- Final version of the basis of design.

- System single-line diagrams.

- As-built sequences of operations, control drawings, and original setpoints.

- Operating instructions for integrated building systems.

- Recommended schedule of maintenance requirements and frequency, if not already included in the project O&M manuals.

- Recommended schedule for retesting of commissioned systems with blank test forms from the original commissioning plan.

- Recommended schedule for calibrating sensors and actuators.

STEP 10

Verify that the requirements for training operating personnel and building occupants have been completed.

This step is required by EA Credit 3, Enhanced Commissioning, but is not mandatory for achievement of EA Prerequisite 1, Fundamental Commissioning of Building Energy Systems.

Establish and document training expectations and needs with the owner. Many common training topics are identified in Table 5. Ensure that operations staff and occupants receive this training and orientation. Pay particular attention to new or uncommon sustainable design features that could be overridden or removed because of a lack of understanding. Document that the training was completed according to the contract documents.

Have a contract in place to review operation with O&M staff and occupants, including a plan for resolution of outstanding commissioning-related issues 10 months after substantial completion.

Table 5. Common Training Topics

Common Training Topics
General purpose of system (design intent).
Use of O&M manuals.
Review of control drawings and schematics.
Startup, normal operation, shutdown, unoccupied operation, seasonal changeover, manual operation, control setup and programming troubleshooting, and alarms.
Interactions with other systems.
Adjustments and optimizing methods for energy conservation.
Health and safety issues.
Special maintenance and replacement sources.
Occupant interaction issues.
System response to different operating conditions.

STEP 11

Complete a summary commissioning report.

After installation inspections and performance verification items have been completed, the

EA	
NC	Prerequisite 1
SCHOOLS	Prerequisite 1
CS	Prerequisite 1

results are tabulated and assembled into a commissioning report. Supporting information can be compiled as a Cx record but is not required in the summary.

The summary commissioning report should include the following:

- Executive summary of the process and the results of the commissioning program, including observations, conclusions, and any outstanding items.

- History of any system deficiencies identified and how they were resolved, including any outstanding issues or seasonal testing scheduled for a later date.

- Systems performance test results and evaluation.

- Confirmation from the CxA indicating whether individual systems meet the owner's project requirements, basis of design, and contract documents.

In addition, for projects pursuing EA Credit 3, Enhanced Commissioning, the summary commissioning report should include the following:

- Summary of the design review process.

- Summary of the submittal review process.

- Summary of the O&M documentation and training process.

Table 6. Commissioning Report Components

Commissioning Report Components
Owner's project requirements.
Project commissioning specifications.
Verification of installation (construction checklist).
Functional performance testing results and forms.
O&M documentation evaluation (EA Credit 3).
Training program evaluation (EA Credit 3).
Description of commissioning process benefits.
Outstanding issues.
Contract and plan for resolution within 10 months of substantial completion (EA Credit 3).

STEP 12

Ensure the involvement by the CxA in reviewing building operation 10 months after substantial completion with O&M staff and occupants. Include a plan for resolving outstanding issues.

This step is required by EA Credit 3, Enhanced Commissioning, but is not mandatory for achievement of EA Prerequisite 1, Fundamental Commissioning of Building Energy Systems.

The CxA should coordinate with the owner and the O&M staff to review the facility and its performance within 10 months of substantial completion. All unresolved construction deficiencies as well as any deficiencies identified in this postoccupancy review should be documented and corrected under manufacturer or contractor warranties.

The CxA review of the building operation with operations staff and occupants should identify any problems in operating the building as originally intended. Any significant issues identified by the CxA that will not be corrected should be recorded in the systems manual.

District Energy Systems

For projects with district energy systems, specific technical guidance can be found on USGBC's Registered Project Tools page (http://www.usgbc.org/projecttools). Follow the guidance in effect at the time of registration.

CS   Not all energy-related systems are installed as part of a Core & Shell project. Energy-related systems include heating, ventilating, air-conditioning, and refrigeration (HVAC&R) systems, associated controls, lighting, daylighting controls, domestic hot water systems, and renewable energy systems (wind, solar, etc.). Commissioning is required for any of these systems that are part of the Core & Shell project. Some commissioning activities will be limited because of the installed systems or components. Systems performance testing procedures are generally designed for complete system installations, and core and shell systems may not be complete. For example, in a core and shell office, the air-handling unit of the variable air volume (VAV) system may be installed, but the VAV boxes and ductwork may not yet be in place in the tenant spaces. Testing procedures may have to be changed or eliminated for systems that are incomplete. Document all the systems that will be installed as part of the Core & Shell project and commission these systems.

The precertification information should be included as a section of the commissioning plan.

6. Calculations
There are no calculations required for this prerequisite.

7. Documentation Guidance
As a first step in preparing to complete the LEED-Online documentation requirements, work through the following measures. Refer to LEED-Online for the complete descriptions of all required documentation.

- Update the commissioning plan at milestones throughout the project. This should happen, at a minimum, during the design development phase, the construction documents phase, and just prior to the kick-off meeting with the general contractor.

- Prepare a systems list that indicates which systems have been included within the scope of commissioning.

- Obtain confirmation that the commissioning authority has documented experience on at least 2 building projects.

- Retain copies of the owner's project requirements, basis of design, commissioning specifications, commissioning report, and systems manual.

	EA
NC	Prerequisite 1
SCHOOLS	Prerequisite 1
CS	Prerequisite 1

8. Examples

EXAMPLE 1

The example below demonstrates the interconnectedness of the owner's project requirements, basis of design, construction documents, commissioning plan, commissioning report, and systems manual.

Building Commissioning Documents

Systems Manual

- Final BOD
- System single line diagrams
- As-built sequence of operation, set points, etc.
- System operating instructions
- Maintenance schedule
- Retesting schedule

(Can also include OPR, record keeping procedures, optimization guidance, training materials, and commissioning process report)

Building Operating Plan
(Owner's Operating Requirements)

EA Prerequisite 1 for LEED for Existing Buildings: Operations & Maintenance

Owner's intent for the project

What is needed to implement the OPR

How the OPR will be physically achieved

Owner's Project

Requirements (OPR)
- Introduction
- Key Requirements (including LEED credit requirements)
- Project Scope/Objectives (including systems to be commissioned)
- Functional Spaces
- Occupancy
- Budget Considerations
- Performance Criteria (measureable and verifiable)
- OPR Revision History

ASHRAE Guideline 0-2005 ANNEX J

Updates and Revisions

Basis of Design (BOD)

- Systems and Assemblies
- Performance Criteria/Assumptions
- Descriptions (general building, envelope, HVAC, electrical, water, other)
- Governing Codes and Standards
- Owner Directives
- Design Development Guidelines (concepts, calculations, decisions, and product selections)
- BOD Revision History

ASHRAE Guideline 0-2005 ANNEX K

Updates and Revisions

Construction Documents (CD's)

- General Commissioning Requirements (The commissioning requirements specified in Division 1)
- Specific Requirements Specific commissioning requirements specified in each of the other applicable divisions of the project specifications

(See Table 4: Commissioning Requirements in Construction Documents)

Issues Log

Commissioning Plan

- Overview
- Commissioning Team
- Description of Commissioning Process Activities (by project phases – predesign, design, construction, occupancy)
- Schedules (Update throughout project)

ASHRAE Guideline 0-2005 ANNEX G

Updates and Revisions

Commissioning Report

- Executive Summary
- Deficiency Resolutions
- Systems Performance Test Results and Evaluation

(May also include summary of commissioning process activities – logs, progress reports, submittals, pre-functional testing, test and balance, functional tests, O&M manuals, and training)

EXAMPLE 2. Summary Report Outline

The outline below is a guide for what can be included in the summary commissioning report. There is no required order of presentation, only that these primary report components (applicable to the commissioning scope) are included in the report.

The final report that goes to the owner should include copies of issue and testing logs, meeting minutes, and interim process reports.

Summary Commissioning Report

Executive Summary

Provide a brief description of project (size, space types, occupancy, etc.), highlighting commissioning goals.

Provide a brief narrative on the scope of commissioning, highlighting the systems to be commissioned, process activities, and examples of significant issues:

1. Predesign activities (if any)

2. Design activities (if any)

3. Construction activities

4. Postoccupancy activities (if any)

Highlight any significant systemic issues that were uncovered during the commissioning process.

Provide recommendations for future project commissioning activities.

Deficiency Resolution

Provide a more detailed summary of the types of issues uncovered and how they were resolved. These issues are best presented in order of project phases (e.g., during design, during construction). A copy of the issues log is typically included as an appendix.

Systems Performance Test Results and Evaluation

Summarize observations on test results and evaluations for prefunctional tests, test and balance, functional tests, and postoccupancy testing (if applicable).

---

9. Exemplary Performance

This prerequisite is not eligible for exemplary performance under the Innovation in Design section.

10. Regional Variations

The significance of commissioning tasks may vary with the climate. For example, in northern regions, the functioning of heating systems, such as boilers, is a critical issue. Suboptimal performance for heating systems in northern climates can result in high utility bills, wasted energy, and added emissions. In the Southeast, humidity is an important consideration. Here, the introduction of hot, humid outside air must be controlled, and suboptimal performance for cooling systems could raise utility bills. In other regions of the country, equipment such as economizers and evaporative cooling will be used for extended periods and must function correctly.

EA	
NC	Prerequisite 1
SCHOOLS	Prerequisite 1
CS	Prerequisite 1

Regional climates tend to drive the selection of systems and the associated commissioning and maintenance decisions. For example, including the commissioning of the building envelope may be more important in certain regions than in others. Adding the commissioning of water systems may be important in arid regions.

Regardless of the types of equipment selected, each project can greatly benefit from a systematic approach to ensuring that the right equipment and systems are specified, ordered, installed, and tested to ensure proper operation and performance.

11. Operations and Maintenance Considerations

So that building systems operate effectively for the life of the building, use the commissioning process and outcomes to develop documents that will help facility managers run the building consistent with the design intent and equipment specifications. These documents should include the following:

- Building operating plan (owner's operating requirements). This plan defines the delivered conditions required by building management and occupants for the successful operation of a building. It identifies the spaces, uses, occupancy types, and required conditions. It includes the time-of-day schedules of every system, the mode of operation for each system when it is running, and the desired indoor conditions or setpoints for each schedule or mode. This information is initially developed in the basis of design.

- Systems narrative. The systems narrative is a summary description of each of the following types of base building systems installed in the project building: space heating, space cooling, ventilation, domestic water heating, humidification and/or dehumidification, and lighting. The description should include summaries of the central plant, distribution, and terminal units, as applicable, as well as the controls associated with these systems.

- Sequence of operations. The sequence of operations represents system-level documentation that defines what operational states are desired under what conditions. This can include which systems are running or idle; whether operations are full-load or part-load; staging or cycling of compressors, fans, or pumps; proper valve positions; desired system water temperatures and duct static air pressures, depending on other variables (e.g., outside air temperatures, room air temperatures, and/or relative humidity); and any reset schedules or occupancy schedules. The sequence of operations should include specific information on operating phases (warmup, occupied, unoccupied), setpoints and controls, and feedback systems to monitor performance.

- Preventive maintenance plan. This plan should reflect manufacturers' recommendations for the ongoing operation of the base building systems.

- Commissioning report. Ensure that the commissioning report adequately identifies problems that are likely to reemerge or merit particular attention on an ongoing basis.

12. Resources

Please see USGBC's LEED Registered Project Tools (http://www.usgbc.org/projecttools) for additional resources and technical information.

Websites

American Society of Heating, Refrigerating and Air-Conditioning Engineers
http://www.ashrae.org
ASHRAE advances the science of heating, ventilation, air conditioning, and refrigeration for the public's benefit through research, standards writing, continuing education, and publications. According to the ASHRAE website, "membership is open to any person associated with the field

including indoor air quality, building design and operation, and environmental control for food processing and industry."

	EA
NC	Prerequisite 1
SCHOOLS	Prerequisite 1
CS	Prerequisite 1

Building Commissioning Association

http://www.bcxa.org/resources/index.htm

BCxA promotes building commissioning practices that maintain high professional standards and fulfill building owners' expectations. The association offers a 5-day intensive course focused on how to implement the commissioning process and that is intended for commissioning authorities with at least 2 years of experience.

California Commissioning Collaborative

http://www.cacx.org

The California Commissioning Collaborative is a group of government, utility, and building services professionals committed to developing and promoting viable building commissioning practices in California. Its online library, available at http://resources.cacx.org/library/, has more than 300 resources, including articles, papers, guides, and sample commissioning documents.

California Department of General Services, Division of the State Architect, Adopting the Commissioning Process for the Successful Procurement of Schools

http://www.chps.net/links/pdfs/CommissioningProcessGuide.pdf

According to its publisher, this guide is "intended to be used by school districts, programmers, design professionals, contractors, operations and maintenance personnel, and commissioning authorities to understand the commissioning process and their role in it."

Energy Design Resources, Cx Assistant Commissioning Tool

http://www.ctg-net.com/edr2002/cx/

This web-based tool provides project-specific building commissioning information to design teams and enables users to evaluate probable commissioning cost, identify appropriate commissioning scope, and access project-related sample commissioning specifications.

Lawrence Berkeley National Laboratory, The Cost-Effectiveness of Commercial Buildings Commissioning: A Meta-Analysis of Existing Buildings and New Construction in the United States

http://eetd.lbl.gov/emills/PUBS/Cx-Costs-Benefits.html

Oregon Office of Energy, Commissioning for Better Buildings in Oregon

http://egov.oregon.gov/ENERGY/CONS/BUS/comm/bldgcx.shtml

This website and document of the same name contain a comprehensive introduction to the commissioning process, including research, financial benefits, and case studies.

Portland Energy Conservation Inc.

http://www.peci.org

PECI develops the field for commissioning services by helping building owners understand the value of commissioning and by producing process and technical information for commissioning providers. Their focus includes owners of private and public buildings and a range of building types. PECI manages the annual National Conference on Building Commissioning.

University of Wisconsin, Madison, Department of Engineering Professional Development

http://www.engr.wisc.edu

This program offers commissioning process training courses for building owners, architects, engineers, operations and maintenance staff, and other interested parties. The program also offers accreditation of commissioning process providers and managers.

Print Media

ASHRAE Guideline 0–2005: The Commissioning Process, (American Society of Heating, Refrigerating and Air-Conditioning Engineers, 2005). http://www.ashrae.org

	EA
NC	Prerequisite 1
SCHOOLS	Prerequisite 1
CS	Prerequisite 1

ASHRAE Guideline 1-1996: The HVAC Commissioning Process, (American Society of Heating, Refrigerating and Air-Conditioning Engineers, 1996). http://www.ashrae.org

ASHRAE Guideline 4-1993: Preparation of Operations & Maintenance Documentation for Building Systems (American Society of Heating, Refrigerating and Air-Conditioning Engineers: 1993). http://www.ashrae.org

The Building Commissioning Handbook, second edition, By John A. Heinz and Rick Casault (The Building Commissioning Association, 2004). http://www.bcxa.org

Commissioning Fact Sheets, Collaborative of High Performance Schools (CHPS). http://www.chps.net/manual/index.htm#com
These fact sheets explore how commissioning can help school districts ensure their schools are built to high performance standards.

Portland Energy Conservation Model Commissioning Plan and Guide Specifications (PECI, 1998). http://www.peci.org

Building Commissioning Guide, Office of Energy Efficiency and Renewable Energy Federal Energy Management Program (U.S. Department of Energy).
http://www.eere.energy.gov

Commissioning for Better Buildings in Oregon (Oregon Office of Energy). http://egov.oregon.gov/ENERGY/CONS/BUS/comm/bldgcx.shtml

13. Definitions

Basis of design includes design information necessary to accomplish the owner's project requirements, including system descriptions, indoor environmental quality criteria, design assumptions, and references to applicable codes, standards, regulations, and guidelines

Commissioning (Cx) is the process of verifying and documenting that a building and all of its systems and assemblies are planned, designed, installed, tested, operated, and maintained to meet the owner's project requirements.

The **commissioning authority (CxA)** is the individual designated to organize, lead, and review the completion of commissioning process activities. The CxA facilitates communication among the owner, designer, and contractor to ensure that complex systems are installed and function in accordance with the owner's project requirements.

The **commissioning plan** is a document that outlines the organization, schedule, allocation of resources, and documentation requirements of the commissioning process.

The **commissioning process** is a systematic quality-focused effort to ensure that building systems are designed, specified, procured, installed, and functioning in accordance with the owner's intent. The process uses planning, documentation, and verification of testing to review and oversee the activities of both designer and constructor.

The **commissioning report** documents the commissioning process, including a commissioning program overview, identification of the commissioning team, and description of the commissioning process activities.

Commissioning specification is the contract language used in the construction documents to detail the objective, scope, and implementation of the construction and acceptance phases of the commissioning process as developed in the design phase of the commissioning plan. This allows the construction contractor to ensure that these activities are considered in proposals for the construction work.

The **commissioning team** includes those people responsible for working together to carry out the commissioning process.

A **district energy system** is a central energy conversion plant and transmission and distribution system that provides thermal energy to a group of buildings (e.g., a central cooling plant on a university campus). Central energy systems that provide only electricity are not included.

Downstream equipment consists of all heating or cooling systems, equipment, and controls located within the project building and site associated with transporting thermal energy into heated or cooled spaces. This includes the thermal connection or interface with the district energy system, secondary distribution systems in the building, and terminal units.

Enhanced commissioning is a set of best practices that go beyond fundamental commissioning to ensure that building systems perform as intended by the owner. These practices include designating a commissioning authority prior to the construction documents phase, conducting commissioning design reviews, reviewing contractor submittals, developing a systems manual, verifying operator training, and performing a postoccupancy operations review.

Fundamental commissioning is a set of essential best practices used to ensure that building performance requirements have been identified early in the project's development and to verify that the designed systems have been installed in compliance with those requirements. These practices include designating a commissioning authority, documenting the owner's project requirements and basis of design, incorporating commissioning requirements into the construction documents, establishing a commissioning plan, verifying installation and performance of specified building systems, and completing a summary commissioning report.

An **installation inspection** examines components of the building systems to determine whether they are installed properly and ready for systems performance testing.

Owner's project requirements is a written document that details the ideas, concepts, and criteria that are determined by the owner to be important to the success of the project.

Systems performance testing is the process of determining the ability of commissioned systems to perform in accordance with the owner's project requirements, the basis of design, and construction documents.

Upstream equipment consists of all heating or cooling systems, equipment, and controls that are associated with a district energy system but are not part of the project building's thermal connection or do not interface with the district energy system. It includes the central energy plant and all transmission and distribution equipment associated with transporting the thermal energy to the project building and site.

Verification is the range of checks and tests carried out to determine whether components, subsystems, systems, and interfaces between systems operate in accordance with the contract documents.

	NC	SCHOOLS	CS
Prerequisite	EA Prerequisite 2	EA Prerequisite 2	EA Prerequisite 2
Points	Required	Required	Required

Intent

To establish the minimum level of energy efficiency for the proposed building and systems to reduce environmental and economic impacts associated with excessive energy use.

Requirements

SCHOOLS

The project must establish an energy performance rating goal for the facility design using EPA's Target Finder rating tool.

OPTION 1. Whole Building Energy Simulation

NC, SCHOOLS & CS

Demonstrate a 10% improvement in the proposed building performance rating for new buildings, or a 5% improvement in the proposed building performance rating for major renovations to existing buildings, compared with the baseline building performance rating.

Calculate the baseline building performance rating according to the building performance rating method in Appendix G of ANSI/ASHRAE/IESNA Standard 90.1-2007 (with errata but without addenda[1]) using a computer simulation model for the whole building project.

Appendix G of Standard 90.1-2007 requires that the energy analysis done for the building performance rating method include all energy costs associated with the building project. To achieve points using this credit, the proposed design must meet the following criteria:

- Comply with the mandatory provisions (Sections 5.4, 6.4, 7.4, 8.4, 9.4 and 10.4) in Standard 90.1-2007 (with errata but without addenda).

- Inclusion of all the energy costs within and associated with the building project.

- Compare against a baseline building that complies with Appendix G of Standard 90.1-2007 (with errata but without addenda[1]). The default process energy cost is 25% of the total energy cost for the baseline building. If the building's process energy cost is less than 25% of the baseline building energy cost, the LEED submittal must include documentation substantiating that process energy inputs are appropriate.

For the purpose of this analysis, process energy is considered to include, but is not limited to, office and general miscellaneous equipment, computers, elevators and escalators, kitchen cooking and refrigeration, laundry washing and drying, lighting exempt from the lighting power allowance (e.g., lighting integral to medical equipment) and other (e.g., waterfall pumps).

NC, SCHOOLS & CS (continued)

Regulated (non-process) energy includes lighting (for the interior, parking garage, surface parking, façade, or building grounds, etc. except as noted above), heating, ventilation and air conditioning (HVAC) (for space heating, space cooling, fans, pumps, toilet exhaust, parking garage ventilation, kitchen hood exhaust, etc.), and service water heating for domestic or space heating purposes.

Process loads must be identical for both the baseline building performance rating and the proposed building performance rating. However, project teams may follow the exceptional calculation method (ANSI/ASHRAE/IESNA Standard 90.1-2007 G2.5) to document measures that reduce process loads. Documentation of process load energy savings must include a list of the assumptions made for both the base and the proposed design, and theoretical or empirical information supporting these assumptions.

Projects in California may use Title 24-2005, Part 6 in place of ANSI/ASHRAE/IESNA Standard 90.1-2007 for Option 1.

OR

OPTION 2. Prescriptive Compliance Path: ASHRAE Advanced Energy Design Guide

NC & CS

Comply with the prescriptive measures of the ASHRAE Advanced Energy Design Guide appropriate to the project scope, outlined below. Project teams must comply with all applicable criteria as established in the Advanced Energy Design Guide for the climate zone in which the building is located.

PATH 1. ASHRAE Advanced Energy Design Guide for Small Office Buildings 2004

The building must meet the following requirements:

- Less than 20,000 square feet.
- Office occupancy.

PATH 2. ASHRAE Advanced Energy Design Guide for Small Retail Buildings 2006

The building must meet the following requirements:

- Less than 20,000 square feet.
- Retail occupancy.

PATH 3. ASHRAE Advanced Energy Design Guide for Small Warehouses and Self Storage Buildings 2008

The building must meet the following requirements:

- Less than 50,000 square feet.
- Warehouse or self-storage occupancy.

OPTION 2. Prescriptive Compliance Path: Advanced Energy Design Guide for K-12 School Buildings

SCHOOLS

Comply with all of the prescriptive measures identified in the Advanced Energy Design Guide for K-12 school buildings. Comply with all applicable criteria as established in the Advanced Energy Design Guide for the climate zone in which the building is located.

Projects using Option 2 must be less than 200,000 square feet.

OR

OPTION 3. Prescriptive Compliance Path: Advanced Buildings™ Core Performance™ Guide

NC, SCHOOLS & CS

Comply with the prescriptive measures identified in the Advanced Buildings™ Core Performance™ Guide developed by the New Buildings Institute. The building must meet the following requirements:

- Less than 100,000 square feet.

- Comply with Section 1: Design Process Strategies, and Section 2: Core Performance Requirements.

- Office, school, public assembly, and retail projects less than 100,000 square feet must comply with Section 1 and Section 2 of the Core Performance Guide.

- Other project types less than 100,000 square feet implement the basic requirements of the Core Performance Guide.

- Health care, warehouse and laboratory projects are ineligible for this path.

	EA
NC	Prerequisite 2
SCHOOLS	Prerequisite 2
CS	Prerequisite 2

1. Benefits and Issues to Consider

Environmental Issues

Energy efficiency reduces the environmental burdens associated with producing and using energy. Fossil fuels, such as coal and oil, are the most common source of energy used in buildings. However, these fuels are also finite resources. The process of extracting and consuming energy from fossil fuels causes many environmental impacts, including air and water pollution, land degradation, solid waste generation, and greenhouse gas emissions. Mounting evidence connects fossil-fuel based energy use with climate change as well as serious risks to environmental and human health and safety. Data from the U.S. Energy Information Administration show that buildings are responsible for almost half (48%) of all energy consumed and greenhouse gases emitted annually.[5] The U.S. Environmental Protection Agency (EPA) estimates that if the energy efficiency of commercial and industrial buildings improved by 10%, the resulting reductions in greenhouse gas emissions would be equivalent to taking about 30 million vehicles off the road.[6]

In addition to fossil fuels, other sources of energy also carry environmental costs. Hydropower activities, for example, can alter aquatic ecosystems and harm endangered species. Nuclear power plants pose an environmental threat when they are decommissioned without appropriate storage sites for spent fuel. Given both the environmental impacts inherent in most energy-production processes and our limited energy supplies, efficiency measures are an important strategy for managing the impacts of energy consumption.

Economic Issues

Optimizing energy performance can reduce overall operating costs. Changing operational strategies to avoid energy use—for example, turning off lights and HVAC systems when the building is unoccupied—can often be done at zero or very low initial cost and rapid payback. Even seemingly small conservation measures can be significant; for instance, replacing a single incandescent lamp with a fluorescent lamp, which uses up to 75% less energy, can save more than $30 in energy costs over the lifetime of the lamp.[7]

2. Related Credits

The LEED for New Construction, Core & Shell, and Schools rating systems address building energy efficiency in 2 places: EA Prerequisite 2, Minimum Energy Performance, and EA Credit 1, Optimize Energy Performance. Energy consumption for the building can be reduced by ensuring that the project exceeds the building code requirements for envelope, lighting, and HVAC systems. Further, energy use can be directly affected through the use of climatically appropriate roofing materials and careful optimization of exterior lighting. Refer to these credits:

- EA Credit 1: Optimize Energy Performance
- SS Credit 7.2: Heat Island Effect—Roof
- SS Credit 8: Light Pollution Reduction

In addition to reducing energy use through efficiency measures, project teams can mitigate energy use impacts by using renewable energy. Refer to these credits:

- EA Credit 2: On-site Renewable Energy
- EA Credit 6: Green Power

Building energy performance and indoor environmental quality issues, such as ventilation, occupant controllability, and the amount of daylight, must be carefully coordinated. Energy-efficient buildings should not compromise the health and well-being of occupants. Increased ventilation in buildings may require additional energy use, which may in turn cause air and water pollution. However, the additional need for energy can be mitigated by using heat-recovery ventilation and/or economizer strategies. Review the strategies in these credits:

	EA
NC	Prerequisite 2
SCHOOLS	Prerequisite 2
CS	Prerequisite 2

- IEQ Prerequisite 1: Minimum Indoor Air Quality Performance

- IEQ Credit 1: Outdoor Air Delivery Monitoring

- IEQ Credit 2: Increased Ventilation

- IEQ Credit 6: Controllability of Systems

- IEQ Credit 7: Thermal Comfort

- IEQ Credit 8: Daylight and Views

Because water use, especially domestic hot water, requires significant energy use, water use reductions can lead to energy savings. Consider meeting the requirements for these credits:

- WE Credit 3: Water Use Reduction

- WE Credit 4: Process Water Use Reduction (LEED for Schools only)

3. Summary of Referenced Standards

ANSI/ASHRAE/IESNA Standard 90.1–2007: Energy Standard for Buildings Except Low-Rise Residential

American National Standards Institute
American Society of Heating, Refrigerating and Air-Conditioning Engineers
Illuminating Engineering Society of North America

ANSI/ASHRAE/IESNA Standard 90.1–2007 was formulated by ASHRAE under an ANSI consensus process. IESNA is a joint sponsor of the standard.

ANSI/ASHRAE/IESNA Standard 90.1–2007 establishes minimum requirements for the energy-efficient design of buildings, with these exceptions: single-family houses; multifamily structures of 3 habitable stories or fewer above grade; manufactured houses (mobile and modular homes); buildings that do not use either electricity or fossil fuel; and equipment and portions of buildings systems that use energy primarily for industrial, manufacturing, or commercial processes. Building envelope requirements are provided for semiheated spaces, such as warehouses.

The standard provides criteria in the general categories shown in Table 1. Within each section tare mandatory provisions and additional prescriptive requirements. Some sections also contain a performance alternative.

The energy cost budget method (Section 11) allows the project team to exceed some of the prescriptive requirements, provided energy cost savings are made in other areas. However, in all cases, the mandatory provisions must still be met.

Table 1. Energy Standard Requirements Addressed by ASHRAE 90.1-2007

ASHRAE 90.1-2007 Components
Section 5. Building envelope (including semiheated spaces, such as warehouses)
Section 6. Heating, ventilation, and air-conditioning (including parking garage ventilation, freeze protection, exhaust air recovery, and condenser heat recovery for service water heating)
Section 7. Service water heating (including swimming pools)
Section 8. Power (including all building power distribution systems)
Section 9. Lighting (including exit signs, building exterior, grounds, and parking garages)
Section 10. Other equipment (including all permanently wired electrical motors)

EA	
NC	Prerequisite 2
SCHOOLS	Prerequisite 2
CS	Prerequisite 2

ASHRAE Advanced Energy Design Guide for Small Office Buildings 2004

http://www.ashrae.org

The *Advanced Energy Design Guide* series provides a sensible approach to achieving advanced levels of energy savings without having to resort to detailed calculations or analysis. This guide is for office buildings up to 20,000 square feet; such buildings make up the bulk of office space in the United States. The strategies provide benefits and savings for the building owner while maintaining the quality and functionality of the office space.

ASHRAE Advanced Energy Design Guide for Small Warehouses and Self Storage Buildings 2008

http://www.ashrae.org

The *Advanced Energy Design Guide* series provides a sensible and easy approach to achieving advanced levels of energy savings without having to resort to detailed calculations or analysis. This guide focuses on warehouses up to 50,000 square feet and self-storage buildings that use unitary heating and air-conditioning equipment; such facilities make up a significant amount of commercial warehouse space in the United States.

ASHRAE Advanced Energy Design Guide for K-12 School Buildings

http://www.ashrae.org

The *Advanced Energy Design Guide* series provides a sensible and easy approach to achieving advanced levels of energy savings without having to resort to detailed calculations or analysis. This guide focuses on elementary, middle and high school buildings, which have a wide variety of heating and air-conditioning requirements. Options for daylighting, an important component in schools, are included.

New Building Institute, Advanced Buildings™ Core Performance™ Guide

The Advanced Building program provides a prescriptive plan for exceeding the energy performance requirements of ASHRAE 90.1–2004. The program was designed to provide a predictable alternative to energy performance modeling and a simple set of criteria for increasing building energy performance significantly.

The Advanced Building Core Performance program updates and replaces the Advanced Building Benchmarked program. Core Performance is calibrated to exceed the requirements of ASHRAE 90.1–2004 in all climate zones.

Information about the Core Performance program requirements and a range of additional reference material is available at http://www.advancedbuildings.net.

Several aspects of the Core Performance program overlap with other LEED credits and prerequisites. Following the Core Performance program is not an alternative path to achieving any LEED credits other than EA Credit 1, Optimize Energy Performance, but Core Performance may facilitate earning other LEED credits and prerequisites.

ENERGY STAR® Program, Target Finder Rating Tool

http://www.energystar.gov/index.cfm?c=new_bldg_design.bus_target_finder

ENERGY STAR is a government-industry partnership managed by the U.S. Environmental Protection Agency and the U.S. Department of Energy. Target Finder is an online tool that can establish energy performance goals for a project. It uses data such as zip code and building type to calculate the estimated total energy use for the building, and then it assigns an energy performance rating on a scale of 1 to 100. The zip code is used to determine the climate conditions that the building would experience in a normal year (based on a 30-year climate average) and estimate energy use intensity for the target based on the energy fuel mix typical in the region. The tool displays the percentage electricity and natural gas assumption used to calculate design targets. The energy use intensity generated by Target Finder reflects the distribution of energy performance in commercial buildings derived from data in the U.S. Department of Energy's Commercial Buildings Energy Consumption Survey.

	EA
NC	Prerequisite 2
SCHOOLS	Prerequisite 2
CS	Prerequisite 2

The ratings generated by Target Finder provide a useful benchmark for estimating and comparing a building's energy use with that of other buildings and for determining a project's goals for energy efficiency. Assessing energy consumption early in the process enables teams to employ a holistic approach in making design decisions that improve the building's performance. Energy performance targets are more easily achieved if all the building's systems enhance one another; attempting to increase energy efficiency after construction is less successful because only small changes are possible without major disruption and additional cost.

Energy Computer Simulation Modeling Basics

As part of the school design process, an energy modeling expert should use approved energy simulation software, such as DOE-2, DOE EnergyPlus, Trane® Trace™700, or Carrier HAP-E20 II, to determine building energy performance. In such programs, the proposed building is first simulated to reflect the structure's current design. Next, following the rules of Appendix G, the proposed building model is modified to reflect a building that "just meets" the prescriptive requirements of ASHRAE 90.1-2007 as well as standard practice. The difference in energy use and cost between these 2 building models is then quantified. Creating such an energy model early in the design of a school informs decision makers about potential materials and systems and their impact on the school's energy performance.

4. Implementation

ASHRAE 90.1-2007 Overview

Each section of ASHRAE 90.1-2007 describes the scope of the provisions (e.g., definitions and relevant building elements), lists the mandatory provisions, and lists the requirements for complying with the standard.

Section 5. Building Envelope Requirements (ASHRAE 90.1-2007)

These requirements apply to enclosed spaces whose heating system has an output capacity of 3.4 Btu/hour/square foot or more, and to spaces whose cooling system has a sensible output capacity of 5 Btu/hour/square foot or more.

ASHRAE 90.1-2007 Section 5.4 describes mandatory provisions for insulation installation (5.4.1); window, skylight, and door ratings (5.4.2); and air leakage (5.4.3). Section 5.5 contains the prescriptive provisions for fenestration and opaque assemblies.

Figure 1. Climate Zones

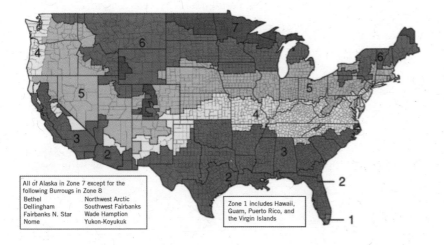

All of Alaska in Zone 7 except for the following Burrougs in Zone 8
Bethel   Northwest Arctic
Dellingham   Southwest Fairbanks
Fairbanks N. Star   Wade Hamption
Nome   Yukon-Koyukuk

Zone 1 includes Hawaii, Guam, Puerto Rico, and the Virgin Islands

	EA
NC	Prerequisite 2
SCHOOLS	Prerequisite 2
CS	Prerequisite 2

Each county in the United States is assigned to 1 of 8 climate zones (ASHRAE 90.1–2007, Table B-1). Climate zone assignments for Canada and other countries can be determined from ASHRAE 90.1–2007, Tables B-2 and B-3.

Prescriptive building envelope requirements are determined based on the building's climate zone classification (ASHRAE Standard 90.1–2007, Tables 5.5-1 to 5.5-8). For projects following the prescriptive compliance method, all building envelope components must meet the minimum insulation and maximum U-factor and solar heat gain coefficients (SHGC) requirements listed for the project's climate zone. Window area must be less than 40% of the gross wall area, and the skylight area must be less than 5% of the gross roof area.

The project may exceed the envelope prescriptive requirements if the project uses an energy simulation model to document points earned for EA Credit 1, Optimize Energy Performance.

Section 6. Heating, Ventilation and Air-Conditioning Requirements (ASHRAE 90.1–2007)

The requirements of Section 6 apply to all building HVAC systems. Mandatory provisions for HVAC performance are documented in ASHRAE 90.1–2007, Section 6.4, and include minimum system efficiency requirements (6.4.1), load calculation requirements (6.4.2), controls requirements (6.4.3), HVAC system construction and insulation requirements (6.4.4), and completion requirements (6.4.5).

ASHRAE 90.1–2007, Section 6.4.3.4, lists minimum control schemes for thermostats (off-hours, including setback and optimum start/stop), stair and elevator vents, outdoor air supply and exhaust vents, heat pump auxiliary heat, humidification and dehumidification, freeze protection, snow- and ice-melting systems, and ventilation for high-occupancy areas.

Because manual control is not addressed by the Appendix G modeling methodology, any manual control features of the project must be submitted under the exceptional calculation methodology for case-by-case review. Be prepared to demonstrate convincingly that a manual control strategy is appropriate and workable for this project.

ASHRAE 90.1–2007, Section 6.5, provides a prescriptive compliance option. Prescriptive provisions are included for air and water economizers (6.5.1); simultaneous heating and cooling limitations (6.5.2); air system design and control, including fan power limitation and variable speed drive control (6.5.3); hydronic system design and control, including variable flow pumping (6.5.4); heat rejection equipment (6.5.5); energy recovery from exhaust air and service water heating systems (6.5.6); kitchen and fume exhaust hoods (6.5.7); radiant heating systems (6.5.8); and hot gas bypass limitations (6.5.9).

Project teams must meet the minimum efficiency requirements for system components listed in ASHRAE 90.1–2007, Tables 6.8.1A-G, even if using the energy cost budget or performance-based compliance methods.

Exceptions

For projects served by existing HVAC systems, such as a central plant on a campus or district heating and cooling, the exception to Section 6.1.1.2 applies. The existing systems and existing equipment are not required to comply with the standard.

Occupant-controlled swirl floor diffusers meet the intent of the ASHRAE 90.1–2007, Section 6.4.3.1, requirement for individually controlled zone controls, similar to operable windows in a naturally ventilated and cooled space.

Section 7. Service Water Heating Requirements (ASHRAE 90.1–2007)

These requirements include mandatory provisions (7.4) and a choice of prescriptive (7.5) or performance-based compliance (Appendix G). Mandatory provisions include requirements for load calculations (7.4.1), efficiency (7.4.2), piping insulation (7.4.3), controls (7.4.4), pool heaters and pool covers (7.4.5), and heat traps for storage tanks (7.4.6).

	EA
NC	Prerequisite 2
SCHOOLS	Prerequisite 2
CS	Prerequisite 2

Section 8. Power Requirements (ASHRAE 90.1-2007, Section 8.4.1)

These requirements address mandatory provisions related to voltage drop.

Section 9. Lighting Requirements (ASHRAE 90.1-2007)

These requirements apply to all lighting installed on the building site, including interior and exterior lighting. Mandatory provisions include minimum requirements for controls (9.4.1), tandem wiring (9.4.2), luminaire source efficacy for exit signs (9.4.3), exterior lighting power definitions (9.4.5), and luminaire source efficacy for exterior lighting fixture (9.4.4). Per 9.4.1.2, occupancy controls are required in classrooms, conference rooms, and employee lunch and break rooms. Interior lighting compliance must be documented using either the building area method (9.5) or the space-by-space method (9.6). See the Implementation and Calculations sections for additional guidance on lighting power calculations.

Section 10. Other Equipment Requirements (ASHRAE 90.1-2007)

This section includes mandatory provisions for electric motors (10.4).

Section 11. Energy Cost Budget Method (ASHRAE 90.1-2007)

The energy cost budget method is no longer an alternative option for compliance with this prerequisite.

Appendix G. The Performance Rating Method (ASHRAE 90.1-2007)

Appendix G demonstrates the required method for EA Credit 1, Optimize Energy Performance. If the project is using the performance rating method to achieve points under EA Credit 1, the EA Credit 1 documentation can be used to prove compliance with the performance requirements (the second part) of this prerequisite. The performance rating method does not exempt the project from also meeting the mandatory ASHRAE 90.1-2007 requirements listed for this prerequisite.

EA Credit 1 includes a more detailed discussion of the performance rating method.

Additional Strategies

In a campus setting with a central plant, improving plant efficiency affects all buildings on the district heating and cooling system. By installing a combined heat and power system designed to meet thermal and electrical base loads, a facility can greatly increase its operational efficiency and decrease energy costs.

Guidance on Combined Heat and Power (CHP) Systems

See EA Credit 1, Optimize Energy Performance, for guidance on CHP systems supplying electricity and/or recovered thermal energy.

Credit for Natural Ventilation Strategies

Projects may be able to take credit for natural ventilation in the energy modeling. However, projects demonstrating natural ventilation savings will be evaluated on a case-by-case basis. To demonstrate the process and the results, be prepared to provide the following:

- Detailed project description.

EA	
NC	Prerequisite 2
SCHOOLS	Prerequisite 2
CS	Prerequisite 2

- Clear identification of the areas with natural ventilation.

- Detailed description or references that document the modeling algorithms and/or methodology for the natural ventilation portion of the energy model.

- All thermostat, fan, infiltration, and other appropriate schedules for naturally ventilated areas.

- Verification that the range of unmet load hours is similar for both the design and the baseline building, to ensure that savings are not claimed for hours outside the control parameters.

The team must clearly demonstrate that the operational schedule used to model the natural ventilation system aligns with occupants' anticipated behavior. For example, the model cannot assume that natural ventilation will occur when no one is in the building to operate the system.

CS   In Core & Shell buildings, not all the components addressed by ASHRAE 90.1–2007 may be designed or defined. For these types of projects, show compliance for the scope of work that is controlled by the core and shell project team. For example, if there is no lighting scope of work in the Core & Shell, the team need not demonstrate compliance with the lighting standard but must show compliance with the other provisions.

5. Timeline and Team

The project team should start the energy simulation modeling early in the design phase to gain insights for design decisions and an indication of how to achieve certain levels of energy cost reductions.

6. Calculations

Follow the calculation and documentation methodology as prescribed in ASHRAE 90.1–2007. Record all calculations on the appropriate forms (Table 2). The forms and further information regarding the calculation methodology are available in the ASHRAE 90.1–2007 User's Guide.

Table 2. Documenting Compliance with ASHRAE 90.1–2007

ASHRAE 90.1–2007 Compliance Forms
Mandatory Measures: All Projects
Building envelope compliance documentation (Part I), mandatory provisions checklist
HVAC compliance documentation (Part II), mandatory provisions checklist
Service water heating compliance documentation (Part I), mandatory provisions checklist
Lighting Compliance Documentation (Part I), Mandatory Provisions Checklist
Prescriptive Requirements: Projects Using Prescriptive Compliance Approach
Building envelope compliance documentation (Part II)
HVAC compliance documentation (Part I, for buildings less than 25,000 square feet using simplified approach, and Part III, for all other buildings
Service water heating compliance documentation
Performance Requirements: Projects Using Performance Compliance Approach
Performance rating report (for EA Credit 1, Optimize Energy Performance)
Table documenting energy-related features included in the design and including all energy features that differ between the baseline design and proposed design models

Area Calculations

A conditioned conservatory or greenhouse space cannot be excluded on the basis of horticultural "process loads" when it qualifies as an amenity for the occupants or users of the facility rather than as the primary facility function (see ASHRAE 90.1–2007's definition of process load). Conditioning for the conservatory space must be included in the energy simulation and savings calculations.

To calculate the gross floor area of a building, include both conditioned and unconditioned spaces. If the area exceeds the 25,000-square-foot maximum stipulated in ASHRAE 90.1–2007, HVAC systems must comply with the mandatory requirements in Section 6.4. However, only those areas that are heated or cooled per Section 2.2(1) of the standard must meet the envelope requirements.

	EA
NC	Prerequisite 2
SCHOOLS	Prerequisite 2
CS	Prerequisite 2

Lighting Power Calculations

Lighting power calculations for performance-based compliance methods must use either the building area method or the space-by-space method. For both methods, the total installed interior lighting power is calculated by summing the luminaire wattages for all permanently installed general, task and furniture lighting, where the luminaire wattage includes lamps, ballasts, current regulators, and control devices.

Building area method calculations can be used only if the project involves the entire building or a single independent occupancy within a multioccupancy building. Allowable lighting power for this method is calculated by multiplying the allowable lighting power density for the given building type (found in ASHRAE 90.1–2007, Table 9.5.1) by the interior building area.

Allowable lighting for the space-by-space method is determined by multiplying the allowable lighting power density for each space function in the building (found in ASHRAE 90.1–2007, Table 9.6.1) by the corresponding area for each space function, then summing the results. The project complies if the total installed interior lighting power is lower than the interior lighting power allowance calculated using either the building area or the space-by-space method.

The exterior lighting power allowance is calculated by multiplying the allowed lighting power for each exterior surface (found in ASHRAE 90.1–2007, Table 9.4.5) by the total area or length associated with that surface, summing the results, and then multiplying this number by 1.05. For nontradable exterior lighting surfaces, the allowed lighting power can be used for the specific application only; it cannot be traded among surfaces or with other exterior lighting.

7. Documentation Guidance

As a first step in preparing to complete the LEED-Online documentation requirements, work through the following measures. Refer to LEED-Online for the complete descriptions of all required documentation.

- For ASHRAE compliance, list any addenda used, and retain copies of ASHRAE compliance forms.

- Determine the climate zone for the project location.

- Calculate energy use by type.

- Maintain a list of energy end uses for the project building (for both the baseline case and the design case).

- If the project is using a computer energy simulation, adhere to Appendix G of ASHRAE 90.1–2007 (or equivalent local code) and retain the final report indicating the annual energy cost of the baseline and design cases.

- If the project is using the prescriptive compliance path, assemble documentation demonstrating that the project meets all applicable requirements.

8. Examples

Energy simulation software packages, such as DOE-2 or EnergyPlus, enable the creation of a representative model. Energy simulation software can be used to demonstrate compliance with the

	EA
NC	Prerequisite 2
SCHOOLS	Prerequisite 2
CS	Prerequisite 2

performance requirements of ASHRAE 90.1-2007, as an alternative to the prescriptive requirements. Figure 2 shows an example of a 3-D building model.

Figure 2. Screenshot from Building Simulation Software

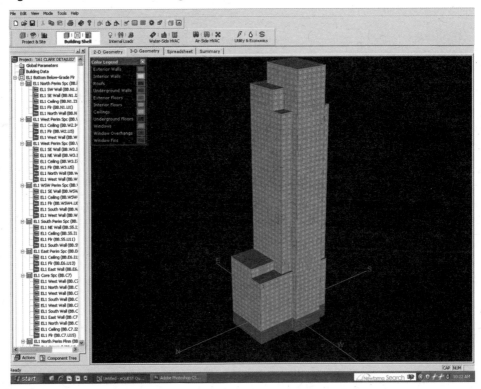

9. Exemplary Performance

This prerequisite is not eligible for exemplary performance under the Innovation in Design section.

10. Regional Variations

Regional variance is already represented in ASHRAE 90.1-2007 under 8 climatic zones and 3 climatic subzones, which account for the climate types and their minimum envelope and glazing property requirements.

11. Operations and Maintenance Considerations

Once the building is completed, it is critical to maintain efforts to support energy efficiency. Ensuring that the building systems are functioning properly and tracking energy use can save energy and operating costs. LEED for Existing Buildings: Operations & Maintenance covers this topic in EA Prerequisite 2, Minimum Energy Efficiency Performance, and EA Credit 1, Optimize Energy Performance.

Promote energy efficiency by ensuring that the building management has a firm grasp of anticipated energy loads as well as the necessary tools for tracking and analysis.

Provide facility management with a breakdown of anticipated end energy uses based on any modeling results. The breakdown will provide a baseline to help operators evaluate ongoing energy consumption patterns and catch any system inefficiencies.

Enable linkages with EPA's ENERGY STAR software tools. Register the building with the ENERGY STAR Portfolio Manager tool and input basic building data (e.g., location, square footage). Analyze anticipated building energy performance using the ENERGY STAR Target Finder tool and make sure the facility owner or manager has access to this analysis.

12. Resources

Please see USGBC's LEED Registered Project Tools (http://www.usgbc.org/projecttools) for additional resources and technical information.

	EA
NC	Prerequisite 2
SCHOOLS	Prerequisite 2
CS	Prerequisite 2

Websites

Advanced Buildings, Technologies and Practices

http://www.advancedbuildings.org

This online resource, supported by Natural Resources Canada, presents energy-efficient technologies, strategies for commercial buildings, and pertinent case studies.

American Council for an Energy-Efficient Economy

http://www.aceee.org

ACEEE is a nonprofit organization dedicated to advancing energy efficiency through technical and policy assessments; advising policymakers and program managers; collaborating with businesses, public interest groups, and other organizations; and providing education and outreach through conferences, workshops, and publications.

ENERGY STAR® Buildings Upgrade Manual

http://www.energystar.gov/index.cfm?c=business.bus_upgrade_manual

This manual is a strategic guide for planning and implementing energy-saving building upgrades. It provides general methods for reviewing and adjusting system control settings, plus procedures for testing and correcting calibration and operation of system components such as sensors, actuators, and controlle devices.

New Buildings Institute, Inc.

http://www.newbuildings.org

The New Buildings Institute is a nonprofit, public-benefits corporation dedicated to making buildings better for people and the environment. Its mission is to promote energy efficiency in buildings through technology research, guidelines, and codes.

U.S. Department of Energy, Building Energy Codes Program

http://www.energycodes.gov

The Building Energy Codes program provides comprehensive resources for states and code users, including news, compliance software, code comparisons and the Status of State Energy Codes database. The database includes state energy contacts, code status, code history, DOE grants awarded, and construction data. The program is also updating the COMCheck-EZ™ compliance tool to include ANSI/ASHRAE/IESNA 90.1–2007. This compliance tool includes the prescriptive path and trade-off compliance methods. The software generates appropriate compliance forms as well.

U.S. Department of Energy, Office of Energy Efficiency and Renewable Energy

http://www.eere.energy.gov

This extensive website for energy efficiency links to DOE-funded sites that address buildings and energy. Of particular interest is the tools directory, which includes the Commercial Buildings Energy Consumption Tool for estimating end-use consumption in commercial buildings. This tool allows the user to define a set of buildings by principal activity, size, vintage, region, climate zone, and fuels (main heat, secondary heat, cooling, and water heating) and view the resulting energy consumption and expenditure estimates in tabular form.

U.S. EPA, Combined Heat and Power Partnership

http://www.epa.gov/chp

Information on cogeneration, also called combined heat and power, is available from EPA through the CHP Partnership. The CHP Partnership is a voluntary program seeking to reduce the environmental impact of power generation by promoting the use of CHP. The Partnership works closely with energy users, the CHP industry, state and local governments, and other clean energy stakeholders to facilitate the development of new projects and to promote their environmental and economic benefits.

Print Media

ANSI/ASHRAE/IESNA Standard 90.1–2007 User's Manual (ASHRAE, 2008).

The ANSI/ASHRAE/IESNA 90.1–2007 User's Manual was developed as a companion document to the ANSI/ASHRAE/IESNA 90.1–2007, Energy Standard for Buildings Except Low-Rise Residential Buildings. The manual explains the new standard and includes sample calculations, useful reference material, and information on the intent and application of the standard. It is abundantly illustrated and contains numerous examples and tables of reference data. It also includes a complete set of compliance forms and worksheets that can be used to document compliance with the standard. The manual is helpful to architects and engineers applying the standard to the design of buildings, plan examiners and field inspectors who must enforce the standard in areas where it is adopted as code, and contractors who must construct buildings in compliance with the standard. A compact disk is included that contains electronic versions of the compliance forms found in the manual.

13. Definitions

Baseline building performance is the annual energy cost for a building design intended for use as a baseline for rating above standard design, as defined in ASHRAE 90.1-2007, Appendix G.

Combined heat and power (**CHP**), or **cogeneration**, generates both electrical power and thermal energy from a single fuel source.

An **economizer** is a device used to make building systems more energy efficient. Examples include HVAC enthalpy controls, which are based on humidity and temperature.

An **energy simulation model**, or **energy model**, is a computer-generated representation of the anticipated energy consumption of a building. It permits a comparison of energy performance, given proposed energy efficiency measures, with the baseline.

An **ENERGY STAR** rating is a measure of a building's energy performance compared with that of similar buildings, as determined by the ENERGY STAR Portfolio Manager. A score of 50 represents average building performance.

Interior lighting power allowance is the maximum lighting power (in watts) allowed for the interior of a building.

Lighting power density is the installed lighting power, per unit area.

Proposed building performance is the annual energy cost calculated for a proposed design, as defined in ASHRAE 90.1-2007, Appendix G.

	NC	SCHOOLS	CS
Prerequisite	EA Prerequisite 3	EA Prerequisite 3	EA Prerequisite 3
Points	Required	Required	Required

Intent

To reduce stratospheric ozone depletion.

Requirements

NC, SCHOOLS & CS

Zero use of chlorofluorocarbon (CFC)-based refrigerants in new base building heating, ventilating, air conditioning and refrigeration (HVAC&R) systems. When reusing existing base building HVAC equipment, complete a comprehensive CFC phase-out conversion prior to project completion. Phase-out plans extending beyond the project completion date will be considered on their merits.

EA	
NC	Prerequisite 3
SCHOOLS	Prerequisite 3
CS	Prerequisite 3

1. Benefits and Issues to Consider

Environmental Issues

Chlorofluorocarbons (CFCs), used in refrigeration equipment, cause significant damage to Earth's protective ozone layer when they are released into the atmosphere. The reaction between CFC and ozone molecules in the stratosphere destroys the ozone and reduces the stratosphere's ability to absorb a portion of the sun's ultraviolet radiation.

As part of the U.S. commitment to implement the Montreal Protocol, EPA has established regulations for responsible management of ozone-depleting substances. In compliance with the Montreal Protocol, CFC production in the United States ended in 1995. Not using CFC-based refrigerants in new equipment and implementing a phase-out of CFC-based refrigerants in existing equipment have helped slow the depletion of the ozone layer.

Economic Issues

The standard practice in new buildings is to install equipment that does not use CFCs. However, existing buildings may already have CFC-based refrigeration equipment. Energy, demand, and maintenance savings realized from upgrading equipment may offset the cost of converting or replacing existing systems. If savings offset costs, a CFC phase-out plan must be implemented to earn this prerequisite. If savings do not offset costs, detailed calculations and the results of a qualified third-party audit must confirm that CFC conversion or replacement is not economically feasible.

2. Related Credits

This prerequisite represents a minimum threshold for refrigerant selection. To achieve greater environmental benefit, install environmentally preferable refrigerants or no refrigerants, as detailed in this credit:

- EA Credit 4: Enhanced Refrigerant Management

3. Summary of Referenced Standard

U.S. EPA Clean Air Act, Title VI, Section 608, Compliance with the Section 608 Refrigerant Recycling Rule
http://www.epa.gov/ozone/title6/608/608fact.html
Under Section 608 of the Clean Air Act, EPA has established regulations on using and recycling ozone-depleting compounds. An overview of the pertinent regulations and information about compliance can be found on this website.

4. Implementation

Replace or retrofit any CFC-based refrigerants in the existing base building HVAC&R and fire-suppression systems. If the building is connected to an existing chilled water system, that system must either be CFC-free or the project team must demonstrate a commitment to phasing out CFC-based refrigerants no later than 5 years after the project is completed. An alternative compliance path for buildings connected to a central chilled water system requires an economic analysis (defined below) showing that system replacement or conversion is not economically feasible. Before phasing out CFC-based refrigerants, or if an economic analysis shows that system replacement or conversion is not feasible, reduce annual leakage of CFC-based refrigerants to 5% or less using EPA Clean Air Act, Title VI, Rule 608 procedures governing refrigerant management and reporting.

Consider the characteristics of various CFC substitutes. Refrigerants have varying applications, lifetimes, ozone-depleting potentials (ODPs), and global-warming potentials (GWPs). **Table 1** shows the ODPs and direct GWPs of many common refrigerants. Choose refrigerants that have short environmental lifetimes, small ODP values, and small GWP values.

No ideal alternative for CFCs has been developed, and some alternatives are not suitable for retrofits. See EPA's list of substitutes for ozone-depleting substances (http://www.epa.gov/ozone/snap).

Table 1. Ozone Depletion and Global Warming Potentials of Refrigerants (100-Year Values)

Chlorofluorocarbons	ODP	GWP	Common Building Applications
CFC-11	1.0	4,680	Centrifugal chillers
CFC-12	1.0	10,720	Refrigerators, chillers
CFC-114	0.94	9,800	Centrifugal chillers
CFC-500	0.605	7,900	Centrifugal chillers, humidifiers
CFC-502	0.221	4,600	Low-temperature refrigeration
Hydrochlorofluorocarbons			
HCFC-22	0.04	1,780	Air-conditioning, chillers
HCFC-123	0.02	76	CFC-11 replacement
Hydrofluorocarbons			
HFC-23	~ 0	12,240	Ultra-low-temperature refrigeration
HFC-134a	~ 0	1,320	CFC-12 or HCFC-22 replacement
HFC-245fa	~ 0	1,020	Insulation agent, centrifugal chillers
HFC-404A	~ 0	3,900	Low-temperature refrigeration
HFC-407C	~ 0	1,700	HCFC-22 replacement
HFC-410A	~ 0	1,890	Air conditioning
HFC-507A	~ 0	3,900	Low-temperature refrigeration
Natural Refrigerants			
Carbon dioxide (CO_2)	0	1.0	
Ammonia (NH_3)	0	0	
Propane	0	3	

Economic Analysis

An alternative compliance path requires an audit by a third party showing that it is not economically feasible to replace or convert the system. (Both replacement and conversion must be assessed.) The replacement or conversion of a chiller is considered not economically feasible if the simple payback of the replacement or conversion will be longer than 10 years. The economic assessment must be performed by a third party, defined as a qualified company that is not otherwise employed by the building owner or property manager.

Minimize Refrigerant Leakage

Refrigerants cannot damage the atmosphere if they are contained and never released to the environment. Unfortunately, in real-world applications, some or all refrigerants in HVAC&R equipment leak out, often undetected, during installation, operation, charging, servicing, or decommissioning of equipment, both indoor and outdoor.

Under Section 608 of the Clean Air Act of 1990, EPA's regulations

- require practices that maximize recycling of ozone-depleting compounds (both CFCs and HCFCs) during the servicing and disposal of air-conditioning and refrigeration equipment;

- set certification requirements for recycling and recovery equipment, technicians, and reclaimers, and prohibit the sale of refrigerant to uncertified technicians;

- require persons servicing or disposing of air-conditioning and refrigeration equipment to confirm with EPA that they have acquired recycling or recovery equipment and are complying with the requirements of the rule;

- require the repair of substantial leaks in air-conditioning and refrigeration equipment with a charge of greater than 50 pounds;

- establish safe disposal requirements to ensure removal of refrigerants from goods that enter the waste stream with the charge intact (e.g., vehicle air-conditioners, home refrigerators, and room air-conditioners); and

- prohibit individuals from knowingly venting ozone-depleting compounds that are used as refrigerants (generally CFCs and HCFCs) into the atmosphere while maintaining, servicing, repairing, or disposing of air-conditioning or refrigeration equipment (including appliances).

Adhering to federal regulation and best practices for refrigerant management and equipment maintenance can minimize refrigerant emissions. Manufacturers may offer leakage rate guarantees for certain types of major HVAC&R equipment (such as chillers) as part of a long-term service contract.

The program used to minimize leakage should specify refrigerant loss-minimization procedures and systems to meet annual loss-minimizing standards and reporting requirements. See EPA's Complying with the Section 608 Refrigerant Recycling rule for guidance.

District Energy Systems

For projects with district energy systems, specific technical guidance can be found on USGBC's Registered Project Tools (http://www.usgbc.org/projecttools). Follow the guidance in effect at the time of registration.

5. Timeline and Team

Consult with a mechanical engineer or HVAC&R specialist to confirm the presence of CFC-based refrigerants in the base building HVAC&R systems. If CFC-based refrigerants are located, the building owner should develop a phase-out plan and convert to less environmentally harmful refrigerants. Do not install any systems with CFC-based refrigerants.

6. Calculations

There are no calculations associated with this prerequisite.

7. Documentation Guidance

As a first step in preparing to complete the LEED-Online documentation requirements, work through the following measures. Refer to LEED-Online for the complete descriptions of all required documentation.

- For major renovations, where applicable, develop and track the phase-out plan.

- Assemble manufacturers' documentation demonstrating the type of refrigerant used by the base building's HVAC&R systems.

8. Examples

There are no examples for this prerequisite.

9. Exemplary Performance

This prerequisite is not eligible for exemplary performance under the Innovation in Design section.

10. Regional Variations

There are no regional variations for this prerequisite.

11. Operations and Maintenance Considerations

Provide facility operators with complete records (such as LEED application materials) for all refrigerant-containing systems, including fire suppression. Ensure that equipment labels are in place and accessible to building operators, and provide them with a copy of any CFC phase-out plan.

	EA
NC	Prerequisite 3
SCHOOLS	Prerequisite 3
CS	Prerequisite 3

12. Resources

Please see USGBC's LEED Registered Project Tools (http://www.usgbc.org/projecttools) for additional resources and technical information.

Websites

ASHRAE Service Life and Maintenance Cost Database

www.ashrae.org/database

This database provides current information on the service life and maintenance costs of typical HVAC equipment.

***Facility Management*, Coping with the CFC Phase-Out**

http://www.facilitymanagement.com

This magazine's website provides various articles on the issues of CFC phase-out.

U.S. EPA, Benefits of CFC Phase-Out

http://www.epa.gov/ozone/geninfo/benefits.html

This EPA document details the benefits of phasing out CFC and includes brief case studies.

U.S. EPA, Building Owners Save Money, Save the Earth; Replace Your CFC Air Conditioning Chiller

http://www.epa.gov/ozone/title6/608/chiller1_07.pdf

This EPA brochure documents the environmental and financial reasons to replace chloro fluorocarbon chillers with new, energy-efficient equipment.

U.S. EPA, Ozone Layer Depletion

http://www.epa.gov/ozone/strathome.html

This website includes information about the science of ozone depletion, EPA's regulatory approach to protecting the ozone layer, and alternatives to ozone-depleting substances.

U.S. EPA, Significant New Alternatives Policy

http://www.epa.gov/ozone/snap/index.html

SNAP is an EPA program to identify alternatives to ozone-depleting substances. The program maintains up-to-date lists of environmentally friendly substitutes for refrigeration and air-conditioning equipment, solvents, fire-suppression systems, adhesives, coatings, and other substances.

Print Media

Building Systems Analysis and Retrofit Manual (SMACNA, 1995).

CFCs, HCFC and Halons: Professional and Practical Guidance on Substances that Deplete the Ozone Layer (CIBSE, 2000).

The Refrigerant Manual: Managing the Phase Out of CFCs (BOMA International, 1993).

13. Definitions

Chlorofluorocarbons (CFCs) are hydrocarbons that are used as refrigerants and cause depletion of the stratospheric ozone layer.

The **leakage rate** is the speed at which an appliance loses refrigerant, measured between refrigerant charges or over 12 months, whichever is shorter. The leakage rate is expressed in terms of the percentage of the appliance's full charge that would be lost over a 12-month period if the rate stabilized. (EPA Clean Air Act, Title VI, Rule 608)

Refrigerants are the working fluids of refrigeration cycles that absorb heat from a reservoir at low temperatures and reject heat at higher temperatures.

OPTIMIZE ENERGY PERFORMANCE

	NC	SCHOOLS	CS
Credit	EA Credit 1	EA Credit 1	EA Credit 1
Points	1-19 points	1-19 points	3-21 points

Intent

To achieve increasing levels of energy performance beyond the prerequisite standard to reduce environmental and economic impacts associated with excessive energy use.

Requirements

NC, SCHOOLS & CS

Select 1 of the 3 compliance path options described below. Project teams documenting achievement using any of the 3 options are assumed to be in compliance with EA Prerequisite 2: Minimum Energy Performance.

OPTION 1. Whole Building Energy Simulation (1-19 points for NC and Schools, 3-21 points for CS)

Demonstrate a percentage improvement in the proposed building performance rating compared with the baseline building performance rating. Calculate the baseline building performance according to Appendix G of ANSI/ASHRAE/IESNA Standard 90.1-2007 (with errata but without addenda[1]) using a computer simulation model for the whole building project. The minimum energy cost savings percentage for each point threshold is as follows:

New Buildings	Existing Building Renovations	Points (NC & Schools)	Points (CS)
12%	8%	1	3
14%	10%	2	4
16%	12%	3	5
18%	14%	4	6
20%	16%	5	7
22%	18%	6	8
24%	20%	7	9
26%	22%	8	10
28%	24%	9	11
30%	26%	10	12
32%	28%	11	13
34%	30%	12	14
36%	32%	13	15
38%	34%	14	16
40%	36%	15	17
42%	38%	16	18
44%	40%	17	19
46%	42%	18	20
48%	44%	19	21

---

1 Project teams wishing to use ASHRAE approved addenda for the purposes of this credit may do so at their discretion. Addenda must be applied consistently across all LEED credits.

NC, SCHOOLS & CS (continued)

Appendix G of Standard 90.1-2007 requires that the energy analysis done for the building performance rating method include all the energy costs associated with the building project. To achieve points under this credit, the proposed design must meet the following criteria:

- Compliance with the mandatory provisions (Sections 5.4, 6.4, 7.4, 8.4, 9.4 and 10.4) in Standard 90.1-2007 (with errata but without addenda).
- Inclusion of all the energy costs within and associated with the building project.
- Comparison against a baseline building that complies with Appendix G of Standard 90.1-2007 (with errata but without addenda). The default process energy cost is 25% of the total energy cost for the baseline building. If the building's process energy cost is less than 25% of the baseline building energy cost, the LEED submittal must include documentation substantiating that process energy inputs are appropriate.

For the purpose of this analysis, process energy is considered to include, but is not limited to, office and general miscellaneous equipment, computers, elevators and escalators, kitchen cooking and refrigeration, laundry washing and drying, lighting exempt from the lighting power allowance (e.g., lighting integral to medical equipment) and other (e.g., waterfall pumps).

Regulated (non-process) energy includes lighting (e.g., for the interior, parking garage, surface parking, façade, or building grounds, etc. except as noted above), heating, ventilating, and air conditioning (HVAC) (e.g., for space heating, space cooling, fans, pumps, toilet exhaust, parking garage ventilation, kitchen hood exhaust, etc.), and service water heating for domestic or space heating purposes.

For this credit, process loads must be identical for both the baseline building performance rating and the proposed building performance rating. However, project teams may follow the exceptional calculation method (ANSI/ASHRAE/IESNA Standard 90.1-2007 G2.5) to document measures that reduce process loads. Documentation of process load energy savings must include a list of the assumptions made for both the base and proposed design, and theoretical or empirical information supporting these assumptions.

Projects in California may use Title 24-2005, Part 6 in place of ANSI/ASHRAE/IESNA Standard 90.1-2007 for Option 1.

OR

NC & CS

OPTION 2. Prescriptive Compliance Path: ASHRAE Advanced Energy Design Guide (1 point)

Comply with the prescriptive measures of the ASHRAE Advanced Energy Design Guide appropriate to the project scope, outlined below. Project teams must comply with all applicable criteria as established in the Advanced Energy Design Guide for the climate zone in which the building is located.

PATH 1. ASHRAE Advanced Energy Design Guide for Small Office Buildings 2004

The building must meet the following requirements:

- Less than 20,000 square feet.
- Office occupancy.

NC & CS (continued)

PATH 2. ASHRAE Advanced Energy Design Guide for Small Retail Buildings 2006

The building must meet the following requirements:

- Less than 20,000 square feet.
- Retail occupancy.

PATH 3. ASHRAE Advanced Energy Design Guide for Small Warehouses and Self Storage Buildings 2008

The building must meet the following requirements:

- Less than 50,000 square feet.
- Warehouse or self-storage occupancy.

SCHOOLS

OPTION 2. Prescriptive Compliance Path: Advanced Energy Design Guide for K-12 School Buildings (1 point)

Comply with all the prescriptive measures identified in the Advanced Energy Design Guide for K-12 School buildings.

- Projects using Option 2 must be less than 200,000 square feet.

OR

NC, SCHOOLS & CS

OPTION 3. Prescriptive Compliance Path: Advanced Buildings™ Core Performance™ Guide (1–3 points)

Comply with the prescriptive measures identified in the Advanced Buildings™ Core Performance™ Guide developed by the New Buildings Institute. The building must meet the following requirements:

- Less than 100,000 square feet.
- Comply with Section 1: Design Process Strategies, and Section 2: Core Performance Requirements.
- Health care, warehouse or laboratory projects are ineligible for this path (for NC & CS Projects).

Points achieved under Option 3 (1 point):

- 1 point is available for all projects (office, school, public assembly, and retail projects) less than 100,000 square feet that comply with Sections 1 and 2 of the Core Performance Guide.

- Up to 2 additional points are available to projects that implement performance strategies listed in Section 3: Enhanced Performance. For every 3 strategies implemented from this section, 1 point is available.

- The following strategies are addressed by other aspects of LEED and are not eligible for additional points under EA Credit 1:
  - 3.1 — Cool Roofs
  - 3.8 — Night Venting
  - 3.13 — Additional Commissioning

	EA
NC	Credit 1
SCHOOLS	Credit 1
CS	Credit 1

1. Benefits and Issues to Consider

Environmental Issues

Energy efficiency reduces the environmental burdens associated with producing and using energy. Fossil fuels, such as coal and oil, are the most common source of energy used in buildings. However, these fuels are also finite resources. The process of extracting and consuming energy from fossil fuels causes many environmental impacts, including air and water pollution, land degradation, solid waste generation, and greenhouse gas emissions. Mounting evidence connects fossil-fuel based energy use with climate change as well as serious risks to environmental and human health and safety. Data from the U.S. Energy Information Administration show that buildings are responsible for almost half (48%) of all energy consumed and greenhouse gases emitted annually.[8] EPA estimates that if the energy efficiency of commercial and industrial buildings improved by 10%, the resulting greenhouse gas reductions would be **equiva**lent to taking about 30 million vehicles off the road.[9]

In addition to fossil fuels, other sources of energy also carry environmental costs. Hydropower activities, for example, can alter aquatic ecosystems and harm endangered species. Nuclear power plants pose an environmental threat when they are decommissioned without appropriate storage sites for spent fuel. Given both the environmental impacts inherent in most energy-production processes and our limited energy supplies, efficiency measures are an important strategy for managing the impacts of energy consumption.

Economic Issues

Some energy-efficiency measures may not require additional first costs. Many measures that do result in higher capital costs may generate savings from lower energy use, smaller equipment, reduced space needs for mechanical and electrical equipment, and utility rebates. These savings may vastly exceed the incremental capital costs associated with the energy-efficiency measures over the life of the project.

Even seemingly small conservation measures can be significant; for instance, replacing 1 incandescent lamp with a fluorescent lamp will save over $30 in energy costs over the operating lifetime of the lamp[10].

2. Related Credits

The LEED for New Construction, Core & Shell, and Schools rating systems address building energy efficiency in 2 places: EA Prerequisite 2, Minimum Energy Performance, and EA Credit 1, Optimize Energy Performance. Energy consumption for the building can be reduced by ensuring that the project exceeds the building code requirements for envelope, lighting, and HVAC systems. Further, energy use can be directly affected through the use of climatically appropriate roofing materials and careful optimization of exterior lighting. Refer to these credits:

- EA Prerequisite 2: Minimum Energy Performance

- SS Credit 7.2: Heat Island Effect—Roof

- SS Credit 8: Light Pollution Reduction

In addition to reducing energy use through efficiency measures, project teams can mitigate energy use impacts by using renewable energy. Refer to these credits:

- EA Credit 2: On-site Renewable Energy

- EA Credit 6: Green Power

Building energy performance and indoor environmental quality issues, such as ventilation, occupant controllability, and the amount of entering daylight, must be carefully coordinated. Energy-efficient buildings should not compromise the health and well-being of occupants. Increased ventilation in buildings may require additional energy use, which may in turn cause air and water pollution. However, the additional need for energy can be mitigated by using heat-recovery ventilation and/or economizer strategies. Review the strategies in these credits:

	EA
NC	Credit 1
SCHOOLS	Credit 1
CS	Credit 1

- IEQ Prerequisite 1: Minimum Indoor Air Quality Performance
- IEQ Credit 1: Outdoor Air Delivery Monitoring
- IEQ Credit 2: Increased Ventilation
- IEQ Credit 6: Controllability of Systems
- IEQ Credit 7: Thermal Comfort
- IEQ Credit 8: Daylight and Views

Because water use, especially domestic hot water, requires significant energy use, water use reductions can lead to energy savings. Consider meeting the requirements for these credits:

- WE Credit 3: Water Use Reduction
- WE Credit 4: Process Water Use Reduction (LEED for Schools only)

3. Summary of Referenced Standards

ANSI/ASHRAE/IESNA Standard 90.1-2007, Energy Standard for Buildings except Low-Rise Residential, and Informative Appendix G, Performance Rating Method
American National Standards Institute
American Society of Heating, Refrigerating and Air-Conditioning Engineers
Illuminating Engineering Society of North America
http://www.ashrae.org
ANSI/ASHRAE/IESNA 90.1-2007 was formulated by ASHRAE under an ANSI consensus process. IESNA is a joint sponsor of the standard.

ANSI/ASHRAE/IESNA 90.1-2007 establishes minimum requirements for the energy-efficient design of buildings, with these exceptions: single-family houses; multifamily structures of 3 habitable stories or fewer above grade; manufactured houses (mobile and modular homes); buildings that do not use either electricity or fossil fuel; and equipment and portions of buildings systems that use energy primarily for industrial, manufacturing, or commercial processes. Building envelope requirements are provided for semiheated spaces such as warehouses. Please refer to ASHRAE 90.1-2007, Section 2 for further details.

Option 1 of EA Prerequisite 2 and EA Credit 1 for LEED for New Construction, Schools, and Core & Shell requires documentation of a percentage savings in energy cost using the ASHRAE 90.1-2007, Appendix G (the performance rating method). Appendix G is an informative document for rating the energy efficiency of building designs, but it does not provide verification that the minimum requirements of the code have been met. Instead, Appendix G is used to "quantify performance that substantially exceeds the requirements of Standard 90.1" (G1.1).

For EA Credit 1, Option 1, LEED relies extensively on the performance rating method explained in Appendix G. The method provides performance criteria for the components listed in Table 1 below.

The performance rating method uses an interactive model that enables project teams to compare the total energy cost for the proposed design with a baseline design. For modeling purposes, this method simplifies climate data and includes a mechanical system and process loads in both designs. See the Calculations section for more information on achieving compliance with the credit.

Table 1. Energy Standard Requirements Addressed by ASHRAE 90.1–2007

ASHRAE 90.1–2007 Components
Section 5. Building envelope (including semiheated spaces, such as warehouses)
Section 6. Heating, ventilation, and air-conditioning (including parking garage ventilation, freeze protection, exhaust air recovery, and condenser heat recovery for service water heating)
Section 7. Service water heating (including swimming pools)
Section 8. Power (including all building power distribution systems)
Section 9. Lighting (including exit signs, building exterior, grounds, and parking garages)
Section 10. Other equipment (including all permanently wired electrical motors)

ASHRAE Advanced Energy Design Guide for Small Office Buildings, 2006

http://www.ashrae.org

This compliance path is available only for LEED for New Construction and Core & Shell projects. ASHRAE developed the Advanced Energy Design Guide for Small Office Buildings 2006 to provide a simplified approach for exceeding ASHRAE 90.1–1999 standards in small office buildings. The guide provides climate-specific recommendations for the building envelope, interior lighting, and HVAC systems; these suggestions will improve building energy performance beyond ASHRAE 90.1–1999 levels by approximately 30%. To demonstrate compliance with this standard, teams must also provide additional documentation such as detailed drawings, cutsheets, mechanical and electrical schedules, and sections of specifications.

ASHRAE Advanced Energy Design Guide for Retail Buildings 2006

http://www.ashrae.org

The *Advanced Energy Design Guide* series provides a sensible and easy approach to achieving advanced levels of energy savings without having to resort to detailed calculations or analysis. This guide focuses on retail buildings up to 20,000 square feet that use unitary heating and air-conditioning equipment; such buildings represent a significant amount of commercial retail space in the United States.

ASHRAE Advanced Energy Design Guide for Small Warehouses and Self Storage Buildings 2008

http://www.ashrae.org

The *Advanced Energy Design Guide* series provides a sensible and easy approach to achieving advanced levels of energy savings without having to resort to detailed calculations or analysis. This guide focuses on warehouses up to 50,000 square feet and self-storage buildings that use unitary heating and air-conditioning equipment; such facilities represent a significant amount of commercial warehouse space in the United States.

ASHRAE Advanced Energy Design Guide for K-12 School Buildings

http://www.ashrae.org

The *Advanced Energy Design Guide* series provides a sensible and easy approach to achieving advanced levels of energy savings without having to resort to detailed calculations or analysis. This guide focuses on elementary, middle, and high school buildings, which have a wide variety of heating and air-conditioning requirements. Options for daylighting, an important component in schools, are included.

New Buildings Institute, Advanced Buildings™ Core Performance™ Guide

The Advanced Building program provides a prescriptive plan for exceeding the energy performance requirements of ASHRAE 90.1–2004. The program was designed to provide a predictable alternative to energy performance modeling and a simple set of criteria for increasing building energy performance significantly. To use this option, projects cannot have a window-to-wall ratio greater than 40%.

The Advanced Building Core Performance program updates and replaces the Advanced Building Benchmarked program. Core Performance is calibrated to exceed the requirements of ASHRAE 90.1–2004 in all climate zones.

	EA
NC	Credit 1
SCHOOLS	Credit 1
CS	Credit 1

Information about the Core Performance program requirements and a range of additional reference material is available at www.advancedbuildings.net.

Several aspects of the Core Performance program overlap with other LEED credits and prerequisites. Following the Core Performance program is not an alternative path to achieving any LEED credits other than EA Credit 1, Optimize Energy Performance, but Core Performance may facilitate earning other LEED credits and prerequisites.

4. Implementation

OPTION 1. Whole Building Energy Simulation

The performance rating method in ASHRAE 90.1-2007, Informative Appendix G, is an effective way to rate building energy performance and compare the costs and benefits of different energy efficiency strategies. The performance rating method described in Appendix G is a modification of the energy cost budget method in Section 11 of ASHRAE 90.1-2007. A model using the energy cost budget method will not be accepted.

The terminology used by the performance rating method is used in this LEED credit. Proposed building performance is the "the annual energy cost calculated for a proposed design." Baseline building performance is "the annual energy cost for a building design intended for use as a baseline for rating above standard design." The energy simulation modeling methodology addressed in Appendix G of ASHRAE 90.1-2007 describes procedures for establishing the proposed building performance and the baseline building performance to evaluate the percentage improvement in energy cost for the project.

The performance rating method requires developing an energy simulation model for the proposed design, which is then used as the basis for generating the baseline design energy simulation model. As the design progresses, any updates made to the proposed design energy simulation model (such as changes to the building orientation, wall area, fenestration area, space function, HVAC system type, and HVAC system sizing) should also be reflected in the baseline design energy simulation model, as dictated by Appendix G.

The performance rating method enables the design team to identify the interactive effects of energy efficiency measures across all building systems. For example, a change to the proposed lighting power affects both heating and cooling energy consumption. When building lighting power density is decreased, the model will indicate how much additional summertime cooling energy is saved (because of lower internal loads) and how much the peak cooling equipment can be downsized (for first-cost savings). The greatest savings will accrue in the hottest climates and the least savings in the coldest climates, but in almost all cases, reducing lighting power density will achieve savings beyond the lighting alone.

The performance rating method requires that annual energy cost expressed in dollars be used to calculate the percentage improvement in energy usage. Annual energy costs are determined using rates for purchased energy, such as electricity, gas, oil, propane, steam, and chilled water, that are based on actual local utility rates or the state average prices published annually by the U.S. Department of Energy's Energy Information Administration, at www.eia.doe.gov.

Strategies

Four fundamental strategies can increase energy performance:

- Reduce demand by optimizing building form and orientation, reducing internal loads

	EA
NC	Credit 1
SCHOOLS	Credit 1
CS	Credit 1

through shell and lighting improvements, and shifting load to off-peak periods.

- Harvest free energy by using site resources such as daylight, ventilation cooling, solar heating and power, and wind energy to satisfy needs for space conditioning, service water heating, and power generation.

- Increase efficiency with a more efficient building envelope, lighting system, and HVAC systems and by using appropriately sized HVAC systems. More efficient systems reduce energy demand and energy use.

- Recover waste energy through exhaust air energy recovery systems, graywater heat recovery systems, and cogeneration. When applying these strategies, establish and document energy goals and expectations and apply appropriate modeling techniques to assess achievement of the goals.

OPTION 2. Prescriptive Compliance Path, ASHRAE Advanced Energy Design Guide

To comply with the prescriptive measures of the ASHRAE Advanced Energy Design Guide, first identify the climate zone where the building is located. Section 3 includes a U.S. map defining the 8 climate zones by county borders.

Then, find the appropriate climate zone table that identifies the recommended roofs, walls, floors, slabs, doors, vertical glazing, skylights, interior lighting, ventilation, ducts, energy recovery, and service water heating. Please refer to the individual LEED rating systems for further details about the compliance requirements, as well as available points under each.

CS To apply for credit under this option, a Core & Shell project must comply with all requirements for the ASHRAE Advanced Energy Design Guidelines, including those that may be in the tenant's scope of work. A sales agreement or tenant lease may be necessary.

NC & CS

ASHRAE Advanced Energy Design Guide for Small Office Buildings 2004

For office buildings smaller than 20,000 square feet, the ASHRAE Advanced Energy Design Guide for Small Office Buildings 2006 provides an effective means of limiting building energy usage and documenting improved building energy performance without using a building energy model. The climate-specific recommendations listed in the guide should be incorporated in the project early in the building design to optimize building performance and minimize costs.

ASHRAE Advanced Energy Design Guide for Small Retail Buildings 2006

The ASHRAE Advanced Energy Design Guide for Small Retail Buildings 2006 applies to retail buildings smaller than 20,000 square feet. Comply with all applicable criteria as established in this guide for the climate zone in which the building is located.

ASHRAE Advanced Energy Design Guide for Small Warehouses and Self-Storage Buildings 2008.

Warehouse and self-storage buildings smaller than 50,000 square feet can use the ASHRAE Advanced Energy Design Guide for Small Warehouses and Self-Storage Buildings 2008. The climate-specific recommendations listed in this guide should be incorporated in the project early in the building design to optimize building performance and minimize capital costs.

SCHOOLS

ASHRAE Advanced Energy Design Guide for K–12 School Buildings.
The ASHRAE Advanced Energy Design Guide for K–12 school buildings is applicable to school buildings smaller than 200,000 square feet.

OPTION 3. Prescriptive Compliance Path, Advanced Buildings™ Core Performance Guide

Comply with the prescriptive measures identified in the Advanced Building Core Performance Guide developed by the New Building Institute. The following restrictions apply:

- The building must be less than 100,000 square feet.

- Health care, warehouse, or laboratory projects are not eligible.

- The building must have a window-to-wall ratio of less than 40%.

- Project teams must fully comply with Section 1, Design Process Strategies, and Section 2, Core Performance Requirements.

OPTION 3 (1 point)

This point is available for all office, school, public assembly, and retail projects smaller than 100,000 square feet that comply with Section 1, Design Process Strategies, and Section 2, Core Performance Requirements, of the Core Performance Guide. The topics addressed in Sections 1 and 2 are as follows:

1.1. — Identify design intent

1.2. — Communicating design intent

1.3. — Building configuration

1.4. — Mechanical system design

1.5. — Construction certification (acceptance testing)

1.6. — Operator training and documentation

1.7. — Performance data review

2.1. — Energy code requirements

2.2. — Air barrier performance

2.3. — Minimum indoor air quality performance

2.4. — Below-grade exterior insulation

2.5. — Opaque envelope performance

2.6. — Fenestration performance

2.7. — Lighting controls

2.8. — Lighting power density

2.9. — Mechanical equipment efficiency requirements

2.10. — Dedicated mechanical systems

2.11. — Demand control ventilation

2.12. — Domestic hot water system efficiency

2.13. — Fundamental economizer performance

	EA
NC	Credit 1
SCHOOLS	Credit 1
CS	Credit 1

OPTION 3 (up to 2 additional points):

These points are available to projects that implement the performance strategies listed in Section 3, Enhanced Performance, of the Core Performance Guide. The strategies that can be implemented for credit under Option 3 are as follows:

3.2. — Daylighting and controls

3.3. — Additional lighting power reductions

3.4. — Plug loads, appliance efficiency

3.5. — Supply air temperature reset (VAV)

3.6. — Indirect evaporative cooling

3.7. — Heat recovery

3.9. — Premium economizer performance

3.10. — Variable speed control

3.11. — Demand-responsive buildings (peak power reduction)

3.12. — On-site supply of renewable energy

3.14. — Fault detection and diagnostics

For every 3 strategies implemented from this section, 1 point is available.

The following strategies are addressed by other aspects of the LEED program and are not eligible for additional points under EA Credit 1:

3.1. — Cool roofs

3.8. — Night venting

3.13. — Additional commissioning

Combined Heat and Power (CHP)

Combined heat and power (CHP) systems capture the heat that would otherwise be wasted in traditional fossil fuel generation of electrical power; these integrated systems are therefore much more efficient than central station power plants and separate thermal systems. CHP systems also produce fewer emissions than traditional generators burning fossil fuels. Other benefits include reductions in peak demand, release of electrical grid system capacity, and reductions in overall electrical system transmission and distribution losses.

CHP systems that supply electricity and/or recovered thermal energy to LEED project buildings are treated under the performance rating method of Appendix G, ASHRAE 90.1-2007. G2.4, Energy Rates, adequately addresses on-site CHP systems but does not provide a methodology for recognizing the potential benefits of district CHP.

CHP Cases and Calculation of Benefit

Table 2. CHP Cases

	EA
NC	Credit 1
SCHOOLS	Credit 1
CS	Credit 1

Case	Ownership of CHP vs. Building	CHP Location	Electricity	Recovered Thermal
1	Same	Inside Building	All in building and/or sold to the grid	All in building
2	Different (3rd party in building)	Inside building	All in building	All in building
3	Same (campus district energy plant)	District energy plant	Campus electrical supply and/or exported to grid	Campus thermal energy supply
4	Different(commercial district energy plant	District energy plant	Campus electrical supply and/or exported to grid	District thermal energy supply

CASE 1. Same ownership, CHP inside building

In accordance with the performance rating method, the parameters of the calculation of the CHP benefit are as follows:

The baseline building's heating and cooling plant utilizes the backup energy source of the design, or electricity if no backup source is present or specified.

When all electricity and thermal outputs (heating or cooling) of the CHP are used within the design building, the electricity produced is considered free, as is the produced thermal energy. The input fuel for the CHP and any additional purchased energy is charged to the design building.

In some cases, some electricity generated by the CHP is sold to the grid or an external customer. Thermal and electrical outputs of the CHP used within the design building are treated as above. All electricity sold externally is a "process," and both the design and the baseline buildings are charged with the input fuel associated with the generation of that electricity. (The sold electricity is irrelevant to the calculations other than for the purpose of determining the associated fuel input.) The thermal output generated from the process and used by the design is considered free.

Considerations for Simulation or Calculation

The performance rating method requires hourly calculation of the CHP performance, either directly through simulation of the system or manual postprocessing of the hourly simulation results. This captures hourly effects of load coincidence and electrical demand reduction, plus any declining block or time-of-day utility rate structures. The approach is used to determine the net design building hourly energy use after the CHP contribution and then apply the prevailing conventional utility rates. However, it may be possible to conduct the calculation on a net annual basis if hourly load, demand, or utility rate relationships are insignificant.

CASE 2. Different ownership, CHP inside the building

The rates charged to a building by a CHP developer or operator for electricity and thermal outputs typically include factors for capital recovery, maintenance, and other nonenergy costs. Since these types of costs are not included in the performance rating method calculation for other energy efficiency equipment and measures within the design building, they are also excluded for the CHP calculation, regardless of who owns the system. Essentially, the CHP system in Case 2 is treated the same as in Case 1, with the input fuel charged to the design building (at the prevailing utility rate as it applies to the design building) for all CHP outputs used within the building, and charged to both the design and the baseline buildings for process electricity sold externally

	EA
NC	Credit 1
SCHOOLS	Credit 1
CS	Credit 1

(again at the prevailing rate). As with Case 1, the design building realizes the benefit of thermal outputs resulting from the process electricity generation.

CASES 3 and 4. District CHP

Projects with district CHP must follow all the requirements in Required Treatment of District Thermal Energy (http://www.usgbc.org/ShowFile.aspx?DocumentID=4176). In principle, Cases 3 and 4 are analogous to Cases 1 and 2 except that a "virtual" CHP system within the design building uses the process electricity defined in the Required Treatment of District Thermal Energy document. As with Cases 1 and 2, the calculation of the CHP benefit considers only energy inputs and outputs and ignores all other nonenergy cost factors. The parameters of the calculation are as follows:

The baseline building's heating and cooling plant uses the backup energy source of the design building, or electricity if no backup source is present (as in Cases 1 and 2).

All electricity and thermal output obtained from the district CHP is considered free. Fuel input is charged as follows:

a) When the amount of virtual CHP electricity associated with the amount of thermal output used by the design building at a given point in time is equal to or less than the amount of electricity actually obtained from the district CHP, then the design building is charged with the input fuel associated with the generation of (all) the electricity obtained from the district CHP. The fuel is charged to the design building at the prevailing rate. Any additional energy used by the design building is also charged at market rates.

b) When the amount of virtual CHP electricity associated with the amount of thermal output used by the design building at a given time exceeds the amount of electricity actually obtained from the district CHP, then the excess virtual electricity generation is deemed to be a process (as in Case 1). The associated (excess) input fuel is charged to both the design and the baseline buildings at the prevailing rate.

Considerations for Simulation or Calculation

Considerations are analogous to Cases 1 and 2. Although hourly calculation is necessary for most cases, either through simulation or manual postprocessing of the hourly simulation results, for Cases 3 or 4 it may be possible to conduct the calculation on a net annual basis if hourly load, demand, and/or utility rate relationships are insignificant.

1. The design building must meet EA Prerequisite 2 without the benefit of CHP.

2. Additionally, to qualify for EA Credit 1 consideration under Case 4 (external ownership of the CHP plant with multiple customers), a project must meet the following criteria:

   a) Long-term commitment from the building owner. The project must have in place a long-term agreement (minimum 10 years) to purchase CHP thermal output from the district CHP system.

   b) Building reliance on district system. The project must be reliant on the district system for 90% of its thermal energy (heating, cooling, or both, depending on district service provided to the building), exclusive of any renewable energy (as defined in EA Credit 2).

District Energy Systems

For projects with district energy systems, specific technical guidance can be found on USGBC's Registered Project Tools page (http://www.usgbc.org/projecttools). Follow the guidance in effect at the time of registration.

5. Timeline and Team

By implementing energy analysis early in the design process, the design team can develop the most effective—and cost-effective—energy conservation strategies.

	EA
NC	Credit 1
SCHOOLS	Credit 1
CS	Credit 1

A simplified model analysis should be done at the end of the schematic design phase to understand the project's overall energy performance. This "shoe-box" analysis will help the architect and the mechanical engineer understand the current building performance and select the energy efficiency measures that can be implemented to achieve the target points.

The next phase of the energy analysis phase is to develop a detailed energy model that can be submitted for review, as required for this credit. The construction documents must be used for performing a detailed energy model. This model must be revised to include all the modified details so that the final energy model reflects the 100% contract documents.

Team members engaged in energy analysis should work closely with other design team members from the early design phases through construction documentation, when the implemented strategies can be validated and revised. The team members involved during the entire process includes energy analyst (the modeler), architect, mechanical engineer, LEED consultant, and commissioning authority.

6. Calculations

Option 1 requires software energy simulation; Options 2 and 3 use a prescriptive approach and do not require modeling.

OPTION 1. Whole Building Simulation

Option 1 relies entirely on the performance rating method in ASHRAE 90.1-2007, Appendix G, and requires extensive calculations using an approved energy simulation program. The performance rating method is different from the energy cost budget method in ASHRAE 90.1-2007, Section 11. A calculation using the energy cost budget method will not be accepted.

Both the baseline building model and the proposed building model must cover all building energy components, including, but not limited to, office and general miscellaneous equipment, computers, elevators and escalators, kitchen cooking and refrigeration, laundry washing and drying, lighting exempt from the lighting power allowance (e.g., lighting integral to medical equipment), and other (e.g., waterfall pumps). Regulated (nonprocess) energy includes lighting (such as for the interior, parking garage, surface parking, façade, or building grounds, except as noted above), HVAC (such as for space heating, space cooling, fans, pumps, toilet exhaust, parking garage ventilation, and kitchen hood exhaust), and service water heating for domestic or space heating purposes.

For EA Credit 1, process loads must be identical for both the baseline building performance rating and the proposed building performance rating. However, project teams may follow the exceptional calculation method (ASHRAE 90.1-2007, G2.5) to document measures that reduce process loads.

Design criteria, including both climate data and interior temperature and humidity setpoints, must be the same for the proposed and baseline building models. Furthermore, both heating and cooling must be modeled in all conditioned spaces of both the proposed and the baseline building, even if no heating or cooling system will be installed.

Modeling Requirements for Baseline and Proposed Case Building

The following table summarizes the modeling requirements from ASHRAE 90.1-2007, Appendix G, for typical projects. Project-specific information will vary; refer to the cited tables and sections of the referenced standard for all applicable details and modeling requirements.

	EA	
NC	Credit 1	
SCHOOLS	Credit 1	
CS	Credit 1	

Baseline Case	LEED for New Construction and LEED for Schools Proposed Case	LEED for Core & Shell Proposed Case
Schedule of Operation		
Same as proposed design. Exception: Schedules may differ from proposed design if proposed design is implementing some nonstandard efficiency measures.	Use actual operating hours for schedule of operation in proposed design. Exception: Schedules can be modified if schedule changes are necessary to model nonstandard efficiency measures such as lighting controls, natural ventilation, demand control ventilation, or service water heating load reductions (Table G3.1.4). Describe any schedule of operation differences between baseline building model and proposed building.	Same as LEED for New Construction and LEED for Schools.
Orientation		
4 baseline design simulations are required for generating baseline building performance. Models are identical except that building orientation for each model is modified as described in Table G3.5.1(a), and window solar heat gain coefficients are revised to reflect minimum ASHRAE building envelope requirements for revised building orientation.	Proposed design models building as designed (with minor exceptions).	Same as LEED for New Construction and LEED for Schools.
Building Envelope		
Model building envelope for baseline design using Table G3.1.5. New buildings Model above-grade walls, roof, and floor assemblies using lightweight assembly types (i.e., steel-framed walls, roofs with insulation entirely above deck, and steel-joist floors). Match values with appropriate assembly maximum U-factors in Tables 5.5-1 through 5.5-8. Existing Buildings Model building envelope using existing (preretrofit) building envelope thermal parameters rather than referenced standard's prescriptive building envelope requirements for specified climate.	Building components must be modeled as shown in architectural drawings. Model any exceptions using Table G3.1.5. Existing Buildings Model must include any renovations in existing building envelope (such as replacing windows or increasing roof insulation).	Same as LEED for New Construction and LEED for Schools.
Match percentage of vertical fenestration in baseline and proposed designs, or use 40% of gross wall area, whichever is less. Distribute windows on each face of building in same proportion as in proposed design. Fenestration U-factor must match appropriate requirements in Tables 5.5-1 through 5.5-8.	Model fenestration location and its properties (U-value, solar heat gain coefficient, and transmittance) as shown on architectural drawings.	Same as LEED for New Construction and LEED for Schools.
Use fixed vertical glazing in baseline design, flush to exterior wall with no shading projections. Do not model manually controlled interior shading devices, such as blinds or curtains, in baseline design.	Shading projections in proposed design, which reduce solar gains on glazing, can also be modeled to demonstrate energy savings compared with baseline. Manually controlled interior shading devices such as blinds and curtains should not be modeled. Automatically controlled interior shading devices can be modeled, as per Appendix G.	Same as LEED for New Construction and LEED for Schools.

			EA	
			NC	Credit 1
			SCHOOLS	Credit 1
			CS	Credit 1

Model all roof surfaces with reflectivity of 0.30.	"Cool roofs" (light-colored roof finishes that have low heat absorption) can be modeled to show impact of reduced heat gains. Model proposed roof with solar reflectance greater than 0.70 and emittance greater than 0.75 with reflectivity of 0.45 (accounting for degradation in actual reflectivity) versus default reflectivity value of 0.30	Same as LEED for New Construction and LEED for Schools.

Lighting Systems

LEED for New Construction and LEED for Schools Model lighting using building area (9.5) or space-by-space (9.6) method depending on proposed design categorization. The baseline design model should also include exterior lighting power allowance (9.4.5). LEED for Core & Shell Model lighting power in core and shell areas as determined by space type classification in Table 9.6.1. Tenant Spaces Model separate electric meters for lighting in core building and tenant spaces. Use lighting power allowances for each space as indicated in Section 9.6.1.	Model proposed design with installed lighting power density for each thermal block and account for all installed lighting on site including interior ambient and task lighting, parking garage lighting, and exterior lighting.	Model proposed design with installed lighting power density and account for all installed lighting on site including interior ambient and task lighting, parking garage lighting and exterior lighting. AND For core and shell project areas where no lighting system has been specified, model these spaces identically in both baseline and design cases as minimally code compliant according to building area method using appropriate space type classification in Table 9.6.1. Tenant Spaces Model separate electric meters for lighting in core building and tenant spaces. If tenant lighting is designed or installed, use as-designed values; otherwise classify space types for building spaces and use lighting power allowances for each space as indicated in Section 9.6.1.
Do not take credit for automatic lighting controls such as daylight controls, occupancy controls, or programmable controls.	Model any daylight responsive lighting control systems directly in proposed design energy simulation. Credit can also be taken for occupant sensor lighting controls (Table G3.1, No. 6) in spaces where they are not mandatory; however, note that such controls are mandatory per Section 9.4.1.2 in classrooms, conference rooms and employee lunch and break rooms.	Same as LEED for New Construction and LEED for Schools.
Excepted interior lighting power allowance is classified as process energy and must be identical to proposed case.	Lighting excepted from interior lighting power allowance should be modeled in proposed design; however, this lighting should be considered process energy (Table G.3.1.6).	Same as LEED for New Construction and LEED for Schools.

HVAC System Selection

Determine HVAC system type using actual building area, usage, quantity of floors, occupancy (residential or nonresidential), and heating fuel source per Tables G3.1.1A and G3.1.1B. As per G3.1.1, use same baseline HVAC system type for entire building except for, areas where occupancy, process loads or schedules differ significantly from rest of building or areas with varying pressurization, cross-contamination requirements	Proposed design HVAC system type, quantities, should reflect actual design parameters except in cases where either heating system or cooling system has not been specified. If no cooling system has been specified, proposed design must include cooling system modeled identically to baseline design cooling system. If no heating system has been specified, proposed design should assume electric heating. For areas of project without heating or cooling systems (such as parking garages), there is no need to model heating or cooling systems in either proposed or baseline designs.	Model building system as described in design documents. If HVAC system is not yet designed, use same HVAC system as baseline case.
HVAC equipment capacities for baseline system should be oversized 15% for cooling, and 25% for heating (G3.1.2.2 and G3.1.2.2.1).	Proposed design HVAC system should reflect actual design capacities and system efficiencies.	Same as LEED for New Construction and LEED for Schools.
Unmet load hours (occupied periods where any zone is outside its temperature setpoints) may not be exceeded by more than 300 hours. Also, unmet load hours for proposed design may not exceed unmet load hours for baseline design by more than 50 (G3.1.2.2).	Same as baseline case.	Same as baseline case.
Outdoor ventilation rates should be identical to proposed case.	Proposed design should reflect actual outdoor ventilation rates.	Same as LEED for New Construction and LEED for Schools.
Operate fan continuously when spaces are occupied and cycle it during unoccupied hours. Except for spaces that have mandated minimum ventilation requirements, fan must remain on during occupied hours for health and safety reasons (G3.1.2.4). Baseline system fan supply air volume should be based on a supply-air-to-room-air temperature difference of 20°F or required ventilation or makeup air, whichever is greater (G3.1.2.8). Use this supply air volume to calculate total fan power for baseline system design (G3.1.2.9). This value reflects sum of power modeled for supply, exhaust, return, and relief fans.	The proposed HVAC design should reflect actual fan operation, fan supply rate and fan motor horse power.	Same as LEED for New Construction and LEED for Schools.
Fan energy must be separated from cooling system. Overall efficiency rating, such as an energy efficiency ratio, must be separated into component energy using coefficient of performance or other conversion (Equations G-A, G-B and G-C, pages G-24 and G-26).	Same as baseline case.	Same as baseline case.
Model economizers and exhaust air energy recovery systems in baseline HVAC systems when required for given climate zone and system parameters (G3.1.2.6 and G3.1.2.10).	Include economizers if indicated in actual design parameters.	Same as LEED for New Construction and LEED for Schools.
Follow HVAC system-specific requirements (chillers, boilers, heat pumps) as indicated in G.3.1.3	System-specific requirements should reflect actual conditions.	System-specific requirements should reflect actual conditions. OR If system-specific requirements are not specified, HVAC system must be identical to baseline case system.

	EA
NC	Credit 1
SCHOOLS	Credit 1
CS	Credit 1

Process Energy

LEED for New Construction and LEED for Schools
Process loads must be identical to proposed building. Occupancy and occupancy schedules may not be changed. However, variations of power requirements, schedules or control sequences are allowed based upon documentation that installed equipment in proposed design represents significant verifiable departure from documented conventional practice.

LEED for Core & Shell
Model separate meters for tenant receptacle loads and process loads.
Use same values for receptacle loads as used in proposed building.

Process energy includes office and general miscellaneous equipment, computers, elevators and escalators, kitchen cooking and refrigeration, laundry washing and drying, lighting exempt from lighting power allowance (e.g., lighting integral to medical equipment), and other (e.g., waterfall pumps).
Table G-B provides acceptable receptacle power densities per occupancy type, which can be incorporated into building energy models. Other process energy inputs such as elevators, escalators, data center and telecom room computing equipment, refrigeration, process lighting, and non-HVAC motors should be modeled based on actual power requirements, and assuming reasonable schedules of operation.
Total process energy cost must be equal to at least 25% of baseline building performance.
For buildings where process energy cost is less than 25% of baseline building energy cost, include documentation substantiating that process energy inputs are appropriate.

Same as LEED for New Construction and LEED for Schools.

Tenant Spaces
Model separate meters for tenant plug loads and process loads.
Use values indicated in Table G-B to model tenant plug loads or provide documentation for modeled loads.

Energy Rates

Use same rates for both baseline and proposed building.

Rates from local utility schedules are default option to compute energy costs. However, intent is to encourage simulations that provide owners value and help them minimize their energy costs.
In absence of local utility rate schedule or energy rate schedules approved by local ASHRAE 90.1-2007 adopting authority, use energy rates listed in state average prices, published annually by Energy Information Administration at http://www.eia.doe.gov. Regardless of source of rate schedule used, same rate schedule must be used in both baseline and proposed simulations.

Same as LEED for New Construction and LEED for Schools.

Tenant Spaces
Energy-using components are metered and apportioned and/or billed to tenant.
Tenant will pay for components.

Service Hot Water System

Service hot water must use same energy sources as proposed building.
System-related specific parameters must be modeled as indicated in Table G.3.11.

Service hot water system type and its related performance parameters must be modeled to reflect actual system installed or designed in design documents.

Same as LEED for New Construction and LEED for Schools.

EA	
NC	Credit 1
SCHOOLS	Credit 1
CS	Credit 1

CS Credit for Tenant-Implemented Efficiency Measures

Under the LEED for Core & Shell Rating System, project teams can claim efficiency improvements and therefore additional points under this credit for measures implemented by a tenant. The measures for which the project team is claiming credit must be included in the tenant's lease agreement and be enforceable by the owner through the lease agreement. The project team must provide a list of such measures, the level of performance expected to be met by the tenant, and a copy of the lease agreement. These credits are available only if the lease agreement is enforceable, not if it is simply a tenant guideline.

Strategies with exceptional modeling requirements

1. Projects with natural ventilation may be able to take credit for natural ventilation in the energy modeling. However, projects demonstrating natural ventilation savings will be evaluated on a case-by-case basis. To adequately demonstrate the process and the results, provide the following:

   ▪ Detailed project description.

   ▪ Clear identification of the areas that qualify for natural ventilation credit.

   ▪ Detailed description or references that document the modeling algorithms and/or methodology for the natural ventilation portion of the energy model.

   ▪ All thermostat, fan, infiltration, and other appropriate schedules for naturally ventilated areas.

   Also demonstrate that the range of unmet load hours is similar for both the proposed and the baseline building, to ensure that savings are not claimed for hours outside the control parameters.

   Clearly demonstrate that the operational schedule for the natural ventilation system as modeled aligns with occupants' anticipated behavior.

   Because manual control is not addressed by the Appendix G modeling methodology, any manual control features must be submitted under the exceptional calculation methodology (see below) for case-by-case review. Be prepared to demonstrate convincingly that a manual control strategy is appropriate and workable.

2. On-site renewable energy and site-recovered energy costs are not included in the proposed case as per ASHRAE 90.1-2007 Section G.2.4; therefore, these systems receive full credit using the performance rating method.

   Examples of on-site renewable energy systems include power generated by photovoltaics or wind turbines, and thermal energy collected by solar panels. Examples of site-recovered energy include heat recovered with chiller heat recovery systems or waste heat recovery units on distributed generation systems.

   When the actual building design incorporates on-site renewable or site-recovered energy, the baseline design should be modeled based on the backup energy source for the actual building design, or electricity if no backup energy source is specified. Proposed building performance can be determined using 1 of the following 2 methods when on-site renewable energy or site-recovered energy is incorporated into the building project:

   1. Model the systems directly in the proposed design energy model. If the building simulation program is capable of modeling the on-site renewable or site-recovered energy systems, these systems can be modeled directly within the building energy model. The model should reflect the cost savings achieved through the on-site renewable or site-recovered energy systems.

2. Model the systems using the exceptional calculation method. If the building simulation program is not capable of modeling the on-site renewable or site-recovered energy systems, the energy saved by these systems can be calculated using the exceptional calculation method. The renewable or site-recovered energy cost can then be subtracted from the proposed building performance.

	EA
NC	Credit 1
SCHOOLS	Credit 1
CS	Credit 1

Exceptional Calculation Method

The exceptional calculation method in ASHRAE 90.1-2007, G2.5, must be used to document any measures that cannot be adequately modeled in a simulation program.

Examples of measures that may be modeled using the exceptional calculation method include improvements to laboratory or kitchen exhaust systems, improved appliance efficiencies in high-rise residential buildings, graywater heat recovery, flat-panel LCD computer monitors, improvements to refrigeration equipment efficiency, and zone variable air volume (VAV) occupant sensor controls.

Documentation of energy savings using the exceptional calculation method must include the following:

- Assumptions made for both the baseline and the proposed design.

- Theoretical or empirical information supporting these assumptions.

- Specific energy cost savings achieved based on the exceptional calculation.

Common mistakes made using the performance rating method

The following is a list of mistakes to avoid when using the performance rating method for EA Credit 1 calculations and submittals:

- Incorrect use of the energy cost budget method (Section 11) rather than the performance rating method (Appendix G).

- Opaque assembly (wall, roof, and slab) values are not correctly accounted for in the baseline case. Appendix G.3.1.5 requires using lightweight assembly type (i.e., steel-framed walls, roofs with insulation entirely above deck, and steel-joist floors).

- Center-of-glass performance is incorrectly used rather than fenestration assembly U-factor and solar heat gain coefficient (SHGC). The building envelope requirements listed for each climate zone (ASHRAE 90.1-2007, Tables 5.5-1 through 5.5-8) refer to fenestration assembly maximum U-factors and SHGCs for glazing (also see ASHRAE 90.1-2007, Sections 5.2.8.4 and 5.2.8.5). The fenestration assembly performance accounts for the effects of both the frame and the glazing. To determine the fenestration assembly U-factor and SHGC, use Tables 8.1A and 8.2. Alternatively, the fenestration U-factors, SHGCs, and visual light transmittance must be certified and labeled in accordance with NFRC 100, 200, and 300, respectively (A8).

- Baseline design window area percentages are not calculated in accordance with the performance rating method.

- Baseline design fenestration is not uniformly distributed as per Appendix G.3.1.5, which requires that fenestration be distributed on each face of the building in the same proportion as in the proposed design.

- Models mistakenly include manually operated shading devices, which are ineligible under this credit; only automatically controlled shades or blinds should be modeled.

- The proposed design does not account for portable (task) lighting.

- Nontradable surfaces (such as building façades) are incorrectly treated as tradable surfaces for determining the exterior lighting power allowance.

	EA
NC	Credit 1
SCHOOLS	Credit 1
CS	Credit 1

- The baseline design is modeled with the automatic lighting controls (such as daylight sensors, occupancy sensor).

- The baseline HVAC system type is incorrectly determined.

- The baseline system capacities, design supply air volume, or total fan power are incorrectly calculated.

- The outdoor air ventilation volume varies between the proposed and the baseline building.

- The manufacturer's overall cooling energy efficiency ratings (EERs) are not separated into the component energy using the coefficient of performance or other conversion factors in accordance with ASHRAE 90.1-2007 requirements. Fan power is not deducted from the packaged equipment's EER values.

- The quantities and/or types of chillers and boilers are not determined in accordance with the performance rating method (ASHRAE 90.1-2007, G3.1.3.2, G3.1.3.7).

- The hot water and chilled water pump powers are not calculated in accordance with the performance rating method (ASHRAE 90.1-2007, G3.1.3.5, G3.1.3.10).

- Insufficient information is provided for energy measures incorporating the exceptional calculation methodology. Please refer the documentation required under exceptional calculations method above.

- Energy consumption is incorrectly used to calculate the percentage improvement rather than energy cost.

- Energy simulation output reports are not included as part of the documentation. Simulation output reports that give a breakdown of the end-use energy consumption by fuel type as well as energy cost are required to document this credit.

- The process loads in the proposed and the baseline designs are not identical. Further, no detailed explanation of the inputs is provided to assess the percentage change.

- Demand control ventilation is modeled as energy efficiency measures, and no information regarding the modeling process is provided.

- The number of unmet load hours for the proposed design exceeds that of the baseline design by more than 50 hours.

Calculating the Percentage Improvement

First, the whole-building simulations are used to produce reports that show the total cost for electricity, gas, and possibly other energy sources, such as steam and chilled water. The total annual energy cost calculated for the proposed design simulation is the proposed building performance. The average total energy cost for the 4 orientations simulated for the baseline design is the baseline building performance. ASHRAE 90.1-2007 also requires that the energy consumption and peak demand be reported for each building end use. In programs based on DOE-2, such as eQUEST or VisualDOE, these data can be found in the BEPS or BEPU and PS-E reports. In Trane® Trace™700, this information is reported in the energy consumption summary. As with the baseline building performance, the average of the 4 baseline building simulation results is used to calculate the energy consumption and peak demand by end use.

The total percentage improvement (energy savings) for the proposed case compared with the baseline case is calculated with this equation:

$$\text{Percentage Improvement} = 100 \times \frac{1 - \text{Proposed Building Performance}}{\text{Baseline Building Performance}}$$

Separate point scales are provided for new and existing buildings in recognition of the constraints inherent in renovating an existing shell compared with new construction.

	EA
NC	Credit 1
SCHOOLS	Credit 1
CS	Credit 1

Calculations for Option 2, Prescriptive Compliance Path

There are no calculations required for Option 2.

Calculations for Option 3, Prescriptive Compliance Path: Advanced Buildings™ Core Performance™ Guide

There are no calculations required for Option 3.

7. Documentation Guidance

As a first step in preparing to complete the LEED-Online documentation requirements, work through the following measures. Refer to LEED-Online for the complete descriptions of all required documentation.

- For ASHRAE compliance, list any addenda used and retain copies of ASHRAE compliance forms.

- Determine the climate zone for the project location.

- Calculate energy use by type.

- List energy end uses for the project building (for both the baseline case and the design case).

- If the project is using a computer energy simulation, adhere to Appendix G of ASHRAE 90.1-2007 (or equivalent local code) and retain the final report indicating the annual energy cost of the baseline and design cases.

- If the project is using the prescriptive compliance path, assemble documentation demonstrating that the project meets all requirements applicable to the selected prescriptive path.

8. Examples

OPTION 1. Whole Building Simulation

The project building is a 100,000-square-foot office building, and the team is using the performance rating method. The design case uses a high-performance envelope with 23% glazing, "Super T8" direct and indirect ambient lighting with supplemental task lighting, a VAV system that receives chilled water from a 400-ton variable-speed electric chiller, and 20 kW of photovoltaic panels installed on the roof. Using the performance rating method system map, the budgeted HVAC system type is modeled as a packaged VAV system with hot water reheat, variable speed fan control, and direct expansion cooling.

To determine the proposed building performance, the energy modeler creates an energy simulation model for the design building using DOE-2, Trane Trace™700, EnergyPlus, Carrier HAP-E20 II, or another hourly load and energy modeling software tool. The model parameters for all loads, including receptacle and process loads and the expected building occupancy profile and schedule, are adjusted to determine central system capacities and energy use by system. Through parametric manipulation, the energy modeler, working with the design team, increases component efficiencies to exceed the referenced standard. The energy generated by the photovoltaic panels is calculated using PV Watts Version 1 software according to the ASHRAE 90.1-2007 exceptional calculations method.

The proposed building performance is calculated as the total projected energy cost for the design energy model minus the energy generated by the photovoltaic panels as calculated in PV Watts Version 1.

	EA
NC	Credit 1
SCHOOLS	Credit 1
CS	Credit 1

The baseline building performance is then calculated by adjusting the model parameters to meet the requirements listed in ASHRAE 90.1-2007, Appendix G. The baseline model includes the same plug and process loads and an identical building occupancy profile and schedule as the proposed design to determine central system capacities and energy use by system.

For the baseline model, the energy modeler redistributes the glazing uniformly across all 4 building orientations but otherwise models the baseline glazing percentage identically to the proposed design because the ratio of window-to-wall area for the proposed design is less than 40%. The energy modeler adjusts the construction assembly types in accordance with ASHRAE 90.1-2007, Table G3.1.5, and to meet minimal building envelope requirements for the building's climate zone. The baseline HVAC system type is modeled as a packaged VAV system with hot water reheat (ASHRAE 90.1-2007, Table G3.1.1.A). The energy modeler uses prescribed ASHRAE 90.1-2007 HVAC system component efficiencies and performs sizing runs to determine the fan supply air volume, and then uses this volume to calculate the total fan brake horsepower and the total fan power of the baseline case.

The energy modeler first performs the baseline design simulation with the actual building orientation, and then with the building rotated 90°, 180°, and 270°. For each of the 4 baseline design orientations, the energy modeler revises the window solar heat gain coefficients to reflect the minimum ASHRAE prescriptive requirements for the revised building orientations. The energy modeler takes the average of the total annual energy cost simulated for the 4 baseline simulations to establish the baseline building performance.

In the example, the general building energy model information is summarized in Table 3, the baseline and proposed design input parameters are summarized in Tables 4 and 5, the baseline performance is calculated in Table 6, and the baseline design and proposed design results, as well as the percentage improvement (Equation 1), are summarized in Table 7. In Tables 6 and 7, energy is reported as site energy, not source energy. These 4 tables illustrate the format required for EA Credit 1 documentation.

Equation 1

$$\text{Percentage Improvement} = 100 \times \frac{1 - \text{Proposed Building Performance}}{\text{Baseline Building Performance}}$$

Table 3. General Project Information

EA	
NC	Credit 1
SCHOOLS	Credit 1
CS	Credit 1

Performance Rating Method Compliance Report – Page 1		
Project Name:	Midrastleton Office Building	
Project Address:	2850 W. Washington Ave.	Date: October 5, 2006
Designer of Record:	Maddlestobum Architects	Telephone: 702-020-0400
Contact Person:	Fenray Constrablik	Telephone: 702-014-9284
City:	Las Vegas, NV	Principal Heating Source: ❑ Fossil Fuel ❑ Electricity ❑ Solar/Site Recovered ❑ Other
Weather Data:	Las Vegas, NV (LAS-VENV.bin)	
Climate Zone:	3B	

Space Summary			
Building Use	**Conditioned Area (sf)**	**Unconditioned (sf)**	**Total (sf)**
1. Office (open plan)	40,000		40,000
2. Office (executive/private)	30,000		30,000
3. Corridor	10,000		10,000
4. Lobby	5,000		5,000
5. Restrooms	5,000		5,000
6. Conference room	4,000		4,000
7. Mechanical/electrical room	4,000		4,000
8. Copy room	2,000		2,000
Total	100,000		100,000

Advisory Messages

	Proposed Building Design	**Budget Building**	**Difference (Proposed Budget)**
Number of hours heating loads not met (system/plant)	0	0	0
Number of hours cooling loads not met (system/plant)	0	0	0
Number of warnings	0	0	0
Number of errors	0	0	0
Number of defaults overridden	1	1	0

Description of differences between the budget building and proposed design not documented on other forms:
❑ Not Applicable ☒ Attached

Additional Building Information

Quantity of floors	Three
Simulation program	eQuest v. 3.55
Utility rate: electricity	Nevada Power Large General Service (average $0.0935/kWh)
Utility rate: natural gas	Southwest Gas Medium General Service (average $1.04/therm)
Utility rate: steam or hot water	
Utility rate: chilled water	
Utility rate: other	

Table 3. General Project Information

Performance Rating Method Compliance Report – Page 2		
Comparison of Proposed Design versus Baseline Design Energy Model Inputs:		
Building Element	**Proposed Design Input**	**Baseline Design Input**
Envelope		
Above grade wall construction(s)	1. Steel-frame Construction, R-19 insulation, 16 in. OC, 6" depth, U-factor = 0.109	Steel-frame Construction, R-13 insulation, U-factor = 0.124
Below grade wall construction	Not Applicable	Not Applicable
Roof construction	Built-up Roof, Insulation entirely above deck, R-30 ci, U-factor = 0.032, Roof Reflectivity = 0.45 (cool roof)	Insulation entirely above deck, R-15ci, U-factor = 0.063, Roof Reflectivity = 0.30
Exterior floor construction	Not applicable	Not applicable
Slab-on-grade construction	Uninsulated, F-0.730	Uninsulated, F-0.730 .
Window-to-gross wall ratio	23%	23%
Fenestration type(s)	1. Dual-pane metal frame tinted low-E glass doors with thermal break 2. Dual-pane metal-frame low-E glass windows with thermal break	1. North orientation 2. South, East, West Orientations
Fenestration assembly u-factor	1. 0.61 2. 0.59	1. 0.57 2. 0.57
Fenestration assembly shgc	1. 0.25 2. 0.25	1. 0.39 2. 0.25
Fenestration visual light transmittance	1. 0.44 2. 0.44	1. 0.44 2. 0.44
Fixed shading devices	1. None	1. None
Automated movable shading devices	None	None
Electrical Systems & Process Loads		
Ambient lighting power density, and lighting design description	Building Area Method: 1.0 w/ft² Office	Building Area Method: 1.0 w/ft² Office
Process lighting	None	None
Lighting occupant sensor controls	Not installed	Not installed
Daylighting controls	None	None
Exterior lighting power (tradable surfaces)	3.7 kW	4.2 kW
Exterior lighting power (non-tradable surfaces)	0.8 kW	0.8 kW
Receptacle equipment	0.75 W/sf	0.75 W/sf
Elevators or escalators	Two elevators operated intermittently (5kW per elevator with 490 equivalent full load hours of operation per elevator)	Two elevators operated intermittently (5kW per elevator with 490 equivalent full load hours of operation per elevator)
Refrigeration equipment	None	None
Other process loads	Telecom rooms, one per floor, 2.3kW peak wirh 3,680 equivalent full load hours of operation	Telecom rooms, one per floor, 2.3kW peak wirh 3,680 equivalent full load hours of operation

Table 4. Proposed and Baseline Summary Table

EA	
NC	Credit 1
SCHOOLS	Credit 1
CS	Credit 1

Performance Rating Method Compliance Report – Page 3		
Comparison of Proposed Design versus Baseline Design Energy Model Inputs:		
Building Element	**Proposed Design Input**	**Baseline Design Input**
Mechanical & Plumbing Systems		
HVAC system type(s)	1. Variable Air Volume with Reheat (one per floor) 2. Packaged single Zone systems with gas furnace (gas furnace not in actual design) serving telecom rooms and elevator equipment room.	System Type 5: Packaged Rooftop Variable Air Volume with Reheat. Packaged with Single Zone systems with gas furnace serving telecom rooms and elevator equipment room
Design supple air temperature differential	23° F	20°
Fan control	VSD Control	VSD Control
Fan power	1. AH-1: 14.0 bhp supply; 5.6 bhp return 2. AH-2: 14.5 bhp supply; 5.8 bhp return 3. AH-3: 14.4 bhp supply; 5.8 bhp return	94.8 total brake horsepower; 75.3kW total fan power (Supply Fans + Return Fans)
Economizer control	Differential TemperatureEconomizers with maximum temperature of 70° F	None
Demand control ventilation	Outside air quantity based on DCV zone sensors; Minimum Outside Air Sizing method set by critical zone	None
Unitary equipment cooling efficiency	1. 2. 12 SEER for two small PSZ systems	1. 8.8 EER for Packaged Rooftop VAV units 2. 12 SEER for two small PSZ systems
Unitary equipment heating efficiency	80% furnace efficiency for two small PSZ units	80% furnace efficiency for two small PSZ units
Chiller type, capacity, and efficiency	One 300-ton VSD centrifugal chiller: 0.58kW/ton full load-efficiency, variable speed control for part-load operation	Not Applicable
Cooling tower	One two-cell cooling tower; each cell has a 15 hp fan with variable speed control	Not Applicable
Boiler efficiency	One 85% efficient boiler, 2.0 MBTUH	Two boilers, 75% thermal efficiency; 1.25 MBTUH each
Chilled water loop and pump parameters	Variable primary flow with 25 hp variable speed pump; Chilled Water Temperature reset from 42° to 50° F	Not Applicable
Condenser water loop and pump parameters	Constant flow with 25 hp variable speed pump; Condenser Water Temperature reset from 70° to 85° F	Not Applicable
Hot water loop and pump parameters	Variable primary flow with 3 hp variable speed pump; Hot Water temperature reset based on load between 150° and 180° F	Variable primary flow with 3 hp constant speed pump; Hot water supply temperature reset based on outdoor dry-bulb temperature using the following schedule: 180° F at 20° F and below, 150° F at 50° F and above, and ramped linearly between 180° F and 150° F at temperatures between 20° F and 50° F
Domestic hot water system(s)	100 gallon storage gas water heater with 80% thermal efficiency, 175,000 btuh capacity, and 1,319 Btuh standby losses	100 gallon storage gas water heater with 80% thermal efficiency, 175,000 btuh capacity, and 1,319 Btuh standby losses

Table 5. Proposed and Baseline Summary Table, Continued

EA	
NC	Credit 1
SCHOOLS	Credit 1
CS	Credit 1

			Performance Rating Method Compliance Report – Page 4										

Baseline Building Performance Table

Baseline Building Energy Summary by End use

End Use	Process?	Energy Type	0° rotation Energy (10⁶ Btu)	0° rotation Peak (10⁶ Btu)	90° rotation Energy (10⁶ Btu)	90° rotation Peak (10⁶ Btu)	180° rotation Energy (10⁶ Btu)	180° rotation Peak (10⁶ Btu)	270° rotation Energy (10⁶ Btu)	270° rotation Peak (10⁶ Btu)	Average Energy (10⁶ Btu)	Average Peak (10⁶ Btu)	Average Cost ($/yr)
Interior lighting		Electricity	1,137.2	418.7	1,137.2	418.7	1,137.2	418.7	1,137.2	418.7	1,137.2	418.7	$31,990
Interior lighting (process)	X	Electricity											$0
Exterior lighting		Electricity	54.4	17.1	54.4	17.1	54.4	17.1	54.4	17.1	54.4	17.1	$1,531
Space heating (fuel 1)		Natural gas	515.8	2,300.0	525.6	2,300.0	486.7	2,300.0	494.3	2,300.0	505.6	2,300.0	$4,916
Space heating (fuel 2)		Electricity											$0
Space cooling		Electricity	1,299.4	836.8	1,308.9	843.8	1,298.1	815.7	1,310.3	812.3	1,304.2	827.1	$36,687
Pumps		Electricity	3.2	3.1	3.3	3.1	2.9	3.1	2.9	3.1	3.1	3.1	$86
Heat rejection		Electricity											$0
Fans - interior		Electricity	222.5	106.9	228.1	108.6	223.8	106.8	223.5	106.5	224.5	107.2	$6,315
Fans - parking garage		Electricity											$0
Service water heating (fuel 1)		Natural gas	57.3	10.4	57.3	10.4	57.3	10.4	57.3	10.4	57.3	10.4	$557
Service water heating (fuel 2)		Electricity											$0
Receptacle equipment	X	Electricity	1,040.7	273.0	1,040.7	273.0	1,040.7	273.0	1,040.7	273.0	1,040.7	273.0	$29,276
Refrigeration (food, etc.)	X	Electricity											$0
Cooking (commercial, fuel 1)	X	Electricity											$0
Cooking (commercial, fuel 2)	X	Electricity											$0
Elevators and escalators	X	Electricity	16.7	17.1	16.7	17.1	16.7	17.1	16.7	17.1	16.7	17.1	$470
Other process	X	Electricity	28.9	7.8	28.9	7.8	28.9	7.8	28.9	7.8	28.9	7.8	$813
Total building consumption/demand			4,376.1	3,990.9	4,401.2	3,999.6	4,346.7	3,969.7	4,366.3	3,965.9	4,372.6	3,981.5	$112,641
Total process energy			1,086.3	297.9	1,086.3	297.9	1,086.3	297.9	1,086.3	297.9	1,086.3	297.9	$30,559

Note: Energy Consumption is listed in units of site energy
10³ Btu = kWh x 3.413   10³ Btu = therms / 100

Table 6. Baseline Summary Table

Energy Type	Baseline Building Energy Cost and Consumption by Fuel Type									
	0° rotation		90° rotation		180° rotation		270° rotation		Average	
	Energy Consumption (10³ Btu)	Energy Cost ($/Yr)	Energy Consumption (10³ Btu)	Energy Cost ($/Yr)	Energy Consumption (10³ Btu)	Energy Cost ($/Yr)	Energy Consumption (10³ Btu)	Energy Cost ($/Yr)	Energy Consumption (10³ Btu)	Energy Cost ($/Yr)
Electricity	3,803.0	$107,174	3,818.3	$107.398	3,802.7	$107,021	3,814.7	$107,079	3,809.7	$107,168
Natural gas	573.1	$5,563	582.9	$5,650	544.0	$5,305	551.6	$5,373	562.9	$5,473
Steam/hot water										
Other										
Total	4,376.1	$112,737	4,401.2	$113,048	4,346.7	$112,326	4,366.3	$112,452	4,372.6	$112,641

The process energy cost is 27% of the Baseline Building Performance. This meets the requirements of LEED EAc1.

Table 6. Summary Table

EA	
NC	Credit 1
SCHOOLS	Credit 1
CS	Credit 1

Performance Rating Method Compliance Report – Page 5						
Perfromance and Rating Table Energy Summary by End Use		EAc1 Points: 5				
		EaA2 Points: 1				
		Proposed Building		**Baseline Building**		
End Use	**Energy Type**	**Energy** (10^6 Btu)	**Peak** (10^3 Btu/h)	**Energy** (10^6 Btu)	**Peak** (10^3 Btu/h)	**Energy** (%)
Interior lighting (ambient)	Electricity	1,137.2	418.7	1,137.2	418.7	0%
Interior lighting (process)	Electricity					
Exterior lighting	Electricity	49.0	15.4	54.4	17.1	10%
Space heating (fuel 1)	Natural gas	360.2	1,600.0	505.6	2,300.0	29%
Space heating (fuel 2)	Electricity					
Space cooling	Electricity	452.0	331.1	1,304.2	827.1	65%
Pumps	Electricity	230.7	79.6	3.1	3.1	-7426%
Heat rejection	Electricity	23.9	20.5			
Fans - interior	Electricity	177.8	76.2	224.5	107.2	21%
Fans - parking garage	Electricity					
Service water heating (fuel 1)	Natural gas	57.3	10.4	57.3	10.4	0%
Service water heating (fuel 2)	Electricity					
Receptacle equipment	Electricity	1,040.7	273.0	1,040.7	273.0	0%
Refrigeration (food, etc.)	Electricity					
Cooking (commercial, fuel 1)	Natural gas					
Cooking (commercial, fuel 2)	Electricity					
Elevators and escalators	Electricity	16.7	17.1	16.7	17.1	0%
Other process	Electricity	28.9	7.8	28.9	7.8	0%
Total Building Consumption		3,573.9	2,849.8	4.372.6	3,981.5	22%

Note: Energy Consumption is listed in units of site energy
10^3 Btu = kWh x 3.413 10^3 Btu = therms / 100

	Proposed Building		**Baseline Building**		**Percentage Improvement**	
Type	**Energy Use** (10^6 Btu)	**Energy Cost** ($/yr)	**Energy Use** (10^6 Btu)	**Energy Cost** ($/yr)	**Energy (%)**	**Cost (%)**
Nonrenewable (Regulated & Unregulated)						
Electricity	3,156.4	$86,453	3,809.7	$107,168	17%	19%
Natural gas	417.5	$4,184	562.9	$5,473	26%	24%
Steam or hot water						
Chilled water						
Other						
Total nonrenewable (regulated & unregulated)	3,573.9	$90,638	4,372.6	$112,641	22%	24%
	Proposed Building		**Baseline Building**		**Percentage Improvement**	
Exceptional Calculation Method Savings (savings indicated as negative numbers)	**Energy Use** (10^6 Btu)	**Energy Cost** ($/yr)	**Energy Use** (10^6 Btu)	**Energy Cost** ($/yr)	**Energy (%)**	**Cost (%)**
Site-generated renewable (REC)	(96.4)	$(2,639)			2%	2%
Site recovered						
Exceptional calculation #1 savings						
Exceptional calculation #2 savings						
Exceptional calculation #3 savings						
Total including exceptional calculations	3,477.5	$87,999	4,372.6	$112,641	25%	26%
Percentage Improvement = 100 x (1 - (Proposed Building Performance / Baseline Building Performance))					21.88%	
Percent Renewable = REC / (Proposed Building Performance + REC)					2.91%	

	EA
NC	Credit 1
SCHOOLS	Credit 1
CS	Credit 1

9. Exemplary Performance

OPTION 1. Whole Building Simulation

Projects that use Option 1 and demonstrate a percentage improvement in the proposed building performance rating compared with the baseline building performance rating per ASHRAE 90.1-2007 by the following minimum energy cost savings percentages will be considered for 1 additional point under the Innovation in Design category:

- New Building: 50%
- Existing Building Renovation: 46%

OPTION 2. Prescriptive Compliance Path

There is no exemplary performance point available for the Option 2.

OPTION 3. Prescriptive Compliance Path: Advanced Buildings™ Core Performance™ Guide

There is no exemplary performance point available for Option 3.

10. Regional Variations

Regional variance is already incorporated in ASHRAE 90.1-2007, which account for 8 climate zones and 3 climate subzones and their minimum envelope and glazing property requirements.

11. Operations and Maintenance Considerations

Ensuring that the building systems are functioning properly and tracking energy use can save energy and operating costs. LEED for Existing Buildings: Operations & Maintenance covers this topic in EA Credit 1, Optimizing Energy Efficiency Performance.

12. Resources

Please see USGBC's LEED Registered Project Tools (http://www.usgbc.org/projecttools) for additional resources and technical information.

Websites

Advanced Buildings Technologies and Practices

http://www.advancedbuildings.org

This online resource, supported by Natural Resources Canada, presents energy-efficient technologies, strategies for commercial buildings, and pertinent case studies.

American Council for an Energy-Efficient Economy

http://www.aceee.org

ACEEE is a nonprofit organization dedicated to advancing energy efficiency through technical and policy assessments; advising policymakers and program managers; collaborating with businesses, public interest groups, and other organizations; and providing education and outreach through conferences, workshops, and publications.

American Society of Heating, Refrigerating and Air-Conditioning Engineers

http://www.ashrae.org

ASHRAE has developed a number of publications on energy use in existing buildings, including Standard 100–1995, Energy Conservation in Existing Buildings. This standard defines methods for energy surveys, provides guidance for operation and maintenance, and describes building and equipment modifications that result in energy conservation. 2 publications referenced by this credit (ANSI/ASHRAE/IESNA 90.1–2007 and ASHRAE Advanced Energy Design Guide for Small Office Buildings 2004) are available through ASHRAE.

Energy Information Agency, Commercial Building Energy Consumption Survey

http://www.eia.doe.gov

	EA
NC	Credit 1
SCHOOLS	Credit 1
CS	Credit 1

ENERGY STAR®

http://www.energystar.gov

ENERGY STAR is a government-industry partnership managed by the U.S. Environmental Protection Agency and the U.S. Department of Energy. The program's website offers energy management strategies, benchmarking software tools for buildings, product procurement guidelines, and lists of ENERGY STAR-labeled products and buildings.

ENERGY STAR® Building Upgrade Manual

http://www.energystar.gov/index.cfm?c=business.bus_upgrade_manual&layout=print

This document is a guide for ENERGY STAR Buildings Partners to use in planning and implementing energy efficiency upgrades in their facilities, and can be used as a comprehensive framework for an energy strategy.

International Energy Agency Solar Heating and Cooling Programme

http://www.iea-shc.org

National Renewable Energy Program, Energy-10™ Energy Simulation Software

http://www.nrel.gov/buildings/energy10.html

http://www.Energy-10.com

ENERGY-10 is an award-winning software tool for designing low-energy buildings. ENERGY-10 integrates daylighting, passive solar heating, and low-energy cooling strategies with energy-efficient shell design and mechanical equipment. The program is applicable to commercial and residential buildings of 10,000 square feet or less.

The Energy-10 software was developed by the National Renewable Energy Laboratory with funding from the Office of Building Technologies, Energy Efficiency and Renewable Energy, U.S. Department of Energy. It is distributed by the Sustainable Buildings Industry Council under license to the Midwest Research Institute.

New Buildings Institute

http://www.newbuildings.org

The New Buildings Institute is a nonprofit, public-benefits corporation dedicated to making buildings better for people and the environment. Its mission is to promote energy efficiency in buildings through technology research, guidelines, and codes.

U.S. Department of Energy, Building Energy Codes Program

http://www.energycodes.gov

The Building Energy Codes program provides comprehensive resources for states and code users, including news, compliance software, code comparisons, and the Status of State Energy Codes database. The database includes state energy contacts, code status, code history, DOE grants awarded, and construction data. The program is also updating the COMcheck-EZ compliance tool to include ANSI/ASHRAE/IESNA 90.1–2007. This compliance tool includes the prescriptive path and trade-off compliance methods. The software generates appropriate compliance forms as well.

DOE-2, Building Energy Use and Cost Analysis Software

http://www.doe2.com

This website includes information from the developers of DOE-2 and DOE-2 products, such as eQUEST, PowerDOE, and COMcheck-Plus.

U.S. Department of Energy, Office of Energy Efficiency and Renewable Energy

http://www.eere.energy.gov/buildings

This extensive website for energy efficiency is linked to a number of DOE-funded sites that address buildings and energy. Of particular interest is the tools directory, which includes the Commercial Buildings Energy Consumption Tool for estimating end-use consumption in commercial buildings. The tool allows the user to define a set of buildings by principal activity, size, vintage, region, climate zone, and fuels (main heat, secondary heat, cooling and water heating) and to view the resulting energy consumption and expenditure estimates in tabular form.

Print Media

ANSI/ASHRAE/IESNA Standard 90.1–2007 User's Manual (ASHRAE).

Advanced Lighting Guidelines, 2003 edition (New Building Institute, Inc., 2003). http://www.newbuildings.org/lighting.htm
These guidelines are available as a free download or can purchased as a printed manual of 390 pages.

ANSI/IESNA RP-1-04, American National Standard Practice for Office Lighting (IESNA).

Daylight in Buildings: A Source Book on Daylighting Systems and Components, Chapter 5, Daylight-Responsive Controls (Lawrence Berkeley National Laboratory). http://gaia.lbl.gov/iea21/

Design Brief: Lighting Controls Energy Design Resources (Southern California Edison). http://www.energydesignresources.com

Electricity Used by Office Equipment and Network Equipment in the United States: Detailed Report and Appendices, by Kawamoto, et al. (Lawrence Berkeley National Laboratory, February 2001). http://enduse.lbl.gov/Projects/InfoTech.html

Illuminating Engineering Society of North America Lighting Handbook, ninth edition (IESNA, 2000).

Mechanical and Electrical Equipment for Buildings, ninth edition, by Benjamin Stein and John S. Reynolds (John Wiley & Sons, 2000).

Sustainable Building Technical Manual (Public Technology Institute, 1996). http://www.pti.org/index.php/ptiee1/inside/C84

13. Definitions

Baseline building performance is the annual energy cost for a building design intended for use as a baseline for rating above standard design, as defined in ASHRAE 90.1-2007, Appendix G.

Daylighting is the controlled admission of natural light into a space, used to reduce or eliminate electric lighting.

A **district energy system** is a central energy conversion plant and transmission and distribution system that provides thermal energy to a group of buildings (e.g., a central cooling plant on a university campus). Central energy systems that provide only electricity are not included.

Downstream equipment consists of all heating or cooling systems, equipment, and controls located within the project building and site associated with transporting thermal energy into heated or cooled spaces. This includes the thermal connection or interface with the district energy system, secondary distribution systems in the building, and terminal units.

An **energy simulation model**, or **energy model**, is a computer-generated representation of the anticipated energy consumption of a building. It permits a comparison of energy performance, given proposed energy efficiency measures, with the baseline.

An **ENERGY STAR** rating is a measure of a building's energy performance compared with that of similar buildings, as determined by the ENERGY STAR Portfolio Manager. A score of 50 represents average building performance.

Lighting power density is the installed lighting power, per unit area.

Percentage improvement measures the energy cost savings for the proposed building performance compared with the baseline building performance.

Plug load is synonymous with **receptacle load.**

Proposed building performance is the annual energy cost calculated for a proposed design, as defined in ASHRAE 90.1-2007, Appendix G.

Receptacle (or plug) load is the current drawn by all equipment that is plugged into the electrical system.

Upstream equipment consists of all heating or cooling systems, equipment, and controls that are associated with a district energy system but are not part of the project building's thermal connection or do not interface with the district energy system. It includes the central energy plant and all transmission and distribution equipment associated with transporting the thermal energy to the project building and site.

	EA
NC	Credit 1
SCHOOLS	Credit 1
CS	Credit 1

ON-SITE RENEWABLE ENERGY

	NC	SCHOOLS	CS
Credit	EA Credit 2	EA Credit 2	EA Credit 2
Points	1-7 points	1-7 points	4 points

Intent

To encourage and recognize increasing levels of on-site renewable energy self-supply to reduce environmental and economic impacts associated with fossil fuel energy use.

Requirements

NC, SCHOOLS & CS

Use on-site renewable energy systems to offset building energy costs. Calculate project performance by expressing the energy produced by the renewable systems as a percentage of the building's annual energy cost and use the table below to determine the number of points achieved.

Use the building annual energy cost calculated in EA Credit 1: Optimize Energy Performance or the U.S. Department of Energy's Commercial Buildings Energy Consumption Survey database to determine the estimated electricity use.

The minimum renewable energy percentage for each point threshold is as follows:

NC & SCHOOLS

Percentage Renewable Energy	Points
1%	1
3%	2
5%	3
7%	4
9%	5
11%	6
13%	7

CS

Percentage Renewable Energy	Points
1%	4

	EA
NC	Credit 2
SCHOOLS	Credit 2
CS	Credit 2

1. Benefits and Issues to Consider

Use of renewable energy instead of fossil fuel–based energy can dramatically improve outdoor environmental quality. Use of renewable energy means reductions in air and water pollution, benefiting all community members. Wind Powering America is an initiative by the U.S. Department of Energy to dramatically increase the use of wind energy in the United States.

Renewable energy has a positive impact on rural communities in particular; siting and operating wind farms and biomass conversion facilities in rural areas enhances economic development. Rural wind generation is providing new sources of income for American farmers, Native Americans, and other rural landowners while meeting the growing demand for clean sources of electricity. However, care must be taken to minimize undesirable noise from wind farms and emissions from combustion at biomass conversion facilities.

Environmental Issues

Energy production from traditional, fossil fuel–based sources is a significant contributor to air pollution in the United States, releasing such pollutants as sulfur dioxide, nitrogen oxide, and carbon dioxide, which have widespread and adverse effects on human health, especially respiratory health, and contribute to acid precipitation, smog, and concentrations of greenhouse gases.

The overall environmental benefit of renewable energy depends on the source of energy and the process by which it is extracted. For example, using biomass can reduce the estimated 136 million tons of woody construction, demolition, and land-clearing waste annually sent to landfills,[11] but if these wastes are not processed properly, their combustion could degrade air quality. Although renewably generated electricity is not entirely benign, it greatly lessens the negative environmental impacts of power generation. Generating renewable energy on-site is an excellent way for owners to reduce the negative environmental impacts associated with a building's energy use.

Economic Issues

Using on-site renewable energy technologies can result in cost savings. Utility rebates are often available to reduce first costs of renewable energy equipment. The initial costs of installing or providing renewable energy sources on-site can be offset by future savings. A life-cycle cost analysis of the potential savings can help project teams in their decision-making process. In some states, initial costs can also be offset by net metering, in which excess energy is sold back to the utility, and through programs that provide incentives for using renewable energy. Project teams should ascertain whether these options are available locally, particularly for the type of renewable energy they plan to use.

Research on the available technologies is essential; consider climatic, geographical, and other regional factors that influence the appropriateness of an on-site renewable source for the building's energy use.

SCHOOLS   On-site renewable energy systems present an opportunity to incorporate sustainable technologies into the school curriculum.

2. Related Credits

The installation of renewable energy generation equipment usually has only a small effect on the achievement of other credits. Renewable energy equipment will change the energy performance of the building and require commissioning as well as measurement and verification. Achievement of EA Credit 2 is determined by the percentage of the building's energy use that is provided by on-site renewable energy generation systems, and therefore is directly tied to the building's energy performance. Additionally, there are synergies with purchasing green power for the project, since on-site energy generation reduces the quantity of green power that must be purchased to offset the building's energy use. Refer to the following prerequisites and credits:

- EA Prerequisite 1: Fundamental Commissioning

- EA Prerequisite 2: Minimum Energy Performance

- EA Credit 1: Optimize Energy Performance

- EA Credit 5: Measurement and Verification

- EA Credit 6: Green Power

	EA
NC	Credit 2
SCHOOLS	Credit 2
CS	Credit 2

3. Summary of Referenced Standard

ANSIASHRAE/IESNA Standard 90.1–2007, Energy Standard for Buildings Except Low-Rise Residential

American Society of Heating, Refrigerating and Air-Conditioning Engineers

http://www.ashrae.org

ANSI/ASHRAE/IESNA 90.1–2007 establishes minimum requirements for the energy-efficient design of buildings, with these exceptions: single-family houses; multifamily structures of 3 habitable stories or fewer above grade; manufactured houses (mobile and modular homes); buildings that do not use either electricity or fossil fuel; and equipment and portions of buildings systems that use energy primarily for industrial, manufacturing, or commercial processes. Building envelope requirements are provided for semiheated spaces such as warehouses.

On-site renewable or site-recovered energy that might be used to earn EA Credit 2 is handled as a special case in the modeling process. Renewable and recovered energy produced on-site are considered free energy in the performance rating method and not included in the design energy cost. See the Calculation section for details.

4. Implementation

Renewable energy systems include technologies designed to capture solar, wind, geothermal, water, or bio-based energy to satisfy on-site electric power demand or to directly offset space heating, space cooling, or water heating energy consumption.

Consider photovoltaics, solar thermal, geothermal, wind, biomass, and biogas energy. Eligible systems produce electric power or thermal energy for use on-site and should, where possible, deliver power to the grid when their output exceeds the site demand. Contact local utilities or electric service providers to determine whether net metering is available,.

Energy savings from the use of on-site renewable energy should be based on either the metered renewable energy produced and used on-site, or the metered renewable energy produced and used on-site or sent to the grid. Energy produced on-site that is not captured and used, whether on-site or via the grid, cannot be included in the credit calculations. For example, if a project building uses photovoltaic panels to generate electricity on-site but does not store energy when output exceeds demand or use net metering, only the portion of renewable electricity actually consumed on-site counts. Renewable energy produced on-site and then sold to the grid is not eligible.

Eligible On-site Systems

On-site renewable energy technologies eligible for EA Credit 2 include the following:

- Photovoltaic systems

- Wind energy systems

- Solar thermal systems

	EA
NC	Credit 2
SCHOOLS	Credit 2
CS	Credit 2

- Biofuel-based electrical systems (see list of eligible biofuels, below)
- Geothermal heating systems
- Geothermal electric systems
- Low-impact hydroelectric power systems
- Wave and tidal power systems

There are some restrictions for geothermal energy systems, solar thermal energy systems, and biofuel-based electrical systems. Geothermal energy systems using deep-earth water or steam sources (but not vapor compression systems for heat transfer) may be eligible for this credit. These systems may either produce electric power or provide thermal energy for primary use at the building.

Active solar thermal energy systems that employ collection panels, heat transfer mechanical components (such as pumps or fans), and defined heat storage systems (such as hot water tanks) are eligible for this credit. Thermo-siphon solar and storage tank "batch heaters" are also eligible.

The following biofuels are considered renewable energy under this credit:

- Untreated wood waste, including mill residues
- Agricultural crops or waste
- Animal waste and other organic waste
- Landfill gas,

Ineligible On-site Systems
These types of on-site systems are not eligible for this credit:

- Architectural features
- Passive solar strategies
- Daylighting strategies
- Geo-exchange systems (ground-source heat pumps)

Architectural passive solar and daylighting strategies provide significant energy savings. Their contributions are reflected in project-wide energy efficiency levels and facilitate the achievement of EA Prerequisite 2 and EA Credit 1.

Geoexchange systems (geothermal or ground-source heat pumps) are earth-coupled HVAC applications use vapor-compression systems for heat transfer and do not obtain significant quantities of deep-earth heat. These systems are not eligible as renewable energy systems. The contributions of these systems are reflected in project-wide energy efficiency levels and facilitate the achievement of EA Prerequisite 2 and EA Credit 1.

Energy production based on the following biofuels are not eligible for this credit:

- Combustion of municipal solid waste,
- Forestry biomass waste other than mill residue,
- Wood coated with paints, plastics, or formica,
- Wood treated for preservation with materials containing halogens, chlorine compounds, halide compounds, chromated copper arsenate, or arsenic. If more than 1% of the wood fuel has been treated with these compounds, the energy system is ineligible.

Retention of Renewable Energy Environmental Attributes

For renewable energy coming from both on-site and off-site sources, the associated environmental attributes must be retained or retired; they cannot be sold. Project teams should understand and value the positive effect of on-site renewables on the surrounding ecosystems. For on-site renewables, energy that exceeds the project building's demand may be sold at fees equivalent to the market rate of nonrenewable energy, but no premium can be charged for the renewable nature of the energy. Such a premium indicates that these attributes have not been retained, and therefore the project team cannot take credit for that energy as renewable.

	EA
NC	Credit 2
SCHOOLS	Credit 2
CS	Credit 2

To encourage the greater development of on-site renewable energy systems, the sale of renewable energy certificates (RECs) is allowed from an on-site renewable energy system that claims this credit if the building owner or energy system owner, either separately or acting together, meets the following conditions:

- RECs equal to 200% of the system's annual rated energy output each year are purchased from another source, which must be Green-e eligible. The system's rated output must reflect all system performance characteristics as well as actual local site conditions (e.g., climate, mounting location and angles, etc.). The rationale for the 1-for-2 ratio is that many states have set renewable portfolio standards and in-state renewable energy targets that can be traded in the form of credits. These in-state RECs are typically more expensive to achieve and typically cost more (e.g., $0.05/kWh for New England wind power vs. $0.01/kWh for RECs from West Texas or Dakotas wind). From an environmental and financial perspective, these are not equivalent for 2 reasons:

  - In-state and out-of-state RECs reduce carbon dioxide emissions by the same amount, but out-of-state RECs result in fewer reductions of other emissions than in-state RECs where the population is concentrated and where RECs are largely purchased.

  - Distant renewable energy generation may be stranded by limited technical and design capacities.

  Given that in-state RECs create more non-CO_2 benefits than out-of-state RECs but are equivalent in their CO_2 impacts, in-state credits may be replaced by out-of-state credits on a 1-for-2 basis. This allows green building projects to capture the value of RECs created by on-site renewables while reducing net CO_2.

- The seller of the on-site RECs must follow all established guidelines for the sale of RECs and not claim any of the environmental attributes for the on-site system.

District Energy Systems

For projects with district energy systems, specific technical guidance can be found on USGBC's registered project tools page (http://www.usgbc.org/projecttools). Follow the guidance in effect at the time of registration.

5. Timeline and Team

The project team, with the owner, architect, and engineer, should first estimate the potential energy use of the building so that renewable technologies with adequate capacity can be identified. Systems producing on-site renewable electrical power should be designed to facilitate net metering back to the grid for periods when the renewable energy system output exceeds the site demand. Ask local utilities and electric service providers about incentive and rebate programs.

6. Calculations

Calculate the amount of energy cost offset by using the energy calculated in EA Credit 1 or based on

	EA
NC	Credit 2
SCHOOLS	Credit 2
CS	Credit 2

the Commercial Buildings Energy Consumption Survey database for the building type. Calculations are based on energy use before the credit for renewable energy is taken.

7. Documentation Guidance

As a first step in preparing to complete the LEED-Online documentation requirements, work through the following measures. Refer to LEED-Online for the complete descriptions of all required documentation.

- Document on-site renewable energy source types, total annual energy generation, and backup energy sources.

- Calculate the energy generated from each on-site renewable energy source.

- Maintain documentation regarding any incentives that were provided to support the installation of on-site renewable energy systems.

8. Example

There are no examples for this credit.

9. Exemplary Performance

NC & SCHOOLS Projects can earn credit for exemplary performance by showing that on-site renewable energy accounts for 15% or more of the annual building energy cost.

CS Projects can earn credit for exemplary performance by showing that on-site renewable energy accounts for 5% or more of the annual building energy cost.

10. Regional Variations

The availability and appropriateness of renewable energy technologies for a building varies by region. Factors like climate, geography, and location can greatly affect the choice of the best renewable source. For example, although solar energy is available across the United States, it is most abundant—and thus solar-based energy generation is most efficient—in the Southwest. Figure 1 illustrates the variation in solar radiation over the United States.

Average Daily Solar Radiation Per Month
ANNUAL

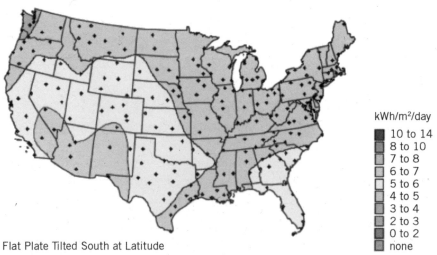

kWh/m²/day

- 10 to 14
- 8 to 10
- 7 to 8
- 6 to 7
- 5 to 6
- 4 to 5
- 3 to 4
- 2 to 3
- 0 to 2
- none

Flat Plate Tilted South at Latitude

Similarly, biomass is likely to be more cost-effective in agricultural regions, and wind power in coastal regions. More information on regional variation of renewable energy sources can be found at http://www1.eere.energy.gov/maps_data.

	EA
NC	Credit 2
SCHOOLS	Credit 2
CS	Credit 2

Although energy efficiency is universally important, it is crucial in regions where coal is used to generate electricity. It is also particularly important to reduce peak energy use because units brought online to meet peak demand tend to be the greatest contributors to greenhouse gas emissions. Replacing fossil fuel with renewable energy for generating electricity during peak periods delivers the greatest benefits in reducing the marginal emissions.

11. Operations and Maintenance Considerations

Confirm that the renewable energy systems have been correctly and appropriately implemented as designed and that the building owner, maintenance personnel, and occupants are given the information they need to understand, maintain, and use systems that may be unfamiliar to them. Provide building operators with the manufacturer's recommendations for operating and maintenance procedures. Operators may need guidance on how to maximize efficiency, including information about the cleaning method and frequency for solar panels.

Specify a way to track energy production from the renewable energy source over the lifespan of the building, to help the facility manager maximize use of the system and accurately determine the savings. Ensure that the renewable energy system is submetered so that energy production and use can be monitored.

12. Resources

Please see USGBC's LEED Registered Project Tools (http://www.usgbc.org/projecttools) for additional resources and technical information.

Websites

American Wind Energy Association

http://www.awea.org

AWEA is a national trade association representing wind power plant developers, wind turbine manufacturers, utilities, consultants, insurers, financiers, researchers, and others involved in the wind energy industry.

ENERGY Guide

http://www.energyguide.com

This website provides information on different power types, including green power, as well as general information on energy efficiency and tools for selecting power providers based on economic, environmental, and other criteria.

National Center for Photovoltaics

http://www.nrel.gov/ncpv/

NCPV provides clearinghouse information on all aspects of photovoltaic systems.

North Carolina Solar Center, Database of State Incentives for Renewable Energy

http://www.dsireusa.org

The DSIRE database collects information on state financial and regulatory incentives (e.g., tax credits, grants, and special utility rates) to promote the application of renewable energy technologies. The database details the incentives on a state-by-state basis.

U.S. Department of Energy, Green Power Partnership

http://www.eere.energy.gov/greenpower

The Green Power Partnership provides news and information on green power markets and related activities. It contains up-to-date information on green power providers, product offerings, consumer issues, and in-depth analyses of issues and policies affecting green power markets. The website is maintained by the National Renewable Energy Laboratory for the Department of Energy.

U.S. Department of Energy, National Renewable Energy Laboratory
http://www.nrel.gov
NREL is a leader in the U.S. Department of Energy's effort to secure for the nation an energy future that is environmentally and economically sustainable.

U.S. Department of Energy, Office of Energy Efficiency and Renewable Energy
http://www.eere.energy.gov
This website is a comprehensive resource for U.S. Department of Energy information on energy efficiency and renewable energy and provides access to energy links and downloadable documents.

U.S. Department of Energy, Energy Efficiency and Renewable Energy, Renewable Energy Maps and Data
http://www1.eere.energy.gov/maps_data
The maps and data section of DOE's EERE website provides information on regional distribution of renewable energy sources and technologies in the United States.

U.S. EPA Green Power Partnership
http://www.epa.gov/greenpower/index.htm
EPA's Green Power Partnership provides assistance and recognition to organizations that demonstrate environmental leadership by choosing green power. It includes a buyer's guide with lists of green power providers in each state.

Print Media

Wind and Solar Power Systems, by Mukund Patel (CRC Press, 1999).
This text offers information about the fundamental elements of wind and solar power generation, conversion, and storage and detailed information about the design, operation, and control methods of stand-alone and grid-connected systems.

Wind Energy Comes of Age, by Paul Gipe (John Wiley & Sons, 1995).
This book provides extensive information on the wind power industry, and is among several books by the author covering general and technical information about wind power.

13. Definitions

Biofuel-based systems are power systems that run on renewable fuels derived from organic materials, such as wood by-products and agricultural waste. Examples of biofuels include untreated wood waste, agricultural crops and residues, animal waste, other organic waste, and landfill gas.

Biomass is plant material from trees, grasses, or crops that can be converted to heat energy to produce electricity.

A **district energy system** is a central energy conversion plant and transmission and distribution system that provides thermal energy to a group of buildings (e.g., a central cooling plant on a university campus). Central energy systems that provide only electricity are not included.

Downstream equipment consists of all heating or cooling systems, equipment, and controls located within the project building and site associated with transporting thermal energy into heated or cooled spaces. This includes the thermal connection or interface with the district energy system, secondary distribution systems in the building, and terminal units.

Geothermal energy is electricity generated by converting hot water or steam from within the earth into electrical power.

Geothermal heating systems use pipes to transfer heat from underground steam or hot water for heating, cooling, and hot water. The system retrieves heat during cool months and returns heat in summer months.

	EA
NC	Credit 2
SCHOOLS	Credit 2
CS	Credit 2

Green-e is a program established by the Center for Resource Solutions to both promote green electricity products and provide consumers with a rigorous and nationally recognized method to identify those products.

Life-cycle cost analysis calculates expected future operating, maintenance, and replacement costs of designs and features used to assist owners in developing a realistic design and budget estimate.

Net metering is a metering and billing arrangement that allows on-site generators to send excess electricity flows to the regional power grid; these flows offset a portion of the energy drawn from the grid.

On-site renewable energy is energy derived from renewable sources located within the project site perimeter.

Renewable energy comes from sources that are not depleted by use. Examples include energy from the sun, wind, and small (low-impact) hydropower, plus geothermal energy and wave and tidal systems. Ways to capture energy from the sun include photovoltaic, solar thermal, and bioenergy systems based on wood waste, agricultural crops or residue, animal and other organic waste, or landfill gas.

Upstream equipment consists of all heating or cooling systems, equipment, and controls that are associated with a district energy system but are not part of the project building's thermal connection or do not interface with the district energy system. It includes the central energy plant and all transmission and distribution equipment associated with transporting the thermal energy to the project building and site.

ENHANCED COMMISSIONING

	NC	SCHOOLS	CS
Credit	EA Credit 3	EA Credit 3	EA Credit 3
Points	2 points	2 points	2 points

Intent

To begin the commissioning process early in the design process and execute additional activities after systems performance verification is completed.

Requirements

NC, SCHOOLS & CS

Implement, or have a contract in place to implement, the following additional commissioning process activities in addition to the requirements of EA Prerequisite 1: Fundamental Commissioning of Building Energy Systems and in accordance with the LEED Reference Guide for Green Building Design and Construction, 2009 Edition:

- Prior to the start of the construction documents phase, designate an independent commissioning authority (CxA) to lead, review, and oversee the completion of all commissioning process activities.

  - The CxA must have documented commissioning authority experience in at least 2 building projects.

  - The individual serving as the CxA:

    - Must be independent of the work of design and construction.

    - Must not be an employee of the design firm, though he or she may be contracted through them.

    - Must not be an employee of, or contracted through, a contractor or construction manager holding construction contracts.

    - May be a qualified employee or consultant of the owner.

    - The CxA must report results, findings and recommendations directly to the owner.

- The CxA must conduct, at a minimum, 1 commissioning design review of the owner's project requirements basis of design, and design documents prior to the mid-construction documents phase and back-check the review comments in the subsequent design submission.

- The CxA must review contractor submittals applicable to systems being commissioned for compliance with the owner's project requirements and basis of design. This review must be concurrent with the review of the architect or engineer of record and submitted to the design team and the owner.

- The CxA or other project team members must develop a systems manual that provides future operating staff the information needed to understand and optimally operate the commissioned systems.

- The CxA or other project team members must verify that the requirements for training operating personnel and building occupants have been completed.

- The CxA must be involved in reviewing the operation of the building with operations and maintenance (O&M) staff and occupants within 10 months after substantial completion. A plan for resolving outstanding commissioning-related issues must be included.

	EA
NC	Credit 3
SCHOOLS	Credit 3
CS	Credit 3

1. Benefits and Issues to Consider

Environmental Issues

Facilities that do not perform as intended may consume significantly more resources over their lifetimes. Commissioning can minimize the negative impacts buildings have on the environment by helping verify that buildings are designed, constructed, and operated as intended and in accordance with the owner's project requirements.

Economic Issues

An effective commissioning process typically increases soft costs and may require additional scheduling for commissioning activities. This investment is generally recouped in improved design and construction coordination, fewer change orders, and reduced operating costs.

Indoor air quality and building occupants' comfort may have tremendous impact on their productivity, health, and well-being, as well as the cost of ownership. Commissioning can significantly reduce repairs, construction change orders, energy costs, and maintenance and operation costs.

2. Related Credits

The commissioning effort can affect many performance-based features encouraged in the LEED Rating System. Consider including in commissioning the energy-using systems addressed by the following credits:

- SS Credit 8: Light Pollution Reduction
- WE Credit 1: Water Efficient Landscaping
- WE Credit 2: Innovative Wastewater Technologies
- WE Credit 3: Water Use Reduction
- EA Credit 1: Optimize Energy Performance
- EA Credit 2: On-site Renewable Energy
- EA Credit 5: Measurement and Verification
- IEQ Prerequisite 1: Minimum Indoor Air Quality Performance
- IEQ Credit 1: Outdoor Air Delivery Monitoring
- IEQ Credit 2: Increased Ventilation
- IEQ Credit 5: Indoor Chemical and Pollutant Source Control
- IEQ Credit 6: Controllability of Systems
- IEQ Credit 7: Thermal Comfort

EA Credit 3, Enhanced Commissioning, goes beyond the minimum threshold for commissioning activities, as defined by the related prerequisite:

- EA Prerequisite 1: Fundamental Commissioning

3. Summary of Referenced Standards

There are no standards referenced for this credit.

4. Implementation

Relationship between Fundamental and Enhanced Commissioning

LEED for New Construction, LEED for Core & Shell, and LEED for Schools address building commissioning in 2 places, EA Prerequisite 1, Fundamental Commissioning of Building Energy Systems, and EA Credit 3, Enhanced Commissioning.

	EA
NC	Credit 3
SCHOOLS	Credit 3
CS	Credit 3

For LEED design and construction projects, the scope of services for the commissioning authority (CxA) and project team should be based on the owner's project requirements. The commissioning process activities must address the commissioned systems noted in the EA Prerequisite 1 requirements. Other systems, such as the building envelope, storm water management systems, water treatment systems, and information technology systems, may also be included in the commissioning process at the owner's discretion. EA Credit 3 requires that the commissioning authority be involved early in the process to help facilitate a commissioning design review and a commissioning documentation review. As the project nears completion, enhanced commissioning requires oversight of staff training, a walk-through 10 months after completion, and the completion of a systems manual.

5. Timeline and Team
Refer to the Timeline and Team section in EA Prerequisite 1.

6. Calculations
There are no calculations required for this credit.

7. Documentation Guidance
As a first step in preparing to complete the LEED-Online documentation requirements, work through the following measures. Refer to LEED-Online for the complete descriptions of all required documentation.

- Update the commissioning plan at milestones throughout the project. This should happen, at a minimum, during the design development phase, the construction documents phase, and just prior to the kick-off meeting with the general contractor.

- Prepare a systems list that indicates which systems have been included within the scope of enhanced commissioning.

- Request confirmation that the commissioning authority has documented experience on at least 2 building projects.

- Create a written schedule of building operator trainings.

- Retain a copy of the commissioning authority's design review, any designer responses to this review, and confirmation of the back-check.

- Retain copies of the owner's project requirements, basis of design, commissioning specifications, commissioning report, and systems manual.

8. Examples
There are no examples for this credit.

9. Exemplary Performance
LEED for New Construction, LEED for Core & Shell, and LEED for Schools projects that conduct comprehensive envelope commissioning may be considered for an innovation credit. These projects will need to demonstrate the standards and protocol by which the envelope was commissioned.

	EA
NC	Credit 3
SCHOOLS	Credit 3
CS	Credit 3

CS LEED for Core & Shell projects that require the full scope of commissioning (both fundamental and enhanced) for all the tenant spaces may be considered for an innovation point.

10. Regional Variations

Refer to EA Prerequisite 1, Regional Variations.

11. Operations and Maintenance Considerations

Refer to the Operations and Maintenance section in EA Prerequisite 1.

12. Resources

Please see USGBC's LEED Registered Project Tools (http://www.usgbc.org/projecttools) for additional resources and technical information.

See also the Resources section of EA Prerequisite 1 for a list of specific commissioning resources.

13. Definitions

Basis of design includes design information necessary to accomplish the owner's project requirements, including system descriptions, indoor environmental quality criteria, design assumptions, and references to applicable codes, standards, regulations, and guidelines.

Commissioning (Cx) is the process of verifying and documenting that a building and all of its systems and assemblies are planned, designed, installed, tested, operated, and maintained to meet the owner's project requirements.

The **commissioning authority (CxA)** is the individual designated to organize, lead, and review the completion of commissioning process activities. The CxA facilitates communication among the owner, designer, and contractor to ensure that complex systems are installed and function in accordance with the owner's project requirements.

The **commissioning plan** is a document that outlines the organization, schedule, allocation of resources, and documentation requirements of the commissioning process.

The **commissioning process** is a systematic quality-focused effort to ensure that building systems are designed, specified, procured, installed, and functioning in accordance with the owner's intent. The process uses planning, documentation, and verification of testing to review and oversee the activities of both designer and constructor.

The **commissioning report** documents the commissioning process, including a commissioning program overview, identification of the commissioning team, and description of the commissioning process activities.

Commissioning specification is the contract language used in the construction documents to detail the objective, scope, and implementation of the construction and acceptance phases of the commissioning process as developed in the design phase of the commissioning plan. This allows the construction contractor to ensure that these activities are considered in proposals for the construction work.

The **commissioning team** includes those people responsible for working together to carry out the commissioning process.

A **district energy system** is a central energy conversion plant and transmission and distribution system that provides thermal energy to a group of buildings (e.g., a central cooling plant on a university campus). Central energy systems that provide only electricity are not included.

Downstream equipment consists of all heating or cooling systems, equipment, and controls located within the project building and site associated with transporting thermal energy into heated or cooled spaces. This includes the thermal connection or interface with the district energy system, secondary distribution systems in the building, and terminal units.

Enhanced commissioning is a set of best practices that go beyond fundamental commissioning to ensure that building systems perform as intended by the owner. These practices include designating a commissioning authority prior to the construction documents phase, conducting commissioning design reviews, reviewing contractor submittals, developing a systems manual, verifying operator training, and performing a postoccupancy operations review.

Fundamental commissioning is a set of essential best practices used to ensure that building performance requirements have been identified early in the project's development and to verify that the designed systems have been installed in compliance with those requirements. These practices include designating a commissioning authority, documenting the owner's project requirements and basis of design, incorporating commissioning requirements into the construction documents, establishing a commissioning plan, verifying installation and performance of specified building systems, and completing a summary commissioning report.

An **installation inspection** examines components of the building systems to determine whether they are installed properly and ready for systems performance testing.

Owner's project requirements is a written document that details the ideas, concepts, and criteria that are determined by the owner to be important to the success of the project.

Systems performance testing is the process of determining the ability of commissioned systems to perform in accordance with the owner's project requirements, the basis of design, and construction documents.

Upstream equipment consists of all heating or cooling systems, equipment, and controls that are associated with a district energy system but are not part of the project building's thermal connection or do not interface with the district energy system. It includes the central energy plant and all transmission and distribution equipment associated with transporting the thermal energy to the project building and site.

Verification is the range of checks and tests carried out to determine whether components, subsystems, systems, and interfaces between systems operate in accordance with the contract documents.

	EA
NC	Credit 3
SCHOOLS	Credit 3
CS	Credit 3

	NC	SCHOOLS	CS
Credit	EA Credit 4	EA Credit 4	EA Credit 4
Points	2 points	1 point	2 points

Intent

To reduce ozone depletion and support early compliance with the Montreal Protocol while minimizing direct contributions to climate change.

Requirements

NC, SCHOOLS & CS

OPTION 1

Do not use refrigerants.

OR

OPTION 2

Select refrigerants and heating, ventilating, air conditioning and refrigeration (HVAC&R) that minimize or eliminate the emission of compounds that contribute to ozone depletion and global climate change. The base building HVAC&R equipment must comply with the following formula, which sets a maximum threshold for the combined contributions to ozone depletion and global warming potential:

$$\text{LCGWP} + \text{LCODP} \times 10^5 \leq 100$$

Calculation definitions for LCGWP + LCODP x $10^5 \leq$ 100
LCODP = [ODPr x (Lr x Life +Mr) x Rc]/Life
LCGWP = [GWPr x (Lr x Life +Mr) x Rc]/Life
LCODP: Lifecycle Ozone Depletion Potential (lb CFC 11/Ton-Year)
LCGWP: Lifecycle Direct Global Warming Potential (lb CO_2/Ton-Year)
GWPr: Global Warming Potential of Refrigerant (0 to 12,000 lb CO_2/lbr)
ODPr: Ozone Depletion Potential of Refrigerant (0 to 0.2 lb CFC 11/lbr)
Lr: Refrigerant Leakage Rate (0.5% to 2.0%; default of 2% unless otherwise demonstrated)
Mr: End-of-life Refrigerant Loss (2% to 10%; default of 10% unless otherwise demonstrated)
Rc: Refrigerant Charge (0.5 to 5.0 lbs of refrigerant per ton of gross ARI rated cooling capacity)
Life: Equipment Life (10 years; default based on equipment type, unless otherwise demonstrated)

For multiple types of equipment, a weighted average of all base building HVAC&R equipment must be calculated using the following formula:

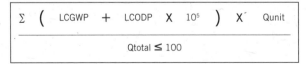

$$\frac{\Sigma \left(\text{LCGWP} + \text{LCODP} \times 10^5 \right) \times \text{Qunit}}{\text{Qtotal}} \leq 100$$

NC, SCHOOLS & CS (continued)

Calculation definitions for [$\sum$ (LCGWP + LCODP x 10^5) x Qunit] / Qtotal $\leq$ 100
Qunit = Gross ARI rated cooling capacity of an individual HVAC or refrigeration unit (Tons)
Qtotal = Total gross ARI rated cooling capacity of all HVAC or refrigeration

ALL OPTIONS

Small HVAC units (defined as containing less than 0.5 pounds of refrigerant) and other equipment, such as standard refrigerators, small water coolers and any other cooling equipment that contains less than 0.5 pounds of refrigerant, are not considered part of the base building system and are not subject to the requirements of this credit.

Do not operate or install fire suppression systems that contain ozone-depleting substances such as CFCs, hydrochlorofluorocarbons (HCFCs) or halons.

1. Benefits and Issues to Consider

	EA
NC	Credit 4
SCHOOLS	Credit 4
CS	Credit 4

Environmental Issues

Some refrigerants used in heating, ventilating, air conditioning, and refrigeration (HVAC&R) systems cause significant damage to Earth's protective ozone layer if they are released into the atmosphere. Others contribute to greenhouse gas emissions, causing global climate change. According to a report issued by the LEED Technical and Scientific Advisory Committee, an objective, scientific analysis of trade-offs between global climate change and ozone depletion is extremely complex and will come only from a full understanding of all interacting pathways and effects on economic activities, human health, and terrestrial and oceanic ecosystems.[12] Refrigerant management to minimize the negative impacts on ozone depletion and climate change requires all of the following strategies to reduce dangerous refrigerant leakage to the environment:

- Designing buildings that do not rely on chemical refrigerants.

- Designing HVAC&R equipment that uses energy efficiently.

- Selecting refrigerants with zero or low ozone depleting potential (ODP) and minimal direct global warming potential (GWP).

- Maintaining HVAC&R equipment to reduce refrigerant leakage to the environment.

Under the Montreal Protocol, an international treaty ratified in 1989, refrigerants with nonzero ODP will be phased out by 2030 in developed countries. This includes the chlorinated refrigerants chlorofluorocarbons (CFCs) and hydrochlorofluorocarbons (HCFCs).

Economic Issues

Passive cooling strategies can greatly decrease the costs associated with mechanical equipment by reducing or eliminating the need for active cooling systems.

Although environmentally preferable refrigerants are becoming standard or available as an option on new air-conditioning equipment, approximately 50% of the water chillers in existing buildings still use CFC-11 as refrigerant. As environmental impacts are factored into the costs of replacement refrigerant, operational cost savings will be realized through installation of HVAC&R equipment with environmentally preferable refrigerants.

2. Related Credits

This credit encourages either the use of no refrigerants or the use of environmentally preferable refrigerants. Because cooling equipment is often a significant percentage of the overall building energy use, the selection of HVAC&R system has a large effect on the overall energy performance of the building. Additionally, the systems addressed by this credit can help meet the thermal comfort needs of the building occupants. It is important to balance refrigerant impact, energy use, and occupants' comfort when selecting HVAC&R systems. Refer to these prerequisites and credits:

- EA Prerequisite 3: Fundamental Refrigerant Management

- EA Prerequisite 2: Minimum Energy Performance

- EA Credit 1: Optimize Energy Performance

- IEQ Credit 7.1 (CS IEQ Credit 7): Thermal Comfort—Design

- IEQ Credit 7.2: Thermal Comfort—Verification

3. Summary of Referenced Standards

There are no standards referenced for this credit.

	EA
NC	Credit 4
SCHOOLS	Credit 4
CS	Credit 4

4. Implementation

Most refrigerants used in building HVAC and refrigeration equipment are stable chemical compounds until they are released to the atmosphere, where they become greenhouse gases that deplete Earth's protective ozone layer and contribute to climate change.

HVAC&R systems also contribute to climate change through their energy consumption and the greenhouse gas emissions associated with the production of energy at power plants. Over the life of the equipment, the indirect global warming impact of HVAC&R equipment may be much greater than the direct impact of releasing the refrigerant into the atmosphere. The indirect impact of running HVAC&R equipment is addressed by EA Credit 1, Optimize Energy Performance, which accounts for the energy savings associated with more energy-efficient equipment. The direct impact of refrigerant selection is addressed in EA Prerequisite 3, Fundamental Refrigerant Management, which requires zero use of CFC-based refrigerants in base building systems, or a reduction in refrigerant leakage if system conversion is not economically feasible. This credit encourages significantly reducing or even eliminating a building's use of refrigerants.

The credit covers base building HVAC&R equipment—any equipment permanently installed in the building that contains more than 0.5 pound of refrigerant. This includes chillers, unitary (split and packaged) HVAC equipment, room or window air-conditioners, computer room air-conditioning units, data and telecommunications room cooling units, and commercial refrigeration equipment. Portable cooling equipment (such as standard refrigerators), temporary cooling equipment, and equipment with less than 0.5 pound of refrigerant (such as small water coolers) may be excluded from the calculations for this credit. For buildings connected to an existing chilled water system, the chilled water supplier must perform the required calculation and submit a letter showing compliance with the requirements.

Do Not Use Refrigerants

Eliminating the use of vapor-compression HVAC&R equipment can help prevent atmospheric damage from refrigerant emissions. LEED projects that use no refrigerants—for example, a naturally ventilated building with no active cooling systems—are awarded this LEED credit without having to submit any calculations or analyses.

Use Only Natural Refrigerants

Some HVAC&R systems use natural refrigerants, including water, carbon dioxide, and ammonia. These naturally occurring compounds generally have much lower potential for atmospheric damage than manufactured chemical refrigerants. Projects that employ natural refrigerants are eligible for this credit.

Select Refrigerants with Low Ozone-depletion and Global-warming Potentials

Selection of the appropriate refrigerant for any given project and HVAC system may be affected by available equipment, energy efficiency, budget, and other factors. If possible, use refrigerants with zero or very little ozone depletion potential (ODP) and global warming potential (GWP). Table 1 shows the ODPs and direct GWPs of many common refrigerants.

Table 1. Ozone Depletion and Global Warming Potentials of Refrigerants (100-Year Values)

Refrigerant	ODP	GWP	Common Building Applications
Chlorofluorocarbons			
CFC-11	1.0	4,680	Centrifugal chillers
CFC-12	1.0	10,720	Refrigerators, chillers
CFC-114	0.94	9,800	Centrifugal chillers
CFC-500	0.605	7,900	Centrifugal chillers, humidifiers
CFC-502	0.221	4,600	Low-temperature refrigeration
Hydrochlorofluorocarbons			
HCFC-22	0.04	1,780	Air-conditioning, chillers
HCFC-123	0.02	76	CFC-11 replacement
Hydrofluorocarbons			
HFC-23	~ 0	12,240	Ultra-low-temperature refrigeration
HFC-134a	~ 0	1,320	CFC-12 or HCFC-22 replacement
HFC-245fa	~ 0	1,020	Insulation agent, centrifugal chillers
HFC-404A	~ 0	3,900	Low-temperature refrigeration
HFC-407C	~ 0	1,700	HCFC-22 replacement
HFC-410A	~ 0	1,890	Air-conditioning
HFC-507A	~ 0	3,900	Low-temperature refrigeration
Natural refrigerants			
Carbon dioxide (CO_2)	0	1.0	
Ammonia (NH_3)	0	0	
Propane	0	3	

The LEED Technical and Scientific Advisory Committee report that provides the basis of this credit notes the following: The ozone-depletion potential (ODP) of the HCFCs (e.g., HCFC-123, HCFC-22) is much smaller than the ODP of the CFCs, but is not negligible. In contrast, the HFCs (e.g., HFC-134a, HFC-410a) have an ODP that is essentially zero, but their global warming potential (GWP) is substantially greater than some of the HCFCs, leading to a direct mechanism when the compound leaks into the atmosphere. Moreover, thermodynamic properties make the HFCs slightly less efficient refrigerants than the HCFCs given idealized equipment design, so the same amount of cooling may require more electricity and thereby causes the indirect release of more CO2 in generating that electricity. The dilemma, therefore, is that some refrigerants cause more ozone depletion than others, but the most ozone-friendly refrigerants cause more climate change.

Minimize Refrigerant Leakage

The refrigerant leakage rate can magnify or minimize the harmful effects of refrigerant use. See EA Prerequisite 3, Fundamental Refrigerant Management, for information about minimizing leakage rates through compliance with refrigerant management regulations and best practices.

In general, refrigerants that operate at low or negative pressure are likely to leak less.

Select Equipment with Efficient Refrigerant Charge

Refrigerant charge is the ratio of refrigerant required (pounds) to gross cooling capacity provided (tons) for a given piece of HVAC&R equipment. Equipment that uses refrigerants efficiently has low refrigerant charge and therefore less potential to contribute to atmospheric damage.

Table 2 shows the maximum refrigerant charge for a single unit of equipment that would comply with this credit, based on default values. Most projects have multiple units of base building HVAC&R equipment, but if each unit is compliant, the project as a whole meets the requirement. The values in

	EA
NC	Credit 4
SCHOOLS	Credit 4
CS	Credit 4

the table assume average refrigerant leak rates of 2% per year and 10% end-of-life losses; if a unit has a higher leakage rates, the maximum allowable refrigerant charge for that equipment would decrease accordingly. For equipment that has a service life greater than 23 years, the allowable refrigerant charge is 1–2% higher.

Table 2. Maximum Refrigerant Charge

Refrigerant	10-Year Life (Room or Window AC, Heat Pumps)	15-Year Life (Unitary, Split, Packaged AC, Heat Pumps)	20-Year Life (Reciprocating or Scroll Compressors, Chillers)	23-Year Life (Screw, Absorption Chillers)
R-22	0.57	0.64	0.69	0.71
R-123	1.60	1.80	1.92	1.97
R-134a	2.52	2.80	3.03	3.10
R-245fa	3.26	3.60	3.92	4.02
R-407c	1.95	2.20	2.35	2.41
R-410a	1.76	1.98	2.11	2.17

Select Equipment with Long Service Life

HVAC&R service equipment with a long service life will generally reduce the potential amount of refrigerant leaked to the environment, because most refrigerant loss occurs during installation and decommissioning of equipment. The 2007 ASHRAE Applications Handbook provides data on the service life of different types of HVAC equipment; see the Calculations section of this credit for the ASHRAE equipment life list.

Select Alternative Fire-Suppression Systems

Halons were widely used in fire-suppression systems prior to their phase-out, which began in 1994 under the Montreal Protocol because of their strong ozone-depleting potential. EPA maintains a list of acceptable alternatives to halon-based fire suppression, but facility managers must determine the suitability of these alternatives for the situation. To achieve this credit, replacement systems must avoid halons, CFCs, and HCFCs.

District Energy Systems

For projects with district energy systems, specific technical guidance can be found on USGBC's Registered Project Tools page (http://www.usgbc.org/projecttools). Follow the guidance in effect at the time of registration.

5. Timeline and Team

Consult with a mechanical engineer or HVAC&R systems specialist during the design phase to identify refrigerant issues and leakage rates.

6. Calculations

The following information is required for each unit of base building HVAC&R equipment:

- Refrigerant charge (Rc) in pounds of refrigerant per ton of gross cooling capacity.

- Refrigerant type (used to determine ODP and GWP).

- Equipment type (used to determine Life).

Table 1 lists ODP and GWP values for many common refrigerants. These values should be used in the calculations.

Assume equipment life as follows (from 2007 ASHRAE Applications Handbook):

- Window air-conditioning units and heat pumps, 10 years.

- Unitary, split, and packaged air-conditioning units and heat pumps, 15 years.

- Reciprocating compressors, scroll compressors, and reciprocating chillers, 20 years.

- Absorption chillers, 23 years.

- Water-cooled packaged air-conditioners, 24 years.

- Centrifugal chillers, 25 years.

Use any updated equipment life assumptions from Abramson (see the ASHRAE Applications Handbook). All other HVAC&R equipment is assumed to have a life of 15 years. Applicants may use alternative values for equipment life if they submit supporting documentation, such as a manufacturer's 30-year guarantee and equivalent long-term service contract for a chiller installation.

Refrigerant leakage rate (Lr) is assumed to be 2%/yr for all equipment types. End-of-life refrigerant loss (Mr) is assumed to be 10% for all equipment types. Applicants may use alternate values for Lr and Mr, provided their alternative values are approved by USGBC. If their alternative values have not yet been reviewed by USGBC, information demonstrating and documenting their alternative values may be considered for approval. Documentation provided for review must include, at a minimum, the following:

- Manufacturers' test data for refrigerant leakage rates (percent per year)

- Refrigerant leak detection equipment in the room where the equipment is located

- Preventive maintenance program for minimizing equipment refrigerant leakage

- Program for recovering and recycling refrigerant at the end of equipment life

Projects may not claim zero leakage over the life of the HVAC&R equipment.

For each piece of HVAC&R equipment, calculate the following values:

$$\text{Life-Cycle Ozone Depletion Potential (LCODP)} = \frac{ODPr \times (Lr \times Life + Mr) \times Rc}{Life}$$

$$\text{Life-Cycle Direct Global Warming Potential (LCGWP)} = \frac{GWPr \times (Lr \times Life + Mr) \times Rc}{Life}$$

If there is only 1 piece of base building HVAC&R equipment, use the following equation to demonstrate compliance:

$$\text{Refrigerant Atmospheric Impact} = LCGWP + LCODP \times 10^5 \leq 100$$

If there are multiple pieces of base building HVAC&R equipment, use a weighted average of all equipment, based on cooling capacity:

$$\text{Average Refrigerant Atmospheric Impact} = \frac{\sum (LCGWP + LCODP \times 10^5) \times Qunit}{Qtotal} \leq 100$$

Where:

- Qunit = Cooling capacity of an individual HVAC or refrigeration unit (tons)

- Qtotal = Total cooling capacity of all HVAC or refrigeration

7. Documentation Guidance

As a first step in preparing to complete the LEED-Online documentation requirements, work through the following measures. Refer to LEED-Online for the complete descriptions of all required documentation.

- List base building systems containing refrigerants and the associated type of refrigerant. Include ODP and GWP in the list.

- Retain manufacturer's documentation, indicating the type and quantity of refrigerant used.

- Compile engineer's or manufacturer's information indicating that halons, CFCs, and HCFCs are not in fire-suppression systems.

8. Examples

Sample calculations are shown below. In the first sample, the school building does not comply with EA Credit 4, Enhanced Refrigerant Management. In the second and third examples, the office building and hotel meet the requirements even though individual units of HVAC&R equipment have refrigerant atmospheric impacts greater than 100.

Sample Calculation 1. School Building

- (12) 5-ton packaged HVAC units with HFC-410A for classrooms

- (1) 2-ton split system HVAC units with HCFC-22 for a data room

- (1) 1-ton window HVAC unit with HCFC-22 for an office

Inputs									Calculations				
Units	Qunit (tons)	Refrigerant	GWPr	ODPr	Rc (lb/ ton)	Life (yrs)	Lr (%)	Mr (%)	Tr Total Leakage (Lr x Life +Mr)	LCGWP (GWPr x Tr x Rc)/ Life	LCODP x 10^5 100,000 x (ODPr x Tr x Rc)/Life	Refrigerant atmospheric impact = LCGWP + LCODP x 10^5	(LCGWP + LCODP x 10^5) x N x Qunit
12	5	R410A	1,890	0	1.8	15	2	10	40%	90.72	0	90.7	5443
1	2	R22	1,780	0.04	3.3	15	2	10	40%	156.6	352.0	508.6	1,017
1	1	R22	1,780	0.04	2.1	10	2	10	30%	112.1	252.0	364.1	364
Qtotal	63											Subtotal	6825
Average refrigerant atmospheric impact = [$\sum$ (LCGWP + LCODP x 10^5) x Qunit] / Qtotal													108.33
Result: Average refrigerant atmospheric impact has a value greater than 100, therefore this project does not earn EA Credit 4.													

Sample Calculation 2. Office Building

- (1) 500-ton absorption chiller with HFC-134a, with manufacturer's data and service contract acceptable to USGBC demonstrating less than 1% per year leakage rate

- (1) 50-ton reciprocating "pony" chiller with HCFC-22

- (5) 10-ton computer room air-conditioning units with HCFC-22

Inputs									Calculations				
Units	Qunit (tons)	Refrigerant	GWPr	ODPr	Rc (lb/ ton)	Life (yrs)	Lr (%)	Mr (%)	Tr Total Leakage (Lr x Life +Mr)	LCGWP (GWPr x Tr x Rc)/ Life	LCODP x 10^5 10,000 x (ODPr x Tr x Rc)/Life	Refrigerant atmospheric impact = LCGWP + LCODP x 10^5	(LCGWP + LCODP x 10^5) x N x Qunit
1	500	R-134a	1,320	0	2	23	1	10	33%	37.9	0	37.9	18,939
1	50	R-22	1,780	0.04	2.1	20	2	10	50%	93.5	210	303	15,173
5	10	R-22	1,780	0.04	2.4	15	2	10	40%	113.9	256.0	369.9	18,496
Qtotal	600											Subtotal	52,608
Average refrigerant atmospheric impact = [$\sum$ (LCGWP + LCODP x 10^5) x Qunit] / Qtotal													87.7
Result: Average refrigerant atmospheric impact has a value ≤ 100, therefore this project earns EA Credit 4.													

Sample Calculation 3. Hotel

- (3) 400-ton absorption chillers with HCFC-123
- (1) 40-ton commercial refrigeration compressor rack with HCFC-22
- (12) 2-ton telephone and data room split-system cooling units with HCFC-22

			EA
NC	Credit 4
SCHOOLS	Credit 4
CS	Credit 4

Inputs									Calculations				
Units	Qunit (tons)	Refrigerant	GWPr	ODPr	Rc (lb/ ton)	Life (yrs)	Lr (%)	Mr (%)	Tr Total Leakage (Lr x Life +Mr)	LCGWP (GWPr x Tr x Rc)/ Life	LCODP x 10⁵ 100,000 x (ODPr x Tr x Rc)/Life	Refrigerant atmospheric impact = LCGWP + LCODP x10⁵	(LCGWP + LCODP x 10⁵) x N x Qunit
3	400	R123	76	0.02	1.63	23	2	10	56%	3.016209	79.37391	82.4	98,868.1
1	40	R22	1,780	0.04	2.1	20	2	10	50%	93.45	210	303.5	12,138.0
12	2	R22	1,780	0.04	3.1	15	2	10	40%	147.1467	330.6667	477.8	11,467.5
Qtotal	1,264											Subtotal	12,2473
Average refrigerant atmospheric impact = [∑ (LCGWP + LCODP x 10⁵) x Qunit] / Qtotal													96.9

Result: Average refrigerant atmospheric impact has a value ≤ 100; therefore this project earns EA Credit 4.

9. Exemplary Performance

This credit is not eligible for exemplary performance under the Innovation in Design section.

10. Regional Variations

There are no regional variations associated with this credit.

11. Operations and Maintenance Consideration

Provide facility operators with complete records (such as LEED application materials) for all refrigerant-containing systems, including fire suppression. Ensure that equipment labels are in place and accessible to building operators.

12. Resources

Please see USGBC's LEED Registered Project Tools (http://www.usgbc.org/projecttools) for additional resources and technical information.

Websites

U.S. EPA Significant New Alternatives Policy

http://www.epa.gov/ozone/snap/index.html

SNAP is an EPA program to identify alternatives to ozone-depleting substances. The program maintains up-to-date lists of environmentally-friendly substitutes for refrigeration and air conditioning equipment, solvents, fire suppression systems, adhesives, coatings, and other substances.

The Treatment by LEED of the Environmental Impact of HVAC Refrigerants (U.S. Green Building Council, 2004).

http://www.usgbc.org/DisplayPage.aspx?CMSPageID=154

This report was prepared under the auspices of the U.S. Green Building Council's LEED Technical and Scientific Advisory Committee. It was created in response to the LEED Steering Committee's charge to the committee to review the atmospheric environmental impacts of the use of halocarbons as refrigerants in building HVAC equipment.

Print Media

Building Systems Analysis and Retrofit Manual (SMACNA, 1995).
This manual provides an overview of topics related to HVAC retrofits, including energy management retrofits and CFC and HCFC retrofits.

CFCs, HCFC and Halons: Professional and Practical Guidance on Substances That Deplete the Ozone Layer (CIBSE, 2000).
The Refrigerant Manual: Managing the Phase-Out of CFCs (BOMA International, 1993).

13. Definitions

Chlorofluorocarbons (**CFCs**) are hydrocarbons that are used as refrigerants and cause depletion of the stratospheric ozone layer.

Greenhouse gases (**GHG**) absorb and emit radiation at specific wavelengths within the spectrum of thermal infrared radiation emitted by Earth's surface, clouds, and the atmosphere itself. Increased concentrations of greenhouse gases are a root cause of global climate change.

Halons are substances, used in fire-suppression systems and fire extinguishers, that deplete the stratospheric ozone layer.

Hydrochlorofluorocarbons (**HCFCs**) are refrigerants that cause significantly less depletion of the stratospheric ozone layer than chlorofluorocarbons.

Hydrofluorocarbons (**HFCs**) are refrigerants that do not deplete the stratospheric ozone layer but may have high global warming potential. HFCs are not considered environmentally benign.

The **leakage rate** is the speed at which an appliance loses refrigerant, measured between refrigerant charges or over 12 months, whichever is shorter. The leakage rate is expressed in terms of the percentage of the appliance's full charge that would be lost over a 12-month period if the rate stabilized. (EPA Clean Air Act, Title VI, Rule 608)

Refrigerants are the working fluids of refrigeration cycles that absorb heat from a reservoir at low temperatures and reject heat at higher temperatures.

	NC	SCHOOLS	CS
Credit	EA Credit 5	EA Credit 5	NA
Points	3 points	2 points	NA

Intent

To provide for the ongoing accountability of building energy consumption over time.

Requirements

NC & SCHOOLS

OPTION 1

Develop and implement a measurement and verification (M&V) plan consistent with Option D: Calibrated Simulation (Savings Estimation Method 2) as specified in the International Performance Measurement & Verification Protocol (IPMVP) Volume III: Concepts and Options for Determining Energy Savings in New Construction, April, 2003.

The M&V period must cover at least 1 year of post-construction occupancy.

Provide a process for corrective action if the results of the M&V plan indicate that energy savings are not being achieved.

OR

OPTION 2

Develop and implement a measurement and verification (M&V) plan consistent with Option B: Energy Conservation Measure Isolation, as specified in the International Performance Measurement & Verification Protocol (IPMVP) Volume III: Concepts and Options for Determining Energy Savings in New Construction, April, 2003.

The M&V period must cover at least 1 year of postconstruction occupancy.

Provide a process for corrective action if the results of the M&V plan indicate that energy savings are not being achieved.

MEASUREMENT AND VERIFICATION—BASE BUILDING

	NC	SCHOOLS	CS
Credit	NA	NA	EA Credit 5.1
Points	NA	NA	3 points

Intent

To provide for the ongoing accountability of building energy consumption over time.

Requirements

OPTION 1

Develop and implement a measurement and verification (M&V) plan consistent with Option D: Calibrated Simulation (Savings Estimation Method 2) as specified by the International Performance Measurement & Verification Protocol (IPMVP), Volume III: Concepts and Options for Determining Energy Savings in New Construction, April 2003.

The documentation must include the following:

- A description of the infrastructure design.
- Existing meter locations.
- Existing meter specifications.
- 1-line electrical schematics identifying end-use circuits.
- Guidelines for carrying out tenant sub-metering.

OR

OPTION 2

Develop a and implement a measurement and verification (M&V) plan consistent with Option B: Energy Conservation Measure Isolation, as specified by the International Performance Measurement & Verification Protocol (IPMVP), Volume III: Concepts and Options for Determining Energy Savings in New Construction, April 2003.

The documentation must include the following:

- A description of the infrastructure design.
- Existing meter locations.
- Existing meter specifications.
- 1-line electrical schematics identifying end-use circuits.
- Guidelines for carrying out tenant sub-metering.

MEASUREMENT AND VERIFICATION—TENANT SUBMETERING

EA CREDIT 5.2

	NC	SCHOOLS	CS
Credit	NA	NA	EA Credit 5.2
Points	NA	NA	3 points

Intent

To provide for ongoing accountability of building electricity consumption performance over time.

Requirements

Include a centrally monitored electronic metering network in the base building design that is capable of being expanded to accommodate the future tenant submetering as required by LEED 2009 for Commercial Interiors Rating System EA Credit 3: Measurement and Verification.

Develop a tenant measurement and verification (M&V) plan that documents and advises future tenants of this opportunity and the means of achievement.

Provide a process for corrective action if the results of the M&V plan indicate that energy savings are not being achieved.

1. Benefits and Issues to Consider

	EA
NC	Credit 5
SCHOOLS	Credit 5
CS	Credit 5.1 & 5.2

Environmental Issues

Measurement and verification of a building's ongoing energy use optimize performance and minimize the economic and environmental impacts associated with its energy-using systems.

Economic Issues

The benefits of optimal building operation, especially in terms of energy performance, are substantial. The lifetime of many buildings is longer than 50 years, and so even minor energy savings are significant when considered in aggregate. Potential long-term benefits often go unrealized because of maintenance personnel changes, aging of building equipment, and changing utility rate structures. Therefore, it is important to institute M&V procedures and continuous monitoring to achieve and maintain optimal performance over the lifetime of the building. The goal of M&V activities is to provide building owners with the tools and data necessary to identify systems that are not functioning as expected and thus optimize building system performance.

The cost to institute an M&V program in a new construction project varies with the complexity of the building's systems and instrumentation and controls in the baseline design. The additional instrumentation and metering equipment, programming of controls, and labor associated with monitoring and processing data can all add to costs. Projects with sophisticated digital controls can often support an effective M&V program without incurring significant additional costs. On the other hand, projects with a series of chillers, air handlers, and simple controls may need to install a significant amount of equipment to generate the necessary data for an effective M&V program. Smaller buildings with packaged HVAC equipment and fewer pieces of equipment overall may have lower costs for instrumentation and metering because there are fewer systems to measure and verify. The cost of an M&V program must be balanced against the potential performance risk. A simple method of estimating performance risk can be based on the project value and technical uncertainty, as illustrated in Table 1.

Table 1. Sample Calculation of Performance Risk

Project	Anticipated Annual Energy Costs	Estimated Savings	Estimated Uncertainty	Performance Risk
Small	$250,000	$50,000	20%	$10,000
Large	$2,000,000	$500,000	30%	$150,000

A capital and operational budget for M&V can be a percentage of the project's performance risk over a suitable time period. A smaller project with predictable technologies has less performance risk (and thus a lower M&V budget) than a larger project that includes less predictable technologies.

In general, higher M&V intensity and rigor mean higher costs, both upfront and over time. The following factors (many of which are interrelated) typically affect M&V accuracy and costs:

- Level of detail and effort associated with verifying postconstruction conditions.
- Number and types of metering points.
- Duration and accuracy of metering activities.
- Number and complexity of dependent and independent variables that must be measured or determined on an ongoing basis.
- Availability of existing data collection systems (e.g., energy management systems).
- Confidence and precision levels specified for the analyses.

CREDIT 5.2: CS The goal of submetering is to give tenants an incentive to save energy. Submetering accounts for their energy consumption so that they can see a return on any conservation investments they make. Enabling tenants to track their electricity use gives them the opportunity to realize savings by reducing energy use or implementing energy efficiency measures.

Submeters are not a major expense. Some municipalities and utilities, however, do not allow a second party to charge for electricity based on submetering. In this case, providing separate utility meters for each tenant may be the best option. Or, for buildings that submeter, electricity cost can be apportioned to the tenants based on usage. The design team should confirm its strategies with both the municipality and the utility provider.

2. Related Credits

Implementation of a measurement and verification plan can help ensure accountability and contribute to realizing optimal energy performance. If system performance is the basis for the funding of the project (as with energy performance contracts), the International Performance Measurement and Verification Protocol (see the Referenced Standards section) will likely be used for verification. Renewable energy generation systems are considered within an M&V plan, and performance of these systems is often tracked to identify any operational issues. Refer to the requirements in the following:

- EA Prerequisite 2: Minimum Energy Performance
- EA Credit 1: Optimize Energy Performance
- EA Credit 2: On-site Renewable Energy

Commissioning often employs measurement devices and capabilities to track building performance. These same devices can serve as the basis for a measurement and verification plan, especially if ongoing commissioning programs have been adopted by the owner. See the following:

- EA Prerequisite 1: Fundamental Commissioning
- EA Credit 3: Enhanced Commissioning

3. Summary of Referenced Standards

International Performance Measurement and Verification Protocol, Volume III, EVO 30000.1–2006, Concepts and Options for Determining Energy Savings in New Construction, effective January, 2006
http://www.evo-world.org

The Efficiency Valuation Organization is a nonprofit organization whose vision is a global marketplace that properly values energy and water efficiency.

IPMVP Volume III provides a concise description of best practice techniques for verifying the energy performance of new construction projects. Chapter 2 describes the process for developing the theoretical baseline for new construction projects and provides examples of relevant applications. Chapter 3 describes the basic concepts and structure of the measurement and verification plan. Chapter 4 describes specific measurement and verification methods for energy conservation measure isolation (Option B) and whole-building calibrated simulation (Option D). Volume III pertains to new construction projects; Volume I relates to retrofit projects in existing facilities.

4. Implementation

IPMVP Volume III presents 4 options for new construction M&V. Of these, Options B and D are appropriate for LEED M&V (Table 2).

Table 2. Measurement and Verification for New Construction

M&V Option	Baseline Energy Use	Typical Applications
Option B, Energy Conservation Measure Isolation		
Determine savings by measuring energy use and operating parameters of system to which measure was applied, separate from rest of facility.	Calculate hypothetical energy performance of baseline system under measured postconstruction operating conditions.	Variable speed control of fan motor; electricity use is measured on continuous basis throughout M&V period.
Option D, Whole-Building Simulation		
Determine savings at whole-building or system level by measuring energy use and comparing it with baseline.	Estimate through whole-building simulation, then subtract energy efficiency measures from measured building performance.	Savings determination for new building performance contract, with baseline defined by local energy code.

IPMVP is not prescriptive about the application of M&V options but instead defers to the professional judgment of the implementer to apply the options in an appropriate manner while still meeting the M&V objective (see Economic Issues). The M&V plan should be based on the owner's needs and described in the owner's project requirements. Other implementation issues are the availability of a building automation system and whether the local utility uses meters that provide hourly or minute-by-minute power consumption data.

Option B addresses M&V at the system or energy conservation measure level. This approach is suitable for small and/or simple buildings that can be monitored by isolating the main energy systems and applying Option B to each system on an individual basis. The savings associated with most types of energy conservation measures can be determined using Option B. However, since each measure may require a meter, the limiting consideration may be cost associated with increased metering complexity. Greater certainty in determining savings, particularly with variable loads, often warrants the higher cost.

The energy savings may be determined from simple spreadsheet calculations using metered data. Deficiencies and operation errors can often be identified at this time. Usually, the ongoing cost of implementation for this option tends to be lower, because once the meters are installed, they provide continuous performance monitoring. Once the system or tracking is in place, monitoring requires minimal effort.

Option B is best applied in these circumstances:

- Interactive effects between energy conservation measures or with other building equipment can be measured or assumed to be insignificant.

- The parameters that affect energy use are not complex or excessively difficult or expensive to monitor.

- If measurement is limited to a few parameters, this option is less costly and is preferable to simulating operation under Option D.

- Meters can serve a dual purpose; for example, submetering is used for both operational feedback and tenant billing.

- Projected baseline energy use can be readily and reliably calculated.

Option D addresses M&V at the whole-building level. This approach is most suitable for buildings with a large number of energy conservation measures or interacting systems, such as those related to the building envelope. The performance of triple-glazed windows, air infiltration control, and highly insulated or mass wall systems is difficult to measure and requires computer simulation. An owner or institution wishing to analyze the effectiveness of such conservation measures should choose this option. Whole-building calibration compares the actual energy use of the building and its systems with the performance predicted by a calibrated computer model (like that developed for the energy simulation model used for EA Credit 1, Option 1). Calibration is achieved by adjusting the energy simulation model to reflect actual operating conditions and parameters. Next, the conservation measures are removed from the model to define the baseline. The energy savings are determined by subtracting the baseline energy simulation from the actual energy use.

	EA
NC	Credit 5
SCHOOLS	Credit 5
CS	Credit 5.1 & 5.2

Option D is useful in these circumstances:

- Calibration of the as-built energy simulation model shows how interactive energy conservation measures affect building energy use.

- Calibration of the as-built energy simulation model develops a breakdown of energy use. The breakdown of specific systems and equipment depends on the simulation software used. The advantages to this breakdown are discussed in the Performance Measurement credit of USGBC's Green Building Operations & Maintenance Reference Guide.

- A breakdown of energy end uses can help determine the most effective areas for energy conservation, such as electrical lighting versus gas water heating.

- The comparison of the calibrated as-built model with the calibrated baseline can show the payback of the capital costs of multiple, interactive conservation measures, such as a continuously insulated wall plus triple-glazed windows.

The M&V plan identifies the options to be applied, defines the baseline (or how it will be determined), identifies metering requirements, and outlines specific methodologies associated with implementing the plan. Responsibility for the design, coordination, and implementation of the M&V plan should reside with 1 entity of the design team. The person(s) responsible for energy engineering and analysis is usually best suited for this role, although third-party verification may be appropriate in some cases. Since the pursuit of this credit is largely affected by the option selected to achieve EA Credit 1, Optimize Energy Performance, the baseline definition will vary. For EA Credit 1, Option 1, ASHRAE 90.1-2007, Appendix G, defines the baseline. The baselines for EA Credit 1, Options 2 and 3, are defined by the respective prescriptive standards, which (in some cases) may be effectively the same as the design. In that case, the M&V plan addresses design performance only. However, it is necessary in all cases to predict the energy performance of the design and/or its systems. For Option B, this can be accomplished through either computer modeling or engineering analysis, depending on the complexity of the systems.

District Energy Systems

For projects with district energy systems, specific technical guidance can be found on USGBC's Registered Project Tools page (http://www.usgbc.org/projecttools). Follow the guidance in effect at the time of registration.

CREDIT 5.1: CS This credit focuses on the energy-using systems (and primarily the electricity-using systems) of the core and shell building. This may include measuring electricity use in the tenant spaces. However, for the purposes of this credit, the electricity use of the tenant spaces does not have to be itemized by the tenant. The submetering of tenant spaces is addressed in EA Credit 5.2.

To achieve this credit, the electricity-using systems in the core and shell building should be addressed in the M&V plan. Decide which electricity uses to focus on and how electricity use will be measured. Infrastructure, such as meters or a building management system, must be provided. If the building does not have any electricity-using equipment, the project is ineligible for this credit. Consider measuring other energy use (i.e., natural gas) to get a complete picture of the energy use of the building.

CREDIT 5.2: CS This credit is designed to create the infrastructure that will enable any tenant in the building to earn EA Credit 3, Energy Use, in LEED for Commercial Interiors. Either the project building or the local utility can install submeters so that tenants can monitor the energy consumption in their leased spaces. In a commercial office building that has a master electric meter, submeters track the actual consumption of individual tenants. In tests of commercial and residential situations, individual tenant responsibility for utility charges has resulted in conservation. For electrical service, the equipment and installation of submeters is not a major expense.

To satisfy the credit requirement, only electricity needs to be submetered. The electricity used for lighting and plug loads and to run HVAC equipment may be measured on a single meter and reported together.

5. Timeline and Team

Table 3. M&V Activities, by Project Phase

Phase	M&V Activities
Design development	
	Develop an energy model of the design.
	Specify number and types of meters.
	Provide trending parameters for controls specifications.
	Design document review.
Construction documents	
	Review meter placement in drawings.
Construction phase	
	Verify controls; contractor sets up required trends.
Postconstruction	
	Begin logging data.
	Re-calibrate base model or estimate base energy use.
	Report on energy savings.
	Provide suggestions for continuous improvement.

Introducing M&V early can alter the design of the mechanical system. Cross-discipline coordination of M&V system implementation can help the design team think about how the building will be operated. The operators of the building should be involved in M&V development, since they will be expected to execute the plan either directly or in partnership with a third party.

M&V begins after occupancy and only once a reasonable degree of operational stability has been achieved. The first phase of M&V lasts 1 year. The information recorded during the first phase helps to establish a protocol for the following:

- Determining the energy use in the building systems or system.

- Verifying the performance of energy conservation measures.

- Determining the energy conservation and associated cost savings over the baseline.

Continuation of M&V after the first year will enable the following:

- Continued performance improvements of the building energy systems.

- Tracking of systems to determine whether the long-term performance goals of the building are being achieved.

The M&V plan may identify additional monitoring opportunities to track and analyze energy use and permit continuous improvement, such as installation of specific diagnostic alerts within the control system for the following:

- Leaking valves in the cooling and heating coils within air-handling units.

- Missed economizer opportunities (e.g., faulty economizer damper controls).

- Software and manual overrides allowing equipment to operate 24/7.

- Equipment operation during unusual circumstances (e.g., boiler on when outside air temperature is above 65°F).

In addition bringing in control diagnostics specialists, consider employing retrocommissioning services or dedicating staff (usually a resource conservation manager) to investigate increases in energy use.

6. Calculations

IPMVP Volume III provides basic formulas as well as quantitative guidelines for error estimation and tolerance for various M&V options (not applicable to Core & Shell EA Credit 5.2, for which there are no calculations).

7. Documentation Guidance

As a first step in preparing to complete the LEED-Online documentation requirements, work through the following measures. Refer to LEED-Online for the complete descriptions of all required documentation.

CREDIT 5: NC & SCHOOLS
CREDIT 5.1: CS

- Develop an IPMVP-compliant measurement and verification plan.

- Diagram the locations of any meters needed for measurement and update as necessary.

CREDIT 5.2: CS

- Decide how the tenants will be accountable for their energy use; include specific indication of how the energy use will be determined and how costs will be incurred.

8. Examples

There are no examples for this credit.

9. Exemplary Performance

This credit is not eligible for exemplary performance under the Innovation in Design section.

10. Regional Variations

There are no regional variations in the M&V methods, but the type of energy conservation measures employed does depend on climate. For example, optimization of heating systems optimization will be more critical in northern regions, and optimization of air-conditioning systems will be more important in the South. Various M&V techniques may become more popular in a given region because of the typical projects employing them. However, IPMVP is based on industry best practices, and the fundamentals of M&V apply to all projects.

EA	
NC	Credit 5
SCHOOLS	Credit 5
CS	Credit 5.1 & 5.2

11. Operations and Maintenance Considerations

Consider submetering major energy end uses to help operators identify any deviations from expected consumption. Ensure that building operators are given the original and recalibrated energy use models so that they can identify unusual or unexpected consumption patterns.

12. Resources

Please see USGBC's LEED Registered Project Tools (http://www.usgbc.org/projecttools) for additional resources and technical information.

Websites

ENERGY STAR® Portfolio Manager

http://www.energystar.gov/benchmark

ENERGY STAR is a government-industry partnership managed by the U.S. Environmental Protection Agency and the U.S. Department of Energy. The program's website offers energy management strategies, benchmarking software tools for buildings, product procurement guidelines, and lists of ENERGY STAR–qualified products and buildings.

Portfolio Manager is an online tool to help track the energy use of commercial buildings. It provides a benchmark number that can be used to assess future energy improvements.

International Performance Measurement and Verification Protocol

http://www.evo-world.org

IPMVP Inc. is a nonprofit organization whose vision is a global marketplace that properly values energy and water efficiency.

13. Definitions

A **district energy system** is a central energy conversion plant and transmission and distribution system that provides thermal energy to a group of buildings (e.g., a central cooling plant on a university campus). Central energy systems that provide only electricity are not included.

Downstream equipment consists of all heating or cooling systems, equipment, and controls located within the project building and site associated with transporting thermal energy into heated or cooled spaces. This includes the thermal connection or interface with the district energy system, secondary distribution systems in the building, and terminal units.

Energy conservation measures are installations or modifications of equipment or systems intended to reduce energy use and costs.

Upstream equipment consists of all heating or cooling systems, equipment, and controls that are associated with a district energy system but are not part of the project building's thermal connection or do not interface with the district energy system. It includes the central energy plant and all transmission and distribution equipment associated with transporting the thermal energy to the project building and site.

Verification is the range of checks and tests carried out to determine whether components, subsystems, systems, and interfaces between systems operate in accordance with the contract documents.

GREEN POWER

	NC	SCHOOLS	CS
Credit	EA Credit 6	EA Credit 6	EA Credit 6
Points	2 points	2 points	2 points

Intent

To encourage the development and use of grid-source, renewable energy technologies on a net zero pollution basis.

Requirements

NC, SCHOOLS & CS

Engage in at least a 2-year renewable energy contract to provide at least 35% of the building's electricity from renewable sources, as defined by the Center for Resource Solutions' Green-e Energy product certification requirements.

All purchases of green power shall be based on the quantity of energy consumed, not the cost.

SCHOOLS Additional Requirement

School districts can purchase green power on a centralized basis and allocate the green power to a specific project. However, the same power cannot be credited to another LEED project. Submit a letter from the company owner attesting to this.

CS Additional Requirement

The core and shell building's electricity is defined as the electricity usage of the core and shell square footage, as defined by the Building Owners and Managers Association (BOMA) Standards, but not less than 15% of the building total gross square footage.

OPTION 1. Determine Baseline Electricity Use

Use the annual electricity consumption from the results of EA Credit 1: Optimize Energy Performance.

OR

OPTION 2. Estimate Baseline Electricity Use

Use the U.S. Department of Energy's Commercial Buildings Energy Consumption Survey database to determine the estimated electricity use.

	EA
NC	Credit 6
SCHOOLS	Credit 6
CS	Credit 6

1. Benefits and Issues to Consider

Environmental Issues

Energy production from traditional sources (such as coal, natural gas, and other fossil fuels) is a significant contributor to air pollution in the United States, releasing such pollutants as sulfur dioxide, nitrogen oxide, and carbon dioxide. These pollutants are primary contributors to acid rain, smog, and climate change. Along with other associated pollutants, they have widespread and adverse effects on human health, especially respiratory health.

Green electricity products reduce the air pollution impacts of electricity generation by relying on renewable energy sources such as solar, water, wind, biomass, and geothermal sources. In addition, the use of ecologically responsive energy sources avoids reliance on nuclear power and large-scale hydropower, which have their own drawbacks—security and environmental issues related to nuclear waste reprocessing, transportation, and storage, and alteration of aquatic habitats in the case of hydroelectric dams. Deregulated energy markets have enabled hydroelectric generators to market their electricity in areas unaffected by the dams' regional impacts.

The overall environmental benefit of renewable energy depends on the source of energy and the process by which it is extracted. For example, using biomass can reduce the estimated 136 million tons of woody construction, demolition, and land-clearing waste sent annually to landfills,[15] but if these wastes are not processed properly, their combustion could degrade air quality. Although green electricity is not entirely benign, it significantly lessens the negative environmental impacts of power generation. Using renewable energy generated either on-site or off-site is an excellent way for owners to reduce the negative environmental impacts on air and water associated with a building's energy requirements.

Renewable energy has a positive impact on rural communities in particular; siting and operating wind farms and biomass conversion facilities in rural areas enhances economic development. Rural wind generation is providing new sources of income for American farmers, Native Americans, and other rural landowners while meeting the growing demand for clean sources of electricity. However, care must be taken to minimize undesirable noise from wind farms and emissions from combustion at biomass conversion facilities.

While acknowledging the difficulty of identifying the exact source of green energy in every region, this credit requires that the renewable energy used for the building and its site be certified as green by the Green-e Energy program or its equivalent. The program was established by the Center for Resource Solutions to promote green electricity and provide consumers with a rigorous and nationally recognized method to identify green electricity products.

Economic Issues

Green power products may cost somewhat more than conventional energy products but are derived, in part, from renewable energy sources with stable energy costs. As the green power market matures and the effects of other power sources on the environment and human health are factored into power costs, renewable energy is expected to become less expensive than conventional power products. Typically, programs are structured such that utility customers can choose the portion of their electricity delivered from renewable sources. In these cases, a premium may be added to the monthly utility bill. Although the source of the green power is different from traditional sources, it reaches end users via the established grid distribution system, and thus project teams can implement green power programs, even in the postdesign phase, with very few design changes and, consequently, fewer maintenance costs. Find out whether the local government sponsors any incentive program or tax benefit for using renewable energy, particularly for the type of renewable energy planned for a project. The Database for State Incentives for Renewables and Efficiency (DSIRE: http://www.

dsireusa.org/) is good source of information on federal and state programs supporting the use of renewable energy.

	EA
NC	Credit 6
SCHOOLS	Credit 6
CS	Credit 6

2. Related Credits

Replacing conventional energy sources with renewable energy sources works synergistically with efforts to reduce energy costs. Refer to the following credit:

- EA Credit 1: Optimize Energy Performance

On-site renewable energy systems can and should be commissioned. Examine the building's roof for structural stability if any rooftop installations are under consideration. Refer to the following credits to appropriately commission and install renewable energy systems:

- SS Credit 7.2: Heat Island Reduction—Roof

- EA Prerequisite 1: Fundamental Commissioning of Building Energy Systems

- EA Credit 3: Enhanced Commissioning

3. Summary of Referenced Standards

Center for Resource Solutions, Green-e Product Certification Requirements
http://www.green-e.org
Green-e Energy is a voluntary certification and verification program for renewable energy products. Green-e certifies products that meet environmental and consumer protection standards developed in conjunction with environmental, energy, and policy organizations. Sellers of Green-e–certified energy must disclose clear and useful information to customers. Three types of renewable energy options are eligible for Green-e certification: renewable energy certificates, utility green-pricing programs, and competitive electricity products. The Green-e standard that went into effect on January 1, 2007, supersedes previous regional and product specific criteria.

Products exhibiting the Green-e logo are greener and cleaner than the average retail electricity product sold in that particular region. To be eligible for the Green-e logo, companies must meet certain criteria. The first criterion is the inclusion of qualified sources of renewable energy content such as solar electric, wind, geothermal, biomass, and small or certified low-impact hydro facilities. Other criteria are the inclusion of new renewable energy content (to support new generation capacity); compliance with emissions regulations for the nonrenewable portion of the energy product; and the absence of nuclear power. Companies must also meet other criteria regarding renewable portfolio standards. Criteria are often specific to a state or region of the United States. Refer to the standard for more details.

4. Implementation

There are 3 approaches for achieving this credit.

1. In a state with an open electricity market, building owners may be able to select a Green-e–certified power provider. Investigate green power and power markets licensed to provide power in the state and secure a 2-year contract for a minimum of 35% of the annual electrical power consumption from a Green-e–certified provider.

2. In a state with a closed electricity market, the governing utility company may have a Green-e–accredited utility program. In this case, enroll the building in the renewable power program for at least 35% of the provided electrical energy. Typically, programs are structured such that utility customers can choose how much of their electricity will be delivered from renewable sources; a premium may be added to the monthly utility bill. Commit to a 2-year enrollment period or use other strategies to accumulate 2 years' worth of renewable energy for the desired

portion of total annual energy use. If the utility does not offer 2-year enrollment options, submit a letter of commitment to stay enrolled in the program for the required period.

3. If Green-e–certified power cannot be purchased through a local utility, the owner and project team can purchase Green-e–accredited renewable energy certificates (RECs). In this case, purchase a quantity of RECs equal to 35% of the predicted annual electricity consumption over a 2-year period either all at once (which is equivalent to 70% of predicted annual electricity consumption if all the RECs are purchased at 1 time) or in contracted installments. These RECs, or "green-tags," compensate Green-e generators for the premium of production over the market rate they sell to the grid. Purchasing Green-e RECs will not affect the cost or procurement of the electricity from the local electrical utility. See the Calculations section below for information on calculating electrical power consumption and determining the 35% threshold.

Establishing Green-e Equivalency

If renewable energy is not Green-e certified, establish that it is equivalent for the 2 major criteria for Green-e Energy certification: (1) the energy source meets the requirements for renewable resources detailed in the current version of the Green-e standard, and (2) the renewable energy supplier has undergone an independent, third-party verification that the standard has been met. The current version of the standard is available on the Green-e website (http://www.green-e.org). The third-party verification process must be as rigorous as that used in the Green-e certification process, and it must be performed annually.

Retention of Renewable Energy Environmental Attributes

For renewable energy coming from both on-site and off-site sources, the associated environmental attributes must be retained or retired; they cannot be sold.

District Energy Systems

For projects with district energy systems, specific technical guidance can be found on USGBC's registered project tools page (http://www.usgbc.org/projecttools). Follow the guidance in effect at the time of registration.

5. Timeline and Team

The project team should estimate the potential energy use of the building during the design phase so that appropriate renewable technologies and potential benefits can be identified.

6. Calculations

Use either of 2 compliance paths to calculate the amount of electrical energy that must be obtained from qualifying providers to achieve compliance with EA Credit 6.

1. Design Energy Cost

The first compliance path is based on the design case annual electricity consumption, which the project team may have calculated as part of compliance with EA Credit 1. The project owner should contract with a Green-e power producer for that amount.

Sample Calculation Based on Design Energy Cost

In the example of the performance rating method for EA Credit 1, Option 1, the building's annual electricity use (including tenant use) was 843,422 kWh. From the Building Owners and Managers Association (BOMA) calculation, above, it is determined that the core and shell square footage is 18% of the total building square footage. The core and shell electricity usage is defined as 18% of the total electricity usage, or 151,816 kWh.

Required Green Power Quantity

	EA
NC	Credit 6
SCHOOLS	Credit 6
CS	Credit 6

151,816 (kWh/yr)	X	35%	X	2 yrs	=	106,271 (kWh)

This project needs to purchase Green-e-certified green power or RECs equal to 106,271 kWh/yr.

If, for example, the project obtained a quote from a REC provider of $0.02/kWh, the total cost to the project to earn EA Credit 6 would be $2,125.

2. Default Electricity Consumption

If an energy model was not performed in EA Credit 1, use the Department of Energy's Commercial Buildings Energy Consumption Survey database to determine the estimated electricity use. This database provides electricity intensity factors (kWh/sf/yr) for various building types in the United States.

Table 1 summarizes median annual electrical intensities (kWh/sf/yr) for different building types, based on data from the latest survey. The energy intensity multiplied by the square footage of the project represents the total amount of green power (in kWh) that would need to be purchased over a 2-year period to qualify for EA Credit 6 using this option.

Table 1: Commercial Buildings Energy Consumption Survey (CBECS) data, from U.S. DOE Energy Information Administration

Building Type	Median Electrical Intensity(kWh/sf-yr)
Education	6.6
Food Sales	58.9
Food Service	28.7
Health Care Inpatient	21.5
Health Care Outpatient	9.7
Lodging	12.6
Retail (Other than Mall)	8.0
Enclosed and Strip Malls	14.5
Office	11.7
Public Assembly	6.8
Public Order and Safety	4.1
Religious Worship	2.5
Service	6.1
Warehouse and Storage	3.0
Other	13.8

	EA
NC	Credit 6
SCHOOLS	Credit 6
CS	Credit 6

Area Calculation

The building's core and shell square footage is the gross square footage (gsf) minus the usable square footage (usf); both are defined in ANSI/BOMA Standard Z65.1–1996.

To calculate the percentage of the building that is core and shell square footage, first calculate the building's gsf. Next calculate the building's usf. The percentage of the building that is core and shell square footage is as follows:

$$\frac{GSF - USF}{GSF} \times 100$$

If the result is less than 15%, use 15% for the calculations.

Sample Calculation Based on Department of Energy Data

The project is a 950,000-square-foot speculative office building. According to the BOMA calculation, the core and shell is 20% of the building total square footage, or 190,000. The calculation for the renewable energy required is based on this figure. To determine how much renewable energy is needed to meet the requirements of EA Credit 6, use Table 1 and the median electricity consumption intensity for offices.

Default Annual Electricity Consumption

$$190,000 \text{ (sf)} \quad X \quad 11.7 \text{ (kWh/sf/yr)} \quad X \quad 2,223,000 \text{ (kWh/yr)}$$

Required Green Power

$$2,223,000 \text{ (kWh/yr)} \quad X \quad 35\% \quad X \quad 2 \text{ yrs} \quad = \quad 1,556,100 \text{ (kWh)}$$

This project needs to purchase Green-e–certified green power or RECs equal to 1,556,100 kWh per year. If the project obtained a quote from a RECs provider of $0.02/kWh, the total cost to the project to earn EA Credit 6 would be $31,122.

7. Documentation Guidance

As a first step in preparing to complete the LEED-Online documentation requirements, work through the following measures. Refer to LEED-Online for the complete descriptions of all required documentation.

- Sign a 2-year contract for the purchase of renewable energy certified by Green-e (or equivalent) and maintain contractual documentation.

- For a campus project, where the certified renewable energy is purchased for the project by others, maintain documentation indicating that the renewable energy was retained on behalf of the project.

8. Examples

There are no examples for this credit.

9. Exemplary Performance

Exemplary performance is available to projects that purchase 100% of their electricity from renewable sources.

10. Regional Variations

Renewable energy certificates (RECs) are now widely available in nearly all the U.S. states. Customers can buy green certificates whether or not they have access to green power through their local utility or a competitive electricity marketer.[14]

	EA
NC	Credit 6
SCHOOLS	Credit 6
CS	Credit 6

11. Operations and Maintenance Considerations

To facilitate the continued purchase of green power beyond the 2-year contract period, give building operators details of the original green power contract.

12. Resources

Please see USGBC's LEED Registered Project Tools (http://www.usgbc.org/projecttools) for additional resources and technical information.

Websites

Center for Resource Solutions, Green-e Program
http://www.green-e.org
See the Referenced Standards section for more information.

North Carolina Solar Center, Database of State Incentives for Renewable Energy
http://www.dsireusa.org
This database collects information on state financial and regulatory incentives (e.g., tax credits, grants, and special utility rates) to promote the application of renewable energy technologies. The database details the incentives on a state-by-state basis.

Union of Concerned Scientists, Clean Energy
http://www.ucsusa.org/clean_energy
This independent nonprofit analyzes and advocates energy solutions that are environmentally and economically sustainable. The site provides news and information on research and public policy.

U.S. Department of Energy, Green Power Network
http://www.eere.energy.gov/greenpower
The Green Power Network provides news and information on green power markets and related activities. It contains up-to-date information on green power providers, product offerings, consumer issues, and in-depth analyses of issues and policies affecting green power markets. The website is maintained by the National Renewable Energy Laboratory for the Department of Energy.

U.S. Department of Energy, Energy Efficiency and Renewable Energy, Green Power
http://apps3.eere.energy.gov/greenpower/buying/buying_power.shtml
This site provides information on the availability of green power in the United States by state. The results include utility green pricing programs, retail green power products offered in competitive electricity markets, and renewable energy certificate products sold separately from electricity.

U.S. EPA, Green Power Partnership
http://www.epa.gov/greenpower
The Green Power Partnership provides news and information on green power markets and related activities. It contains up-to-date information on green power providers, product offerings, consumer issues, and in-depth analyses of issues and policies affecting green power markets. The website is maintained by the National Renewable Energy Laboratory for the Department of Energy.

13. Definitions

Biofuel-based systems are power systems that run on renewable fuels derived from organic materials, such as wood by-products and agricultural waste. Examples of biofuels include untreated wood waste, agricultural crops and residues, animal waste, other organic waste, and landfill gas.

	EA
NC	Credit 6
SCHOOLS	Credit 6
CS	Credit 6

Biomass is plant material from trees, grasses, or crops that can be converted to heat energy to produce electricity.

Geothermal energy is electricity generated by converting hot water or steam from within the earth into electrical power.

Geothermal heating systems use pipes to transfer heat from underground steam or hot water for heating, cooling, and hot water. The system retrieves heat during cool months and returns heat in summer months.

Green power is synonymous with renewable energy.

Hydropower is electricity produced from the downhill flow of water from rivers or lakes.

Photovoltaic (PV) energy is electricity from photovoltaic cells that convert the energy in sunlight into electricity.

Renewable energy comes from sources that are not depleted by use. Examples include energy from the sun, wind, and small (low-impact) hydropower, plus geothermal energy and wave and tidal systems. Ways to capture energy from the sun include photovoltaic, solar thermal, and bioenergy systems based on wood waste, agricultural crops or residue, animal and other organic waste, or landfill gas.

Renewable energy certificates (RECs) are tradable commodities representing proof that a unit of electricity was generated from a renewable energy resource. RECs are sold separately from electricity itself and thus allow the purchase of green power by a user of conventionally generated electricity.

Solar thermal systems collect or absorb sunlight via solar collectors to heat water that is then circulated to the building's hot water tank. Solar thermal systems can be used to warm swimming pools or heat water for residential and commercial use.

Wave and tidal power systems capture energy from waves and the diurnal flux of tidal power, respectively. The captured energy is commonly used for desalination, water pumping, and electricity generation.

Wind energy is electricity generated by wind turbines.

Endnotes

[1] U.S. Department of Energy, Office of Energy Efficiency and Renewable Energy. "Table 1.1.1 U.S. Residential and Commercial Buildings Total Primary Energy Consumption (Quadrillion Btu and Percent of Total), 2006." 2008 Buildings Energy Data Book. 2008. http://buildingsdatabook.eren.doe.gov (accessed November 2008).

[2] Ibid.

[3] U.S. Environmental Protection Agency. "Clean Energy: Air Emissions." http://www.epa.gov/cleanenergy/energy-and-you/affect/air-emissions.html (accessed November 2008).

[4] U.S. Environmental Protection Agency, Office of Air and Radiation. "Six Common Air Pollutants: SO2: What is it? Where does it come from?". http://www.epa.gov/air/urbanair/so2/what1.html (accessed November 2008).

[5] Architecture 2030. "The Building Sector: A Hidden Culprit." http://www.architecture2030.org/current_situation/building_sector.html (accessed November 2008).

[6] U.S. Environmental Protection Agency. "Facts About Energy Use in Commercial and Industrial Facilities." http://www.energystar.gov/index.cfm?c=learn_more.fast_facts (accessed November 2008).

7 U.S. Environmental Protection Agency. "ENERGY STAR® Home Improvement Tips." http://www.energystar.gov/index.cfm?c=cfls.pr_cfls (accessed November 2008).

8 Architecture 2030. "The Building Sector: A Hidden Culprit." http://www.architecture2030.org/current_situation/building_sector.html (accessed November 2008).

9 U.S. Environmental Protection Agency. "Facts About Energy Use in Commercial and Industrial Facilities." http://www.energystar.gov/index.cfm?c=learn_more.fast_facts (accessed November 2008).

10 Ibid.

11 U.S. Environmental Protection Agency, Office of Solid Waste. "Wastes — Non-Hazardous Waste — Industrial Waste: Basic Information." http://www.epa.gov/osw/nonhaz/industrial/cd/basic.htm (accessed November 2008).

12 U.S. Green Building Council LEED Steering Committee. *The Treatment by LEED® of the Environmental Impact of HVAC Refrigerants.* 2004. https://www.usgbc.org/Docs/LEED_tsac/TSAC_Refrig_Report_Final-Approved.pdf.

13 U.S. Environmental Protection Agency, Office of Solid Waste. "Wastes — Resource Conservation — Reduce, Reuse, Recycle — Construction & Demolition Materials." http://www.epa.gov/osw/conserve/rrr/imr/cdm/ (accessed November 13, 2008).

14 U.S. Department of Energy, Office of Energy Efficiency and Renewable Energy. "Renewable Energy Certificates." http://apps3.eere.energy.gov/greenpower/markets/certificates.shtml?page=0.

Overview

Building operations generate a large amount of waste on a daily basis. Meeting the LEED Materials and Resources (MR) credits can reduce the quantity of waste while improving the building environment through responsible waste management and materials selection. The credits in this section focus on 2 main issues: the environmental impact of materials brought into the project building, and the minimization of landfill and incinerator disposal for materials that leave the project building.

This credit category addresses the environmental concerns relating to materials selection, waste disposal, and waste reduction. The LEED for New Construction, LEED for Core & Shell, and LEED for Schools Materials and Resources prerequisites and credits promote the following measures:

Selecting Sustainable Materials

Materials selection plays a significant role in sustainable building operations. During the life cycle of a material, its extraction, processing, transportation, use, and disposal can have negative health and environmental consequences, polluting water and air, destroying native habitats, and depleting natural resources. Environmentally responsible procurement policies can significantly reduce these impacts. Consider the relative environmental, social, and health benefits of the available choices when purchasing materials and supplies. For example, the purchase of products containing recycled content expands markets for recycled materials, slows the consumption of raw materials, and reduces the amount of waste entering landfills. Use of materials from local sources supports local economies while reducing transportation impacts.

Practicing Waste Reduction

Maintaining occupancy rates in existing buildings reduces redundant development and the associated environmental impact of producing and delivering new materials. Construction waste disposal through landfilling or incineration contributes significantly to the negative environmental impacts of a building. Construction and demolition wastes constitute about 40% of the total solid waste stream in the United States. In its solid waste management hierarchy, the U.S. Environmental Protection Agency (EPA) ranks source reduction, reuse, and recycling as the 3 preferred strategies for reducing waste.[1] Source reduction appears at the top of EPA's hierarchy because it minimizes environmental impacts throughout the material's life cycle, from the supply chain and use to recycling and waste disposal. Reuse of materials is ranked second because reused materials are diverted from the waste stream and substitute for other materials with greater environmental impacts. Recycling does not have all the same benefits as source reduction and reuse, but it diverts waste from landfills and incinerators and lessens the demand for virgin materials.

Reducing Waste at Its Source

Source reduction, which includes reducing the overall demand for products, is the most economical way to reduce waste. In 2006, U.S. residents, businesses, and institutions produced more than 251 million tons of solid waste, a 65% increase since 1980. That amount is roughly equivalent to 4.6 pounds per person per day, a 25% increase since 1980.[2] In addition, 7.6 billion tons of industrial solid waste are generated each year[3]. Waste generation raises building costs in 2 ways. First, unnecessary materials (such as packaging) add to the cost of products purchased, and second, fees for waste collection and disposal rise as the amount of waste increases.

Reducing the amount of waste is an important component of sustainable construction practices. A construction waste management plan is the first step in managing construction waste because it requires contractors to establish a system for tracking waste generation and disposal during construction.

Reusing and Recycling

Reuse of existing buildings, versus building new structures, is one of the most effective strategies for minimizing environmental impacts. By reusing existing building components, waste can be reduced and diverted from landfills. Reuse of an existing building results in less habitat disturbance and, typically, less new infrastructure, such as utilities and roads. An effective way to reuse interior components is to specify them in construction documents. By reusing or recycling these materials, an increasing number of public and private waste management operations have reduced the volume of construction debris. Recovery typically begins on the jobsite with separation of debris into bins or disposal areas. Some regions have access to mixed waste processing facilities. EPA reports that in 2007 there were 34 mixed waste processing facilities in the United States handling about 43 millions tons of waste per day.[4]

When selecting materials, it is important to evaluate new and alternative sources. Salvaged materials can be substituted for new materials, saving costs and adding character to the building. Recycled-content materials reuse waste that would otherwise be disposed in landfills or incinerators. Use of local materials supports the local economy and reduces transportation impacts. Using rapidly renewable materials may minimize natural resource consumption with the harvest cycle of the resource potentially matching the life of the material in buildings. Use of third-party certified wood improves the stewardship of forests and related ecosystems.

Recycling construction, demolition, and land-clearing debris reduces demand for virgin resources and has the potential to lessen the environmental and health burdens associated with resource extraction, processing, and transportation. Debris recycling also reduces dependence on landfills, which may contaminate groundwater and encroach upon valuable open space. In addition, it lessens disposal in incinerators, which may contaminate groundwater and pollute the air. Effective construction waste management can extend the life of existing landfills, which in turn reduces the need for expansion or development of new landfills.

Over the past few decades, recycling has increased in the United States. In 1960, only 6.4% of U.S. waste was recycled. By 2006, the amount climbed to 32.5%.[5] Curbside recycling is now standard in many communities, and recycling facilities are available throughout the nation. In addition, many businesses, nonprofit organizations, and manufacturers have successful recycling programs that divert a wide range of materials from the waste stream.

Recycling provides materials for new products that would otherwise be manufactured from virgin materials. It avoids the extraction of raw materials and preserves landfill space. Recycling certain products, such as batteries and fluorescent light bulbs, prevents toxic materials from polluting the air and ground water.

Reuse and recycling can also save money. Effective waste management benefits organizations by reducing the cost of waste disposal and generating revenue from recycling or resale proceeds.

Summary

A sustainable building requires policies for responsible construction and materials selection as well as effective waste management. The Materials and Resources prerequisites and credits establish the foundation for developing, implementing, and documenting these policies. In LEED for Schools, many possibilities exist for integrating topics such as resource life cycle, waste reduction, and recycling into the curriculum and for motivating students to become actively involved in conservation efforts at school and in the community.

Operations and building management can effectively reduce a building's overall impact on the environment with waste management programs and purchasing policies that reduce waste and specify less harmful materials and supplies.

Materials and Resources Credit Characteristics

Table 1 shows the metrics used to determine compliance with each credit, such as area, weight, and cost, and materials that should be included and excluded in the calculations. Materials that are blacked out in the table are excluded from the corresponding credit calculations.

Calculating Materials Costs to Achieve MR Credits

Project teams are encouraged to determine the actual total materials cost (excluding labor and equipment) from Construction Specification Institute (CSI) MasterFormat™ Divisions 03–10, 31 (Section 31.60.00 Foundations) and 32 (Sections 32.10.00 Paving, 32.30.00 Site Improvements, and 32.90.00 Planting). However, LEED for New Construction, LEED for Core & Shell, and LEED for Schools allow project teams to apply a 45% factor to total construction costs (including labor and equipment) from Construction Specification Institute (CSI) MasterFormat™ Divisions 03–10, 31 (Section 31.60.00 Foundations) and 32 (Sections 32.10.00 Paving, 32.30.00 Site Improvements, and 32.90.00 Planting) to establish a default total materials cost for the project. Table 2 contains guidance regarding specification sections included in the cost calculation. The approach selected by the project team (actual materials cost or LEED default materials cost) must be consistent across all credits based on total materials cost. A project team may include materials costs from Construction Specification Institute MasterFormat™ Division 12—Furniture and Furnishings as long as this is done consistently across all MR credits. LEED Core & Shell project teams that use tenant sales or lease agreements to assist with credit compliance must also do so consistently across all MR credits.

Materials calculated toward materials reuse cannot be applied to MR credits for building reuse, construction waste management, recycled content, rapidly renewable materials, or certified wood.

Table 1. MR Credit Metrics

Material	MRc1: Building Reuse	MRc2: Construction Waste Management	MRc3: Materials Reuse	MRc4: Recycled Content	MRc5: Regional Materials	MRc6: Rapidly Renewable Materials	MRc7: Certified Wood
CSI Divisions 3 thru 10	Based on Area	Based on weight or volume. Include demolition and construction waste	Based on replacement value ($)	Based on cost of qualifying materials as a percent of overall materials cost for Divisions 3-10 ($)			Based on cost of FSC wood as a percentage of all new wood ($)
Mechanical							
Electrical							
Plumbing							
Furniture & Furnishings (CSI Division 12)			May be included with Divisions 3-10, if done consistently for credits 3-7				

MR OVERVIEW

CREDIT	TITLE	NC	SCHOOLS	CS
MR Prerequisite 1	Storage and Collection of Recyclables	Required	Required	Required
MR Credit 1.1	Building Reuse—Maintain Existing Walls, Floors, and Roof	1-3 points	1-2 points	NA
MR Credit 1	Building Reuse—Maintain Existing Walls, Floors, and Roof	NA	NA	1-5 points
MR Credit 1.2	Building Reuse—Maintain Interior Nonstructural Elements	1 point	1 point	NA
MR Credit 2	Construction Waste Management	1-2 points	1-2 points	1-2 points
MR Credit 3	Materials Reuse	1-2 points	1-2 points	1 point
MR Credit 4	Recycled Content	1-2 points	1-2 points	1-2 points
MR Credit 5	Regional Materials	1-2 points	1-2 points	1-2 points
MR Credit 6	Rapidly Renewable Materials	1 point	1 point	NA
MR Credit 7	Certified Wood	1 point	1 point	NA
MR Credit 6	Certified Wood	NA	NA	1 point

STORAGE AND COLLECTION OF RECYCLABLES

	NC	SCHOOLS	CS
Prerequisite	MR Prerequisite 1	MR Prerequisite 1	MR Prerequisite 1
Points	Required	Required	Required

Intent

To facilitate the reduction of waste generated by building occupants that is hauled to and disposed of in landfills.

Requirements

NC, SCHOOLS & CS

Provide an easily-accessible dedicated area or for the collection and storage materials for recycling for the entire building. Materials must include at a minimum paper, corrugated cardboard, glass, plastics and metals.

	MR
NC	Prerequisite 1
SCHOOLS	Prerequisite 1
CS	Prerequisite 1

1. Benefits and Issues To Consider

Environmental Issues

By creating convenient recycling opportunities for all building occupants, a significant portion of the solid waste stream can be diverted from landfills. Recycling of paper, metals, glass, cardboard, and plastics reduces the need to extract virgin natural resources. For example, recycling 1 ton of paper prevents the processing of 17 trees and saves 3 cubic yards of landfill space.[6] Recycled aluminum requires only 5% of the energy required to produce virgin aluminum from bauxite, its raw material form.[7] Diverting waste from landfills can help minimize land, water, and air pollution. An occupant education program that addresses the environmental and financial benefits of recycling can encourage occupants to participate in preserving the environment.

Economic Issues

Many communities sponsor and promote recycling programs to reduce the amount of waste sent to landfills. Community recycling efforts return valuable resources to local production processes and may spur increases in employment in the recycling industry. Community-wide participation results in higher recycling rates and, in turn, more stable markets for recycled materials.

Recycling infrastructure, such as storage areas and bins, may add to project costs and take up floor area that could be used for other purposes. However, recycling offers significant savings through reduced landfill disposal costs or tipping fees. In larger projects, processing equipment (can crushers, cardboard balers) can minimize the space required for recycling activities. Some recyclables can generate revenue that offsets collection and processing costs.

2. Related Credits

Project teams seeking an Innovation in Design credit for educational outreach can create signage and displays to inform building occupants and visitors about on-site recycling.

> **CS** Core & Shell project teams should address recycling within tenant guidelines. The tenant guidelines should include information regarding the building's recycling policy and procedures. The project team should encourage activities to reduce and reuse materials before recycling to decrease the volume of recyclables handled.

3. Summary of Referenced Standards

There are no standards referenced for this credit.

4. Implementation

Building owners and designers must determine the best way to create a dedicated recycling collection and storage area that is easily accessible within the building and encourages recycling yet is accessible to the waste hauler. Recyclable material collection and storage space might increase the project footprint in some instances. Consider how recycling activities might affect a building's indoor environmental quality. Activities that create odors, noise, and air contaminants should be isolated or performed during nonoccupant hours. The requirements of this prerequisite do not regulate the size of the recycling area. However, Table 1 provides guidelines for the recycling storage area based on overall building square footage, including corridors, elevators, stairwells, and shaft spaces. These guidelines will help the design team determine the appropriate size for recycling facilities according to specific building operations.

Table 1. Recycling Area Guidelines

Commercial Building (sf)	Minimum Recycling Area (sf)
0 to 5,000	82
5,001 to 15,000	125
15,001 to 50,000	175
50,001 to 100,000	225
100,001 to 200,000	275
200,001 or greater	500

	MR
NC	Prerequisite 1
SCHOOLS	Prerequisite 1
CS	Prerequisite 1

In places where the materials specified in this prerequisite are not recycled, a building should still have designated space to collect and store those materials in anticipation of recycling infrastructure for the materials becoming available in the future.

Designate and visibly mark central collection and storage areas for recyclables, including paper, cardboard, glass, plastic, and metals. The central collection and storage area should provide easy access for both maintenance staff and collection vehicles. A central collection area designed to consolidate a building's recyclables meets the credit requirements as long as the intent of the credit and the recycling needs of the occupants are met. For projects with larger site areas, it may be possible to create a central collection area that is outside the building footprint or project site boundary. In this case, document how the recyclable materials will be transported to the separate collection area. For projects with landscaping, consider designating an area for collecting plant debris.

Establish recycling collection points within common areas, such as classrooms, break rooms, open offices, and any location where occupants may need to recycle.

Design considerations for recycling areas should include signage to discourage contamination, protection from the elements, and security for high-value materials. Design security for the recyclable collection areas to discourage illegal disposal.

If possible, teach occupants, maintenance personnel, and other building users about recycling procedures. Consider using a recycling manual or educational program. Activities to reduce and reuse materials before recycling will reduce the volume of recyclables. For instance, building occupants can reduce the solid waste stream by using reusable bottles, bags, and other containers. Maintenance personnel can reduce waste by purchasing cleaners in bulk or concentrated form. Consider employing cardboard balers, aluminum can crushers, recycling chutes, and other waste management technologies to further improve the recycling program.

SCHOOLS For schools and other institutional projects, a student- or occupant-run recycling team that transports materials from small collection bins to a central collection point provides opportunities for learning and collaboration.

CS Core & Shell project teams need to consider the maintenance and waste management practices for the entire building, including tenant spaces. Depending on the region, market, business practices, and customs, core and shell building owners may approach waste management differently. Building owners who provide cleaning services for all tenants can control both the space needs and the procedures for removing, storing, and hauling recyclables. In these instances, the space needs should be evaluated based on how frequently waste and recyclables are collected from tenant spaces. In buildings where tenants contract their own cleaning services, provide adequate space for recyclable storage and include specific instructions for use within tenant guidelines.

If cleaning services are contracted directly by the tenants, consider providing several recycling collection points within the building. For example, building owners with multiple tenant floors or large floor plates may want to provide collection points in the building core areas that tenants can easily access. Recyclables can then be collected and removed as needed by the building owner's contracted recycling service.

5. Timeline and Team

Early in the design phase, to ensure that proper space is allocated for a centralized collection point, seek input from the local hauler who will be providing waste management services to the site. Attention should be given to the accessibility and convenience of the waste and recycling collection locations. Prior to occupancy, the owner or owner's representative should ensure that sufficient recycling bins are in place. Postoccupancy, the project team should educate occupants on the benefits of recycling, as well as the location of facilities. Most importantly, the project team should educate the facilities staff on the proper recycling procedures. This is critical to ongoing success and improvements in waste management.

6. Calculations

There are no calculations required for this credit. However, project teams should refer to Table 1 for sizing recycling areas. The values in this table were developed by the City of Seattle in support of an ordinance requiring minimum areas for recycling and storage of recyclables in commercial buildings. The ordinance is based on the total square footage of the building. Minimum areas for residential buildings are also specified. The requirements of this prerequisite do not regulate the size of the recycling area; the intent is for the design team to size the facilities appropriately for the specific building operations.

Another source of guidelines for sizing recycling areas is the California Integrated Waste Management Board's (CIWMB) 2004 Statewide Waste Characterization Study,[8] which gives quantity and composition estimates for commercial, residential, and self-hauled waste streams. The study examines material disposal rates of rigid plastic packaging containers and California redemption value containers in more detail beyond the 1999 report (see the References section).

7. Documentation Guidance

As a first step in preparing to complete the LEED-Online documentation requirements, work through the following measures. Refer to LEED-Online for the complete descriptions of all required documentation.

- Keep a record of the recycling plan's size and accessibility to occupants and facility staff; based on expected volume for the entire building (pickup frequency of commingling, etc.), consider whether the planned approach will be adequate.

- Prepare documentation such as floor plans and site plans that highlight all recycling storage areas.

8. Examples

Figure 1 shows a typical breakdown of waste stream materials. The 5 materials required for collection— paper, glass, plastics, cardboard, and metals—make up 59% of the waste stream.

Figure 1. Municipal Solid Waste Generation
Data from U.S. Environmental Protection Agency, 2006.

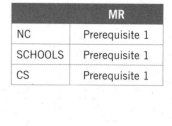

	MR
NC	Prerequisite 1
SCHOOLS	Prerequisite 1
CS	Prerequisite 1

TOTAL MUNICIPAL SOLID WASTE GENERATION, 2006 - 251 MILLION TONS (BEFORE RECYCLING)

GLASS 5%

METALS 8%

PLASTICS 12%

PAPER / CARDBOARD 34%

YARD TRIMMINGS 13%

FOOD SCRAPS 12%

WOOD 6%

OTHER 3%

TEXTILES, LEATHER & RUBBER 7%

■ LEED REQUIRED RECYCLABLES COLLECTION (59% OF TOTAL)

■ ENCOURAGED TO BE COMPOSTED ON-SITE, WHEN POSSIBLE (25% OF TOTAL)

▫ OTHER

9. Exemplary Performance

This prerequisite is not eligible for exemplary performance under the Innovation in Design section.

10. Regional Variations

Dense urban areas typically have public or private recycling infrastructure in place, but some less populated areas may not. Research local recycling programs to find the best method of diverting recyclable materials from the waste stream. Space needs can vary depending on collection strategies used by the hauler, and whether recyclables are commingled or separated at the source. For example, if the local hauler accepts commingled recyclables, it may be possible to reduce the area needed for separate collection bins.

11. Operations and Maintenance Considerations

Consider developing a commercial waste and recycling policy and education program for occupants. The policy should outline the protocol for collection and processing that the facility staff will follow and detail the signage for collection areas. The education component should explain the environmental and financial benefits of recycling to all building occupants.

MR	
NC	Prerequisite 1
SCHOOLS	Prerequisite 1
CS	Prerequisite 1

Postoccupancy, the recycling program should be reviewed as needed and any problems addressed. Conduct periodic reviews of building waste collection points and adjust the number and size of recycling bins. Provide additional on-site recycling resources and occupant training if needed. Owners should consider a waste stream audit to identify the types and amounts of building waste. Many schools have students conduct such waste stream audits as part of an effort to teach the benefits of effective recycling.

12. Resources

Please see USGBC's LEED Registered Project Tools (http://www.usgbc.org/projecttools) for additional resources and technical information.

Websites

California Integrated Waste Management Board

http://www.ciwmb.ca.gov

The California Integrated Waste Management Board (CIWMB) offers information about waste reduction, recycling and solid waste characterization, as well as generation rates for offices, schools, and residences.

Earth 911

http://earth911.com

Earth 911 offers information and education programs on recycling as well as links to local recyclers.

U.S. Conference of Mayors, Recycling at Work

http://www.usmayors.org/recycle

The U.S. Conference of Mayors provides information on workplace recycling efforts.

Inform: Strategies for a Better Environment, Waste at Work

http://www.informinc.org/wasteatwork.php

This is an online document from Inform, Inc., and the New York City Council on the Environment on strategies and case studies designed to reduce workplace waste generation.

Go Green Initiative

http://www.gogreeninitiative.org

The Go Green Initiative is a comprehensive environmental action plan that promotes conservation and environmental education in schools. The website contains a variety of resources for developing environmental stewardship programs and curriculum about recycling, waste, and other environmental topics.

California Integrated Waste Management Board, School Waste Management Education and Assistance

http://www.ciwmb.ca.gov/Schools/WasteReduce/

This site offers resources for helping schools develop waste management programs and curricula

Print Media

Composting and Recycling Municipal Solid Waste, by Luis Diaz et al. (CRC Press, 1993).

McGraw-Hill Recycling Handbook, by Herbert F. Lund (McGraw-Hill, 2000).

13. Definitions

Landfills are waste disposal sites for solid waste from human activities.

Occupants in a commercial building are workers who either have a permanent office or workstation in the building or typically spend a minimum of 10 hours per week in the building. In a residential building, occupants also include all persons who live in the building. In schools, occupants also include students, faculty, support staff, administration, and maintenance employees.

Recycling is the collection, reprocessing, marketing, and use of materials that were diverted or recovered from the solid waste stream.

A **recycling collection** area is located in regularly occupied space in the building for the collection of occupants' recyclables. A building may have numerous collection areas from which recyclable materials are typically removed to a central collection and storage area.

Reuse returns materials to active use in the same or a related capacity as their original use, thus extending the lifetime of materials that would otherwise be discarded.

Source reduction reduces the amount of unnecessary material brought into a building. Examples include purchasing products with less packaging.

Tipping fees are charged by a landfill for disposal of waste, typically quoted per ton.

Waste comprises all materials that flow from the building to final disposal. Examples include paper, grass trimmings, food scraps, and plastics. In LEED, waste refers to all materials that are capable of being diverted from the building's waste stream through waste reduction.

Waste disposal eliminates waste by means of burial in a landfill, combustion in an incinerator, dumping at sea, or any other way that is not recycling or reuse.

Waste diversion is a management activity that disposes of waste other than through incineration or the use of landfills. Examples include reuse and recycling.

Waste reduction includes both source reduction and waste diversion through reuse or recycling.

The **waste stream** is the overall flow of waste from the building to a landfill, incinerator, or other disposal site.

	MR
NC	Prerequisite 1
SCHOOLS	Prerequisite 1
CS	Prerequisite 1

LEED REFERENCE GUIDE FOR GREEN BUILDING DESIGN AND CONSTRUCTION

BUILDING REUSE—MAINTAIN EXISTING WALLS, FLOORS, AND ROOF

	NC	SCHOOLS	CS
Credit	MR Credit 1.1	MR Credit 1.1	MR Credit 1
Points	1-3 points	1-2 points	1-5 points

Intent

To extend the life cycle of existing building stock, conserve resources, retain cultural resources, reduce waste and reduce environmental impacts of new buildings as they relate to materials manufacturing and transport.

Requirements

NC, SCHOOLS & CS

Maintain the existing building structure (including structural floor and roof decking) and envelope (the exterior skin and framing, excluding window assemblies and nonstructural roofing material).

Hazardous materials that are remediated as a part of the project must be excluded from the calculation of the percentage maintained.

The minimum percentage building reuse for each point threshold is as follows:

NC

Building Reuse	Points
55%	1
75%	2
95%	3

SCHOOLS

Building Reuse	Points
75%	1
95%	2

CS

Building Reuse	Points
25%	1
33%	2
42%	3
50%	4
75%	5

If the project includes an addition that is more than 6 times (for Core & Shell) and 2 times (for New Construction and Schools) the square footage of the existing building, this credit is not applicable.

1. Benefits and Issues to Consider

Environmental Issues

Building reuse is a very effective strategy for reducing the overall environmental impact of construction. Reusing existing buildings significantly reduces the energy use associated with the demolition process as well as construction waste. Reuse strategies also reduce environmental impacts associated with raw material extraction, manufacturing, and transportation.

Economic Issues

Although retrofitting an existing building to accommodate new programmatic and LEED requirements can add to the complexity of design and construction—reflected in the project's soft costs—reuse of existing components can reduce the cost of construction substantially.

2. Related Credits

When working on an adaptive reuse project, assess the site early on to determine which areas and materials would be valuable to reincorporate into the new development. Inventory the areas and square footage of the existing site and incorporate a reuse strategy into the initial design charrettes. Review these 2 credits:

- MR Credit 2: Construction Waste Management
- MR Credit 3: Materials Reuse.

The development of a comprehensive reuse management plan that evaluates the anticipated materials saved will determine whether the project meets the requirements of MR Credit 1, Building Reuse. If reuse is not enough to achieve credit compliance, the materials can still contribute toward MR Credit 2, Construction Waste Management, if the material has not been applied to MR Credit 1.

3. Summary of Referenced Standards

There are no standards referenced for this credit.

4. Implementation

If the project will reuse part of an existing building, inventory the existing conditions. The architect should develop a floor plan showing the location of existing structural components, exterior and party walls, and exterior windows and doors. The drawings should be detailed enough to determine the surface area of all elements to be reused.

Confirm that the structural and envelope elements designated for reuse can be reused and take the necessary steps to retain and maintain them. Projects that incorporate part of an existing building but do not meet the requirements for MR Credit 1 may apply the reused portion toward the achievement of MR Credit 2, Construction Waste Management. To do so, determine an approximate weight or volume for existing building elements.

5. Timeline and Team

As a design strategy, building reuse has significant impact on all phases of a project, from schematic design through bidding and construction.

At site selection, the owner and project team should identify a project site that will utilize an existing building. In predesign, the project team should analyze the cost savings associated with building reuse. During schematic design, the project team should consider how to reuse as much of the building as possible. The specifications for bid, developed by the architect in consultation with the owner, should outline measures to preserve the building during construction, and these should be implemented with project team oversight.

6. Calculations

This credit is based on the surface areas of major existing structural and envelope elements. Structural support elements such as columns and beams are considered part of the larger surfaces they support, so they are not quantified separately. Prepare a spreadsheet listing all envelope and structural elements within the building. Quantify each item, listing the square footage of both the existing area and the retained area. Determine the percentage of existing elements that are retained by dividing the square footage of the total retained materials area by the square footage of the total existing materials area.

Take measurements as if preparing a bid for construction of a building. For structural floors and roof decking, calculate the square footage of each component. For existing exterior walls and existing walls adjoining other buildings or additions, calculate the square footage of the exterior wall only and subtract the area of exterior windows and exterior doors from both the existing and the reused area tallies. For interior structural walls (e.g., shear walls), calculate the square footage of 1 side of the existing wall element. Table 1 provides an example of the calculations for MR Credit 1.1.

Table 1. Sample Building Structure and Envelope Reuse Calculation

Structure/Envelope Element	Exisiting Area (sf)	Reused Area (sf)	Percentage Rused (%)
Foundation/Slab on Grade	11,520	11,520	100
2nd Floor Deck	11,520	10,000	87
1st Floor Interior Structural Walls	240	240	100
2nd Floor Interior Structural Walls	136	136	100
Roof Deck	11,520	11,520	100
North Exterior Wall (excl. windows)	8,235	7,150	87
South Exterior Wall (excl. windows)	8,235	8,235	100
East Exterior Wall (excl. windows)	6,535	6,535	100
West Exterior Wall (excl. windows)	6,535	5,820	81
Total	64,476	61,156	95

Exclude the following items from this calculation: nonstructural roofing material, window assemblies, structural and envelope materials that are deemed structurally unsound, hazardous materials, and materials that pose a contamination risk to building occupants.

7. Documentation Guidance

As a first step in preparing to complete the LEED-Online documentation requirements, work through the following measures. Refer to LEED-Online for the complete descriptions of all required documentation.

- For an existing building major renovation and/or addition, prepare a list of shell attributes; include element IDs and the total area of new, existing, and reused elements..

- Be able to explain why any existing building elements were excluded.

8. Examples

See Table 1 for an example of a typical building structure and envelope reuse calculation.

9. Exemplary Performance

CS Project teams may earn an Innovation in Design credit for exemplary performance by maintaining 95% or more of the existing walls, floors, and roof.

MR	
NC	Credit 1.1
SCHOOLS	Credit 1.1
CS	Credit 1

10. Regional Variations

This credit may have particular importance in areas with historic structures and neighborhoods. Building reuse can encourage new development while preserving the history and character of an area. Reuse can also be a strategy for development in areas in need of inner-city investment. Where there is pressure to demolish existing structures and build larger buildings, renovations of existing buildings and building additions can become models of how to preserve and incorporate original structures and achieve associated environmental and financial benefits.

11. Operations and Maintenance Considerations

The project team should communicate to building operators any special maintenance practices required by the reused materials, or any differences in life expectancy or durability compared with new materials.

12. Resources

Please see USGBC's LEED Registered Project Tools (http://www.usgbc.org/projecttools) for additional resources and technical information.

Print Media

How Buildings Learn: What Happens after They're Built, by Stewart Brand (Viking Press, 1994).

13. Definitions

Adaptive reuse is the renovation of a space for a purpose different from the original.

Existing area is the total area of the building structure, core, and envelope that existed when the project area was selected. Exterior windows and doors are not included.

Prior condition is the state of the project space at the time it was selected.

Prior condition area is the total area of finished ceilings, floors, and full-height walls that existed when the project area was selected. It does not include exterior windows and doors.

Retained components are portions of the finished ceilings, finished floors, full-height walls and demountable partitions, interior doors, and built-in case goods that existed in the prior condition area and remain in the completed design.

Reused area is the total area of the building structure, core, and envelope that existed in the prior condition and remains in the completed design.

BUILDING REUSE—MAINTAIN INTERIOR NONSTRUCTURAL ELEMENTS

	NC	SCHOOLS	CS
Credit	MR Credit 1.2	MR Credit 1.2	NA
Points	1 point	1 point	NA

Intent

To extend the life cycle of existing building stock, conserve resources, retain cultural resources, reduce waste and reduce environmental impacts of new buildings as they relate to materials manufacturing and transport.

Requirements

NC & SCHOOLS

Use existing interior nonstructural elements (e.g., interior walls, doors, floor coverings and ceiling systems) in at least 50% (by area) of the completed building, including additions. If the project includes an addition with square footage more than 2 times the square footage of the existing building, this credit is not applicable.

1. Benefits and Issues to Consider

Environmental Issues

Building reuse is a very beneficial strategy for reducing the overall environmental impact of construction. Reusing existing buildings significantly reduces the energy use associated with the demolition process as well as construction waste. Reuse strategies also reduce environmental impacts associated with raw material extraction, manufacturing, and transportation. Building reuse maintains the vital link between neighborhoods of the past and present, reduces emissions and waste, and preserves open space. Projects that reuse a high percentage of nonstructural components serve as examples of the value of preservation.

Economic Issues

Although retrofitting an existing building to accommodate new programmatic and LEED requirements may add to the complexity of design and construction—reflected in the project's soft costs—reuse of existing components can reduce overall construction costs by reducing costs associated with demolition, hauling fees, purchase of new construction materials, and labor.

2. Related Credits

Refer to the Related Credits section of MR Credit 1.1, Building Reuse—Maintain Existing Walls, Floors, and Roofs.

If reuse is not enough to achieve credit compliance, the materials can still contribute toward MR Credit 2, Construction Waste Management, or MR Credit 3, Materials Reuse (but not both) if the material has not been applied to MR Credit 1.

3. Summary of Referenced Standards

There are no standards referenced for this credit.

4. Implementation

Confirm that the items designated for reuse can be reused and take the necessary steps to retain and maintain them in the finished work. Fixed items, such as nonstructural walls and doors, are included in this credit and count toward the percentage of reuse when they perform the same function (e.g., doors reused as doors). If materials are used for another purpose (e.g., doors made into tables), they can count toward the achievement of MR Credit 3, Materials Reuse, but they cannot count toward both credits.

Projects that incorporate part of an existing building but do not meet the requirements for MR Credit 1 may apply the reused portion toward the achievement of MR Credit 2, Construction Waste Management. To do so, determine an approximate weight or volume for existing building elements.

5. Timeline and Team

As a design strategy, building reuse has significant impact on all phases of a project, from schematic design through bidding and construction.

During schematic design, the architect and owner should identify nonstructural building materials that can be retained and reused. The specifications for bid, developed by the architect in consultation with the owner, should outline measures to preserve the building during the construction process, and these should be implemented with project-team oversight.

Inventory the existing conditions. The architect should develop a floor plan showing the location of finished ceilings and flooring, interior wall partitions, doors within the interior walls, exterior and party walls, and exterior windows and doors. If existing built-in case goods will be reused, they should be documented as well. The architectural drawings should provide the detail needed to determine the surface area of all elements to be reused.

6. Calculations

Achievement of MR Credit 1.1 is not required for projects pursuing MR Credit 1.2.

This credit focuses on reuse of interior, nonstructural elements and compares the retained and reused elements with the total completed area of interior elements. It is not necessary to calculate the total area of existing interior nonstructural elements prior to demolition.

Prepare a spreadsheet listing all interior nonstructural elements within the building. Quantify each item and then determine the total area, including new construction and the area of retained elements, in square feet. Determine the percentage of existing elements that are retained by dividing the total area of all retained interior nonstructural elements by the total area of interior nonstructural elements.

$$\text{Percentage Existing Elements} = \frac{\text{Area (sf) of All Retained Interior Nonstructural Elements}}{\text{Total Area (sf) of Interior Nonstructural Elements}} \times 100$$

If the total area of existing and/or reused nonstructural interior components is a minimum of 50% of the area of all interior nonstructural building elements, the project earns 1 point.

Take measurements as if preparing a bid for flooring, ceiling, or painting:

- Finished ceilings and flooring areas (tile, carpeting, etc.). Use square footage to determine area.

- Interior nonstructural walls. Determine the finished area between floor and ceiling and count both sides.

- Exterior structural and party walls. If the interior finishes (e.g., drywall and plaster) have been reused, count only 1 side.

- Interior doors. Count surface area once.

- Interior casework. Calculate the visible surface area of the assembly; see the example in Figure 1.

Include items that have been saved but may have been relocated, such as full-height demountable walls and doors that were rehung. Items counted for this credit cannot be included in MR Credit 3.

Table 1 illustrates a spreadsheet for determining credit compliance. The total area of all new and existing building materials (following construction) is determined. The total area of only the existing and reused components is then entered. The sum of the existing materials is then divided by the sum of the total building materials to obtain the overall percentage of retained components. Since the overall percentage of reused nonstructural interior materials exceeds 50% of the total area of all nonstructural interior building materials, the project earns 1 point.

Table 1. Sample Interior Nonstructural Reuse Calculation

Interior Non-Structural Element	Total Area* (sf)	Existing/Reused (sf)	Percentage Reused (%)
Gypsum Board Wall Partitions – Full Height	5,400	3,600	67%
Gypsum Board Wall Partitions – Partial Height	650	650	100%
Carpeting	10,000	0	0%
Resilient Flooring	350	350	100%
Ceramic Tile	150	150	100%
Suspended Ceiling Systems	10,400	10,400	100%
Gypsum Board Ceilings	350	350	100%
Interior Doors (Wood)	525	420	80%
Interior Windows / Sidelights	56	56	100%
Interior Doors (Metal)	42	42	100%
Interior Casework / Cabinetry	235	150	64%
Totals	28,158	16,168	57%

* Note: The Total Area calculation includes both new and existing/reused materials.

Figure 1. Area Calculation for Existing Casework

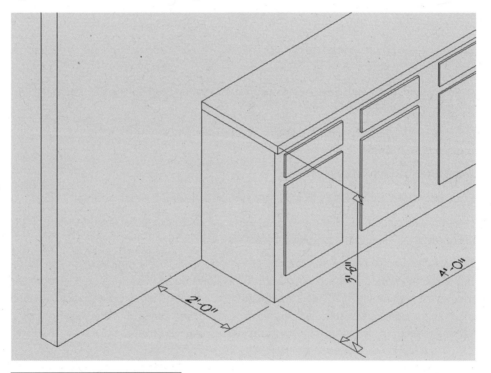

Surface	Area (sf)
Top	8
Left Side	7
Front	14
Rear	0
Right Side	0
Total Reused Casework	29

7. Documentation Guidelines

As a first step in preparing to complete the LEED-Online documentation requirements, work through the following measure. Refer to LEED-Online for the complete descriptions of all required documentation.

- For an existing building major renovation and/or addition, prepare a list of interior nonstructural elements; include element IDs and the total area of new, existing, and reused elements.

8. Examples

Projects should evaluate the interior nonstructural components to determine what can be reused. Figure 2 illustrates the eligible components.

Figure 2. Eligible Components for MR Credit 1.2

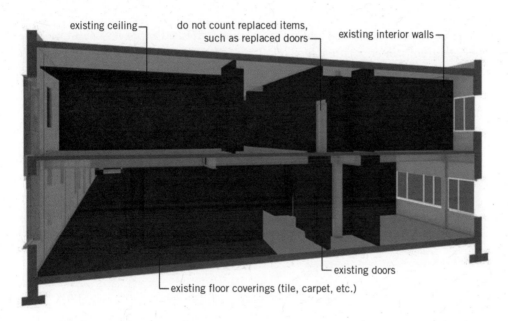

existing ceiling

do not count replaced items, such as replaced doors

existing interior walls

existing doors

existing floor coverings (tile, carpet, etc.)

■ surfaces that can be counted toward area for this credit

9. Exemplary Performance

This credit is not eligible for exemplary performance under the Innovation in Design section.

10. Regional Variations

This credit may have particular importance in areas with historic structures, where reuse of components can preserve the history and character of a building and its location. When deciding what interior structures to preserve, the project team should consider not only the nature of the building and whether the materials will enhance the character of the project, but also the local historical context. Reuse of interior materials to divert waste from landfills can be particularly important in areas with constrained landfill space.

11. Operations and Maintenance Considerations

The project team should communicate to building operators any special maintenance practices required by the reused materials, or any differences in life expectancy or durability compared with new materials.

12. Resources

Please see USGBC's LEED Registered Project Tools (http://www.usgbc.org/projecttools) for additional resources and technical information.

Print Media

How Buildings Learn: What Happens after They're Built, by Stewart Brand (Viking Press, 1994).

13. Definitions

Adaptive reuse is the renovation of a space for a purpose different from the original.

Existing area is the total area of the building structure, core, and envelope that existed when the project area was selected. Exterior windows and doors are not included.

Interior nonstructural components reuse is determined by dividing the area of retained components by the larger of (1) the area of the prior condition or (2) the area of the completed design.

Retained components are portions of the finished ceilings, finished floors, full-height walls and demountable partitions, interior doors, and built-in case goods that existed in the prior condition area and remain in the completed design.

Soft costs are expense items that are not considered direct construction costs. Examples include architectural, engineering, financing, and legal fees.

CONSTRUCTION WASTE MANAGEMENT

	NC	SCHOOLS	CS
Credit	MR Credit 2	MR Credit 2	MR Credit 2
Points	1-2 points	1-2 points	1-2 points

Intent

To divert construction and demolition debris from disposal in landfills and incineration facilities. Redirect recyclable recovered resources back to the manufacturing process and reusable materials to appropriate sites.

Requirements

NC, SCHOOLS & CS

Recycle and/or salvage nonhazardous construction and demolition debris. Develop and implement a construction waste management plan that, at a minimum, identifies the materials to be diverted from disposal and whether the materials will be sorted on-site or comingled. Excavated soil and land-clearing debris do not contribute to this credit. Calculations can be done by weight or volume, but must be consistent throughout. The minimum percentage debris to be recycled or salvaged for each point threshold is as follows:

Recycled or Salvaged	Points
50%	1
75%	2

	MR
NC	Credit 2
SCHOOLS	Credit 2
CS	Credit 2

1. Benefits and Issues to Consider

Environmental Issues

Construction and demolition generate enormous quantities of solid waste. EPA estimates that 136 million tons of such debris was generated in 1996, 57% of it from nonresidential sources.[9] Commercial construction generates between 2 and 2.5 pounds of solid waste per square foot, and the majority of this waste could be recycled.[10]

The greatest environmental benefit is achieved through source control—reducing the total waste generated. Use design strategies that minimize waste, such as shop fabrication of component parts, modular construction, and the ordering of materials cut to size. Work with manufacturers to minimize unnecessary packaging and making arrangements for pallets to be reclaimed after use can also reduce waste volumes and waste management costs. Extending the lifetime of existing landfills through effective construction waste management can avoid the need for expansion or new landfill sites.

Recycling of construction and demolition debris reduces demand for virgin resources and reduces the environmental impacts associated with resource extraction, processing and, in many cases, transportation.

Economic Issues

In the past, when landfill capacity was readily available and disposal fees were low, recycling or reuse of construction waste was not economically feasible. Construction materials were less expensive than labor, and construction site managers focused on worker productivity rather than on materials conservation. In addition, recycling infrastructure and recycled-materials marketplaces that process and resell construction debris did not exist. The economics of recycling has improved in recent years, particularly with the advent of international competition for both raw and recycled materials, and disposal costs have increased. More stringent waste disposal regulations coupled with ever-decreasing landfill capacity have changed the waste management equation.

Waste management plans require time and money to draft and implement; in the long term, however, they provide guidance to achieve substantial savings throughout the construction process.

Recyclable materials have differing market values, depending on the presence of local recycling facilities, reprocessing costs, and the availability of virgin materials on the market. In general, it is economically beneficial to recycle metals, concrete, asphalt, and cardboard. Market values normally fluctuate from month to month, so track the values and project different cost recapturing scenarios. When no revenue is received for materials, as is often the case for scrap wood and gypsum wallboard, it is still possible to benefit from recycling by avoiding landfill tipping fees.

2. Related Credits

Projects that reuse existing buildings but do not meet the threshold requirements for MR Credit 1 may apply the reused building portions toward achievement of MR Credit 2, Construction Waste Management:

- MR Credit 1: Building Reuse

If an existing building is found to contain contaminated substances, such as lead or asbestos, these materials should be remediated as required by EPA; see the following credit:

- SS Credit 3: Brownfield Redevelopment

3. Summary of Referenced Standards

There are no standards referenced for this credit.

4. Implementation

This credit addresses how much waste material leaving the site is diverted from landfills. The percentage requirement represents the amount diverted through recycling and salvage divided by the total waste generated by the construction project.

	MR
NC	Credit 2
SCHOOLS	Credit 2
CS	Credit 2

Identify construction haulers and recyclers to handle the designated materials; they often serve as valuable partners in this effort. Make sure that job-site personnel understand and participate in construction debris recycling, and ask them to provide updates throughout the construction process. Obtain and retain verification records (e.g., waste haul receipts, waste management reports, and spreadsheets) to confirm that the diverted materials have been recycled or salvaged as intended. Diversion may include salvaged materials such as furniture, computers and equipment, white boards, lockers, doors, lighting, and plumbing fixtures. Salvaged material can be donated to charitable organizations such as Habitat for Humanity, reuse centers, nonprofit organizations, or other buildings. Materials sold to the community can also be counted.

A project may choose to separate construction waste on-site or have commingled construction waste sorted at an off-site facility. On-site separation provides immediate feedback of the ongoing waste diversion efforts, but may require additional labor. Although commingled recycling can increase recycling costs, it might also simplify the waste management effort on-site and ensure that diversion rates will be high. This option is especially useful for projects with tight space constraints and no room for multiple collection bins.

5. Timeline and Team

After researching regional recycling options, the project team should create a construction waste management plan during the design phase. The general contractor should identify on-site recycling locations and review recycling requirements with all subcontractors to ensure that the plan is implemented. During construction, the contractor should remind subcontractors of the plan requirements and confirm that the plan is implemented on the site. The contractor should continuously track construction waste and report to the project team. At the end of construction the contractor should complete the documentation and submit detailed records to the project team.

6. Calculations

Calculations for this credit are based on the amount of waste diverted from landfill or incineration compared with the total amount of waste generated on-site. Convert all materials to either weight or volume to calculate the percentage. Exclude excavated soil and land-clearing debris from calculations. Projects that crush and reuse existing concrete, masonry, or asphalt on-site should include the weight or volume of these materials in the calculations Any construction debris processed into a recycled content commodity that has an open-market value (e.g., alternative daily cover material) may be applied to the construction waste calculation. Projects that use commingled recycling rather than on-site separation should obtain summaries of diversion rates from the recycler. Typically, the recycler should provide monthly reports.

Hazardous waste should be excluded from calculations and should be disposed of according to relevant regulations.

Table 1 provides an example of a summary calculation for waste diversion. If exact material weights are not available, use the conversion factors from Table 2 or another defensible conversion metric to estimate the weight of construction waste.

MR	
NC	Credit 2
SCHOOLS	Credit 2
CS	Credit 2

Table 1. Sample Construction Waste Management Diversion Summary

Diversion/Recycling Materials Description	Diversion/Recycling Hauler or Location	Quantity of Diverted/ Recycled Waste	Units (tons/cy)
Concrete	ABC Recycling	138.0	tons
Wood	Z-Construction Reuse	10.2	tons
Gypsum Wallboard	ABC Recycling	6.3	tons
Steel	Re-Cycle Steel Collectors	1.1	tons
Crushed Asphalt	On-Site Reuse	98.2	tons
Masonry	ABC Recycling	6.8	tons
Cardboard	ABC Recycling	1.6	tons
Total Construction Waste Diverted		262.2	tons
Landfill Materials Description	**Landfill Hauler or Location**	**Quantity of Diverted/ Recycled Waste**	**Units (tons/cy)**
General Mixed Waste	XYZ Landfill	52.3	tons
Total Construction Waste Sent to Landfill			52.3 tons
Total of All Construction Waste			314.5 tons
Percentage of Construction Waste Diverted From Landfill			83.4%

Table 2. Solid Waste Conversion Factors

Material	Density (lbs/cy)
Cardboard	100
Gypsum Wallboard	500
Mixed Waste	350
Rubble	1,400
Steel	1,000
Wood	300

7. Documentation Guidance

As a first step in preparing to complete the LEED-Online documentation requirements, work through the following measures. Refer to LEED-Online for the complete descriptions of all required documentation.

- Track and keep a summary log of all construction waste generated by type, the quantities of each type that were diverted and landfilled, and the total percentage of waste diverted from landfill disposal.

- A project's construction waste management plan should, at a minimum, identify the diversion goals, relevant construction debris and materials to be diverted, implementation protocols, and parties responsible for implementing the plan.

8. Examples

A contractor is preparing for partial demolition of a 5,400-square-foot urban structure built in 1918. The new owner intends to keep the structural components of the building but remove the existing interior walls and floors. The contractor, prior to construction, developed a construction waste management plan to aid in the demolition and construction process. The plan outlines the staging of waste materials during demolition to be sorted within the building before being delivered to local recycling facilities.

		MR
NC		Credit 2
SCHOOLS		Credit 2
CS		Credit 2

- Existing wood will be treated with care as it is removed from the building so that it can be reused by another local contractor or donated to a reuse store.
- Gypsum board from a previous building remodel will be composted.
- Existing doors will be removed, restored, and stored off-site before being reinstalled during construction.
- The construction waste will be commingled and sorted off-site because the site does not have enough room for sorting materials.
- All cardboard, wood, plastic, and metals will be placed in the same bins.
- The construction waste management plan outlines the responsibility of each subcontractor to recycle lunch waste in a separate, smaller container, to prevent contaminating the construction waste.
- The construction office is instructed to sort paper, plastic, cans, and bottles within the office.
- The contractor takes responsibility for enforcing the plan throughout the construction process.

Because most of the construction waste is sorted off-site, the contractor can document a construction waste diversion rate of 96%.

9. Exemplary Performance

Project teams may earn an Innovation in Design credit for exemplary performance by diverting 95% or more of total construction waste.

10. Regional Variations

Recycling opportunities are expanding rapidly in many communities. Metal, vegetation, concrete, and asphalt recycling has long been available and affordable in most communities. Recycling options for paper, corrugated cardboard, plastics, and clean wood markets vary with regional and local recycling infrastructure. Some materials, such as gypsum wallboard, can be recycled only in communities that have reprocessing plants exist or where soil can handle the material as a stabilizing agent. The recyclability of a demolished material often depends on the extent of contamination. Demolished wood, for instance, is often not reusable or recyclable unless it is taken apart and the nails removed.

In urban areas, recycling resources are frequently more developed, and project managers can decide whether to separate waste on-site or hire a commingled waste recycler. In more rural and remote areas, recyclers may be harder to find. The environmental benefits of recycling in these cases need to be balanced against the environmental impacts of transporting waste long distances to recycling centers.

Other regional variances that affect the treatment of construction waste include landfill space, waste diversion options, and tipping fees.

11. Operations and Maintenance Considerations

A challenging aspect of managing and diverting construction waste is identifying appropriate entities to receive the diverse waste types generated. Owners should develop policies for future remodeling, with specific construction waste recycling targets and end sources. General contractors should implement waste diversion strategies in their own company structure. Lessons learned from the project experience can be used to develop a company policy and education program for all employees.

12. Resources

Please see USGBC's LEED Registered Project Tools (http://www.usgbc.org/projecttools) for additional resources and technical information.

Government Resources

Check with the solid waste authority or natural resources department in your city or county. Many local governments provide information about regional recycling opportunities.

Websites

California Integrated Waste Management Board Construction and Demolition Debris Recycling Information

http://www.ciwmb.ca.gov/ConDemo

The CIWMB offers case studies, fact sheets, and links to additional resources for construction and demolition debris recycling.

Construction Materials Recycling Association

http://www.cdrecycling.org

The Construction Materials Recycling Association is a nonprofit organization dedicated to information exchange within the North American construction waste and demolition debris processing and recycling industries.

Smart Growth Online, Construction Waste Management Handbook

http://www.smartgrowth.org/library/articles.asp?art=15

This report by the National Association of Home Builders Research Center discusses residential construction waste management for a housing development in Homestead, Florida.

Resource Venture, Construction Waste Management Guide

http://www.resourceventure.org/free-resources/get-started/green-building-publications/CWM%20Guide.pdf/view?searchterm=construction%20waste%20prevention

This is a guidebook on waste prevention during construction.

King County, WA, Recycling and Waste Management during Construction

http://www.metrokc.gov/procure/green/wastemgt.htm

View specification language from the city of Seattle and Portland metro projects on construction waste management.

A Sourcebook for Green and Sustainable Building, Construction Waste

http://www.greenbuilder.com/sourcebook/ConstructionWaste.html

This website offers a guide to waste management during construction.

U.S. EPA, Environmental Specifications for Research Triangle Park

http://www.epa.gov/rtp/campus/environmental/s_01120.htm

Learn about waste management and other specifications from EPA.

Triangle J Council of Governments, Waste Spec: Model Specifications for Construction Waste Reduction, Reuse, and Recycling

ftp://ftp.tjcog.org/pub/tjcog/regplan/solidwst/wastspec.pdf

This organization has developed model specifications for North Carolina. 10 case studies show the results of using the specifications.

13. Definitions

Alternative daily cover is material (other than earthen material) that is placed on the surface of the active face of a municipal solid waste landfill at the end of each operating day to control vectors, fires, odors, blowing litter, and scavenging.

Construction and demolition debris includes waste and recyclables generated from construction and from the renovation, demolition, or deconstruction of preexisting structures. It does not include land-clearing debris, such as soil, vegetation, and rocks.

Recycling is the collection, reprocessing, marketing, and use of materials that were diverted or recovered from the solid waste stream.

Reuse returns materials to active use in the same or a related capacity as their original use, thus extending the lifetime of materials that would otherwise be discarded.

Tipping fees are charged by a landfill for disposal of waste, typically quoted per ton.

MATERIALS REUSE

	NC	SCHOOLS	CS
Credit	MR Credit 3	MR Credit 3	MR Credit 3
Points	1-2 points	1-2 points	1 point

Intent

To reuse building materials and products to reduce demand for virgin materials and reduce waste, thereby lessening impacts associated with the extraction and processing of virgin resources.

Requirements

NC & SCHOOLS

Use salvaged, refurbished or reused materials, the sum of which constitutes at least 5% or 10%, based on cost, of the total value of materials on the project. The minimum percentage materials reused for each point threshold is as follows:

Reused Materials	Points
5%	1
10%	2

CS

Use salvaged, refurbished or reused materials, the sum of which constitutes at least 5%, based on cost, of the total value of materials on the project.

NC, SCHOOLS & CS

Mechanical, electrical and plumbing components, and specialty items such as elevators and equipment cannot be included in this calculation. Include only materials permanently installed in the project. Furniture may be included if it is included consistently in MR Credit 3: Materials Reuse through MR Credit 7: Certified Wood (MR Credit 6 in Core & Shell).

	MR
NC	Credit 3
SCHOOLS	Credit 3
CS	Credit 3

1. Benefits and Issues to Consider

Environmental Issues

Many existing materials can be salvaged, refurbished, or reused. Reuse strategies divert material from the construction waste stream, reducing the need for landfill space and environmental impacts from associated water and air contamination. Use of salvaged materials also avoids the environmental impacts of producing new construction products and materials. These impacts are significant because buildings account for a large portion of natural resource consumption, including 40% of raw stone, gravel, and sand as well as 25% of virgin wood.[11]

Economic Issues

Although some salvaged materials are more costly than new materials because of the high cost of labor involved in recovering and refurbishing processes, local demolition companies may be willing to sell materials recovered from existing buildings to avoid landfill tipping fees and to generate income. In some areas, municipalities and waste management companies have established facilities for selling salvaged building materials at landfill sites. Sometimes, salvaged materials are offered at prices that appear to be cost-effective but may include hidden costs, such as the need for reprocessing, excessive transportation costs, or liabilities associated with toxic contamination. Conversely, certain salvaged materials may be impossible to duplicate (e.g., turn-of-the century lumber and casework) and may be worth the higher cost compared with new materials.

Because a school can function as the center of its community, prominent use of reclaimed materials in a schools project helps people understand environmental issues. In some instances, it may be possible to choose materials with historical significance to the community, providing meaningful architectural context for the school and increasing students' awareness of local history.

2. Related Credits

The development of a comprehensive reuse management plan that evaluates the anticipated materials saved will help determine whether the project meets the requirements of the following credits:

- MR Credit 1: Building Reuse
- MR Credit 2: Construction Waste Management

Remanufactured materials are not considered a reuse of the material and do not contribute toward this credit. However, these materials can contribute toward the following credits:

- MR Credit 2: Construction Waste Management
- MR Credit 4: Recycled Materials

The project materials costs used here need to be consistent with those used in the following credits:

- MR Credit 4: Recycled Content
- MR Credit 5: Regional Materials
- MR Credit 6: Rapidly Renewable Materials

3. Summary of Referenced Standards

There are no standards referenced for this credit.

4. Implementation

Using salvaged and refurbished materials in building projects extends the life of materials and can reduce overall initial costs. Use of salvaged materials can also add character to the building and can be used effectively as architectural details.

	MR
NC	Credit 3
SCHOOLS	Credit 3
CS	Credit 3

Reused Materials Found On-site

Items that were "fixed" components on-site before construction began. To qualify as reused for this credit, these items must no longer be able to serve their original functions and must then be installed for a different use or in a different location. An example would be a door removed and modified to serve as the countertop for the receptionist station.

Walls, ceilings, and flooring. If such items continue to serve their original functions in the new building, they are excluded from this credit but are covered by MR Credit 1.2, Building Reuse—Maintain Interior Nonstructural Components.

Other reused materials found on-site. Components that are retained and continue to serve their original function, such as door hardware, are eligible for this credit.

Reused Materials Found Off-site

Reusable materials eligible for this credit are not limited to items found within the project building. Materials obtained off-site qualify as reused if they have been previously used. These materials may be purchased as salvaged, similar to any other project material, or they may be relocated from another facility, including ones previously used by the occupant. The salvaged materials from both on-site and off-site can be applied to MR Credit 5, Regional Materials, if they comply with the requirements of that credit. Materials qualifying as reused for MR Credit 3 cannot be applied to MR Credits 1, 2, 4, 6, or 7.

This credit applies primarily to CSI MasterFormat™ 2004 Edition Divisions 03-10, 31 (Section 31.60.00 Foundations) and 32 (Sections 32.10.00 Paving, 32.30.00 Site Improvements, and 32.90.00 Planting). Do not include mechanical, electrical, and plumbing components or appliances and equipment in the calculations for this credit. This exclusion is consistent with MR Credits 4 and 5. Exclude furniture and furnishings (CSI Division 12 components) unless they are included consistently across MR Credits 3–7.

For salvaged furniture taken from the occupant's previous facility or location, demonstrate that these materials were purchased at least 2 years prior to the project's initiation. For example, if the owner is moving to a new construction, core and shell, or school project, furniture and furnishings relocated to the new site can contribute to this credit because their reuse will eliminate the need for purchasing new furniture and furnishings.

Generally, opportunities to reuse building materials may be limited. Core materials that may be eligible include salvaged brick, structural timber, stone, and pavers. While considering the potential to reuse salvaged materials, confirm that they do not contain toxic substances, such as lead or asbestos.

5. Timeline and Team

The incorporation of materials reuse as a design strategy affects cost estimates, the demolition phase (if salvaging from the project site), and the ultimate design development of the project. Coordination among the owner, architect or design team, and contractor should begin early in the predesign phase and continue through design development so that knowledge of the site and building areas to be salvaged and reused can be creatively and efficiently worked into the basis of design, and opportunities to bring in salvaged materials from off-site can be incorporated into the project. Documentation should likewise begin early.

	MR
NC	Credit 3
SCHOOLS	Credit 3
CS	Credit 3

During predesign, the project team should assess opportunities for materials reuse and the extent of site demolition involved, and set goals accordingly. In the design phase, the architect should incorporate salvaged or reused materials into the design and then, during the construction documents and specifications development phase, identify sources and outline measures for their use. The contractor should locate sources for these materials and document and track their cost and quantity during construction. This recordkeeping will aid the project team in the credit submittal process.

6. Calculations

List the reused or salvaged materials used and their cost Table 1 provides an example of a salvaged materials tracking log.

Determine the cost of each material. This cost will be the actual cost paid or, if the material came from on-site, the replacement value. The replacement value can be determined by pricing a comparable material in the local market; exclude labor and shipping. If a project team receives a discount from a vendor, the replacement value should reflect the discounted price as opposed to the list value. When the actual cost paid for the reused or salvaged material is below the cost of an equivalent new item, use the higher value (actual cost) in the calculations. When the cost to reclaim an item found on-site is less than the cost of an equivalent new item, use the cost of the new item (or replacement cost).

Table 1. Sample Salvaged Materials Tracking Log

Salvaged/Reused Material Description	Source for Salvaged/Reused Material	Value / Product Cost ($)
Salvaged Brick	ABC Salvage Suppliers	$62,500
Salvaged Wood Floor	Salvage Company Y	$24,200
Remanufactured Wood Doors (Used as Built-in Countertops)	On-Site Salvage / Remanufacture	$4,200
Sub-Total Salvaged/Reused Materials		$90,900
Total Construction Materials Cost – or 45% Default Materials Value		$1,665,498
Salvaged/Reused Materials as a Percentage of Total Materials Cost		5.5%

Determine the total materials cost by multiplying the total construction cost (hard costs only in CSI MasterFormat™ 2004 Edition Divisions 03–10, 31 (Section 31.60.00 Foundations) and 32 (Sections 32.10.00 Paving, 32.30.00 Site Improvements, and 32.90.00 Planting) by 0.45. Alternatively, the total materials cost may be a tally of actual materials cost in CSI MasterFormat™ 2004 Edition Divisions 03–10, 31 (Section 31.60.00 Foundations) and 32 (Sections 32.10.00 Paving, 32.30.00 Site Improvements, and 32.90.00 Planting) from the project schedule of values or a similar document. The benefit of using actual materials costs, as opposed to the default 45%, is that projects with less than 45% materials cost can more easily achieve the credit thresholds because total materials cost is in the denominator of the equation below. Furniture and furnishings (CSI Division 12 components) are excluded from the calculations for this credit unless they are included consistently across MR Credits 3–7.

Calculate the percentage of reuse materials according to Equation 1.

Equation 1

$$\text{Percentage Reused Materials} = \frac{\text{Cost of Reused Material (\$)}}{\text{Total Materials Cost (\$)}} \times 100$$

7. Documentation Guidance

As a first step in preparing to complete the LEED-Online documentation requirements, work through the following measures. Refer to LEED-Online for the complete descriptions of all required documentation.

- Maintain a list of reused and salvaged materials and their corresponding costs. Include construction costs for materials in CSI MasterFormat™ 2004 Edition Divisions 03–10, 31 (section 31.60.00 Foundations) and 32 (sections 32.10.00 Paving, 32.30.00 Site Improvements, and 32.90.00 Planting).

	MR
NC	Credit 3
SCHOOLS	Credit 3
CS	Credit 3

OR

- Maintain a list of actual materials costs, excluding labor and equipment.

8. Examples

There are no examples for this credit.

9. Exemplary Performance

NC & SCHOOLS An Innovation in Design credit for exemplary performance is available when a project team documents that the value of salvaged or reused materials used on the project is 15% or more of the total materials cost.

CS An Innovation in Design credit for exemplary performance is available if the value of salvaged or reused materials used on the project is equal to at least 10% of the total materials cost.

10. Regional Variations

This credit may have particular importance in areas with historic structures and neighborhoods, or in offering the benefits of a nonvirgin source of building material. New England, the Pacific Northwest, and California, have well-developed markets for salvaged material. Project teams should research rebuilding centers in their region, using the resources listed in this section. Where salvage markets are not as readily available, consider using deconstruction techniques. By increasing the demand for used materials, teams might encourage the development of a regional salvage market that would expand economic opportunities while diverting waste. Building reuse can encourage new development while preserving the history and character of an area, and materials reuse can work in tandem with this strategy.

11. Operations and Maintenance Considerations

There are no operations and maintenance considerations specific to reused or refurbished materials.

12. Resources

Please see USGBC's LEED Registered Project Tools (http://www.usgbc.org/projecttools) for additional resources and technical information.

Websites

Builders' Guide to Reuse and Recycling

http://www.mwcog.org/buildersrecyclingguide

The Builders' Guide to Reuse and Recycling is a directory for construction and demolition materials in the Metropolitan Washington, D.C., region, produced by the Metropolitan Washington Council of Governments. The website includes a searchable database for sources of salvaged materials.

California Integrated Waste Management Board, California Materials Exchange

http://www.ciwmb.ca.gov/CalMAX

The California Materials Exchange is a program of the CIWMB. This site enables users to exchange nonhazardous materials online.

	MR
NC	Credit 3
SCHOOLS	Credit 3
CS	Credit 3

Government Resources

Check with the solid waste authority or natural resources department in your city or county. Many local governments provide information about regional materials exchanges and other sources.

King County, Washington, Industrial Materials Exchange Local Hazardous Waste Management Program, Materials Exchanges on the Web

http://www.govlink.org/hazwaste

The Local Hazardous Waste Management Program is a regional program of local governments working together to protect public health and environmental quality by reducing the threat posed by the production, use, storage, and disposal of hazardous materials.

Reuse Development Organization

http://www.redo.org

ReDO is a national nonprofit in Baltimore that promotes reuse as an environmentally sound, socially beneficial, and economical means of managing surplus and discarded materials. See the list of ReDO subscribers for contacts around the United States.

Green Building Resource Guide, Sa vaged Building Materials Exchange

http://www.greenguide.com/exchange/search.html

The Green Building Resource Guide is a database of more than 600 green building materials and products selected specifically for their usefulness to the design and building professions.

Building Materials Reuse Association (formerly Used Building Materials Association)

http://www.bmra.org

The Building Materials Reuse Association is a nonprofit, membership-based organization that represents companies and organizations involved in the acquisition and/or redistribution of used building materials.

Used Building Materials Exchange

http://www.build.recycle.net

The Used Building Materials Exchange is a free marketplace for buying and selling recyclables and salvaged materials.

The Greater Vancouver Regional District, Old to New: Design Guide, Salvaged Building Materials in New Construction

http://www.lifecyclebuilding.org/files/Old%20to%20New%20Design%20Guide.pdf

This useful and detailed guidebook reviews the use of salvaged materials in real-life case studies.

13. Definitions

Refurbished materials are products that could have been disposed of as solid waste. These products have completed their life cycle as consumer items and are then refurbished for reuse without substantial alteration of their form. Refurbishing includes renovating, repairing, restoring, or generally improving the appearance, performance, quality, functionality, or value of a product.

Remanufactured materials are items that are made into other products. One example is concrete that is crushed and used as subbase.

Salvaged materials or **reused materials** are construction materials recovered from existing buildings or construction sites and reused. Common salvaged materials include structural beams and posts, flooring, doors, cabinetry, brick, and decorative items.

RECYCLED CONTENT

	NC	SCHOOLS	CS
Credit	MR Credit 4	MR Credit 4	MR Credit 4
Points	1-2 points	1-2 points	1-2 points

Intent

To increase demand for building products that incorporate recycled content materials, thereby reducing impacts resulting from extraction and processing of virgin materials.

Requirements

NC, SCHOOLS & CS

Use materials with recycled content[1] such that the sum of postconsumer[2] recycled content plus 1/2 of the preconsumer[3] content constitutes at least 10% or 20%, based on cost, of the total value of the materials in the project. The minimum percentage materials recycled for each point threshold is as follows:

Recycled Content	Points
10%	1
20%	2

The recycled content value of a material assembly is determined by weight. The recycled fraction of the assembly is then multiplied by the cost of assembly to determine the recycled content value.

Mechanical, electrical and plumbing components, and specialty items such as elevators cannot be included in this calculation. Include only materials permanently installed in the project. Furniture may be included if it is included consistently in MR Credit 3: Materials Reuse through MR Credit 7: Certified Wood (MR Credit 6 in Core & Shell).

---

1   Recycled content is defined in accordance with the International Organization of Standards document, ISO 14021 — Environmental labels and declarations — Self-declared environmental claims (Type II environmental labeling).

2   Postconsumer material is defined as waste material generated by households or by commercial, industrial and institutional facilities in their role as end-users of the product, which can no longer be used for its intended purpose.

3   Preconsumer material is defined as material diverted from the waste stream during the manufacturing process. Reutilization of materials (i.e., rework, regrind or scrap generated in a process and capable of being reclaimed within the same process that generated it) is excluded.

	MR
NC	Credit 4
SCHOOLS	Credit 4
CS	Credit 4

1. Benefits and Issues to Consider

Environmental Issues

Products with recycled content reduce virgin materials use and solid waste volumes. As the number of building products containing recycled content grows, the marketplace for recycled materials develops.

Postconsumer recycled content is derived from materials that can no longer be used for their original purpose, and preconsumer recycled content consists of raw material diverted from the waste stream during the manufacturing process. Although the use of both types of recycled content is encouraged, postconsumer recycled content is accorded greater value because of its increased environmental benefit over the life cycle of the product.

Economic Issues

Many commonly used products are now available with recycled content, including metals, concrete, masonry, gypsum wallboard, acoustic tile, carpet, ceramic tile, rubber flooring and wall base, and insulation. Research all recycled-content materials for environmental considerations. For example, if the recycled-content product is not as durable as its conventional counterpart, the environmental benefits may be compromised by the need for more frequent replacement. Most recycled-content products, however, exhibit performance similar to products containing only virgin materials and can be incorporated into building projects with ease and little to no cost premium.

2. Related Credits

Coordinate recycled material procurement with a construction waste management plan to make use of on-site salvaged deconstruction and demolition waste. There are opportunities for synergies with the following credits:

- MR Credit 2: Construction Waste Management
- MR Credit 3: Materials Reuse

When purchasing new materials, look for recycled-content materials that use local waste products and are remanufactured locally to take advantage of synergies with MR Credit 5, Regional Materials.

Check recycled-content materials for problematic air emissions, especially with synthetic products such as plastic, rubber, or polyester. Make sure that any recycled-content materials are considered in the planning and execution of IEQ Credit 4, Low-Emitting Materials.

The project materials costs used here need to be consistent with those used in the following credits:

- MR Credit 3: Materials Reuse
- MR Credit 5: Regional Materials
- MR Credit 6: Rapidly Renewable Materials

3. Summary of Referenced Standard

International Standard ISO 14021–1999, Environmental Labels and Declarations—Self-Declared Environmental Claims (Type II Environmental Labeling)

International Organization for Standardization (ISO)
http://www.iso.org
This International Standard specifies requirements for self-declared environmental claims including statements, symbols, and graphics, for products. It further describes selected terms commonly used

in environmental claims and gives qualifications for their use. It also describes a general evaluation and verification methodology for self-declared environmental claims and specific evaluation and verification methods for the selected claims.

	MR
NC	Credit 4
SCHOOLS	Credit 4
CS	Credit 4

4. Implementation

Establish goals for recycled content during the design phase and include them in the project specifications. Doing so is not a LEED requirement, but it can help in achieving the credit. To establish recycled content goals, first add a LEED general requirements section to Division 01 to allow for writing LEED performance requirements for overlapping work sections (such as building envelope and structure). Then, specify products and materials according to CSI MasterFormat 2004 classifications for Division 01 recycled-content requirements. Careful research may be required to determine the percentages of recycled content that can realistically be expected in specific products and materials.

Many standard materials contain recycled content because of how they are manufactured; examples are steel, gypsum board, and acoustical ceiling tile. Design and construction teams may need to research which materials contain high levels of recycled content or verify which models of a certain product line feature the desired recycled content; examples include carpet and ceramic tile.

Reusing materials reclaimed from the same process in which they are generated—though good practice—does not contribute toward the recycled content of the material. In other words, putting waste back into the same manufacturing process from which it came is not considered recycling because it was not diverted from the waste stream. Reuse of materials includes rework, regrind, or scrap product (ISO 14021); examples are glass culls, which are often reused in the making of new glass, as well as planer shavings, plytrim, sawdust, chips, bagasse, sunflower seed hulls, walnut shells, culls, trimmed materials, print overruns, over-issue publications, and obsolete inventories.

Distinguish between postconsumer and preconsumer recycled content when tracking materials for the purpose of credit calculations (see Definitions, below).

CS Because interior construction is not part of a Core & Shell project, look for opportunities to meet this credit by evaluating the major structural and envelope materials.

5. Timeline and Team

Run preliminary calculations during the design phase, as soon as a project budget is available, to set appropriate recycled-content targets. Identification of materials that contain recycled content should begin during the preconstruction phase, whenever possible. All project team members, including the general contractor and subcontractors, should consult with suppliers prior to the buy-out phase to determine the availability of materials and the specific amount of postconsumer and preconsumer recycled content within each type of material. Careful planning before construction can minimize capital expenses and enable the project team to verify whether the procured building materials contain the desired amount of recycled content.

The architect should identify and then specify products with recycled content. The contractor is responsible for ensuring the appropriate installation of these materials, documenting and tracking the cost and quantity of recycled materials, and providing this documentation to the project team

	MR
NC	Credit 4
SCHOOLS	Credit 4
CS	Credit 4

6. Calculations

Determine the total materials cost for the project by multiplying the total construction cost (hard costs only in CSI MasterFormat™ 2004 Edition Divisions 03–10, 31 (Section 31.60.00 Foundations) and 32 (Sections 32.10.00 Paving, 32.30.00 Site Improvements, and 32.90.00 Planting) by 0.45. Alternatively, the total materials cost may be a tally of actual materials cost in CSI MasterFormat™ 2004 Edition Divisions 03–10, 31 (Section 31.60.00 Foundations) and 32 (Sections 32.10.00 Paving, 32.30.00 Site Improvements, and 32.90.00 Planting) from the project schedule of values or a similar document. The benefit of using actual materials costs, as opposed to the default 45%, is that projects with less than 45% materials cost can more easily achieve the 10% and 20% credit thresholds. The purpose of the default value is to streamline the documentation process because it can be challenging to separate the materials costs from labor and equipment costs for all materials on the project.

Materials costs include all expenses to deliver the material to the project site. Materials costs should account for all taxes and transportation costs incurred by the contractor but exclude any cost for labor and equipment once the material has been delivered to the site.

Determine the Recycled-Content Value

To calculate the percentage of recycled-content materials used on a project, list all recycled-content materials and products and their costs.

For each product, identify the percentage of postconsumer and/or preconsumer recycled content by weight, and list the recycled content information source. LEED requires that the information be from a reliable, verifiable source.

Postconsumer Recycled Content

Postconsumer recycled content is consumer waste, much of which comes from residential curbside recycling programs for aluminum, glass, plastic, and paper. To be a feedstock, the raw materials must have served a useful purpose in the consumer market before being used again. Other postconsumer feedstock is generated when construction and demolition debris is recycled.

Preconsumer Recycled Content

Preconsumer (or postindustrial) recycled content comes from process waste that an industry has sold or traded with another through the marketplace. For instance, a composite board manufacturer may obtain sawdust from a lumber mill or waste straw from a wheat farm. This definition does not include in-house industrial scrap or trimmings, which are normally fed back into the same manufacturing process.

Calculate the recycled-content value of each material according to Equation 1.

Equation 1

$$\text{Recycled Content Value (\$)} = \left(\% \text{ Postconsumer Recycled Content} \times \text{Materials Cost} \right) + 0.5 \left(\% \text{ Preconsumer Recycled Content} \times \text{Materials Cost} \right)$$

Calculate the project's percentage recycled content according to Equation 2.

Equation 2

$$\text{Percentage Recycled Content} = \frac{\text{Total Recycled Content Value (\$)}}{\text{Total Materials Cost}} \times 100$$

Exclude furniture and furnishings (CSI Division 12 components) from the calculations for this credit unless they are included consistently across MR Credits 3–7. This credit applies primarily to CSI MasterFormat™ 2004 Edition Divisions 03–10, 31 (Section 31.60.00 Foundations) and 32 (Sections 32.10.00 Paving, 32.30.00 Site Improvements, and 32.90.00 Planting). Do not include mechanical, electrical, and plumbing components or appliances and equipment in the calculations for this credit. Compared with structural and finish materials, mechanical and electrical equipment tends to have a high dollar value relative to the amount of material it contains. That high dollar value would skew the results of the calculation.

Default Recycled Content

For steel products where no recycled content information is available, assume the recycled content to be 25% postconsumer. No other material has been recognized as having a similarly consistent minimum recycled content. Many steel products contain 90% or higher recycled content if manufactured by the electric arc furnace process, so it may be beneficial to obtain actual information from the manufacturer rather than relying on the default value.

Calculating Assembly Recycled Content

An assembly can be either a product formulated from multiple materials (e.g., a composite wood panel) or a product made up of subcomponents (e.g., a window system). For assembly recycled content values, determine the percentage by weight of the postconsumer recycled content and the preconsumer recycled content. For subcomponents, determine the percentages of postconsumer and preconsumer recycled content by using the weights of the component elements. No consideration is given to relative costs of the materials or the subcomponents when calculating these percentages of recycled content. For example, a pound of steel in a window assembly is of equal significance in determining recycled content as a pound of fabric on a movable wall panel.

To incorporate assembly recycled content into Equation 2, use Equation 3 and add the resulting value to Equations 2's total recycled content value:

Equation 3

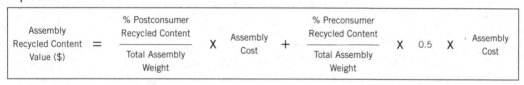

$$\text{Assembly Recycled Content Value (\$)} = \frac{\text{\% Postconsumer Recycled Content}}{\text{Total Assembly Weight}} \times \text{Assembly Cost} + \frac{\text{\% Preconsumer Recycled Content}}{\text{Total Assembly Weight}} \times 0.5 \times \text{Assembly Cost}$$

Supplementary Cementitious Materials

In the case of supplementary cementitious materials (SCMs) used in concrete recycled from other operations, the recycled content value can be based on the mass of the cementitious materials only, rather than on the entire concrete mix. For example, if 150 pounds of coal fly ash is used per yard of concrete, the fly ash would represent only a small fraction (5%) of the roughly 3,000 pounds of concrete. The project team can choose instead to calculate it as a fraction of the cementitious materials by obtaining the value of the cementitious materials (separate from the total cost of the concrete) from the concrete supplier (Example 1). Fly ash is a preconsumer recycled-content material.

Example 1. Sample Supplementary Cementitious Materials Calculation

Mix #	Mass of Portland Cement* (lbs)	Mass of recycled SCMs (lbs)	Mass of total cementitious materials (lbs)	SCMs as a percentage of total cementitious materials (%)	Dollar value of all cementitious materials (from concrete supplier)	Recycled content value per yard [(SCM/2) x dollar value]
2	200	50	250	20%	$35	$3.50
3	300	100	400	25%	$45	$5.63
*This column also includes any other cementitious ingredients that are not recycled.						

	MR
NC	Credit 4
SCHOOLS	Credit 4
CS	Credit 4

7. Documentation Guidance

As a first step in preparing to complete the LEED-Online documentation requirements, work through the following measures. Refer to LEED-Online for the complete descriptions of all required documentation.

- Record product names, manufacturers' names, costs, percentage postconsumer content, and percentage preconsumer content.

- Collect cutsheets or manufacturers' letters to document the listed products' recycled content.

- Where appropriate, maintain a list of actual materials costs, excluding labor and equipment for CSI Division 03–10, 31 (Section 31.60.00 Foundations) and 32 (Sections 32.10.00 Paving, 32.30.00 Site Improvements, and 32.90.00 Planting) only; including Division 12 is optional.

8. Examples

The total construction cost for an office building is $600,000. Using the default materials calcuations, the total cost of materials (excluding labor and equipment) is $600,000 x 0.45 = $270,000. Table 1 lists recycled-content material purchased for the project. In this example, the combined value of postconsumer content plus half the preconsumer content as a percentage of total cost of all materials is 11.31%. The project earns 1 point for MR Credit 4.

Table 1. Sample Calculations for Recycled Content

Total Construction Cost						$600,000
Default Total Materials Cost (45% of Total Construction Cost)						$270,000
Product Name	**Vendor**	**Product Cost**	**% Postconumer**	**% Preconsumer**	**Recycled Content Value (Equation 1)**	**Recycled Content Information Source**
Structural steel	Multi Steel	$40,000	10.00%	85.00%	$21,000	Structural manufacturer
Underlay aggregate	ABC Foundation	$21,000	20.00%		$4,200	Concrete manufacturer
Particleboard	Sol's Big Boards	$4,000		100.00%	$2,000	Manufacturer
Gypsum board	Gypsum R Us	$8,550		78.00%	$3,335	Manufacturer
Combined Value of Postconsumer + 1/2 Preconsumer Content (Total Recycled Content Value)						$30,535
Combined Value of Postconsumer + 1/2 Preconsumer Content, as a Percentage of Default Total Materials Cost (Total Percent Recycled Content) (Equation 2)						11.31%
Total Points Documented						1

Figure 1. Preconsumer versus Postconsumer Recycled Content

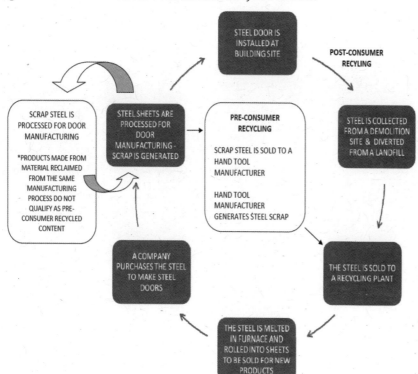

9. Exemplary Performance

Project teams may earn an Innovation in Design credit for exemplary performance by achieving a total recycled-content value of 30% or more.

10. Regional Variations

The location of the project site affects the availability of locally sourced materials. Availability of building materials containing recycled content may vary by region based on the proximity of suppliers. Some materials, such as structural steel, will be readily available for any project site; others may be manufactured or distributed in specific regions only. A project team might need to decide whether it is more sustainable to use a local material containing virgin content or to import materials containing recycled-content from a long distance.

11. Operations and Maintenance Considerations

Recycled-content materials may require different maintenance practices than conventional products. When specifying recycled products, request maintenance recommendations from the manufacturer and give this information to the operations team.

The duplication, replacement, and repair of recycled-content materials will be easier if information about the installed products has been maintained. Encourage the creation of a sustainable purchasing plan and provide building operators with lists of the installed products and their manufacturers, such as the documentation used in the LEED application.

	MR
NC	Credit 4
SCHOOLS	Credit 4
CS	Credit 4

12. Resources

Please see USGBC's LEED Registered Project Tools (http://www.usgbc.org/projecttools) for additional resources and technical information.

Government Resources

Check with the solid waste authority or natural resources department in your city or county. Many local governments provide information on recyclers and recycled content product manufacturers within their region.

Websites

U.S. Federal Trade Commission, Guides for the Use of Environmental Marketing Claims, 16 CFR 260.7 (e)
http://www.ftc.gov/bcp/grnrule/guides980427.htm
The guides provided on this site represent administrative interpretation of Section 5 of the FTC Act to environmental advertising and marketing practices.

BuildingGreen, Inc., GreenSpec
http://www.buildinggreen.com/menus/index.cfm
GreenSpec contains detailed listings for more than 2,000 green building products, and each entry includes environmental data, manufacturer information, and links to additional resources.

California Integrated Waste Management Board, Recycled Content Product Directory
http://www.ciwmb.ca.gov/rcp
Developed by the CIWMB, the Recycled Content Product Directory is a searchable database for recycled content products.

Center for Resourceful Building Technology, Guide to Resource-Efficient Building Elements
http://crbt.ncat.org/
The directory of environmentally responsible building products is a resource that provides introductory discussions for each topic and contact information for specific products, including salvaged materials. (The CRBT project is no longer active, and the CRBT website is no longer updated. The National Center for Appropriate Technology is providing this website for archival purposes only.)

Oikos
http://www.oikos.com
Oikos is a searchable directory of efficient building products and sustainable design resources.

Recycled Content: What Is It, and What Is It Worth? Environmental Building News, February 2005.
http://www.buildinggreen.com/auth/article.cfm?filename=140201a.xml

U.S. EPA Comprehensive Procurement Guidelines Program
http://www.epa.gov/cpg/products.htm
The Comprehensive Procurement Guidelines Program contains EPA information on recycled-content materials with guidelines for recycled percentages. It also includes a searchable database of suppliers.

Construction Specifications Institute (CSI), Green Format
http://www.greenformat.com
This database features a standardized format for manufacturers to report recycled content as well other environmental and sustainable attributes. The website is based on principles of ISO 14021,–Environmental Labels and Declarations—Self-Declared Environmental Claims (Type II Environmental Labeling), and ASTM E 2129, Standard Practice for Data Collection for Sustainability Assessment of Building Products.

13. Definitions

	MR
NC	Credit 4
SCHOOLS	Credit 4
CS	Credit 4

Assembly recycled content is the percentage of material in a product that is either postconsumer or preconsumer recycled content. It is determined by dividing the weight of the recycled content by the overall weight of the assembly.

Fly ash is the solid residue derived from incineration processes. Fly ash can be used as a substitute for Portland cement in concrete.

Postconsumer recycled content is the percentage of material in a product that was consumer waste. The recycled material was generated by household, commercial, industrial, or institutional end-users and can no longer be used for its intended purpose. It includes returns of materials from the distribution chain (ISO 14021). Examples include construction and demolition debris, materials collected through recycling programs, discarded products (e.g., furniture, cabinetry, decking), and landscaping waste (e.g., leaves, grass clippings, tree trimmings).

Preconsumer recycled content, formerly known as postindustrial content, is the percentage of material in a product that is recycled from manufacturing waste. Examples include planer shavings, sawdust, bagasse, walnut shells, culls, trimmed materials, overissue publications, and obsolete inventories. Excluded are rework, regrind, or scrap materials capable of being reclaimed within the same process that generated them (ISO 14021).

Recycled content is the proportion, by mass, of preconsumer or postconsumer recycled material in a product (ISO 14021).

REGIONAL MATERIALS

	NC	SCHOOLS	CS
Credit	MR Credit 5	MR Credit 5	MR Credit 5
Points	1-2 points	1-2 points	1-2 points

Intent

To increase demand for building materials and products that are extracted and manufactured within the region, thereby supporting the use of indigenous resources and reducing the environmental impacts resulting from transportation.

Requirements

NC, SCHOOLS & CS

Use building materials or products that have been extracted, harvested or recovered, as well as manufactured, within 500 miles of the project site for a minimum of 10% or 20%, based on cost, of the total materials value. If only a fraction of a product or material is extracted, harvested, or recovered and manufactured locally, then only that percentage (by weight) must contribute to the regional value. The minimum percentage regional materials for each point threshold is as follows:

Regional Materials	Points
10%	1
20%	2

Mechanical, electrical and plumbing components, and specialty items such as elevators and equipment must not be included in this calculation. Include only materials permanently installed in the project. Furniture may be included if it is included consistently in MR Credit 3: Materials Reuse through MR Credit 7: Certified Wood (MR Credit 6 in Core & Shell).

	MR
NC	Credit 5
SCHOOLS	Credit 5
CS	Credit 5

1. Benefits and Issues To Consider

Environmental Issues

The use of regional building materials reduces transportation activities and associated pollution. Trucks, trains, ships, and other vehicles deplete finite reserves of fossil fuels and generate air pollution. It also is important to address the source of raw materials used to manufacture building products; some are harvested or extracted far from the point of manufacture, also contributing to air and water pollution associated with transportation.

Economic Issues

The availability of regionally manufactured building materials depends on the project location. In some areas, the majority of products needed for the project can be obtained within a 500-mile radius. In other areas, only a small portion or no building materials can be sourced locally. However, the purchase of regional building materials is generally more cost-effective because of reduced transportation costs. Also, the support of regional manufacturers and labor forces retains capital in the community, contributing to a more stable tax base and a healthier local economy, as well as showcases the resources and skills of the region.

2. Related Credits

Specifying regional materials to achieve this credit may affect the levels of achievement for the following credits:

- MR Credit 3: Materials Reuse
- MR Credit 4: Recycled Content
- MR Credit 6: Rapidly Renewable Materials

Set goals early for materials use; assess the availability of regional materials and determine the best available products to minimize the project's environmental impact. The use of life-cycle assessment tools may be employed in the decision-making process.

The project materials costs used in this credit need to be consistent with those used in the following credits:

- MR Credit 3: Materials Reuse
- MR Credit 4: Recycled Content
- MR Credit 6: Rapidly Renewable Materials

3. Summary of Referenced Standards

There are no standards referenced for this credit.

4. Implementation

The point of manufacture is considered the place of final assembly of components into the building product that is furnished and installed by the tradesworkers. For example, if the hardware comes from Dallas, the lumber comes from Vancouver, and the joist is assembled in Kent, Washington, then the location of the final assembly is Kent, Washington.

It may require careful research to determine what local products are available, so evaluate this credit early in the design process. This credit is achieved by summing the cost of all materials that are extracted and manufactured within 500 miles of the construction site. If the material contains components that were sourced from a place within 500 miles but the final assembly was farther away, the product cannot be counted toward the credit. In cases where products and construction components are assembled on-site, the individual components that are extracted within 500 miles of the site will be counted toward this credit.

	MR
NC	Credit 5
SCHOOLS	Credit 5
CS	Credit 5

The general contractor should work with subcontractors and suppliers to verify availability of materials that are extracted, harvested, or recovered and manufactured locally. The contractor should run preliminary calculations based on the construction budget or schedule of values during the preconstruction phase. This will allow the construction team to focus on those materials with the greatest contribution to this credit as early as possible.

5. Timeline and Team

Run preliminary calculations, as soon as a project budget is available, to set appropriate regional materials targets. Architects should specify in the construction documents products that are extracted/harvested/recovered and manufactured within 500 miles and work with the general contractor on approved alternatives that meet the requirements of this credit. During construction, the general contractor is typically responsible for documenting the amounts and values of regionally harvested and manufactured materials used on the project. The general contractor must track the materials cost of each locally harvested and manufactured product that will be applied to this credit.

6. Calculations

Determine the total materials cost for the project by multiplying the total construction cost (hard costs only in CSI MasterFormat™ 2004 Edition Divisions 03–10, 31 (Section 31.60.00 Foundations) and 32 (sections 32.10.00 Paving, 32.30.00 Site Improvements, and 32.90.00 Planting) by 0.45. Alternatively, the total materials cost may be a tally of actual materials cost in CSI MasterFormat™ 2004 Edition Divisions 03–10, 31 (Section 31.60.00 Foundations) and 32 (Sections 32.10.00 Paving, 32.30.00 Site Improvements, and 32.90.00 Planting) from the project schedule of values or a similar document. The benefit to using actual materials costs, as opposed to the default 45%, is that projects with less than 45% materials cost will find it easier to achieve the 10% and 20% credit thresholds, since total materials cost is in the denominator of the equation below. The purpose of the default value is to streamline the documentation process, since it is often challenging to break out the materials costs from labor and equipment costs for all materials on the project.

Materials costs include all expenses to deliver the material to the project site. Materials costs should account for all taxes and transportation costs incurred by the contractor but exclude any cost for labor and equipment once the material has been delivered to the site.

List those products that are extracted, harvested, or recovered and manufactured within 500 miles of the project site. Indicate the manufacturer, the product cost, the distance between the project site and the manufacturer location, and the distance between the project site and the extraction site for each raw material in each product.

Calculate the percentage local materials according to Equation 1.

Equation 1

$$\text{Percentage Local Materials} = \frac{\text{Total Cost of Local Materials (\$)}}{\text{Total Materials Cost (\$)}} \times 100$$

The project achieves 1 point when the percentage of local material is 10% or greater, and 2 points when the percentage of local material is 20% or greater.

Table 1 lists sample materials and components eligible for this credit.

MR	
NC	Credit 5
SCHOOLS	Credit 5
CS	Credit 5

Table 1. Sample Regional Materials

Distance to Point of Harvest or Extraction	Distance to Point of Manufacture or Assembly	Product Included in MR 5 Calculations?
Flooring: Timber harvested, 450 miles	Flooring mill, 400 miles	Yes
I Beams: Steel extraction, 1,000 miles	Steel mill, 300 miles	No
Concrete: Cement, 650 miles Aggregate, 150 miles	Cement plant, 600 miles Aggregate and sand, 100 miles	No for cement Yes for aggregate and sand
Drywall: Gypsum factory, 200 miles	Drywall supplier, 600 miles	No

Furniture and furnishings (CSI Division 12) are excluded from the calculations for this credit, unless they are considered consistently across MR Credits 3–7. This credit applies primarily to CSI MasterFormat™ 2004 Edition Divisions 03–10, 31 (Section 31.60.00 Foundations) and 32 (Sections 32.10.00 Paving, 32.30.00 Site Improvements, and 32.90.00 Planting).

Do not include mechanical, electrical, and plumbing components or appliances and equipment in the calculations for this credit. Compared with structural and finish materials, mechanical and electrical equipment tends to have a high dollar value relative to the amount of material it contains and that high dollar value would skew the results of the calculation.

Reused and Salvaged Materials

Reused and salvaged materials that satisfy the requirements of MR Credit 3 may also contribute to MR Credit 5. Use the location from which they were salvaged as the point of extraction, and use the location of the salvaged goods vendor as the point of manufacture. On-site salvaged materials automatically qualify.

For materials with more than 1 point of manufacture or extraction, all within the 500-mile radius, list the component with the greatest distance. If a portion of the material was either manufactured or extracted beyond the 500-mile radius, list only that portion and associated cost satisfying the credit requirement.

For assemblies or products manufactured within the 500-mile radius that contain some components extracted farther away, use multiple lines when listing purchases. Base the proportionality of such products' costs on the weight of their various components (see the example for concrete in Tables 2 and 3.)

Table 2. Sample Assembly Percentage Regionally Extracted Calculation for Concrete

Components	Weight (lbs)	Distance between Project & Extraction Site (miles)	Weight Contributing to Regional Extraction (lbs)
Cement	282	1,250	0
Fly Ash	282	125	282
Water	275	1	275
Slag	750	370	750
Recycled Concrete & Aggregate	1,000	8	1,000
Sand	1,200	18	1,200
Component Totals	3,789	NA	3,507
Percent Regionally Extracted Materials (3,507/3,789)			92.6%

Table 3. Sample Spreadsheet for Regional Materials

		MR
NC		Credit 5
SCHOOLS		Credit 5
CS		Credit 5

Product	Manufacturer	Distance between Project & Manufcaurer (miles)	Distance between Project & Extraction/ Harvest (miles)	Product Cost ($)	Value Qualifying as Regional	Information Source
Plant material	Green's Landscape	5	5	$6,770	$6,770	Contractor submittal
Concrete	Joe's Concrete	15	15	$21,000	$21,000	Contractor submittal
Insulation	UR Warm	105	1,080	$9,250	-	Product cut sheet
Gypsum	Gypsum R Us	75	288	$8,550	$8,550	Letter from manufacturer
Carpet	Fiber Good	355	721	$15,333	-	Letter from manufacturer
Casework	Top Counter	18	320	$12,200	$12,200	Contractor submittal
Lumber	My Mill	110	320	$38,990	$38,990	Contractor submittal
Wood Doors	Closeby	71	320	$7,000	$7,000	Contractor submittal

Total Cost of Regional Materials	$94,510
Total Materials Cost (Divisions 2–10)	$751,000
Percent Regional Materials	13%
Points Earned	1

7. Documentation Guidance

As a first step in preparing to complete the LEED-Online documentation requirements, work through the following measures. Refer to LEED-Online for the complete descriptions of all required documentation.

- Compile a list of product purchases manufactured, extracted, or harvested regionally.

- Record manufacturers' names, product costs, distances between the project and manufacturer, and distances between the project and the extraction site.

- Where appropriate, retain cutsheets that document material origin and manufacture within a 500-mile radius of the project site.

- Where appropriate, maintain a list of materials costs, excluding labor and equipment, for CSI Divisions 03–10, 31 (Section 31.60.00 Foundations) and 32 (Sections 32.10.00 Paving, 32.30.00 Site Improvements, and 32.90.00 Planting) only; including Division 12 is optional.

8. Examples

EXAMPLE 1

Figure 2 illustrates an example for a hypothetical slag concrete material that is extracted, processed, and manufactured within 500 miles of a project site.

Figure 2. Extraction and Manufacturing Location of Fly Ash Concrete

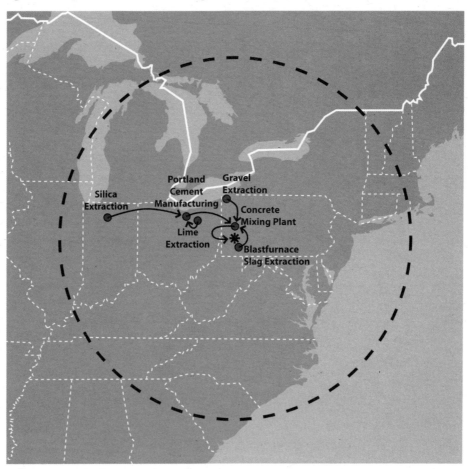

* Project Site Location
● Location of Harvesting, Extraction, & Manufacturing

EXAMPLE 2

The total construction costs for a library building are $600,000. Using the default materials calculations, the total cost of materials excluding labor and equipment is $600,000 x 0.45 = $270,000. Table 4 lists the regional materials purchased for the project. In this example, the cost of regionally harvested and manufactured products as a percentage of the total cost of materials is 27.89%. The project earns 2 points.

Table 4. Sample Calculation for Regional Material

					MR
				NC	Credit 5
				SCHOOLS	Credit 5
				CS	Credit 5

Total construction cost					$ 600,000
for default total materials cost; OR					$ 600,000
Provide total materials cost (exclude labor, equipment)					$ 270,000

Product name	Vendor	Product Cost ($)	Distance between project and manufacturer (miles)	Distance between project and extraction site (miles)	Regional content information source
Plant Material	Green Landscaping	$6,770	25	5	Manufacturer
Concrete aggregate	Joe's Concrete	$21,000	5	15	Concrete manufacturer
Gypsum board	Gypsum R Us	$8,550	75	288	Manufacturer
Wood flooring	Lumber Specialists	$38,990	119	320	Mill

Combined value of postconsumer and half of preconsumer content	$ 30,535
Total cost of locally manufactured and extracted materials	$75,310
Cost of regionally manufactured products as a percentage of the cost of all materials	27.89%

Points documented	
10% regional materials	1
20% regional materials	1
Total points documented	2

EXAMPLE 3

Concrete dry mix is provided by a subcontractor. The dry mix contains cement, aggregate, sand, water, and admixtures with a definite proportion. While the concrete is manufactured within 20 miles from the project site, the aggregate is mined from a town 100 miles away, the cement plant is 600 miles away, and the sand is from 550 miles away. In this case, only the aggregate will qualify for the regional material credit. The cost of the aggregate material can either be provided by the subcontractor or calculated on the basis of the percentage of aggregate and total cost of the concrete mix. If the concrete mix was $100,000 and the aggregate was 10% by weight of the concrete, the aggregate cost will be assumed to be $10,000. Therefore, the concrete will account for $10,000 to the regional material credit.

9. Exemplary Performance

Project teams may earn an Innovation in Design credit for exemplary performance by achieving a total value of regionally harvested, extracted, and manufactured materials of 30% or more.

10. Regional Variations

Local availability of materials will vary by region. Regional building materials are often consistent with regional design aesthetics and may be more stable in the local climate than materials from other regions. Consider the local architecture and adopt a design that incorporates locally produced materials wherever possible. Those project sites near sources for material origin and manufacture will have an advantage in the achievement of this credit.

	MR
NC	Credit 5
SCHOOLS	Credit 5
CS	Credit 5

11. Operations and Maintenance Considerations

The duplication, replacement, and repair of regional materials will be easier if information about the installed products has been maintained. Encourage the creation of a sustainable purchasing plan and provide building operators with lists of the installed products and their manufacturers, such as the documentation used in the LEED application.

12. Resources

Please see USGBC's LEED Registered Project Tools (http://www.usgbc.org/projecttools) for additional resources and technical information.

Government Resources

Check with the local chamber of commerce or regional and state economic development agencies for building materials manufacturers in the region.

13. Definitions

Manufacturing refers to the final assembly of components into the building product that is furnished and installed by the tradesworkers.

Regionally extracted materials are raw materials taken from within a 500-mile radius of the project site.

Regionally manufactured materials are assembled as finished products within a 500-mile radius of the project site. Assembly does not include on-site assembly, erection, or installation of finished components.

RAPIDLY RENEWABLE MATERIALS

	NC	SCHOOLS	CS
Credit	MR Credit 6	MR Credit 6	NA
Points	1 point	1 point	NA

Intent

To reduce the use and depletion of finite raw materials and long-cycle renewable materials by replacing them with rapidly renewable materials.

Requirements

NC & SCHOOLS

Use rapidly renewable building materials and products for 2.5% of the total value of all building materials and products used in the project, based on cost. Rapidly renewable building materials and products are made from plants that are typically harvested within a 10-year or shorter cycle.

	MR
NC	Credit 6
SCHOOLS	Credit 6
CS	NA

1. Benefits and Issues to Consider

Environmental Issues

Many conventional building materials require large inputs of land, natural resources, capital, and time to produce. Conversely, rapidly renewable materials generally require fewer of these inputs and are likely to have fewer environmental impacts. Rapidly renewable resources are replenished faster than traditional materials—they are planted and harvested in a cycle of 10 years or less.

Sourcing rapidly renewable materials reduces the use of raw materials whose extraction and processing have greater environmental impacts. A common example is the use of agricultural fiber such as wheat in composite panels as a substitute for wood products, reducing the overall consumption of wood. Irresponsible forestry practices cause ecosystem and habitat destruction, soil erosion, and stream sedimentation; replacing wood products with rapidly renewable resources reduces a product's overall environmental impact. Because of their intensive production and shorter growing cycles, rapidly renewable crops also require significantly less land to produce the same amount of end product; some are byproducts that are otherwise considered waste. Bio-based plastics (e.g., from corn starch) and other rapidly renewable resources are beginning to provide alternatives to some petroleum-based plastics.

Many products made from rapidly renewable materials have interesting visual or tactile qualities. Using these materials in a visually prominent way provides opportunities for learning about manufacturing processes, economics, environmental impacts, and embodied energy.

For schools, such opportunities help students connect everyday products to their sources in nature and understand the importance of resource conservation.

Economic Issues

Land saved by the use of rapidly renewable materials will be available for a variety of other uses, including open space and food crops Because rapidly renewable resources can be harvested more quickly, they tend to give faster payback on investment for producers. Although rapidly renewable materials can carry a price premium over their conventional counterparts, as demand increases, they are expected to become cost-competitive with conventional materials.

2. Related Credits

Rapidly renewable materials like cork or bamboo plywood may come from distant sources and may impact achievement of the following credit:

- MR Credit 5: Regional Materials

To reduce the detrimental effects some materials have on IAQ, project teams should follow the guidelines of IEQ Credit 4: Low Emitting Materials and specify materials and furnishings that do not release harmful or irritating chemicals, such as volatile organic compounds (VOCs), from paints and solvents.

The project materials costs used in this credit need to be consistent with those used in the following credits:

- MR Credit 3: Materials Reuse
- MR Credit 4: Recycled Content
- MR Credit 5: Regional Materials

3. Summary of Referenced Standards

There are no standards referenced for this credit.

4. Implementation

Establish a goal for the use of rapidly renewable materials early in the design phase, identify possible building materials that may be substituted with rapidly renewable products, and find vendors that can achieve this goal. Table 1 provides examples of common rapidly renewable building materials, and Figure 1 illustrates the typical harvest rate of sample materials. Identify products and vendors in the project specifications and plans and work with the general contractor to source acceptable alternatives. During construction, make sure that the specified rapidly renewable materials are installed.

Examples of rapidly renewable materials include bamboo flooring and plywood, cotton batt insulation, linoleum flooring, sunflower seed board panels, wheatboard cabinetry, wool carpeting, cork flooring, bio-based paints, geotextile fabrics such as coir and jute, soy-based insulation and form-release agent, and straw bales.

	MR
NC	Credit 6
SCHOOLS	Credit 6
CS	NA

Figure 1. Harvest Rate of Sample Materials

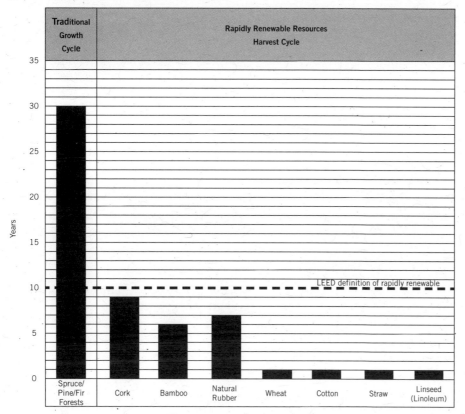

5. Timeline and Team

Run preliminary calculations during the early design phase, as soon as a project budget is available, to determine the feasibility of achieving this credit and identify the quantity of material (by cost) that must be purchased to meet the 2.5% threshold (refer to the Examples and Calculations sections). Research the availability and cost of rapidly renewable materials. The architect should specify these materials. During construction, the general contractor should ensure that the specified rapidly renewable materials are properly installed and collect product documentation from manufacturers to give to the project team.

	MR
NC	Credit 6
SCHOOLS	Credit 6
CS	NA

6. Calculations

Determine the total materials cost for the project. by multiplying the total construction cost (hard costs only in CSI MasterFormat™ 2004 Edition Divisions 03–10, 31 (Section 31.60.00 Foundations) and 32 (Sections 32.10.00 Paving, 32.30.00 Site Improvements, and 32.90.00 Planting) by 0.45. Alternatively, the total materials cost may be a tally of actual materials cost in CSI MasterFormat™ 2004 Edition Divisions 03–10, 31 (Section 31.60.00 Foundations) and 32 (Sections 32.10.00 Paving, 32.30.00 Site Improvements, and 32.90.00 Planting) from the project schedule of values or a similar document. The benefit to using actual materials costs, as opposed to the default 45%, is that projects with less than 45% materials cost will find it easier to achieve the credit thresholds, since total materials cost is in the denominator of the equation below. The purpose of the default value is to streamline the documentation process, since it is often challenging to break out the materials costs from labor and equipment costs for all materials on the project.

Materials costs include all expenses to deliver the material to the project site. Materials costs should account for all taxes and transportation costs incurred by the contractor but exclude any cost for labor and equipment once the material has been delivered to the site.

Identify those products that are considered rapidly renewable and their materials costs.

Calculate the percentage of rapidly renewable materials using Equation 1.

Equation 1

$$\text{Percent of Rapidly Renewable Materials} = \frac{\text{Total Cost of Rapidly Renewable Material (\$)}}{\text{Total Materials Cost (\$)}} \times 100$$

The project achieves MR Credit 6 when rapidly renewable building materials and products account for 2.5% of the total materials cost of all building materials and products used in the project.

Furniture and furnishings (CSI MasterFormat 2004 Division 12 components) are excluded from the calculations for this credit unless they are included consistently across MR Credits 3–7. This credit applies primarily to CSI MasterFormat™ 2004 Edition Divisions 03–10, 31 (Section 31.60.00 Foundations) and 32 (Sections 32.10.00 Paving, 32.30.00 Site Improvements, and 32.90.00 Planting). Mechanical, electrical and plumbing components, along with appliances and equipment, cannot be included in calculations for this credit. These are excluded because, when compared with structural and finish materials, mechanical and electrical equipment tend to have a high dollar value relative to the amount of material they contain.

Assembly Rapidly Renewable Content

Assemblies are products made of multiple materials, either in their formulation (e.g., particle board), or in their manufacture (e.g., workstation components). For assembly rapidly renewable content, the fraction of the assembly that is considered rapidly renewable is determined by weight. That fraction is then applied to the materials cost to determine the rapidly renewable materials cost for that assembly.

7. Documentation Guidance

As a first step in preparing to complete the LEED-Online documentation requirements, work through the following measures. Refer to LEED-Online for the complete descriptions of all required documentation.

- Compile a list of rapidly renewable product purchases.

- Record manufacturers' names, materials costs, the percentage of each product that is rapidly renewable criteria (by weight), and each compliant value.

- Retain cutsheets to document rapidly renewable criteria.
- Where appropriate, maintain a list of actual materials costs, excluding labor and equipment for CSI Divisions 03–10, 31 (Section 31.60.00 Foundations) and 32 (Sections 32.10.00 Paving, 32.30.00 Site Improvements, and 32.90.00 Planting) only; including Division 12 is optional.

	MR
NC	Credit 6
SCHOOLS	Credit 6
CS	NA

8. Examples

The total construction cost for a school building is $600,000. Using the default materials calcuations, the total cost of materials (excluding labor and equipment) is $600,000 x 0.45 = $270,000. Table 2 lists rapidly renewable materials purchased for the project. In this example, the total percentage of rapidly renewable content to total cost of all materials is 4.86%. The project earns 1 point.

Table 2. Sample Calculations for Rapidly Renewable Material

Total construction cost for default total materials cost; OR					$ 600,000
Provide total materials cost (exclude labor, equipment)					$ 270,000
Product name	Vendor Name	Assembly Product Cost	% Rapidly Renewable Content (if part of an assembly)	Value of Rapidly Renewable Content	Recycled content information source
Countertop wheatboard	Rho Company	$6,700	30.00%	$2,010.00	Vendor
Linoleum flooring	Tau Floors	$882	50.00%	$441.00	Manufacturer letter
Bamboo window blinds	Upsilion Shades	$14,079	75.00%	$10,559.25	Website
Totals		$21,661		$13,010.25	
Value of rapidly renewable content					$13,010
Percentage cost of rapidly renewable content total cost of all materials					4.86%
Points documented					1

9. Exemplary Performance

Project teams may earn an Innovation in Design credit for exemplary performance by achieving a rapidly renewable materials content of 5% or more.

10. Regional Variations

Assess the availability of rapidly renewable materials that also contribute to MR Credit 5, Regional Materials, and select products manufactured from rapidly renewable resources located within 500 miles of the project site.

11. Operations and Maintenance Considerations

Some rapidly renewable materials may require different maintenance practices. For example, bamboo and cork generally should not be exposed to excessive moisture from damp mopping and other common janitorial or maintenance actiities. When sourcing rapidly renewable products, request maintenance recommendations from the manufacturer and give this information to the operations team.

The duplication, replacement, and repair of rapidly renewable materials will be easier if information about the installed products has been maintained. Encourage the creation of a sustainable purchasing plan and provide building operators with lists of the installed products and their manufacturers, such as the documentation used in the LEED application.

12. Resources

Please see USGBC's LEED Registered Project Tools (http://www.usgbc.org/projecttools) for additional resources and technical information.

	MR
NC	Credit 6
SCHOOLS	Credit 6
CS	NA

BuildingGreen, Inc., Environmental Building News

http://www.buildinggreen.com/products/bamboo.html

Read an article in Environmental Building News on bamboo flooring that includes a listing of bamboo flooring suppliers.

Environmental Design + Construction, Highlights of Environmental Flooring

http://www.edcmag.com

Read an Environmental Design + Construction article with information on bamboo flooring, linoleum, and wool carpeting.

BuildingGreen, Inc., GreenSpec

http://www.buildinggreen.com/menus/index.cfm

GreenSpec contains detailed listings for more than 2,000 green building products that include environmental data, manufacturer information, and links to additional resources.

Oikos

http://www.oikos.com

Oikos is a searchable directory of efficient building products and sustainable design resources.

13. Definitions

Embodied energy is the energy used during the entire life cycle of a product, including its manufacture, transportation, and disposal, as well as the inherent energy captured within the product itself.

Life cycle assessment is an analysis of the environmental aspects and potential impacts associated with a product, process, or service.

Rapidly renewable materials are agricultural products, both fiber and animal, that take 10 years or less to grow or raise and can be harvested in a sustainable fashion.

CERTIFIED WOOD

	NC	SCHOOLS	CS
Credit	MR Credit 7	MR Credit 7	MR Credit 6
Points	1 point	1 point	1 point

Intent

To encourage environmentally responsible forest management.

Requirements

NC, SCHOOLS & CS

Use a minimum of 50% (based on cost) of wood-based materials and products that are certified in accordance with the Forest Stewardship Council's principles and criteria, for wood building components. These components include at a minimum, structural framing and general dimensional framing, flooring, sub-flooring, wood doors and finishes.

Include only materials permanently installed in the project. Wood products purchased for temporary use on the project (e.g., formwork, bracing, scaffolding, sidewalk protection, and guard rails) may be included in the calculation at the project team's discretion. If any such materials are included, all such materials must be included in the calculation. If such materials are purchased for use on multiple projects, the applicant may include these materials for only one project, at its discretion. Furniture may be included if it is included consistently in MR Credits 3. Materials Reuse, through MR Credit 7: Certified Wood (MR Credit 6 for Core & Shell projects).

	MR
NC	Credit 7
SCHOOLS	Credit 7
CS	Credit 6

1. Benefits and Issues to Consider

Environmental Issues

The negative environmental impacts of irresponsible forest practices can include forest destruction, wildlife habitat loss, soil erosion and stream sedimentation, water and air pollution, and waste generation. The Forest Stewardship Council (FSC) standard incorporates many criteria that contribute to the long-term health and integrity of forest ecosystems. From an environmental perspective, the elements of responsible FSC-certified forestry include sustainable timber harvesting (i.e., not removing more timber volume than replaces itself over the cutting interval, or rotation), preserving wildlife habitat and biodiversity, maintaining soil and water quality, minimizing the use of harmful chemicals, and conserving forests of high conservation value (e.g., endangered and old-growth forests).

Economic Issues

As more developing countries enter world forest product markets and their growing economies drive domestic consumption, the protection of forests will become a critical issue. As of 2007, FSC-certified forests represent the equivalent of 7% of the world's productive forests.[12] Currently, the costs of FSC-certified wood products are equal to or higher than conventional wood products, and availability varies by region. The price of FSC-certified wood products is expected to become more competitive with conventional wood products as the world's forest resources are depleted and the forest industry adopts more sustainable business principles.

Because irresponsible logging practices can have harmful social as well as environmental impacts, the socioeconomic and political components of FSC certification include respecting indigenous people's rights and adhering to all applicable laws and treaties. Certification also involves forest workers and forest-dependent communities as stakeholders and beneficiaries of responsible forest management. Responsible forest practices help stabilize economies and preserve forestland for future generations.

2. Related Credits

Project teams pursuing this credit may find opportunities to achieve other MR credits. An FSC strategy should be developed early to determine whether certified wood can be sourced and manufactured within 500 miles of the site. Additionally, when specifying mixed FSC materials and pursuing IEQ Credit 4.4, determine whether the finished product will be free of urea-formaldehyde. Refer to the following credits:

- MR Credit 5: Regional Materials
- IEQ Credit 4.4: Low-Emitting Materials—Composite Wood and Agrifiber Products

3. Summary of Referenced Standard

Forest Stewardship Council Principles and Criteria

http://www.fscus.org

Certification by the Forest Stewardship Council (FSC) is a seal of approval awarded to forest managers who adopt environmentally and socially responsible forest management practices and to companies that manufacture and sell products made from certified wood. This seal enables consumers, including architects and specifiers, to identify and procure wood products from well-managed sources and thereby use their purchasing power to influence and reward improved forest management activities around the world.

LEED accepts certification according to the comprehensive system established by the internationally recognized Forest Stewardship Council. FSC was created in 1993 to establish international forest management standards, known as the FSC principles and criteria, to ensure that forestry practices are environmentally responsible, socially beneficial, and economically viable. These principles and criteria are also intended to ensure the long-term health and productivity of forests for timber production, wildlife habitat, clean air and water supplies, climate stabilization, spiritual renewal, and social benefit. These global principles and criteria are translated into meaningful standards at a local level through region-specific standard-setting processes.

	MR
NC	Credit 7
SCHOOLS	Credit 7
CS	Credit 6

FSC also accredits and monitors certification organizations. The certifiers are independent, third-party auditors that are qualified to annually evaluate compliance with FSC standards on the ground and to award certifications. There are 2 types of certification:

- **Forest management certification** is awarded to responsible forest managers after their operations successfully complete audits of forestry practices and plans.

- **Chain-of-custody (COC) certification** is awarded to companies that process, manufacture, and/or sell products made of certified wood and who successfully complete audits to ensure proper use of the FSC name and logo; segregation of certified and noncertified materials in manufacturing and distribution systems; and observation of other relevant FSC rules (e.g., meeting minimum requirements for FSC fiber content in assembled and composite wood products).

The majority of FSC certification audits performed in North America are conducted by SmartWood and Scientific Certification Systems (SCS), which are based in the United States. A limited number are performed by SGS, which is based in Europe.

4. Implementation

Establish a project goal for FSC-certified wood products and identify suppliers that can achieve this goal. Research the availability of the wood species and products that they want to use, and make sure that they are available from FSC-certified sources. Another method for lowering the impact of wood resources is to research and specify quality grades that are most readily available from well-managed forests. Using lower grades of wood can dramatically reduce pressure on forests, which produce only limited quantities of top-grade timber (i.e., Architectural Woodwork Institute (AWI) Grades 2 or 3 for lumber or veneer rather than Grade 1).

Contact local vendors, suppliers, and manufacturers that provide FSC-certified products as early as possible. Design teams should provide project bidders with a list of certified vendors and encourage them to make contact early in the project to establish product availability and pricing. Consult the Resources section for information about product databases and boilerplate forms. Since the availability of certain certified wood products may vary over the life of a project, teams should consider having the owner prepurchase, store, and supply particular items to the contractor ("furnished by the owner, installed by the contractor," or FOIC). Finding a storage location that matches the final ambient moisture of the space will ensure proper installation. Because ambient moisture is usually higher during construction, a job site is not the best location to store wood.

The design team should specify in contract documents that wood products must come from forests that are certified as well-managed according to the rules of the FSC, and the team should require chain-of-custody documentation. Wherever possible, use a line-item strategy based on the current availability of specific products rather than a blanket approach.

Figure 1 is based on information from FSC's website (http://www.fsc.org/) and outlines the FSC process, explains when chain-of-custody documentation is required, and describes what types of information a project should collect.

	MR
NC	Credit 7
SCHOOLS	Credit 7
CS	Credit 6

Figure 1. FSC Certification Process and Categories

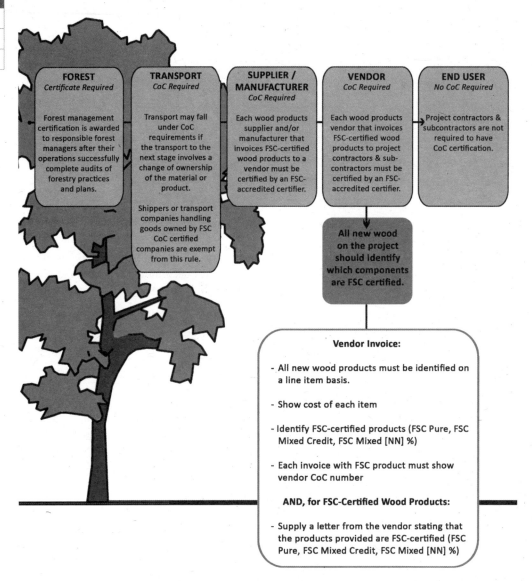

FOREST
Certificate Required

Forest management certification is awarded to responsible forest managers after their operations successfully complete audits of forestry practices and plans.

TRANSPORT
CoC Required

Transport may fall under CoC requirements if the transport to the next stage involves a change of ownership of the material or product.

Shippers or transport companies handling goods owned by FSC CoC certified companies are exempt from this rule.

SUPPLIER / MANUFACTURER
CoC Required

Each wood products supplier and/or manufacturer that invoices FSC-certified wood products to a vendor must be certified by an FSC-accredited certifier.

VENDOR
CoC Required

Each wood products vendor that invoices FSC-certified wood products to project contractors & sub-contractors must be certified by an FSC-accredited certifier.

END USER
No CoC Required

Project contractors & subcontractors are not required to have CoC certification.

All new wood on the project should identify which components are FSC certified.

Vendor Invoice:

- All new wood products must be identified on a line item basis.

- Show cost of each item

- Identify FSC-certified products (FSC Pure, FSC Mixed Credit, FSC Mixed [NN] %)

- Each invoice with FSC product must show vendor CoC number

AND, for FSC-Certified Wood Products:

- Supply a letter from the vendor stating that the products provided are FSC-certified (FSC Pure, FSC Mixed Credit, FSC Mixed [NN] %)

Chain-of-Custody Requirements

Collect all vendor invoices for permanently installed wood products, FSC certified or not, purchased by the project contractor and subcontractors. Vendors are defined as those companies that sell products to the project contractor or subcontractors.

Each vendor invoice must conform to the following requirements (except as noted below):

- Each wood product must be identified on a line-item basis.

- FSC products must be identified as such on a line-item basis.

- The dollar value of each line item must be shown.

- The vendor's COC certificate number must be shown on any invoice that includes FSC products.

Each wood product's vendor that invoices FSC certified products must be COC certified by an FSC-accredited certifier.

Exceptions: In some rare instances, it may not be practical for a vendor to invoice wood products on a line-item basis because the invoice would be dozens of pages long. In such cases, the invoice should indicate the aggregate value of wood products sold by the vendor. If the wood products are FSC certified, comply with the following requirements:

- The vendor's COC number must be shown on the invoice.

- The invoice must be supplemented by a letter from the vendor stating that the products invoiced are FSC certified.

- The invoice or the letter must state whether the products are FSC Pure, FSC Mixed Credit, or FSC Mixed (NN)%.

	MR
NC	Credit 7
SCHOOLS	Credit 7
CS	Credit 6

5. Timeline and Team

The incorporation of FSC-certified building materials will affect the financial planning stage, design development, and installation schedules of the project. Coordination among the owner, architect or design team, and contractor should begin early in the design development phase so that the availability, costs, and lead times of FSC-certified products can be anticipated and their purchase coordinated with the construction schedule.

During the design phase, the architect should incorporate certified wood products into the project plans and specifications. During construction, the contractor should review the project cost to verify that 50% of wood costs are FSC-certified. As materials are purchased during construction, the general contractor must obtain and retain COC certificates. At the end of construction, the general contractor should provide the documentation needed for the LEED certification application.

6. Calculations

List all new wood products (not reclaimed, salvaged, or recycled) on the project and identify which components are FSC certified. The cost of all new wood products, both FSC certified and not, must be tallied. Develop a spreadsheet to calculate the amount of new wood and the amount of FSC-certified wood permanently installed on the project. Wood products that are not FSC certified and those that are identified on invoices as FSC Pure and FSC Mixed Credit should be valued at 100% of the product cost. Wood products identified as FSC Mixed (NN)% should be valued at the indicated percentage of their cost, For example, a product identified as FSC Mixed 75% should be valued at 75% of the cost.

Wood products identified as FSC Recycled or FSC Recycled Credit do not count toward MR Credit 7, Certified Wood. They qualify instead as recycled-content products that may contribute to MR Credit 4, Recycled Content.

Using Equation 1, determine the percentage of FSC-certified wood.

Equation 1

$$\text{Certified Wood Material Percentage} = \frac{\text{FSC-certified Wood Material Value (\$)}}{\text{Total New Wood Material Value (\$)}} \times 100$$

FSC wood products purchased for temporary use on the project may be included in the credit calculation at the project team's discretion. If any such materials are included, all such materials must be included in the calculation. Examples of products used for temporary assemblies include formwork, bracing, scaffolding, sidewalk protection, and guard rails. If such materials are purchased for multiple projects, the project team may include these materials on 1—and only 1—project at its discretion.

Assemblies

In the case of manufactured products, such as windows and furniture systems that combine wood and nonwood materials, only the new wood portion can be applied toward the credit. To determine the value of the wood component(s), calculate the amount of new wood as a percentage of the total weight, volume, or cost, and the amount of FSC-certified wood as a percentage of the total weight, volume, or cost. Multiply these figures by the total value of the product as invoiced to project contractors, subcontractors, or buying agents.

Develop a separate spreadsheet for each assembly to calculate the amount of new wood and amount of FSC-certified wood for assemblies and enter the summary data as 1 line item on the comprehensive spreadsheet used to calculate the percentage of certified wood used in the project.

To incorporate assembly FSC-certified and new wood content into Equation 1, use Equations 2 and 3 and add the result to the appropriate category.

Equation 2

$$\text{Assembly FSC Certified Wood Material Value} = \frac{\text{Weight of FSC-certified Wood in Assembly}}{\text{Weight of Assembly}} \times \text{Assembly Value (\$)}$$

Equation 3

$$\text{Assembly New Wood Material Value} = \frac{\text{Weight of New Wood in Assembly}}{\text{Weight of Assembly}} \times \text{Assembly Value (\$)}$$

7. Documentation Guidance

As a first step in preparing to complete the LEED-Online documentation requirements, work through the following measures. Refer to LEED-Online for the complete descriptions of all required documentation.

- Track certified wood purchases and retain associated COC documentation.

- Collect copies of vendor invoices for each certified wood product.

- Maintain a list that identifies the percentage of certified wood in each purchase.

8. Examples

See Table 1 for a sample calculation.

Table 1. Sample Assembly Percentage Wood-Based Content for BIFMA Typical Configuration.

Manufacturer		Lambda Furniture		
Product Line		High End Workstations		
BIFMA Typical Configuration		Workstation Configuration 0010		
Component	Weight (lbs)	Less Postconsumer Weight (lbs)	Wood-based Component Weight (lbs)	FSC Certified Wood Weight (lbs)
Wheat Board	28.0		28.0	28.0
Top Veneer	4.0	.	4.0	0.0
Other Wood	3.0	-1.1	1.9	1.5
Non-wood content	718.0		0.0	0.0
Total	753.0		33.9	29.5
Percent Wood (33.9/753.0)				4.5%
Percent FSC Certified Wood (29.5/753.0)				3.9%

9. Exemplary Performance

Project teams may earn an Innovation in Design credit for exemplary performance by achieving an FSC-certified wood content of 95% or more of the project's total new wood.

	MR
NC	Credit 7
SCHOOLS	Credit 7
CS	Credit 6

10. Regional Variations

This credit may have particular importance in areas with poor forestry practices or high forest conversion rates. Encouraging the development of local FSC markets and assigning economic value to responsible forestry practices will promote the retention of local, indigenous animal and plant species, the preservation of open space, the improvement of local air quality, and the reduction of heat-island effects for areas of developed infrastructure.

11. Operations and Maintenance Considerations

The duplication, replacement, and repair of certified wood products will be easier if information about the installed products has been maintained. Encourage the creation of a sustainable purchasing plan and provide building operators with lists of the installed products, their manufacturers, and COC certificates, such as the documentation used in the LEED application.

12. Resources

Please see USGBC's LEED Registered Project Tools (http://www.usgbc.org/projecttools) for additional resources and other technical information.

Websites

Forest Stewardship Council, United States

http://www.fscus.org/green_building

For information and practical tools such as databases of certified product suppliers, referral services, specification language, and the "Designing and Building with FSC" guide and forms.

Print Media

Sustainable Forestry: Philosophy, Science, and Economics, by Chris Maser (St. Lucie Press, 1994).

The Business of Sustainable Forestry: Strategies for an Industry in Transition, by Michael B. Jenkins and Emily T. Smith (Island Press, 1999).

Governing Through Markets: Forest Certification and the Emergence of Non-State Authority, by Deanna Newsom, Benjamin Cashore, and Graeme Auld (Yale University Press, 2004).

Tapping the Green Market: Certification & Management of Non-Timber Forest Products, edited by Patricia Shanley, Alan R. Pierce, Sarah A. Laird and Abraham Guillén (Earthscan Publications, 2002).

13. Definitions

Chain-of-custody (COC) is a tracking procedure for a product from the point of harvest or extraction to its end use, including all successive stages of processing, transformation, manufacturing, and distribution.

Chain-of-custody certification is awarded to companies that produce, sell, promote, or trade forest products after audits verify proper accounting of material flows and proper use of the Forest Stewardship Council name and logo. The COC certificate number is listed on invoices for nonlabeled products to document that an entity has followed FSC guidelines for product accounting.

Sustainable forestry is the practice of managing forest resources to meet the long-term forest product needs of humans while maintaining the biodiversity of forested landscapes. The primary goal is to restore, enhance, and sustain a full range of forest values, including economic, social, and ecological considerations.

	MR
NC	Credit 7
SCHOOLS	Credit 7
CS	Credit 6

A **vendor** of certified wood is the company that supplies wood products to contractors or subcontractors for on-site installation. A vendor needs a chain-of-custody number if it is selling FSC-certified products that are not individually labeled; this includes most lumber.

Endnotes

[1] U.S. Environmental Protection Agency, Office of Solid Waste. Municipal Solid Waste Generation, Recycling, and Disposal in the United States: Facts and Figures for 2005. 2006. http://www.epa.gov/osw/rcc/resources/msw-2005.pdf (accessed November 2008).

[2] U.S. Environmental Protection Agency, Office of Solid Waste. Municipal Solid Waste Generation, Recycling, and Disposal in the United States: Facts and Figures for 2005. 2006. http://www.epa.gov/osw/rcc/resources/msw-2005.pdf (accessed May 2008).

[3] U.S. Environmental Protection Agency. "Guide for Industrial Waste Management." http://www.epa.gov/wastes/nonhaz/industrial/guide/index.htm (accessed November 2008).

[4] U.S. Environmental Protection Agency. Municipal Solid Waste: 2007 Facts and Figures. 2008. http://www.epa.gov/osw/nonhaz/municipal/pubs/msw07-rpt.pdf (accessed November 2008).

[5] Ibid.

[6] Oberlin College Recycling Program. "Recycling Facts." http://www.oberlin.edu/recycle/facts.html (accessed November 2008).

[7] The Aluminum Association. "Aluminum Industry Vision." http://www1.eere.energy.gov/industry/aluminum/pdfs/alum_vision.pdf (accessed November 2008).

[8] Contractor's Report to the Board: Statewide Waste Characterization Study, December 2004. http://www.ciwmb.ca.gov/Publications/LocalAsst/34004005.pdf (accessed December 2008)

[9] U.S. Environmental Protection Agency, Office of Solid Waste. Municipal Solid Waste Generation, Recycling, and Disposal in the United States: Facts and Figures for 2006. 2007. http://www.epa.gov/epawaste/nonhaz/municipal/pubs/msw06.pdf (accessed November 2008).

[10] Department of Natural Resources, Northeast Region. "Building Green at DNR—Northeast Region Headquarters Construction Waste & Recycling." http://dnr.wi.gov/org/land/facilities/greenbldg/gbhqwaste.html (accessed November 2008).

[11] County of San Mateo, California. San Mateo Countywide Guide Sustainable Buildings. 2004. www.recycleworks.org/pdf/GB-guide-2-23.pdf (accessed November 2008).

[12] Forest Stewardship Council. "FSC: Facts & Figures." http://www.fsc.org/facts-figures.html (accessed November 2008).

Overview

Americans spend an average of 90% of their time indoors, so the quality of the indoor environment has a significant influence on their well-being, productivity, and quality of life.[1] The U.S. Environmental Protection Agency (EPA) reports that pollutant levels of indoor environments may run 2 to 5 times—and occasionally more than 100 times—higher than outdoor levels.[2] Similarly, the World Health Organization (WHO) reported in its Air Quality Guidelines for Europe, 2nd edition, that most of an individual's exposure to air pollutants comes through inhalation of indoor air. Following the release in 1987[3] and 1990[4] of EPA reports that designated indoor air pollution as a top environmental risk to public health, assessing and managing indoor pollutants have become the focus of integrated governmental and private efforts. Recent increases in building-related illnesses and "sick building syndrome," as well as an increasing number of related legal cases, have further heightened awareness of indoor air quality (IAQ) among building owners and occupants.[5] Strategies to improve indoor environmental quality have the potential to reduce liability for building owners, increase the resale value of the building, and improve the health of building occupants.

For schools and schoolchildren, indoor environmental quality issues are even more urgent. Many pollutants cause adverse health reactions in the estimated 7 million children and adolescents who suffer from asthma,[6] contributing to 14.7 million days of absence in schools each year.[7] In fact, asthma is the leading chronic illness and chief cause of absenteeism among school-aged children.[8] In the United States, more than 56 million children[9] and 7.1 million teachers[10] spend a considerable amount of time in school buildings. The indoor environmental quality in these buildings can have a significant effect on the health and well-being of students and staff, as well as on the quality and effectiveness of the learning environment.

Compared with adults, children are at greater risk of exposure to and possible illness from environmental hazards because of their greater sensitivity during development and growth. In addition to upper respiratory infections and asthma, continuous exposure to pollutants can cause symptoms such as nausea, dizziness, headaches, lethargy, inattentiveness, and irritation of the eyes, nose, and throat. Continuous exposure to hazardous substances can also lead to learning disabilities, cancers, and illnesses caused by damage to the nervous system.

In addition to health and liability concerns, productivity gains also drive indoor environmental quality improvements. With employees' salaries a significant cost in any commercial building, it makes good business sense to keep staff healthy and productive by improving and maintaining the quality of the indoor environment. The potential annual savings and productivity gains from improved indoor environmental quality in the United States are estimated at $6 billion to $14 billion from reduced respiratory disease, $1 billion to $4 billion from reduced allergies and asthma, $10 billion to $30 billion from reduced sick building syndrome symptoms, and $20 billion to $160 billion from direct improvements in worker performance that are unrelated to health.[11]

Over the past 20 years, research and experience have improved our understanding of what is involved in attaining high indoor environmental quality and revealed manufacturing and construction practices that can prevent many indoor environmental quality problems. The use of better products and practices has reduced potential liability for design team members and building owners, increased market value for buildings with exemplary indoor environmental quality, and boosted the productivity of building occupants. In a case study included in the 1994 publication, "Greening the Building and the Bottom Line," the Rocky Mountain Institute highlights how improved indoor environmental quality increased worker productivity by 16%, netting a rapid payback on the capital investment.[12]

This credit category addresses environmental concerns relating to indoor environmental quality; occupants' health, safety, and comfort; energy consumption; air change effectiveness; and air contaminant management. The following are important strategies for addressing these concerns and improving indoor environmental quality:

Improving Ventilation

Actions that affect employee attendance and productivity will affect an organization's bottom line. One study estimates a 283% return on investment associated with increased ventilation in less than 6 months.[13]

Specify building systems that will provide a high level of indoor air quality. Increased ventilation in buildings may require additional energy use, but the need for additional energy can be mitigated by using heat-recovery ventilation and/or economizing strategies. Indoor air quality design can help take advantage of regional climate characteristics and reduce energy costs. In regions with significant heating and/or cooling loads, for example, using exhaust air to heat or cool the incoming air can significantly reduce energy use and operating costs.

Managing Air Contaminants

Protecting indoor environments from contaminants is essential for maintaining a healthy space for building occupants. Several indoor air contaminants should be reduced to optimize tenants' comfort and health. There are 3 basic contaminants:

Environmental tobacco smoke (ETS), or secondhand smoke, is both the smoke given off by ignited tobacco products and the smoke exhaled by smokers. Environmental tobacco smoke contains thousands of chemicals, more than 50 of which are carcinogenic.[14] Exposure to environmental tobacco smoke is linked to an increased risk of lung cancer and heart disease in nonsmoking adults[15] and associated with increased risk of sudden infant death syndrome and asthma, bronchitis, and pneumonia in children.[16] Smoking should be eliminated in all indoor building spaces and limited to designated outdoor areas.

Carbon dioxide (CO_2) concentrations can be measured to determine and maintain adequate outdoor air ventilation rates in buildings. CO_2 concentrations are an indicator of air change effectiveness. Elevated levels suggest inadequate ventilation and possible buildup of indoor air pollutants. CO_2 levels should be measured to validate indications that ventilation rates need to be adjusted. Although relatively high concentrations of CO_2 alone are not known to cause serious health problems, they can lead to drowsiness and lethargy in building occupants.[17]

Particulate matter in the air degrades the indoor environment. Airborne particles in indoor environments include lint, dirt, carpet fibers, dust, dust mites, mold, bacteria, pollen, and animal dander. These particles can exacerbate respiratory problems such as allergies, asthma, emphysema, and chronic lung disease.[18] Air filtration reduces the exposure of building occupants to these airborne contaminants, and high-efficiency filters greatly improve indoor air quality. Protecting air handling systems during construction and flushing the building before occupancy further reduce the potential for problems to arise once the building is occupied.

Specifying Less Harmful Materials

Preventing indoor environmental quality problems is generally much more effective and less expensive than identifying and solving them after they occur. A practical way to prevent indoor environmental quality problems is to specify materials that release fewer and less harmful chemical compounds. Adhesives, paints, carpets, composite wood products, and furniture with low levels of potentially irritating off-gassing can reduce occupants' exposure and harm. Appropriate scheduling of deliveries and sequencing of construction activities can reduce material exposure to moisture and absorption of off-gassed contaminants.

Allowing Occupants to Control Desired Settings

Working with building occupants to assess their needs will help improve building efficiencies. Providing individual lighting controls and area thermostats can improve occupants' comfort and productivity and save energy. Individual controls enable occupants to set light levels appropriate to tasks, time of day, personal preferences, and individual variations in visual acuity. Individual thermostats enable them to more accurately meet their heating and cooling needs during different seasons.

Providing Daylight and Views

Daylighting reduces the need for electric lighting, which lowers energy use and thereby decreases the environmental effects of energy production and consumption. Natural daylight also increases occupants' productivity and reduces absenteeism and illness. Studies have shown that providing daylight and exterior views can measurably increase academic performance in schools. Courtyards, atria, clerestory windows, skylights, interior light shelves, exterior fins, louvers, and adjustable blinds, used alone or in combination, are effective strategies to achieve deep daylight penetration. The desired amount of daylight depends on the tasks in a given space. Daylit buildings often have several daylight zones with differing target light levels. In addition to light levels, daylighting strategies affect interior color schemes, direct beam penetration, and integration with the electric lighting system.

Building occupants with access to outside views have an increased sense of well-being, leading to higher productivity and increased job satisfaction. Important considerations for providing views include building orientation, window size and spacing, glass selection, and locations of interior walls.

CS In their design and construction, core and shell projects can affect indoor air quality in 2 ways. First, the design and construction teams can influence the quality of interior spaces, such as lobbies, central circulation areas, and building cores. Second, and more important, Core & Shell design and construction decisions can directly affect the indoor environmental quality of tenant spaces outside the control of the Core & Shell submittal. Examples include ventilation design and careful design consideration for tenants' ability to optimize daylight and views. Design and construction teams in Core & Shell projects should consider how their decisions could enable tenant fit-outs to deliver high indoor environmental quality to building occupants.

SCHOOLS

Reduce Background Noise and Provide Good Acoustics in Schools

Creating a high-performance acoustic environment is important in learning spaces because human communication is a primary foundation of learning. Minimizing background noise and optimizing acoustics through careful design and material choices enable effective teacher-to-student and student-to-student communication.

Compliant Space Types for Indoor Environmental Quality Credits

The following list identifies school spaces considered to be regularly occupied for applicability to indoor environmental quality credits. In these spaces, daylight, views, thermal comfort, and/or acoustics affect the quality of occupants' regular use. LEED will evaluate exceptions to these classifications on a case-by-case basis for spaces with atypical uses or those in which the strategies required for compliance may compromise the function of the space.

Regularly Occupied Spaces: Classroom and Core Learning

This category consists of spaces that are used for at least 1 hour per day for educational activities where the primary functions are teaching and learning:

- art
- band
- biology lab
- chemistry lab
- chorus
- classroom
- computer lab
- gymnasium
- instructional technology
- instrument instruction
- language lab or arts
- library
- media center
- observatory
- physical education
- physics lab
- vocational arts
- voice instruction

Other Regularly Occupied Spaces

This category includes all nonlearning spaces that are used by occupants for 1 or more hours per day to perform work-related activities:

- administrative conference room
- administrative office
- administrative staff room
- cafeteria, cafetorium
- counseling conference room
- counselor's office
- custodial office
- faculty office
- faculty workroom
- kitchen
- maintenance staff room
- natatorium
- school nurse's office
- school nurse's treatment room
- school security office
- staff dining room
- staff lounge

Spaces Not Regularly Occupied

Spaces considered not regularly occupied are those that occupants pass through and those that are not regularly used for at least 1 hour per day:

- administration waiting room
- auditorium
- back stage
- corridor
- greenhouse
- locker room
- main entrance
- receiving area
- secondary entrance
- stage
- stairs
- students' activity room
- students' locker area

Summary

Ensuring excellent indoor environmental quality requires the joint efforts of the building owner, design team, contractors, subcontractors, and suppliers. To provide optimal indoor environmental quality, automatic sensors and individual controls can be integrated with the building systems to adjust temperature, humidity, and ventilation. Sensors can measure building CO_2 levels and indicate the need for increased outdoor airflow to eliminate high leels of volatile organic compounds (VOCs) and other air contaminants. Other indoor environmental quality issues addressed by the LEED New Construction, Core & Shell, and Schools rating systems include daylighting and lighting quality, thermal comfort, acoustics, and access to views. These issues all have the potential to enhance the indoor environment and optimize interior spaces for building occupants.

CREDIT	TITLE	NC	SCHOOLS	CS
IEQ Prerequisite 1	Minimum Indoor Air Quality Performance	Required	Required	Required
IEQ Prerequisite 2	Environmental Tobacco Smoke (ETS) Control	Required	Required	Required
IEQ Prerequisite 3	Minimum Acoustical Performance	NA	Required	NA
IEQ Credit 1	Outdoor Air Delivery Monitoring	1 point	1 point	1 point
IEQ Credit 2	Increased Ventilation	1 point	1 point	1 point
IEQ Credit 3.1	Construction Indoor Air Quality Management Plan During Construction	1 point	1 point	NA
IEQ Credit 3	Construction Indoor Air Quality Management Plan During Construction	NA	NA	1 point
IEQ Credit 3.2	Construction Indoor Air Quality Management Plan Before Occupancy	1 point	1 point	NA
IEQ Credit 4.1	Low-Emitting Materials—Adhesives and Sealants	1 point	1 point*	1 point
IEQ Credit 4.2	Low-Emitting Materials—Paints and Coatings	1 point	1 point*	1 point
IEQ Credit 4.3	Low-Emitting Materials—Flooring Systems	1 point	1 point*	1 point
IEQ Credit 4.4	Low-Emitting Materials—Composite Wood and Agrifiber Products	1 point	1 point*	1 point
IEQ Credit 4.5	Low-Emitting Materials—Furniture and Furnishings	NA	1 point*	NA
IEQ Credit 4.6	Low-Emitting Materials—Ceiling and Wall Systems	NA	1 point*	NA
IEQ Credit 5	Indoor Chemical and Pollutant Source Control	1 point	1 point	1 point
IEQ Credit 6.1	Controllability of Systems—Lighting	1 point	1 point	NA
IEQ Credit 6.2	Controllability of Systems—Thermal Comfort	1 point	1 point	NA
IEQ Credit 6	Controllability of Systems—Thermal Comfort	NA	NA	1 point
IEQ Credit 7.1	Thermal Comfort—Design	1 point	1 point	NA
IEQ Credit 7	Thermal Comfort—Design	NA	NA	1 point
IEQ Credit 7.2	Thermal Comfort—Verification	1 point	1 point	NA
IEQ Credit 8.1	Daylight and Views—Daylight	1 point	1-3 points	1 point
IEQ Credit 8.2	Daylight and Views—Views	1 point	1-3 points	1 point
IEQ Credit 9	Enhanced Acoustical Performance	NA	1 point	NA
IEQ Credit 10	Mold Prevention	NA	1 point	NA

* note: Schools projects may choose from IEQ Credits 4.1-4.6 for a maximum of 4 points.

MINIMUM INDOOR AIR QUALITY PERFORMANCE

	NC	SCHOOLS	CS
Prerequisite	IEQ Prerequisite 1	IEQ Prerequisite 1	IEQ Prerequisite 1
Points	Required	Required	Required

Intent

To establish minimum indoor air quality (IAQ) performance to enhance indoor air quality in buildings, thus contributing to the comfort and well-being of the occupants.

Requirements

NC, SCHOOLS & CS

CASE 1. Mechanically Ventilated Spaces

Meet the minimum requirements of Sections 4 through 7 of ASHRAE Standard 62.1-2007, Ventilation for Acceptable Indoor Air Quality (with errata but without addenda[1]). Mechanical ventilation systems must be designed using the ventilation rate procedure or the applicable local code, whichever is more stringent.

CS Additional Requirement

Mechanical ventilation systems installed during core and shell construction must be capable of meeting projected ventilation levels based on anticipated future tenant requirements.

CASE 2. Naturally Ventilated Spaces

Naturally ventilated buildings must comply with ASHRAE Standard 62.1-2007, Paragraph 5.1 (with errata but without addenda[1]).

---

1   Project teams wishing to use ASHRAE approved addenda for the purposes of this prerequisite may do so at their discretion. Addenda must be applied consistently across all LEED credits.

	IEQ
NC	Prerequisite 1
SCHOOLS	Prerequisite 1
CS	Prerequisite 1

1. Benefits and Issues to Consider

Minimum indoor air quality (IAQ) performance in buildings improves occupant comfort, well-being, and productivity compared with buildings with poor IAQ performance. Key strategies for maintaining minimum IAQ include limiting potential indoor contaminant sources, limiting the introduction of contaminants from potential outdoor sources, and—most importantly—determining and maintaining at least the minimum zone outdoor airflow and the minimum outdoor air intake flow required by the ventilation rate procedure of Standard 62.1–2007.

Environmental Issues

Providing minimum IAQ performance improves IAQ generally. Doing so can require higher energy use to operate compliant HVAC systems compared with systems that do not meet the ventilation guidelines of ASHRAE 62.1–2007. Compared with the personnel costs of the occupants, any premium associated with ensuring IAQ is insignificant. Poor IAQ can cause occupant illness, and the additional energy cost of ensuring IAQ may be offset by improved occupant productivity and lower absentee rates. The USGBC website (http://www.usgbc.org) provides links to recent studies on this issue.

Economic Issues

Because ASHRAE 62.1–2007 is the required standard for ventilation design for many areas, no additional design effort or cost will be required to meet this prerequisite in general. Its successful implementation reduces potential liability regarding IAQ issues for architects, builders, owners, building operators, and occupants.

2. Related Credits

Some IAQ problems can be solved by diluting contaminant concentration, but this strategy may affect indoor thermal comfort and increase energy use. The building commissioning and measurement and verification processes are tools that can be used to improve IAQ while minimizing energy efficiency losses, as described in the following:

- EA Prerequisite 1: Fundamental Commissioning
- EA Credit 3: Enhanced Commissioning
- EA Credit 5: Measurement and Verification

Dense neighborhoods and heavy traffic as well as existing site contamination can adversely affect the quality of outside air for ventilation. Refer to these 2 credits:

- SS Credit 4: Alternative Transportation,
- SS Credit 3: Brownfield Redevelopment

To reduce the detrimental effects some materials have on IAQ, follow the guidelines of the prerequisites and credits below and specify materials and furnishings that do not release harmful or irritating chemicals, such as volatile organic compounds (VOCs) from paints and solvents. Occupants' activities such as chemical handling and smoking can also affect air quality.

- IEQ Credits 4: Low-Emitting Materials
- IEQ Credit 5: Indoor Chemical and Pollutant Source Control
- IEQ Prerequisite 2: Environmental Tobacco Smoke (ETS) Control

3. Summary of Referenced Standard

American National Standards Institute (ANIS)/ ASHRAE Standard 62.1–2007: Ventilation for Acceptable Indoor Air Quality

American Society of Heating, Refrigerating, and Air-Conditioning Engineers

This standard specifies minimum ventilation rates and IAQ levels so as to reduce the potential for adverse health effects. The standard specifies that ventilation systems be designed to prevent uptake of contaminants, minimize growth and dissemination of microorganisms, and if necessary, filter particulates.

The standard outlines a ventilation rate procedure and an IAQ procedure for compliance. The ventilation rate procedure prescribes outdoor air quality levels acceptable for ventilation; treatment measures for contaminated outdoor air; and ventilation rates for residential, commercial, institutional, vehicular, and industrial spaces. The IAQ procedure is a performance-based design approach in which the building and its ventilation system maintain concentrations of specific contaminants at or below certain determined limits to achieve an indoor air quality acceptable to building occupants and/or visitors. For the purposes of this procedure, acceptable perceived indoor air quality means there is no dissatisfaction related to thermal comfort, noise and vibration, lighting, and psychological stressors. The IAQ procedure also includes criteria for the following situations: reducing outdoor air quantities when recirculated air is treated by contaminant-removal equipment, and ventilating when a space's air volume is used as a reservoir to dilute contaminants. The IAQ procedure incorporates quantitative and subjective evaluation and restricts contaminant concentrations to acceptable levels.

ASHRAE updated the standard in 2007 to include requirements for buildings that allow smoking in designated areas to separate areas with environmental tobacco smoke (ETS) from those without ETS. The standard now also clarifies how designers must analyze mechanical cooling systems to limit indoor relative humidity that would cause dampness-related problems such as mold and microbial growth.

	IEQ
NC	Prerequisite 1
SCHOOLS	Prerequisite 1
CS	Prerequisite 1

4. Implementation

Local code can be used in lieu of ASHRAE when the local code is more stringent. For the purposes of this credit, the code that requires providing more outside air is considered more stringent. Mechanical and natural ventilation systems should provide adequate outside air to building occupants. Underventilated buildings may be stuffy, odorous, uncomfortable, and/or unhealthful for occupants. ASHRAE 62.1–2007 establishes minimum requirements for ventilation air rates in various types of occupied zones and building ventilation systems. The standard takes into account an area's square footage, number of occupants and their activities, and the ventilation system.

Strategies

There are 3 basic methods for ventilating buildings:

- mechanical ventilation (i.e., active ventilation);

- natural ventilation (i.e., passive ventilation); and

- mixed-mode ventilation (i.e., both mechanical and natural ventilation).

Mechanically Ventilated Spaces: Ventilation Rate Procedure

For mechanical ventilation systems, ASHRAE 62.1–2007, Section 6, explains how to determine the minimum required ventilation rates for various applications, using either the ventilation rate procedure or the indoor air quality procedure. The ventilation rate procedure is easier to apply and used more frequently and is the prescribed approach for this prerequisite.

The ventilation rate procedure methodology is found in Section 6.2 of ASHRAE 62.1–2007. The standard's Table 6-1, Minimum Ventilation Rates in Breathing Zone, explains how to determine both the amount of outdoor air needed to ventilate people-related source contaminants and area-related source contaminants for various by occupancy categories. The outdoor air rate for people-related

IEQ	
NC	Prerequisite 1
SCHOOLS	Prerequisite 1
CS	Prerequisite 1

source contaminants takes into account the number of occupants and their activities. The area-related sources portion accounts for background off-gassing from building materials, furniture, and materials typically found in that particular occupancy. Finally, the required zone outdoor airflow is the breathing zone outdoor airflow adjusted to reflect the "zone air distribution effectiveness" using adjustment factors in Table 6-2 of the standard. For multiple-zone systems, outdoor air intake flow is adjusted to reflect the "system ventilation efficiency" of the air distribution configuration, using adjustment factors in Table 6-3 of the standard.

If an occupancy category is not included in ASHRAE 62.1–2007, it is up to the the designer to choose 1 that best corresponds to the usage of the space. Explain the rationale for the selection in the submission. Spaces that do not qualify as occupiable spaces are not necessarily excluded from ventilation rate procedure calculations. Additional ventilation and odor or pollutant control might be necessary to meet this prerequisite.

Naturally Ventilated Spaces

ASHRAE 62.1–2007, Section 5.1, provides requirements on the location and size of ventilation openings for naturally ventilated buildings. All naturally ventilated spaces must be within 25 feet of (and permanently open to) operable wall or roof openings to the outdoors; the operable area also must be at least 4% of the space's net occupiable floor area. Interior spaces without direct openings to the outdoors can be ventilated through adjoining rooms if the openings between rooms are unobstructed and at least 8% or 25 square feet of the area is free. As appropriate, all other nonventilation-related requirements (e.g., exhaust for combustion appliances, outdoor air assessment, and outdoor air intakes) in the standard must be met.

An engineered natural ventilation system can show compliance with acceptable engineering calculations or multinodal bulk airflow simulation.

Mixed-Mode Ventilated Spaces

For mixed-mode ventilated spaces and hybrid ventilation systems, meet the minimum ventilation rates required by Chapter 6 of ASHRAE 62.1–2007 regardless of ventilation mode (natural ventilation, mechanical ventilation, or both mechanical and natural ventilation). Project teams can use any acceptable engineering calculation methodology to demonstrate compliance.

CS Core & Shell buildings may not have final occupancy counts. Projects that do not have occupancy counts must use the default occupant densities provided in ASHRAE 62.1–2007 Table 6-1, based on the intended use of the space. Projects that do have tenant occupancy counts must use these numbers as long as the gross square footage per occupant is not greater than that in the default occupant density in Table 6.1.

Sometimes both occupancy of the building and distribution of occupancy are unknown. Occupancy distribution is for calculating the percentage of outside air on a system level under ASHRAE 62.1–2007. For the Core & Shell project, it is usually necessary to determine the system level outside air without the distribution of people. For example, a typical office building has office and conference room space, and the conference rooms require more outdoor air than the offices. If these spaces are all on the same system, the system-level outside air must be increased to account for the outside air requirements of the conference rooms. The location of conference rooms and other densely occupied spaces will be unknown in a core and shell building. For the sake of the calculations, assume a reasonable distribution of people.

5. Timeline and Team

Early in the design process, the architect and mechanical engineer teams determine and design the most appropriate ventilation system for the project building. The design team may include the building owner, tenants, facility manager, and maintenance personnel as applicable; these team members should be present in the design meetings to share ideas on the building owner's needs, special requirement areas, zone categories, occupant density, and occupant needs.

6. Calculations

For mechanically ventilated spaces, calculations pertaining to the ventilation rate procedure (VRP) methodology are found in Section 6.2 of ASHRAE 62.1–2007. The breathing zone outdoor airflow is equal to the sum of the outdoor airflow rate required per person times the zone population, plus the outdoor airflow rate required per unit area times the zone floor area.

Breathing zone outdoor airflow is the design outdoor airflow required in the breathing zone of the occupied space or spaces in a zone and is calculated as follows:

$$V_{bz} = R_p \times P_z + R_a \times A_z$$

Where:

R_p = outdoor airflow rate required per person as determined from Table 6-1 in ASHRAE 62.1–2007;

P_z = zone population; the largest number of people expected to occupy the zone during typical usage;

R_a = outdoor airflow rate required per unit area as determined from Table 6-1 in ASHRAE 62.1–2007; and

A_z = zone floor area; the net occupied floor area of the zone.

Zone outdoor airflow is the outdoor airflow that must be provided to the zone by the supply air distribution system and is calculated as follows:

$$V_{oz} = \frac{V_{bz}}{E_z}$$

Where:

E_z = Zone air distribution effectiveness as determined from Table 6-2 in ASHRAE 62.1–2007.

For **single-zone systems**, in which 1 air handler supplies a mixture of outdoor air and recirculated air to only 1 zone, the **outdoor air intake flow** is $(V_{ot}) = V_{oz}$.

For 100% **outdoor air systems**, in which 1 air handler supplies only outdoor air to 1 or more zones, $V_{ot} = \sum$ all zones x V_{oz}.

For **multiple-zone recirculating systems**, in which 1 air handler supplies a mixture of outdoor air and recirculated return air to more than 1 zone, calculate the **outdoor air intake flow** (V_{ot}) as follows:

- Determine the **zone primary outdoor air fraction** $(Z_p) = V_{oz}/V_{pz}$, where **Vpz** is the **zone primary airflow** (i.e., the primary airflow to the zone from the air handler, including outdoor air and recirculated air). For VAV systems, V_{pz} is the minimum expected primary airflow for design purposes.

- Determine the **system ventilation efficiency** (**Ev**) from Table 6-3 in ASHRAE 62.1–2007.

- Determine the **uncorrected outdoor air intake** (**Vou**) = $D \sum$all zones $(R_p)(P_z) + \sum$all zones R_aA_z, where the **occupant diversity** (**D**) may be used to account for variations in occupancy within zones served by the same system: $D = P_s / \sum$all zones P_z, and where P_s is the **system population**, the total population in the area served by the system.

The outdoor air intake flow for the multiple-zone recirculating system may then be determined by this calculation:

$$V_{ot} = \frac{V_{ou}}{E_v}$$

7. Documentation Guidance

As a first step in preparing to complete the LEED-Online documentation requirements, work through the following measures. Refer to LEED-Online for the complete descriptions of all required documentation.

- Demonstrate compliance with the applicable sections of ASHRAE 62.1–2007; see Calculations.

- For Core & Shell projects, create a description of future tenants, space types, and expected uses.

8. Examples

The following are examples of the ASHRAE 62.1–2007 ventilation rate procedure calculations. Refer to the ASHRAE standard for project-specific applications.

Table 1. Sample Summary Calculations for Determining Outdoor Air Ventilation Rates

Zone	Occupancy Category	Outdoor Airflow Rate Required per Person (Rp)	Zone Population (Pz)	Outdoor Airflow Rate Required per Unit Area (Ra)	Zone Floor Area (Az)	Zone Air Distribution Effectiveness (Ez)	Breathing Zone Outdoor Airflow (Vbz)
VAV-1	Office space	5	8	0.06	310	1.0	59
VAV-2	Conference room	5	10	0.06	270	1.0	66

Table 2. Ventilation Rate Procedure for Multiple-Zone, Variable-Volume System

Inputs for Potentially Critical Zones

Zone Name			Corner Open Office	North Conference Room
		Zone title turns purple italic for critical zones(s)		
Zone Tag			VAV-1	VAV-2
Space type		Select from pull-down list	Office space	Conference meeting
Floor Area of zone	Az	sf	310	270
Design population of zone	Pz	P (default value listed; may be overridden)	8	7
Design discharge airflow to zone (total primary plus local recirculated)	Vdzd	cfm	590	30
Induction Terminal Unit, Dual Fan Dual Duct or Transfer Fan?		Select from pull-down list or leave blank if N/A	ITU	ITU
Local recirc. air fraction representative of ave system return air	Er		0.50	0.5
Inputs for Operating Condition Analyzed				
Percent of total design airflow rate at conditioned analyzed	Ds	%	100%	100%
Air distribution type at conditioned anlayzed		Select from pull-down list	CS	CS
Zone air distribution effectiveness at conditioned analyzed	Ez		1.00	1.00
Primary air fraction of supply air at conditioned analyzed	Ep		.95	.9

Potentially Critical Zones										
North Conference Room	North Private Office	Corner Open Office	South Private Office	Reception	West Open Office	East Private Office	Interior Private Office	Interior Private Office	Interior Conference Room	Server Room
VAV-2	VAV-3	VAV-4	VAV-5	VAV-6	VAV-7	VAV-8	VAV-9	VAV-10	VAV-11	VAV12
conference/meeting	Office Space	Office Space	Office Space	Reception areas	Office Space	Office Space	Office Space	Office Space	Conference/meeting	Computer (not printing)
270	107	310	165	258	347	140	65	65	220	140
10	1	8	1	3.5	5	1	1	1	8	0
300	120	465	215	250	450	155	50	50	200	50
ITU	ITU	ITU	ITU	ITU	ITU	ITU	ITU	ITU	ITU	ITU
.50	.50	.50	.50	.50	.50	.50	.50	.50	.50	.50
100%	100%	100%	100%	100%	100%	100%	100%	100%	100%	100%
CS	CS	CS	CS	CS	CS	CS	CS	CS	CS	CS
1.00	1.00	1.00	1.00	1.00	1.00	1.00	1.00	1.00	1.00	1.00
0.90	0.90	0.90	0.90	0.90	0.90	0.80	0.70	0.70	0.75	0.80

Table 3. Results from Ventilation Rate Procedure

Results		
System Ventilation Efficiency	Ev	0.78
Outdoor air intake airflow rate required at condition analyzed	Vot	331 cfm
Outdoor air intake rate per unit floor area	Vot/As	0.14 cfm/sf
Outdoor air intake rate per person served by system (including diversity)	Vot/Ps	14.4 cfm/p
Outdoor air intake rate as a % of design primary supply air	Vot/Vpsd	13%
Uncorrected outdoor air intake airflow rate	Vou	259 cfm

	IEQ
NC	Prerequisite 1
SCHOOLS	Prerequisite 1
CS	Prerequisite 1

Table 4. Sample Summary Calculations for Naturally Ventilated Spaces

Zone	Floor Area (sf)	Natural Ventilation Opening Area (sf)	Opening Areas as Percentage of Floor Area	Is Distance to Opening 25 Feet or Less?
General office	8,000	336	4.20	Yes
Training room	750	32	4.30	Yes
Break room	216	12	5.60	Yes

9. Exemplary Performance

This prerequisite is not eligible for exemplary performance under the Innovation in Design section.

10. Regional Variations

There are no regional variations associated with this prerequisite.

11. Operations and Maintenance Considerations

For mechanically ventilated systems, provide the building operator with copies of the ventilation rate procedure calculations for each zone used to show compliance with ASHRAE 62.1–2007. Over the building's life, these can be updated with actual occupancy values to adjust delivered ventilation rates as appropriate.

Provide maintenance personnel with the information needed to understand, maintain, and adjust the ventilation system, and retain mechanical design documents showing zone configurations. Include appropriate setpoints, control sequences, and recommendations for typical corrective actions in the facility's building operating plan and sequence of operations document. Establish procedures and schedules for testing and maintaining exhaust systems and include them in the building's preventive maintenance plan.

12. Resources

Please see USGBC's LEED Registered Project Tools (http://www.usgbc.org/projecttools) for additional resources and technical information.

Websites
American Society of Heating, Refrigerating, and Air-Conditioning Engineers (ASHRAE)
http://www.ashrae.org
ASHRAE advances the science of heating, ventilation, air conditioning, and refrigeration for the public's benefit through research, standards writing, continuing education, and publications. To purchase ASHRAE standards and guidelines, visit the bookstore on the ASHRAE website.

U.S. EPA's Indoor Air Quality website

http://www.epa.gov/iaq

EPA's IAQ website includes a variety of tools, publications, and links to address IAQ concerns in schools and large buildings.

13. Definitions

Active ventilation is synonymous with mechanical ventilation.

Air-conditioning is the process of treating air to meet the requirements of a conditioned space by controlling its temperature, humidity, cleanliness, and distribution. (ASHRAE 62.1–2007)

The **breathing zone** is the region within an occupied space between 3 and 6 feet above the floor and more than 2 feet from walls or fixed air-conditioning equipment. (AHSRAE 62.1–2007)

Contaminants are unwanted airborne elements that may reduce air quality. (ASHRAE 62.1–2007)

Indoor air quality (**IAQ**) is the nature of air inside a building that affects the health and well-being of building occupants. It is considered acceptable when there are no known contaminants at harmful concentrations as determined by cognizant authorities and with which a substantial majority (80% or more) of the people exposed do not express dissatisfaction. (ASHRAE 62.1–2007)

Mechanical ventilation, or active ventilation, is provided by mechanically powered equipment such as motor-driven fans and blowers, but not by devices such as wind-driven turbine ventilators and mechanically operated windows. (ASHRAE 62.1–2007)

Mixed-mode ventilation combines mechanical and natural ventilation methods.

Natural ventilation, or passive ventilation, is provided by thermal, wind, or diffusion effects through doors, windows, or other intentional openings in the building. (ASHRAE 62.1–2007)

Off-gassing is the emission of volatile organic compounds (VOCs) from synthetic and natural products.

Outdoor air is the ambient air that enters a building through a ventilation system, either through natural ventilation or by infiltration (ASHRAE 62.1–2007).

Passive ventilation uses the building layout, fabric, and form to provide natural ventilation to a conditioned space using nonmechanical forms of heat transfer and air movement.

Thermal comfort exists when occupants express satisfaction with the thermal environment.

Ventilation is the process of supplying air to or removing air from a space for the purpose of controlling air contaminant levels, humidity, or temperature within the space. (ASHRAE 62.1-2007).

	NC	SCHOOLS	CS
Prerequisite	IEQ Prerequisite 2	IEQ Prerequisite 2	IEQ Prerequisite 2
Points	Required	Required	Required

Intent

NC & CS

To prevent or minimize exposure of building occupants, indoor surfaces and ventilation air distribution systems to environmental tobacco smoke (ETS).

SCHOOLS

To eliminate exposure of building occupants, indoor surfaces, and ventilation air distribution systems to environmental tobacco smoke (ETS).

Requirements

NC & CS

CASE 1. All Projects

OPTION 1

Prohibit smoking in the building.

Prohibit on-property smoking within 25 feet of entries, outdoor air intakes and operable windows. Provide signage to allow smoking in designated areas, prohibit smoking in designated areas or prohibit smoking on the entire property.

OR

OPTION 2

Prohibit smoking in the building except in designated smoking areas.

Prohibit on-property smoking within 25 feet of entries, outdoor air intakes and operable windows. Provide signage to allow smoking in designated areas, prohibit smoking in designated areas or prohibit smoking on the entire property.

Provide designated smoking rooms designed to contain, capture and remove ETS from the building. At a minimum, the smoking room must be directly exhausted to the outdoors, away from air intakes and building entry paths, with no recirculation of ETS-containing air to nonsmoking areas and enclosed with impermeable deck-to-deck partitions. Operate exhaust sufficient to create a negative pressure differential with the surrounding spaces of at least an average of 5 Pascals (Pa) (0.02 inches of water gauge) and a minimum of 1 Pa (0.004 inches of water gauge) when the doors to the smoking rooms are closed.

Verify performance of the smoking rooms' differential air pressures by conducting 15 minutes of measurement, with a minimum of 1 measurement every 10 seconds, of the differential pressure in the smoking room with respect to each adjacent area and in each adjacent vertical chase with the doors to the smoking room closed. Conduct the testing with each space configured for worst-case conditions of transport of air from the smoking rooms (with closed doors) to adjacent spaces.

CASE 2. Residential and Hospitality Projects Only

Prohibit smoking in all common areas of the building.

Locate any exterior designated smoking areas, including balconies where smoking is permitted, at least 25 feet from entries, outdoor air intakes and operable windows opening to common areas.

Prohibit on-property smoking within 25 feet of entries, outdoor air intakes and operable windows. Provide signage to allow smoking in designated areas, prohibit smoking in designated areas or prohibit smoking on the entire property.

Weather-strip all exterior doors and operable windows in the residential units to minimize leakage from outdoors.

Minimize uncontrolled pathways for ETS transfer between individual residential units by sealing penetrations in walls, ceilings and floors in the residential units and by sealing vertical chases adjacent to the units.

Weather-strip all doors in the residential units leading to common hallways to minimize air leakage into the hallway[1].

Demonstrate acceptable sealing of residential units by a blower door test conducted in accordance with ANSI/ASTM-E779-03, Standard Test Method for Determining Air Leakage Rate By Fan Pressurization.

Use the progressive sampling methodology defined in Chapter 4 (Compliance Through Quality Construction) of the Residential Manual for Compliance with California's 2001 Energy Efficiency Standards (http://www.energy.ca.gov/title24/residential_manual). Residential units must demonstrate less than 1.25 square inches leakage area per 100 square feet of enclosure area (i.e., sum of all wall, ceiling and floor areas).

Prohibit smoking in the building.

Prohibit on-property smoking within 25 feet from entries, outdoor air intakes and operable windows. Provide signage to allow smoking in designated areas, prohibit smoking in designated areas or prohibit smoking on the entire property.

1   If the common hallways are pressurized with respect to the residential units then doors in the residential units leading to the common hallways need not be weather-stripped provided that the positive differential pressure is demonstrated as in Case 1, Option 2 above, considering the residential unit as the smoking room.

1. Benefits and Issues to Consider

The purpose of this prerequisite is to limit the exposure of building occupants to Environmental Tobacco Smoke (ETS), or secondhand smoke. ETS is produced by burning cigarettes, pipes, or cigars. It contains thousands of different compounds, many of which are known carcinogens.[19] By prohibiting smoking indoors, occupants will have less exposure to ETS. Smoking boundaries will increase the quality of air inside the building and around the building perimeter, and will decrease risk to occupants' health.

The relationship between smoking and various health risks, including lung disease, cancer, and heart disease, is well documented. A strong link between ETS and similar health risks has also been demonstrated.

The most effective way to avoid health problems associated with ETS is to prohibit smoking indoors. If this cannot be accomplished, indoor smoking areas must be isolated from nonsmoking areas and have separate ventilation systems to prevent the introduction of tobacco smoke contaminants to nonsmoking areas.

	IEQ
NC	Prerequisite 2
SCHOOLS	Prerequisite 2
CS	Prerequisite 2

Environmental Issues

Separate smoking areas occupy additional space and may result in a larger building, greater material use, and increased energy for ventilation. However, these environmental impacts can be offset by the gains in health and well-being of building occupants who are more comfortable, have higher productivity rates, lower absenteeism, and less illness.

Economic Issues

Providing separate smoking areas adds to the design and construction costs of most projects, and maintaining designated smoking areas also adds to lease and operating costs. Prohibiting indoor smoking can increase the useful life of interior fixtures and furnishings.

Smoking within a building contaminates indoor air and can cause occupant reactions, including irritation, illness, and decreased productivity. These problems increase expenses and liability for building owners, tenants, operators, and insurance companies. Strict no-smoking policies improve the health of the community as a whole, resulting in lower health care and insurance costs.

2. Related Credits

The use of separate ventilation systems to isolate smoking areas from the rest of the building requires additional energy and commissioning, as well as measurement and verification efforts. This prerequisite is related to the following prerequisites and credits:

- EA Prerequisite 1: Fundamental Commissioning
- EA Credit 1: Optimize Energy Performance
- EA Credit 3: Enhanced Commissioning
- EA Credit 5: Measurement and Verification

Because smoking, both indoors and outdoors, affects the IAQ performance of the building, this prerequisite is also related to the following prerequisites and credits:

- IEQ Prerequisite 1: Minimum Indoor Air Quality Performance
- IEQ Credit 1: Outdoor Air Delivery Monitoring
- IEQ Credit 2: Increased Ventilation

Project teams may wish to address smoking-related contaminants in the building in conjunction with other sources of air pollutants, as outlined in the following credits:

IEQ	
NC	Prerequisite 2
SCHOOLS	Prerequisite 2
CS	Prerequisite 2

- IEQ Credit 4: Low-Emitting Materials

- IEQ Credit 5: Indoor Chemical and Pollutant Source Control

3. Summary of Referenced Standards

American National Standards Institute (ANSI)/ASTME-779-03, Standard Test Method for Determining Air Leakage Rate by Fan Pressurization

To purchase this standard, go to: http://www.astm.org

This test method covers a standardized technique for measuring air leakage rates through a building envelope under controlled pressurization and depressurization; it should produce a measurement of the air tightness of a building envelope.

Residential Manual for Compliance with California's 2001 Energy Efficiency Standards (For Low Rise Residential Buildings), Chapter 4

www.energy.ca.gov/title24/archive/2001standards/residential_manual/res_manual_chapter4.PDF

According to this chapter of the manual, "The *Standards* require quality design and construction of mechanical ventilation systems and air distribution systems. They also offer compliance credit for the construction of less leaky building envelopes. With the 2001 *Standards*, testing of ducts, refrigerant charge, and airflow was added to the prescriptive requirements (Package D) and is assumed as part of the standard design in performance calculations. Many of the compliance credit options require installer diagnostic testing and certification, and independent diagnostic testing and field verification by a certified home energy rater."

4. Implementation

Prohibit smoking in the building. Provide appropriately located designated smoking areas outside the building away from building entrances, operable windows, and ventilation systems. These designated areas should also be located away from concentrations of building occupants or pedestrian traffic. Post information about the building's nonsmoking policy for all occupants to read.

If interior smoking areas are incorporated within the building, install separate ventilation systems must be installed test their effectiveness to ensure that they are isolated from the nonsmoking portions of the building.

The design criteria and instructions for Case 1 Option 2 and Case 2 Option 3 are detailed in the credit requirements and the referenced standard for Case 2 Option 3.

CS In many regions of North America, municipal regulations prohibit indoor smoking. In regions where indoor smoking is allowed and a building owner allows some indoor smoking, the smoking area in a core and shell building must carefully follow all of the requirements for smoking areas listed in this prerequisite. It is important to protect other tenants from the environmental tobacco smoke (ETS), so make sure that the smoking area functions as intended. Air from the smoking area must not return to a common HVAC system. The building must accommodate a separate exhaust system that removes ETS from the smoking area. In many buildings, the space for mechanical equipment and chases is limited, so extra space for a separate exhaust system may be difficult to find.

SCHOOLS Providing designated indoor smoking areas is not acceptable for a schools project. School buildings must always be nonsmoking facilities; it is recommended that smoking be prohibited at the site exterior as well.

5. Timeline and Team

The building smoking policy and site smoking policy should be drafted by the facility manager and signed by the facility manager, property manager, or owner. This policy should be in place over the life of the building. Enforcing the building policy is the responsibility of the facility manager. Enforcing the site policy is the responsibility of the groundskeeper. Any building modifications made to accommodate new smoking rooms should be coordinated by the facility manager in consultation with the building owner.

6. Calculations

There are no calculations required for this prerequisite.

7. Documentation Guidance

As a first step in preparing to complete the LEED-Online documentation requirements, work through the following measures. Refer to LEED-Online for the complete descriptions of all required documentation.

- Develop an environmental tobacco smoke policy that details areas where smoking is prohibited.

- Maintain documentation (e.g., site plans and renderings) that visually indicates how the smoking policy has been implemented on-site.

- Track and record testing data for any interior smoking rooms to verify that there is no cross contamination to adjacent spaces.

8. Examples

Figure 1. Compliant Smoking Room

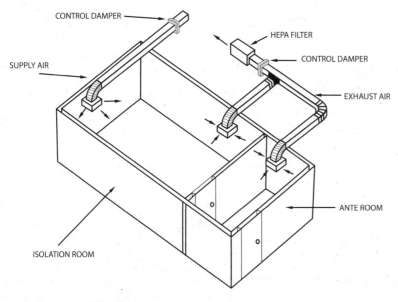

Figure 1 illustrates the degree of isolation required to comply with this prerequisite. The anteroom helps prevent pollutants from entering the rest of the building. Air enters and exits the designated smoking room through control dampers, maintaining a constant flow. Upon exiting, the air may or may not be filtered before exiting the building. Air recirculated into the room is filtered.

9. Exemplary Performance

This credit is not eligible for exemplary performance under the Innovation in Design section.

	IEQ
NC	Prerequisite 2
SCHOOLS	Prerequisite 2
CS	Prerequisite 2

10. Regional Variations

Figure 2. Smoking Bans, by State[20]

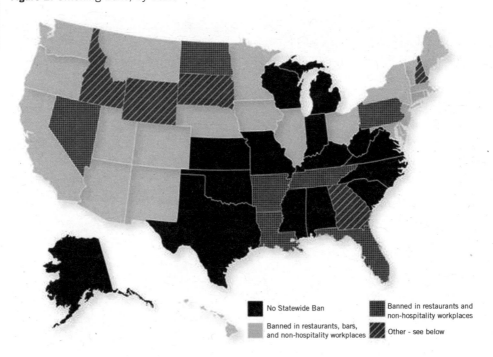

Figure 2 shows how the U.S. states regulate smoking. Idaho has a statewide ban on smoking in restaurants, as does Georgia. South Dakota has a statewide ban on smoking in nonhospitality workplaces. New Hampshire bans smoking in restaurants and bars. Individual cities, counties, or towns may have their own laws on smoking. Consult these laws before establishing a smoking policy for the project building.

11. Operations and Maintenance Considerations

Communicate the building's smoking policy to all occupants, establish a plan for enforcement, and designate the person responsible for implementing the policy.

12. Resources

Please see USGBC's LEED Registered Project Tools (http://www.usgbc.org/projecttools) for additional resources and technical information.

Websites

American National Standards Institute (ANSI)/ASTM–E779–03, Standard Test Method for Determining Air Leakage Rate by Fan Pressurization
To purchase this standard go to: http://www.astm.org
This test method covers a standardized technique for measuring air leakage rates through a building envelope under controlled pressurization and depressurization; it should produce a measurement of the air tightness of a building envelope

California Low-Rise Residential Alternative Calculation Method Approval Manual, Energy Rating Systems (HERS) Required Verification and Diagnostic Testing,
California Energy Commission
http://www.energy.ca.gov/HERS/

Isolation Rooms and Pressurization Control

http://www.engr.psu.edu/AE/iec/abe/control/isolation.asp

Thisdocument describes the engineering involved in negative pressure rooms.

	IEQ
NC	Prerequisite 2
SCHOOLS	Prerequisite 2
CS	Prerequisite 2

Setting the Record Straight: Secondhand Smoke Is a Preventable Health Risk

U.S. EPA

http://www.epa.gov/smokefree/pubs/strsfs.html

This EPA document reviews laboratory research on ETS and federal legislation aimed at curbing ETS-related problems.

Smoke-Free Lists, Maps, and Data

http://www.no-smoke.org/goingsmokefree.php?id=519

These publications from the American Nonsmokers' Rights Foundation describe all of the tobacco control ordinances, by-laws, and board of health regulations.

Secondhand Smoke: What You Can Do about Secondhand Smoke as Parents, Decision Makers, and Building Occupants

U.S. EPA

http://www.ehso.com/ehshome/SmokingEPAFacts.htm

http://www.epa.gov/iedweb00/pubs/#Environmental%20Tobacco%20Smoke (800) 438-4318

This EPA document (reprinted by Environment, Health, and Safety Online) describes the effects of ETS and measures for reducing human exposure to it.

Print Media

The Chemistry of Environmental Tobacco Smoke: Composition and Measurement, 2nd edition, by R.A. Jenkins, B.A. Tomkins, et al. (CRC Press & Lewis Publishers, 2000).

The Smoke-Free Guide: How to Eliminate Tobacco Smoke from Your Environment, by Arlene Galloway (Gordon Soules Book Publishers, 1988).

13. Definitions

Environmental tobacco smoke (**ETS**), or secondhand smoke, consists of airborne particles emitted from the burning end of cigarettes, pipes, and cigars, and is exhaled by smokers. These particles contain about 4,000 different compounds, up to 50 of which are known to cause cancer.

Mechanical ventilation is ventilation provided by mechanically powered equipment, such as motor-driven fans and blowers, but not by devices such as wind-driven turbine ventilators and mechanically operated windows (ASHRAE 62.1–2007).

Ventilation is the process of supplying air to or removing air from a space for the purpose of controlling air contaminant levels, humidity, or temperature within the space. (ASHRAE 62.1-2007).

	NC	SCHOOLS	CS
Prerequisite	NA	IEQ Prerequisite 3	NA
Points	NA	Required	NA

Intent

To provide classrooms that are quiet so that teachers can speak to the class without straining their voices and students can effectively communicate with each other and the teacher.

Requirements

SCHOOLS

Design classrooms and other core learning spaces to include sufficient sound-absorptive finishes for compliance with reverberation time requirements as specified in ANSI Standard S12.60-2002, Acoustical Performance Criteria, Design Requirements and Guidelines for Schools.

Achieve a maximum background noise level[1] from heating, ventilating and air conditioning (HVAC) systems in classrooms and other core learning spaces of 45 dBA.

AND

CASE 1. Classrooms and Core Learning Spaces < 20,000 Cubic Feet

For classrooms and core learning spaces less than 20,000 cubic feet, options for compliance include, but are not limited to the following:

OPTION 1

Confirm that 100% of all ceiling areas (excluding lights, diffusers and grilles) in all classrooms and core learning spaces are finished with a material that has a Noise Reduction Coefficient (NRC) of 0.70 or higher.

OR

OPTION 2

Confirm that the total area of acoustical wall panels, ceiling finishes, and other sound-absorbent finishes equals or exceeds the total ceiling area of the room (excluding lights, diffusers and grilles) Materials must have an NRC of 0.70 or higher to be included in the calculation.

CASE 2. Classrooms and Core Learning Spaces ≥ 20,000 Cubic Feet

For classrooms and core learning spaces 20,000 cubic feet or greater:

Confirm through calculations described in ANSI Standard S12.60-2002 that all classrooms and core learning spaces greater than or equal to 20,000 cubic feet are designed to have a reverberation time of 1.5 seconds or less.

---

1 Recommended methodologies and best practices for mechanical system noise control are described in Annex B of ANSI Standard S12.60-2002 and the 2007 HVAC Applications ASHRAE Handbook, Chapter 47 on Sound and Vibration Control (with errata but without addenda).

	IEQ
NC	NA
SCHOOLS	Prerequisite 3
CS	NA

1. Benefits and Issues to Consider

Environmental Issues

Acoustics is an important consideration in the design of classrooms because it can affect students' learning and performance. Background noise and reverberation tend not to bother adults but have a very different effect on children, whose ability to distinguish sounds is not fully developed.[21] Students who cannot hear effectively are more likely to become distracted, have difficulty retaining information, and have trouble engaging in learning.

Poor classroom acoustics are an additional educational barrier for children with hearing loss and for those who have cochlear implants. Assistive technologies amplify both wanted and unwanted sound and do not improve student-to-teacher or student-to-student communication. According to the Centers for Disease Control and Prevention, children with temporary hearing loss, who account for some 15% of the school-age population, are especially affected, as are children who have speech impairments or learning disabilities.[22]

Economic Issues

Although planning for an effective acoustic environment may require more design attention and additional materials, any increase in cost should be weighed against the significant long-term benefits. These include improved teacher effectiveness and higher levels of student performance, for a higher quality of educational experience. The costs of poor acoustics include teachers' vocal fatigue and absenteeism, and remedial instruction and repeating school years for underperforming students.

Many schools can achieve a healthy acoustical environment with no additional cost. This may be more challenging in urban areas and in schools adjacent to traffic, construction, and other sources of noise.

2. Related Credits

A related credit outlines additional strategies and measures to achieve effective acoustical performance in school buildings:

- IEQ Credit 9: Enhanced Acoustical Performance

3. Summary of Referenced Standards

American National Standards Institute (ANSI)/ASHRAE Standard S12.60–2002, Acoustical Performance Criteria, Design Requirements, and Guidelines for Schools

This standard provides acoustical performance criteria and design requirements for classrooms and other learning spaces. Annexes provide information on good design and construction practices, installation methods, and optional procedures to demonstrate conformance to the acoustical performance and design requirements of this standard. This standard seeks to provide design flexibility without compromising the goal of obtaining adequate speech intelligibility for all students and teachers in classrooms and learning spaces. This standard is available at no charge from the Acoustical Society of America Online Store: http://asastore.aip.org.

ASHRAE Handbook, Chapter 47, Sound and Vibration Control, 2003 HVAC Applications

Because mechanical equipment is a major source of sound in a building, the sound generated by mechanical equipment and its effects on the overall acoustical environment in a building must be considered. Mechanical equipment should be selected and equipment spaces designed with both an emphasis on the intended uses of the equipment and the goal of providing acceptable sound and vibration levels in occupied spaces of the building. This chapter is available separately from the full handbook in the online ASHRAE bookstore at http://www.ashrae.org.

4. Implementation

To provide an acoustical environment that meets the requirements of this prerequisite, designers need to consider 2 primary areas of performance:

	IEQ
NC	NA
SCHOOLS	Prerequisite 3
CS	NA

- low background noise inside the core learning space; and
- reverberation time for core learning spaces.

One measure of acoustical performance is the A-weighted decibel (dBA) measurement of background noise levels. Because noise is measured on a nonlinear scale, an increase of 10 dBA means that noise levels are perceived to be about twice as loud as the previous level. For example, a busy school cafeteria may have a sound level of 80 dBA, and 90 dBA is typical of a jackhammer—twice the volume.

ANSI S12.60-2002 should be used as the guiding document for acoustical design. The standard describes effective methods and strategies for HVAC noise control and for reverberation time calculation and design.

Background Noise Levels

HVAC systems are often the most significant sources of noise inside a building. One way to reduce noise in classrooms is not to install fans, compressors, and other HVAC machinery in or near classrooms. If HVAC units operate inside the building, prevent noise transmission to adjacent rooms. The best way to isolate HVAC noise depends on the type and location of mechanical equipment; these variables should be considered during the design phase of the project. Selecting quieter HVAC systems and locating HVAC units centrally are among the more effective ways to prevent equipment-related noise. Simple ducting of the supply air path and, to a lesser extent, the return-air path will help meet the background noise criteria. Additionally, using acoustic liner in ductwork minimizes sound transmission. The 2007 HVAC Applications ASHRAE Handbook, Chapter 47, Sound and Vibration Control provides detailed methods for reducing noise transmission from HVAC systems.

Other sources of background noise may include light fixtures, classroom computers, plumbing systems, audiovisual equipment, and the building occupants themselves. With careful planning, selection, and design of building systems, background noise can be kept to a minimum.

Reverberation

Too much reverberation in a room causes an echo effect that makes words difficult to understand. Reverberation time (RT) is the time it takes for sound to decay by 60 dB after the sound has stopped. RT has the most effect on speech intelligibility in the 500, 1,000, and 2,000 Hz frequency bands. ANSI S12.60–2002 requires calculation of RT at each of these 3 frequencies.

An appropriate reverberation time can be confirmed in the design phase through calculation, or it can be achieved prescriptively by using sufficient quantities of materials with a specified noise reduction coefficient (NRC). The NRC is a single-number rating for the sound-absorptive properties of a material. It is the arithmetic average of sound absorption coefficients for a material at frequencies of 250, 500, 1,000, and 2,000 Hz. The requirements for NRC rating and quantities of material in classrooms smaller than 20,000 cubic are specified as Option 1 and Option 2 in the Requirements section of this prerequisite.

The following information is required for calculating the RT of a room:

- volume (cubic feet)
- interior surface area (square feet)

- sound absorption coefficient at frequencies of 500, 1,000, and 2,000 Hz for each interior fixed element

- surface area of each interior fixed element

Hard surfaces raise reverberation time in a room, reducing speech intelligibility and increasing overall loudness levels. Hard parallel surfaces, such as 2 walls or a floor and hard-finish ceiling, can cause "flutter echoes" as the sound bounces back and forth between them. Adding absorptive materials to 1 or both surfaces helps reduce flutter echoes. Absorptive materials can be alternated with sections of bare wall on parallel surfaces, with each section of bare wall facing a section of absorptive material on the other wall. Adding materials for diffusing sound to the back wall of the room can also help reduce unwanted sound reflections. ANSI S12.60–2002, Annex C, provides design guidelines for controlling reverberation in classrooms that can augment a design. Included in the standard is guidance for determining the amount of sound absorption needed in a classroom of known volume.

Reverberation time must not exceed 1.5 seconds at 500, 1,000, and 2,000 Hz in rooms of 20,000 cubic feet or larger. As with standard classrooms, overall reverberation can be effectively controlled with sufficient quantities of sound-absorbing materials. However, placement of the sound-absorbing materials can be more critical for acoustical performance in large spaces, particularly lecture halls and performing arts spaces. Such spaces must be carefully designed for acoustical conditions that meet all intended uses. See ANSI S12.60–2002, Annex C, Section C3, for further guidance on placement of sound-absorbent materials and treatments.

Sound Transmission

Specific sound transmission performance is not required for compliance with this prerequisite. For information on sound transmission, see IEQ Credit 9, Enhanced Acoustical Performance.

Suggested Ways to Reduce Reverberation

- Replace existing low-NRC acoustical ceiling tiles with high-NRC acoustical tiles.

- Add new suspended acoustical tile ceiling if room height permits; if not, mount high-NRC acoustical tiles to the ceiling with the maximum possible air space behind the tiles.

- Add sound-absorbing panels high on the walls at the sides and rear of room.

- If the classroom has a very high ceiling (>11 feet), acoustical panels on both ceiling and walls may be needed. Carpet adds little to reverberation control but is useful for controlling self-noise (chair movement, footfalls, etc.), especially in preschool and lower grade levels.

Suggested Ways to Reduce Background Noise

For compliance with the acoustics prerequisite, background noise is defined as noise from HVAC systems only. However, other background noise sources can be reduced with the following strategies:

- Add storm windows.

- Replace existing windows with new thermal insulating units (this will improve energy performance, too). Such windows may also have sound transmission class (STC) ratings from the manufacturer; select windows with the highest affordable rating.

- Install specially fabricated sound-reducing windows, particularly near traffic arterials and airports and in dense urban locations.

- Check doors for gaps larger than 1/16 inch.

- Add good-quality drop seals and gaskets.

- Install tight-fitting solid-core doors with seals and gaskets.
- Install special sound-control doors if adjacent spaces are very noisy.

	IEQ
NC	NA
SCHOOLS	Prerequisite 3
CS	NA

Suggested Ways to Reduce HVAC Noise

HVAC equipment is typically the primary source of noise in classrooms. In the past, it has been common practice to install fan coils and similar through-the-wall heating and cooling units in classrooms. This puts the fan and compressor right in the room with the students. Children with hearing loss should not be seated near an HVAC unit or diffuser. Noisy through-wall, through-roof, or under-window units in the classroom should first be serviced and balanced to be sure they are operating as intended. Additional strategies:

- Add a custom-built sound enclosure around each unit.
- Add sound-lined ductwork to the unit to attenuate air distribution noise.
- Replace the unit with quieter split systems or through-wall models.
- Increase the open area at grilles and diffusers.
- Rebalance the system to reduce air volume delivered to the classroom.
- Relocate ductwork and diffusers away from teaching locations.
- Add separate duct runs to eliminate noise from common use.
- Add duct length to attenuate noise.
- Add sound lining to ducts.

Additional Suggestions for Reducing Room Noise

- Arrange seating so that students are distant from noise sources (fans, HVAC units, etc.).
- Put tennis balls or rubber tips on the chair legs.
- Avoid open classrooms, including temporary or sliding walls that separate instructional areas.
- Diminish the sound from computer keyboards by underlaying them with rubber pads or carpeting.
- Whenever possible, locate all large pieces of computer equipment (servers, audiovisual controls, printers, plotters) in a separate room.

5. Timeline and Team

Since architectural proportions and finish materials affect reverberation time and overall acoustical performance, project teams should consider acoustics in the schematic design phase of planning. Early in the design phases (and no later than design development), design teams should coordinate with mechanical engineers, electrical engineers, and contractors to specify methods to reduce background noise and achieve acoustical performance goals. In the schematic phase, locate noisy equipment and high-activity areas away from classrooms and other spaces where quiet is required. Develop mechanical system schemes that significantly reduce potential mechanical noise. For example, use centralized mechanical systems rather than in-room units, place VAV boxes and other mechanical equipment in corridors rather than above classrooms, and route ductwork outside classrooms. Involve an acoustical consultant, if necessary, as early as possible in the design process.

During schematic design, teachers and staff should educate the architects on the physical and spatial aspects of learning. Architects, designers, and materials specifiers must understand the different methods of teaching and learning that a single classroom might accommodate. For example, the same space might be used for collaborative projects, individual student work, lectures, and demonstrations.

6. Calculations

CASE 1. Noise Reduction Coefficient and Ceiling Area

OPTION 1

Calculate the volume of the classroom to confirm that total enclosed volume is less than 20,000 cubic feet.

Specify ceiling finish materials with an NRC of 0.70 or higher for 100% of the ceiling area, excluding diffusers, grilles, and light fixtures. NRC ratings for acoustical ceiling tile, ceiling panels, and other acoustical materials are available from manufacturers.

OPTION 2

Calculate the volume of the classroom to confirm that the total enclosed volume is less than 20,000 cubic feet.

Calculate the total ceiling area for the classroom, excluding diffusers, grilles, and light fixtures.

Specify ceiling and wall finish materials with an NRC of 0.70, such that the total acoustical ceiling and wall area is equal to or greater than 100% of ceiling area, excluding diffusers, grilles, and light fixtures. NRC ratings for acoustical ceiling tile, ceiling panels, wall panels, and other acoustical materials are available from manufacturers.

CASE 2. Reverberation Time

Core learning spaces with an enclosed volume of 20,000 cubic feet or larger must meet an RT of 1.5 seconds. For each core learning space, the RT must be calculated separately for the 500 Hz, 1,000 Hz, and 2,000 Hz bands; all 3 RT values must meet the stated requirement.

To calculate the RT for a room, use the following methodology:

Determine the sound absorption coefficient for each material inside the space at 500, 1,000, and 2,000 Hz frequencies. The sound absorption coefficients for any highly absorbent surface, such as acoustical ceiling tile or acoustical panels, should be obtained from the manufacturer.

Many manufacturers publish only the noise reduction coefficient on their data sheets. To obtain an NRC value, the test standards require measurement of sound absorption coefficients at 250 Hz, 500 Hz, 1,000 Hz, and 2,000 Hz. These data should be readily available from the manufacturer. Sound absorption coefficients for many common building materials are available in textbooks on architectural acoustics; see Table 1.

Table 1. Sound Absorption Coefficients for Common Materials

	IEQ
NC	NA
SCHOOLS	Prerequisite 3
CS	NA

Material	Coefficient (α)			Material	Coefficient (α)		
	500HZ	1000HZ	2000HZ		500Hz	1000Hz	2000HZ
Walls				**Floor**			
Brick, unglazed	.03	.04	.05	Concrete or Terrazzo	.015	.02	.02
Brick, unglazed, painted	.02	.02	.02	Linoleum, asphalt, rubber, or cork tile on concrete	.03	.03	.03
Plaster, gypsum, or lime, smooth finish on tile or brick	.02	.03	.04	Wood	.10	.07	.06
Plaster, gypsum, or lime, rough or smooth finish on lath	.06	.05	.04	Wood parquet in asphalt on concrete	.07	.06	.06
Concrete block, light, porous	.31	.29	.39	Carpet, heavy, on concrete	.14	.37	.60
Concrete block, dense, painted	.06	.07	.09	Same, on 40 oz hairfelt or foam rubber	.57	.69	.71
Gypsum boards. 1/2-inch nailed to 2x4s, 16 inches o.c.	.05	.04	.07	Same, with impermeable latex backing on 40 oz hairfelt or foam rubber	.39	.34	.48
Plywood paneling, 3/8-inch thick	.17	.09	.10	Marble or glaze tile	.01	.01	.02
Large panes of heavy plate glass	.04	.03	.02	**Fabrics**			
Ordinary window glass	.18	.12	.07	Light velour, 10 oz per sq yd, hung straight, in contact with walll	.11	.17	.24
Misc				Medium velour, 14 oz per sq yd, draped to half area	.49	.75	.70
Chairs, metal or wood seats, each, unoccupied	.22	.39	.38	Heavy velour, 18 oz per sq yd, draped to half area	.55	.72	.70

Use Equation 1 to determine the total sound absorption for the room at 500, 1,000, and 2,000 Hz. Each frequency must be calculated separately.

Equation 1

$$A = (\alpha_1 S_1 + \alpha_2 S_2 + \alpha_3 S_3 + \ldots\ldots\alpha_n S_n)$$

Where α_1 is the sound absorption coefficient at 500, 1,000, or 2,000 Hz for a material, and s_1 is the total surface area for that material in square feet The total sound absorption for the room is the sum of absorption coefficients times surface areas at each frequency (500, 1,000, and 2,000 Hz). Equation 1 must be calculated separately for each frequency. The calculation should include all finish materials in the room.

Use Equation 2 to calculate the reverberation time for the room at each of the 3 frequencies.

Equation 2

$$RT = 0.049 \times \frac{V}{A}$$

Where V is the room volume in cubic feet, and A is the total sound absorption in the room at 500, 1,000, and 2,000 Hz (from Equation 1). The result is 3 reverberation times; all must meet the specified RT requirement.

Project teams may elect to measure RT after construction by using the methodology described in Section E4 of ANSI S12.60–2002, Verifying Reverberation Times. Measurement is not required for compliance with the prerequisite.

Background Noise Level

Background noise level can be calculated through analysis of mechanical system noise source levels, sound paths (ducts, diffusers, etc.) between sources and receiving rooms, and receiving room acoustical conditions (wall and ceiling constructions, room sound absorption, etc.).

Recommended methodologies and best practices for mechanical system noise control are described in Annex B of ANSI Standard S12.60–2002. Best practices and calculation methods are described in the 2007 HVAC Applications ASHRAE Handbook, Chapter 47, Sound and Vibration Control.

The required calculations can be conducted by a mechanical engineer familiar with the methodologies in the 2007 HVAC Applications ASHRAE Handbook, Chapter 47, Sound and Vibration Control, or by a qualified acoustical consultant.

7. Documentation Guidance

As a first step in preparing to complete the LEED-Online documentation requirements, work through the following measures. Refer to LEED-Online for the complete descriptions of all required documentation.

- Maintain manufacturer documentation for the noise reduction coefficient of each acoustical finish material.

- Document the installed surface areas of sound-absorptive materials on interior elevations.

- Record reverberation times.

- Document the means by which the background noise level in classrooms and other primary spaces was kept below 45 dBA by following ANSI S12.60 methodology or using software based on the 2007 HVAC Applications ASHRAE Handbook, Chapter 47, Sound and Vibration Control.

8. Examples

Figure 1. CASE 1, OPTION 1. 100% of Ceiling Area = NRC 0.70 or Higher

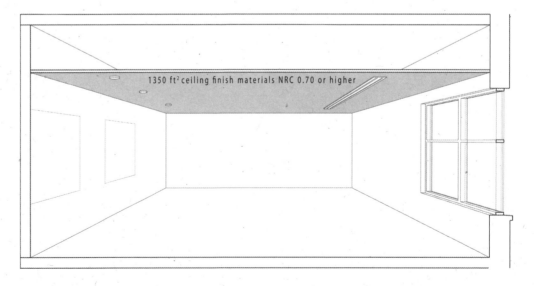

1350 ft² ceiling finish materials NRC 0.70 or higher

Figure 2. CASE 1, OPTION 2. Total Area with NRC 0.70 or Higher = Ceiling Area

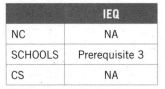

	IEQ
NC	NA
SCHOOLS	Prerequisite 3
CS	NA

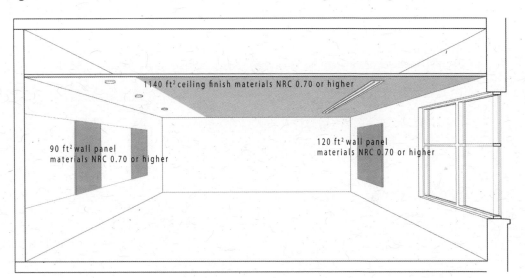

1140 ft² ceiling finish materials NRC 0.70 or higher

90 ft² wall panel materials NRC 0.70 or higher

120 ft² wall panel materials NRC 0.70 or higher

CASE 2. Calculated Reverberation Time

The following example of calculating the reverberation time uses the room in Figure 1. The RT must be calculated for 500, 1,000, and 2,000 Hz.

Determine room volume (V) from the room dimensions:

38' L	X	35.5' W	X	10' H	=	13,490 cubic feet

Determine total absorption (A) from the room materials: gypsum board walls on studs, linoleum floor, ordinary window glass, and acoustical ceiling tiles (NRC = 0.70; sound absorption coefficient at 500 Hz = 0.72, from manufacturer's data).

500 Hz calculation data:

Table 2. Surface Areas and Absorption Coefficients (α)

Surface	Area (sf)	α (500 hz)
End wall 1	35.5 x 10 = 355	0.05*
End wall 2	35.5 x 10 = 355	0.05*
Side wall 1	38 x 10 = 380	0.05*
Side wall 2	38 x 10 = 380 (minus 60 sf window) = 320	0.05*
Window	6 x 10 = 60	0.18*
Floor	38 x 35.5 = 1349	0.03*
Ceiling	38 x 35.5 = 1349	0.72**

* from Table 1
** from manufacturer's data

Total absorption (A) @ 500 Hz = (355 x 0.05) + (355 x 0.05) + (380 x 0.05) +

(320 x 0.05) + (60 x 0.18) + (1349 x 0.03) + (1349 x 0.72) = 1093 sabins

Determine reverberation time (RT) at 500 Hz:

$$RT = 0.049 \times \frac{V}{A}$$

$$RT = 0.049 \times \frac{13490}{1093} = 0.60 \text{ seconds @ 500 Hz}$$

Repeat the calculations using sound absorption coefficients for 1,000 and 2,000 Hz to confirm that all RTs are 0.60 seconds at each frequency, or as required for larger room volumes.

The RT calculation can also be applied to a classroom smaller than 20,000 cubic feet to demonstrate compliance.

9. Exemplary Performance

This prerequisite is not eligible for exemplary performance under the Innovation in Design section.

10. Regional Variations

Project teams should pay attention to regional factors that can influence ambient noise around school buildings. For example, wind may be an issue in the Midwest. Atmospheric fog and water vapor in coastal regions may also affect environmental sound transmission. The use of natural ventilation may require additional noise control design because of open pathways between exterior and interior spaces.

11. Operations and Maintenance Considerations

Establish a policy for the continued use of acoustical best practices during the building's operation, and help building operators find acoustically appropriate products and materials for repairs or alterations by providing them with a list of compliant products.

Consider equipping operating personnel with a sound level meter so that they can perform periodic acoustical assessments and correct any deficiencies.

12. Resources

Please see USGBC's LEED Registered Project Tools (http://www.usgbc.org/projecttools) for additional resources and technical information.

Websites
Acoustical Society of America
http://asa.aip.org/
The Acoustical Society of America (ASA) is an international scientific society dedicated to increasing and diffusing the knowledge of acoustics and its practical applications. ASA's website contains a variety of resources, including publications, standards information, and links. Of special note are the 2 ASA booklets on classroom acoustics at http://asa.aip.org/classroom/booklet.html and http://asa.aip.org/classroom/bookletII.pdf.

Collaborative for High Performance Schools Best Practices Manual, 2006
http://www.chps.net/manual/index.htm
The Collaborative for High Performance Schools (CHPS) Best Practices Manual contains guidelines and strategies for effective acoustical performance in school buildings.

Classroom Acoustics: Implementing a New Standard
United States Access Board
http://www.access-board.gov/acoustic/index.htm
This websiteprovides background information on the development of a classroom acoustics standard and lists states, local jurisdictions, and boards of education that have taken action to improveclassroom acoustics.

Education Resources Information Center (ERIC)

http://www.eric.ed.gov/

ERIC provides free access to more than 1.2 million bibliographic records of journal articles and other education-related materials and includes links to full text, if available. The U.S. Department of Education's Institute of Education Sciences (IES) sponors ERIC. The center has posted many studies that show the impact of acoustics on learning, including the effects on students with hearing disabilities, and also has posted studies and papers on good acoustical design in classrooms.

Maryland Classroom Acoustics Guidelines

www.marylandpublicschools.org/NR/rdonlyres/FCB60C1D-6CC2-4270-BDAA-153D67247324/10128/ClassroomAcousticsGuidelines.pdf

This resource, developed by the state of Maryland, discusses the components and importance of good classroom acoustics, the American National Standards Institute (ANSI) Standard S12.60–2002 for classroom acoustics, typical existing classroom conditions, and the cost impact of the standard. The guidelines cover planning, design, furnishings, equipment, HVAC systems, plumbing noise, construction practices, postoccupancy inspection, sound field amplification systems, indoor air quality considerations, and portable classrooms.

Quiet Classrooms

http://www.quietclassrooms.org/

Quiet Classrooms is an alliance of nonprofit organizations working to create better learning environments in schools by reducing noise. Negligible background noise levels and good classroom acoustics are important for learning by all students and especially those who are hearing-impaired. The alliance's website is a resource for schools, school boards, PTAs, principals, parents, teachers, students, and school architects.

Whole Building Design Guide, Acoustic Comfort

www.wbdg.org/resources/acoustic.php?r=ieq

This section of the Whole Building Design Guide focuses on acoustic comfort in offices, classrooms, and conference rooms and discusses the following issues: site selection, glazing, HVAC noise issues, natural ventilation, sound masking, emerging issues, relevant codes and standards, and additional resources.

13. Definitions

Core learning spaces are spaces for educational activities where the primary functions are teaching and learning. (ANSI S12.60–2002)

Hertz (Hz) is the unit used to describe the frequency of vibrations (cycles) per second. One Hz equals 1 cycle per second.

HVAC systems are equipment, distribution systems, and terminals that provide the processes of heating, ventilating, or air conditioning to a building or portion of a building. (ASHRAE 90.1–2007)

Noise reduction coefficient (NRC) is the arithmetic average of absorption coefficients at 250, 500, 1,000, and 2,000 Hz for a material. The NRC is often published by manufacturers in product specifications, particularly for acoustical ceiling tiles and acoustical wall panels.

Reverberation is an acoustical phenomenon that occurs when sound persists in an enclosed space because of its repeated reflection or scattering upon the enclosing surfaces or objects within the space. (ANSI S12.60–2002)

Reverberation time (RT) is a measure of the amount of reverberation in a space and equal to the time required for the level of a steady sound to decay by 60 dB after the sound has stopped. The decay rate depends on the amount of sound absorption in a room, the room geometry and the frequency of the sound. RT is expressed in seconds. (ANSI S12.60–2002).

	IEQ
NC	NA
SCHOOLS	Prerequisite 3
CS	NA

IEQ	
NC	NA
SCHOOLS	Prerequisite 3
CS	NA

Sound absorption is the portion of sound energy striking a surface that is not returned as sound energy. (ANSI S12.60–2002)

Sound absorption coefficient describes the ability of a material to absorb sound, expressed as a fraction of incident sound. The sound absorption coefficient is frequency-specific and ranges from 0.00 to 1.00. For example, a material may have an absorption coefficient of 0.50 at 250 Hz, and 0.80 at 1,000 Hz. This indicates that the material absorbs 50% of incident sound at 250 Hz, and 80% of incident sound at 1,000 Hz. The arithmetic average of absorption coefficients at midfrequencies is the NRC.

Sound transmission class (**STC**) is a single-number rating for the acoustic attenuation of airborne sound passing through a partition or other building element, such as a wall, roof, or door, as measured in an acoustical testing laboratory following accepted industry practice. A higher STC rating provides more sound attenuation through a partition. (ANSI S12.60–2002)

A **weighted decibel** (**dBA**) is a sound pressure level measured with a conventional frequency weighting that roughly approximates how the human ear hears different frequency components of sounds at typical listening levels for speech. (ANSI S12.60–2002)

OUTDOOR AIR DELIVERY MONITORING

	NC	SCHOOLS	CS
Credit	IEQ Credit 1	IEQ Credit 1	IEQ Credit 1
Points	1 point	1 point	1 point

Intent

To provide capacity for ventilation system monitoring to help promote occupant comfort and well-being.

Requirements

NC, SCHOOLS & CS

Install permanent monitoring systems to ensure that ventilation systems maintain design minimum requirements. Configure all monitoring equipment to generate an alarm when the airflow values or carbon dioxide (CO_2) levels vary by 10% or more from the design values via either a building automation system alarm to the building operator or a visual or audible alert to the building occupants.

AND

CASE 1. Mechanically Ventilated Spaces

Monitor CO_2 concentrations within all densely occupied spaces (those with a design occupant density of 25 people or more per 1,000 square feet). CO_2 monitors must be between 3 and 6 feet above the floor.

Provide a direct outdoor airflow measurement device capable of measuring the minimum outdoor air intake flow with an accuracy of plus or minus 15% of the design minimum outdoor air rate, as defined by ASHRAE 62.1-2007 (with errata but without addenda[1]) for mechanical ventilation systems where 20% or more of the design supply airflow serves nondensely occupied spaces.

CASE 2. Naturally Ventilated Spaces

Monitor CO_2 concentrations within all naturally ventilated spaces. CO_2 monitors must be between 3 and 6 feet above the floor. One CO_2 sensor may be used to monitor multiple spaces if the natural ventilation design uses passive stack(s) or other means to induce airflow through those spaces equally and simultaneously without intervention by building occupants.[2]

---

1. Project teams wishing to use ASHRAE approved addenda for the purposes of this credit may do so at their discretion. Addenda must be applied consistently across all LEED credits.
2. CO_2 monitoring is required in densely occupied spaces, in addition to outdoor air intake flow measurement.

	IEQ
NC	Credit 1
SCHOOLS	Credit 1
CS	Credit 1

1. Benefits and Issues to Consider

Environmental Issues

Measuring CO_2 concentrations to determine and maintain adequate outdoor air ventilation rates in buildings is 1 recommended method for achieving better indoor air quality (IAQ). Increasing ventilation rates may require additional energy inputs, which generate additional air and water pollution.

CO_2 concentrations are an indicator of air-change effectiveness, with elevated levels suggesting inadequate ventilation and possible buildup of indoor air pollutants. Although CO_2 alone is not harmful, high concentrations in indoor environments displace oxygen and therefore can lead to headaches, dizziness, and increased heart rate.[23]

Ambient outdoor CO_2 concentrations may fluctuate between approximately 300 and 500 ppm, depending on local and regional factors,. Time-of-day fluctuations (e.g., from nearby major highways) and annual fluctuations, if any, should also be considered.

Economic Issues

Installing CO_2 and ventilation rate monitoring systems requires an investment in equipment, installation, annual calibration, and maintenance. However, these systems enable building owners, facility managers, maintenance personnel, and occupants to detect air quality problems quickly so that corrective action can be taken. Reduced absenteeism and increased occupant productivity, though difficult to quantify, are important factors when evaluating investment in these systems. Effective air quality monitoring can also extend the life of a building's HVAC system and reduce energy use by ensuring that the amount of makeup air provided accurately reflects building occupancy loads.

CO_2 and ventilation rate monitoring systems increase initial construction costs compared to less efficiently and effectively controlled spaces. Capital and annual costs for air-flow monitoring equipment maintenance and calibration procedures may be offset by reduced absenteeism, increased occupant productivity, and reduced HVAC energy use.

2. Related Credits

Monitoring of airflow can allow for performance trending and alert building operators about potential IAQ problems. The monitoring capability can help inform the commissioning process and enable robust measurement and verification, both to maximize energy performance and to ensure consistent indoor air quality. The following credits and prerequisite are related to this credit:

- IEQ Credit 2: Increased Ventilation

- EA Prerequisite 1: Fundamental Building Commissioning

- EA Credit 3: Enhanced Commissioning

- EA Credit 5: Measurement and Verification

CO_2 is commonly mitigated within indoor spaces by increasing the ventilation rates. However, the quantity of outside air required to mitigate high CO_2 depends on the concentration of CO_2 in the outside air. Dense neighborhoods, heavy traffic, and existing site contamination can raise CO_2 levels and lower the quality of outside air available for ventilation purposes. Alternative transportation amenities, such as bicycle corridors or public transportation, can reduce the need for single-occupant vehicles and decrease CO_2 concentrations. Refer to this credit:

- SS Credit 4: Alternative Transportation

3. Summary of Referenced Standards

American National Standards Institute (ANSI)/ASHRAE Standard 62.1–2007: Ventilation for Acceptable Indoor Air Quality

American Society of Heating, Refrigerating, and Air-Conditioning Engineers (ASHRAE)
http://www.ashrae.org

	IEQ
NC	Credit 1
SCHOOLS	Credit 1
CS	Credit 1

This standard specifies minimum ventilation rates and IAQ levels so as to reduce the potential for adverse health effects. The standard specifies that ventilation systems be designed to prevent uptake of contaminants, minimize growth and dissemination of microorganisms, and, if necessary, filter particulates.

The standard outlines a ventilation rate procedure and an IAQ procedure for compliance. The ventilation rate procedure prescribes outdoor air quality levels acceptable for ventilation; treatment measures for contaminated outdoor air; and ventilation rates for residential, commercial, institutional, vehicular, and industrial spaces. The IAQ Procedure is a performance-based design approach in which the building and its ventilation system maintain concentrations of specific contaminants at or below certain previously determined limits in order to achieve an indoor air quality acceptable to building occupants and/or visitors. For the purposes of this procedure, acceptable perceived indoor air quality excludes dissatisfaction related to thermal comfort, noise and vibration, lighting, and psychological stressors. The IAQ procedure also includes criteria for the following situations: reducing outdoor air quantities when recirculated air is treated by contaminant-removal equipment and ventilating when a space's air volume is used as a reservoir to dilute contaminants. The IAQ procedure incorporates quantitative and subjective evaluation and restricts contaminant concentrations to acceptable levels.

ASHRAE updated the standard in 2007 to include requirements for buildings that allow smoking in designated areas to separate areas with environmental tobacco smoke (ETS) from those without ETS . The standard now also clarifies how designers must analyze mechanical cooling systems to limit indoor relative humidity that would cause dampness-related problems such as mold and microbial growth.

Project teams wishing to use ASHRAE-approved addenda for the purposes of this credit may do so at their own discretion. Apply addenda consistently across all LEED credits.

4. Implementation

Building HVAC systems are designed to flush out indoor airborne contaminants by exhausting old air and replacing it with outdoor air. The rate of ventilation air exchange is usually determined during the design phase, and is based on space density and type of occupancy. Many conventional ventilation systems do not directly measure the amount of outdoor air that is delivered. Implementation of the following strategies is recommended to achieve this credit.

Outdoor Air Flow Monitoring

Monitoring the outdoor air flow rate confirms that the HVAC equipment is providing the required ventilation rate. Air balance control methodologies, such as fan-tracking and measuring building-pressurization, do not directly prove that appropriate ventilation air is being provided and do not satisfy the credit requirement. The ventilation rate can be measured at the outdoor air intake of an air distribution system using a variety of airflow devices, including Pitot tubes, Venturi meters, rotating vane anemometers, and mass air flow sensors. These sensors must be installed according to the manufacturer's best practices guidelines. The ventilation rate for a particular HVAC system can be accurately determined from a mass balance calculation if both supply air flow and return air flow are directly measured with air flow monitoring devices. To satisfy the requirements of this credit, the measurement devices must detect when the system is 15% below the design minimum outdoor air rate. When the ventilation system fails to provide the required levels of outside air, the

IEQ	
NC	Credit 1
SCHOOLS	Credit 1
CS	Credit 1

monitoring system should be configured to deliver a visible or audible alert to the system operator to indicate that operational adjustments might be necessary.

The minimum outdoor air rate might change based on the design and modes of the HVAC system. Constant volume systems with steady-state design occupancy conditions usually have different outdoor air rates for weekdays and nighttime or off-peak conditions. In variable air volume systems, the rate of outdoor air needs to stay above the design minimum, even when the supply air flow is decreased because of reduced thermal load conditions.

CO_2 Monitoring

CO_2 monitors can also measure the effectiveness of the ventilation system in delivering outdoor air. Properly placed CO_2 monitors can confirm that a ventilation system is functioning properly. There are 2 typical system configurations that generally meet the requirements of this credit.

The first approach involves CO_2 sensors that use measured concentration to provide an alert if the ventilation system is not functioning properly. An indoor concentration of 1000 parts per million (ppm) was commonly used in the past as the set point for the alarm, but a higher alarm concentration may be appropriate when the design complies with Standard 62.1–2007, because the effective ventilation rate per person has been reduced significantly for some zones. ASHRAE 62.1–2007, Users Manual Appendix A, provides more information about CO_2 sensors, including demand control ventilation.

Locate CO_2 monitors so that they provide accurate representative readings of the CO_2 concentrations in occupied spaces. Multiple CO_2 monitoring stations throughout occupied spaces provide better information and control than a single CO_2 monitor for the entire system. A single CO_2 monitor, typically installed in the return air duct, is less expensive and easier to use than providing multiple sensors, but it may not be able to identify underventilated areas in the building.

The second approach for buildings with HVAC systems that have limited airflow monitoring capabilities (small capacity air handling units or split systems) is to use differential CO_2 monitoring to satisfy the credit requirements. This approach requires CO_2 monitors in all occupied spaces, an outdoor CO_2 monitor, and a means by which the air handling units can provide a greater amount of outside air if the CO_2 delta between the spaces reaches or exceeds 530 ppm.

For outdoor CO_2 sensors, use reliable measurement data to determine conservative set points based on an ambient CO_2 concentration. Alternatively, use 400 ppm for the assumed constant outdoor CO_2 value, because it is a conservative assumption and supported in California's Title 24 energy code.

NC & SCHOOLS

CO_2 Monitoring in Densely Occupied Spaces

The CO_2 level for each densely occupied space in a mechanically ventilated building needs to be monitored to satisfy the credit requirements. The density factor is 25 people per 1000 square feet; for example, a 240-square-foot conference room that accommodates 6 or more people would need a CO_2 monitor. CO_2 monitors in densely occupied spaces should be mounted within the space's vertical breathing zone (between 3 and 6 feet above the floor).

Ventilation Air Flow Monitoring in Non-Densely Occupied Spaces

For mechanically ventilated spaces with an occupant density of less than 25 people per 1000 square feet, this LEED for New Construction credit requires that the outdoor ventilation rate be directly measured and compared against the minimum required ventilation rate.

Typically, air flow monitoring stations located in the outdoor air intakes of each central HVAC air distribution system will provide those measurements. The direct outdoor airflow measurement device must be capable of measuring the outdoor airflow rate at all expected system operating conditions, within an accuracy of plus or minus 15% of the design minimum outdoor air rate.

CO_2 Monitoring in Naturally Ventilated Spaces

Monitoring CO_2 levels in the occupied spaces in naturally ventilated buildings gives building occupants and operators feedback so that they can adjust the ventilation by, for example, opening windows. The CO_2 monitors in naturally ventilated spaces should be mounted in the vertical breathing zone (between 3 and 6 feet above the floor).

Building Type

Airflow and CO_2 monitoring systems can be applied to any building or HVAC system type, including both mechanically and naturally ventilated buildings. In addition to ventilation alarms, these systems can provide building operators and automated control systems with information about making necessary operational adjustments, such as increasing or decreasing intake airflow rates.

For naturally ventilated buildings and spaces served by HVAC systems that do not permit active control of ventilation rates, CO_2 monitors in the occupied spaces can provide building occupants and facilities staff with useful information that enables operational adjustments, such as opening windows or adjusting fixed ventilation rates in under-ventilated areas.

CS

Ventilation Air Flow Monitoring

The outdoor ventilation rate in mechanically ventilated spaces must be measured and compared to the minimum required ventilation. Typically, air flow monitoring stations, located in the outdoor intakes of each central HVAC air distribution system, will measure the outdoor ventilation rate. The direct outdoor airflow measurement device must be capable of measuring the outdoor airflow rate at all expected system operating conditions within an accuracy of plus or minus 15% of the design minimum outdoor air rate.

Ventilation Air Flow Monitoring Considerations

Providing the required amount of outside air to occupied spaces is very important for core and shell buildings. Sufficient outside air must be provided to the tenant spaces at all times. Airflow monitoring stations can measure and track outdoor air quantities, which helps ensure that proper ventilation is provided.

Project teams may want to include measures that enable building occupants to monitor the CO_2 in their spaces. The control system can be specified to include expansion capability so that occupants can use CO_2 monitors and earn points in the LEED for Commercial Interiors rating system.

5. Timeline and Team

The placement of outdoor air sensors and intakes should be coordinated with the design team before construction documents are prepared. Engage a mechanical engineer to work on the issues of outdoor air delivery monitoring no later than the design development phase.

6. Calculations

There are no calculations required for this credit.

7. Documentation Guidance

As a first step in preparing to complete the LEED-Online documentation requirements, work through the following measures. Refer to LEED-Online for the complete descriptions of all required documentation.

- Incorporate airflow monitors and CO_2 sensors into floor plans, schematics, elevations (where applicable), and mechanical schedules.

- Commission ventilation systems to monitor for excess energy use.

- Alarm systems should be checked to verify settings according to ANSI/ASHRAE 62.1–2007 for mechanical ventilation systems.

- Any automated building systems used for the project should be calibrated according to manufacturer guidelines. Routine function checks of alarm systems are recommended.

8. Examples

There are no examples for this credit.

9. Exemplary Performance

This credit is not eligible for exemplary performance under the Innovation in Design section.

10. Regional Variations

Ambient outdoor CO_2 concentrations may fluctuate between approximately 300 and 500 ppm based on local and regional factors. Project teams should consider time-of-day fluctuations near major congested highways and any annual fluctuations. High ambient CO_2 concentrations typically indicate combustion or other contaminant sources. Low ventilation rates may yield a sense of stuffiness or general dissatisfaction with IAQ.

11. Operations and Maintenance Considerations

Provide the building owner and facility manager with the information needed to understand, maintain, and use the monitoring system. Establish appropriate setpoints and control sequences, as well as recommendations for typical corrective actions, in the facility's operating plan and sequence of operations document.

Establish procedures and schedules for inspecting CO_2 monitors and airflow monitoring stations, recalibrating sensors based on the manufacturer's requirements, and testing and maintaining the exhaust systems, and include them in the building's preventive maintenance plan.

Use CO_2 sensors that require recalibration no less than every 5 years. A CO_2 monitor that has fallen out of calibration may indicate that indoor CO_2 concentrations are lower or higher than they actually are, leading to underventilation or overventilation of the space.

12. Resources

Please see USGBC's LEED Registered Project Tools (http://www.usgbc.org/projecttools) for additional resources and technical information.

Websites
ASHRAE 62.1–2007 Users Manual, Appendix A
http://www.ashrae.org
This manual provides information on CO_2 sensors including demand-controlled ventilation.

American Society of Heating, Refrigerating, and Air-Conditioning Engineers (ASHRAE)

This organization advances the science of heating, ventilation, air conditioning, and refrigeration for the public's benefit through research, standards writing, continuing education, and publications. To purchase ASHRAE standards and guidelines, visit the bookstore on the ASHRAE website.

	IEQ
NC	Credit 1
SCHOOLS	Credit 1
CS	Credit 1

Building Air Quality: A Guide for Building Owners and Facility Managers

http://www.epa.gov/iaq/largebldgs/baqtoc.html

This EPA publication details IAQ sources in buildings and methods to prevent and resolve IAQ problems.

Print Media

Air Handling Systems Design, by Tseng-Yao Sun (McGraw Hill, 1992).

ASHRAE 55–2004: Thermal Environmental Conditions for Human Occupancy (ASHRAE, 2004).

ASHRAE 62.1–2007: Ventilation for Acceptable Indoor Air Quality (ASHRAE, 2007).

ASHRAE 62.2–2004: Ventilation for Acceptable Indoor Air Quality in Low-Rise Residential Buildings (ASHRAE, 2004).

ASTM–D–6245–1998: Standard Guide for Using Indoor Carbon Dioxide Concentrations to Evaluate Indoor Air Quality and Ventilation (ASTM, 1998).

Efficient Building Design Series, Volume 2: Heating, Ventilating, and Air Conditioning, by J. Trost and Frederick Trost (Prentice Hall, 1998).

13. Definitions

The **breathing zone** is the region within an occupied space between 3 and 6 feet above the floor and more than 2 feet from the walls or fixed air-conditioning equipment. (AHSRAE 62.1–2007)

CO2 is carbon dioxide.

Demand control ventilation is the automatic reduction of outside air to a level below design rates when occupancy is less than design determined by occupancy indicators; such as, time-of-day schedules, a direct count of occupants, or an estimate of occupancy or ventilation rate per person using occupancy sensors.

Densely occupied space is an area with a design occupant density of 25 people or more per 1,000 square feet (40 square feet or less per person).

HVAC systems are equipment, distribution systems, and terminals that provide the processes of heating, ventilating, or air-conditioning. (ASHRAE 90.1-2007)

Indoor air quality (**IAQ**) is the nature of air inside a building that affects the health and well-being of building occupants. It is considered acceptable when there are no known contaminants at harmful concentrations as determined by cognizant authorities and with which a substantial majority (80% or more) of the people exposed do not express dissatisfaction. (ASHRAE 62.1–2007)

Mechanical ventilation is provided by mechanically powered equipment, such as motor-driven fans and blowers, but not by devices such as wind-driven turbine ventilators and mechanically operated windows. (ASHRAE 62.1–2007)

Natural ventilation is provided by thermal, wind, or diffusion effects through doors, windows, or other intentional openings in the building. (ASHRAE 62.1–2007)

Occupants in a commercial building are workers who either have a permanent office or workstation in the building or typically spend a minimum of 10 hours per week in the building In a residential building, occupants also include all persons who live in the building.

	IEQ
NC	Credit 1
SCHOOLS	Credit 1
CS	Credit 1

Outdoor air is the ambient air that enters a building through a ventilation system, either through intentional openings for natural ventilation or by infiltration. (ASHRAE 62.1–2007)

ppm is parts per million.

Return air is removed from a space and then recirculated or exhausted. (ASHRAE 62.1–2007)

Thermal comfort exists when occupants express satisfaction with the thermal environment.

Ventilation is the process of supplying air to or removing air from a space for the purpose of controlling air contaminant levels, humidity, or temperature within the space. (ASHRAE 62.1-2007).

Volatile organic compounds (**VOCs**) are carbon compounds that participate in atmospheric photochemical reactions (excluding carbon monoxide, carbon dioxide, carbonic acid, metallic carbides and carbonates, and ammonium carbonate). The compounds vaporize at normal room temperatures.

	NC	SCHOOLS	CS
Credit	IEQ Credit 2	IEQ Credit 2	IEQ Credit 2
Points	1 point	1 point	1 point

Intent

To provide additional outdoor air ventilation to improve indoor air quality (IAQ) and promote occupant comfort, well-being and productivity.

Requirements

NC, SCHOOLS & CS

CASE 1. Mechanically Ventilated Spaces

Increase breathing zone outdoor air ventilation rates to all occupied spaces by at least 30% above the minimum rates required by ASHRAE Standard 62.1-2007 (with errata but without addenda[1]) as determined by IEQ Prerequisite 1: Minimum Indoor Air Quality Performance.

CASE 2. Naturally Ventilated Spaces[2]

Design natural ventilation systems for occupied spaces to meet the recommendations set forth in the Carbon Trust "Good Practice Guide 237" (1998). Determine that natural ventilation is an effective strategy for the project by following the flow diagram process shown in Figure 1.18 of the Chartered Institution of Building Services Engineers (CIBSE) Applications Manual 10: 2005, Natural Ventilation in Non-domestic Buildings.

AND

OPTION 1

Use diagrams and calculations to show that the design of the natural ventilation systems meets the recommendations set forth in the CIBSE Applications Manual 10: 2005, Natural Ventilation in Non-domestic Buildings.

OR

OPTION 2

Use a macroscopic, multizone, analytic model to predict that room-by-room airflows will effectively naturally ventilate, defined as providing the minimum ventilation rates required by ASHRAE Standard 62.1-2007 Chapter 6 (with errata but without addenda[1]), for at least 90% of occupied spaces.

---

1 Project teams wishing to use ASHRAE approved addenda for the purposes of this credit may do so at their discretion. Addenda must be applied consistently across all LEED credits.
2 The core and shell buildings that are designed to be naturally ventilated must provide the capability for the tenant build-out to meet the requirements of this credit.

	IEQ
NC	Credit 2
SCHOOLS	Credit 2
CS	Credit 2

1. Benefits and Issues to Consider

Environmental Issues

Americans spend about 90% of their time indoors, where concentrations of pollutants are often much higher than those outside. Of the thousands of chemicals and biological pollutants found indoors, many are known to have significant health impacts. Risks include asthma, cancer, and reproductive and developmental problems.[24] Increasing ventilation above minimum standards improves the indoor air quality (IAQ) of a building's occupied spaces and directly benefits occupants' health and well-being.

Economic Issues

Depending on the climate, increasing ventilation rates by 30% beyond ASHRAE 62.1–2007 can yield higher HVAC energy costs and potentially greater HVAC capacity needs than those associated with the minimum ventilation rates established in the standard. This increase in HVAC capacity and energy use will be more pronounced in extreme climates than in mild, temperate climates. Some projects may choose to increase the outdoor air intake rate and accept higher HVAC equipment and energy costs because research indicates that the resulting IAQ is associated with improved employee health, welfare, well-being, and productivity. The use of heat transfer equipment, like heat recovery wheels, can precondition intake air and minimize the extent to which increased ventilation requires additional energy to heat and cool intake air.

Although a naturally ventilated building may have less equipment than a comparable mechanically ventilated building, natural ventilation designs may require additional costs for operable windows, increased thermal mass, and other architectural elements that enable passive ventilation and space conditioning. Energy and maintenance costs for naturally ventilated buildings tend to be lower than for comparable mechanically ventilated spaces.

For mechanically ventilated and air-conditioned buildings, increasing ventilation rates will require somewhat greater HVAC system capacity and energy use, adding to both capital and operational costs. Natural ventilation systems can provide increased ventilation rates and good IAQ. They also allow for individual occupant control over thermal comfort and ventilation via operable windows while potentially reducing operating costs compared to mechanical ventilation systems.

 CS Increased outdoor air rates may result in improved tenant attraction and retention.

2. Related Credits

Ventilation strategies influence the overall energy performance of the building and require commissioning as well as measurement and verification. Increased ventilation, particularly when delivered by mechanical ventilation systems, can increase energy consumption. Installing a permanent ventilation performance monitoring system can facilitate the achievement and maintenance of increased ventilation. For these reasons, increased ventilation is related to the following other credits:

- EA Prerequisite 1: Fundamental Commissioning
- EA Prerequisite 2: Minimum Energy Performance
- EA Credit 1: Optimize Energy Performance
- EA Credit 3: Enhanced Commissioning
- EA Credit 5: Measurement and Verification
- IEQ Credit 1: Outdoor Air Delivery Monitoring

3. Summary of Referenced Standards
American National Standards Institute (ANIS)/ ASHRAE Standard 62.1–2007: Ventilation For Acceptable Indoor Air Quality
American Society of Heating, Refrigerating, and Air-Conditioning Engineers (ASHRAE)
http://www.ashrae.org

	IEQ
NC	Credit 2
SCHOOLS	Credit 2
CS	Credit 2

This standard specifies minimum ventilation rates and IAQ levels so as to reduce the potential for adverse health effects. The standard specifies that ventilation systems be designed to prevent uptake of contaminants, minimize growth and dissemination of microorganisms, and, if necessary, filter particulates.

The standard outlines a ventilation rate procedure and an IAQ procedure for compliance. The ventilation rate procedure prescribes outdoor air quality levels acceptable for ventilation; treatment measures for contaminated outdoor air; and ventilation rates for residential, commercial, institutional, vehicular, and industrial spaces. The IAQ Procedure is a performance-based design approach in which the building and its ventilation system maintain concentrations of specific contaminants at or below certain previously determined limits in order to achieve an indoor air quality acceptable to building occupants and/or visitors. For the purposes of this procedure, acceptable perceived indoor air quality excludes dissatisfaction related to thermal comfort, noise and vibration, lighting, and psychological stressors. The IAQ procedure also includes criteria for the following situations: reducing outdoor air quantities when recirculated air is treated by contaminant-removal equipment and ventilating when a space's air volume is used as a reservoir to dilute contaminants. The IAQ procedure incorporates quantitative and subjective evaluation and restricts contaminant concentrations to acceptable levels.

ASHRAE updated the standard in 2007 to include requirements for buildings that allow smoking in designated areas to separate areas with environmental tobacco smoke (ETS) from those without ETS . The standard now also clarifies how designers must analyze mechanical cooling systems to limit indoor relative humidity that would cause dampness-related problems such as mold and microbial growth.

Project teams wishing to use ASHRAE-approved addenda for the purposes of this credit may do so at their own discretion. Apply addenda consistently across all LEED credits.

Chartered Institute of Building Services Engineers (CIBSE) Applications Manual 10–2005, Natural Ventilation in Non-Domestic Buildings
CIBSE, London
http://www.cibse.org

CIBSE Applications Manual 10–2005 provides guidance for implementing natural ventilation in nonresidential buildings. It provides detailed information on how to adopt natural ventilation as the sole servicing strategy for a building or as an element in a mixed mode design. According to the publisher, this manual "is a major revision of the Applications Manual (AM) first published in 1997. At the time, there was a significant expansion of interest in the application of engineered natural ventilation to the design of non-domestic buildings. The original AM10 sought to capture the state of knowledge as it existed in the mid-90s and present it in a form suited to the needs of every member of the design team. Some 10 years on from the time when the initial manual was conceived, the state of knowledge has increased, and experience in the design and operation of naturally ventilated buildings has grown. This revision of AM10 is therefore a timely opportunity to update and enhance the guidance offered to designers and users of naturally ventilated buildings."

4. Implementation
A green building should provide its occupants with superior indoor air quality (IAQ) to support their productivity and well-being. Providing adequate ventilation rates is key to maintaining superior IAQ. Underventilated buildings may be stuffy, odorous, uncomfortable and/or unhealthy.

IEQ	
NC	Credit 2
SCHOOLS	Credit 2
CS	Credit 2

Building ventilation systems, including both active HVAC systems and natural ventilation systems, are designed and installed to introduce fresh outside air into the building while exhausting an equal amount of building air. HVAC systems also typically provide thermal comfort. Building conditioning systems that provide enhanced ventilation air as efficiently and effectively as possible will help to maintain a high standard of indoor air quality in the building.

Strategies

There are 3 basic methods for ventilating buildings:

- mechanical ventilation (i.e., active ventilation);
- natural ventilation (i.e., passive ventilation); and
- mixed-mode ventilation (i.e., both mechanical and natural ventilation).

Projects employing both mechanical and natural ventilation (i.e., mixed-mode ventilation) must exceed the minimum ventilation rates required by ASHRAE 62.1–2007, Chapter 6, by at least 30%.

Mechanically Ventilated Spaces: Ventilation Rate Procedure

Section 6 of ASHRAE 62.1–2007 outlines guidelines for determining ventilation rates for various applications of mechanical ventilation systems, using either the ventilation rate procedure or the IAQ procedure. The ventilation rate procedure is easier to apply and used more frequently than the IAQ procedure. It is the recommended approach in IEQ Prerequisite 1, Minimum Indoor Air Quality Performance.

When following the ventilation rate procedure, use the methodology found in Section 6.2 of ASHRAE 62.1–2007. The breathing zone outdoor airflow is equal to the sum of the outdoor airflow rate required per person times the zone population, plus the outdoor airflow rate required per unit area times the zone floor area. The standard's Table 6-1, Minimum Ventilation Rates in Breathing Zone, provides information by occupancy category to determine both the amount of outdoor air needed to ventilate people-related source contaminants and area-related source contaminants. The people-related sources figure of the outdoor air rate addresses actual occupancy density and activity. The area-related sources figure accounts for background off-gassing from building materials, furniture, and materials typically found in that particular occupancy. Finally, the required zone outdoor airflow is the breathing zone outdoor airflow adjusted to reflect the "zone air distribution effectiveness" using adjustment factors in Table 6-2 of the standard. For multiple-zone systems, outdoor air intake flow is adjusted to reflect the "system ventilation efficiency" for the air distribution configuration, using adjustment factors in Table 6-3 of the standard.

Naturally Ventilated Spaces

When choosing natural ventilation, there are 2 ways to demonstrate credit compliance: 1 is by using the compliance path found in Chapter 2 of the CIBSE Applications Manual 10–2005 (AM10); the other is to provide documentation using a macroscopic, multizone, analytic model that predicts room-by-room air flow rates.

When using AM10 (see Figure 2-1), begin by establishing the required flow rates through each space. There is an acceptable average rate needed for IAQ and thermal comfort; exceeding this rate results in wasted energy during heating seasons. Additional ventilation is needed for summer cooling requirements. There are several ways to determine the acceptable average rate needed for IAQ and thermal comfort, such as by using a separate manual or simulation software listed in AM10; project teams should explain their choice. Submittals must include a narrative with information on the building, its orientation, and the glazing ratios. Include a summary of the internal heat gains and weather conditions; explain the ventilation strategy, including the airflow paths, rates planned for different operational periods during the day and night, peak internal temperatures, and means of shading for summer solar gains; provide sample calculations on how the opening size for operable windows, trickle vents and louvers was determined; and include the calculations for the driving pressure, showing the effects of both wind and stack-induced pressure differentials.

When using a macroscopic, multizone, analytic model that predicts room-by-room air flow rates, provide a narrative with the same information listed above and demonstrate that 90% of the occupied areas meet the room-by-room airflow rates. Indicate what standard was used, such as Volume A of the CIBSE Guide, ASHRAE 62.1–2007, Section 6.2, or other.

For a multiunit residential building, exhaust fans in kitchens and bathrooms can sometimes provide required ventilation rates.

	IEQ
NC	Credit 2
SCHOOLS	Credit 2
CS	Credit 2

CS In some instances, project teams may not know who will be the final occupants of core and shell buildings. In that case, use the default occupancy counts provided in Appendix 1. These numbers can be used for projects where occupancy is unknown as long as the gross square foot per occupant is no greater than that in the default occupancy count table. Other numbers can be used if justification is provided.

Core & Shell projects with multiple-zoned systems should use a "system ventilation efficiency," that reflects the expected occupant distribution. A tenant fit test or sample plan can be used to approximate the occupant distribution and estimate the "system ventilation efficiency." Not accounting for spaces with a high occupant density can lead to undersized ventilation systems and can affect compliance with ASHRAE 62.1–2007.

LEED for Core & Shell requires that applicants demonstrate that the delivered minimum zone outdoor airflow is at least 30% higher than the minimum airflow required by ASHRAE 62.1–2007 for each zone.

Table 1 shows how the sample space used in IEQ Prerequisite 1 has attained the 30% increase.

Table 1. ASHRAE 62.1–2007 Ventilation Rate Procedure

Zone				Table 6-1		Standard Case: ASHRAE 62.1–2007 Verification Rate Procedure	Table 6-2		Table 6-3				Design Case		
Zone	Occupancy Category	Area (sf)	People Outdoor Air Rate (cfm/ person)	Area Outdoor Air Rate (cfm/sf)	Occupant Density (#/ 1000 sf)	Breathing Zone Outdoor Air Flow Vbz (cfm)	Zone Air Distribution Effectiveness Ez	Zone Outdoor Air Flow Voz (cfm)	System Ventilation Efficiency Ev	Minimum Outdoor Air Intake Flow Vot (cfm)	Design Outdoor Air Intake Flow (cfm)	Zone Primary Air Flow Faction Vpz (cfm)	Primary Outdoor Air Fraction Zp = Voz/Vpz	% Increase Over Standard
General Office	Office Space	8000	5	0.06	5	680	1.0	680	1.0	680	900	8000	0.09	32%
Training Room	Lecture Classroom	750	7.5	0.06	65	411	1.2	342	0.9	380	500	1400	0.24	32%
Break Room	Conference Meeting	250	5	0.06	50	63	1.0	63	1.0	63	85	500	0.13	36%
Total		9000				1154		1085		1123	1485	9900		32%
Notes:	For the general office space, air distribution is overhead, hence Ez = 1. Outdoor air fraction, Zp, < 0.15, hence system ventilation efficiency is 1.0. For the training room, air distribution is underfloor, hence Ez = 1.2. Outdoor air fraction, Zp < 0.25, hence system ventilation efficiency is 0.9. For the break room, air distribution is overhead, hence Ez = 1. Outdoor air fraction, Zp, < 0.15, hence system ventilation efficiency is 1.0.													

	IEQ
NC	Credit 2
SCHOOLS	Credit 2
CS	Credit 2

Figure 1. Selecting Natural Ventilation for Nondomestic Buildings

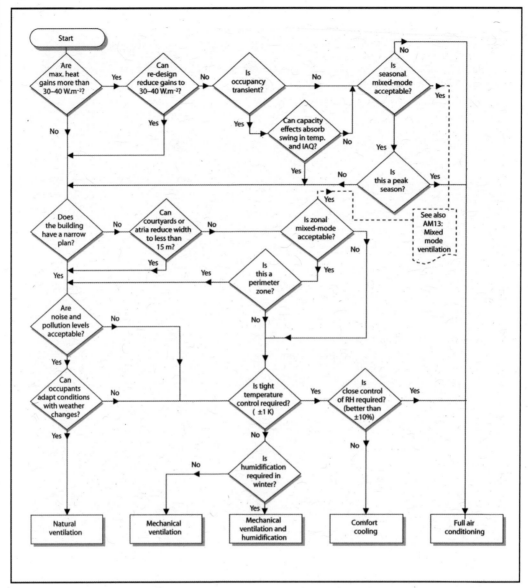

From CIBSE Applications Manual 10–2005. Reproduced with permission from the Chartered Institute of Building Services Engineers, London.

5. Timeline and Team

Most project teams decide early on whether to have a mechanical ventilation system, a passive ventilation system, or a combination. This decision might be influenced by the building size and type, as well as climatic, economic, and organizational considerations. Figure 1, from CIBSE AM–10, provides a decision diagram to help teams make an informed evaluation. In addition, project teams considering natural ventilation should evaluate site conditions and building design. Potential IAQ problems might arise from traffic exhaust, nearby polluting industries, and neighboring waste management sites.

For mechanical ventilation, the design and operating setpoints of the HVAC system will largely determine ventilation rates. Building owners and designers should determine whether increasing ventilation rates beyond ASHRAE 62.1–2007 requirements is a good idea for the facility. If so, the HVAC design and sizing should account for increased ventilation rates.

Occupants generally take a primary role in managing ventilation conditions in naturally ventilated buildings by opening and closing windows. Naturally ventilated buildings generally have somewhat more variable ventilation rates than actively conditioned buildings.

In addition to designing the HVAC systems properly and selecting appropriate building materials, the project team may choose to increase ventilation rates beyond standard practice as 1 way of providing superior indoor air quality. Managing IAQ concerns during construction and operation is also appropriate for many green building projects.

6. Calculations

Mechanically Ventilated Spaces

To show compliance in mechanically ventilated spaces, use the calculations in the ASHRAE User Manual and the IEQ Prerequisite 1 calculators, available for free download on the LEED Registered Project Tools page of the USGBC website. The same calculations are used to document IEQ Prerequisite 1.

Naturally Ventilated Spaces

Determine the opening sizes for operable windows, trickle vents, and louvers in accordance with CIBSE Applications Manual 10–2005. Alternatively, for project teams using a macroscopic, multizone, analytic model that predicts room-by-room airflow rates, provide the room-by-room outdoor airflow rates predicted by the analysis and a comparison with minimum ventilation rates required by ASHRAE 62.1–2007, Section 6.

7. Documentation Guidance

As a first step in preparing to complete the LEED-Online documentation requirements, work through the following measures. Refer to LEED-Online for the complete descriptions of all required documentation.

- Size mechanical equipment to accommodate increased ventilation rates.

- For naturally ventilated projects, maintain appropriate visual documentation (e.g., plans) of open areas within the project.

8. Examples

Ventilation rates as specified by ASHRAE must be determined for each space. The example in Table 2 calculates the percentage increase in ventilation for 3 sample spaces, each of which provides increased ventilation sufficient to meet the credit requirements.

Table 2. Sample Summary Calculations for Increased Mechanical Ventilation

Zone	Occupancy	Area (sf)	Standard Zone Outdoor Airflow Voz(cfm/sf)	Design Zone Outdoor Airflow (cfm/sf)	Percentage Increase
General office	Office space	8,000	0.088	0.115	30.7
Training room	Lecture hall	750	0.460	0.600	32.6
Break room	Conference, meeting	216	0.338	0.440	30.2

9. Exemplary Performance

This credit is not eligible for exemplary performance under the Innovation in Design section.

10. Regional Variations

Additional ventilation is more practical for mild climates, where increasing ventilation beyond the ASHRAE 62.1–2007 minimum rates will not have as great an impact on HVAC systems' capacity and energy consumption as in hot, humid, or cold climates. Natural ventilation and passive conditioning approaches are also more typical in mild and temperate climates, although there are precedents for passively conditioned buildings in all climates. There may be variable conditions in naturally ventilated buildings, but occupants are satisfied because they control their environment.

11. Operations and Maintenance Considerations

For mechanically ventilated systems, provide the building operator with copies of the ventilation rate procedure calculations for each zone used to show compliance with ASHRAE 62.1–2007. Over the building's life, these can be updated with actual occupancy values to adjust delivered ventilation rates as appropriate.

Provide maintenance personnel with the information needed to understand, maintain, and use the ventilation system and retain mechanical design documents showing zone configurations. Establish appropriate setpoints and control sequences, as well as recommendations for typical corrective actions, and include them in the facility's building operating plan and sequence of operations document. Establish procedures and schedules for testing and maintaining exhaust systems, and include them in the building's preventive maintenance plan.

12. Resources

Please see USGBC's LEED Registered Project Tools (http://www.usgbc.org/projecttools) for additional resources and technical information.

Websites
American National Standards Institute (ANSI)/ ASHRAE Standard 62.1–2007: Ventilation For Acceptable Indoor Air Quality
ASHRAE
http://www.ashrae.org
ASHRAE advances the science of heating, ventilation, air conditioning, and refrigeration for the public's benefit through research, standards writing, continuing education, and publications. To purchase ASHRAE standards and guidelines, visit the bookstore on the ASHRAE website.

Chartered Institute of Building Services Engineers (CIBSE) Applications Manual 10–2005, Natural Ventilation in Non-domestic Buildings
CIBSE, London
http://www.cibse.org
CIBSE Applications Manual 10–2005 provides guidance for implementing natural ventilation in nonresidential buildings. It provides detailed information on how to adopt natural ventilation as the sole servicing strategy for a building or as an element in a mixed mode design. According to the publisher, this manual "is a major revision of the Applications Manual (AM) first published in 1997. At the time, there was a significant expansion of interest in the application of engineered natural ventilation to the design of nondomestic buildings. The original AM10 sought to capture the state of knowledge as it existed in the mid-90s and present it in a form suited to the needs of every member of the design team. Some 10 years on from the time when the initial manual was conceived, the state of knowledge has increased, and experience in the design and operation of naturally ventilated

buildings has grown. This revision of AM10 is therefore a timely opportunity to update and enhance the guidance offered to designers and users of naturally ventilated buildings."

Building Assessment, Survey, and Evaluation Study
U.S. EnviroEPA
http://www.epa.gov/iaq/largebldgs/base_page.htm

Building Air Quality Action Plan
U.S. EPA
http://www.epa.gov/iaq/largebldgs/#Building%20Air%20Quality%20Action%20Plan

The Chartered Institution of Building Services Engineers (CIBSE)
http://www.cibse.org
Located in London, this organization publishes a series of guides on ventilation, including natural ventilation, on its own and in collaboration with other entities.

13. Definitions

Air-conditioning is the process of treating air to meet the requirements of a conditioned space by controlling its temperature, humidity, cleanliness, and distribution (ASHRAE 62.1–2007).

The **breathing zone** is the region within an occupied space between 3 and 6 feet above the floor and more than 2 feet from the walls or fixed air-conditioning equipment.

Conditioned space is the part of a building that is heated or cooled, or both, for the comfort of occupants. (ASHRAE 62.1–2007)

Contaminants are an unwanted airborne elements that may reduce air quality. (ASHRAE 62.1–2007)

Exfiltration is air leakage through cracks and interstices and through the ceilings, floors, and walls.

Exhaust air is removed from a space and discharged outside the building by means of mechanical or natural ventilation systems.

HVAC systems are equipment, distribution systems, and terminals that provide the processes of heating, ventilating, or air-conditioning. (ASHRAE 90.1-2007)

Indoor air quality (IAQ) is the nature of air inside a building that affects the health and well-being of building occupants. It is considered acceptable when there are no known contaminants at harmful concentrations as determined by cognizant authorities and with which a substantial majority (80% or more) of the people exposed do not express dissatisfaction. (ASHRAE 62.1–2007)

Infiltration is air leakage into conditioned spaces through cracks and interstices in ceilings, floors, and walls. (ASHRAE 62.1–2007).

Mechanical ventilation is provided by mechanically powered equipment, such as motor-driven fans and blowers, but not by devices such as wind-driven turbine ventilators and mechanically operated windows (ASHRAE 62.1–2007).

Mixed-mode ventilation combines mechanical and natural ventilation methods.

Natural ventilation is provided by thermal, wind, or diffusion effects through doors, windows, or other intentional openings in the building.

Off-gassing is the emission of volatile organic compounds (VOCs) from synthetic and natural products.

Outdoor air is the ambient air that enters a building through a ventilation system, either through natural ventilation or by infiltration. (ASHRAE 62.1–2007)

	IEQ
NC	Credit 2
SCHOOLS	Credit 2
CS	Credit 2

Recirculated air is removed from a space and reused as supply air, delivered by mechanical or natural ventilation.

Supply air is air delivered by mechanical or natural ventilation to a space, composed of any combination of outdoor air, recirculated air, or transfer air. (ASHRAE 62.1–2007)

Ventilation is the process of supplying air to or removing air from a space for the purpose of controlling air contaminant levels, humidity, or temperature within the space. (ASHRAE 62.1-2007).

CONSTRUCTION INDOOR AIR QUALITY MANAGEMENT PLAN— DURING CONSTRUCTION

	NC	SCHOOLS	CS
Credit	IEQ Credit 3.1	IEQ Credit 3.1	IEQ Credit 3
Points	1 point	1 point	1 point

Intent

To reduce indoor air quality (IAQ) problems resulting from construction or renovation and promote the comfort and well-being of construction workers and building occupants.

Requirements

NC, SCHOOLS & CS

Develop and implement an IAQ management plan for the construction and preoccupancy phases of the building as follows:

- During construction, meet or exceed the recommended control measures of the Sheet Metal and Air Conditioning National Contractors Association (SMACNA) IAQ Guidelines For Occupied Buildings Under Construction, 2nd Edition 2007, ANSI/ SMACNA 008-2008 (Chapter 3).

- Protect stored on-site and installed absorptive materials from moisture damage.

- If permanently installed air handlers are used during construction, filtration media with a minimum efficiency reporting value (MERV) of 8 must be used at each return air grille, as determined by ASHRAE Standard 52.2-1999 (with errata but without addenda). Replace all filtration media immediately prior to occupancy.

SCHOOLS Additional Requirement

- Prohibit smoking inside the building and within 25 feet of building entrances once the building is enclosed.

	IEQ
NC	Credit 3.1
SCHOOLS	Credit 3.1
CS	Credit 3

This credit seeks to recognize construction practices that help ensure high indoor air quality (IAQ) during construction and into occupancy.

1. Benefits and Issues to Consider

Environmental Issues

Reducing indoor air contaminants improves comfort levels, lowers absenteeism, and increases productivity. Demolition and construction practices lead to increased exposure to indoor air pollutants through the introduction of synthetic building materials, power equipment and vehicles, new furnishings, and finish materials. The negative effects of the construction process on indoor air quality can be heightened by reduced ventilation rates (typical during the construction phase) and a lack of attention to pollutant source control. If unaddressed, the contamination can result in poor IAQ extending over the lifetime of the building. Fortunately, there are IAQ management strategies that, if instituted during construction and before occupancy, will minimize potential problems (see Implementation).

Economic Issues

Consider the time and labor required to maintain a clean construction site. Protecting the ventilation system and isolating work that involves power equipment are critical methods to preventing the introduction of indoor air contaminants. Clean ventilation systems and building spaces can also extend the lifetime of the ventilation system and improve its efficiency, resulting in reduced energy use. Construction schedule disruption can be avoided through the proper sequencing of material installation, so as to reduce contamination and maintain the project schedule. Early coordination between the design team, contractor and subcontractors can minimize or eliminate scheduling delays.

CS For some Core & Shell building types, ongoing construction may overlap with tenant space build-out—often when the building is fully enclosed and major building systems are in place. Core & Shell project teams should carefully consider coordinating the construction IAQ management plan with tenants' plans and, ideally, a tenant IAQ management plan.

2. Related Credits

Construction activities can affect the IAQ of the building long after occupancy. Successfully implementing a construction IAQ management plan, selecting low-emitting finish materials and furnishings, and isolating indoor pollutant sources will reduce levels of indoor contaminants. The following credits relate to IAQ management before occupancy:

- IEQ Credit 3.2: Construction Indoor Air Quality Management Plan—Before Occupancy
- IEQ Credit 4: Low-Emitting Materials
- IEQ Credit 5: Indoor Chemical and Pollutant Source Control

CS Core & Shell projects are eligible for exemplary performance under the Innovation in Design section when project teams enforce a construction indoor air quality management plan for 100% of the tenant spaces. The following credits are therefore related when tenants pursue LEED for Commercial Interiors Certification. It is important to note that there are a number of credit synergies between LEED for Core & Shell and LEED for Commercial Interiors rating systems. This is intentional to encourage tenants within a Core & Shell-certified project to pursue LEED for Commercial Interiors certification.

- IEQ Credit 3.1: Construction IAQ Management Plan—During Construction
- IEQ Credit 3.2: Construction IAQ Management Plan—Before Occupancy
- IEQ Credit 4: Low-Emitting Materials
- IEQ Credit 5: Indoor Chemical and Pollutant Source Control

3. Summary of Referenced Standards

Sheet Metal and Air Conditioning Contractors National Association (SMACNA) IAQ Guidelines for Occupied Buildings under Construction, 2nd edition, Chapter 3, November 2007
http://www.smacna.org

The Sheet Metal and Air Conditioning Contractors National Association (SMACNA) is an international organization that developed guidelines for maintaining healthful indoor air quality during demolitions, renovations, and construction. The full document covers air pollutant sources, control measures, IAQ process management, quality control and documentation, interpersonal communication , sample projects, tables, references, resources, and checklists.

American National Standards Institute (ANSI)/ASHRAE Standard 52.2–1999: Method of Testing General Ventilation Air-Cleaning Devices for Removal Efficiency by Particle Size
ASHRAE ·

http://www.ashrae.org

This standard presents methods for testing air cleaners for 2 performance characteristics: the device's capacity for removing particles from the air stream and the device's resistance to airflow. The minimum efficiency reporting value (MERV) is based on 3 composite average particle size removal efficiency points. Consult the standard for a complete explanation of MERV calculations.

4. Implementation

Complete the construction IAQ management plan before construction begins. The plan should include agenda items to be discussed regularly at preconstruction and construction meetings. Continually educating subcontractors and field personnel and giving them the proper resources (e.g., collection bins, cleaning tools and materials) reinforce the importance of following the plan's procedures and encourage their compliance. When possible, the design team should select a member of the contractor's team to serve as the indoor air quality manager and take responsibility for identifying problems and implementing solutions. The referenced SMACNA standard recommends control measures in 5 areas: HVAC protection, source control, pathway interruption, housekeeping, and scheduling. Review the applicability of each control measure and include those that apply in the final construction IAQ management plan. The control measures are as follows:

HVAC Protection

Ideally during demolition and construction, the permanently installed HVAC systems should not be used because the systems can become contaminated and damaged. In most cases, using the HVAC system during construction activates the clock on the manufacturer's warranty, exposing the contractor to potential out-of-pocket costs if problems occur when the manufacturer's warranty has expired but the warranty for the building has not. Using temporary ventilation units is feasible, practical and generally not costly. Using temporary ventilation units is 1 strategy to meet the SMACNA control measure for HVAC protection. However, it does not satisfy all of the requirements of this credit on its own. Other strategies to mitigate contamination of both HVAC equipment and occupied spaces during construction are detailed below.

The contractor should protect all HVAC equipment from both dust and odors and seal all duct and equipment openings with plastic. If the system must be operated to maintain service to other occupied portions of the building or to protect finished work, the contractor should be sure to protect

IEQ	
NC	Credit 3.1
SCHOOLS	Credit 3.1
CS	Credit 3

the return/negative pressure side of the system. If the returns cannot be closed, the construction team should install and maintain temporary filters over grilles and openings. To comply with the credit requirements, the filtration medium must have a rating of MERV 8 or better. If an unducted plenum over the construction zone must be used, the team should isolate it by having all ceiling tiles in place. The construction team should check for leaks in the return ducts and air handlers and make needed repairs promptly. The contractor should avoid using the mechanical rooms for construction storage.

The contractor should replace all filtration media just before occupancy, installing only a single set of final filtration media. Note that the requirement for MERV 13 rated filters has been moved to IEQ Credit 5: Indoor Chemical and Pollutant Source Control. This credit does not regulate the efficiency of the filters used for the long-term operation of the building.

Source Control

The architect or designer should specify finish materials such as paints, carpet, composite wood, adhesives and sealants that have low-toxicity levels or none at all. (Note that the selection of low-emitting materials is covered under IEQ Credit 4: Low-Emitting Materials). The Construction IAQ Management Plan should specify the control measures for materials containing VOCs. The construction team should recover, isolate and ventilate containers housing toxic materials. Finally, exhaust fumes from idling vehicles and gasoline-fueled tools. Finally, exhaust fumes from idling vehicles and gasoline-fueled tools to the exterior of the building through the use of funnels or temporary piping.

Pathway Interruption

During construction, the contractor must isolate areas of work to prevent contamination of clean or occupied spaces. Depending on weather conditions, the contractor should ventilate using 100% outside air to exhaust contaminated air directly to the outside during installation of VOC-emitting materials. Depressurizing the work area will allow the air pressure differential between construction and clean areas to contain dust and odors. The contractor should provide temporary barriers that contain the construction area.

Housekeeping

The project and building maintenance teams should institute cleaning activities designed to control contaminants in building spaces during construction and before occupancy. The maintenance team should protect all porous building materials from exposure to moisture and store them in a clean area before installation. The team should use vacuum cleaners with high-efficiency particulate filters, increase cleaning frequency and use wetting agents for dust.

Scheduling

The contractor and the project team should coordinate construction activities to minimize or eliminate disruption of operations in the occupied portions of the building. The contractor should sequence construction activities carefully over the duration of the project to minimize the impact on IAQ. It might be necessary to conduct activities with high pollution potential during off hours, such as weekends or evenings, to allow time for new materials to air out. The contractor should plan adequate time to conduct flush-out and IAQ test procedures before occupancy. Upon completion of construction, the contractor should replace all filtration media just before occupancy, and coordinate this activity with the activities and requirements addressed in IEQ Credit 3.2: Construction IAQ Management—Before Occupancy and IEQ Credit 5: Indoor Chemical and Pollution Source Control.

	IEQ
NC	Credit 3.1
SCHOOLS	Credit 3.1
CS	Credit 3

CS While future tenant fit-outs are not addressed in LEED for Core & Shell, minimizing cross contamination of existing tenant spaces as future tenants build out their spaces should also be considered. The Sheet Metal and Air Conditioning Contractors' National Association's (SMACNA's) IAQ Guidelines for Occupied Buildings under Construction details many measures to help improve the indoor air quality of occupied buildings under construction. One measure is to seal off the return air system from the construction site. Another measure is to exhaust contaminants directly from construction to the building's exterior. A comprehensive building IAQ management plan can help minimize health risks to existing tenants during construction of new tenant space.

5. Timeline and Team

Scheduling aspects of this credit are related to the sequencing of demolition and construction procedures as well as the installation of finish materials. It is best to select low-emitting materials and install any products that emit VOCs before installing absorbent materials, such as ceiling tiles, gypsum wallboard, fabric furnishings, carpet, and insulation. If possible, store these materials in an isolated area to minimize contamination.

Give subcontractors and field personnel copies of the construction IAQ management plan prior to the initiation of work, and contractually require them to implement the applicable plan components. Post a copy of the plan in an obvious location on the job site and conduct periodic visual inspections to help enforce compliance. Maintaining a regular photo log of the prescribe strategies is advised.

6. Calculations

There are no calculations required for this credit.

7. Documentation Guidance

As a first step in preparing to complete the LEED-Online documentation requirements, work through the following measures. Refer to LEED-Online for the complete descriptions of all required documentation.

- Create a written construction IAQ management plan for use during demolition and construction.

- Maintain a detailed photo log of the construction IAQ management plan practices followed during construction.

8. Examples

Indoor Air Quality Management Plan (Facility Alterations)

1. Goals and Scope

   To limit indoor air quality problems resulting from construction or renovation projects, (Building) must implement this Indoor Air Quality (IAQ) management plan to sustain the comfort and well-being of occupants and construction workers.

2. SMACNA Guidelines: The following is a list of example procedures. The project team should create a Construction IAQ Management Plan appropriate to the scope of work being completed.

   The following Construction IAQ Management Plan measures must be implemented throughout the construction and occupancy phase of any project.

   A. HVAC Protection: Provide project-specific measures to be employed.
      - When possible, HVAC system should be shut down during construction.
   B. Source Control: Provide project-specific measures to be employed.
      - Product substitution: low emitting paints, adhesives, sealants,and carpets must be used when feasible.
   C. Pathway Interruption: Provide project specific measures to be employed.
   D. Housekeeping: Provide project-specific measures to be employed.
      - Services must utilize best practices for minimizing IAQ problems, such as dust suppression, cleaning frequency, cleaning efficiency, water and spill cleanup, protection of on-site or installed absorptive and porous material.
   E. Scheduling: Provide project specific measures to be employed.

      - Building flush out: After construction ends and all interior finishes have been installed, new filtration media must be installed and a flush out of the construction area must be performed. The flush out must comply with the procedure listed within the LEED Rating System

3. Responsible Party

   Teams and individuals involved in activities pertaining to the policy:

   Facility Manager

   General Contractor

   Building Owner

4. Guidance for Resources and Implementation

   A. Sheet Metal and Air Conditioning National Contractors Association (SMACNA) IAQ Guidelines for Occupied Buildings under Construction, second edition, November 2007, Chapter 3

5. Quality Assurance and Quality Control Processes

   During any construction or renovation project the following strategies must be utilized to ensure the implementation of this plan:

   A. A list of filtration media utilized, including the manufacturer, model number, MERV rating, date of installation, and date of replacement.
   B. Photographs documenting the IAQ control measures implemented at 3 time periods during the project (e.g., beginning, middle, and end). The photos will be labeled to highlight the approach taken.
   C. Narrative documenting the flush-out procedure utilized, including airflow and duration.

---

9. Exemplary Performance

NC & SCHOOLS This credit is not eligible for exemplary performance under the Innovation in Design section.

CS Projects that require and enforce a construction indoor air quality management plan for 100% of tenant spaces are eligible for exemplary performance under the Innovation in Design section.

10. Regional Variations

There are no regional variations applicable to this credit.

11. Operations and Maintenance Considerations

Provide the facility manager with a copy of the IAQ management plan used during construction to facilitate adoption of similar practices during future alterations or additions.

12. Resources

Please see USGBC's LEED Registered Project Tools (http://www.usgbc.org/projecttools) for additional resources and technical information.

Websites

Controlling Pollutants and Sources

U.S. EPA

http://www.epa.gov/iaq/schooldesign/controlling.html

The EPA website provides information regarding typical sources of indoor and outdoor pollutants and methods for resolving indoor air quality concerns. Find detailed information on exhaust or spot ventilation practices during construction .

Indoor Air Pollution Report, July 2005

California Air Resources Board

http://www.arb.ca.gov/research/indoor/ab1173/finalreport.htm

This report, released in July 2005, covers the significant health effects caused by indoor air pollution, including respiratory illness and disease, asthma attacks, cancer, and premature death. The report describes the health effects, sources, and concentrations of indoor air pollutants; existing regulations, guidelines, and practices for indoor air pollution; and ways to prevent and reduce indoor air pollution.

The State of Washington Program and IAQ Standards

http://www.aerias.org/DesktopModules/ArticleDetail.aspx?articleId=85

This standard was the first state-initiated program to ensure the design of buildings with acceptable IAQ.

Sheet Metal and Air Conditioning Contractors' National Association, Inc. (SMACNA)

http://www.smacna.org

SMACNA is an international organization that developed guidelines for maintaining healthful indoor air quality during demolitions, renovations, and construction. The professional trade association publishes the referenced standard as well as Indoor Air Quality: A Systems Approach, a comprehensive document that covers air pollutant sources, control measures, IAQ process management, quality control and documentation, interpersonal communication , sample projects, tables, references, resources, and checklists.

Print Media

Indoor Air Quality: A Facility Manager's Guide, published by the Construction Technology Centre Atlantic, is written as a comprehensive review of indoor air quality issues and solutions. Purchase the report online at http://ctca.unb.ca/CTCA/communication/IAQ/Order_IAQ.htm.

13. Definitions

A **construction IAQ management plan** outlines measures to minimize contamination in a specific project building during construction and describes procedures to flush the building of contaminants prior to occupancy.

HVAC systems are equipment, distribution systems, and terminals that provide the processes of heating, ventilating, or air-conditioning. (ASHRAE 90.1–2007)

Indoor air quality (**IAQ**) is the nature of air inside a building that affects the health and well-being of building occupants. It is considered acceptable when there are no known contaminants at harmful concentrations as determined by cognizant authorities and with which a substantial majority (80% or more) of the people exposed do not express dissatisfaction. (ASHRAE 62.1–2007)

Minimum efficiency reporting value (**MERV**) is a filter rating established by the American Society of Heating, Refrigerating, and Air-Conditioning Engineers (ASHRAE 52.2–1999, Method of Testing General Ventilation Air Cleaning Devices for Removal Efficiency by Particle Size). MERV categories range from 1 (very low efficiency) to 16 (very high).

CONSTRUCTION INDOOR AIR QUALITY MANAGEMENT PLAN— BEFORE OCCUPANCY

	NC	SCHOOLS	CS
Credit	IEQ Credit 3.2	IEQ Credit 3.2	NA
Points	1 point	1 point	NA

Intent

To reduce indoor air quality (IAQ) problems resulting from construction or renovation to promote the comfort and well-being of construction workers and building occupants.

Requirements

NC & SCHOOLS

Develop an (IAQ) management plan and implement it after all finishes have been installed and the building has been completely cleaned before occupancy.

OPTION 1. Flush-Out[1]

PATH 1

> After construction ends, prior to occupancy and with all interior finishes installed, install new filtration media and perform a building flush-out by supplying a total air volume of 14,000 cubic feet of outdoor air per square foot of floor area while maintaining an internal temperature of at least 60° F and relative humidity no higher than 60%.

OR

PATH 2

> If occupancy is desired prior to completion of the flush-out, the space may be occupied following delivery of a minimum of 3,500 cubic feet of outdoor air per square foot of floor area. Once the space is occupied, it must be ventilated at a minimum rate of 0.30 cubic feet per minute (cfm) per square foot of outside air or the design minimum outside air rate determined in IEQ Prerequisite 1: Minimum Indoor Air Quality Performance, whichever is greater. During each day of the flush-out period, ventilation must begin a minimum of 3 hours prior to occupancy and continue during occupancy. These conditions must be maintained until a total of 14,000 cubic feet per square foot of outside air has been delivered to the space.

OR

OPTION 2. Air Testing

> Conduct baseline IAQ testing, after construction ends and prior to occupancy, using testing protocols consistent with the EPA Compendium of Methods for the Determination of Air Pollutants in Indoor Air and as additionally detailed in the LEED Reference Guide for Green Building Design and Construction, 2009 Edition.

1 All finishes must be installed prior to flush-out.

NC & SCHOOLS (continued)

Demonstrate that the contaminant maximum concentrations listed below are not exceeded.

Contaminant	Maximum Concentration
Formaldehyde	27 parts per billion
Particulates (PM10)	50 micrograms per cubic meter
Total volatile organic compounds (TVOCs)	500 micrograms per cubic meter
4-Phenylcyclohexene (4-PCH)*	6.5 micrograms per cubic meter
Carbon monoxide (CO)	9 part per million and no greater than 2 parts per million above outdoor levels

*This test is required only if carpets and fabrics with styrene butadiene rubber (SBR) latex backing are installed as part of the base building systems.

For each sampling point where the maximum concentration limits are exceeded, conduct an additional flush-out with outside air and retest the noncompliant concentrations. Repeat until all requirements are met. When retesting noncompliant building areas, take samples from the same locations as in the first test, although it is not required.

Conduct the air sample testing as follows:

- All measurements must be conducted prior to occupancy, but during normal occupied hours with the building ventilation system started at the normal daily start time and operated at the minimum outside air flow rate for the occupied mode throughout the test.

- All interior finishes must be installed, including but not limited to millwork, doors, paint, carpet and acoustic tiles. Movable furnishings such as workstations and partitions should be in place for the testing, although it is not required.

- The number of sampling locations willdependon the size of the building and number of ventilation systems. For each portion of the building served by a separate ventilation system, the number of sampling points must not be less than 1 per 25,000 square feet or for each contiguous floor area, whichever is larger. Include areas with the least ventilation and greatest presumed source strength.

- Air samples must be collected between 3 and 6 feet from the floor to represent the breathing zone of occupants, and over a minimum 4-hour period.

This credit seeks to recognize postconstruction practices that help ensure high indoor air quality during occupancy.

	IEQ
NC	Credit 3.2
SCHOOLS	Credit 3.2
CS	NA

1. Benefits and Issues to Consider

Environmental Issues

Reducing contaminants inside buildings results in greater occupants comfort, lower absenteeism, and improved productivity. Construction inevitably introduces contaminants to building interiors. If unaddressed, contamination can result in poor IAQ extending over the lifetime of a building. Fortunately, there are IAQ management strategies that, if instituted during construction and before occupancy, will minimize potential problems (see Implementation).

Economic Issues

Additional time and labor may be required during construction to protect and clean ventilation systems and building spaces. These actions can extend the lifetime of ventilation systems and improve their efficiency, resulting in reduced energy use. The sequencing of material installation so as to reduce contamination may require additional time and could potentially delay occupancy. However, early coordination between the design team, contractor, and subcontractors can minimize or eliminate scheduling delays.

2. Related Credits

Comprehensive construction IAQ management consists of best practices both during construction and after construction prior to occupancy. These activities are typically governed by the same management plan. The following credit also requires development and implementation of a construction IAQ management plan:

- IEQ Credit 3.1: Construction Indoor Air Quality Management Plan During Construction

The materials that are specified and installed within the external moisture barrier of the building, as well as filtration, can directly affect air quality and influence the results for air quality testing. Refer also to the following credits:

- IEQ Credit 4: Low-Emitting Materials

- IEQ Credit 5: Indoor Chemical and Pollutant Source Control

Dilution of indoor air contaminants can typically be achieved by introducing outdoor air. The following credit and prerequisite deal with ventilation rates:

- IEQ Prerequisite 1: Minimum Indoor Air Quality Performance

- IEQ Credit 2: Increased Ventilation

3. Summary of Referenced Standard

U.S. Environmental Protection Agency Compendium of Methods for the Determination of Air Pollutants in Indoor Air

This standard is available from NTIS (800) 553-6847 with the ordering number PB90200288. According to the Compendium, the EPA created this document to "provide regional, state and local environmental regulatory agencies with step-by-step sampling and analysis procedures for the determination of selected pollutants in indoor air. Determination of pollutants in indoor air is a complex task, primarily because of the wide variety of compounds of interest and the lack of standardized sampling and analysis procedures. The Compendium has been prepared to provide a standardized format for such analytical procedures. A core set of 10 chapters with each chapter containing 1 or more methods are presented in the current document. Compendium covers a variety

	IEQ
NC	Credit 3.2
SCHOOLS	Credit 3.2
CS	NA

of active and passive sampling procedures, as well as several analytical techniques both on and off site..."

4. Implementation

Flush-Out Procedure

This compliance path uses the building HVAC system to evacuate airborne contaminants. The flush-out can begin only after all construction work, including punch-list items, is completed. Finalize all cleaning, complete the final test and balancing of HVAC systems, and make sure the HVAC control is functional prior to the flush out. (This is especially important if the occupants will be moving in during the second phase of the flush-out.) Commissioning can occur during the flush-out if it does not introduce any additional contaminants into the building.

The flush-out procedure discussed below assumes that the building's HVAC system will be used, but alternatives are acceptable if they meet the air quantity, temperature, and humidity requirements.

One approach uses temporary supply and exhaust systems placed into windows or window openings. EPA's Indoor Air Quality for Schools website provides information on exhaust and spot ventilation during construction that can be helpful for design teams who are considering using this approach. Make sure that the airflow is not short-circuited, which could leave remote corners of the project spaces with inadequate circulation or cause unanticipated increases in other parts of the building other parts of the building (such as a stack effect up elevator shafts).

If the space's central HVAC system is used, remove any temporary filters and duct coverings installed as part of the construction IAQ management plan. Replace the HVAC filtration media with new media; if the system is configured to filter only outside air, the filters do not need to be replaced. New filters that meet the design specification and that were installed prior to the start of the flush-out will also satisfy the requirements of IEQ Credit 3.1, Construction IAQ Management Plan During Construction. When attempting to earn IEQ Credit 5, Indoor Chemical and Pollution Source Control, these filters must be MERV 13 or better. Depending on their condition following the flush-out, some or all of the filters might be ready for replacement, but this is not a condition for satisfying the credit requirements.

Outside air is used to dilute and remove off-gassed contaminants. The quantity of outside air that must be introduced to the project space for the flush-out is 14,000 cubic feet of air per square foot of floor area. Occupants may move in only after the initial flush-out phase, when 3,500 cubic feet of air per square foot has been replaced (Figure 3.2-1). However, the initial flush-out phase does not signal the completion of the flush-out: A total of 14,000 cubic feet of outside air must be supplied per square foot of floor area before the HVAC system is switched to its normal operational mode.

Figure 1. Sample Air Quantity for Flush-Out

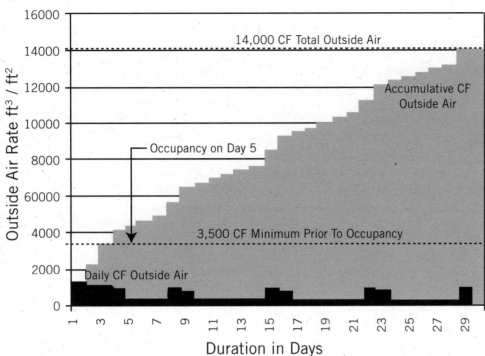

	IEQ
NC	Credit 3.2
SCHOOLS	Credit 3.2
CS	NA

Not all outside air is equal. Depending upon geography and season, outside air can be very cold or damp. Because of this, prudent limits have been set to ensure that no harm comes to the building and its occupants. The rate of outside air should not cause the interior temperature to drop below 60°F, and relative humidity should not exceed 60%.

During an occupied flush-out phase, a minimum ventilation rate must begin at least 3 hours before daily occupancy and continue while the space is occupied. The rate of outside air must be at least 0.30 cubic feet per minute per square foot or the design minimum outside air rate, whichever is greater. The design minimum outside air rate should be determined using ASHRAE 62.1–2007, the same criteria for IEQ Prerequisite 1, Minimum Indoor Air Quality Performance, or the applicable local code if it is more stringent. The 0.30 cubic feet per minute per square foot rate may be several times the ASHRAE 62.1–2007 requirement for a project's planned occupancy. As a result, consider the minimum flush-out rate during the early stages of HVAC design.

There are other thermal comfort, expense, and operational considerations to evaluate when preparing to occupy a space before the end of the flush-out. Check to make sure the HVAC system can maintain temperatures within a range that is comfortable for the occupants; opinions formed during this period may last long after the system is operating normally.

There are numerous expense and operational issues to consider, such as the rent or lease details or the existing HVAC system capacity to accommodate the flush-out criteria. Input from the entire project team will help determine the best approach. When completed, make the evaluation and the resulting flush-out strategy part of the IAQ management plan.

When there are multiple HVAC systems that can operate independently, it is acceptable to flush out portions of the building as they are completed, but no additional construction work can occur once the flush-out of an area begins. Isolate completed areas from those under construction per SMACNA IAQ Guidelines for Occupied Buildings under Construction.

	IEQ
NC	Credit 3.2
SCHOOLS	Credit 3.2
CS	NA

Air Quality Testing

The baseline IAQ testing approach is meant to confirm that major contaminants are below recognized acceptable levels before occupancy. While the list included in the credit is not intended to be all-inclusive, it approximates the major forms of postconstruction airborne constituents.

Testing results that meet the credit requirements indicate that the project has implemented a successful construction IAQ management plan; low-emitting materials have been specified; cleanup has been thorough; and the HVAC system is providing adequate ventilation. They can also mean that occupancy can potentially occur sooner than what might be possible if the flush-out compliance path had been followed. Ideally the groundwork should be laid for baseline testing during the design process by making sure the testing requirements are included in Division 1 of the project construction specifications. This credit does not establish qualifications for the laboratory or those conducting the sampling; however, the project team should evaluate the capabilities of the IAQ specialist, industrial hygienist, and testing facility being considered for field sampling of IAQ in buildings.

During construction, be vigilant about avoiding substitutions for the specified low-emitting materials. Use low-VOC cleaning supplies to prevent short-term high-VOC levels that may affect test results. Vacuum cleaners with HEPA filtration will help capture particulates.

Projects also following the requirements of IEQ Credit 3.1, Construction IAQ Management Plan During Construction, should replace all filtration media after the final cleaning and complete the air test and balancing of the HVAC system before beginning the baseline IAQ testing. The IAQ maximum contaminant levels are dependent on the HVAC system operating under normal conditions with minimum outdoor airflow rates; that way, the air tested will be as similar as possible to what the occupants will be breathing. The protocols described in the referenced publication, EPA's Compendium of Methods for the Determination of Air Pollutants in Indoor Air, are recommended, but others may be used valid justification is provided. Select the sampling locations carefully to find the concentrations in areas with the least ventilation and, potentially, the greatest presumed contaminant source strength. Take at least 1 sample per 25,000 square feet in each portion of the building served by a separate ventilation system. For example, in a 20,000-square-foot tenant space served by 3 rooftop units—1 each for the north and south elevations (general office area) and the third for a training room and conference rooms—take samples in at least 3 places, even though 2 units serve 1 general office area. Take the samples in the breathing zone, between 3 feet and 6 feet above the floor, during normal occupied hours with the HVAC system operating at normal daily start times and at the minimum outside airflow rate. Follow-up samples might be needed, so record the exact sample locations. If a test sample exceeds the maximum concentration level, flush out the space by increasing the rate of outside air. While the credit requirements do not prescribe the duration of the flush-out, those responsible for testing should make an evaluation based on the contaminant, its concentration, and the potential source. Off-gassing characteristics of sources differ; some deplete rapidly, while others emit at a steady rate over an extended period. Resample and confirm compliance before allowing occupancy. The retest may be limited to the chemical contaminants that produced excessive chemical concentration levels in the initial test.

5. Timeline and Team

During the design phase, include language requiring the general contractor to develop and implement a construction IAQ management plan that includes a flush-out procedure and/or air quality testing that meets the requirements of this credit.

After construction and installation of all finishes (including furniture and furnishings), conduct indoor air quality testing and/or a flush-out per the construction IAQ management plan and in accordance with the requirements of this credit.

Some additional time and labor may be required during and after construction to protect and clean ventilation systems. With early coordination for the sequencing of material installation and coordination between the contractor and subcontractors, the team can minimize or eliminate scheduling delays.

6. Calculations

If a building flush-out is performed before occupancy, the total quantity of outdoor air that must be delivered to the space is calculated as follows:

Phased flush-out:

Phase 1

Building Area (sf)	X	3,500 ft of Outdoor Air	=	Cubic Feet of Air Needed Prior to Occupancy

Phase 2

Building Area (sf)	X	10,500 ft of Outdoor Air	=	Cubic Feet of Air Needed to Complete Flush-Out

Nonphased flush-out:

Building Area (sf)	X	14,000 ft of Outdoor Air	=	Cubic Feet of Air Needed Prior to Occupancy

Note: feet of outdoor air = cubic feet per square foot

7. Documentation Guidance

As a first step in preparing to complete the LEED-Online documentation requirements, work through the following measures. Refer to LEED-Online for the complete descriptions of all required documentation.

- Maintain a written construction IAQ management plan.

- For projects completing a flush-out procedure, record dates, occupancy, outdoor air delivery rates, internal temperature, and humidity, as well as any special considerations.

- For projects completing IAQ testing, maintain a copy of the testing report and verify that all required contaminants are accounted for and reported in the correct unit of measure.

8. Examples

Table 1. Time for Flush-Out Options

	Square Foot of Office	Outdoor Air Required for Flush-Out (cfm/sf)	Volume of Air Required Before Occupancy (cu. ft.)	Time Before Occupancy (days)	Minimum Outdoor Air Delivery Rate Post-Occupancy (cfm)	Time to Complete Flush-Out @ Minimum Delivery Rate (days)
Pre-Occupancy Option	50,000	14,000	700,000,000	32.4	0	0
Post-Occupancy Option	50,000	14,000	175,000,000	8.1	15,000	24.3

Note: Assuming the building has a 15,000 cfm air handler, capable of operating at 100% OA while maintaining 60° F and 60% RH 24 hr/day

9. Exemplary Performance

This credit is not eligible for exemplary performance under the Innovation in Design section.

	IEQ
NC	Credit 3.2
SCHOOLS	Credit 3.2
CS	NA

10. Regional Variations

For projects that pursue this credit through the flush-out options in regions where there may be humid or cold outdoor air, maintain the indoor air temperature at or above 60°F and maintain the relative humidity at or below 60%. When weather conditions may affect the ability to sufficiently heat, cool, or dehumidify the supply air, careful coordination between the project schedule and seasonal variations is crucial.

11. Operations and Maintenance Considerations

Minimize potential sources of indoor air contamination. If such sources must be introduced, consider flushing out the affected areas of the building before those areas are occupied.

Use periodic IAQ testing to verify safe, healthful conditions.

If applicable, provide building operators with information about the flush-out procedures used during construction to facilitate adoption of similar practices following future alterations or additions.

12. Resources

Please see USGBC's LEED Registered Project Tools (http://www.usgbc.org/projecttools) for additional resources and technical information.

Websites
Indoor Air Pollution Report, July, 2005
California Air Resources Board
http://www.arb.ca.gov/research/indoor/ab1173/finalreport.htm

Controlling Pollutants and Sources, IAQ Design for Schools
U.S. EPA
http://www.epa.gov/iaq/schooldesign/controlling.html
This EPA website offers detailed information on exhaust or spot ventilation practices during construction activity.

State of Washington Program and IAQ Standards
http://www.aerias.org/DesktopModules/ArticleDetail.aspx?articleId=85
This standard was the first state-initiated program to ensure the design of buildings with acceptable IAQ.

Sheet Metal and Air Conditioning Contractors' National Association
http://www.smacna.org
SMACNA is an international organization that developed guidelines for maintaining healthful indoor air quality during demolitions, renovations, and construction. They publish *Indoor Air Quality: A Systems Approach,* which covers air pollutant sources, control measures, IAQ process management, quality control and documentation, interpersonal communication , sample projects, tables, references, resources, and checklists.

Print Media
Indoor Air Quality: A Facility Manager's Guide, Construction Technology Centre Atlantic, is written as a comprehensive review of IAQ issues and solutions. Purchase the report online at http://ctca.unb.ca/CTCA/communication/IAQ/Order_IAQ.htm or call (506) 453-5000.

Compendium of Methods for the Determination of Inorganic Compounds in Ambient Air, U.S. EPA
This standard is available for purchase from NTIS. To order, call (800) 553-6847 and use order number PB90200288.

13. Definitions

	IEQ
NC	Credit 3.2
SCHOOLS	Credit 3.2
CS	NA

A **construction IAQ management plan** outlines measures to minimize contamination in a specific building during construction and to flush the building of contaminants before occupancy.

Contaminants are unwanted airborne elements that may reduce air quality. (ASHRAE 62.1–2007)

HVAC systems are equipment, distribution systems, and terminals that provide the processes of heating, ventilating, or air-conditioning. (ASHRAE 90.1-2007)

Indoor air quality (**IAQ**) is the nature of air inside a building that affects the health and well-being of building occupants. It is considered acceptable when there are no known contaminants at harmful concentrations as determined by cognizant authorities and with which a substantial majority (80% or more) of the people exposed do not express dissatisfaction. (ASHRAE 62.1–2007)

Off-gassing is the emission of volatile organic compounds (VOCs) from synthetic and natural products.

Outdoor air is the ambient air that enters a building through a ventilation system, either through natural ventilation or by infiltration. (ASHRAE 62.1–2007)

Thermal comfort exists when occupants express satisfaction with the thermal environment.

Ventilation is the process of supplying air to or removing air from a space for the purpose of controlling air contaminant levels, humidity, or temperature within the space. (ASHRAE 62.1-2007).

LOW-EMITTING MATERIALS—ADHESIVES AND SEALANTS

	NC	SCHOOLS	CS
Credit	IEQ Credit 4.1	IEQ Credit 4.1	IEQ Credit 4.1
Points	1 point	1 point	1 point

Intent

To reduce the quantity of indoor air contaminants that are odorous, irritating and/or harmful to the comfort and well-being of installers and occupants.

Requirements

NC & CS

All adhesives and sealants used on the interior of the building (i.e., inside of the weatherproofing system and applied on-site) must comply with the following requirements as applicable to the project scope[1]:

- Adhesives, Sealants and Sealant Primers must comply with South Coast Air Quality Management District (SCAQMD) Rule #1168. Volatile organic compound (VOC) limits listed in the table below correspond to an effective date of July 1, 2005 and rule amendment date of January 7, 2005.

Architectural Applications	VOC Limit (g/L less water)	Specialty Applications	VOC Limit (g/L less water)
Indoor carpet adhesives	50	PVC welding	510
Carpet pad adhesives	50	CPVC welding	490
Wood flooring adhesives	100	ABS welding	325
Rubber floor adhesives	60	Plastic cement welding	250
Subfloor adhesives	50	Adhesive primer for plastic	550
Ceramic tile adhesives	65	Contact adhesive	80
VCT and asphalt adhesives	50	Special purpose contact adhesive	250
Drywall and panel adhesives	50	Structural wood member adhesive	140
Cove base adhesives	50	Sheet applied rubber lining operations	850
Multipurpose construction adhesives	70	Top and trim adhesive	250
Structural glazing adhesives	100		
Substrate Specific Applications	**VOC Limit (g/L less water)**	**Sealants**	**VOC Limit (g/L less water)**
Metal to metal	30	Architectural	250
Plastic foams	50	Nonmembrane roof	300
Porous material (except wood)	50	Roadway	250
Wood	30	Single-ply roof membrane	450
Fiberglass	80	Other	420
Sealant Primers	**VOC Limit (g/L less water)**		
Architectural, nonporous	250		
Architectural, porous	775		
Other	750		

1   The use of a VOC budget is permissible for compliance with this credit.

NC & CS (continued)

- Aerosol Adhesives must comply with Green Seal Standard for Commercial Adhesives GS-36 requirements in effect on October 19, 2000.

Aerosol Adhesives	VOC Limit
General purpose mist spray	65% VOCs by weight
General purpose web spray	55% VOCs by weight
Special purpose aerosol adhesives (all types)	70% VOCs by weight

SCHOOLS

All adhesives and sealants installed in the building interior (defined as inside the weatherproofing system and applied on-site) must meet the testing and product requirements of the California Department of Health Services Standard Practice for the Testing of Volatile Organic Emissions from Various Sources Using Small-Scale Environmental Chambers, including 2004 Addenda.

Schools projects may choose from IEQ Credits 4.1-4.6 for a maximum of 4 points.

1. Benefits and Issues to Consider

Many building products contain compounds that have a negative impact on indoor air quality (IAQ) and the Earth's atmosphere. The most prominent of these compounds—volatile organic compounds (VOCs)—contribute to smog generation and air pollution as well as adversely affect the well-being of building occupants. Low-emitting materials have a positive impact on both outdoor and indoor air quality.

	IEQ
NC	Credit 4.1
SCHOOLS	Credit 4.1
CS	Credit 4.1

Environmental Issues

VOCs react with sunlight and nitrogen oxides (NOx) in the atmosphere to form ground-level ozone, a chemical that has detrimental effects on human health, agricultural crops, forests, and ecosystems.[25] This ground-level ozone damages lung tissue, reduces lung function, and sensitizes the lungs to other irritants. Additionally, ground-level ozone is also a major component of smog.

Economic Issues

Healthy occupants are more productive and have less illness-related absenteeism. Materials with high-VOC content can threaten occupants' health and may decrease their productivity, increasing expenses and liability for building owners, operators, and insurance companies. Because of these issues, the construction market is driving product manufacturers to offer low-VOC alternatives to conventional building products. Costs for these products are generally competitive with conventional materials; however, some low-VOC materials are more expensive, particularly when the products are new to the marketplace. Low-VOC alternatives may also be difficult to obtain for some product types. These issues likely will fade as use of low-VOC products become more commonplace.

2. Related Credits

Because the intent of this credit is to reduce odorous, irritating, and/or harmful indoor air contaminants, the following other credits may be applicable:

- IEQ Credit 4.2: Low Emitting Materials—Paints and Coatings
- IEQ Credit 4.3: Low Emitting Materials—Flooring Systems
- IEQ Credit 4.4: Low Emitting Materials—Composite Wood and Agrifiber Products
- IEQ Credit 4.5: Low Emitting Materials—Furniture and Furnishings (Specific to Schools)
- IEQ Credit 4.6: Low Emitting Materials—Ceiling and Wall Systems (Specific to Schools)

SCHOOLS Acoustical elements within the building may require special installation considerations, which can necessitate careful coordination between acoustical concerns and the materials specifier. Indoor environmental quality also encompasses occupants' auditory comfort and well-being, which are covered under these 2 credits:

- IEQ Prerequisite 3: Minimum Acoustical Performance
- IEQ Credit 9: Enhanced Acoustical Performance

Scheduling strategies and the use and tracking of building materials are also addressed in the contractor orientation training, covered under these 2 credits:

- IEQ Credit 3.1: Construction IAQ Management Plan During Construction
- IEQ Credit 3.2: Construction IAQ Management Plan Before Occupancy

Indoor air quality is affected by sources generated within the building itself and introduced into its spaces. Both sources are addressed in the following prerequisite and credit:

- IEQ Prerequisite 2: Environmental Tobacco Smoke (ETS) Control
- IEQ Credit 5: Indoor Chemical and Pollutant Source Control

3. Summary of Referenced Standards

South Coast Air Quality Management District (SCAQMD) Amendment to South Coast Rule 1168, VOC Limits, effective January 7, 2005

South Coast Air Quality Management District

http://www.aqmd.gov/rules/reg/reg11/r1168.pdf

The South Coast Air Quality Management District is a governmental organization in southern California with the mission to maintain healthful air quality for its residents. The organization established source-specific standards to reduce air quality impacts.

Adhesives, sealants and sealant primers must comply with South Coast Air Quality Management District (SCAQMD) Rule 1168. VOC limits listed in the table below correspond to an effective date of July 1, 2005, and rule amendment date of January 7, 2005.

Table 1. VOC Limits for Adhesives and Sealants

Architectural Applications	VOC Limit (g/L less water)	Specialty Applications	VOC Limit (g/L less water)
Indoor carpet adhesives	50	PVC welding	510
Carpet pad adhesives	50	CPVC welding	490
Wood flooring adhesives	100	ABS welding	325
Rubber floor adhesives	60	Plastic cement welding	250
Subfloor adhesives	50	Adhesive primer for plastic	550
Ceramic tile adhesives	65	Contact adhesive	80
VCT and asphalt adhesives	50	Special purpose contact adhesive	250
Drywall and panel adhesives	50	Structural wood member adhesive	140
Cove base adhesives	50	Sheet applied rubber lining operations	850
Multipurpose construction adhesives	70	Top and trim adhesive	250
Structural glazing adhesives	100		
Substrate Specific Applications	**VOC Limit (g/L less water)**	**Sealants**	**VOC Limit (g/L less water)**
Metal to metal	30	Architectural	250
Plastic foams	50	Nonmembrane roof	300
Porous material (except wood)	50	Roadway	250
Wood	30	Single-ply roof membrane	450
Fiberglass	80	Other	420
Sealant Primers	**VOC Limit (g/L less water)**		
Architectural, nonporous	250		
Architectural, porous	775		
Other	750		

Aerosol adhesives must comply with Green Seal Standard for Commercial Adhesives GS–36 requirements that went in effect on October 19, 2000.

Green Seal Standard 36 (GS–36), effective October 19, 2000

http://www.greenseal.org/certification/standards/commercial_adhesives_GS_36.cfm

Green Seal is an independent, nonprofit organization that strives to achieve a healthier and cleaner environment by identifying and promoting products and services that cause less toxic pollution and waste, conserve resources and habitats, and minimize global warming and ozone depletion. GS–36 sets VOC limits for commercial adhesives.

Green Seal Standard for Commercial Adhesives GS–36 requirements went into effect on October 19, 2000.

IEQ	
NC	Credit 4.1
SCHOOLS	Credit 4.1
CS	Credit 4.1

Table 2. VOC Limits for Aerosol Adhesives

Aerosol Adhesives	VOC Limit
General purpose mist spray	65% VOCs by weight
General purpose web spray	55% VOCs by weight
Special purpose aerosol adhesives (all types)	70% VOCs by weight

SCHOOLS

California Department of Health Services Standard Practice for the Testing of Volatile Organic Emissions from Various Sources Using Small-Scale Environmental Chambers, including 2004 Addenda

California Department of Health Services

http://www.cal-iaq.org/VOC/Section01350_7_15_2004_FINAL_PLUS_ADDENDUM-2004-01.pdf

This standard practice applies to any newly manufactured material generally used within an enclosed indoor environment. However, the testing practice excludes all products that cannot be tested whole or by representative sample in small-scale environmental chambers.

The testing practice establishes the procedures for product sample collection, emissions testing, indoor concentration modeling, and documentation requirements associated with the analyzing the emissions of VOCs from various sources using small-scale environmental chambers. In addition, the testing practice lists target chemicals and their maximum allowable concentrations.

4. Implementation

The sections under IEQ Credit 4, Low-Emitting Materials, apply to products and installation processes that have the potential to adversely affect the IAQ of a project space and, subsequently, those occupants exposed to the off-gassing of contaminants from these materials.

Composition Limits

All materials that emit contaminants that might enter the indoor air are considered indoor contaminant sources. They include all surfaces in contact with indoor air, such as flooring; walls; ceilings; interior furnishings; suspended ceiling systems and the materials above those suspended ceilings; ventilation system components that contact the ventilation supply or return air; and all materials inside wall cavities, ceiling cavities, floor cavities, or horizontal or vertical chases. This includes caulking materials for windows and ceiling or wall insulation. An example of a material that has little or no potential to contact indoor air is siding on the exterior of waterproofing membrane. In this approach, the formulation of a product is controlled. The amount of VOCs permitted in a given volume of a product is limited. The threshold limits and content within a particular product are generally expressed in grams per liter (g/L). 3 IEQ credits use this approach: 4.1, Low-Emitting

Materials—Adhesives and Sealants; 4.2, Low-Emitting Materials—Paints and Coatings; and 4.3, Low-Emitting Materials—Flooring Systems. IEQ Credit 4.4, Low-Emitting Materials—Composite Wood and Agrifiber Products, also controls formulation by not allowing any added urea-formaldehyde resins.

CS Because core and shell buildings do not have direct control over tenant spaces, the owner or developer has limited control over the building's overall indoor air quality through the selection of low-VOC materials and products. Core and shell building owners are encouraged to explain the benefits of low-VOC materials to their tenants through tenant design and construction guidelines. Consider exceeding the guidelines and mandating specific materials with proven VOC off-gassing performance as requirements for the build-out of all tenant spaces.

SCHOOLS

Emissions Factors

California Department of Health Services Standard Practice for the Testing of Volatile Organic Emissions from Various Sources Using Small-Scale Environmental Chambers, including 2004 Addenda

This standard sets a limit on the rate that off-gassing may occur. The rate is stated as the mass of contaminant that may be off-gassed by a given unit quantity of the product in a set period of time. This approach is used in IEQ Credit 4.3, Low-Emitting Materials—Flooring Systems, for carpet where the rate is expressed as micrograms of contaminant per square meter of carpet per hour. Additionally, this approach is used for IEQ Credit 4.5: Low-Emitting Materials—Furniture and Furnishings, and IEQ Credit 4.6, Low-Emitting Materials—Ceiling and Wall Systems. It is required for all options under LEED for Schools. These tests, which are now being conducted on a variety of product types, place precisely sized samples in test chambers.

Air samples are drawn off at set times, generally over several days, and analyzed. Extensive protocols are established to make the testing representative of actual conditions on a project site and consistent between similar products from multiple manufactures. The Carpet and Rug Institute (CRI) Green Label Plus program uses emission factor test results for its certifications.

5. Timeline and Team

The requirements for products and activities covered in IEQ Credit 4, Low-Emitting Materials, should be noted in the project specifications and, ideally, within the specific section applicable to a particular trade or supplier.

Clearly state the credit requirements in project specifications. Refer to the credit requirements in both Division 1 and in the technical divisions. Indicate what must be provided in the way of cut sheets, MSD sheets, certificates, and test reports. Consider making submittal of this compliance documentation a condition of product approval.

The requirements for IEQ Credit 4, Low-Emitting Materials, are not typical practice for all construction teams and suppliers. Consider asking the project owner to stress the importance of meeting the LEED requirements during prebid meetings and again at the time of contract award. During these sessions, have LEED Accredited Professionals available and ask for questions. Include requirements in subcontracts and purchase orders. Determine whether the VOC budget approach will be necessary and track materials accordingly.

Consider providing LEED project signage alongside the project safety signage. In progress meetings, address topics relevant to low-emitting materials and the LEED requirements. Finally, provide leadership and ensure compliance.

	IEQ
NC	Credit 4.1
SCHOOLS	Credit 4.1
CS	Credit 4.1

6. Calculations

VOC Budget Methodology

Determining a VOC budget is one way to achieve compliance under IEQ Credit 4.1, Low-Emitting Materials—Adhesives and Sealants. To demonstrate that the overall low-VOC performance has been attained for paints and adhesives separately, not in combination, compare the baseline case and the design case. When the design (or actual) is less than the baseline, the credit requirement is satisfied. The values used in the comparison calculation are the total VOCs contained in the products (e.g., sealants) used on the project. To determine total VOCs, multiply the volume of the product used by the threshold VOC level for the baseline case and actual product VOC level for the design case. The baseline application rate should not be greater than that used in the design case. As the term budget implies, this compliance path involves an up-front decision. If a product with high VOC levels is used unintentionally, use the VOC budget approach to determine whether compliance can nevertheless be attained.

7. Documentation Guidance

As a first step in preparing to complete the LEED-Online documentation requirements, work through the following measures. Refer to LEED-Online for the complete descriptions of all required documentation.

- Maintain a list of each indoor aerosol adhesive product, sealants and sealant primers used on a project. Include the manufacturer's name, product name, and specific VOC data (g/L, less water) for each product, as well as the corresponding allowable VOC from the referenced standard.

- Track the amount of product used if the VOC budget approach is taken.

8. Examples

There are no examples for this credit.

9. Exemplary Performance

This credit is not eligible for exemplary performance under the Innovation in Design section.

10. Regional Variations

There are no regional variations for this credit.

11. Operations and Maintenance Considerations

Use low-emitting materials during building operations and instruct building operators to use low-emitting products when performing repairs or alterations. Provide repair teams and contractors with a list of compliant products used during the initial construction process.

12. Resources

Please see USGBC's LEED Registered Project Tools (http://www.usgbc.org/projecttools) for additional resources and technical information.

Websites

South Coast Air Quality Management District (SCAQMD) **Rule 1168**
South Coast Air Quality Management District
http://www.aqmd.gov/rules/reg/reg11/r1168.pdf

Green Seal Standard 36 (GS–36)
http://www.greenseal.org/certification/standards/commercial_adhesives_GS_36.cfm
Green Seal is an independent, nonprofit organization that strives to achieve a healthier and cleaner environment by identifying and promoting products and services that cause less toxic pollution and waste, conserve resources and habitats, and minimize global warming and ozone depletion. GS–36 sets VOC limits for commercial adhesives.

SCHOOLS

Collaborative for High Performance Schools Best Practices Manual, 2006, Low-Emitting Materials Table
Collaborative for High-Performance Schools
http://www.chps.net/manual/lem_table.htm
The Collaborative for High Performance Schools (CHPS) Best Practices Manual contains guidelines and strategies for effective acoustical performance in school buildings. According to CHPS, "this table lists products that have been certified by its manufacturer and an independent laboratory to meet the CHPS Low-Emitting Materials criteria Section 01350 for use in a typical classroom."

California Department of Health Services Standard Practice for The Testing Of Volatile Organic Emissions From Various Sources Using Small-Scale Environmental Chambers, including 2004 Addenda
California Department of Health Services
http://www.cal-iaq.org/VOC/Section01350_7_15_2004_FINAL_PLUS_ADDENDUM-2004-01.pdf

This standard practice applies to any newly manufactured material generally used within an enclosed indoor environment. However, the testing practice excludes all products that cannot be tested whole or by representative sample in small-scale environmental chambers.

The testing practice establishes the procedures for product sample collection, emissions testing, indoor concentration modeling, and documentation requirements associated with the analyzing the emissions of VOCs from various sources using small-scale environmental chambers. In addition, the testing practice lists target chemicals and their maximum allowable concentrations.

13. Definitions

An **adhesive** is any substance that is used to bond 1 surface to another by attachment. Adhesives include bonding primers, adhesive primers, and adhesive primers for plastics. (SCAQMD Rule 1168).

Aerosol adhesive is an aerosol product in which the spray mechanism is permanently housed in a nonrefillable can. Designed for hand-held application, these products do not need ancillary hoses or spray equipment. Aerosol adhesives include special-purpose spray adhesives, mist spray adhesives, and web spray adhesives. (SCAQMD Rule 1168)

Architectural nonporous sealant primer is a substance used as a sealant primer on nonporous materials.

Architectural porous sealant primer is a substance used as a sealant on porous materials.

Contaminants are unwanted airborne elements that may reduce air quality (ASHRAE 62.1–2007).

Indoor adhesive, sealant, or sealant primer product is defined as an adhesive or sealant product applied on-site, inside the building's weatherproofing system.

	IEQ
NC	Credit 4.1
SCHOOLS	Credit 4.1
CS	Credit 4.1

Indoor air quality (IAQ) is the nature of air inside a building that affects the health and well-being of building occupants. It is considered acceptable when there are no known contaminants at harmful concentrations as determined by cognizant authorities and with which a substantial majority (80% or more) of the people exposed do not express dissatisfaction. (ASHRAE 62.1–2007)

Nonporous sealant is a substance used as a sealant on nonporous materials. Nonporous materials, such as plastic and metal, do not have openings in which fluids may be absorbed or discharged.

Occupants in a commercial building are workers who either have a permanent office or workstation in the building or typically spend a minimum of 10 hours per week in the building. In a residential building, occupants also include all persons who live in the building.

Off-gassing is the emission of volatile organic compounds (VOCs) from synthetic and natural products.

Ozone (O3) is a gas composed of 3 oxygen atoms. It is not usualy emitted directly into the air, but at ground-level is created by a chemical reaction between oxides of nitrogen (NOx) and volatile organic compounds (VOCs) in the presence of sunlight. Ozone has the same chemical structure whether it occurs miles above the earth or at ground-level and can have positive or negative effects, depending on its location in the atmosphere. (U.S. Environmental Protection Agency)

Porous materials have tiny openings, often microscopic, which can absorb or discharge fluids. Examples include wood, fabric, paper, corrugated paperboard, and plastic foam. (SCAQMD Rule 1168)

A **sealant** has adhesive properties and is formulated primarily to fill, seal, or waterproof gaps or joints between 2 surfaces. Sealants include sealant primers and caulks. (SCAQMD Rule 1168)

A **sealant primer** is applied to a substrate, prior to the application of a sealant, to enhance the bonding surface. (SCAQMD Rule 1168)

Volatile organic compounds (VOCs) are carbon compounds that participate in atmospheric photochemical reactions (excluding carbon monoxide, carbon dioxide, carbonic acid, metallic carbides and carbonates, and ammonium carbonate). The compounds vaporize at normal room temperatures.

LOW-EMITTING MATERIALS—PAINTS AND COATINGS

	NC	SCHOOLS	CS
Credit	IEQ Credit 4.2	IEQ Credit 4.2	IEQ Credit 4.2
Points	1 point	1 point	1 point

Intent

To reduce the quantity of indoor air contaminants that are odorous, irritating and/or harmful to the comfort and well-being of installers and occupants.

Requirements

NC & CS

Paints and coatings used on the interior of the building (i.e., inside of the weatherproofing system and applied on-site) must comply with the following criteria as applicable to the project scope[1]:

- Architectural paints and coatings applied to interior walls and ceilings must not exceed the volatile organic compound (VOC) content limits established in Green Seal Standard GS-11, Paints, 1st Edition, May 20, 1993.

- Anti-corrosive and anti-rust paints applied to interior ferrous metal substrates must not exceed the VOC content limit of 250 g/L established in Green Seal Standard GC-03, Anti-Corrosive Paints, 2nd Edition, January 7, 1997.

- Clear wood finishes, floor coatings, stains, primers, and shellacs applied to interior elements mustl not exceed the VOC content limits established in South Coast Air Quality Management District (SCAQMD) Rule 1113, Architectural Coatings, rules in effect on January 1, 2004.

SCHOOLS

All paints and coatings installed in the building interior must meet the testing and product requirements of the California Department of Health Services Standard Practice for the Testing of Volatile Organic Emissions from Various Sources Using Small-Scale Environmental Chambers, including 2004 Addenda.

Schools projects may choose from IEQ Credits 4.1-4.6 for a maximum of 4 points.

---

1 The use of a VOC budget is permissible for compliance with this credit.

IEQ	
NC	Credit 4.2
SCHOOLS	Credit 4.2
CS	Credit 4.2

1. Benefits and Issues to Consider

Refer to the Benefits and Issues section of IEQ Credit 4.1: Low-Emitting Materials—Adhesives and Sealants.

2. Related Credits

Because the intent of this credit is to reduce odorous, irritating, or harmful indoor air contaminants, the following other credits may be applicable:

- IEQ Credit 4.1: Low-Emitting Materials—Adhesives and Sealants
- IEQ Credit 4.3: Low-Emitting Materials—Flooring Systems
- IEQ Credit 4.4: Low-Emitting Materials—Composite Wood and Agrifiber Products
- IEQ Credit 4.5: Low-Emitting Materials—Furniture and Furnishings (Specific to Schools)
- IEQ Credit 4.6: Low-Emitting Materials—Ceiling and Wall Systems (Specific to Schools)

Scheduling strategies and the use and tracking of building materials are also addressed in the contractor orientation training, covered under these 2 credits:

- IEQ Credit 3.1: Construction IAQ Management Plan—During Construction
- IEQ Credit 3.2: Construction IAQ Management Plan—Before Occupancy

Indoor air quality is affected by sources generated within the building itself and introduced into its spaces. Both sources are addressed in the following prerequisite and credit:

- IEQ Prerequisite 2: Environmental Tobacco Smoke (ETS) Control
- IEQ Credit 5: Indoor Chemical and Pollutant Source Control

SCHOOLS Acoustical elements within the building may require specialty installation considerations, which can necessitate careful coordination between acoustical concerns and the materials specifier. Indoor environmental quality also encompasses occupants' auditory comfort and well-being, which are covered under these 2 credits:

- IEQ Prerequisite 3: Minimum Acoustical Performance
- IEQ Credit 9: Enhanced Acoustical Performance

3. Summary of Referenced Standards

Green Seal Standard GS–11

http://www.greenseal.org/certification/standards/paints_and_coatings.pdf

Green Seal is an independent, nonprofit organization that strives to achieve a healthier and cleaner environment by identifying and promoting products and services that cause less toxic pollution and waste, conserve resources and habitats, and minimize global warming and ozone depletion. GS–11 sets VOC limits for commercial flat and nonflat paints Tables 1 and 2 summarize Green Seal Standard GS–11.

Green Seal Standard GC–03

http://www.greenseal.org/certification/standards/anti-corrosivepaints.pdf

GC–03 sets VOC limits for anti-corrosive and anti-rust paints.

Chemical Component Limitations— VOC: the manufacturer shall demonstrate that the paint is not formulated to exceed the VOC concentrations listed below:

Coating Type	(g/L) minus water
Gloss	250
Semi-Gloss	250
Flat	250

South Coast Air Quality Management District (SCAQMD) Rule 1113, Architectural Coatings

http://www.aqmd.gov/rules/reg/reg11/r1113.pdf

The South Coast Air Quality Management District is a governmental organization in southern California with the mission to maintain healthful air quality for its residents. The organization established source-specific standards to reduce air quality impacts.

Table 1. Standard VOC Limits

VOCs (g/L minus water, minus exempt compounds)

Coating	Ceiling Limit*	Current Limit	Effective Date					
			1/1/03	1/1/04	1/1/05	7/1/06	7/1/07	7/1/08
Bond breakers	350							
Clear Wood finishes	350							
– Varnish	350					275		
– Sanding	350					275		
Sealers	680	550			275	275		
– Lacquer								
Clear brushing lacquer	680				275			
Concrete-curing compounds	350						100	
Concrete-curing compounds for roadways and bridges**	350							
Dry-fog coatings	400						150	
Fire-proofing exterior coatings	450	350						
Fire-retardant coatings***								
– Clear	650							
– Pigmented	350							
Flats	250	100						50
Floor coatings	420		100					50
Graphic arts (sign) coatings	500							
Industrial maintenance (im) coatings	420			250		100		
High temperature im coatings			420			100		
Zinc-rich im primers	420		340					
Japans/faux finishing coatings	700	350						
Magnesite cement coatings	600	450						
Mastic coatings	300							
Metallic Pigmented coatings	500							
Multicolor coatings	420	250						
Nonflat coatings	250	150				50		
Nonflat high gloss	250		150				50	
Pigmented lacquer	680	550			275			
Pretreatment wash primers	780		420					
Primers, sealers, undercoaters	350		200			100		
Primers, sealers, undercoaters	350		200			100		
Quick-dry enamels	400		250			150	50	
Quick-dry primers, sealers, undercoaters	350		200			100		
Recycled coatings			250					
Roof coatings	300		250	50				
Aluminum roof coatings	500			100				
Roof primers, bituminous	350		350					
Rust: preventive coatings	420		400			100		
Shellac								
– Clear	730							
– Pigmented	550							
Specialty primers	350					250	100	
Stains	350		250				100	
– Interior	250							
Swimming pool coatings								
– Repair	650							
– Other	340		340					
Traffic coatings	250	150					100	
Waterproofing sealers	400		250			100		
Waterproofing concrete, masonry sealers	400					100		
Wood preservatives – Below-ground	350							
Other	350							

* The specified limits remain in effect until revised.

** Does not include compounds used for curbs and gutters, sidewalks, islands, driveways, and other miscellaneous concrete areas.

*** The fire-retardant coating category was eliminated on January 1, 2007, and subsumed by the coating category for which it was formulated.

IEQ	
NC	Credit 4.2
SCHOOLS	Credit 4.2
CS	Credit 4.2

Table 2. Standard VOC Limits

Coating	Limit VOCs (g/L)
Low-solids coating	27 parts per billion

SCHOOLS

California Department of Health Services Standard Practice for the Testing of Volatile Organic Emissions from Various Sources Using Small-Scale Environmental Chambers, including 2004 Addenda
California Department of Health Services
http://www.cal-iaq.org/VOC/Section01350_7_15_2004_FINAL_PLUS_ADDENDUM-2004-01.pdfw

The above standard practice applies to any newly manufactured material generally used within an enclosed indoor environment. However, the testing practice excludes all products that cannot be tested whole or by representative sample in small-scale environmental chambers.

The testing practice establishes the procedures for product sample collection, emissions testing, indoor concentration modeling, and documentation requirements associated with analyzing the emissions of volatile organic chemicals from various sources using small-scale environmental chambers. In addition, the testing practice lists target chemicals and their maximum allowable concentrations.

---

4. Implementation

Refer to the Implementation section of IEQ Credit 4.1, Low-Emitting Materials—Adhesives and Sealants.

5. Timeline and Team

Refer to the Timeline and Team section of IEQ Credit 4.1, Low-Emitting Materials—Adhesives and Sealants.

6. Calculations

Refer to the Calculations section of IEQ Credit 4.1, Low-Emitting Materials—Adhesives and Sealants.

7. Documentation Guidance

As a first step in preparing to complete the LEED-Online documentation requirements, work through the following measures. Refer to LEED-Online for the complete descriptions of all required documentation.

- Maintain a list of each indoor paint and coating product used. Include the manufacturer's name, product name, and specific VOC data (in g/L, less water) for each product, as well as the corresponding allowable VOC from the referenced standard.

- Track the amount of product used if the VOC budget approach is taken.

8. Examples

There are no examples for this credit.

9. Exemplary Performance

This credit is not eligible for exemplary performance under the Innovation in Design section.

10. Regional Variations

There are no regional variations for this credit.

	IEQ
NC	Credit 4.2
SCHOOLS	Credit 4.2
CS	Credit 4.2

11. Operations and Maintenance Considerations

Establish a sustainable purchasing policy for the continued use of low-emitting materials during the building's operation. Help building operators find low-emitting products for repairs or alterations by providing them with a list of compliant products. Provide maintenance personnel with information about original products to aid in color matching. Using fewer types of paint and coating products in the design makes maintenance easier.

12. Resources

Please see USGBC's LEED Registered Project Tools (http://www.usgbc.org/projecttools) for additional resources and technical information.

Websites

Green Seal

http://www.greenseal.org

Green Seal is an independent, nonprofit organization that strives to achieve a healthier and cleaner environment by identifying and promoting products and services that cause less toxic pollution and waste, conserve resources and habitats, and minimize global warming and ozone depletion.

South Coast Air Quality Management District

http://www.aqmd.gov

SCHOOLS

Collaborative for High Performance Schools (CHPS) Manual, 2006, Low-Emitting Materials (LEM) Table

Collaborative for High Performance Schools (CHPS)

http://www.chps.net/manual/lem_table.htm

The Collaborative for High Performance Schools (CHPS) Best Practices Manual contains guidelines and strategies for effective acoustical performance in school buildings. According to CHPS, "this table lists products that have been certified by its manufacturer and an independent laboratory to meet the CHPS Low-Emitting Materials criteria Section 01350 for use in a typical classroom."

13. Definitions

Anticorrosive paints are coatings formulated and recommended for use in preventing the corrosion of ferrous metal substrates.

A **coating** is applied to beautify, protect, or provide a barrier to a surface. (SCAQMD Rule 1113)

Contaminants are unwanted airborne elements that may reduce air quality. (ASHRAE 62.1–2007)

Indoor air quality (**IAQ**) is the nature of air inside a building that affects the health and well-being of building occupants. It is considered acceptable when there are no known contaminants at harmful concentrations as determined by cognizant authorities and with which a substantial majority (80% or more) of the people exposed do not express dissatisfaction. (ASHRAE 62.1–2007)

Indoor paints or **coating products** are applied inside a building's weatherproofing system.

Occupants in a commercial building are workers who either have a permanent office or workstation in the building or typically spend a minimum of 10 hours per week in the building. In a residential building, occupants also include all persons who live in the building.

	IEQ
NC	Credit 4.2
SCHOOLS	Credit 4.2
CS	Credit 4.2

Paint is a liquid, liquefiable, or mastic composition that is converted to a solid protective, decorative, or functional adherent film after application as a thin layer. These coatings are intended for application to interior or exterior surfaces of residential, commercial, institutional, or industrial buildings.

A **primer** is a material applied to a substrate to improve adhesion of subsequently applied coats.

Volatile organic compounds (**VOCs**) are carbon compounds that participate in atmospheric photochemical reactions (excluding carbon monoxide, carbon dioxide, carbonic acid, metallic carbides and carbonates, and ammonium carbonate). The compounds vaporize at normal room temperatures.

LOW-EMITTING MATERIALS—FLOORING SYSTEMS

	NC	SCHOOLS	CS
Credit	IEQ Credit 4.3	IEQ Credit 4.3	IEQ Credit 4.3
Points	1 point	1 point	1 point

Intent

To reduce the quantity of indoor air contaminants that are odorous, irritating and/or harmful to the comfort and well-being of installers and occupants.

Requirements

NC & CS

OPTION 1

All flooring must comply with the following as applicable to the project scope:

- All carpet installed in the building interior must meet the testing and product requirements of the Carpet and Rug Institute Green Label Plus program.

- All carpet cushion installed in the building interior must meet the requirements of the Carpet and Rug Institute Green Label[1] program.

- All carpet adhesive must meet the requirements of IEQ Credit 4.1: Adhesives and Sealants, which includes a volatile organic compound (VOC) limit of 50 g/L.

- All hard surface flooring must be certified as compliant with the FloorScore[2] standard (current as of the date of this rating system, or more stringent version) by an independent third-party. Flooring products covered by FloorScore include vinyl, linoleum, laminate flooring, wood flooring, ceramic flooring, rubber flooring and wall base.

- An alternative compliance path using FloorScore is acceptable for credit achievement: 100% of the non-carpet finished flooring must be FloorScore-certified and must constitute at least 25% of the finished floor area. Examples of unfinished flooring include floors in mechanical rooms, electrical rooms and elevator service rooms.

- Concrete, wood, bamboo and cork floor finishes such as sealer, stain and finish must meet the requirements of South Coast Air Quality Management District (SCAQMD) Rule 1113, Architectural Coatings, rules in effect on January 1, 2004.

- Tile setting adhesives and grout must meet South Coast Air Quality Management District (SCAQMD) Rule 1168. VOC limits correspond to an effective date of July 1, 2005 and rule amendment date of January 7, 2005.

---

1 The Green Label Plus program for carpets and its associated VOC emission criteria in micrograms per square meter per hour, along with information on testing method and sample collection developed by the Carpet & Rug Institute (CRI) in coordination with California's Sustainable Building Task Force and the California Department of Public Health, are described in Section 9, Acceptable Emissions Testing for Carpet, DHS Standard Practice CA/DHS/EHLB/R-174, dated 07/15/04. This document is available at: http://www.dhs.ca.gov/ps/deodc/ehlb/iaq/ VOCS/Section01350_7_15_2004_FINAL_PLUS_ADDENDUM-2004-01.pdf (also published as Section 01350 Section 9 [dated 2004] by the Collaborative for High Performance Schools [www.chps.net]).

2 FloorScore is a voluntary, independent certification program that tests and certifies hard surface flooring and associated products for compliance with criteria adopted in California for indoor air emissions of VOCs with potential health effects. The program uses a small-scale chamber test protocol and incorporates VOC emissions criteria, which are widely known as Section 1350, developed by the California Department of Health Services.

OR

NC, SCHOOLS & CS

OPTION 2

All flooring elements installed in the building interior must meet the testing and product requirements of the California Department of Health Services Standard Practice for the Testing of Volatile Organic Emissions from Various Sources Using Small-Scale Environmental Chambers, including 2004 Addenda.

Schools projects may choose from IEQ Credits 4.1-4.6 for a maximum of 4 points.

1. Benefits and Issues to Consider

Refer to the Benefits and Issues section of IEQ Credit 4.1, Low-Emitting Materials—Adhesives and Sealants.

	IEQ
NC	Credit 4.3
SCHOOLS	Credit 4.3
CS	Credit 4.3

2. Related Credits

Because the intent of this credit is to reduce odorous, irritating, or harmful indoor air contaminants, the following other credits may be applicable:

- IEQ Credit 4.1: Low-Emitting Materials—Adhesives and Sealants

- IEQ Credit 4.2: Low-Emitting Materials—Paints and Coatings

- IEQ Credit 4.4: Low-Emitting Materials—Composite Wood and Agrifiber Products

- IEQ Credit 4.5: Low-Emitting Materials—Furniture and Furnishings (Specific to Schools)

- IEQ Credit 4.6: Low-Emitting Materials—Ceiling and Wall Systems (Specific to Schools)

Scheduling strategies and the use and tracking of building materials are also addressed in the contractor orientation training, covered under these 2 credits:

- IEQ Credit 3.1: Construction IAQ Management Plan During Construction

- IEQ Credit 3.2: Construction IAQ Management Plan Before Occupancy

Indoor air quality is affected by sources generated within the building itself and introduced into its spaces. Both sources are addressed in the following prerequisite and credit:

- IEQ Prerequisite 2: Environmental Tobacco Smoke (ETS) Control

- IEQ Credit 5: Indoor Chemical and Pollutant Source Control

SCHOOLS Acoustical elements within the building may require specialty installation considerations, which can necessitate careful coordination between acoustical concerns and the materials specifier. Indoor environmental quality also encompasses occupants' auditory comfort and well-being, which are covered under these 2 credits:

- IEQ Prerequisite 3: Minimum Acoustical Performance

- IEQ Credit 9: Enhanced Acoustical Performance

3. Summary of Referenced Standards

Carpet and Rug Institute (CRI) Green Label Plus Testing Program

Carpet and Rug Institute

http://www.carpet-rug.com

The Carpet and Rug Institute (CRI) is a trade organization representing the carpet and rug industry. Green Label Plus is an independent testing program that identifies carpets with very low VOC emissions. The CRI website describes the program and the associated VOC emission criteria in micrograms per square meter per hour. These criteria were developed by the Carpet and Rug Institute (CRI) in coordination with California's Sustainable Building Task Force and the California Department of Health Services (DHS). In the CRI "Green Label Plus Program," emission rates must be verified by annual tests. Approved certification numbers can be reviewed on the CRI website under Indoor Air Quality/Green Label Plus/Approved companies. Approved products are listed under the company heading.

South Coast Air Quality Management District (SCAQMD) Rule 1168, VOC Limits

http://www.aqmd.gov/rules/reg/reg11/r1168.pdf

The South Coast Air Quality Management District is a governmental organization in southern

California with the mission to maintain healthful air quality for its residents. The organization established source specific standards to reduce air quality impacts. The South Coast Rule 1168 VOC limits for adhesives are summarized in Table 1, in IEQ Credit 4.1.

South Coast Air Quality Management District (SCAQMD) Rule 1113, Architectural Coatings
http://www.aqmd.gov/rules/reg/reg11/r1113.pdf
The South Coast Air Quality Management District is a governmental organization in Southern California with the mission to maintain healthful air quality for its residents. The organization established source-specific standards to reduce air quality impacts. Table 1, in IEQ Credit 4.1.

FloorScore™ Program
Resilient Floor Covering Institute
http://www.rfci.com/int_FloorScore.htm
According to its website, "The FloorScore program, developed by the Resilient Floor Covering Institute (RFCI) in conjunction with Scientific Certification Systems (SCS), tests and certifies flooring products for compliance with indoor air quality emission requirements adopted in California. Flooring products include vinyl, linoleum, laminate flooring, wood flooring, ceramic flooring, rubber flooring, wall base, and associated sundries."

California Department of Health Services Standard Practice for the Testing of Volatile Organic Emissions from Various Sources Using Small-Scale Environmental Chambers, including 2004 Addenda
California Department of Health Services
http://www.cal-iaq.org/VOC/Section01350_7_15_2004_FINAL_PLUS_ADDENDUM-2004-01.pdf
This practice applies to any newly manufactured material generally used within an enclosed indoor environment. However, the testing practice excludes all products that cannot be tested whole or by representative sample in small-scale environmental chambers.

The testing practice establishes the procedures for product sample collection, emissions testing, indoor concentration modeling, and documentation requirements associated with the analyzing the emissions of VOCs from various sources using small-scale environmental chambers. In addition, the testing practice lists target chemicals and their maximum allowable concentrations.

State of California Standard 1350, Section 9, Standard Practice for the Testing of Volatile Organic Emissions from Various Sources Using Small-Scale Environmental Chambers, Testing Criteria
http://www.dhs.ca.gov/ps/deodc/ehlb/iaq/VOCS/Section01350_7_15_2004_FINAL_PLUS_ADDENDUM-2004-01.pdfw
This standard practice document specifies testing criteria for carpet emissions that will satisfy the credit requirements.

According to the criteria, carpet must not exceed the maximum target emission factors used in the CRI Green Label program and follow the test protocol used by Green Label Plus. Test results submitted must be no more than 2 years old at the time of submission.

4. Implementation
Refer to the Implementation section of IEQ Credit 4.1, Low-Emitting Materials—Adhesives and Sealants.

5. Timeline and Team
Refer to the Timeline and Team section of IEQ Credit 4.1, Low-Emitting Materials—Adhesives and Sealants.

6. Calculations

There are no calculations required for this credit.

7. Documentation Guidance

As a first step in preparing to complete the LEED-Online documentation requirements, work through the following measures. Refer to LEED-Online for the complete descriptions of all required documentation.

- Maintain a list of each carpet, carpet cushion, and carpet adhesive installed in the building interior. Record the VOC content for each adhesive.

- Maintain a list of each hard surface flooring product, tile setting adhesive, finishes, and grout installed in the building interior. Record the VOC content for each tile setting adhesive and grout.

8. Examples

Figure 1. Sample Product Information for CRI Green Label Plus Carpeting

Style Number 1111	
Specifications	
Construction	Textured loop pattern
Yarn content	Nylon with 25% recycled content
Dye method	Solution
Machine gauge	1/10 in (39.4 col/10 cm)
Stitch count	11 S.P.I. (43.3/10 cm)
Finished pile thickness	0.124 in (3.15 mm)
Average density	8,710
Yarn weight tufted	30 oz/yd^2 (1085 g/m^2)
Primary backing	Polypropylene
Secondary backing	Woven polypropylene with postconsumer recycled content
Width	12 ft (3.66 m)
Pattern repeat	0.40 in w x .047 in l (1.01 cm x 1.19 cm)
Total recycled content	2.43%
Performance	
Flameresistance	Passes (DOC FF-1-70)
Flooring radiant panel	Class 1(ASTM E-662)
Smoke density	Less than 450 (ASTM E-662)
CRI Green Label Plus	Certification # GLP 0000
Warranties	
Example nylon warranty	Lifetime carpet static warranty
Example nylon warranty	Lifetime carpet wear, limited warranty
Example nylon certification	Class III, extra heavy traffic
Example nylon content	Minimum 25% recycled content
Example nylon recycling	Available
Additional Information	
Custom colors	Contact sales representative
Coordinating styles	Multiple

9. Exemplary Performance

This credit is not eligible for exemplary performance under the Innovation in Design section.

10. Regional Variations

There are no regional variations for this credit.

11. Operations and Maintenance Considerations

Establish a sustainable purchasing policy for the continued use of low-emitting materials during the building's operation. Help building operators find low-emitting products for repairs or alterations by providing a list of compliant products.

Use of carpet tiles saves materials over the life of the building because individual tiles can be replaced as the carpet wears. Using fewer flooring products in the design makes maintenance easier. If specialized flooring materials are specified, request maintenance information from product manufacturers or installers and give this information to the operations team.

12. Resources

Please see USGBC's LEED Registered Project Tools (http://www.usgbc.org/projecttools) for additional resources and technical information.

Websites
Carpet and Rug Institute (CRI)
http://www.carpet-rug.org

Floorscore
http://www.rfci.com/int_FloorScore.htm
http://www.scscertified.com/ecoproducts/indoorairquality/floorscore.html

GreenGuard
http://www.greenguard.org/

Scientific Certification System, Inc.
http://www.scscertified.com/

South Coast Air Quality Management District
http://www.aqmd.gov/rules

SCHOOLS

Collaborative for High Performance Schools Best Practices Manual, 2006, Low-Emitting Materials (LEM) Table
Collaborative for High Performance Schools
http://www.chps.net/manual/lem_table.htm
The Collaborative for High Performance Schools (CHPS) Best Practices Manual contains guidelines and strategies for effective acoustical performance in school buildings. According to CHPS, "this table lists products that have been certified by its manufacturer and an independent laboratory to meet the CHPS Low-Emitting Materials criteria Section 01350 for use in a typical classroom."

13. Definitions

Contaminants are unwanted airborne elements that may reduce air quality. (ASHRAE 62.1–2007)

Hard surface flooring includes vinyl, linoleum, laminate flooring, wood flooring, rubber flooring, wall base, and associated sundries.

Indoor carpet systems are carpet, carpet adhesive, or carpet cushion products installed inside the building's weatherproofing system.

Indoor air quality (**IAQ**) is the nature of air inside a building that affects the health and well-being of building occupants. It is considered acceptable when there are no known contaminants at harmful concentrations as determined by cognizant authorities and with which a substantial majority (80% or more) of the people exposed do not express dissatisfaction. (ASHRAE 62.1–2007)

Occupants in a commercial building are workers who either have a permanent office or workstation in the building or typically spend a minimum of 10 hours per week in the building. In a residential building, occupants also include all persons who live in the building.

Volatile organic compounds (**VOCs**) are carbon compounds that participate in atmospheric photochemical reactions (excluding carbon monoxide, carbon dioxide, carbonic acid, metallic carbides and carbonates, and ammonium carbonate). The compounds vaporize at normal room temperatures.

	IEQ
NC	Credit 4.3
SCHOOLS	Credit 4.3
CS	Credit 4.3

LOW-EMITTING MATERIALS—COMPOSITE WOOD AND AGRIFIBER PRODUCTS

	NC	SCHOOLS	CS
Credit	IEQ Credit 4.4	IEQ Credit 4.4	IEQ Credit 4.4
Points	1 point	1 point	1 point

Intent

To reduce the quantity of indoor air contaminants that are odorous, irritating and/or harmful to the comfort and well-being of installers and occupants.

Requirements

NC & CS

Composite wood and agrifiber products used on the interior of the building (i.e., inside the weatherproofing system) must contain no added urea-formaldehyde resins. Laminating adhesives used to fabricate on-site and shop-applied composite wood and agrifiber assemblies must not contain added urea-formaldehyde resins.

Composite wood and agrifiber products are defined as particleboard, medium density fiberboard (MDF), plywood, wheatboard, strawboard, panel substrates and door cores. Materials considered fixtures, furniture and equipment (FF&E) are not considered base building elements and are not included.

SCHOOLS

All composite wood and agrifiber products installed in the building interior must meet the testing and product requirements of the California Department of Health Services Standard Practice for the Testing of Volatile Organic Emissions from Various Sources Using Small-Scale Environmental Chambers, including 2004 Addenda.

Schools projects may choose from IEQ Credits 4.1-4.6 for a maximum of 4 points.

	IEQ
NC	Credit 4.4
SCHOOLS	Credit 4.4
CS	Credit 4.4

1. Benefits and Issues to Consider

Refer to the Benefits and Issues section of IEQ Credit 4.1, Low-Emitting Materials—Adhesives and Sealants.

2. Related Credits

Because the intent of this credit is to reduce odorous, irritating, or harmful indoor air contaminants, the following other credits may be applicable:

- IEQ Credit 4.1: Low-Emitting Materials—Adhesives and Sealants
- IEQ Credit 4.2: Low-Emitting Materials—Paints and Coatings
- IEQ Credit 4.3: Low-Emitting Materials—Flooring Systems
- IEQ Credit 4.5: Low-Emitting Materials—Furniture and Furnishings (Specific to Schools)
- IEQ Credit 4.6: Low-Emitting Materials—Ceiling and Wall Systems (Specific to Schools)

Scheduling strategies and the use and tracking of building materials are also addressed in the contractor orientation training, covered under these 2 credits:

- IEQ Credit 3.1: Construction IAQ Management Plan During Construction
- IEQ Credit 3.2: Construction IAQ Management Plan Before Occupancy

Indoor air quality is affected by sources generated within the building itself and introduced into its spaces. Both sources are addressed in the following prerequisite and credit:

- IEQ Prerequisite 2: Environmental Tobacco Smoke (ETS) Control
- IEQ Credit 5: Indoor Chemical and Pollutant Source Control

SCHOOLS Acoustical elements within the building may require specialty installation considerations, which can necessitate careful coordination between acoustical concerns and the materials specifier. Indoor environmental quality also encompasses occupants' auditory comfort and well-being, which are covered under these 2 credits:

- IEQ Prerequisite 3: Minimum Acoustical Performance
- IEQ Credit 9: Enhanced Acoustical Performance

3. Summary of Referenced Standards

SCHOOLS

California Department of Health Services Standard Practice for the Testing of Volatile Organic Emissions from Various Sources Using Small-Scale Environmental Chambers, including 2004 Addenda
California Department of Health Services
http://www.cal-iaq.org/VOC/Section01350_7_15_2004_FINAL_PLUS_ADDENDUM-2004-01.pdfw
This standard practice applies to any newly manufactured material generally used within an enclosed indoor environment. However, the testing practice excludes all products that cannot be tested whole or by representative sample in small-scale environmental chambers.

The testing practice establishes the procedures for product sample collection, emissions testing, indoor concentration modeling, and documentation requirements associated with the analyzing the emissions of volatile organic chemicals from various sources using small-scale environmental chambers. In addition, the testing practice lists target chemicals and their maximum allowable concentrations.

4. Implementation

Refer to the Implementation section of IEQ Credit 4.1: Low-Emitting Materials—Adhesives and Sealants.

	IEQ
NC	Credit 4.4
SCHOOLS	Credit 4.4
CS	Credit 4.4

5. Timeline and Team

Refer to the Timeline and Team section of IEQ Credit 4.1, Low-Emitting Materials—Adhesives and Sealants.

6. Calculations

There are no calculations required for this credit.

7. Documentation Guidance

As a first step in preparing to complete the LEED-Online documentation requirements, work through the following measures. Refer to LEED-Online for the complete descriptions of all required documentation.

- Maintain a list of each composite wood and agrifiber product installed in the building interior. Confirm that each product does not contain any added urea-formaldehyde.

8. Examples

There are no examples for this credit.

9. Exemplary Performance

This credit is not eligible for exemplary performance under the Innovation in Design section.

10. Regional Variations

There are no regional variations for this credit.

11. Operations and Maintenance Considerations

Establish a sustainable purchasing policy for the continued use of low-emitting materials during the building's operation. Help building operators find low-emitting products for repairs or alterations by providing them with a list of compliant products.

If specialized composite wood or agrifiber materials are specified, request maintenance information from product manufacturers and installers and give this information to the operations team.

12. Resources

Please see USGBC's LEED Registered Project Tools (http://www.usgbc.org/projecttools) for additional resources and technical information.

Websites

An Update on Formaldehyde
Consumer Product Safety Commission
http://www.cpsc.gov/CPSCPUB/PUBS/725.html
This informational document is from the Consumer Product Safety Commission.

	IEQ
NC	Credit 4.4
SCHOOLS	Credit 4.4
CS	Credit 4.4

13. Definitions

Agrifiber board is a composite panel product derived from recovered agricultural waste fiber from sources cereal straw, sugarcane bagasse, sunflower husk, walnut shells, coconut husks, and agricultural prunings. The raw fibers are processed and mixed with resins to produce panel products with characteristics similar to those derived from wood fiber. The following conditions describe which products must comply with the requirements:

1. The product is inside the building's waterproofing system.

2. Composite components used in assemblies are to be included (e.g., door cores, panel substrates).

3. The product is part of the base building systems.

Composite wood consists of wood or plant particles or fibers bonded together by a synthetic resin or binder. Examples include plywood, particle-board, oriented-strand board (OSB), medium-density fiberboard (MDF), and composite door cores. The following conditions describe which products must comply with the credit requirements:

1. The product is inside the building's waterproofing system.

2. Composite wood components used in assemblies are included (e.g., door cores, panel substrates, plywood sections of I-beams).

3. The product is part of the base building systems.

Contaminants are unwanted airborne elements that may reduce air quality. (ASHRAE 62.1–2007)

Formaldehyde is a naturally occurring VOC found in small amounts in animals and plants, but is carcinogenic and an irritant to most people when present in high concentrations, causing headaches, dizziness, mental impairment, and other symptoms. When present in the air at levels above 0.1 ppm parts of air, it can cause watery eyes, burning sensations in the eyes, nose and throat; nausea, coughing, chest tightness, wheezing, skin rashes, and asthmatic and allergic reactions.

Indoor composite wood or agrifiber is a product installed inside the building's weatherproofing system.

Indoor air quality (IAQ) is the nature of air inside a building that affects the health and well-being of building occupants. It is considered acceptable when there are no known contaminants at harmful concentrations as determined by cognizant authorities and with which a substantial majority (80% or more) of the people exposed do not express dissatisfaction. (ASHRAE 62.1–2007)

Laminate adhesive is used in wood or agrifiber products (veneered panels, composite wood products contained in engineered lumber, door assemblies, etc.).

Off-gassing is the emission of volatile organic compounds (VOCs) from synthetic and natural products.

Urea-formaldehyde is a combination of urea and formaldehyde that is used in some glues and may emit formaldehyde at room temperature.

Pheno-formaldehyde, which off-gasses only at high temperature, is used for exterior products, although many of those products are suitable for interior applications.

	IEQ
NC	Credit 4.4
SCHOOLS	Credit 4.4
CS	Credit 4.4

	NC	SCHOOLS	CS
Credit	NA	IEQ Credit 4.5	NA
Points	NA	1 point	NA

Intent

To reduce the quantity of indoor air contaminants that are odorous, irritating and/ or harmful to the comfort and well-being of installers and occupants.

Requirements

SCHOOLS

Classroom furniture including all student and teacher desks, tables and seats that was manufactured, refurbished or refinished within 1 year prior to occupancy must meet 1 of the requirements below. Salvaged and used furniture that is more than 1 year old at the time of occupancy is excluded from the credit requirements.

OPTION 1

Furniture and seating must be GREENGUARD Children and Schools certified

OR

OPTION 2

Calculated indoor air concentrations that are less than or equal to those listed in Table 1 for furniture systems and seating determined by a procedure based on the EPA Environmental Technology Verification (ETV) Large Chamber Test Protocol for Measuring Emissions of VOCs and Aldehydes (September 1999) testing protocol conducted in an independent air quality testing laboratory.

Table 1. Maximum Indoor Air Concentrations

Chemical Contaminant	Classroom Furniture	Seating
Total VOCs	0.5 mg/m^3	0.25 mg/m^3
Formaldehyde	50 parts per billion	25 parts per billion
Total aldehydes	100 parts per billion	50 parts per billion
4—Phenylcyclohexene (4-PCH)	0.0065 mg/m^3	0.00325 mg/m^3

OR

OPTION 3

Calculated indoor air concentrations that are less than or equal to those established in Table 1 for furniture systems and seating determined by a procedure based on ANSI/BIFMA M7.1-2007 and ANSI/BIFMA X7.1-2007 testing protocol conducted in an independent third-party air quality testing laboratory.

Schools projects may choose from IEQ Credits 4.1-4.6 for a maximum of 4 points.

	IEQ
NC	NA
SCHOOLS	Credit 4.5
CS	NA

1. Benefits and Issues to Consider

Refer to the Benefits and Issues section of IEQ Credit 4.1, Low-Emitting Materials—Adhesives and Sealants.

2. Related Credits

Because the intent of this credit is to reduce odorous, irritating, or harmful indoor air contaminants, the following other credits may be applicable:

- IEQ Credit 4.1: Low-Emitting Materials—Adhesives and Sealants
- IEQ Credit 4.2: Low-Emitting Materials—Paints and Coatings
- IEQ Credit 4.3: Low-Emitting Materials—Flooring Systems
- IEQ Credit 4.4: Low-Emitting Materials—Composite Wood and Agrifiber Products
- IEQ Credit 4.6: Low-Emitting Materials—Ceiling and Wall Systems (Specific to Schools)

Scheduling strategies and the use and tracking of building materials are also addressed in the contractor orientation training, covered under these 2 credits:

- IEQ Credit 3.1: Construction IAQ Management Plan During Construction
- IEQ Credit 3.2: Construction IAQ Management Plan Before Occupancy

Indoor air quality is affected by sources generated within the building itself and introduced into its spaces. Both sources are addressed in the following prerequisite and credit:

- IEQ Prerequisite 2: Environmental Tobacco Smoke (ETS) Control
- IEQ Credit 5: Indoor Chemical and Pollutant Source Control

3. Summary of Referenced Standards

American National Standards Institute (ANSI)/Business and Institutional Furniture Makers' Association (BIFMA) X7.1–2007 Standard for Formaldehyde and TVOC Emissions of Low-Emitting Office Furniture Systems and Seating

BIFMA International
http://www.bifma.org/standards/standards.html
ANSI/BIFMA X7.1–2007 "defines the criteria for office furniture VOC emissions to be classified as low-emitting product." Us it in conjunction with the ANSI/BIFMA M7.1-2007.

Environmental Technology Verification (ETV) Large Chamber Test Protocol for Measuring Emissions of VOCs and Aldehydes, effectiveSeptember 1999
Research Triangle Institute and U.S. EPA
http://www.epa.gov/etv/pdfs/vp/07_vp_furniture.pdf
Under the leadership of EPA, a testing protocol committee developed the referenced standards . The protocol requires the placement of the seating product or furniture assembly to be tested in a climatically controlled chamber. A controlled quantity of conditioned air is drawn through the chamber, and emission concentrations are measured at set intervals over a 4-day period.

GREENGUARD™ Certification Program
GreenguardEnvironmental Institute
http://www.greenguard.org
GEI has "established performance-based standards to define goods with low chemical and particle emissions for use indoors," primarily for building materials; interior furnishings; furniture; electronics; and cleaning, maintenance, and personal care products. The standard establishes certification procedures that include "test methods, allowable emissions levels, product sample

collection and handling, testing type and frequency, and program application processes and acceptance."

4. Implementation

The sections under IEQ Credit 4, Low-Emitting Materials, apply to products and installation processes that might adversely affect the IAQ of a project space and, consequently, those occupants exposed to the off-gassing of contaminants.

LEED for Schools IEQ Credit 4 employs 3 approaches to limit off-gassing, composition limits, emissions factors, and performance-based standards. For IEQ Credit 4.5, Low-Emitting Materials—Furniture and Furnishings, the performance-based standards approach applies.

Performance-Based Standards

This approach calculates the concentrations of contaminants that each product will add to the air. The protocols are very similar to those for emission factor testing, but are crafted to allow for testing of more complex assemblies (such as systems furniture). Again, groups of products are placed in a test chamber. Air is circulated in the chamber, simulating the conditions where the product would normally be used. At set intervals, samples of the air are taken and analyzed. The results are reported in the same units of measure established for air quality and used in the IAQ testing procedure of IEQ Credit 3.2, Construction Indoor Air Quality Management Plan Before Occupancy—parts per million, parts per billion, or micrograms per cubic meter of air. The performance-based standards approach is used in IEQ Credit 4.5, Low-Emitting Materials—Furniture and Furnishings. The Greenguard Institute testing program for systems furniture and classroom uses performance-based standards. Using products listed as Greenguard certified is 1 means of compliance for IEQ Credit 4.5, Low-Emitting Materials—Furniture and Furnishings. They are certified as having test results below the threshold contaminant amounts.

In the selection of systems furniture and multiple office seating, confirm that the desired product will meet the testing requirements at the time it is manufactured.

The Greenguard Environmental Institute provides a list of the products it has certified. Additional manufacturers may also have met the testing requirements set out in this credit.

Performance-Based Emissions Limits

By satisfying the test results referenced in LEED for Schools IEQ Credit 4.5, Low-Emitting Materials—Furniture and Furnishings, the product should not increase the concentration of contaminants in the air around it by any more than the threshold limits; the values are expressed as either mg/m3 or parts per billion (ppb).

The testing protocol that covers systems furniture uses a large chamber where a full workstation is assembled. The workstation size, mix of components, and types of materials (including fabrics and finishes) are intended to be representative of what is most commonly used in actual installations. Confer with the manufacturer when considering substitutions or if the density of the components will be higher than in a normal application.

For the performance-based standard used in this credit to apply to the project site, other considerations must be satisfied. The air velocity and outdoor air rate introduced into the classroom should meet ASHRAE 62.1–2007, the same standard referenced in IEQ Prerequisite 1, Minimum Indoor Air Quality Performance. Adequate ventilation during installation helps dissipate early off-gassing. The flush-out period called for in IEQ Credit 3.2, Construction IAQ Management Plan Before occupancy, should not begin until furniture installation is complete.

	IEQ
NC	NA
SCHOOLS	Credit 4.5
CS	NA

Remember that systems furniture may be either a panel-based workstation comprising modular interconnecting panels, hang-on components, and drawer/filing components, or a free-standing grouping of furniture items and their components that have been designed to work together. Seating covered by this credit is defined as task and guest chairs used with systems furniture.

Work tools often attached to systems furniture are not included in the credit requirement. Other furniture is considered as occasional furniture and does not need to be included in the credit documentation. Also, salvaged and used furniture that is more than 1 year old at the time of occupancy is excluded from the credit. Refurbishment of systems furniture or multiple office seating occurring within the 12-month period prior to occupancy must meet the credit requirements.

5. Timeline and Team

Refer to the Timeline and Team section of IEQ Credit 4.1, Low-Emitting Materials—Adhesives and Sealants.

6. Calculations

There are no calculations required for this credit.

7. Documentation Guidance

As a first step in preparing to complete the LEED-Online documentation requirements, work through the following measures. Refer to LEED-Online for the complete descriptions of all required documentation.

- Maintain documentation that confirms furniture and seating products are GREENGUARD™ Children and Schools CertifiedSM, comply with EPA's Environmental Technology Verification (ETV) Large Chamber Test Protocol for Measuring Emissions of VOCs and Aldehydes (September 1999) testing protocol, or comply with ANSI/BIFMA M7.1–2007 and ANSI/BIFMA X7.1–2007 testing protocol.

8. Examples

There are no examples for this credit.

9. Exemplary Performance

This credit is not eligible for exemplary performance under the Innovation in Design section.

10. Regional Variations

There are no regional variations for this credit.

11. Operations and Maintenance Considerations

Establish a policy for the continued use of low-emitting materials during the building's operation. Help building operators find low-emitting products for repairs or alterations by providing them with a list of compliant products.

12. Resources

Please see USGBC's LEED Registered Project Tools (http://www.usgbc.org/projecttools) for additional resources and technical information.

Websites

There are no websites for this credit.

13. Definitions

Contaminants are unwanted airborne elements that may reduce air quality. (ASHRAE 62.1–2007)

Indoor air quality (**IAQ**) is the nature of air inside a building that affects the health and well-being of building occupants. It is considered acceptable when there are no known contaminants at harmful concentrations as determined by cognizant authorities and with which a substantial majority (80% or more) of the people exposed do not express dissatisfaction. (ASHRAE 62.1–2007)

Occupants in an educational building are students, teachers, and administrators who either spend time in a classroom, have a permanent office, or typically spend a minimum of 10 hours per week in the building.

Off-gassing is the emission of volatile organic compounds (VOCs) from synthetic and natural products.

Volatile organic compounds (**VOCs**) are carbon compounds that participate in atmospheric photochemical reactions (excluding carbon monoxide, carbon dioxide, carbonic acid, metallic carbides and carbonates, and ammonium carbonate). The compounds vaporize at normal room temperatures.

	IEQ
NC	NA
SCHOOLS	Credit 4.5
CS —	NA

	NC	SCHOOLS	CS
Credit	NA	IEQ Credit 4.6	NA
Points	NA	1 point	NA

Intent

To reduce the quantity of indoor air contaminants that are odorous, irritating, and/or harmful to the comfort and well-being of installers and occupants.

Requirements

SCHOOLS

All gypsum board, insulation, acoustical ceiling systems and wall coverings installed in the building interior must meet the testing and product requirements of the California Department of Health Services Standard Practice for the Testing of Volatile Organic Emissions from Various Sources Using Small-Scale Environmental Chambers, including 2004 Addenda.

Schools projects may choose from IEQ Credits 4.1-4.6 for a maximum of 4 points.

	IEQ
NC	NA
SCHOOLS	Credit 4.6
CS	NA

1. Benefits and Issues to Consider

Refer to the Benefits and Issues section of IEQ Credit 4.1, Low-Emitting Materials—Adhesives and Sealants.

2. Related Credits

Because the intent of this credit is to reduce odorous, irritating, or harmful indoor air contaminants, the following other credits may be applicable:

- IEQ Credit 4.1: Low-Emitting Materials—Adhesives and Sealants
- IEQ Credit 4.2: Low-Emitting Materials—Paints and Coatings
- IEQ Credit 4.3: Low-Emitting Materials—Flooring Systems
- IEQ Credit 4.4: Low-Emitting Materials—Composite Wood and Agrifiber Products
- IEQ Credit 4.5: Low-Emitting Materials—Furniture and Furnishings (Specific to Schools)

Scheduling strategies and the use and tracking of building materials are also addressed in the contractor orientation training, covered under these 2 credits:

- IEQ Credit 3.1: Construction IAQ Management Plan During Construction
- IEQ Credit 3.2: Construction IAQ Management Plan Before Occupancy

Indoor air quality is affected by sources generated within the building itself and introduced into its spaces. Both sources are addressed in the following prerequisite and credit:

- IEQ Prerequisite 2: Environmental Tobacco Smoke (ETS) Control
- IEQ Credit 5: Indoor Chemical and Pollutant Source Control

Acoustical elements within the building may require specialty installation considerations, which can necessitate careful coordination between acoustical concerns and the materials specifier. Indoor environmental quality also encompasses occupants' auditory comfort and well-being, which are covered under these 2 credits:

- IEQ Prerequisite 3: Minimum Acoustical Performance
- IEQ Credit 9: Enhanced Acoustical Performance

3. Summary of Referenced Standard

California Department of Health Services Standard Practice for the Testing of Volatile Organic Emissions from Various Sources Using Small-Scale Environmental Chambers, including 2004 Addenda
California Department of Health Services
http://www.cal-iaq.org/VOC/Section01350_7_15_2004_FINAL_PLUS_ADDENDUM-2004-01.pdf
This standard practice applies to any newly manufactured material generally used within an enclosed indoor environment. However, the testing practice excludes all products that cannot be tested whole or by representative sample in small-scale environmental chambers.

The testing practice establishes the procedures for product sample collection, emissions testing, indoor concentration modeling, and documentation requirements associated with the analyzing the emissions of VOCs from various sources using small-scale environmental chambers. In addition, the testing practice lists target chemicals and their maximum allowable concentrations.

4. Implementation

Refer to the Implementation section of IEQ Credit 4.1, Low-Emitting Materials—Adhesives and Sealants.

5. Timeline and Team

Refer to the Timeline and Team section of IEQ Credit 4.1, Low-Emitting Materials—Adhesives and Sealants.

6. Calculations

There are no calculations required for this credit.

7. Documentation Guidance

As a first step in preparing to complete the LEED-Online documentation requirements, work through the following measures. Refer to LEED-Online for the complete descriptions of all required documentation.

- Maintain documentation that confirms all gypsum board, insulation, acoustical ceiling systems, and wall coverings installed in the building interior meet the testing and product requirements of the California Department of Health Services *Standard Practice for The Testing Of Volatile Organic Emissions From Various Sources Using Small-Scale Environmental Chambers*, including 2004 Addenda.

8. Examples

There are no examples for this credit.

9. Exemplary Performance

This credit is not eligible for exemplary performance under the Innovation in Design section.

10. Regional Variations

There are no regional variations for this credit.

11. Operations and Maintenance Considerations

Establish a policy for the continued use of low-emitting materials during the building's operation. Help building operators find low-emitting products for repairs or alterations by providing them with a list of compliant products.

12. Resources

Please see USGBC's LEED Registered Project Tools (http://www.usgbc.org/projecttools) for additional resources and technical information.

Websites

Refer to the websites listed for IEQ Credits 4.1–4.4.

13. Definitions

Agrifiber board is a composite panel product derived from recovered agricultural waste fiber from such sources as cereal straw, sugarcane bagasse, sunflower husk, walnut shells, coconut husks, and agricultural prunings. The raw fibers are processed and mixed with resins to produce panel products with characteristics similar to those derived from wood fiber. The following conditions describe which products must comply with the credit requirements:

1. The product is inside the building's waterproofing system.

2. Composite components used in assemblies are to be included (e.g., door cores, panel substrates, etc.)

3. The product is part of the base building systems.

	IEQ
NC	NA
SCHOOLS	Credit 4.6
CS	NA

Composite wood consists of wood or plant particles or fibers bonded together by a synthetic resin or binder. Examples include plywood, particle board, oriented-strand board (OSB), medium-density fiberboard (MDF), and composite door cores. The following conditions describe which products must comply with the credit requirements:

1. The product is inside the building's waterproofing system.

2. Composite wood components used in assemblies are included (e.g., door cores, panel substrates, plywood sections of I-beams).

3. The product is part of the base building systems.

Contaminants are unwanted airborne elements that may reduce air quality. (ASHRAE 62.1–2007)

Indoor air quality (**IAQ**) is the nature of air inside a building that affects the health and well-being of building occupants. It is considered acceptable when there are no known contaminants at harmful concentrations as determined by cognizant authorities and with which a substantial majority (80% or more) of the people exposed do not express dissatisfaction. (ASHRAE 62.1–2007)

Occupants in an educational building are students, teachers, and administrators who either spend time in a classroom, have a permanent office, or typically spend a minimum of 10 hours per week in the building.

Off-gassing is the emission of volatile organic compounds (VOCs) from synthetic and natural products.

Volatile organic compounds (**VOCs**) are carbon compounds that participate in atmospheric photochemical reactions (excluding carbon monoxide, carbon dioxide, carbonic acid, metallic carbides and carbonates, and ammonium carbonate). The compounds vaporize at normal room temperatures.

	NC	SCHOOLS	CS
Credit	IEQ Credit 5	IEQ Credit 5	IEQ Credit 5
Points	1 point	1 point	1 point

Intent

To minimize building occupant exposure to potentially hazardous particulates and chemical pollutants.

Requirements

NC, SCHOOLS & CS

Design to minimize and control the entry of pollutants into buildings and later cross-contamination of regularly occupied areas through the following strategies:

- Employ permanent entryway systems at least 10 feet long in the primary direction of travel to capture dirt and particulates entering the building at regularly used exterior entrances. Acceptable entryway systems include permanently installed grates, grills and slotted systems that allow for cleaning underneath. Roll-out mats are acceptable only when maintained on a weekly basis by a contracted service organization (or school maintenance staff for school projects). Core & Shell projects that do not have entryway systems cannot achieve this credit.

- Sufficiently exhaust each space where hazardous gases or chemicals may be present or used (e.g. garages, housekeeping and laundry areas, science laboratories, prep rooms, art rooms, shops of any kind, and copying and printing rooms) to create negative pressure with respect to adjacent spaces when the doors to the room are closed. For each of these spaces, provide self-closing doors and deck-to-deck partitions or a hard-lid ceiling. The exhaust rate must be at least 0.50 cubic feet per minute (cfm) per/square foot, with no air recirculation. The pressure differential with the surrounding spaces must be at least 5 Pascals (Pa) (0.02 inches of water gauge) on average and 1 Pa (0.004 inches of water) at a minimum when the doors to the rooms are closed.

- In mechanically ventilated buildings, install new air filtration media in regularly occupied areas prior to occupancy; these filters must provide a minimum efficiency reporting value (MERV) of 13 or higher. Filtration should be applied to process both return and outside air that is delivered as supply air.

- Provide containment (i.e. a closed container for storage for off-site disposal in a regulatory compliant storage area, preferably outside the building) for appropriate disposal of hazardous liquid wastes in places where water and chemical concentrate mixing occurs (e.g., housekeeping, janitorial and science laboratories).

	IEQ
NC	Credit 5
SCHOOLS	Credit 5
CS	Credit 5

1. Benefits and Issues to Consider

Environmental Issues

This credit recognizes projects that reduce or mitigate human contact with airborne chemicals and particles. Although additional materials and energy may be required to provide entryway systems and isolated chemical-use areas, proper management of hazardous chemicals used for building operations and maintenance is important. With proper maintenance, harmful chemical spills and accidents can be avoided.

Economic Issues

Additional sinks, drains, room separations, and separate exhaust systems for copying and housekeeping areas can increase the project's overall initial cost. Dedicated ventilation and exhaust systems may require additional ductwork and associated installation costs. Clean air can promote occupants' productivity, increasing profitability for the company. Reducing the potential for spills can avoid costly environmental cleanups. An environmentally sound building also supports the well-being of occupants, which may contribute to lower health insurance rates and health care costs.

CS The level of control a building owner or developer has over different spaces in a multiuse building. For example, a commercial office building may have a retail component at the ground level. The final location of each tenant's entry will be determined by their needs and demands, outside the direct control of the Core & Shell owner. Even in these cases, the project team is required to install permanent entryway systems or properly maintained walk-off mats to comply with the credit. As is the case for all LEED Core & Shell credits, the requirements of a credit exclude the fit-out of tenant spaces. Tenant space activities such as use of copiers, fax machines, and printers are not considered within the scope of the LEED Core & Shell program; however, consider including compliance specifications in tenant design and construction guidelines. Because the decisions of 1 tenant can affect the indoor environmental quality of other tenants, LEED Core & Shell projects should include the requirements of tenant lease agreements.

2. Related Credits

Filtration media can remove contaminants from the air during construction as well as during operation. To ensure that the systems will accommodate high-efficiency filtration, refer to these credits:

- IEQ Credit 3.1: Construction IAQ Management Plan During Construction
- IEQ Credit 3.2: Construction IAQ Management Plan Before Occupancy

Exhausting indoor air in areas where chemicals are used is important to maintaining acceptable indoor air quality but can require additional fan energy. These exhaust systems will require commissioning, relating to the credits below:

- EA Credit 1: Optimized Energy Performance
- EA Prerequisite 2: Minimum Energy Performance
- EA Prerequisite 1: Fundamental Commissioning
- EA Credit 3: Enhanced Commissioning

Ventilation systems must be capable of accommodating the filtration media required for credit compliance. Refer to the following prerequisite and credit:

- IEQ Prerequisite 1: Minimum Indoor Air Quality Performance
- IEQ Credit 1: Outdoor Air Delivery Monitoring

3. Summary of Referenced Standard

American National Standards Institute (ANSI)/ASHRAE Standard 52.2–1999: Method of Testing General Ventilation Air-Cleaning Devices for Removal Efficiency by Particle Size

ASHRAE

www.ashrae.org

	IEQ
NC	Credit 5
SCHOOLS	Credit 5
CS	Credit 5

This standard presents methods for testing air cleaners for 2 performance characteristics: the device's capacity for removing particles from the air stream and the device's resistance to airflow. The minimum efficiency reporting value (MERV) is based on 3 composite average particle size removal efficiency points. Consult the standard for a complete explanation of MERV calculations. Table 1 summarizes the requirements for a MERV value of 13.

Table 1. Requirements for MERV 13

Composite Average Particle Size Efficiency (%)				Minimum Final Resistance (in. of water)
0.30 - 0.10 μm	1.0 - 3.0 μm	3.0 - 10.0 μm	(Pa)	
<75%	≥90%	≥90%	350	1.4

4. Implementation

The indoor air quality (IAQ) of buildings can be adversely affected by daily occupancy and operations. Occupants and building visitors contribute to indoor IAQ issues by introducing contaminants via shoes and clothing. Daily copier, fax, and printer operations add contaminants to the building's interior environment; in addition, the storage, mixing and disposal of housekeeping liquids may adversely affect human health. This credit seeks to improve a building's IAQ and limit the amount of particulate, chemical, and biological contaminants that occupants are exposed to.

Entryway Systems

Incorporate permanent entryway systems at all high-traffic exterior to interior access points to reduce the amount of contaminants tracked into the occupied space. The entryway systems should be designed to capture and remove particles from shoes without allowing buildup of contaminants.

High-traffic exterior access points will always include, but may not be limited to, the main building entry. Building entrances from structured parking areas will be used frequently. In some instances, these entry points are inside a parking garage. While a covered garage does provide protection from the elements, it is also a source of possible contaminants, and it functions as a direct connection to the outdoors. Buildings that have distinct employee and visitor entry points should include permanent entryway systems in these locations as well. Evaluate all building entry points to determine whether permanent entryway systems should be incorporated.

Equip all exterior to interior entrances with entryway systems (e.g., grilles, grates, or mats) to catch and hold dirt particles and prevent contamination of the building interior. Entryway systems must extend 10 feet from the building entrance into the building interior. Open grates and grilles or other entryway systems that have a recessed collection area are generally thought to be most effective.

Mat systems should be appropriate for the climate. For example, durable coarse mats with large open loops are appropriate for capturing sand, mud, or snow and should have a Class I fire-retardant rating.

High void volume within mat fibers provides space for trapping dirt below the mat surface and enables water to spread to a larger area for improved drying. This inhibits dirt retracing and mold and mildew growth. High-void-volume mats are also easier to vacuum or shake out. Fiber height provides maximum scraping surface at the shoe and mat interface and improves vacuuming efficiency.

Entryway mats with solid backings capture dirt and moisture and help to prevent dirt from collecting

	IEQ
NC	Credit 5
SCHOOLS	Credit 5
CS	Credit 5

underneath. A nonporous backing inhibits mold and mildew growth. The use of mold- and mildew-resistant materials in the mat construction can also prevent mold and mildew growth within the materials. Other recommended performance features in an entryway system include the following:

- Fire-retardant ratings that exceed DOC-FF-1-70, such as National Fire Protection Association (NFPA) -253 Class I and II, which can reduce insurance costs

- Electrostatic propensity levels of less than 2.5 kV, which means that the mat should not produce an electrical discharge when a user touches other people or objects

Entryway systems constructed with recycled content and rubber backings are preferable.

Hazardous Chemical Areas

Locate high-volume copy, print, and fax equipment in enclosed rooms away from regularly occupied spaces. In order to effectively remove airborne contaminants generated by this type of equipment, the rooms must be physically separated from adjacent spaces. This may be accomplished through installation of deck-to-deck partitions or sealed gypsum board enclosures. Rooms with large openings but no doors will not meet the credit requirement. Installation of a self-closing door is an option for such spaces. To remove airborne contaminants and prevent cross-contamination of nearby occupied spaces, equip the copy, print, and fax rooms with a dedicated exhaust system that creates negative pressure within the room to meet the requirements of this credit. If possible, convenience copier and printer use should be minimized. Although encouraged, designing exhaust systems that account for convenience copier and printer use is not required for this credit.

Chemical storage and mixing areas, such as janitor's closets and photo labs, should be located away from occupant work areas. Additionally, these rooms must be physically separated from adjacent spaces via installation of deck-to-deck partitions or sealed gypsum board enclosures. Rooms must be equipped with a dedicated exhaust system that creates the required negative pressurization to ensure that nearby occupied spaces will not be cross-contaminated. Drywall ceilings may be used in place of full-height partitions, but acoustical lay-in ceilings are not adequate.

The definition of convenience printers and copiers, which are not required to be segregated in a chemical use area, is left to the discretion of the design team; convenience machines are generally smaller units shared by many office personnel for short print and copy jobs.

Battery banks used to provide temporary back-up power must be segregated to satisfy this credit's requirements.

Housekeeping facilities that are part of a common laundry room in residential or hospitality buildings must meet the chemical storage requirements.

Rooms where chemicals are mixed and disposed of should be isolated. These rooms should include sinks and/or drains in appropriate locations to ensure that chemicals are disposed of properly and are not dumped into inadequate spaces (e.g., restrooms). Local codes requiring separate drain lines must be followed.

Additional ventilation systems to mitigate contaminating adjacent spaces can affect building energy performance; in these situations, the building may require additional commissioning, measurement, and verification to earn this credit. Ventilation system design must ensure that installed systems are capable of accommodating the filtration media that is required for this credit. This may be difficult to achieve for spaces with low-capacity packaged air handling systems because of the size of these filters and their associated pressure drop. The selected space layout may prohibit deck-to-deck separation and separate ventilation systems for chemical use areas. Storage areas for recyclable materials may also be considered contaminant sources, depending on the items recycled. Poorly chosen janitorial supplies can negatively affect IAQ.

Give special consideration to the design and installation of containment drains to ensure that hazardous waste is disposed of properly and to prevent environmental damage or contamination of water systems.

In addition, sources of outdoor air pollution (such as trash dumpsters or areas where vehicles tend to idle) should be located away from outdoor ventilation air intakes.

	IEQ
NC	Credit 5
SCHOOLS	Credit 5
CS	Credit 5

CS In some instances the tenant, not the developer, will determine the location of the exterior entries. In such cases, properly maintained interior walk-off mats are a viable solution.

SCHOOLS In science laboratories, fans should be used to exhaust chemicals from the space, but separate air handling units are not required.

5. Timeline and Team

During the early planning stage of a project, the design team should document the client's equipment requirements and usage patterns. This information will be critical in determining whether dedicated, isolated rooms will be required to house copy, fax, and print equipment.

During the design phase, the architect should consider the location and type of entryway systems and allow adequate space for entryway systems. During the schematic design phase, the team should confirm the locations of areas where chemicals and high-volume copy, fax, and print equipment will be used. It may be possible to locate such rooms above or adjacent to 1 another to make individual exhaust systems unnecessary and minimize exhaust ductwork and drainage piping. Also confirm that chemical and equipment rooms are properly isolated from adjacent spaces. The mechanical engineer should incorporate MERV 13 filters, dedicated exhaust systems, and separate drainage piping into the drawings and specifications; these elements will affect the fan sizing, shaft layout, and underground coordination.

Install and then commission the space exhaust systems to ensure that they meet the owner's requirements and the design intent.

6. Calculations

There are no calculations required for this credit.

7. Documentation Guidance

As a first step in preparing to complete the LEED-Online documentation requirements, work through the following measures. Refer to LEED-Online for the complete descriptions of all required documentation.

- Retain visual documentation of the location and size of all permanent entryway systems and walk-off mats.
- Create a table listing entryway systems.
- Create a building maintenance plan that includes a description of cleaning and maintenance for permanent entryway systems and walk-off mats necessary to manage contaminants brought into the building.
- Create a list of rooms or areas that require separation.
- Detail deck-to-deck partitions or hard-lid conditions at rooms known to have contaminants.

	IEQ
NC	Credit 5
SCHOOLS	Credit 5
CS	Credit 5

- As the project evolves, review negative pressure calculations at hazardous chemical areas to assure proper depressurization.

- Maintain product literature for MERV 13, or higher filters.

8. Examples

Figure 1. Requirements for Isolation Areas for Hazardous Gases or Chemicals

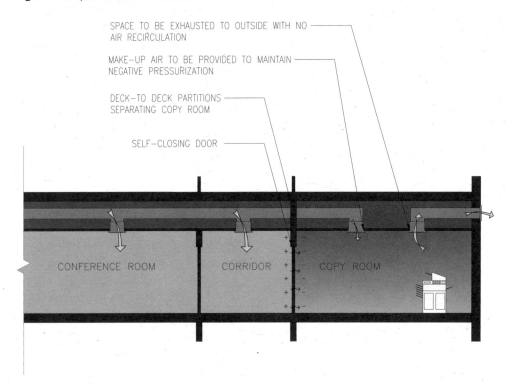

9. Exemplary Performance

This credit is not eligible for exemplary performance under the Innovation in Design section.

10. Regional Variations

Local weather conditions should be factored into determining the location and type of entryway systems. For example, in areas receive heavy rain or snow, it may be prudent to locate entryway systems in an enclosed vestibule or inside the building. A floor drain to remove collected moisture may also be necessary.

11. Operations and Maintenance Considerations

Establish procedures and schedules for replacing filtration media and testing and maintaining exhaust systems and include them in the building's preventive maintenance plan.

Systems that require regular maintenance should be designed to be easily accessible to operations staff. Ensure that protocols for selecting, storing, and handling hazardous waste are clearly communicated to building operators.

Develop, document, and record entryway maintenance practices in accordance with the manufacturer's specifications. These practices should specify cleaning strategies for the exterior and interior of entryways, general maintenance of entryway systems, and cleaning during inclement weather. Operations staff can reduce maintenance and replacement needs for entryway systems by keeping exterior walkways clean and using high-quality mats. Cleaning mats frequently can prolong the life of carpets and other flooring materials.

12. Resources

Please see USGBC's LEED Registered Project Tools (http://www.usgbc.org/projecttools) for additional resources and technical information.

Websites

Green Seal

http://www.greenseal.org/findaproduct/index.cfm

Green Seal is an independent, nonprofit organization that strives to achieve a healthier and cleaner environment by identifying and promoting products and services that cause less toxic pollution and waste, conserve resources and habitats, and minimize global warming and ozone depletion.

Janitorial Products Pollution Prevention Project

http://www.westp2net.org/janitorial/jp4.cfm

The Janitorial Products Pollution Prevention Project is a governmental and nonprofit project that provides fact sheets, tools, and links.

Environmentally Preferable Purchasing Information

U.S. EPA

http://www.epa.gov/opptintr/epp/

This page includes a database of environmental information on more than 600 products, including janitorial and pest control products.

Design Tools for Schools

U.S. EPA

http://www.epa.gov/iaq/schooldesign

According to the website, IAQ Design Tools for Schools "provides both detailed guidance as well as links to other information resources to help design new schools as well as repair, renovate, and maintain existing facilities. Though its primary focus is on indoor air quality, it is also intended to encourage school districts to embrace the concept of designing High Performance Schools, an integrated, whole building approach to addressing a myriad of important—and sometimes competing—priorities, such as energy efficiency, indoor air quality, daylighting, materials efficiency, and safety, and doing so in the context of tight budgets and limited staff."

Print Media

Clean and Green: The Complete Guide to Non-Toxic and Environmentally Safe Housekeeping, by Annie Berthold-Bond (Ceres Press, 1994).

13. Definitions

Air-handling units are mechanically indirect heating, ventilating, or air conditioning systems in which air is treated or handled by equipment located outside the space served, and conveyed to and from the space by means of a fan and duct system. (NEEB 1997 edition)

Entryway systems can be open floor grates or grilles with a recessed area designed to capture dirt and other debris from people entering the building.

Indoor air quality (IAQ) is the nature of air inside a building that affects the health and well-being of building occupants. It is considered acceptable when there are no known contaminants at harmful concentrations as determined by cognizant authorities and with which a substantial majority (80% or more) of the people exposed do not express dissatisfaction. (ASHRAE 62.1–2007)

Minimum efficiency reporting value (MERV) is a filter rating established by the American Society of Heating, Refrigerating, and Air-Conditioning Engineers (ASHRAE 52.2–1999, Method of Testing General Ventilation Air Cleaning Devices for Removal Efficiency by Particle Size). MERV categories range from 1 (very low efficiency) to 16 (very high).

	IEQ
NC	Credit 5
SCHOOLS	Credit 5
CS	Credit 5

Regularly occupied spaces in commercial buildings are areas where people sit or stand as they work. In residential applications these spaces include all living and family rooms and exclude bathrooms, closets, or other storage or utility areas. In schools, they are areas where students, teachers, or administrators are seated or standing as they work or study.

Walk-off mats are placed inside building entrances to capture dirt, water, and other materials tracked inside by people and equipment.

CONTROLLABILITY OF SYSTEMS—LIGHTING

	NC	SCHOOLS	CS
Credit	IEQ Credit 6.1	IEQ Credit 6.1	NA
Points	1 point	1 point	NA

Intent

To provide a high level of lighting system control by individual occupants or groups in multi-occupant spaces (e.g., classrooms and conference areas) and promote their productivity, comfort and well-being.

Requirements

NC

Provide individual lighting controls for 90% (minimum) of the building occupants to enable adjustments to suit individual task needs and preferences

Provide lighting system controls for all shared multi-occupant spaces to enable adjustments that meet group needs and preferences.

SCHOOLS

CASE 1. Administrative Offices and Other Regularly Occupied Spaces

Provide individual lighting controls for 90% (minimum) of the building occupants to enable adjustments to suit individual task needs and preferences

AND

Provide lighting system controls for all learning spaces including classrooms, chemistry laboratories, art rooms, shops, music rooms, gymnasiums and dance and exercise studios to enable adjustments that meet group needs and preferences.

CASE 2. Classrooms

In classrooms, provide a lighting system that operates in at least 2 modes: general illumination and A/V.

IEQ	
NC	Credit 6.1
SCHOOLS	Credit 6.1
CS	NA

1. Benefits and Issues to Consider

Environmental Issues

Providing individual controls for lighting increases occupants' comfort by enabling them to adjust the workspace to their individual needs. Individual controls also allow for multiple lighting possibilities—lighting for specific taks, general overhead lighting, lighting with consideration for A/V needs, and lecture style lighting with emphasis on the learning walls or presentation screens, for example. By balancing ambient light levels and providing user-controlled, flexible, task-appropriate lighting, project teams can reduce the overall lighting energy consumption and the heat loads associated with unnecessarily high or uneven levels of indoor lighting.

Effective lighting is important to human comfort, productivity, and communication. In classroom and presentation settings, building occupants must be able to see material on which they are working, as well as material that is presented on white boards and projected onto screens.

SCHOOLS Lighting controls should be easily accessible to teachers. Consider locations close to teaching walls so that students' attention is not interrupted. Dimming controls provide the greatest flexibility with the least disruption, especially in classrooms. Multiple lighting options that are easy to use and accessible can enhance learning environments.

Economic Issues

Additional task lights and lighting controls might increase initial costs for the project. These costs are generally offset by a reduced heat load and may enable designers to minimize ambient light levels as well as the number of installed fixtures and lamps. It is important to educate occupants on the design and function of system controls, because abuse of personal controls, such as leaving task lights on when not in classrooms or offices, has the potential to increase energy costs. Integrating individual controls with occupancy sensors provides project teams with an opportunity to reduce the overall energy cost. Integrating light-reflecting (or light-absorbing) surface materials with lighting design may create opportunities to reduce the number of installed luminaries, resulting in potential energy savings.

2. Related Credits

Lighting systems are affected by window placement, glazing selection for daylight and views, and zoning strategies employed for thermal comfort controllability. Lighting systems in turn affect energy performance: Giving occupants the ability to turn down or turn off lights when they are not needed can reduce electricity use. As with all control systems, the lighting controls need to be included within the scope of commissioning. For all these reasons, lighting is related to the following credits and prerequisites:

- IEQ Credit 8: Daylight and Views
- IEQ Credit 6.2: Controllability of Systems—Thermal Comfort
- EA Prerequisite 2: Minimum Energy Performance
- EA Credit 1: Optimize Energy Performance
- EA Prerequisite 1: Fundamental Commissioning of the Building Energy Systems
- EA Credit 3: Enhanced Commissioning

3. Summary of Referenced Standards

There are no referenced standards for this credit.

4. Implementation

Many conventional buildings have only fixed-intensity general lighting systems that illuminate indoor spaces without consideration for specific tasks and individual occupant comfort or needs. A better approach provides uniform general ambient lighting, augmented with individually controlled task fixtures.

	IEQ
NC	Credit 6.1
SCHOOLS	Credit 6.1
CS	NA

To comply with ANSI/ASHRAE/IESNA 90.1–2007, task lighting must be included in the lighting allowance. Daylighting can be integrated with this credit by using technologies and strategies to compensate for the reduced illuminance levels, as detailed in IEQ Credit 8. It is important to determine if any installed lighting systems or controls will require special calibration, commissioning, or occupant training.

Task lights come in several varieties, from desk-top lamps to fixtures that are permanently attached to workstations or laboratory benches. Ideally these task lights will have multiple lighting levels and automatic shutoff switching. Task lighting does not need to be hardwired to meet the requirements of this credit: outlet-powered task lighting provides a simple and effective way to add control.

To ensure maintenance of adequate light levels, consider strategies to address output depreciation and address relamping programs with the owner. Internal sensors may be available to make small adjustments to a light fixture as lamp output diminishes over time.

Remember that the operation of automatic occupancy sensors, daylight sensors, and other lighting controls might be adversely affected by items such as office equipment and furnishings that are installed during and after construction. Coordinate the final calibration of these items with the installer and commissioning agent early in the construction phase to ensure that the system operates as intended and provides lighting controls to 90% of occupants. Lighting system designs should comply with average illumination levels recommended by the Illuminating Engineering Society of North America (IESNA).

Increased uniformity will reduce the perception of decreased light levels in open spaces by minimizing high-contrast areas. Designers should investigate the benefits of direct/indirect or pendant mounted systems paired with high-reflectance ceiling surfaces and finishes. Integration of surface materials selection and lighting design may create opportunities to reduce the number of installed lighting fixtures and could result in saving energy.

Document the anticipated space uses, as well as any special needs or preferences regarding illuminance levels of the expected building users, give them to the lighting designer. This will enable the designer to allow all users to be able to match the light levels to their needs and desires.

5. Timeline and Team

During design, the layout of lighting and controls is the responsibility of the architect or lighting designer in consultation with the owner. Consider occupants' lighting needs and desires. Document the tasks specific to each space and the tools and equipment that occupants will use on a daily basis. A large open space, such as a 24-hour data center, might have special design needs because of round-the-clock use. Ensuring consistent, ergonomic, and operable lighting is a fundamental part of design decision making and project infrastructure.

In design development, project teams should involve electrical engineers and coordinate power and circuitry requirements. Design should include lighting professionals and electrical engineers to ensure white boards and screens are free from glare. Improperly lit surfaces can prevent participants from seeing important information. Lighting for audiovisual presentations should be dark enough that images are clearly visible on the screen but not so dark that the audience cannot take notes.

Once fixtures have been installed, coordinate the final calibration of the lighting controls with the installer and commissioning agent to ensure that the system operates as intended.

During building operation, the owner should provide training for building maintenance staff in calibration of systems and relamping. Property management and building engineers should periodically review lighting systems, as well as conduct surveys to ensure that occupants' needs are met and that lighting is working according to design.

Design should include lighting professionals and electrical engineers to ensure that material presented on white boards or on screens is free of glare. White boards and video displays can create glare if improperly lighted, preventing participants in some parts of the room from easily viewing the information presented on them. Lighting during A/V presentations should be dark enough to view images clearly on the screen but not so dark as to prevent building occupants from taking notes, if necessary.

6. Calculations

Adjustable Task Lighting

Identify workstation locations intended for individual use. Include every individual workspace (e.g., private offices, open plan workstations, reception stations, ticket booths). Confirm that 90% or more of the occupants of these spaces have task lighting that enables adjustment to suit individual needs. At a minimum, the occupant must be able to turn the fixture on and off. Ideally, the occupant can easily reposition the fixture and have multiple light levels. The fixture should be appropriate for the task.

Shared Multioccupant Spaces

In conference rooms, classrooms, lounges, and indoor spaces used for presentations and training, the group should have access to adequate controls to suit their activities. Specific types or numbers of controls are not listed in the credit requirements to allow for flexibility in designing to the specific uses of each project. Meeting spaces must be designed so that occupants have control of their individual area; subdivide these spaces with movable walls or partitions. In residential applications, switched receptacles are appropriate to provide a variety of lighting options within the space. When daylighting is used as a component of an ambient lighting scheme in either type of space, provide glare control, lighting level controls, and room-darkening shades if appropriate.

Offices and Other Regularly Occupied Spaces

Count the workstations intended for individual use. The office and equipment layout should be carefully analyzed to ensure that 90% or more of these occupants have individual lighting controls that enable adjustment to suit individual needs. At a minimum, occupants must be able to turn the fixture on and off.

Many types of luminaires are available; select those with a high level of flexibility and control. One effective way to meet the requirement is to use suspended luminaries that have 2 compartments, 1 for downlighting and 1 for general illumination, with separate switches for each. Occupants can quickly switch from 1 lighting scenario to the other without using dimmers, and 1 light is automatically turned off when the other is turned on. Dimming controls provide the greatest flexibility with the least disruption. Audiovisual rooms require a lower light level and should be easy to adjust to maintain optimum contrast levels on projection screens.

Ceilings should be white or light in color and extend at least 9 1/2 feet from the floor. If acoustical tiles or paint are used, select materials with 90% or greater reflectivity.

When using daylighting strategies in these spaces, install window treatments that provide appropriate light levels for audiovisual uses.

Individual Workstation Lighting Controls

Include private offices and cubicles when counting workstations for the following calculation:

$$\text{Workstations with Controls (\%)} = \frac{\text{Individual Workstations with Lighting Controls}}{\text{Total Individual Workstations}}$$

SCHOOLS   Shared multioccupant spaces in schools should meet the lighting needs of classrooms and core learning spaces, which might vary depending on the activities hosted in each room. The lighting should be appropriate for the activity and adjustable to provide optimum conditions for both working at desks and viewing projection screens, as needed.

7. Documentation Guidance

As a first step in preparing to complete the LEED-Online documentation requirements, work through the following measures. Refer to LEED-Online for the complete descriptions of all required documentation.

- Maintain a floor plan that indicates the location, zoning, and type of lighting controls. The floor plan should include furniture layout, indicating individual and shared work areas.

- Retain design information on task lighting, sensors, and lighting controls.

8. Examples

Figure 1. Workstations with Individually Adjustable Task Lighting

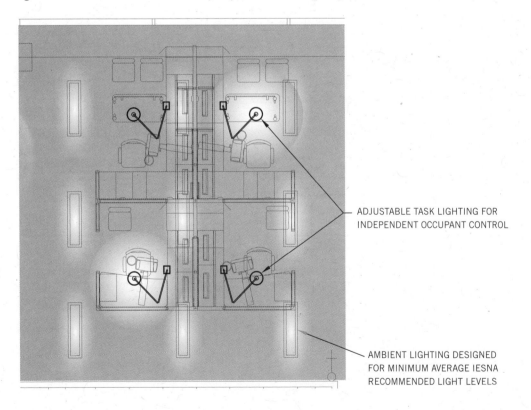

ADJUSTABLE TASK LIGHTING FOR INDEPENDENT OCCUPANT CONTROL

AMBIENT LIGHTING DESIGNED FOR MINIMUM AVERAGE IESNA RECOMMENDED LIGHT LEVELS

	IEQ
NC	Credit 6.1
SCHOOLS	Credit 6.1
CS	NA

Figure 2. Shared Multioccupant Space with Access to Lighting Controls

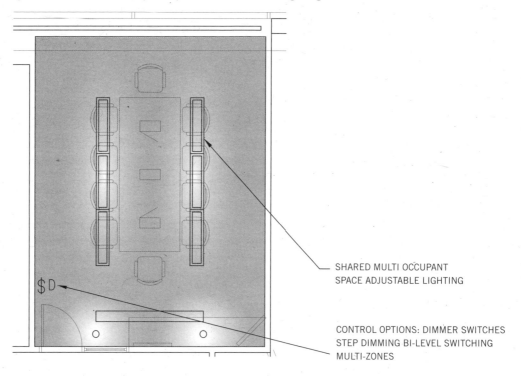

SHARED MULTI OCCUPANT
SPACE ADJUSTABLE LIGHTING

CONTROL OPTIONS: DIMMER SWITCHES
STEP DIMMING BI-LEVEL SWITCHING
MULTI-ZONES

Daylight harvesting and lighting control have been linked to higher productivity and lower energy bills. A lighting control system that either is remotely programmed or uses occupancy sensors (with a delay) to turn lamps on and off can save energy when areas are not in use.

9. Exemplary Performance

This credit is not eligible for exemplary performance under the Innovation in Design section.

10. Regional Variations

Buildings in regions with strong sunlight may use less artificial lighting by day but require greater controllability in their lighting systems. Because daylight levels may range from the low to the intense during the course of a day, building occupants may experience discomfort if light levels fluctuate widely. Project teams in these regions should consider incorporating passive design strategies, such as good building orientation and the use of light-shielding devices like canopies, to control daylight. Daylight sensors that automatically adjust artificial lighting to compensate are also effective.

11. Operations and Maintenance Considerations

Building owners and architects should specify for lighting engineers and operators the number and type of lighting controls installed.

For automatic controls, provide appropriate setpoints and schedules in the facility's building operation plan. Establish procedures and schedules for recalibrating sensors, based on the manufacturer's requirements, and include them in the building's preventive maintenance plan.

When specifying automatic controls, consider the intended space use, and choose an option suited to expected conditions. A utility room, for example, may have moving parts that can falsely trigger motion-based sensors.

12. Resources

Please see USGBC's LEED Registered Project Tools (http://www.usgbc.org/projecttools) for additional resources and technical information.

	IEQ
NC	Credit 6.1
SCHOOLS	Credit 6.1
CS	NA

Websites

A Field Study of Personal Environmental Module Performance in Bank of America's San Francisco Office Buildings

http://www.cbe.berkeley.edu/research/pdf_files/bauman1998_bofa.pdf%20

This University of California, Berkeley research center, provides information about underfloor air distribution technologies and other topics.

Do Green Buildings Enhance the Well-being of Workers? Yes

Environmental Design + Construction

http://www.edcmag.com/Articles/Cover_Story/fb077b7338697010VgnVCM100000f932a8c0

This article by Judith Heerwagen in the July/August 2000 edition of Environmental Design + Construction quantifies the effects of green building environments on productivity.

Association of Lighting and Mercury Recyclers

http://www.almr.org

Energy-10™

National Renewable Energy Laboratory

http://www.nrel.gov/buildings/energy10.html

Print Media

Controls and Automation for Facilities Managers: Applications Engineering, by Viktor Boed (CRC Press, 1998).

Advanced Lighting Guidelines, 2003 edition, by New Buildings Institute (NBI, 2003).

Collaborative for High Performance Schools Best Practices Manual, 2006 edition: http://www.chps.net/manual/index.htm.

IESNA Lighting for Educational Facilities, by Illuminating Engineering Society of North America (IESNA, 2006): Document ID RP-3-00 at http://www.iesna.org.

IESNA Lighting Handbook, 9th edition, by Illuminating Engineering Society of North America (IESNA, 2000): Document ID # HB-9-00 at http://www.iesna.org.

13. Definitions

Audiovisual (A/V) media are slides, film, video, sound recordings, and other such devices used to present information.

Core learning spaces are spaces for educational activities where the primary functions are teaching and learning (ANSI S12.60-2002).

Commissioning is the process of verifying and documenting that the facility and all of its systems and assemblies are planned, designed, installed, tested, operated, and maintained to meet the owner's operating requirements.

Controls are operating mechanisms that enable a person to turn on or off devices (e.g., lights, heaters) or adjust systems within a range (e.g., lighting, temperature).

Daylighting is the controlled admission of natural light into a space, used to reduce or eliminate electric lighting.

	IEQ
NC	Credit 6.1
SCHOOLS	Credit 6.1
CS	NA

Glare is any excessively bright source of light within the visual field that creates discomfort or loss in visibility.

In **individual occupant spaces,** workers use standard workstations to conduct individual tasks. Examples are private offices and open office areas with multiple workers.

Nonoccupied spaces include all rooms used by maintenance personnel that are not open for use by occupants. Examples are closets and janitorial, storage, and equipment rooms.

Outdoor air is the ambient air that enters a building through a ventilation system, either through natural ventilation or by infiltration. (ASHRAE 62.1–2007)

Group multioccupant spaces include conference rooms, classrooms, and other indoor spaces used as places of congregation.

Sensors are devices that undergo a measurable change in response to environmental changes and communicate this to the appropriate equipment or control system.

CONTROLLABILITY OF SYSTEMS—THERMAL COMFORT

	NC	SCHOOLS	CS
Credit	IEQ Credit 6.2	IEQ Credit 6.2	IEQ Credit 6
Points	1 point	1 point	1 point

Intent

To provide a high level of thermal comfort system control[1] by individual occupants or groups in multi-occupant spaces (e.g., classrooms or conference areas) and promote their productivity, comfort and well-being.

Requirements

NC, SCHOOLS & CS

Provide individual comfort controls for 50% (minimum) of the building occupants to enable adjustments (for workspaces only in Schools projects) to meet individual needs and preferences. Operable windows may be used in lieu of controls for occupants located 20 feet inside and 10 feet to either side of the operable part of a window. The areas of operable window must meet the requirements of ASHRAE Standard 62.1-2007 paragraph 5.1 Natural Ventilation (with errata but without addenda[2]).

Provide comfort system controls for all shared multi-occupant spaces to enable adjustments that meet group needs and preferences.

Conditions for thermal comfort are described in ASHRAE Standard 55-2004 (with errata but without addenda[2]) and include the primary factors of air temperature, radiant temperature, air speed and humidity.

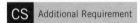 Additional Requirement

Core and shell projects that do not purchase and/or install the mechanical system or operable windows (or a combination of both) have not met the intent of this credit.

See Appendix 1 — Default Occupancy Counts for occupancy count requirements and guidance.

---

1 For the purposes of this credit, comfort system control is defined as control over at least 1 of the following primary factors in the occupant's vicinity: air temperature, radiant temperature, air speed and humidity.
2 Project teams wishing to use ASHRAE approved addenda for the purposes of this credit may do so at their discretion. Addenda must be applied consistently across all LEED credits.

	IEQ
NC	Credit 6.2
SCHOOLS	Credit 6.2
CS	Credit 6

1. Benefits and Issues to Consider

Providing temperature controls for individuals and spaces will increase occupant comfort while simultaneously saving energy.

Economic Issues

Occupant complaints frequently include thermal discomfort. Greater thermal comfort may increase occupant performance and attendance and, at least, will reduce complaints. As noted in a report published by the Center for the Built Environment,[26] studies have shown that individual occupant controls can potentially increase occupant satisfaction and productivity. The financial implications of such improvements can be extremely large. Additional controllability may add to a project's initial costs, however, these costs are generally offset by energy savings from lower-conditioned temperatures, automatic occupancy detectors, natural ventilation, and shading devices. Conversely, abuse of personal controls, such as setting thermostats too high or leaving windows open during nonworking hours, increases energy costs. Therefore, it is important to educate occupants on the design and function of system controls. Alteration of ventilation and temperature schemes may change the energy performance of a building and may require commissioning and measurement and verification attention.

CS Core & Shell HVAC duct design for tenant spaces are typically incomplete. The intent of this credit in LEED Core & Shell is to provide building HVAC systems that can be expanded to allow for a high degree of occupant control. Some system types make this credit easier to achieve and document than others. An underfloor air system that allows tenants to use individual diffusers can offer a high degree of tenant controllability. Buildings that use an overhead variable air volume system will have to demonstrate that it is possible for the system to provide enough control points for 50% of the occupants.

2. Related Credits

The intent of this credit is to enable individuals and, in multioccupant spaces, groups to control their thermal comfort. The following prerequisites and credits also address building occupants' ability to control systems, maintenance, and other factors:

- EA Prerequisite 1: Fundamental Commissioning of Building Systems
- EA Prerequisite 2: Minimum Energy Performance
- EA Credit 1: Optimize Energy Performance
- EA Credit 3: Enhanced Commissioning
- EA Credit 5: Measurement and Verification
- IEQ Credit 5: Indoor Chemical and Pollutant Source Control
- IEQ Credit 6.1: Controllability of Systems—Lighting (New Construction and Schools only)
- IEQ Credit 8: Daylight and Views

3. Summary of Referenced Standards

American National Standards Institute (ANSI)/ASHRAE Standard 62.1–2007: Ventilation for Acceptable Indoor Air Quality
ASHRAE
http://www.ashrae.org
Section 5.1 of the standard provides minimum requirements for operable openings. The portion of the window that can be opened must be 4% of the net inhabitable floor area. Building occupants must have ready access to the means of opening the windows.

American National Standards Institute ANSI/ASHRAE Standard 55-2004: Thermal Environmental Conditions for Human Occupancy

ASHRAE 55-2004 identifies the factors of thermal comfort and the process for developing comfort criteria for a building space and its occupants. ASHRAE states, "this standard specifies the combinations of indoor space environment and personal factors that will produce thermal environmental conditions acceptable to 80% or more of the occupants within a space. The environmental factors addressed are temperature, thermal radiation, humidity and air speed; the personal factors are those of activity and clothing."

	IEQ
NC	Credit 6.2
SCHOOLS	Credit 6.2
CS	Credit 6

4. Implementation

Many conventional buildings are built as sealed spaces in which the occupants have no control over thermal conditions. A better approach gives individuals the controls to adjust thermal conditions for a more comfortable environment. Individual thermal comfort can depend on air velocity, the direction and temperature of indoor air, and moisture content. The design team should determine the level of individual control desired, and should design the building with comfort controls to suit both individual needs and those of groups in shared spaces.

Consider including designs with operable windows, hybrid designs incorporating operable windows and mechanical systems, or mechanical systems alone. Individual control of comfort with mechanical systems may be integrated into the overall systems design by enabling individual adjustment of selected comfort parameters, such as individual thermostats, individual diffusers (located at the floor, desk, or overhead level) and individual radiant panels. Occupancy sensors can also be integrated in the design to automatically turn down the thermostat and reduce airflow when occupants are away, helping reduce energy use.

Educate occupants on their individual control of their environment. Additionally, train key maintenance staff in the operations of the HVAC equipment and any installed controls. Provide at least 1 thermal control per residential unit to be eligible for this credit. Common areas in residential projects are considered multioccupant spaces and are subject to the same requirement as other projects.

Individual Thermal Comfort

To satisfy this portion of the requirement, start by identifying workstation locations that are intended for individual use, including private offices, open plan workstations, reception stations, ticket booths, etc. Confirm that 50% or more of individuals occupying these locations have at least 1 means of individual control over thermal comfort.

Operable windows may be used in lieu of individual controls for those occupants located within 20 feet of the exterior wall and within 10 feet of either side of the operable part of the window. The operable portion of the window will need to comply with the free-opening size criteria of ANSI/ASHRAE 62.1-2007 section 5.1. The minimum area of the window opening may be 4% of the net occupiable area for ventilation purposes; however, larger opening areas may be required for thermal comfort under a wide range of outside conditions. For example, in an area 20 feet by 20 feet, the opening size per window would need to be 16 square feet to meet the limits used in this credit

Multioccupant Spaces

Start by identifying areas where groups occasionally congregate, such as conference rooms, break rooms, and lecture halls. Specific types or numbers of controls are not listed in the credit requirements to allow for flexibility in designing to the unique uses of each project. Confirm that there is at least 1 accessible means of control over thermal comfort in the space. Meeting spaces that can be subdivided, as with a movable wall in a convention hall, must be designed so that occupants in each area have control of their individual area.

5. Timeline and Team

During schematic design, building designers should evaluate the building's orientation and consider how heat gain or loss will affect the occupants. Designers should also consider whether site-specific conditions, such as wind, sound, and odors, may affect the location of operable windows. During design development, locate the thermal comfort controls with electrical and mechanical engineers as well as the construction or development manager. Consider thermal comfort needs as they pertain to ANSI/ASHRAE 55–2004 requirements; survey future occupants' desires. Evaluate the controls for each space, considering the specific tools and equipment that occupants will use on a daily basis. When evaluating shared occupant spaces, consider the occupancy schedule.

Postinstallation commissioning of all thermal comfort systems will ensure proper operation. During building operation, the owner should provide training for building maintenance staff in using the controls. Property management and building engineers should periodically review of comfort control systems to ensure that occupants' needs are met and that controls are working according to design.

6. Calculations

Individual Thermal Comfort

Identify workstations intended for individual use, such as private offices, open-plan workstations, reception stations, and ticket booths. Confirm that 50% or more of individuals occupying these locations have at least 1 means of individual control over thermal comfort.

Operable windows may be used in lieu of individual controls for occupants located within 20 feet of the exterior wall and within 10 feet of either side of the operable part of the window. The operable portion of the window must comply with the free-opening size criterion of ANSI/ASHRAE 62.1–2007, Section 5.1; the minimum area of the window that may be opened is 4% of the net floor area. For the limits used in this credit (i.e., an area 20 feet by 20 feet per window), the opening size would need to be 16 square feet.

Shared Multioccupant Spaces

For conference rooms and lecture halls, confirm that there is at least 1 accessible means of control over thermal comfort. For meeting spaces that can be subdivided, such as a convention hall with a movable wall, occupants in each area should have control of their individual area.

7. Documentation Guidance

As a first step in preparing to complete the LEED-Online documentation requirements, work through the following measures. Refer to LEED-Online for the complete descriptions of all required documentation.

- For individual workstation controls, maintain a list of the total number of individual workstations and thermal controls.

- For shared multioccupant space control, maintain a list of a project's group multioccupant spaces and a description of the installed thermal controls.

CS

- Record the number of expected occupants on a floor-by-floor basis. See Appendix 1 for the default occupancy counts. State which systems serve each floor.

8. Examples

Figure 1. Underfloor Air Distribution System with Individual Controls for Air Velocity and Temperature

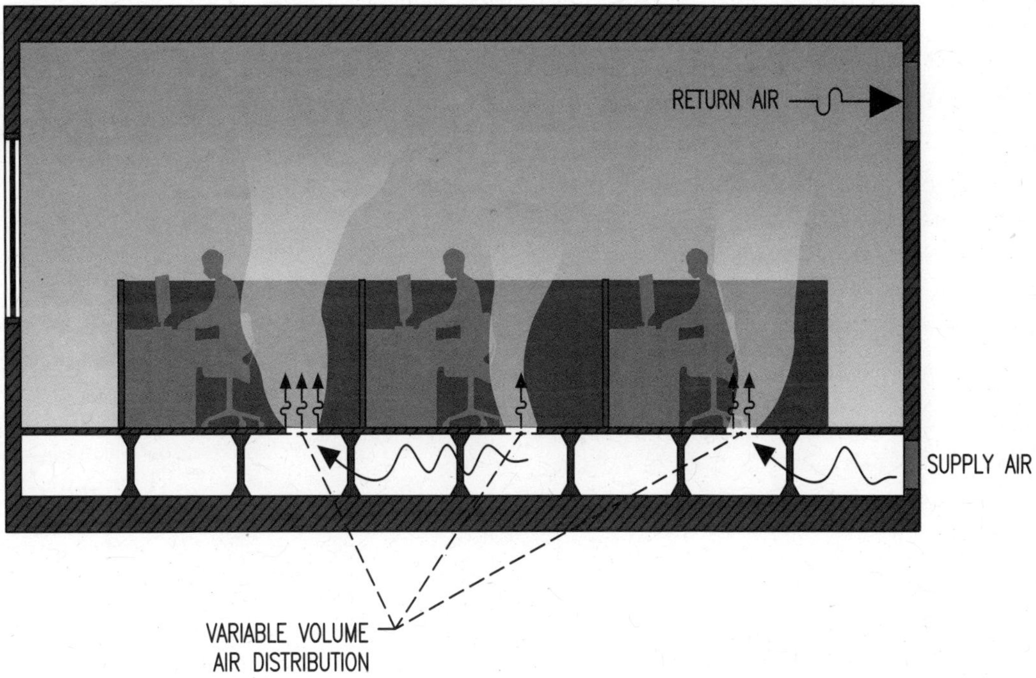

	IEQ
NC	Credit 6.2
SCHOOLS	Credit 6.2
CS	Credit 6

RETURN AIR

SUPPLY AIR

VARIABLE VOLUME
AIR DISTRIBUTION

Some examples to help achieve thermal comfort for building occupants include thermostat controls; local diffusers at the floor, desk, or overhead levels; or control of individual radiant panels. Radiant heating may be a good option to pursue. More specifically, room thermostats, natural ventilation actuators, and ceiling fans can have the capability for local occupant override or bypass.

9. Exemplary Performance

This credit is not eligible for exemplary performance under the Innovation in Design section.

10. Regional Variations

Local weather and ambient air conditions must be considered when determining the feasibility of operable windows for projects. For example, in areas that are prone to extreme temperatures for a majority of the year, or urban areas where traffic and air pollution are problematic, operable windows may not be an appropriate addition to a building.

11. Operations and Maintenance Considerations

Inform building operators about the number and type of thermal comfort controls installed.

Include the default setpoints and schedules in the facility's building operation plan. Establish procedures and schedules for recalibrating controls, based on the manufacturer's recommendations, and include them in the building's preventive maintenance plan. Train building operators in using and maintaining specialty equipment. Maintenance staff should plan to clean or replace HVAC filters more frequently if building occupants use operable windows.

12. Resources

Please see USGBC's LEED Registered Project Tools (http://www.usgbc.org/projecttools) for additional resources and technical information.

Websites

Center for the Built Environment

http://www.cbe.berkeley.edu

This University of California, Berkeley research center provides information on underfloor air distribution technologies and other topics. See the publications page for articles such as A Field Study of Personal Environmental Module (PEM) Performance in Bank of America's San Francisco Office Buildings.

Do Green Buildings Enhance the Well-Being of Workers? Yes

Environmental Design + Construction

http://www.edcmag.com/Articles/Cover_Story/fb077b7338697010VgnVCM100000f932a8co

An article by Judith Heerwagen, in the July/August 2000 edition, of *Environmental Design + Construction* quantifies the effects of green building environments on productivity.

Print Media

Controls and Automation for Facilities Managers: Applications Engineering, by Viktor Boed (CRC Press, 1998).

Giving Occupants What They Want: Guidelines for Implementing Personal Environmental Control in Your Building, by Fred S. Bauman(Center for the Built Environment, 1999).

Using Advanced Office Technology to Increase Productivity: The Impact of Environmentally Responsive Workstations (ERWs) on Productivity and Worker Attitude, by W. Kroner, J. Stark-Martin, and T. Willemain (Rensselaer Polytechnic Institute, 1992).

13. Definitions

The **building envelope,** or shell, is the exterior surface of a building's construction—the walls, windows, roof, and floor.

Comfort criteria are the specific original design conditions that at minimum include temperature, humidity, and air speed as well as outdoor temperature design conditions, outdoor humidity design conditions, clothing, and expected activity. (ASHRAE 55–2004)

Commissioning is the process of verifying and documenting that the facility and all of its systems and assemblies are planned, designed, installed, tested, operated, and maintained to meet the owner's operating requirements.

Controls are operating mechanisms that enable a person to turn on or off devices (e.g., lights, heaters) or adjust systems within a range (e.g., lighting, temperature).

Daylighting is the controlled admission of natural light into a space to reduce or eliminate electric lighting.

HVAC systems are equipment, distribution systems, and terminals that provide the processes of heating, ventilating, or air-conditioning. (ASHRAE 90.1–2007)

In **individual occupant spaces,** workers use standard workstations to conduct individual tasks. Examples are private offices and open office areas with multiple workers.

Natural ventilation is provided by thermal, wind, or diffusion effects through doors, windows, or other intentional openings in the building.

Nonoccupied spaces include all rooms used by maintenance personnel that are not open for use by occupants. Examples are closets and janitorial, storage, and equipment rooms.

Outdoor air is the ambient air that enters a building through a ventilation system, either through natural ventilation or by infiltration (ASHRAE 62.1–2007).

Regularly occupied spaces in commercial buildings are areas where people sit or stand as they work. In residential applications these spaces include all living and family rooms and exclude bathrooms, closets, or other storage or utility areas. In schools, they are areas where students, teachers, or administrators are seated or standing as they work or study.

Group multioccupant spaces include conference rooms, classrooms, and other indoor spaces used as places of congregation.

Sensors are devices that undergo a measurable change in response to environmental changes and communicate this to the appropriate equipment or control system.

Thermal comfort exists when occupants express satisfaction with the thermal environment.

	IEQ
NC	Credit 6.2
SCHOOLS	Credit 6.2
CS	Credit 6

THERMAL COMFORT—DESIGN

	NC	SCHOOLS	CS
Credit	IEQ Credit 7.1	IEQ Credit 7.1	IEQ Credit 7
Points	1 point	1 point	1 point

Intent

To provide a comfortable thermal environment that promotes occupant productivity and well-being.

Requirements

NC, SCHOOLS & CS

Design heating, ventilating and air conditioning (HVAC) systems and the building envelope to meet the requirements of ASHRAE Standard 55-2004, Thermal Environmental Conditions for Human Occupancy (with errata but without addenda[1]). Demonstrate design compliance in accordance with the Section 6.1.1 documentation.

SCHOOLS Additional Requirement

For natatoriums, demonstrate compliance with the "Typical Natatorium Design Conditions" defined in Chapter 4 (Places of Assembly) of the ASHRAE HVAC Applications Handbook, 2003 edition (with errata but without addenda[1]).

CS Additional Requirement

The core and shell base building mechanical system must allow for the tenant build-out to meet the requirements of this credit. Project teams that design their project for mechanical ventilation that do not purchase or install the mechanical system are not eligible achieve this credit.

See Appendix 1 — Default Occupancy Counts for occupancy count requirements and guidance.

---

[1] Project teams wishing to use ASHRAE approved addenda for the purposes of this credit may do so at their discretion. Addenda must be applied consistently across all LEED credits.

	IEQ
NC	Credit 7.1
SCHOOLS	Credit 7.1
CS	Credit 7

1. Benefits and Issues to Consider

Environmental Issues

Maintaining an acceptable level of thermal comfort for building occupants should be considered a necessity for any building or space with regular occupancy. Studies have shown that people who are comfortable are more productive and generally happier. In a work environment, increases in productivity can reduce the amount of time and energy required for an individual task. Over the course of a year, that can translate to fewer hours running equipment such as computers or task lighting, resulting in energy savings that reduce the strain on the environment.

Economic Issues

Generally, HVAC and building envelope systems that do not adequately address the thermal comfort of occupants are less energy efficient than their more robust counterparts—with the exception of passive or naturally ventilated spaces. Mechanical systems relying on natural ventilation typically have lower capital and construction costs and use less energy than mechanically ventilated systems. In climates with extreme seasonal temperature swings, occupants' comfort can suffer in a naturally ventilated building, but a well-designed building envelope and HVAC system can help compensate. Buildings with poor envelopes might struggle to maintain a comfortable environment for occupants near the building perimeter. The building HVAC system will expend more energy trying to maintain a comfortable environment for those occupants on the perimeter, increasing the annual energy cost of the building.

HVAC systems with poorly located or inadequate numbers of thermostats or control zones can significantly affect occupants' comfort. Occupants using areas that could otherwise have been provided individual temperature controls may have to share a thermostat or may use space heaters, which can increase energy use. When spaces have not been properly thermally zoned, occupants may try to heat and cool the same area at the same time, potentially resulting in greater energy use and additional costs to operate the building.

2. Related Credits

The thermal comfort of building occupants is affected by environmental conditions (air temperature, radiant temperature, relative humidity, and air speed), personal factors (metabolic rate and clothing), and personal preferences. Thermal comfort can be controlled through both active (HVAC) and passive systems (natural ventilation). The best results are often achieved through a combination of the 2 systems: Using both can help reduce the building's energy consumption, as well as achieve optimum comfort levels. For all these reasons, this credit is related to the following other prerequisites and credits:

- EA Prerequisite 2: Minimum Energy Performance
- EA Credit 1: Optimize Energy Performance
- EA Credit 5: Measurement and Verification

To address the issue of commissioning thermal comfort features, refer to the following prerequisite and credit:

- EA Prerequisite 1: Fundamental Commissioning
- EA Credit 3: Enhanced Commissioning

The following prerequisite and credits also pertain to occupants' comfort:

- IEQ Prerequisite 1: Minimum Indoor Air Quality Performance
- IEQ Credit 2: Increased Ventilation

- IEQ Credit 6.2: Controllability of Thermal Systems—Thermal Comfort

- IEQ Credit 7.2: Thermal Comfort—Verification

	IEQ
NC	Credit 7.1
SCHOOLS	Credit 7.1
CS	Credit 7

3. Summary of Referenced Standards

American National Standards Institute (ANSI)/ASHRAE Standard 55–2004, Thermal Comfort Conditions for Human Occupancy

ASHRAE

http://www.ashrae.org

According to ASHRAE, this standard "specifies the combinations of indoor space environment and personal factors that will produce thermal environmental conditions acceptable to 80% or more of the occupants within a space. The environmental factors addressed are temperature, thermal radiation, humidity and air speed; the personal factors are those of activity and clothing."

Chartered Institute of Building Services Engineers (CIBSE) Applications Manual 10–2005, Natural Ventilation in Non-Domestic Buildings

CIBSE, London

http://www.cibse.org

CIBSE Applications Manual 10–2005 provides guidance for implementing natural ventilation in nonresidential buildings. It provides detailed information on how to adopt natural ventilation as the sole servicing strategy for a building or as an element in a mixed mode design. According to the publisher, this manual "is a major revision of the Applications Manual (AM) first published in 1997. At the time, there was a significant expansion of interest in the application of engineered natural ventilation to the design of non-domestic buildings. The original AM10 sought to capture the state of knowledge as it existed in the mid-90s and present it in a form suited to the needs of every member of the design team. Some 10 years on from the time when the initial manual was conceived, the state of knowledge has increased, and experience in the design and operation of naturally ventilated buildings has grown. This revision of AM10 is therefore a timely opportunity to update and enhance the guidance offered to designers and users of naturally ventilated buildings."

SCHOOLS

ASHRAE HVAC Applications Handbook, 2003 edition, Chapter 4 (Places of Assembly), Typical Natatorium Design Conditions

ASHRAE

http://www.ashrae.org

ASHRAE advances the science of heating, ventilation, air conditioning, and refrigeration for the public's benefit through research, standards writing, continuing education, and publications. The 2003 edition of ASHRAE Handbook—HVAC Applications contains "chapters on a broad range of applications, written to help design engineers use equipment and systems described in other handbook volumes."

4. Implementation

A green building should provide its occupants with comfortable indoor conditions that support their productivity and well-being. Although often associated only with air temperature, thermal comfort is a complex issue, affected by environmental conditions (e.g., air temperature, radiant temperature, humidity, and air speed) and personal factors (e.g., metabolic rate. clothing, and preferencesl). There are 3 basic approaches to providing thermal comfort within a project space:

- mechanical ventilation (i.e., active ventilation);

- natural ventilation (i.e., passive ventilation); and

- mixed-mode ventilation (i.e., both mechanical and natural ventilation).

	IEQ
NC	Credit 7.1
SCHOOLS	Credit 7.1
CS	Credit 7

The owner and project team should make a decision as to which of the conditioning approaches are appropriate for the building. ASHRAE 55–2004 provides thermal comfort standards, with an optional alternate approach specifically for naturally ventilated spaces.

ASHRAE 55–2004 is based on the predicted mean vote comfort model, which incorporates heat balance principles to relate the personal and environmental thermal comfort factors based on the thermal sensation scale that shows 7 levels ranging from +3 (hot) to -3 (cold). The model is applicable to air speeds not greater than 0.20 m/s (40 fpm).

For naturally ventilated spaces, field experiments have shown that occupants' thermal responses depend in part on the outdoor climate and may differ from thermal responses in buildings with centralized HVAC systems. This is primarily because of the different thermal experiences, changes in clothing, availability of control, and shifts in occupant expectations. The standard provides an optional method of compliance that is intended for naturally ventilated spaces. This optional method (section 5.3 of the standard) provides broad indoor temperature ranges as a function of mean monthly outdoor temperatures, assuming light and sedentary activity but independent of humidity, air speed, and clothing considerations.

5. Timeline and Team

Using ASHRAE 55–2004, the design team and the owner should determine how to achieve the desired thermal comfort in the project space and identify the appropriate conditioning systems (whether active or passive). This decision might be influenced by the local climate, the size and type of the proposed building, and the nature of the operations it will host.

There are many well-established HVAC load calculation methods to assist designers in sizing and selecting HVAC equipment to provide thermal comfort conditions. Lighting and other internal HVAC loads are integrated into the calculations to enable adequate system capacity and meet thermal comfort criteria without oversizing the HVAC system.

A natural ventilation approach may be more difficult to evaluate in design and require more intensive analysis and/or reliance on experience and precedents. For naturally ventilated buildings, CIBSE AM10 presents design strategies to maintain comfort and health.

For mechanical conditioning, the operating setpoints and parameters of the HVAC system will largely determine thermal comfort conditions. Many facility operators in mechanically air-conditioned spaces spend significant effort and time adjusting thermostat setpoints and other operational parameters to limit complaints associated with poor thermal comfort. Giving individual occupants some control over temperature and/or air movement reduces thermal comfort complaints.

The maxim "passive buildings, active occupants" fits the natural ventilation model well. Occupants generally take a primary role in managing thermal comfort conditions in naturally ventilated buildings by opening and closing windows as necessary and appropriate. Thermal comfort in naturally conditioned buildings is also somewhat more variable than in mechanically conditioned buildings, where systems are often designed to maintain relatively consistent conditions through all periods of occupancy.

6. Calculations

There are no calculations required for this credit; however, project teams should be able to describe how thermal comfort conditions were established for the project and how the design of conditioning systems addresses the thermal comfort design.

7. Documentation Guidance

As a first step in preparing to complete the LEED-Online documentation requirements, work through the following measures. Refer to LEED-Online for the complete descriptions of all required documentation.

- Document the owner's project requirements. This should indicate the intended comfort criteria for the building and state assumptions regarding activity level and occupant clothing.

- Summarize operational procedures for building systems, including building controls and other environmental control systems. Teams should also include general information, seasonal set point recommendations, changeover schedules, maintenance and operation instructions, and a maintenance and inspection schedule.

- Document the mechanical designer's basis of design; include design assumptions, including diversity considerations, and HVAC load calculations.

- Maintain documentation (e.g., design plans, lists) of all registers and terminal units that includes the type and flow, or radiant value. Additionally, include any elements that significantly affect thermal comfort, indication of spaces outside comfort-controlled areas, and locations of all occupant-adjustable controls.

8. Examples

Figure 1. Thermal Transfer between Person and Environment.

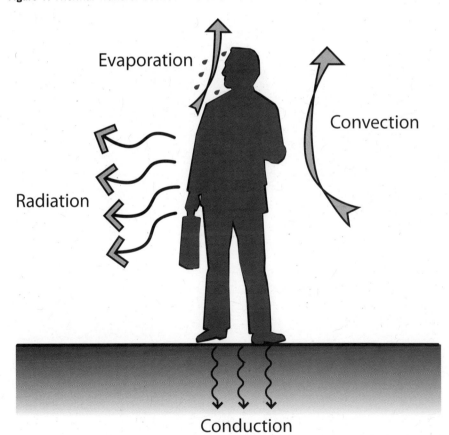

IEQ	
NC	Credit 7.1
SCHOOLS	Credit 7.1
CS	Credit 7

Figure 2. Six Primary Comfort Factors (ASHRAE 55–2004)

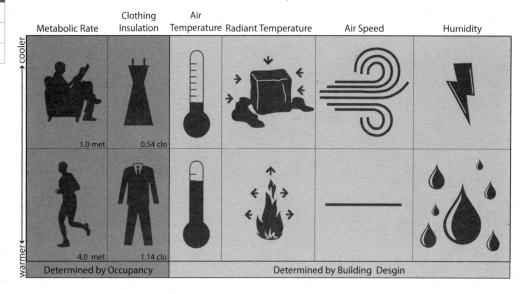

Figure 3. Acceptable Operative Temperature and Humidity Ratio (ASHRAE 55-2004)

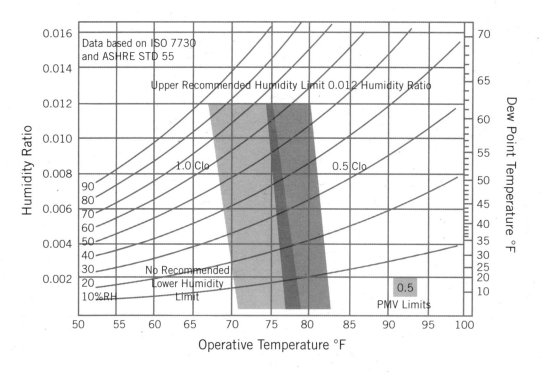

The charts take temperature and humidity into consideration and are most applicable to occupants who are appropriately dressed and involved in light work (e.g., office workers). Variations are based on the assumption that occupants are dressed according to the seasons.

Figure 4. Comfort Zones (ASHRAE 55-2004)

	IEQ
NC	Credit 7.1
SCHOOLS	Credit 7.1
CS	Credit 7

Summer Comfort Zone

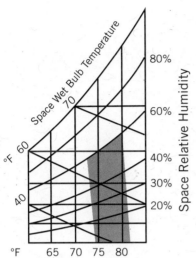

Winter Comfort Zone

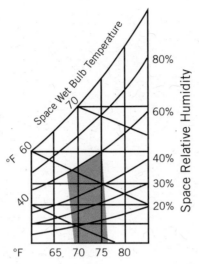

Use Figure 4 to identify optimum interior comfort levels as well as deviations in thermal comfort that are specific to the building, the occupants, and the type of work they do.

9. Exemplary Performance

This credit is not eligible for exemplary performance under the Innovation in Design section.

10. Regional Variations

When considering occupant comfort, anticipate how climate and seasonal variations will affect thermal comfort levels. Climate variations play an important role in passively ventilated buildings because of the introduction of unconditioned outside air. In mechanically ventilated buildings, regional variations have an impact on the temperature range that an occupant considers comfortable. Warmer climates typically have higher design temperatures than colder climates to match the conditions that would normally be considered comfortable.

11. Operations and Maintenance Considerations

Provide the building owner, maintenance personnel, and occupants with the information needed to understand, maintain, and adjust the HVAC system for thermal comfort. Establish appropriate setpoints and control sequences, as well as recommendations for typical corrective actions, and include them in the building operating plan and sequence of operations document.

Establish procedures and schedules for inspecting and recalibrating sensors and controls, based on the manufacturer's recommendations, and include them in the building's preventive maintenance plan.

12. Resources

Please see USGBC's LEED Registered Project Tools (http://www.usgbc.org/projecttools) for additional resources and technical information.

Websites

The Whole Building Design Guide, Enhance IEQ

http://www.wbdg.org/design/ieq.php

The IEQ section provides a wealth of resources including definitions, fundamentals, materials, and tools.

Print Media

ASHRAE 62.1 –2007: Ventilation for Acceptable Indoor Air Quality (ASHRAE, 2007).

Humidity Control Design Guide, by L. Harriman, G.W. Brundett, and R. Kittler (ASHRAE, 2000).

The Impact of Part-Load Air-Conditioner Operation on Dehumidification Performance: Thermal Comfort, by P.O. Fanger (Mc-Graw Hill, 1973).

Thermal Delight in Architecture, by Lisa Heschong (MIT Press, 1979).

13. Definitions

Comfort criteria are the specific original design conditions that at a minimum include temperature, humidity, and air speed as well as outdoor temperature design conditions, outdoor humidity design conditions, clothing, and expected activity. (ASHRAE 55-2004)

Commissioning is the process of verifying and documenting that the facility and all of its systems and assemblies are planned, designed, installed, tested, operated, and maintained to meet the owner's operating requirements.

Mechanical ventilation is provided by mechanically powered equipment, such as motor-driven fans and blowers, but not by devices such as wind-driven turbine ventilators and mechanically operated windows (ASHRAE 62.1-2004).

Mixed-mode ventilation combines mechanical and natural ventilation methods.

Natural ventilation is provided by thermal, wind, or diffusion effects through doors, windows, or other intentional openings in the building. (ASHRAE 62.1–2007)

Occupants in a commercial building are workers who either have a permanent office or workstation in the building or typically spend a minimum of 10 hours per week in the building. In a residential building, occupants also include all persons who live in the building.

Predicted mean vote is an empirical equation for predicting the mean vote on a rating scale of thermal comfort of a large population of people exposed to a certain environment.

Relative humidity is the ratio of partial density of airborne water vapor to the saturation density of water vapor at the same temperature and total pressure.

Thermal comfort exists when occupants express satisfaction with the thermal environment.

	NC	SCHOOLS	CS
Credit	IEQ Credit 7.2	IEQ Credit 7.2	NA
Points	1 point*	1 point*	NA

*1 point in addition to IEQ credit 7.1

Intent

To provide for the assessment of building occupants' thermal comfort over time.

Requirements

NC & SCHOOLS

Achieve IEQ Credit 7.1: Thermal Comfort—Design

Agree to conduct a thermal comfort survey of building occupants (adults and students of grades 6 and above) within 6 to 18 months after occupancy. This survey should collect anonymous responses about thermal comfort in the building, including an assessment of overall satisfaction with thermal performance and identification of thermal comfort problems. Agree to develop a plan for corrective action if the survey results indicate that more than 20% of occupants are dissatisfied with thermal comfort in the building. This plan should include measurement of relevant environmental variables in problem areas in accordance with ASHRAE Standard 55-2004 (with errata but without addenda).

NC Additional Requirement

Provide a permanent monitoring system to ensure that building performance meets the desired comfort criteria as determined by IEQ Credit 7.1: Thermal Comfort—Design.

Residential projects are not eligible for this credit.

---

1   Project teams wishing to use ASHRAE approved addenda for the purposes of this credit may do so at their discretion. Addenda must be applied consistently across all LEED credits.

	IEQ
NC	Credit 7.2
SCHOOLS	Credit 7.2
CS	NA

1. Benefits and Issues to Consider

Environmental Issues

For many facilities, the HVAC systems that maintain indoor thermal comfort are the largest energy users. A successful green building should minimize the energy use associated with building conditioning—along with the associated energy cost, fuel consumption and air emissions—while maintaining thermal comfort conditions that enhance occupant well-being.

Economic Issues

Monitoring, managing, and maintaining thermal comfort conditions in a building might increase or decrease operating costs slightly. Thermal comfort complaints are among the most prevalent from occupants. Maintaining thermal comfort could help operations and maintenance staff to focus on other facility issues by reducing the need to respond to such complaints.

2. Related Credits

The thermal comfort of building occupants is affected by factors such as environmental conditions (air temperature, radiant temperature, relative humidity, and air speed), personal factors (metabolic rate and clothing), and personal preference. Refer to the following related prerequisites and credits:

- EA Credit 5: Measurement and Verification

- EA Prerequisite 1: Fundamental Commissioning

- EA Credit 3: Enhanced Commissioning

The following prerequisite and credits also pertain to occupants' comfort:

- IEQ Prerequisite 1: Minimum IAQ Performance

- IEQ Credit 2: Increased Ventilation

- IEQ Credit 6.2: Controllability of Thermal Systems—Thermal Comfort

- IEQ Credit 7.1: Thermal Comfort—Design

3. Summary of Referenced Standard

American National Standards Institute (ANSI)/ASHRAE Standard 55-2004, Thermal Comfort Conditions for Human Occupancy
ASHRAE
http://www.ashrae.org
According to ASHRAE, "This standard specifies the combinations of indoor space environment and personal factors that will produce thermal environmental conditions acceptable to 80% or more of the occupants within a space. The environmental factors addressed are temperature, thermal radiation, humidity and air speed; the personal factors are those of activity and clothing."

4. Implementation

IEQ Credit 7.2, Thermal Comfort—Verification, is contingent on achieving IEQ Credit 7.1, Thermal Comfort—Design.

Poor thermal comfort is the main occupant complaint in many facilities. A well-managed and responsive green building should have systems in place to determine if occupant comfort is being maintained or can be improved.

Since thermal comfort is inherently subjective and is psychological as much as physiological, surveying occupants regularly is the best way to determine whether a facility is comfortable. Sporadic occupant complaints about thermal comfort may not be an appropriate indicator of overall thermal comfort, but it might indicate local or personal dissatisfaction. Providing a systematic process and mechanism for all occupants to provide feedback about their thermal comfort will help building operators adjust and maintain thermal comfort in their buildings. Temperature, humidity, and other environmental monitoring systems provide facility operators with objective data to determine if the building space conditions meet the design intent and if they are being consistently maintained.

	IEQ
NC	Credit 7.2
SCHOOLS	Credit 7.2
CS	NA

Planning and Design Phase

Once the project has identified appropriate thermal comfort criteria (as part of compliance with IEQ Credit 7.1: Thermal Comfort—Design) and determined the appropriate conditioning system to meet the criteria, identify the key areas of focus for the occupant survey. Anticipate provisions for the analysis of environmental variables if the survey identifies problems.

Survey Occupants

Facility operators or outside consultants should develop procedures to survey building occupants about thermal comfort conditions. The main parameter to be measured in the occupant survey is satisfaction with thermal environment (e.g., "How satisfied are you with the temperature in your workspace?"). The answer is rated according to a 7-point scale format from very satisfied (+3) to very dissatisfied (-3) with the center (0) signifying the neutral point. Survey respondents identify their approximate location by building nominal zone and can specify their exact location voluntarily. The survey must include follow-up questions that are asked if the respondent indicates dissatisfaction, to identify the nature and cause of the problem. Sources of sample surveys include, but are not limited to, the Center for the Built Environment and the Usable Buildings Trust (see Resources).

This survey may be administered in person, over the phone, over networked computers, or on paper, but should be consistently applied and available for participation by all regular occupants. Percent dissatisfied will be the percentage of respondents who answer "dissatisfied" (any of the lower 3 points of the 7-point scale).

The survey may encompass other indoor environmental quality considerations (such as lighting or acoustics), although their inclusion is not required for this credit.

Plan for Corrective Action

The survey responses will identify the nature and location of any thermal environmental problems. Use respondent suggestions to help guide corrective actions. Corrective actions typically include control adjustments (e.g., temperature setpoints, schedules, operating modes), diffuser airflow adjustments, and solar control.

Thermal discomfort in buildings is often caused by local variations in the thermal environment. It is impractical to have monitoring systems in every workstation capable of monitoring and diagnosing thermal comfort problems. The design team and facility operations and maintenance staff can use their discretion to decide how to resolve performance failure. Short-term monitoring and spot measurements of environmental variables with temporary equipment should be done once problem areas have been identified through the occupant survey.

5. Timeline and Team

The design team is primarily responsible for achieving this credit, which is based on the requirements of ASHRAE 55–2004. Additionally, a member of the building operations team, an owner agent, or a commissioning authority should administer the postoccupancy survey to meet the requirements of this credit.

6. Calculations

There are no calculations associated with this credit.

7. Documentation Guidance

As a first step in preparing to complete the LEED-Online documentation requirements, work through the following measures. Refer to LEED-Online for the complete descriptions of all required documentation.

- Create a written plan for corrective action if 20% or more of building occupants are dissatisfied with thermal comfort in the building.

- Create a thermal comfort survey to administer to building occupants.

8. Examples

There are no examples for this credit.

9. Exemplary Performance

This credit is not eligible for exemplary performance under the Innovation in Design section.

10. Regional Variations

Regional climate and seasonal variations significantly affect the thermal comfort of occupants. Climate variations play an important role in passively ventilated buildings because of the introduction of unconditioned outside air. In mechanically ventilated buildings, regional variations affect the temperature range that an occupant considers comfortable. Warmer climates typically have higher design temperatures than colder climates, matching the conditions that would normally be considered comfortable for the occupants.

11. Operations and Maintenance Considerations

Provide the building owner, maintenance personnel, and occupants with the information needed to understand, maintain, and adjust the HVAC system for thermal comfort. Establish appropriate setpoints and control sequences, as well as recommendations for typical corrective actions, and include them in the building operating plan and sequence of operations document.

Establish procedures and schedules for inspecting and recalibrating sensors and controls, based on the manufacturer's recommendations, and include them in the building's preventive maintenance plan.

12. Resources

Please see USGBC's LEED Registered Project Tools (http://www.usgbc.org/projecttools) for additional resources and technical information.

Websites
Center for the Built Environment
http://www.cbesurvey.org
This University of California, Berkeley, research center provides information on underfloor air distribution technologies and other topics. This website serves as an introduction to CBE's online IEQ survey.

The Usable Buildings Trust
http://www.usablebuildings.co.uk/
The Usable Buildings Trust promotes better buildings through the effective use of feedback. As the home of the Post-Occupancy Review of Buildings and Their Engineering (PROBE) studies, it includes an occupant survey that addresses thermal comfort and other IEQ issues.

Print Media

Unplanned Airflows and Moisture Problems, by T. Brennan, J. Cummings, and J. Lstiburek, *ASHRAE Journal* (November 2000).

Federal Facilities Council, Technical Report 145: Learning From our Buildings: A State-of-the-Practice Summary of Post-Occupancy Evaluation, (National Academy Press, 2001).

	IEQ
NC	Credit 7.2
SCHOOLS	Credit 7.2
CS	NA

13. Definitions

Comfort criteria are the specific original design conditions that at a minimum include temperature, humidity, and air speed as well as outdoor temperature design conditions, outdoor humidity design conditions, clothing, and expected activity. (ASHRAE 55–2004)

Commissioning is the process of verifying and documenting that the facility and all of its systems and assemblies are planned, designed, installed, tested, operated, and maintained to meet the owner's operating requirements.

Mechanical ventilation is provided by mechanically powered equipment, such as motor-driven fans and blowers, but not by devices such as wind-driven turbine ventilators and mechanically operated windows. (ASHRAE 62.1–2004)

Mixed-mode ventilation combines mechanical and natural ventilation methods.

Natural ventilation is provided by thermal, wind, or diffusion effects through doors, windows, or other intentional openings in the building.

Occupants in a commercial building are workers who either have a permanent office or workstation in the building or typically spend a minimum of 10 hours per week in the building. In a residential building, occupants also include all persons who live in the building.

Predicted mean vote is an empirical equation for predicting the mean vote on a rating scale of thermal comfort of a large population of people exposed to a certain environment.

Relative humidity is the ratio of partial density of airborne water vapor in the air to the saturation density of water vapor at the same temperature and total pressure.

Thermal comfort exists when occupants express satisfaction with the thermal environment.

DAYLIGHT AND VIEWS—DAYLIGHT

	NC	SCHOOLS	CS
Credit	IEQ Credit 8.1	IEQ Credit 8.1	IEQ Credit 8.1
Points	1 point	1-3 points	1 point

Intent

To provide for the building occupants with a connection between indoor spaces and the outdoors through the introduction of daylight and views into the regularly occupied areas of the building.

Requirements

Through 1 of the 4 options, achieve daylighting in at least the following spaces:

SCHOOLS

Classroom Spaces	Points
75%	1
90%	2

OR

- 75% of all other regularly occupied spaces (1 additional point). Project teams can achieve a point for these other spaces only if they have also achieved at least 1 point for classroom spaces.

NC & CS

Regularly Occupied Spaces	Points
75%	1

NC, SCHOOLS & CS

OPTION 1. Simulation

Demonstrate through computer simulations that 75% (NC, Schools & CS) or 90% (Schools Only) or more of all regularly occupied spaces achieve daylight illuminance levels of a minimum of 25 footcandles (fc) and a maximum of 500 fc in a clear sky condition on September 21 at 9 a.m. and 3 p.m.; areas with illuminance levels below or above the range do not comply. However, designs that incorporate view-preserving automated shades for glare control may demonstrate compliance for only the minimum 25 fc illuminance level.

OR

OPTION 2. Prescriptive

For the Side-lighting daylight zone (see diagram below):

- Achieve a value, calculated as the product of the visible light transmittance (VLT) and window-to-floor area ratio (WFR) of daylight zone 0.150 and 0.180. The window area included in the calculation must be at least 30 inches above the floor.

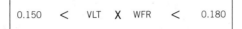

$$0.150 \; < \; VLT \; X \; WFR \; < \; 0.180$$

- The ceiling must not obstruct a line in section that joins the window-head to a line on the floor that is parallel to the plane of the window; Is twice the height of the window-head above the floor in, distance from the plane of the glass as measured perpendicular to the plane of the glass.

- Provide sunlight redirection and/or glare control devices to ensure daylight effectiveness.

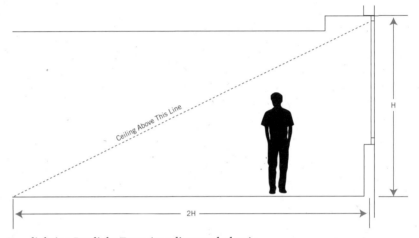

For Top-lighting Daylight Zone (see diagram below):

- The daylit zone under a skylight is the outline of the opening beneath the skylight, plus in each direction the lesser of:

    - 70% of the ceiling height,

    OR

    - 1/2 the distance to the edge of the nearest skylight,

    OR

    - The distance to any permanent opaque partition (if transparent show VLT) that is farther than 70% of the distance between the top of the partition and the ceiling.

- Achieve skylight roof coverage between 3% and 6% of the roof area with a minimum 0.5 VLT.

- The distance between the skylights must not be more than 1.4 times the ceiling height.

- A skylight diffuser, if used, must have a measured haze value of greater than 90% when tested according to ASTM D1003. Avoid direct line of sight to the skylight diffuser.

Exceptions for areas where tasks would be hindered by the use of daylight will be considered on their merits.

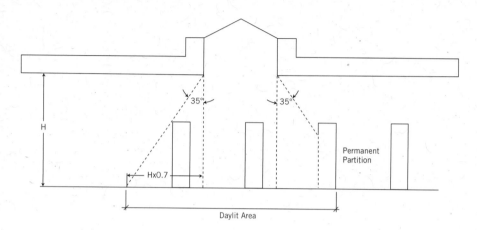

OR

OPTION 3. Measurement

Demonstrate through records of indoor light measurements that a minimum daylight illumination level of 25 fc has been achieved in at least 75% (1 point) or 90% (2 points) of all regularly occupied areas. Measurements must be taken on a 10-foot grid for all occupied spaces and shall be recorded on building floor plans.

Only the square footage associated with the portions of rooms or spaces meeting the minimum illumination requirements may be counted in the calculations.

For all projects pursuing this option, provide daylight redirection and/or glare control devices to avoid high-contrast situations that could impede visual tasks. Exceptions for areas where tasks would be hindered by daylight will be considered on their merits.

OR

OPTION 4. Combination

Any of the above calculation methods may be combined to document the minimum daylight illumination in at least 75% (1 point) or 90% (2 points) of all regularly occupied spaces. The different methods used in each space must be clearly recorded on all building plans.

In all cases, only the square footage associated with the portions of rooms or spaces meeting the requirements can be applied toward the total area calculation required to qualify for this credit.

In all cases, provide glare control devices to avoid high-contrast situations that could impede visual tasks. Exceptions for areas where tasks would be hindered by the use of daylight will be considered on their merits.

1. Benefits and Issues to Consider

This credit addresses the availability of daylight to a building's occupants. When designing for maximum daylight, designers must evaluate and balance a number of environmental factors, such as heat gain and loss, glare control, visual quality, and variations in daylight availability.

Environmental Issues

Buildings emphasizing daylighting may need larger daylighting apertures. Daylighting reduces the need for electric lighting of building interiors, which, if integrated into the overall approach to lighting, can result in decreased energy use. A well-designed daylit building is estimated to reduce lighting energy use by 50% to 80%.[27] This conserves natural resources and reduces air pollution impacts due to energy production and consumption.

Daylighting design involves a careful balance of heat gain and loss, glare control, visual quality, and variations in daylight availability. Shading devices, light shelves, courtyards, atriums, and window glazing are all strategies employed in daylighting design. Important considerations include the selected building's orientation, window size and spacing, glass selection, reflectance of interior finishes, and locations of interior walls.

Large expanses of unfragmented or untreated glazing can give the illusion of transparency or reflect sky and habitat, causing birds in flight to collide into the windows. See the Implementation sections for measures to reduce bird collisions.

Economic Issues

Specialized glazing can increase initial costs for a project and can lead to excessive heat gain if not designed properly. Glazing provides less insulating effects compared to standard walls, resulting in higher energy use and requiring additional maintenance. However, offices with sufficient natural daylight and a visual connection to outdoor environments have been proven to increase occupant productivity and comfort, leading to better employee retention. In most cases, employee compensation significantly outweighs the initial costs of incorporating daylighting measures into a building design.

2. Related Credits

Increasing the area of vision glazing is likely to provide greater access to views from the building interior, which is covered under the following credit:

- IEQ Credit 8.2: Daylight and Views

The increased window-to-wall ratio in a design can alter energy performance and has a direct correlation to lighting design strategies to conserve energy. The interior lighting design can be used to maximize the energy savings by providing daylighting controls. Refer to the following:

- EA Credit 1: Optimize Energy Performance

- EA Prerequisite 2: Minimum Energy Performance

- IEQ Credit 6: Controllability of Systems

3. Summary of Referenced Standard

ASTM D1003 - 07e1, Standard Test Method for Haze and Luminous Transmittance of Transparent Plastics

http://www.astm.org

This test method covers the evaluation of specific light-transmitting and wide-angle-light-scattering properties of planar sections of materials such as essentially transparent plastic.

4. Implementation

A building may have limited daylighting potential because of site constraints that restrict the orientation of the building and limit the number and size of building openings. Vertical site elements, such as neighboring buildings and trees, might reduce the potential for daylighting. The design of the exterior envelope and the depth of the floor plate can allow more daylight into the building, and are critical for credit achievement.

Evaluate the impact of the selected building's orientation on possible daylighting options, and opt for designs with shallow floor plates, courtyards, atriums, clerestory windows, or skylights. Consider adding interior light shelves, exterior fins, louvers, and adjustable blinds if possible. See Figure 1, which illustrates several daylighting strategies.

Attention to daylight should also be addressed during the design phase of the building. Furniture systems, wall partitions, surface color, and texture all have the ability to reflect daylight into the space. Reflective surfaces should also be considered, as they can either hinder or enhance occupants' thermal and visual comfort.

Figure 1. Daylighting Strategies

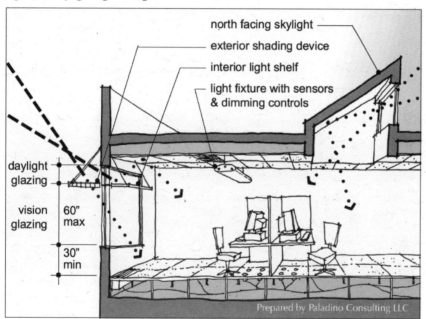

The desired amount of daylight will differ depending on how each space is used. Daylit buildings often have several daylight zones with differing target light levels. In addition to light levels, daylighting strategies should address interior color schemes, direct beam penetration, and integration with the electric lighting system. Glare control is perhaps the most common failure in daylighting strategies. Large windows provide generous amounts of daylight . If not controlled, properly, this daylight can produce unwanted glare and affect interior lighting quality. Measures to control glare include light shelves, louvers, blinds, fins, and shades. Typically, low-luminance ratios and lighting primary surfaces will enhance visual quality. Glare control is required for each window.

Computer modeling software can be used to simulate daylighting conditions and can provide valuable input into the development of an effective, integrated daylighting strategy. Daylighting software simulates the daylighting conditions of interior spaces at various times during the day and shows the combined effects of multiple windows within a daylit space.

Photo-responsive controls for electric lighting can be incorporated into daylighting strategies to maintain consistent light levels and to minimize occupant perception of the transition from natural light to artificial light. These controls help save energy by reducing electric lighting in high-daylight conditions while preserving foot-candle levels on the task surface. These types of automatic controls require commissioning, as well as measurement and verification attention.

Despite the known benefits of views in buildings, 1 clear downside is the increased likelihood that birds may fly into the windows. Perhaps as many as 1 billion birds die in this way each year. Larger areas of unfragmented or untreated glazing increase the risk. To reduce these collisions, consider treating the window glazing. Use exterior shading devices, introduce etched or fritt patterns, and/or create appropriate visual markers, such as differentiated planes, materials, textures, colors, opacity, or other features that help fragment glass reflections and reduce apparent overall transparency and reflectivity.

To control glare, use any of the following common strategies:

- Fixed exterior shading devices
- Exterior light shelves
- Interior light shelves
- Interior blinds and louvers
- Operable draperies and blinds
- Fritted glazing
- Electronic blackout glazing

CS The decisions of the Core & Shell project design team may affect the ability of future tenants to optimize the daylighting of their spaces. Decisions made by the team designing the core and shell can, in some cases, preclude the tenant from achieving this credit in LEED for Commercial Interiors.

5. Timeline and Team

During the predesign stage, the owner, architect, and engineers should discuss general lighting design and the goals for occupants' work environment. Specific daylighting performance criteria should be included in the owner's project requirements.

During schematic design, the architect, civil engineer, and landscape architect should orient the building on its site to allow for passive solar strategies. Daylighting simulations should be run early to ensure effective daylighting while minimizing potential for glare and any undesirable window and building solar exposure. Consider the preservation of existing topography and landscape features that shade the building and minimize glare. Also consider proximity to neighboring buildings and their effect on the daylighting approach. Determine how best to allocate the interior building spaces and consider locating regularly used spaces at the building perimeter, toward sources of daylight. The architect and engineers should evaluate the building footprint, the structural floor to floor height, and finished ceiling clearances to ensure an adequate ratio of window to floor area. Consider strategies to increase the amount of daylight glazing when designing the massing of the building, and carefully weigh the effects of the envelope design on energy efficiency. In addition, identify initial glare control strategies.

During the preparation of construction documents, the LEED calculations and/or computer simulation model should be developed in greater detail to inform the design decisions and verify compliance of the design. Refer again to the owner's project requirements. Use preliminary calculations to guide specifications for glare control devices. Once the design is complete, finalize the LEED calculations and supporting documentation.

During construction, the design and construction team should confirm that the submitted products and systems meet the owner's project requirements, the design performance specifications, and the original design intent.

	IEQ
NC	Credit 8.1
SCHOOLS	Credit 8.1
CS	Credit 8.1

During building operations, the owner should verify that occupants are not subject to glare and ensure that the installed glare control devices are performing as intended. Facility managers should be advised on proper maintenance of interior and exterior light shelves and other shading devices to ensure performance.

6. Calculations

To calculate the daylighting zone percentage, divide the aggregate of all daylit regularly occupied spaces by the aggregate area of all regularly occupied spaces in the project, both daylit and noncompliant areas.

Calculating Regularly Occupied Areas

Identify all regularly occupied spaces within the project and calculate their associated floor areas. For veterinary, boarding, or animal shelter facilities, include the area regularly occupied by the animals. Any spaces dedicated to tasks that would be compromised or hindered by the inclusion of daylighting should be identified and the reason for their exclusion should be explained, for documentation purposes, in a supporting narrative. Any exclusion must be based solely on the basis of the task performed in the space, not the length of time an occupant will spend there. In addition, exceptions to the requirement are solely based on visual considerations, not based on sound.

For consistency across LEED projects, the regularly occupied spaces and total area calculated for this credit should be consistent with the regularly occupied areas identified in other credits, such as IEQ Credit 8.2. However, exceptions for specialized areas dedicated to tasks that would be hindered by the use of daylight will be considered on their merits.

Calculating Daylighting Performance

The requirement can be met even if 100% of each room does not meet the minimum 25 footcandle requirement when using the daylight simulation and/or measurement methodologies. The portion of the room with a 25 footcandle minimum illumination counts toward the percentage of compliant area, and the portion of the space not meeting the illumination criterion is included in the calculation of total area. For the calculation spreadsheet, enter the space portion that meets the illumination criterion and the space portion that does not. The square footage of all compliant spaces is tallied and then divided by the total square footage of all regularly occupied spaces. If the percentage is 75% or more, then the project qualifies for 1 point under this credit. If the percentage is 90% or more, the project qualifies for 2 points. See Table 3.

OPTION 1. Simulation

- Create a daylight simulation model for the building, or each regularly occupied space with glazing. The model should include approximate glazing properties, as well as representative surface reflectance settings for interior finishes.

- For each applicable area, include a horizontal calculation grid at 30 inches above the floor, or measured at the appropriate desk or work height level for the intended use of the space. This represents the typical work plane height. The calculation grid should be set at a maximum of 5-foot intervals to provide a detailed illumination diagram for each area.

- Calculate the daylight illumination for each applicable space using the following daylight criterion: clear-sky conditions at both 9:00 a.m. and 3:00 p.m. on the equinox (March 21 or September 21) for the project's geographic location. Figure 2 illustrates a sample daylight analysis for an office space.

- Identify all regularly occupied rooms or areas. Determine the floor area of each space using construction documents and enter the information on a spreadsheet. Provide illumination levels (in footcandles), determined through the simulation model, for each space.

- If the illumination for a room/area is a minimum of 25 footcandles and a maximum of 500 footcandles, the square footage of the space counts toward the credit. If the project uses automated shades, the maximum footcandle requirement does not apply.

- Dedicated theater spaces (not multipurpose rooms) must meet an illuminance of 10 footcandles, as recommended in the IESNA Lighting Handbook Reference and Application.

- Multipurpose rooms must be included in the credit calculations. Because some activities in these spaces may be hindered by daylight, effective shades and lighting controls should be included in the design.

- Sum the square footage of all daylit rooms or areas and divide by the total square footage of all applicable spaces. If this percentage is 75% or more, the project qualifies for 1 or more points under this credit.

- Note that glare control is also required for each window. Create another spreadsheet entry that identifies the type of glare control applied to each window type. The type of glare control selected for each window does not affect the daylight calculations. See the list of common glare control strategies in the Implementation section.

OPTION 2. Prescriptive

Side Lighting

This option provides a relatively simple method of determining whether the daylighting requirements are met. It is applicable to many standard building designs, primarily rectangular floor plates with a central core. The project team needs the following basic information to determine compliance:

- Window head height

- Window sill height

- Window width (per bay)

- Bay width

- Bay depth to core

- Visible light transmittance (T_{vis})

- Floor area (per bay)

Perform the following calculation for each bay condition in the building (north-south, east-west, and corner):

- Determine the window area (WA) for the bay. This is the window head height less the window sill height 30 inches or more above the floor, multiplied by the window width(s) per bay.

- Determine whether the window head height can contribute to this credit, or if an adjusted head height must be used. Draw a 63-degree angle from the vertical, in section, from the window head to the floor. If the ceiling obstructs this line, a modified head height must be used. Draw a 63-degree angle from the vertical, in section, using the ceiling corner that obstructed the previous line as a starting point. The point at which this line intersects the window is the modified head height. See Figure 3.

- Determine the floor area (FA) for the typical bay—that is, the bay width multiplied by the bay depth to core.

- Determine the ratio of the window area to the floor area (WFR)—that is, WA/FA.

- Determine the ratio of visible light transmittance to window to floor area—that is, (T_{vis}) (WFR).

- If the result is between 0.150 and 0.180, the bay counts toward meeting the requirement.

- Each bay condition in the building must meet this requirement.

Figure 2. Sample Modified Window Head Height and Daylight Zone

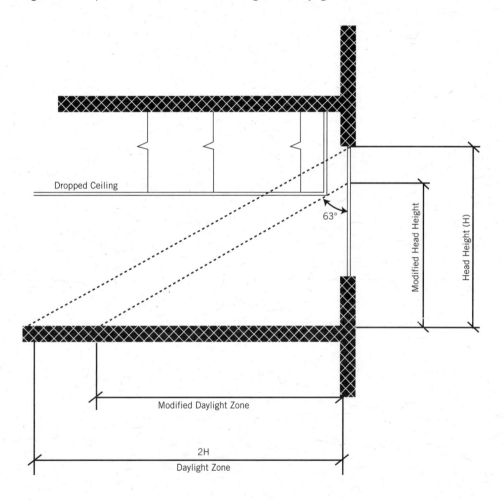

An example of this calculation is shown in Table 2.

		IEQ
NC		Credit 8.1
SCHOOLS		Credit 8.1
CS		Credit 8.1

Table 2. Sample Prescriptive Calculation

	N/S bay	E/W bay	Corner Bay
Window head height	10	10	10
Window sill height	2.5	2.5	2.5
Window Width (per bay)	19	19	78
Bay width	20	20	40
Bay width to core	40	40	40
VLT (T_{vis})	0.86	0.86	0.45
WA			
Window daylight height	7.5	7.5	7.5
Window area (WA)	142.5	142.5	585
FA			
Floor area (FA)	800	800	1600
WFR=(WA/FA)	0.178125	0.178125	
(VLT) (WFR)	0.1531875	0.1531875	
Area effected by glare			
	North façade Nov/Dec mornings	East façade all morning	Refer to N/S/E/W notes
	South façade almost entire day	West façade all afternoon	
Glare control measure			
(refer to wall section details)	north façade - interior adjustable blinds specified for all windows facing north		
	south façade - exterior light shelves and interior adjustable blinds at full length of façade		
	east façade - interior adjustable blinds specified for all windows facing east		
	west façade - exterior light shelves and interior adjustable blinds at full length of façade		

Top-Lighting Daylight Zone

This method is applicable for many standard building designs and might be particularly useful for single-floor retail developments. The project team needs the following basic information to determine compliance:

- Area of skylights (SA) VLT (T_{vis}) of skylights
- Roof area (TA)
- Distance between skylights
- Measured haze value of skylight diffuser

Perform the following calculation for a typical building condition:

- Determine the skylight roof coverage, which is the ratio of area of skylights to area of roof—that is, (SA/RA) (100).
- Confirm that the skylight diffuser is greater than 90%.
- Determine the daylight zone(s) in square feet below the skylight, based on the prescriptive criteria.
- Evaluate the total area (in square feet) of the daylight zone(s). If this total area is 75% or more of the area of the regularly occupied spaces in the building, the requirement has been met.

Figure 3. Top-Lighting Daylight Zone

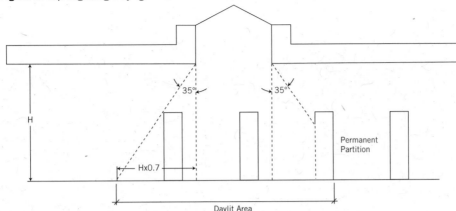

Combined Side-Lighting and Top-Lighting Daylight Zone

For buildings that have both side-lighting and top-lighting conditions, a combination of the above 2 methodologies can be utilized to demonstrate compliance.

OPTION 3

Only the square footage associated with the portions of rooms or spaces meeting the minimum illumination requirements may be counted in the calculations.

Projects pursuing this option must provide daylight redirection and/or glare control devices to avoid high-contrast situations that could impede visual tasks. Exceptions for areas where tasks would be hindered by daylight will be considered on their merits.

- Create a spreadsheet that identifies all regularly occupied rooms or areas. Determine the floor area of each space using construction documents.

- Take field measurements of footcandle levels at 30 inches above the floor within all regularly occupied areas, or measured at the appropriate desk or work height level for the intended use of the space.

- Record indoor light measurements of all regularly occupied spaces on a maximum 10-foot grid on project floor plans. Include room identification labels and/or notes regarding intended uses on the plans to match the spaces listed on the spreadsheet.

- Enter the illumination level (in footcandles), determined using the field measurements for each space. Areas with a minimum 25-footcandle illumination contribute toward credit compliance. See Table 4.

- Sum the square footage of all daylit spaces and divide by the total square footage of all regularly occupied spaces. If this percentage is 75% or more, the project qualifies for 1 point under this credit.

- Glare control is also required for each window. Create another spreadsheet entry that identifies the type of glare control applied to each window type. The type of glare control selected for each window does not affect the daylight factor calculations.

Dedicated theater spaces (not multipurpose rooms) must meet an illuminance of 10 footcandles, as recommended in the IESNA Lighting Handbook Reference and Application.

Include multipurpose rooms in the credit calculations. Because some activities in these spaces may be hindered by daylight, effective shades and lighting controls should be included in the design.

Table 3. Sample Daylighting Measurement

	SF within Grid	Foot candle	Compliant (sf)
Room 101			
point 1	100	60	100
point 2	100	60	100
point 3	75	34	75
point 4	37	24	0
Room 102			
point 1	100	55	100
point 2	57	21	0
point 3	100	25	100
Total	569		475
			83%

	IEQ
NC	Credit 8.1
SCHOOLS	Credit 8.1
CS	Credit 8.1

OPTION 4

The above calculation methods may be combined to document the minimum daylight illumination in at least 75% of all regularly occupied spaces. For all projects using this option, only the square footage of the compliant portions of rooms or spaces applies toward the 75% minimum. The methods used in each space must be clearly recorded on a minimum 10-foot grid on all building plans.

Provide glare control devices to avoid high-contrast situations that could impede visual tasks. Exceptions for areas where tasks would be hindered by the use of daylight will be considered on their merits.

7. Documentation Guidance

As a first step in preparing to complete the LEED-Online documentation requirements, work through the following measures. Refer to LEED-Online for the complete descriptions of all required documentation.

- Develop documentation—such as floor plans, sections, and elevations—showing the glare control methods used on the project.

- Maintain documentation—such as floor plans, sections, and elevations—showing the location of regularly occupied spaces with a qualifying amount of daylight.

- To account for changes in design, develop a spreadsheet documenting the daylight factors outlined in the Calculations section.

- If using daylight simulation, update the computer model as the design progresses.

8. Examples

To optimize daylighting, select glazing with a high visible transmittance (T_{vis}). See Figure 4 for glass characteristics.

Figure 4. Glass Characteristics

	IEQ
NC	Credit 8.1
SCHOOLS	Credit 8.1
CS	Credit 8.1

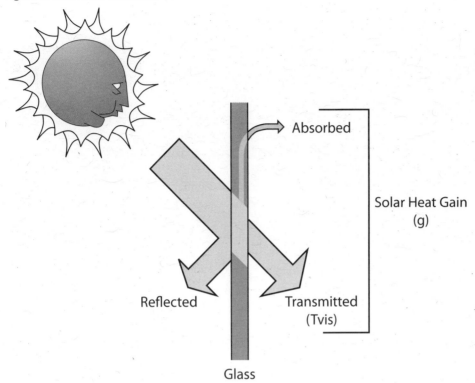

Figure 5 provides an example of a daylight simulation model.

Figure 5. Sample Daylight Simulation Model Output

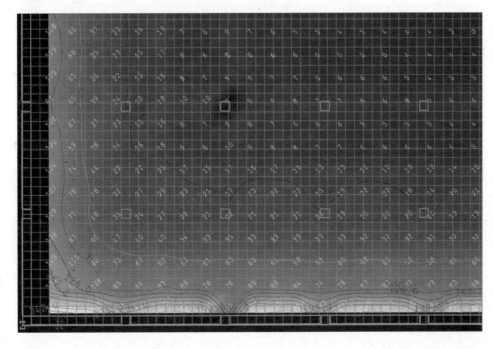

9. Exemplary Performance

NC & CS This credit may be eligible for exemplary performance under the Innovation in Design section if the project achieves 95% daylighting based on the credit requirements and guidelines.

SCHOOLS This credit may be eligible for exemplary performance under the Innovation in Design section if the project achieves daylighting for 90% of all classrooms and 95% daylighting in all other regularly occupied nonclassroom spaces based on the credit requirements and guidelines.

10. Regional Variations

The building site orientation and its specific regional location will directly influence the available daylight throughout the day and during the year. For instance, in northern latitudes, winter days are short, and building occupants might spend the entire period of daylight inside. Seasonal variances in the sun's daily path should be evaluated during the project design development to minimize the potential for glare inside the building while maximizing the use of functional daylighting. The consistent availability of adequate daylight at a particular project site will also affect the potential for reduction in lighting power demand through the use of daylighting strategies, such as incorporation of photoresponsive controls for perimeter lighting zones. When selecting glazing systems, balance the visible light transmittance with overall building energy performance goals to minimize undesirable heat loss and/or gain through the glazing.

11. Operations and Maintenance Considerations

Glazing and shading systems should be regularly cleaned and maintained. Windows and skylights require periodic sealant and flashing inspections to ensure water tightness.

Alterations or additions, both interior and exterior, can directly affect the daylight that reaches the building interior. Care should be taken during tenant build out to minimize obstruction of daylight.

12. Resources

Please see USGBC's LEED Registered Project Tools (http://www.usgbc.org/projecttools) for additional resources and technical information.

Websites
Analysis of the Performance of Students in Daylit Schools
http://www.innovativedesign.net/studentperformance.htm
This website details Innovative Design researchers Michael Nicklas and Gary Bailey's 1996 study of 3 daylit schools in North Carolina.

The Art of Daylighting
http://www.edcmag.com/Articles/Feature_Article/10e5869a47697010VgnVCM100000f932a8c0
This Environmental Design + Construction article provides a solid introduction to daylighting.

New Buildings Institute's Productivity and Building Science Program
http://www.newbuildings.org/downloads/photometrics/5D5.3.5a_photometry.pdf
This report provides case studies and information on the benefits of daylighting.

Radiance Software

http://radsite.lbl.gov/radiance/

This site offers free daylighting simulation software from the Lawrence Berkeley National Laboratory.

Whole Building Design Guide, Daylighting

http://www.wbdg.org/resources/daylighting.php

Whole Building Design Guide, Electric Lighting Controls

http://www.wbdg.org/resources/electriclighting.php?r=school_library

The Daylighting and Electric Lighting Controls sections provide a wealth of resources including definitions, fundamentals, materials, and tools.

American Bird Conservancy (ABC)

http://www.abcbirds.org

ABC is a national leader in reducing human effects on birds and wildlife. ABC's bird collision program supports national efforts to reduce bird mortality through education and advocacy.

City of Chicago, Department of Environment

http://www.cityofchicago.org/Environment/BirdMigration/sub/main.html

In 1 of the first cities to implement a mandatory lights-out program, Chicago's Department of Environment has many resources for bird-friendly design.

Fatal Light Awareness Program (FLAP)

http://www.flap.org

Initiated the Bird-Friendly Building Development Program for the City of Toronto, FLAP monitors and promotes bird-friendly design.

New York City Audubon

http://www.nycaudubon.org

This Audubon chapter takes a leadership role in reducing bird collisions with buildings. The chapter publishes Bird-Safe Building Guidelines, conducts monitoring, and, through its Project Safe Flight, promotes bird-friendly design.

Print Media

Architectural Lighting, second edition by M. David Egan and Victor Olgyay (McGraw-Hill, 2002).

Daylighting Design, by Benjamin Evans, *Time-Saver Standards for Architectural Design Data,* (McGraw-Hill, Inc., 1997).

Daylighting Performance and Design, by Gregg D. Ander (John Wiley & Sons, 1997).

Daylighting for Sustainable Design, by Mary Guzowski (McGraw-Hill, Inc., 1999).

Sustainable Building Technical Manual, Public Technology Institute (Public Technology Institute, 1996): http://www.pti.org.

Biophilic Design: The Theory, Science and Practice of Bringing Buildings to Life, by Kellert, Heerwagen, and Mador (John Wiley & Sons, 2008).

Avian Collisions at Communication Towers, second edition, by Joelle Gehring and Paul Kerlinger (Curry & Kerlinger, 2007).

Bird Density and Mortality at Windows, by Stephen B. Hager, Heidi Trudell, Kelly J. McKay, Stephanie M. Crandall, and Lance Mayer, Wilson Journal of Ornithology 120(3) (2008): 550-564.

	IEQ
NC	Credit 8.1
SCHOOLS	Credit 8.1
CS	Credit 8.1

	IEQ
NC	Credit 8.1
SCHOOLS	Credit 8.1
CS	Credit 8.1

13. Definitions

Daylighting is the controlled admission of natural light into a space, used to eliminate electric lighting.

Daylighting zone is the total floor area that meets the performance requirements for daylighting.

Glare is any excessively bright source of light within the visual field that creates discomfort or loss in visibility.

Regularly occupied spaces in commercial buildings are areas where people sit or stand as they work. In residential applications these spaces include all living and family rooms and exclude bathrooms, closets, or other storage or utility areas. In schools, they are areas where students, teachers, or administrators are seated or standing as they work or study.

Visible light transmittance (T_{vis}) is the ratio of total transmitted light to total incident light. (I.e., the amount of visible spectrum light passing through a glazing surface divided by the amount of light striking the glazing surface. The higher T_{vis} value, the more incident light passes through the glazing.

Vision glazing is that portion of exterior windows between 30 and 90 inches above the floor that permits a view to the exterior of the project space.

Window-to-floor ratio (**WFR**) is the total area of the window (measured vertically from 30 inches above the finished floor to the top of the glass, multiplied by the width of the glass) divided by the floor area.

	NC	SCHOOLS	CS
Credit	IEQ Credit 8.2	IEQ Credit 8.2	IEQ Credit 8.2
Points	1 point	1 point	1 point

Intent

To provide building occupants a connection to the outdoors through the introduction of daylight and views into the regularly occupied areas of the building.

Requirements

NC, SCHOOLS & CS

Achieve a direct line of sight to the outdoor environment via vision glazing between 30 inches and 90 inches above the finish floor for building occupants in 90% of all regularly occupied areas. Determine the area with direct line of sight by totaling the regularly occupied square footage that meets the following criteria:

- In plan view, the area is within sight lines drawn from perimeter vision glazing.

- In section view, a direct sight line can be drawn from the area to perimeter vision glazing.

The line of sight may be drawn through interior glazing. For private offices, the entire square footage of the office may be counted if 75% or more of the area has a direct line of sight to perimeter vision glazing. For classrooms and other multi-occupant spaces, the actual square footage with a direct line of sight to perimeter vision glazing is counted.

CS Additional Requirement

The core and shell design must incorporate a feasible tenant layout(s) per the default occupancy counts (or some other justifiable occupancy count) that can be used in the analysis of this credit.

	IEQ
NC	Credit 8.2
SCHOOLS	Credit 8.2
CS	Credit 8.2

1. Benefits and Issues to Consider

Environmental Issues

Providing access to views of the outdoors through the incorporation of vision glazing enables building occupants to maintain a visual connection to the surrounding environment. The additional glazed area may reduce the need for interior electric lighting, resulting in decreased energy use. This conserves natural resources and reduces air pollution impacts due to energy production and consumption.

When designing for maximum views and daylighting, designers must evaluate and balance a number of environmental factors, including heat gain and loss, glare control, visual quality, and variations in daylight availability. Appropriate interior or exterior shading devices to control glare will provide a high level of visual comfort.

Economic Issues

Additional glazing required to provide access to views can increase initial costs for a project and can lead to increased heat gain if not designed properly. Glazing provides less insulating effects compared to standard walls, resulting in higher energy use and requiring additional maintenance. However, offices with sufficient natural daylight and a visual connection to outdoor environments have been proven to increase occupant productivity and comfort, leading to increased worker production and increased employee retention.

2. Related Credits

Increasing the area of vision glazing is likely to provide greater access to daylight. The following credit has related requirements:

- IEQ Credit 8.1: Daylight and Views—Daylight

The increased window-to-wall ratio in a design can alter energy performance and has a direct correlation to lighting design strategies to conserve energy. The interior lighting design can be used to maximize the energy savings by providing daylighting controls. Refer to the following:

- EA Credit 1: Optimize Energy Performance

- EA Prerequisite 2: Minimum Energy Performance

- IEQ Credit 6: Controllability of Systems

3. Summary of Referenced Standards

There are no standards referenced for this credit.

4. Implementation

One successful design strategy is for designers to locate open plan areas, including classrooms, along the exterior walls, while placing private offices and areas not regularly occupied at the core of the building. This design maintains the optimum number of available views. The line of sight used for the determination of horizontal views is assumed to be 42 inches for the average seated adult, but is lower for students. Design teams may want to use alternate view heights for areas with nontypical functions. Maintaining the views for spaces near the core is an important design objective. See Figure 1.

Figure 1. Horizontal View at Eye Height

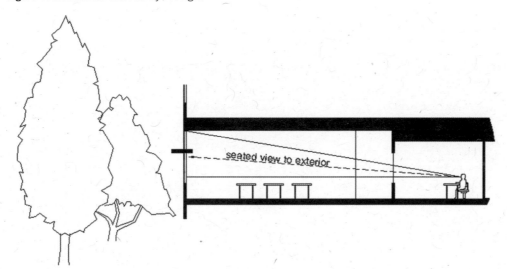

	IEQ
NC	Credit 8.2
SCHOOLS	Credit 8.2
CS	Credit 8.2

Regularly occupied spaces include office spaces, conference rooms, classrooms, core learning spaces, and cafeterias. Areas that do not need to be considered include support areas for copying, storage, mechanical equipment, laundry, and restrooms.

Despite the known benefits of views in buildings, 1 clear downside is the increased likelihood that birds may fly into the windows. Perhaps as many as 1 billion birds die in this way each year. Larger areas of unfragmented or untreated glazing increase the risk. To reduce these collisions, consider treating the window glazing. Use exterior shading devices, introduce etched or fritt patterns, and/or create appropriate visual markers, such as differentiated planes, materials, textures, colors, opacity, or other features that help fragment glass reflections and reduce apparent overall transparency and reflectivity.

5. Timeline and Team

During schematic design, the architect, civil engineer, and landscape architect should orient the building on its site to to incorporate desirable views. During the building programming efforts, spaces and rooms that are regularly occupied should be identified as primary candidates for access to views. Determine how best to allocate interior building spaces and consider locating regularly occupied spaces along the building perimeter, with access to views. The owner, architect, and interior designer should assess the needs for views in all regularly occupied spaces.

6. Calculations

Two calculations are required to determine compliance. One, using the direct line of sight to perimeter glazing, determines whether 90% of the regularly occupied area has the potential for views. It is based on vision glazing between 30 inches and 90 inches above the floor and the location of full-height interior partitions. Movable furniture and partitions are included in the scope of this credit calculation. See Figure 2. The other uses the horizontal view at a typical seated eye height to determine access to views.

	IEQ
NC	Credit 8.2
SCHOOLS	Credit 8.2
CS	Credit 8.2

Figure 2. Direct Line of Sight to Perimeter Glazing

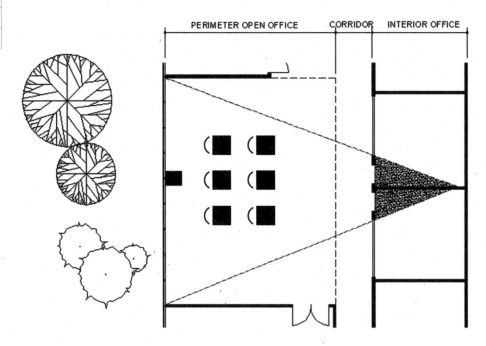

Determining Direct Line of Sight to Perimeter Glazing

- Create a spreadsheet and identify all regularly occupied areas. Determine the floor area (square footage) of each applicable space using construction documents.

- Using a floor plan, determine the fraction of the regularly occupied area that has direct line of sight to the outdoors for each window. The line of sight can pass through 2 interior glazing surfaces but not through doorways with solid doors. See Table 1.

- For private offices, if the percentage of floor area with direct line of sight is 75% or more (i.e., only the corners are noncompliant), enter the entire square footage of that room in the spreadsheet (Table 1) as meeting the credit requirement. If less than 75% of the room has a direct line of sight, estimate the compliant floor area and enter that value.

- For multioccupant spaces, such as conference rooms and classrooms, estimate the actual square footage with direct line of sight to perimeter vision glazing.

Determining Horizontal View at Appropriate Eye Height

- Using representative building sections, draw a line at 42 inches (typical seated eye height) across the section to establish eye height and any obstruction to the perimeter glazing. Draw 1 or more representative sight lines from a point at eye height in the regularly occupied space to the perimeter vision glazing (Figure 1).

- For each space with a horizontal view at seated eye height, enter yes in the spreadsheet (Table 1). If a room has direct line of sight on the floor plan but does not have an unobstructed view at eye height, the floor area does not count toward the requirement; enter no.

- Total the areas that meet all the above criteria and divide the sum by the total regularly occupied area to determine whether the building meets the 90% access to views requirement.

CS Develop a feasible tenant layout(s) per the default occupancy counts (or some other justifiable occupancy count) that can be used in the analysis of this credit.

Table 1. Determination of Compliance

Room	Regularly Occupied Floor Area (sf)	Plan Area of Direct Line of Sight to Perimeter Vision Glazing (sf)	Calculated Area of Direct Line of Sight to Perimeter Vision Glazing (sf)	Horizoinatal View at 42 Inches (Yes/No)	Compliant Area (sf)
101 Office	820	790	820	Yes	820
102 Office	330	280	330	Yes	330
103 Open office	4,935	4,641	4,641	Yes	4,641
104 Office	250	201	250	No	0
105 Office	250	175	175	Yes	175
Total	6,585				5,966
Percent access to views (5,966/6,585)					90.5% credit earned

7. Documentation Guidance

As a first step in preparing to complete the LEED-Online documentation requirements, work through the following measures. Refer to LEED-Online for the complete descriptions of all required documentation.

- Maintain documentation—floor plans, sections, and elevations—showing the location of regularly occupied spaces with views.

- Maintain a spreadsheet documenting the view area as outlined in the Calculations section to account for any changes in design.

8. Examples

The following example demonstrates the percentage of spaces with access to views that could be realized for an 80,000 square foot office building. The floor plan was designed to locate private offices toward the inside the building. In the example, 96% of views are achieved, which meets the threshold for this credit.

	IEQ
NC	Credit 8.2
SCHOOLS	Credit 8.2
CS	Credit 8.2

Figure 3. View Lines

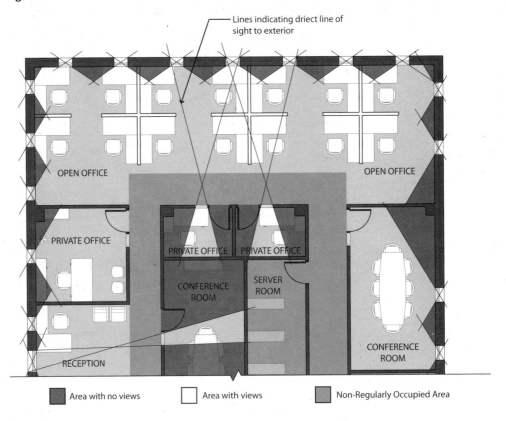

Lines indicating direct line of sight to exterior

OPEN OFFICE

OPEN OFFICE

PRIVATE OFFICE

PRIVATE OFFICE · PRIVATE OFFICE

CONFERENCE ROOM

SERVER ROOM

CONFERENCE ROOM

RECEPTION

Area with no views · Area with views · Non-Regularly Occupied Area

Figure 4. Direct Line of Sight through Interior Window over Low Partition

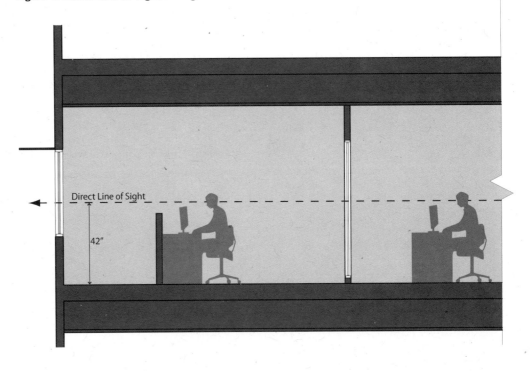

Direct Line of Sight

42"

Table 2. Sample Calculation

Room	Descripton	Floor area (sf)	Horizontal view at 42"	Views (sf)
216	Open office	4,405	Y	4,405
220	Office	136	Y	136
222	Office	115	Y	115
223	Conference	198	Y	197
224	Office	115	Y	115
225	Open office	224	Y	0
226	Office	120	Y	120
227	Conference	169	Y	161
232	Office	132	Y	132
Totals		5,634		5,381
Percentages of Area with Views: (5,381/5,634)				96%

IEQ	
NC	Credit 8.2
SCHOOLS	Credit 8.2
CS	Credit 8.2

9. Exemplary Performance

Exemplary performance may be demonstrated for this credit by meeting 2 of the following 4 measures:

1. 90% or more of regularly occupied spaces have multiple lines of sight to vision glazing in different directions at least 90 degrees apart.

2. 90% or more of regularly occupied spaces have views that include views of at least 2 of the following 3 options: 1) vegetation, 2) human activity, or 3) objects at least 70 feet from the exterior of the glazing.

3. 90% or more of regularly occupied spaces have access to unobstructed views located within the distance of 3 times the head height of the vision glazing.

4. 90% or more of regularly occupied spaces have access to views with a view factor of 3 or greater.

Measures determined per the Heschong Mahone Group study, Windows and Offices; A Study of Office Worker Performance and the Indoor Environment. Refer to page 47, for their Primary View (seated at workstation, facing computer screen). See: http://h-m-g.com/downloads/Daylighting/day_registration_form.htm to download the report.

10. Regional Variations

Available duration and potency of solar radiation can directly affect the heat gain and loss through glazing systems. Consideration should be given when selecting glazing systems to minimize undesirable heat loss and gain through the glazing. The visual appeal of the exterior environment greatly affects the subjective quality of the views.

11. Operations and Maintenance Considerations

Glazing and shading systems should be regularly cleaned and maintained. Windows and skylights require periodic sealant and flashing inspections to ensure water tightness. Additionally, any landscaping that may provide for high-quality views should be well maintained.

Future modifications to the building, both interior and exterior, can directly affect occupants' access to views. Care should be taken during tenant build-out to protect views.

12. Resources

Please see USGBC's LEED Registered Project Tools (http://www.usgbc.org/projecttools) for additional resources and technical information.

Websites

Analysis of the Performance of Students in Daylit Schools

http://www.innovativedesign.net/studentperformance.htm

This website details Innovative Design researchers Michael Nicklas and Gary Bailey's 1996 study of 3 daylit schools in North Carolina.

The Art of Daylighting

http://www.edcmag.com/Articles/Feature_Article/10e5869a47697010VgnVCM100000f932a8c0

This Environmental Design + Construction article provides a solid introduction to daylighting.

New Buildings Institute's Productivity and Building Science Program

http://www.newbuildings.org/downloads/photometrics/5D5.3.5a_photometry.pdf

This report provides case studies and information on the benefits of daylighting.

Radiance Software

http://radsite.lbl.gov/radiance/

This site offers free daylighting simulation software from the Lawrence Berkeley National Laboratory.

Whole Building Design Guide, Daylighting

http://www.wbdg.org/resources/daylighting.php

Whole Building Design Guide, Electric Lighting Controls

http://www.wbdg.org/resources/electriclighting.php?r=school_library

The Daylighting and Electric Lighting Controls sections provide a wealth of resources including definitions, fundamentals, materials, and tools.

American Bird Conservancy (ABC)

http://www.abcbirds.org

ABC is a national leader in reducing human effects on birds and wildlife. ABC's bird collision program supports national efforts to reduce bird mortality through education and advocacy.

City of Chicago, Department of Environment

http://www.cityofchicago.org/Environment/BirdMigration/sub/main.html

In 1 of the first cities to implement a mandatory lights-out program, Chicago's Department of Environment has many resources for bird-friendly design.

Fatal Light Awareness Program (FLAP)

http://www.flap.org

Initiated the Bird-Friendly Building Development Program for the City of Toronto, FLAP monitors and promotes bird-friendly design.

New York City Audubon

http://www.nycaudubon.org

This Audubon chapter takes a leadership role in reducing bird collisions with buildings. The chapter publishes Bird-Safe Building Guidelines, conducts monitoring, and, through its Project Safe Flight, promotes bird-friendly design..

Print Media

Sustainable Building Technical Manual, Public Technology Institute (Public Technology Institute, 1996): http://www.pti.org.

Biophilic Design: The Theory, Science and Practice of Bringing Buildings to Life, by Kellert, Heerwagen, and Mador (John Wiley & Sons, 2008).

Avian Collisions at Communication Towers, second edition, by Joelle Gehring and Paul Kerlinger (Curry & Kerlinger, 2007).

Bird Density and Mortality at Windows, by Stephen B. Hager, Heidi Trudell, Kelly J. McKay, Stephanie M. Crandall, and Lance Mayer, Wilson Journal of Ornithology 120(3) (2008): 550-564.

	IEQ
NC	Credit 8.2
SCHOOLS	Credit 8.2
CS	Credit 8.2

13. Definitions

Core learning spaces are spaces for educational activities where the primary functions are teaching and learning (ANSI S12.60–2002).

Daylighting is the controlled admission of natural light into a space to reduce or eliminate electric lighting.

Direct Line of Sight to Perimeter Vision Glazing is the approach used to determine the calculated area of regularly occupied areas with direct line of sight to perimeter vision glazing. The area determination includes full height partitions and other fixed construction prior to installation of furniture.

Glare is any excessively bright source of light within the visual field that creates discomfort or loss in visibility.

Regularly occupied spaces in commercial buildings are areas where people sit or stand as they work. In residential applications these spaces include all living and family rooms and exclude bathrooms, closets, or other storage or utility areas. In schools, they are areas where students, teachers, or administrators are seated or standing as they work or study.

Vision glazing is that portion of exterior windows above 30 inches and below 90 inches that permits a view to the outside.

	NC	SCHOOLS	CS
Credit	NA	IEQ Credit 9	NA
Points	NA	1 point	NA

Intent

To provide classrooms that facilitates better teacher-to-student and student-to-student communications through effective acoustical design.

Requirements

SCHOOLS

Sound Transmission

Design the building shell, classroom partitions and other core learning space partitions to meet the Sound Transmission Class (STC) requirements of ANSI Standard S12.60-2002, Acoustical Performance Criteria, Design Requirements and Guidelines for Schools, except windows, which must meet an STC rating of at least 35.

AND

Background Noise

Reduce background noise level[1] to 40 dBA or less from heating, ventilating and air conditioning (HVAC) systems in classrooms and other core learning spaces.

---

1 Recommended methodologies and best practices for mechanical system noise control are described in Annex B of ANSI Standard S12.60-2002, and the 2007 HVAC Applications ASHRAE Handbook, Chapter 47 on Sound and Vibration Control (with errata but without addenda).

	IEQ
NC	NA
SCHOOLS	Credit 9
CS	NA

1. Benefits and Issues to Consider

Environmental Issues

Acoustics is an important consideration in the design of classrooms because it can affect students' learning and performance. Background noise and reverberation tend not to bother adults but have a very different effect on children, whose ability to distinguish sounds is not fully developed. Students who cannot hear effectively are more likely to become distracted, have difficulty retaining information, and have trouble engaging in learning.

Poor classroom acoustics are an additional educational barrier for children with hearing loss and for those who have cochlear implants. Assistive technologies amplify both wanted and unwanted sound and do not improve student-to-teacher or student-to-student communication. According to the Centers for Disease Control and Prevention, children with temporary hearing loss, who account for some 15% of the school-age population, are especially affected, as are children who have speech impairments or learning disabilities.

Economic Issues

Although planning for an effective acoustic environment may require more design attention and additional materials, any increase in cost should be weighed against the significant long-term benefits. These include improved teacher effectiveness and higher levels of student performance, for a higher quality of educational experience. The costs of poor acoustics include teachers' vocal fatigue and absenteeism, and remedial instruction and repeating school years for underperforming students.

Many schools can achieve a healthy acoustical environment with no additional cost. This may be more challenging in urban areas and in schools adjacent to traffic, construction, and other sources of noise.

2. Related Credits

This credit is directly related to strategies and measures to achieve effective acoustical performance in school buildings, which are covered in the following prerequisite:

- IEQ Prerequisite 3: Minimum Acoustical Performance

3. Summary of Referenced Standards

American National Standards Institute (ANSI)/ASHRAE Standard S12.60-2002, Acoustical Performance Criteria, Design Requirements and Guidelines for Schools

This standard provides acoustical performance criteria and design requirements for classrooms and other learning spaces. Annexes provide information on good design and construction practices, installation methods, and optional procedures to demonstrate conformance to the acoustical performance and design requirements of this standard. This standard seeks to provide design flexibility without compromising the goal of obtaining adequate speech intelligibility for all students and teachers in classrooms and learning spaces within the scope of the standard. This standard is available at no charge from the Acoustical Society of America Online Store, at asastore.aip.org.

ASHRAE Handbook, Chapter 47, Sound and Vibration Control, 2003 HVAC Applications

Because mechanical equipment is 1 of the major sources of noise in a building, the sound generated by mechanical equipment and its effects on the overall acoustical environment in a building must be considered. Mechanical equipment should be selected and equipment spaces designed with an emphasis on both the intended uses of the equipment and the goal of providing acceptable sound and vibration levels in occupied spaces of the building. This chapter is available separately from the full handbook in the online ASHRAE bookstore, at http://www.ashrae.org.

4. Implementation

To provide an acoustical environment that meets the requirements of this credit, designers need to consider 2 primary areas of performance:

- low background noise inside the core learning space; and

- appropriate sound isolation for core learning spaces from interior and exterior noise sources.

One measure of acoustical performance is is the A-weighted decibel (dBA) measurement of background noise levels. Because noise is measured on a nonlinear scale, an increase of 10 dBA means that noise levels are perceived to be about twice as loud as the previous level. For example, a busy school cafeteria may have a sound level of 80 dBA, and 90 dBA is typical of a jackhammer—twice the volume.

A primary metric for sound isolation is sound transmission class (STC), which is a single-number rating for the sound attenuation properties of a wall, roof, or other building element. A higher STC rating provides a higher level of sound attenuation.

The ANSI S12.60–2002 methodology should be used as the guiding document for acoustical design. The standard describes effective methods and strategies for HVAC noise control and sound isolation design. In addition, the 2007 HVAC Applications ASHRAE Handbook, Chapter 47, Sound and Vibration Control, provides detailed methods for reducing noise transmission from HVAC systems.

Exterior Background Noise

The exterior noise control requirements for IEQ Credit 9 are defined as STC ratings for exterior building elements in ANSI S12.60–2002. In addition to meeting STC requirements, design teams should also be aware of any potentially intrusive exterior sources of background noise, such as high-volume traffic, aircraft, mechanical and electrical equipment, and construction activities. In these high-noise environments, project teams should measure on-site background noise levels before construction to identify noise levels that may require additional control measures. Sites with outdoor noise levels of 75 dBA or more might prove to be particularly difficult. Designs should take outdoor noise sources, such as major roads, into consideration. Consider locating classrooms and core learning spaces away from these sources. In addition, consider the possibility that current outdoor sound levels could increase with future development.

Consider site options for reducing exterior noise transmission. Effective strategies include building orientation and the use of sound barriers or berms. The majority of exterior noise reduction, however, will likely occur through the building envelope's design. The STC requirements for IEQ Credit 9 may not be sufficient for high-noise environments; additional noise control measures should be taken as required.

Interior Background Noise

HVAC systems are often the most significant sources of noise inside a building. One way to reduce noise in classrooms is not to install fans, compressors, and other HVAC machinery in or near classrooms. If HVAC units operate inside the building, prevent noise transmission to adjacent rooms. The best way to isolate HVAC noise depends on the type and location of mechanical equipment; these variables should be considered during the design phase of the project. Selecting quieter HVAC systems and locating HVAC units centrally are among the more effective ways to prevent equipment-related noise. Simple ducting of the supply air path and, to a lesser extent, the return-air path will provide significant value in meeting background noise criteria. Additionally, using acoustic liner in ductwork minimizes sound transmission. The 2007 HVAC Applications ASHRAE

	IEQ
NC	NA
SCHOOLS	Credit 9
CS	NA

Handbook, Chapter 47, Sound and Vibration Control, provides detailed methods for reducing noise transmission from HVAC systems.

Other sources of background noise may include light fixtures, classroom computers, plumbing systems, audiovisual equipment, and the building occupants themselves. With careful planning, selection, and design of building systems, background noise can be kept to a minimum.

Reverberation

Control of reverberation time is required in IEQ Prerequisite 3, Minimal Acoustical Performance; see the Implementation section for reverberation time design and compliance requirements.

Sound Transmission

Classrooms should be designed to prevent the transmission of sound from adjacent spaces through walls and ceilings, especially when adjacent spaces are cafeterias, mechanical rooms, corridors, or other noisy areas. A fundamental metric for defining the sound isolation properties of a building element is the STC rating. The higher a material's STC rating, the more effectively it blocks sound transmission. STC ratings for several wall assemblies are published in acoustical references, fire code guides, and manufacturer's performance data. Determination of the STC rating for composite assemblies (i.e., combinations of walls, windows, and other elements) is described in Section D2.4 of ANSI S12.60–2002. The STC ratings for exterior windows are as noted in the Requirements section of this credit; STC ratings for classroom entrance doors are as noted in Section 4.5.5 of ANSI S12.60–2002.

In addition to ensuring that the required STC rating is maintained, all penetrations (ducts, piping, recessed cabinets, etc.) in the assemblies should be sealed and treated during construction to maintain the required ratings. All construction elements in a room must comply with the STC ratings listed in ANSI Standard S12.60–2002, either singly or as a component in a system that meets the STC requirements as a composite assembly.

5. Timeline and Team

Since architectural elements, building layout, and mechanical system design are primary drivers of sound isolation and mechanical noise control, project teams should consider acoustics in the schematic design phase of planning. Early in the design phase and no later than design development, design teams should coordinate with mechanical engineers, electrical engineers, and contractors to specify methods to achieve goals for interior background noise. In the schematic phase, locate noisy equipment and high-activity areas away from classrooms and other spaces where quiet is required. Develop mechanical system schemes that significantly reduce potential mechanical noise. For example, use centralized mechanical systems rather than in-room units, place VAV boxes and other mechanical equipment in corridors rather than above classrooms, and route ductwork outside classrooms. Involve an acoustical consultant, if necessary, as early as possible in the design process.

Early in the design, allocate the spaces and develop wall types and other noise isolation elements accordingly.

During schematic design, teachers and staff should educate the architects on the physical and spatial aspects of learning. Architects, designers, and materials specifiers must understand the different methods of teaching and learning that a single classroom might accommodate. For example, the same space might be used for collaborative projects, individual student work, lectures, and demonstrations.

6. Calculations

Sound Transmission Class

An STC rating must be determined for every wall, floor, and ceiling assembly that may affect interior noise levels in a core learning space. The STC ratings for several wall assemblies are published in acoustical references, fire code guides, and manufacturer's performance data. To calculate the STC rating for composite assemblies, use the methodology described in Section D2.4 of ANSI S12.60–2002. STC requirements are shown in Table 1.

Table 1. STC Requirements for Classroom Assemblies

Adjacent Space Type	Minimum STC Rating
Other Classrooms	50
Outdoors	50
Bathrooms	53
Corridor	45
Offices, Conference Rooms	45
Music Rooms	60
Mechanical Equipment Room	60
Cafeteria, Gym, Natatorium	60

In addition to employing the appropriate STC ratings, all penetrations (ducts, piping, recessed cabinets, etc.) in the assemblies should be sealed and treated during construction to optimize sound isolation and control sound leakage ("flanking") paths. Sound isolation can also be compromised by connecting ductwork ("crosstalk"), open return air plenums, and classroom doors with large undercuts. Any air leak between spaces is a sound leak; review plans to identify open pathways and take measures to eliminate sound leakage between instructional spaces.

If the project team chooses to measure STC levels for all assemblies after construction, it must use the methodology described in Section E5.1 of ANSI S12.60–2002.

Background Noise Level

Background noise level can be calculated through analysis of mechanical system noise source levels, sound path(s) between sources and receiving room (ducts, diffusers, etc.), and receiving room acoustical conditions (wall and ceiling constructions, room sound absorption, etc.).

Recommended methodologies and best practices for mechanical system noise control are described in Annex B of ANSI Standard S12.60–2002. Best practices and calculation methods are provided in the 2007 HVAC Applications ASHRAE Handbook, Chapter 47, Sound and Vibration Control.

The required calculations can be conducted by a mechanical engineer familiar with the methodologies in the 2007 HVAC Applications ASHRAE Handbook, Chapter 47, Sound and Vibration Control, or by a qualified acoustical consultant.

7. Documentation Guidance

As a first step in preparing to complete the LEED-Online documentation requirements, work through the following measures. Refer to LEED-Online for the complete descriptions of all required documentation.

- Maintain accurate copies of the project building plan; denote STC ratings for wall, ceiling, and floor assemblies. Describe treatments used for sound control where ductwork or other passages connect classroom spaces, and note them on the plan.

	IEQ
NC	NA
SCHOOLS	Credit 9
CS	NA

- Document the means by which the background noise level in classrooms and other primary spaces was kept below 45 dBA by following ANSI S12.60 methodology or using software that is based on the 2007 HVAC Applications ASHRAE Handbook, Chapter 47: Sound and Vibration Control.

8. Examples

There is no example for this credit.

9. Exemplary Performance

This credit may be eligible for exemplary performance under the Innovation in Design section if the project achieves an outdoor background noise level of 55 dBA for playgrounds and 60 dBA for athletic fields and all other school grounds, or an indoor noise level of 35 dBA.

10. Regional Variations

Pay attention to regional factors that can influence ambient noise around school buildings. For example, wind may be an issue in the Midwest. Atmospheric fog and water vapor in coastal regions may also affect environmental sound transmission. The use of natural ventilation may require additional noise control design because of the open pathways between exterior and interior spaces.

11. Operations and Maintenance Considerations

Establish a policy for the continued use of acoustical best practices during the building's operation. Help building operators find acoustically appropriate products and materials for repairs or alterations by providing them with a list of compliant products.

Consider equipping operating personnel with a sound level meter so that they can perform periodic acoustical assessments and correct any deficiencies.

Reducing Background Noise

For compliance with this credit, background noise is defined as noise from HVAC systems only.

Heating, Ventilating, and Air-Conditioning HVAC

HVAC noise results in noisy classrooms. In the past, it has been common practice to install fan-coil and similar through-the-wall heating and cooling units in classrooms. This puts the fan and compressor right in the room with the students. Children with hearing loss should not be seated near an HVAC unit or diffuser. Noisy through-wall, through-roof, or under-window units in the classroom should first be serviced and balanced to be sure they are operating as intended. Additional strategies:

- Add a custom-built sound enclosure around each unit.

- Add sound-lined ductwork to the unit to attenuate air distribution noise.

- Replace the unit with quieter split systems or through-wall models.

- Increase the open area at grilles and diffusers.

- Rebalance the system to reduce air volume delivered to the classroom.

- Relocate ductwork and diffusers away from teaching locations.

- Add separate duct runs to eliminate noise from common use.

- Add duct length to attenuate noise.

- Add sound lining to ducts.

Additional Suggestions for Reducing Room Noise

	IEQ
NC	NA
SCHOOLS	Credit 9
CS	NA

- Arrange seating so that students are distant from noise sources (fans, HVAC units, etc.).

- Put tennis balls or rubber tips on the chair legs.

- Avoid open classrooms, including temporary or sliding walls that separate instructional areas.

- Diminish the sound from computer keyboards by underlaying them with rubber pads or carpeting.

- Whenever possible, locate all large pieces of computer equipment (servers, audiovisual controls, printers, plotters) in a separate room.

Background noise levels from sources other than HVAC systems can be reduced with the following steps:

- Add storm windows.

- Replace existing windows with new thermal insulating units (this will improve energy performance, too). Such windows may also have sound transmission class (STC) ratings from the manufacturer; select windows with the highest affordable rating.

- Install specially fabricated sound-reducing windows, particularly near traffic arterials and airports and in dense urban locations.

- Check doors for gaps larger than 1/16 inch.

- Add good-quality drop seals and gaskets.

- Install tight-fitting solid-core doors with seals and gaskets.

- Install special sound-control doors if adjacent spaces are very noisy.

12. Resources

Please see USGBC's LEED Registered Project Tools (http://www.usgbc.org/projecttools) for additional resources and technical information.

Websites

Acoustical Society of America

http://asa.aip.org/

The Acoustical Society of America (ASA) is an international scientific society dedicated to increasing and diffusing the knowledge of acoustics and its practical applications. ASA's website contains a variety of resources, including publications, standards information, and links. Of special note are the 2 ASA booklets on classroom acoustics at http://asa.aip.org/classroom/booklet.html and http://asa.aip.org/classroom/bookletII.pdf.

Education Resources Information Center (ERIC)

http://www.eric.ed.gov/

ERIC provides free access to more than 1.2 million bibliographic records of journal articles and other education-related materials and includes links to full text, if available. The U.S. Department of Education's Institute of Education Sciences (IES) sponsors ERIC. The center has posted many studies that show the impact of acoustics on learning, including the effects on students with hearing disabilities, and also has posted studies and papers on good acoustical design in classrooms.

	IEQ
NC	NA
SCHOOLS	Credit 9
CS	NA

Maryland Classroom Acoustics Guidelines

www.marylandpublicschools.org/NR/rdonlyres/FCB60C1D-6CC2-4270-BDAA-153D67247324/10128/ClassroomAcousticsGuidelines.pdf

This resource, developed by the state of Maryland, discusses the components and importance of good classroom acoustics, the American National Standards Institute (ANSI) Standard S12.60–2002 for classroom acoustics, typical existing classroom conditions, and the cost impact of the standard. The guidelines cover planning, design, furnishings, equipment, HVAC systems, plumbing noise, construction practices, postoccupancy inspection, sound field amplification systems, indoor air quality considerations, and portable classrooms.

Quiet Classrooms

http://www.quietclassrooms.org/

Quiet Classrooms is an alliance of nonprofit organizations working to create better learning environments in schools by reducing noise. Negligible background noise levels and good classroom acoustics are important for learning by all students and especially those who are hearing-impaired. The alliance's website is a resource for schools, school boards, PTAs, principals, parents, teachers, students, and school architects.

Whole Building Design Guide, Acoustic Comfort

www.wbdg.org/resources/acoustic.php?r=ieq

This section of the Whole Building Design Guide focuses on acoustic comfort in offices, classrooms, and conference rooms and discusses the following issues: site selection, glazing, HVAC noise issues, natural ventilation, sound masking, emerging issues, relevant codes and standards, and additional resources.

13. Definitions

A **building envelope** is the exterior surface of a building's construction—the walls, windows, roof, and floor.

Core learning spaces are spaces for educational activities where the primary functions are teaching and learning. (ANSI S12.60–2002)

Reverberation is an acoustical phenomenon that occurs when sound persists in an enclosed space because of its repeated reflection or scattering upon the enclosing surfaces or objects within the space (ANSI S12.60-2002).

Reverberation time (**RT**) is a measure of the amount of reverberation in a space and equal to the time required for the level of a steady sound to decay by 60 dB after it has been made. The decay rate depends on the amount of sound absorption in a room, the room geometry and the frequency of the sound. RT is expressed in seconds. (ANSI S12.60–2002)

Sound absorption is the portion of sound energy striking a surface that is not returned as sound energy (ANSI S12.60–2002).

Sound transmission class (**STC**) is a single number rating for the acoustic attenuation of airborne sound passing through a partition or any other building element such as a wall, roof, or door as measured in an acoustical testing laboratory following accepted industry practice. A higher STC rating provides more sound attenuation through a partition. (ANSI S12.60–2002)

A **weighted decibel** (**dBA**) is a sound pressure level measured with a conventional frequency weighting that roughly approximates how the human ear hears different frequency components of sounds at typical listening levels for speech. (ANSI S12.60–2002)

MOLD PREVENTION

IEQ CREDIT 10

	NC	SCHOOLS	CS
Credit	NA	IEQ Credit 10	NA
Points	NA	1 point	NA

Intent

To reduce the potential presence of mold in schools through preventive design and construction measures.

Requirements

SCHOOLS

Project teams must achieve the following credits:

- IEQ Credit 3.1: Construction Indoor Air Quality Management Plan—During Construction

- IEQ Credit 7.1: Thermal Comfort—Compliance

- IEQ Credit 7.2: Thermal Comfort—Verification

Provide heating, ventilating and air conditioning (HVAC) systems and controls designed to limit space relative humidity to 60% or less during all load conditions, both occupied and unoccupied.

Develop and implement on an ongoing basis an IAQ management program for buildings based on the U.S. Environmental Protection Agency (EPA) document, Building Air Quality: A Guide for Building Owners and Facility Managers, EPA reference number 402-F-91-102, December 1991.

	IEQ
NC	NA
SCHOOLS	Credit 10
CS	NA

1. Benefits and Issues to Consider

Environmental Issues

The presence of mold inside a building can lead to serious health problems for occupants. There are many different kinds of mold, and sensitivity to them varies by the individual, as well as by the type of mold. Even those who are not sensitive to mold initially can develop increased sensitivity through repeated exposure[28]. Symptoms can range from those resembling hay fever (sneezing, runny nose, headache) to asthma attacks. Some molds produce substances called mycotoxins, which have been linked to a range of health issues. Potential effects range from relatively mild symptoms such as nausea and irritation of the skin, eyes, throat, lungs and mucous membranes to serious and chronic conditions including suppressed immunity, liver damage, central nervous system damage and cancer. Given that students normally spend up to 8 hours a day in school, with more time spent in after-school programs, mold prevention should be a high priority.

Economic Issues

Sickness due to mold exposure may result in increased visits to health care providers, both on and off the campus. Mold-related illness can add significant burden to health care costs for the district as well as students, faculty, and staff. Mold-related illness can also increase absenteeism and decrease productivity.

Besides the health-related costs associated with mold problems, remediation can be a costly maintenance expense.

2. Related Credits

Abating mold through preventive design and construction measures is treated in the following other credits:

- IEQ Credit 3.1: Construction IAQ Management Plan—During Construction
- IEQ Credit 7.1: Thermal Comfort—Design
- IEQ Credit 7.2: Thermal Comfort—Verification

3. Summary of Referenced Standard

Building Air Quality: A Guide for Building Owners and Facility Managers, EPA Reference Number 402–F–91–102, effective December 1991
http://www.epa.gov/iaq/largebldgs/baqtoc.html
Developed by EPA and the National Institute for Occupational Safety and Health, this EPA publication details IAQ sources in buildings and methods to prevent and resolve IAQ problems.

According to EPA, this guide provides information on factors affecting IAQ and describes how to develop and manage an IAQ profile. It offers strategies for identifying causes of IAQ problems, assessing alternative mitigation strategies, determining if a problem has been resolved, and deciding whether to consult outside technical specialists. Other topics included in the guide are "key problem-causing factors; air quality sampling; heating, ventilation, and air conditioning (HVAC) systems; moisture problems; and additional sources of information."

4. Implementation

Mold spores exist in a wide variety of places, both indoors and outdoors. Although there are thousands of species, fewer than ten are commonly associated with chronic illness in the built environment. These types of mold flourish because they enjoy the same living conditions as humans. They become problematic when concentrations (measured in colony-forming units) exceed our immune systems' ability to ward them off.

Mold needs 3 things to grow: oxygen, food, and moisture. Because it is impossible to eliminate oxygen and almost equally as difficult to remove all food sources, the key to mold prevention is moisture control. This is achieved by addressing the following issues in school building design, construction, and maintenance:

Eliminate the Potential for Condensation

Condensation occurs in buildings when moist air comes into contact with surfaces that are at or below the dewpoint temperature, which causes water vapor to revert to liquid. The relationship of surface temperature to humidity is a crucial element in creating the damp conditions that enable mold growth. Cold pipe surfaces and roof drains may have surface temperatures well below the dewpoint, which may allow moisture to reach interior wall and ceiling cavities. The building envelope should be constructed with an effective vapor barrier, overall U value, and minimum infiltration. Keeping the relative humidity below 60% in interior spaces is important in preventing mold growth inside the building. Spaces where humidity is elevated—such as restrooms, locker rooms, natatoriums, and crawl spaces—present special challenges because surfaces can be significantly warmer and still be conducive to condensation and mold growth. Providing appropriate ventilation in high-moisture areas helps exhaust moisture and prevent condensation. Displacement ventilation may be effective in many areas, especially in classrooms.

Pay Special Attention to Known Generators of Condensation

HVAC systems generate condensation during dehumidification. Pans and drains are common hosts found in space conditioning, refrigeration, and food service equipment. Ductwork is another place where mold is commonly found, especially where in-duct humidifiers are present. Rooftop HVAC equipment that is exposed to the elements is problematic because ductwork is often subject to moisture penetration. Mold can grow easily in many acoustic duct linings and duct insulation materials; it can then be circulated throughout the building. It is essential to keep these systems properly maintained. Check air handling units regularly to ensure they are draining properly and that there is no standing water. Clean and maintain humidifiers regularly to make sure they do not distribute mold.

Prevent Mold during Unoccupied Periods

Where HVAC systems operate at significantly reduced capacity or are idle completely during school breaks, mold can increase dramatically in ductwork, on coil surfaces, and in condensate pans. Restarting idled HVAC equipment often releases significant levels of mold into the air. These conditions are best avoided by comprehensive commissioning and periodic inspections of potential trouble spots. If neglected, seasonally dormant systems can foster potentially harmful levels of mold growth. The problem can be exacerbated if outside air intakes are near sources of mold, such as rotting leaves, waste receptacles, and chronically damp soil or roof surfaces. Potential mold areas should be avoided when installing air inlets, operable windows, and other building penetrations.

Address Floods and Leaky or Failed Equipment

Accumulation of water from storms, flooding, leaking pipes, or failed plumbing fixtures can lead to mold growth. Damage can be severe and may require professional remediation to restore the building to acceptable conditions.

Design for Mold Prevention

During the initial design phase, pay special attention to the site and orientation of the building, along with the local climatic conditions. Identify and minimize areas where moisture will likely accumulate. Design the building and landscaping to direct water away from the foundation. Design stormwater management systems to prevent standing water from damaging the roof and creating

	IEQ
NC	NA
SCHOOLS	Credit 10
CS	NA

leaks. Material choices can also play a significant role in mold prevention. Both the interior and exterior of the school will benefit from careful consideration of the building's location and use, since some materials are more resistant to moisture buildup than others. Water is regularly tracked into buildings from the outdoors, so choosing appropriate flooring materials is important. Do not use carpet in areas of high moisture. Water trapped underneath carpet provides an ideal climate for mold to thrive and can be difficult to remove.

Portable classrooms and modular classroom units may require additional measures for mold prevention. These structures may not be sufficiently well built or properly space conditioned to permit the strategies outlined above.

5. Timeline and Team

In the design phases, the mechanical engineer should identify and eliminate potential sources of mold. The lead building engineer is responsible for ongoing efforts to prevent mold during building operation and maintenance.

6. Calculations

There are no calculations to support this credit.

7. Documentation Guidance

As a first step in preparing to complete the LEED-Online documentation requirements, work through the following measures. Refer to LEED-Online for the complete descriptions of all required documentation.

- Document the method used to limit space relative humidity to 60% or less.

- Maintain a written IAQ management plan that addresses operational and maintenance issues.

8. Examples

Apart from the factors mentioned above, schools should pay attention to materials and construction methods. Some examples of mold-resistant materials are gypsum panels, glass-fiber reinforced concrete, precast concrete, fiber reinforced polymers and epoxy concretes. Additionally, mold-resistant coating can also provide the required benefits in controlling mold.

9. Exemplary Performance

This credit may be eligible for exemplary performance under the Innovation in Design section; however, there is no prescribed threshold for determination of exemplary performance. Projects will be evaluated on a case-by-case basis.

10. Regional Variations

Mold issues are more prevalent in regions with warm, humid climates. Because temperature and humidity management may be required, a building may use more energy to cool and dehumidify the air.

11. Operations and Maintenance Considerations

Consult with the building owner and maintenance personnel on the maintenance of the HVAC system's humidity control components. Establish appropriate setpoints and control sequences, as well as recommendations for typical corrective actions, and include them in the facility's building operation plan and sequence of operations document. Establish procedures and schedules for inclusion in the building's preventive maintenance plan.

Designate responsible parties for implementing the ongoing IAQ management program, and provide proper training and resources. EPA's Indoor Air Quality Building Education and Assessment Model (I-BEAM) provides comprehensive guidance for building professionals and others responsible for IAQ in commercial buildings. I-BEAM updates and expands EPA's Building Air Quality guidance (available at http://www.epa.gov/iaq/largebldgs/baqtoc.html); it contains text, animation, visual, interactive, and calculation components for diverse tasks.

	IEQ
NC	NA
SCHOOLS	Credit 10
CS	NA

12. Resources

Please see USGBC's LEED Registered Project Tools (http://www.usgbc.org/projecttools) for additional resources and technical information.

Websites

Center for School Mold Help

http://www.schoolmoldhelp.org

Established to educate the public about school mold in order to help prevent, address, and end this major health threat to students and school staff, the Center for School Mold Health (SMH) provides educational and scientific information about school mold and sick building disorders related to damp buildings," explains the SMH website.

Collaborative for High Performance Schools Best Practices Manual, 2006

http://www.chps.net/manual/index.htm

The Collaborative for High Performance Schools (CHPS) Best Practices Manual contains guidelines and strategies for mold prevention in school buildings.

Flood Cleanup: Avoiding Indoor Air Quality Problems

U.S. EPA

http://www.epa.gov/mold/pdfs/floods.pdf

EPA Publication 402-F-93-005, Revised October 2003

According to EPA, "this fact sheet discusses problems caused by microbial growth, as well as other potential effects of flooding, on long-term IAQ and the steps to take to reduce these effects. Although the information contained here emphasizes residential flood cleanup, it applies to other types of buildings."

Fungal Contamination of Elementary Schools: A New Environmental Hazard

http://www.ncbi.nlm.nih.gov/pubmed/12602667

According to the study's objective, it "evaluates the health effects of mold-contaminated schools on students and teachers. A discussion of the effectiveness of current methods for evaluating these schools, with a focus on the importance of using total mold spore counts, is also provided."

GREENGUARD Mold Protection Program™

GREENGUARD Environmental Institute

http://www.greenguard.org/Default.aspx?tabid=111

According to its website, GEI has "developed a standard of best practices for preventing mold in newly constructed buildings that is currently under consideration as a national standard. The GREENGUARD Mold Protection Program certifies buildings that meet this standard and monitors their compliance throughout the term of the loan or building life."

Health Effects of Mold Exposure in Public Schools

http://www.bio-reveal.com/articles/health-effect-mold-in-schools.pdf

According to this website, this paper "profiles the impact of mold exposure on the health of students, teachers, and staff in 2 public elementary schools in Connecticut and explains how the air quality in each school was tested and how the health of teachers and students was assessed. It also proposes standards for testing IAQ and evaluating the health impact of indoor mold exposure on students, teachers, and staff members".

	IEQ
NC	NA
SCHOOLS	Credit 10
CS	NA

IAQ Design Tools for Schools

U.S. EPA

http://www.epa.gov/iaq/schooldesign

"IAQ Design Tools for Schools provides both detailed guidance and links to other information resources to help design new schools as well as repair, renovate and maintain existing facilities. Although its primary focus is on IAQ, it is also intended to encourage school districts to embrace the concept of designing high-performance schools."

Mold in My School: What Do I Do?

California Department of Health Services

http://www.edfacilities.org/pubs/mold.html

"This publication states that it "provides information on the most important indoor mold-related health concerns and discusses how school districts can keep facilities mold-free and avoid these problems.""

Mold Remediation in Schools and Commercial Buildings

U.S EPA

http://www.epa.gov/mold/pdfs/moldremediation.pdf

EPA Document 402-K-01-001, 2001

According to EPA, this document "presents guidelines for the remediation andcleanup of mold and moisture problems in schools and commercial buildings; these guidelines include measures designed to protect the health of building occupants" and cleaners.

Centers for Disease Control and Prevention, Mold

http://www.cdc.gov/mold

CDC's mold website "provides information on mold and health; an inventory of state IAQ programs; advice on assessment, cleanup efforts, and prevention of mold growth; and links to resources."

California Research Bureau Molds, Toxic Molds, and Indoor Air Quality

California State Library

http://www.library.ca.gov/crb/01/notes/v8n1.pdf

According to the paper, it "provides background information on molds, their potential health effects, and how they relate to IAQ."

Occurrence and Characteristics of Moisture Damage in School Buildings

National Public Health Institute, Department of Environmental Health, Kuopio, Finland

http://www.chps.net/info/iaq_papers/PaperV.5.pdf

According the study, it was "made as a part of exposure assessment in a study program to find links between moisture damage and microbial growth in school buildings and respiratory heath of the students."

Respiratory Infections among Children in Moisture Damaged Schools

National Public Health Institute, Dept. of Environmental Health, Kuopio, Finland

http://www.chps.net/info/iaq_papers/PaperI.1.pdf

According the study, the aim...was to find out whether respiratory infections among school-aged children differed in schools with visible moisture and mold problems compared to non-damaged schools."

School Advanced Ventilation Engineering Software

U.S. EPA

http://www.epa.gov/iaq/schooldesign/saves.html

According to EPA, "SAVES is a free software package that architects, engineers, school officials, and others can use to determine which type of ventilation equipment provides the best advantages for their specific applications."

13. Definitions

	IEQ
NC	NA
SCHOOLS	Credit 10
CS	NA

The **building envelope** is the exterior surface of a building's construction—the walls, windows, roof, and floor.

The **dew point** is the temperature to which air must be cooled for the water vapor it contains to revert to a liquid state.

Displacement ventilation provides buoyancy-driven air flow rather than conventional forced methods. Air is introduced at a low level and at a temperature slightly below the room ambient, in order to provide a local cooled environment around occupants and heat sources, thus eliminating the need to temper the entire space. (CIBSE Guide F–2008)

Infiltration is air leakage into conditioned spaces through cracks and interstices in ceilings, floors, and walls from unconditioned spaces or the outdoors. (ASHRAE 62.1–2007)

Mycotoxins are toxic substances produced by fungus such as mushrooms, molds, and yeasts.

Relative humidity is the ratio of the density of airborne water vapor to the density of a sample of air saturated with water at the same temperature and pressure. (ASHRAE 2005 Fundamentals)

Spores are microscopic cells used by molds to reproduce, which continually travel through the air and land on various surfaces where they may produce mold if moisture is present.

U value is the measure of heat flow through materials that separate the building façade, slab, or roof from the exterior environment in units.

Vapor barrier is any material used to prevent moisture penetration through wall, ceiling, and floor assemblies and potential condensation that can result from differences between a building's interior and exterior temperatures.

Endnotes

[1] U.S. Environmental Protection Agency. Healthy Buildings, Healthy People: A Vision for the 21st Century. 2001. http://www.epa.gov/iaq/hbhp/hbhptoc.html (accessed May 2008).

[2] Ibid.

[3] U.S. Environmental Protection Agency. Unfinished Business: A Comparative Assessment of Environmental Problems. Washington, DC: U.S. EPA, 1987.

[4] U.S. Environmental Protection Agency. Reducing Risk: Setting Priorities and Strategies for Environmental Protection. Washington, DC: U.S. EPA, 1990.

[5] U.S. Environmental Protection Agency. Indoor Air in Large Buildings. 2002. http://www.epa.gov/iaq/largebldgs/i-beam/text/budgets_accounts.html (accessed May 2008).

[6] American Academy of Allergy, Asthma & Immunology (AAAAI). Promoting Best Practice: Guide for Managing Asthma in Children. Pediatric Asthma, 2004.

[7] Centers for Disease Control and Prevention, National Center for Health Statistics. "Asthma Prevalence, Health Care Use and Mortality, 2002." http://www.cdc.gov/nchs/products/pubs/pubd/hestats/asthma/asthma.htm (accessed November 2008).

[8] Asthma and Allergy Foundation of America. "Asthma Facts and Figures." http://www.aafa.org/display.cfm?id=8&sub=42#_ftnref20 (accessed November 2008).

[9] United States Census Bureau. School Enrollment in the United States: 2006. 2008. http://www.census.gov/prod/2008pubs/p20-559.pdf (accessed November 2008).

[10] United States Census Bureau. "Facts for Features: Teacher Appreciation Week (May2-8)." U.S. Census Bureau News Release (April 22, 2004), http://www.census.gov/Press-Release/www/releases/archives/facts_for_features_special_editions/001737.html (accessed November 2008).

[11] Environmental Health, Safety and Quality Management Services for Business and Industry, and Federal, State and Local Government, IAQ Fact Sheet. March 9, 2006.

[12] Rocky Mountain Institute. "Greening the Building and the Bottom Line." http://www.rmi.org/images/PDFs/BuildingsLand/D94-27_GBBL.pdf (accessed November 2008).

[13] This assumes that $100,000 in indoor air quality improvements are invested. Damiano, Leonard, and David Dougan. The Big Carrots: Productivity and Health. Ebtron, Inc., 2003. http://www.automatedbuildings.com/news/apr03/articles/ebtron/ebtron.htm (accessed May 2008).

[14] U.S. Department of Health and Human Services, National Institutes of Health, National Cancer Institute. "Smoking and Tobacco Control Monograph 10." Health Effects of Exposure to Environmental Tobacco Smoke. NIH, 1999. http://cancercontrol.cancer.gov/tcrb/monographs/10/m10_complete.pdf (accessed May 2008).

[15] Ibid.

[16] U.S. Department of Health and Human Services, Public Health Service, Office of the Surgeon General. Women and Smoking: A Report of the Surgeon General. 2001. http://www.cdc.gov/tobacco/sgr/sgr_forwomen/index.htm (accessed May 2008).

[17] Prill, Rich. Why Measure Carbon Dioxide in Buildings? Washington State University Extension Energy Program. 2000. http://www.energy.wsu.edu/documents/building/iaq/CO2inbuildings.pdf (accessed November 2008).

[18] Goren, A., S. Hellman, A. Gabbay, S. Brenner. "Respiratory problems associated with exposure to airborne particles in the community." Archives of Environmental Health 54 (1999).

[19] Department of Health and Human Services, National Institutes of Health, National Cancer Institute. Health Effects of Exposure to Environmental Tobacco Smoke—Smoking and Tobacco Control Monograph 10. 1999. http://cancercontrol.cancer.gov/tcrb/monographs/10/m10_complete.pdf (accessed May 2008).

[20] Americans for Non-Smokers' Rights. "Americans for Non-Smokers' Rights: Smokefree Lists, Maps and Data." http://www.no-smoke.org/goingsmokefree.php?id=519 (accessed September 2008).

[21] Acoustical Society of America. American National Standard: Acoustical Performance Criteria, Design Requirements, and Guidelines for Schools. 2007. http://www.caslpa.ca/PDF/noise%20in%20classroom/ASA%20Acoustic%20requirements%20for%20schools.pdf (accessed November 2008).

[22] Center for Disease Control. National Workshop on Mild and Unilaterial Hearing Loss. 2005. http://www.cdc.gov/ncbddd/ehdi/documents/unilateralhl/Mild_Uni_2005%20Workshop_Proceedings.pdf (accessed November 2008).

[23] Canadian Centre for Occupational Health and Safety. "Health Effects of Carbon Dioxide Gas." http://www.ccohs.ca/oshanswers/chemicals/chem_profiles/carbon_dioxide/health_cd.html.

[24] U.S. Environmental Protection Agency. "Why Study Human Health Indoors?" Healthy Buildings, Healthy People: A Vision for the 21st Century. 2001. http://www.epa.gov/iaq/hbhp/section_1.pdf (accessed May 2008).

[25] U.S. Environmental Protection Agency. "Ozone and Your Patients' Health: Training for Health Care Providers." http://www.epa.gov/o3healthtraining/population.html#other (accessed November 2008).

[26] Bauman, F.S. "Giving Occupants What They Want: Guidelines for Implementing Personal Environmental Control in Your Building." Center for the Built Environment, 1999.

[27] Abraham, Loren E. Sustainable Building Technical Manual: Green Building Design, Construction, and Operations. Public Technology Inc. and U.S. Green Building Council, 1996.

[28] U.S. Environmental Protection Agency. "Mold Remediation in Schools and Commercial Buildings." http://www.epa.gov/mold/append_b.html (accessed November 2008).

Overview

Sustainable design strategies and measures are constantly evolving and improving. New technologies are continually introduced to the marketplace, and up-to-date scientific research influences building design strategies. The purpose of this LEED category is to recognize projects for innovative building features and sustainable building practices and strategies.

Occasionally, a strategy results in building performance that greatly exceeds what is required in an existing LEED credit. Other strategies may not be addressed by any LEED prerequisite or credit but warrant consideration for their sustainability benefits. In addition, LEED is most effectively implemented as part of an integrated design process, and this category addresses the role of a LEED Accredited Professional in facilitating that process.

Implementing New Technologies and Methods

As the building design and construction industry introduces new strategies for sustainable development, opportunities leading to additional environmental benefits will continue to emerge. Opportunities that are not currently addressed by LEED for New Construction, Schools, or Core & Shell may include environmental solutions specific to a particular location, condition, or region. With all sustainable strategies and measures, it is important to consider related environmental impacts. Project teams must be prepared to demonstrate the environmental benefits of innovative strategies and are encouraged to pursue opportunities that provide benefits of particular significance. Project teams can earn exemplary performance points for implementing strategies that result in performance that greatly exceeds the level or scope required by an existing LEED prerequisite or credit. Exemplary performance opportunities are noted throughout this reference guide.

CREDIT	TITLE
ID Credit 1	Innovation in Design
ID Credit 2	LEED® Accredited Professional
ID Credit 3	The School as a Teaching Tool

	NC	SCHOOLS	CS
Credit	ID Credit 1	ID Credit 1	ID Credit 1
Points	1-5 points	1-4 points	1-5 points

Intent

To provide design teams and projects the opportunity to achieve exceptional performance above the requirements set by the LEED Green Building Rating System and/or innovative performance in Green Building categories not specifically addressed by the LEED Green Building Rating System.

Requirements

NC, SCHOOLS & CS

Credit can be achieved through any combination of the paths below:

PATH 1. Innovation in Design (1-5 points for NC and CS, 1-4 points for Schools)

in the LEED 2009 for New Construction and Major Renovations, LEED 2009 for Core and Shell Development, or LEED 2009 for Schools Rating Systems.

One point is awarded for each innovation achieved. No more than 5 points (for NC and CS) and 4 points (for Schools) under IDc1 may be earned through PATH 1—Innovation in Design.

Identify the following in writing:

- The intent of the proposed innovation credit.

- The proposed requirement for compliance.

- The proposed submittals to demonstrate compliance.

- The design approach (strategies) used to meet the requirements.

PATH 2. Exemplary Performance (1-3 points)

Achieve exemplary performance in an existing LEED 2009 for Schools prerequisite or credit that allows exemplary performance as specified in the LEED Reference Guide for Green Building Design & Construction, 2009 Edition. An exemplary performance point may be earned for achieving double the credit requirements and/or achieving the next incremental percentage threshold of an existing credit in LEED.

One point is awarded for each exemplary performance achieved. No more than 3 points under IDc1 may be earned through PATH 2— Exemplary Performance."

	ID
NC	Credit 1
SCHOOLS	Credit 1
CS	Credit 1

1. Benefits and Issues to Consider

Sustainable design comes from innovative strategies and thinking. Institutional measures to reward such thinking—like the achievement of this credit—benefit our environment. Recognition of the exceptional will spur further innovation.

2. Related Credits

Every LEED for New Construction (NC), LEED for Core & Shell (C&S), and LEED for Schools credit holds ideas for Innovation in Design (ID) points and strategies. Refer to the Exemplary Performance section of each credit in this reference guide.

3. Summary of Referenced Standards

There is no standard referenced for this credit. Please refer to the Summary of Referenced Standards section in each credit for relevant standards.

4. Implementation

Credits in this section may be earned by documenting increased benefits to the environment in 1 of 2 ways:

Exemplary Performance Strategy

Exemplary performance strategies result in performance that greatly exceeds the level or scope required by existing LEED NC, LEED C&S, and LEED for Schools prerequisites or credits.

As a rule of thumb, ID credits for exemplary performance are awarded for doubling the credit requirements and/or achieving the next incremental percentage threshold. For instance, to achieve an ID credit for exemplary performance in MR Credit 4, Recycled Content (LEED NC), the total recycled value must be 30% or greater.

Exemplary performance is not available for all credits in LEED NC, LEED C&S, and LEED for Schools. Credits that allow exemplary performance through a predetermined approach are noted throughout this reference guide and the LEED-Online credit templates. A maximum of 3 ID points can be earned for exemplary performance.

Innovative Strategies

Innovative strategies are those that are not addressed by any existing LEED credits. Only those strategies that demonstrate a comprehensive approach and have significant, measurable environmental benefits are applicable.

There are 3 basic criteria for achieving an innovation credit for a category not specifically addressed by LEED:

1. The project must demonstrate quantitative performance improvements for environmental benefit (establishing a baseline of standard performance for comparison with the final design).

2. The process or specification must be comprehensive. For example, a team that is considering applying for an innovation credit for a green housekeeping program would need to demonstrate that the program applies to the entire project being certified under LEED. Measures that address a limited portion of a project or are not comprehensive in other ways are not eligible.

3. The concept the project team develops for the innovation credit must be applicable to other projects and must be significantly better than standard sustainable design practices.

ID credits awarded for 1 project at a specific point in time do not constitute automatic approval for similar strategies in a future project.

ID credits are not awarded for the use of a particular product or design strategy if the technology aids in the achievement of an existing LEED credit.

Approved ID credits may be pursued by any LEED project, but the project team must sufficiently document the achievement using the LEED credit equivalence process.

	ID
NC	Credit 1
SCHOOLS	Credit 1
CS	Credit 1

CS Core & Shell projects pursuing ID credits must implement a comprehensive strategy. In many instances, this will mean that strategies must apply to the whole building and include both the core and shell scope and common areas, as well as the tenant spaces. For example, a LEED for Core & Shell project who is pursuing an innovation credit for a green housekeeping program or integrated pest management, the base building management must either control the cleaning or pest management of both the base building and tenant spaces or enforce the requirements through a legally binding sales agreement or tenant lease for the areas not controlled by the base building management.

5. Timeline and Team

Innovation in Design ideally begins at a project's conception, but it can enter at any step of the process and come from any member of the project team. Open-mindedness, creativity, and rigor in follow-through are the critical ingredients. Options for innovation may come from the spheres of the technological—for example, an inventive wall section for climate control—or the general, such as educational outreach measures. Thus, team members with a variety of skills and interests will be able to contribute to the achievement of this credit.

6. Calculations

For exemplary performance, please refer to the Calculations section within each applicable credit.

7. Documentation Guidance

The Documentation Guidance section helps project teams prepare for formal certification application and complete the LEED-Online documentation requirements. Refer to LEED-Online for the complete descriptions of all required documentation.

- Document the process by which the project team has worked to develop and/or implement environmental benefits beyond the requirements set by the LEED Green Building Rating System and/or innovative performance in other areas.

- Track development and implementation of the specific exceptional and innovative strategies used.

- For Core & Shell projects, state the scope of the building that the innovation credit covers.

8. Examples

The level of effort involved in achieving an ID credit should be extraordinary. For example, installing a single green product or addressing a single aspect of a sustainability issue is not a sufficient level of effort. An environmental educational program consisting of simple signage in a building would not by itself be considered a significant benefit. Conversely, a visitor's center interactive display, coupled with an educational website and video highlighting the project's environmental strategies, would be eligible for an ID credit.

Suggested Topics for Innovation Credits

The following list illustrates sample actions and concepts that may be viable candidates for an ID credit, given appropriate implementation and documentation. It is the responsibility of the project team to determine the feasibility of possible ID-related programs or initiatives, develop

	ID
NC	Credit 1
SCHOOLS	Credit 1
CS	Credit 1

and execute the program in a manner that yields a meaningful environmental benefit, and provide documentation and calculations that substantiate the validity of the project team's approach and implementation. Project teams are encouraged to explore the full range of innovative opportunities within their buildings.

This list provides examples only and does not constitute formal preapproval of any ID strategy. Project teams desiring formal preapproval of an ID strategy must explain the proposal in detail through LEED-Online.

- Provide an educational program on the environmental and human health benefits of green building practices and how building occupants or the public can help improve green performance. Evaluate results and refine the program to increase its impact and audience as appropriate. The program must be actively instructional and include at least 2 instructional initiatives that have ongoing components. Types of initiatives might include the following:

    1. A comprehensive signage program or displays inside the building to educate occupants and visitors on the benefits of green buildings. Examples include windows to view energy-saving mechanical equipment, signs that call attention to water-conserving landscape features, and digital screens showing real-time energy consumption or building performance data.

    2. A case study highlighting the successes of the LEED project that could be used to inform the operations of other buildings.

    3. Guided tours focusing on sustainability, using the project as an example.

    4. An educational outreach program that engages occupants or the public through periodic events covering green building topics.

    5. A website or electronic newsletter that informs building occupants and visitors about the building's features and green strategies they can practice at home.

- Evaluate a substantial quantity of products or materials being used (or being considered for use in the building) on the basis of an ISO 14040 life-cycle assessment.

- Divert significant volumes of waste generated from sources other than the project building site and associated grounds via expanded waste management and diversion programs. For example, provide a collection and recycling program that allows building occupants or members of the community to bring in end-of-life home electronic equipment for recycling.

CS

- Core & Shell projects also have the option of developing legally binding performance criteria, based on existing LEED credits for tenants, that require buyers or tenants to design and construct in accordance with LEED credit requirements. For example, to encourage improved indoor air quality, a LEED for Core & Shell project can achieve an innovation point by requiring all tenants to install low-emitting materials for their spaces.

9. Regional Variations

ID credits may have regional content. For example, in temperate climates, eliminating HVAC systems and emphasizing use of natural ventilation might be worthy of an ID point.

Extraordinary designs that use the vernacular architectural strategies of the region may be among the most environmentally sound. Project teams should look to the characteristic buildings of their region as a source for innovation.

LEED® ACCREDITED PROFESSIONAL

	NC	SCHOOLS	CS
Credit	ID Credit 2	ID Credit 2	ID Credit 2
Points	1 point	1 point	1 point

Intent

To support and encourage the design integration required by LEED to streamline the application and certification process.

Requirements

NC, SCHOOLS & CS

At least 1 principal participant of the project team shall be a LEED Accredited Professional (AP).

	ID
NC	Credit 2
SCHOOLS	Credit 2
CS	Credit 2

1. Benefits and Issues to Consider

LEED APs have the expertise required to design a building to LEED standards and to coordinate the documentation process that is necessary for LEED certification. The LEED AP understands the importance of integrated design and the need to consider interactions between the prerequisites and credits and their respective criteria. Architects, engineers, consultants, owners, and others who have a strong interest in sustainable building design are all appropriate candidates for accreditation. The LEED AP should champion the project's LEED application and be an integral member of the project team. The LEED AP can also educate other team members about LEED and green buildings.

2. Related Credits

There are no related credits for the achievement of this credit.

3. Summary of Referenced Standards

LEED Accredited Professional
Green Building Certification Institute
www.gbci.org

Individuals who successfully complete the LEED professional accreditation exam are LEED APs. Accreditation certifies that the individual has the knowledge and skills necessary to participate in the LEED application and certification process, holds a firm understanding of green building practices and principles, and is familiar with LEED requirements, resources, and processes. The Green Building Certification Institute (GBCI), established with the support of the U.S. Green Building Council (USGBC), handles exam development and delivery to ensure objective and balanced management of the credentialing program.

4. Implementation

A LEED AP is a valuable resource in the LEED design and construction process. Although not required, the presence of a LEED AP aids the project team in understanding the elements of the rating system, the importance of considering interactions among the prerequisites and credits, and the LEED application process.

Including a LEED AP on the project team meets the credit requirements and can be accomplished in either of 2 ways:

- Engaging an individual within the organization who is already a LEED AP to participate in the certification application process.

- Hiring a LEED AP to support the project. Consider selecting a LEED AP experienced with LEED for New Construction, Core & Shell, or Schools and industry best green practices in design and construction.

5. Timeline and Team

There is no guidance for this credit.

6. Calculations

There are no calculations associated with this credit.

7. Documentation Guidance

As a first step in preparing to complete the LEED-Online documentation requirements, work through the following measures. Refer to LEED-Online for the complete descriptions of all required documentation.

- Obtain confirmation from team members who are LEED APs or are planning to become LEED APs.

8. Resources

Please see USGBC's LEED Registered Project Tools (http://www.usgbc.org/projecttools) for additional resources and other technical information.

Websites

Green Building Certification Institute

www.gbci.org

GBCI administers the LEED Professional Accreditation program to ensure objective management of the credential. GBCI manages exam development, registration, and delivery. It was established as a separately incorporated entity with the support of the USGBC. See the GBCI website for more information on workshops, testing locations, fees, and topics covered on the accreditation exam.

9. Definitions

LEED **Accredited Professionals** (**APs**) are individuals who have successfully completed the LEED professional accreditation exam.

	ID
NC	Credit 2
SCHOOLS	Credit 2
CS	Credit 2

	NC	SCHOOLS	CS
Credit	NA	ID Credit 3	NA
Points	NA	1 point	NA

Intent

To integrate the sustainable features of a school facility with the school's educational mission.

Requirements

SCHOOLS

Design a curriculum based on the high-performance features of the building, and commit to implementing the curriculum within 10 months of LEED certification. The curriculum should not just describe the features themselves, but explore the relationship between human ecology, natural ecology and the building. Curriculum must meet local or state curriculum standards, be approved by school administrators and provide 10 or more hours of classroom instruction per year, per full-time student.

	ID
NC	NA
SCHOOLS	Credit 3
CS	NA

This credit seeks to encourage integrating the sustainable attributes of the school building and broader ecological principles into the curriculum.

1. Benefits and Issues to Consider

Environmental Issues

Using a green school as a teaching tool will heighten students' awareness of environmental issues. Understanding the energy, material, and nutrient flows through a community and how the ecological footprint of the school influences them promotes environmental stewardship. The hands-on learning experience engages students in meaningful and relevant ways. This facilitates deeper understanding of the intent and application of these concepts and gives students a sense of ownership over their education. Studies have shown that this type of hands-on learning can lead to greater comprehension and retention of subject matter.

2. Related Credits

There are no related credits for the achievement of this credit.

3. Summary of Referenced Standards

There are no standards referenced for this credit.

4. Implementation

This credit promotes environmental education and raises awareness of the impact of the built environment on the health of ecosystems, using the physical school environment as an educational interface. School facilities represent myriad opportunities to enhance the academic experience through hands-on learning. Using the school as a teaching tool allows students to interact with the everyday functions of their facility in ways that raise their awareness of energy conservation, resource consumption, waste generation, and the influence of the microclimate on building systems and human comfort.

5. Timeline and Team

Involving teachers early on in the development of the curriculum is crucial. The curriculum may be designed as an individual course or included as a component of other coursework but must include at least 10 hours of instruction per year for each full-time student. Any school administrators and teachers involved in the project should assess the options for integrating the building into the curriculum and ensure that the new content is approved by all necessary groups (those who regulate local and state curriculum standards and administration). The project team should provide input on curriculum development, especially in determining the concepts and objectives of the coursework.

6. Calculations

There are no calculations required for this credit.

7. Documentation Guidance

As a first step in preparing to complete the LEED-Online documentation requirements, work through the following measures. Refer to LEED-Online for the complete descriptions of all required documentation.

- Document the process by which the project team has worked to develop and/or implement curriculum based on the high-performance features of the building.

- Maintain confirmation that the curriculum has been reviewed and approved by school administrators and meets applicable local and state curriculum standards.

8. Examples

The following examples illustrate some of the learning opportunities a green school can provide.

	ID
NC	NA
SCHOOLS	Credit 3
CS	NA

- Water gardens can be used for explorations of natural habitats in aquatic ecology studies—without needing a bus for field trips. Rain collection and distribution systems can be used to teach students about the water cycle.

- Constructed wetlands can filter wastewater from the building while teaching students about the biological processes, habitats, and importance of these ecosystems in nature. Such lessons can be applied to biology, chemistry, and other subjects.

- A green roof or open space on the site can provide space for growing food, which can be used to teach students about food sources, agricultural practices, and nutrition. Compost from standard composting bins and vermiculture (worm composting) can provide opportunities to learn about plant ecosystems, biology, and nutrient cycles and also be used in school vegetable gardens.

- A sundial can be used to teach astronomy and math.

- Renewable energy systems—wind and/or photovoltaics—can be used to teach material science and energy production. Math classes can use the systems for estimation and economics to determine cost-effectiveness.

- Prominently displayed meters for measuring high-performance features' inputs and/or outputs, such as water flow or energy production, can be checked by students on a daily, weekly, and seasonal basis.

- Visual and/or physical access to building infrastructure (e.g., HVAC equipment) can be viewed through windows in halls or integrated into the structure of the building. Students can track the performance of these systems based on outside weather conditions.

9. Exemplary Performance

This credit is not eligible for exemplary performance.

10. Operations and Maintenance Considerations

If high-performance features become part of the curriculum, they will need to be well-maintained so that they continually provide the planned educational opportunities. In some cases the students can engage in the operations and maintenance activities. For example, students can assist in the on-going monitoring of the performance of a renewable energy system, or in the care of the water gardens or green roofs.

11. Resources

Please see USGBC's LEED Registered Project Tools (http://www.usgbc.org/projecttools) for additional resources and other technical information.

Websites

Alliance to Save Energy's Green Schools Campaign
http://www.ase.org/section/program/greenschl/gsresources
Alliance's Green Schools Program engages students in creating energy-saving activities in their schools using hands-on, real-world projects. Lesson plans for different age groups can be downloaded for free on this website.

	ID
NC	NA
SCHOOLS	Credit 3
CS	NA

Association for Supervision and Curriculum Development

www.ascd.org

ASCD is a nonprofit organization of 175,000 educators worldwide. Its website offers numerous resources addressing aspects of effective teaching and learning.

Center for Ecoliteracy

www.ecoliteracy.org

The Center for Ecoliteracy promotes sustainability education through systems thinking and place-based learning. Specific curriculum guidelines emphasize food systems and watersheds, but the website also offers useful articles and resources concerning systems thinking, environmental education, and ecological literacy.

Center for Understanding the Built Environment

www.cubekc.org

The Center for Understanding the Built Environment specializes in community-based education, which brings together educators, children, and community partners to effect change. The center provides courses, workshops, newsletters, and teaching guides to help students appreciate good design, preservation, and planning. Curricula can be adapted to any site or grade level.

Closing the Loop: Exploring Integrated Waste Management and Resource Conservation
California Integrated Waste Management Board Office of Education and the Environment

www.ciwmb.ca.gov/Schools/curriculum/CTL

Closing the Loop is a compilation of 50 lessons to help students discover and nurture an environmental ethic and stewardship for natural resources. The activities focus on solid waste and environmental awareness topics including landfills, recycling, packaging, resource conservation, waste prevention, worm composting, and more.

EnergySmart Schools
U.S. Department of Energy

http://www1.eere.energy.gov/buildings/energysmartschools/

The EnergySmart Schools website serves as a mechanism to provide education and information about energy-efficient, healthy, high-performance K-12 schools. The website includes resources for teachers, including a digitized version of the Get Smart about Energy CD-Rom, a curriculum enhancement tool containing 350 inquiry-based lessons aligned to National Science Education Standards.

Earth Day Network, K–12 Environmental Education Program

www.earthday.net

Earth Day Network's Environmental Education Program provides curriculum resources, games, interactive quizzes, and other tools for integrating environmental issues into core curriculum subjects.

The EIC Model™, Using the Environment as an Integrating Context for Improving Student Learning
State Education & Environment Roundtable

www.seer.org/index.html

"The EIC Model™ is a system of specific, interconnected educational practices and encompasses professional development and program evaluation. Learning based on the EIC Model™ is about using a school's surroundings and community as a framework within which students can construct their own learning, guided by teachers and administrators using proven educational practices."

Energy Kid's Page
Energy Information Agency

www.eia.doe.gov/kids/onlineresources.html

This website contains energy-related materials such as history, facts, games, hands-on activities, an energy calculator, and research articles for different age groups.

	ID
NC	NA
SCHOOLS	Credit 3
CS	NA

Environmental Protection Agency Teaching Center

www.epa.gov/teachers/teachresources.htm

The EPA Teacher Resources website contains curricula and links to help educators teach environmental topics, from waste and recycling to local environmental cleanup. Curricula for a variety of age groups are available.

Florida Solar Energy Center

www.fsec.ucf.edu/en/education/k-12/index.htm

The Florida Solar Energy Center has developed several environment and energy curricula for use by teachers. The curriculum units list and adhere to Florida's Sunshine State Education Standards. They focus on a wide variety of topics including conservation, alternative energy technologies, and understanding of the natural systems around us.

Green Schools Energy Project: A Step-by-Step Manual
Youth for Environmental Sanity

http://www.yesworld.org/info/GreenSchoolsManual.pdf

A simple step-by-step guide to help students perform energy audits on their schools and then lobby for change.

Indoor Air Quality Tools for Schools Curriculum
U.S. Environmental Protection Agency

www.epa.gov/region01/eco/iaq

Designed for grades K–3, this free curriculum, offered by EPA's Region 1 (headquartered in Boston), supplements the principles and materials in the IAQ Tools for Schools Action Kit.

National Energy Foundation

http://www.nef1.org/educators.html

The National Energy Foundation provides curricula, training, and materials that promote a better understanding of energy, natural resources, and the environment. Resources include workshops, activities, and materials that can be ordered online.

National Renewable Energy Laboratory (NREL)

www.nrel.gov/education

NREL promotes excellence in teaching and learning and contributes to improving critical elements of the science, mathematics, and technology education system. It offers a variety of educational opportunities, from teacher training in renewable energy technologies to student resources and competitions.

The NEED Project

www.need.org

The NEED program includes innovative curriculum materials, professional development, evaluation tools, and recognition for schools that have implemented NEED-oriented curricula. NEED teaches the scientific concepts of energy and provides objective information about conventional and emerging energy sources—and their use and effect on the environment, economy, and society. NEED materials are available for all grade levels.

School Building Week, School of the Future Student Design Competition

sbw.cefpifoundation.org

School Building Week, under the aegis of the CEFPI Foundation & Charitable Trust, is a weeklong commemoration creating greater public awareness of the importance of well-planned, high-performance, healthy, safe, and sustainable school buildings that enhance student performance and community vitality. The Student Design Competition program challenges students to plan

	ID
NC	NA
SCHOOLS	Credit 3
CS	NA

and design school buildings that enhance their own academic performance and the vitality of the communities they serve. Curriculum for this design competition addresses the national math standards for middle schools and provides an opportunity to apply mathematical concepts relevant to students' lives.

Print Media

Environment-based Education: Creating High Performance Schools and Students. The National Environmental Education & Training Foundation, Washington, DC, September 2002.

Overview

Because some environmental issues are unique to a locale, USGBC regional councils have identified distinct environmental zones within their areas and allocated six credits to encourage design teams to focus on regional priorities. A project that earns a Regional Priority credit automatically earns one point in addition to any points awarded for that credit. Up to four extra points can be earned in this way.

Go to www.usgbc.org to learn more about the Regional Priority credits in your area.

CREDIT	TITLE
RP Credit 1	Regional Priority

	NC	SCHOOLS	CS
Credit	RP Credit 1	RP Credit 1	RP Credit 1
Points	1-4 points	1-4 points	1-4 points

Intent

To provide an incentive for the achievement of credits that address geographically specific environmental priorities.

Requirements

NC, SCHOOLS & CS

Earn 1-4 of the 6 Regional Priority credits identified by the USGBC regional councils and chapters as having environmental importance for a project's region. A database of Regional Priority credits and their geographic applicability is available on the USGBC website; http://www.usgbc.org.

One point is awarded for each Regional Priority credit achieved; no more than 4 credits identified as Regional Priority credits may be earned. Projects outside of the U.S. are not eligible for Regional Priority credits.

	RP
NC	Credit 1
SCHOOLS	Credit 1
CS	Credit 1

1. Benefits and Issues to Consider

Refer to the Benefits and Issues section under a particular Regional Priority credit.

2. Related Credits

For a list of applicable credits, visit the Regional Priority database at www.usgbc.org.

3. Summary of Referenced Standards

Refer to the standards for a particular Regional Priority credit.

4. Implementation

Refer to the Implementation section under a particular Regional Priority credit.

5. Timeline & Team

Identify Regional Priority credits early in the project timeline.

6. Calculations

Refer to the Calculations section under a particular Regional Priority credit.

7. Documentation Guidance

The Documentation Guidance section helps project teams prepare for formal certification application and complete the LEED-Online documentation requirements. Refer to the Documentation Guidance section under each Regional Priority credit and refer to LEED-Online for complete descriptions of all required documentation.

8. Examples

Refer to the Examples section under a particular Regional Priority credit.

9. Regional Variations

Refer to the Regional Variations section under a particular Regional Priority credit.

10. Operations & Maintenance Considerations

Refer to the Operations and Maintenance section under a particular Regional Priority credit.

11. Resources

See USGBC's LEED Registered Project Tools (www.usgbc.org/projecttools) for additional resources and technical information.

12. Definitions

Refer to the Definitions section under a particular Regional Priority credit.

DEFAULT OCCUPANCY COUNTS

Because of the speculative nature of core and shell construction, a project team may not know the final occupant count during the LEED certification process. Determining and demonstrating compliance with some LEED credits can prove challenging and complex. For projects that do not know the final occupant count, a default table has been developed.

Core & Shell projects that do not have final occupancy counts must utilize the default occupancy counts provided in this appendix. Projects that know the tenant occupancy must use the actual numbers, as long as the gross square foot per employee is not greater than that in the default occupancy count table. If code requirements is required gross square foot per occupant is less than those in the table, this is also acceptable. Default occupancy counts are provided for typical core and shell project types. If the buildings and circumstances are not covered in this appendix, provide documentation for comparable buildings demonstrating average gross square foot per occupant when estimating the core and shell's building occupancy.

Table 1. Default Occupancy Numbers

	Gross Square Feet per Occupant	
	Employees	Transients
General office	250	0
Retail, general	550	130
Retail or service (e.g., financial, auto)	600	130
Restaurant	435	95
Grocery store	550	115
Medical office	225	330
R&D or laboratory	400	0
Warehouse, distribution	2,500	0
Warehouse, storage	20,000	0
Hotel	1,500	700
Educational, daycare	630	105
Educational, K–12	1,300	140
Educational, postsecondary	2,100	150

Sources:
ANSI/ASHRAE/IESNA Standard 90.1–2004 (Atlanta, GA, 2004).
2001 Uniform Plumbing Code (Los Angeles, CA)
California Public Utilities Commission, 2004–2005 Database for Energy Efficiency Resources (DEER) Update Study (2008).
California State University, Capital Planning, Design and Construction Section VI, Standards for Campus Development Programs (Long Beach, CA, 2002).
City of Boulder Planning Department, Projecting Future Employment—How Much Space per Person (Boulder, 2002).
Metro, 1999 Employment Density Study (Portland, OR 1999).
American Hotel and Lodging Association, Lodging Industry Profile Washington, DC, 2008.
LEED for Core & Shell Core Committee, personal communication (2003 - 2006).
LEED for Retail Core Committee, personal communication (2007)
OWP/P, Medical Office Building Project Averages (Chicago, 2008).
OWP/P, University Master Plan Projects (Chicago, 2008).
U.S. General Services Administration, Childcare Center Design Guide (Washington, DC,2003).

The figures above may be used to determine occupancy for the following credits:

- SS Credit 4.2: Alternative Transportation, Bicycle Storage and Changing Rooms
- SS Credit 4.4: Alternative Transportation—Parking Capacity
- WE Prerequisite 1: Water Use Reduction
- WE Credit 2: Innovative Wastewater Technologies
- WE Credit 3: Water Use Reduction
- EA Prerequisite 2: Minimum Energy Performance
- EA Credit 1: Optimized Energy Performance
- IEQ Prerequisite 1: Minimum Indoor Air Quality Performance
- IEQ Credit 1: Outdoor Air Delivery Monitoring
- IEQ Credit 2: Increased Ventilation
- IEQ Credit 6: Controllability of Systems—Thermal Comfort
- IEQ Credit 7: Thermal Comfort—Design
- IEQ Credit 8: Daylight and Views

The defaults provided above are based on gross square foot per occupant and not net or leasable square foot per occupant. Gross square footage is defined as the sum of all areas on all floors of a building included within the outside faces of the exterior wall including all floor penetrations that connect one floor to another. This can be determined by taking the building foot print and multiplying it by the number of floors in the building. Projects which contain underground and/or structured parking, may exclude that area from the gross square footage used for the calculation. Other spaces such as common areas, mechanical spaces, and circulation should be included in the gross square footage of the building.

Determining FTE Occupants

If the occupancy count for full-time equivalents (FTEs) is not known, calculate the default occupancy using Equation 1. If the tenant occupancy is known, calculate the FTE for both full- and part-time employees, assuming that an 8-hour occupant has a FTE value of 1.0; part-time occupants have a FTE value based on their hours per day divided by the standard occupancy period (typically 8 hours; other durations may be used if appropriate). Use Equation 2.

Equation 1

$$\text{FTE Occupants} = \frac{\text{Building Gross Square Feet}}{\text{Gross Square Feet per FTE}}$$

Equation 2

$$\text{FTE Occupants} = \frac{\text{Occupant Hours}}{8\ \text{Hours}}$$

EXAMPLE

A mixed-used retail and commercial office building of 620,000 gross square feet has a single-shift occupancy. The transient occupant numbers used below are taken from the default data in Table 1.

Step 1. Determine the area for each occupancy type in the building, and then the gross square feet per FTE and transient occupants.

Table 2. Sample Calculations for Area per Occupancy Type

Occupancy Type	Area (sf)		
	Total	Per FTE	Per Transient Occupant
Commercial office	550,000	250	0
Retail space	50,000	550	130
Restaurant	20,000	225	95
Total Building			620,000

STEP 2

Calculate the FTE occupancy and transient occupancy for each occupancy type.

FTE Occupants

Commercial: $\dfrac{550,000}{250} = 2,200$

Retail space: $\dfrac{50,000}{550} = 90.9,\text{ or }91$

Restaurant: $\dfrac{20,000}{225} = 88.8,\text{ or }89$

Transient Occupants

Retail space: $\dfrac{50,000}{130} = 384.6,\text{ or }385$

Restaurant: $\dfrac{20,000}{95} = 211$

STEP 3

Add the FTE and transient occupants for each space to determine whole building occupancy.

Commercial:	2,200	+	0		
Retail space:	91	+	385		
Restaurant:	89	+	211		
Total	2,380	+	596	=	2976

CORE & SHELL ENERGY MODELING GUIDELINES

These guidelines are intended to ensure that projects in different markets approach the energy modeling requirements in a similar manner, and to establish a minimum benchmark for energy optimization. The energy modeling is based on the ANSI/ASHRAE/IESNA 90.1–2007 Building Performance Rating Method. This can be used for developing a whole building model when the core and shell work is known but the tenant space development is unknown.

Tenant space is defined as an area that meets all the following conditions:

- It is served by separate, exclusive components.

- Its components are specifically designed for the area.

- All appropriate energy-using components are metered and apportioned and/or billed to the tenant.

- The tenant will pay for these components.

The core and shell building is defined as the parts of the building that are not tenant space. Any constraints or guidance issued to the tenant, such as a maximum level of lighting density or restrictions on occupancy type, must be outlined in the tenant lease or sales agreement (see Appendix 4).

Step 1. Model the proposed building.

Core and Shell Building

- Model the heating, ventilation, and air-conditioning (HVAC) system as described in the design documents. If the HVAC system is not yet designed, use the same HVAC system as the baseline model, per ANSI/ASHRAE/IESNA Standard 90.1–2007, Table G3.1.1A.

- Model the building envelope as shown in the architectural drawings.

- Model the lighting power as shown in the design documents for all core and shell spaces.

Tenant Spaces

- If the team is pursuing any additional energy-saving opportunities not associated with the core and shell areas, outline the opportunities or requirements in the tenant lease or sales agreement (see Appendix 4). Tenant space occupancy numbers must be determined by using the default space occupancies outlined in Appendix 1.

- Model electric meters for lighting power in tenant spaces. Choose a space type classification for the building spaces in Appendix 1. Use lighting levels shown in ANSI/ASHRAE/IESNA 90.1–2007, Table 9.6.1 for the space type classification, or Table 9.5.1 for overall building type. If the tenant lighting is designed and installed as part of the core and shell work, the project team may model the designed lighting systems.

- Model separate meters for tenant plug loads and process loads. Use the values in Table 1 to model tenant plug loads, or provide documentation for the modeled loads (see the process energy section of EA Credit 1). These default plug loads do not necessarily reflect all process loads; the values are recommended but not required to achieve the 25% process loads.

CS APPENDIX 2

Table 1. Default Tenant Receptacle Loads, by Occupancy Type

Occupancy Type	Receptacle Load (W/sf)
General office	1.5
Retail, general	1.35
Retail, service	1.35
Restaurant	0.8
Grocery store	2.5
Medical office building	1.5
R&D or laboratory building	1.4
Warehouse, distribution	0.65

Source: Derived from energy modeling exercises undertaken by OWP/P.

STEP 2. Model the baseline building.

Core & Shell Building

- Model the baseline building HVAC system per ANSI/ASHRAE/IESNA 90.1–2007, Table G3.1.1A.

- For the building envelope, comply with the prescriptive requirements of ANSI/ASHRAE/IESNA 90.1–2007.

- Model the lighting power by the space type classification of ANSI/ASHRAE/IESNA 90.1–2007, Chart 9.6.1.

Tenant Spaces

- Model separate electric meters for the lighting in the tenant spaces. Use the same lighting power as modeled in the proposed building, unless efficiencies can be supported by a tenant sales or lease agreement.

- Model separate meters for receptacle loads and process loads in the tenant scope. Use the same values for receptacle loads as used in the proposed building.

STEP 3. Perform energy simulations of the proposed building and the baseline building.

STEP 4. Compare the resulting annual energy costs.

From the simulation, determine the annual energy costs of the budget building and the design building, then calculate the percentage savings for annual energy costs.

Verify that at least 25% of the overall energy cost is process load. If process loads are less than 25% of overall energy cost, prepare supporting documentation or increase plug loads in the energy model to meet the requirement. Process loads greater than 25% are acceptable.

Renewable energy should be included in the energy model or accounted for using the exceptional calculation method.

LEED FOR CORE & SHELL PROJECT SCOPE

The checklist below represents an interactive LEED-Online checklist that helps project teams identify and document the scope of Core & Shell projects. The checklist is a summary description of the building occupancy and its full-time equivalent (FTE) employees and transient occupants.

The checklist also identifies who has control of each building system—that is, the party that has design control and oversight of the construction activities for a given system. The core and shell developer may have sole control over a system, or the tenant may have independent control over a system; alternatively, the tenant may have control over a system but the developer may enforce system requirements through a sales agreement or tenant lease, thereby influencing its design and/or construction. Refer to Appendix 4, Tenant Lease and Sales Agreement, for further information on this option.

Portions of systems may be controlled by both the core and shell developer and the tenant, or the systems listed may not be a part of the project at all. Complete the checklist to reflect varied conditions; a team may check zero, one, or multiple boxes for each system listed below.

Building Use and Occupancy

Project name	
Size (gross sf)	

Occupancy Type	Percentage of Total Building	Occupancy Type Area (gross sf)	Area per FTE (gross sf)	FTEs	Area per Transient (gross sf)	Transients
General office						
Retail, general						
Retail, service						
Restaurant						
Grocery store						
Medical office building						
R&D or laboratory building						
Warehouse, distribution						
Warehouse, storage						
Hotel						
Educational, daycare						
Educational, K–12						
Educational, postsecondary						
Other (specify):						
Total building occupancy						
Total FTEs						
Total transients						

Control of Building Systems

Fill in the table below based on the division of work throughout the project. In some cases, multiple or no boxes may be checked.

	Main Lobby			Main Corridor			Secondary Lobby, Corridors			Buildouts			HVAC			Electrical			Plumbing		
Floor finishes																					
Wall finishes																					
Ceiling finishes																					
Air terminal equipment																					
Air inlets and outlets																					
Light fixtures																					
Lighting controls																					
AHUs/RTUs/ Air supply equipment																					
Chillers																					
Cooling tower																					
Boilers																					
Primary ductwork																					
Electrical panels																					
Switchgear																					
Bus duct																					
Water closets																					
Urinals																					
Showers																					
Public lavatory faucets, aerators																					
Public metering lavatory faucets, aerators																					
Kitchen sinks																					
Janitor sinks																					
Metering faucets																					
	Owner/Developer	Tenant	Lease Agreement	Owner/Developer	Tenant	Lease Agreement	Owner/Developer	Tenant	Lease Agreement	Owner/Developer	Tenant	Lease Agreement	Owner/Developer	Tenant	Lease Agreement	Owner/Developer	Tenant	Lease Agreement	Owner/Developer	Tenant	Lease Agreement

TENANT LEASE OR SALES AGREEMENT

Overview

In a LEED for Core & Shell building, tenants can choose whether to pursue LEED for Commercial Interiors without affecting the building's LEED for Core & Shell certification. However, if a developer makes technical requirements from the LEED for Core & Shell Rating System part of a binding lease or sales agreement, the project may be able to earn additional points for credits with technical requirements not addressed in the Core & Shell project design and construction scope. By encouraging green building practices in the tenant's scope of work, Core & Shell projects with a limited scope can achieve credits for activities that would otherwise be beyond their design and construction control.

Compliance through a binding tenant lease or sales agreement can be pursued as an alternative to or in conjunction with the standard approach to LEED for Core & Shell credit documentation. Clearly identify which components of the credit will be implemented as part of the developer's scope of work, and which portions will be part of the tenants' scope of work and enforced through binding tenant lease or sales agreements.

Requirements

The technical credit requirements must be incorporated into a legally binding document signed by both the developer and the tenant. The document must explicitly state performance requirements for the tenant work, such as lighting power density (watts per square foot), plumbing fixture flow rates, or bike racks and showers. Refer to the requirements and LEED-Online submittal documentation for the chosen credits.

Guidelines, such as the tenant design and construction guidelines required for SS Credit 9, and other nonbinding documents do not meet the requirements for this compliance method. Although all projects are encouraged to develop design and construction guidelines that help tenants adopt green practices, only legally binding documents satisfy the requirements of the Tenant Lease or Sales Agreement compliance method.

Documentation Guidance

Submit sample agreements when applying for precertification as well as certification.

For specific documentation requirements, refer to the selected credits in LEED-Online.

Applicable Credits

CASE A

> Submittal documentation for Case A credits must include data from the entire project building, including tenant-occupied spaces. When documenting compliance with Case A credits, project teams should treat anticipated tenant work as neutral. Or, if claiming performance improvements based on anticipated tenant work, such data must be supported by tenant sales and/or lease agreements.
>
> - WE Prerequisite 1
> - WE Credit 3
> - EA Prerequisite 2
> - EA Credit 1 (performance path only)

CASE B

Submittal documentation for Case B credits need only include data from the Core & Shell project scope. If the project team wishes to claim performance improvements based on anticipated tenant work, such data must be supported by tenant sales and/or lease agreements.

- WE Credit 2
- EA Credit 2

CASE C

Submittal documentation for Case C credits must include data from the entire project building. In some cases, the Core & Shell project will be limited such that compliance cannot be documented without including data from anticipated tenant work. In this instance, such data must be supported by tenant sales and/or lease agreements.

- SS Credit 4.2
- EA Prerequisite 3
- EA Credit 4
- IEQ Prerequisite 1
- IEQ Credit 1
- IEQ Prerequisite 2
- IEQ Credit 2
- IEQ Credit 5
- IEQ Credit 6

Exemplary Performance

Developers can achieve an Innovation in Design point for exemplary performance by requiring their tenants to achieve exemplary performance in certain credits. To earn points this way with a lease or sales agreement, first achieve the credit requirements for the Core & Shell submittal. Additionally, provide documentation and meet the requirements of the Tenant Lease or Sales Agreement compliance path outlined above.

Exemplary performance under Tenant Lease or Sales Agreement is available for the following credits:

- SS Credit 8: Light Pollution Reduction. Require automatic controls within 100% of the tenant space.

- EA Credit 2: On-site Renewable Energy. Require the tenant to achieve 5% on-site renewable energy.

- IEQ Credit 3: Construction IAQ Management Plan. Require the tenant to adhere to a construction IAQ management plan.

- IEQ Credit 4: Low-Emitting Materials. Require the tenant to comply with the requirements in IEQ Credit 4 (4.1, 4.2, 4.3, and 4.4) throughout the tenant space.

LEED FOR CORE & SHELL PRECERTIFICATION GUIDANCE

Overview

Precertification is formal recognition by GBCI that the owner or developer has established LEED for Core & Shell certification as a goal. Precertification is unique to LEED for Core & Shell, and projects may pursue it at their discretion. It gives core and shell building owners and developers a marketing tool to attract potential tenants and financiers who recognize the benefits of a LEED-certified building. Precertification generally occurs early in the design process and is based on declared goals and the intent to use green features, not actual achievement of these features.

Process

Once a project is registered under the LEED for Core & Shell Rating System, the project team may apply for precertification. It is not required, however, and precertification is not certification itself or a promise of eventual certification.

Because much of the value of precertification occurs early in a project's development, both the documentation and the review processes are less comprehensive than for a full certification application. Teams should set carefully considered, realistic goals for the project. They must confirm that the intended design and construction strategies meet the requirements of each LEED Core & Shell prerequisite and credit that is pursued. As with the LEED certification process, achievement of all prerequisites is required to earn LEED precertification.

As with full certification, project teams complete documentation for each prerequisite and credit in LEED-Online. Precertification documentation requirements differ, however, in that they are focused on verification of design intentions rather than actions. Project teams will be required to demonstrate their intentions through narratives, projected calculations, and declarations. In addition, projects must provide general project data and representative project drawings. LEED-Online contains complete precertification documentation requirements for each Core & Shell prerequisite and credit.

Precertification reviews occur in two phases, the preliminary review and the final review. After the preliminary review, project teams have the chance to respond to initial review comments and update any documentation as necessary.

LEED for Core & Shell precertification can be awarded at the project's expected certification level (Certified, Silver, Gold or Platinum). A project approved for LEED for Core & Shell precertification receives a certificate and letter.

Adapted (or introduced) plants reliably grow well in a given habitat with minimal winter protection, pest control, fertilization, or irrigation once their root systems are established. Adapted plants are considered low maintenance and not invasive.

Adaptive reuse is the renovation of a space for a purpose different from the original.

An **adhesive** is any substance used to bond 1 surface to another by attachment. Adhesives include bonding primers, adhesive primers, and adhesive primers for plastics. (SCAQMD Rule 1168)

Aerosol adhesive is an aerosol product in which the spray mechanism is permanently housed in a nonrefillable can. Designed for hand-held application, these products do not need ancillary hoses or spray equipment. Aerosol adhesives include special-purpose spray adhesives, mist spray adhesives, and web spray adhesives. (SCAQMD Rule 1168)

Agrifiber products are made from agricultural fiber. Examples include particleboard, medium-density fiberboard (MDF), plywood, oriented-strand board (OSB), wheatboard, and strawboard.

Air-conditioning is the process of treating air to meet the requirements of a conditioned space by controlling its temperature, humidity, cleanliness, and distribution. (ASHRAE 62.1–2007)

Air-handling units (AHUs) are mechanical indirect heating, ventilating, or air-conditioning systems in which the air is treated or handled by equipment located outside the rooms served, usually at a central location, and conveyed to and from the rooms by a fan and a system of distributing ducts. (NEEB, 1997 edition)

Albedo is synonymous with **solar reflectance.**

Alternative daily cover is material (other than earthen material) that is placed on the surface of the active face of a municipal solid waste landfill at the end of each operating day to control vectors, fires, odors, blowing litter, and scavenging.

Alternative-fuel vehicles use low-polluting, nongasoline fuels such as electricity, hydrogen, propane, compressed natural gas, liquid natural gas, methanol, and ethanol. In LEED, efficient gas-electric hybrid vehicles are included in this group.

Anticorrosive paints are coatings formulated and recommended for use in preventing the corrosion of ferrous metal substrates.

Aquatic systems are ecologically designed treatment systems in which a diverse community of biological organisms (e.g., bacteria, plants, fish) treat wastewater.

An **aquifer** is an underground water-bearing rock formation or group of formations that supply groundwater, wells, or springs.

Architectural porous sealant primer is a substance used as a sealant on porous materials.

An **area-weighted SRI is** a weighted average calculation that may be performed for buildings with multiple roof surfaces to demonstrate that the total roof area has an average solar reflectance index equal to or greater than that of a theoretical roof 75% of whose surfaces have an SRI of 78 and 25% have an SRI of 30.

An **assembly** can be either a product formulated from multiple materials (e.g., concrete) or a product made up of subcomponents (e.g., a workstation).

GLOSSARY

Assembly recycled content is the percentage of material in a product that is either postconsumer or preconsumer recycled content. It is determined by dividing the weight of the recycled content by the overall weight of the assembly.

The **attendance boundary** is used by school districts to determine which students attend what school based on where they live.

Audiovisual (A/V) media are slides, film, video, sound recordings, and other such devices used to present information.

Automatic fixture sensors are motion detectors that automatically turn on and turn off lavatories, sinks, water closets, and urinals. Sensors can be hard wired or battery operated.

Baseline building performance is the annual energy cost for a building design intended for use as a baseline for rating above standard design, as defined in ANSI/ASHRAE/IESNA Standard 90.1–2007, Informative Appendix G.

Baseline irrigation water use is the amount of water used by conventional irrigation in the region.

Basis of design includes design information necessary to accomplish the owner's project requirements, including system descriptions, indoor environmental quality criteria, design assumptions, and references to applicable codes, standards, regulations, and guidelines.

Bicycle racks, in LEED, include outdoor bicycle racks, bicycle lockers, and indoor bicycle storage rooms.

Biochemical oxygen demand is a measure of how fast biological organisms use up oxygen in a body of water. It is used in water quality management and assessment, ecology, and environmental science.

Biodiversity is the variety of life in all forms, levels, and combinations, including ecosystem diversity, species diversity, and genetic diversity.

Biofuel-based energy systems are electrical power systems that run on renewable fuels derived from organic materials, such as wood by-products and agricultural waste. In LEED, biofuels include untreated wood waste (e.g., mill residues), agricultural crops or waste, animal waste and other organic waste, and landfill gas.

Biofuel-based systems are power systems that run on renewable fuels derived from organic materials, such as wood by-products and agricultural waste. Examples of biofuels include untreated wood waste, agricultural crops and residues, animal waste, other organic waste, and landfill gas.

Biological control is the use of chemical or physical water treatments to inhibit bacterial growth in cooling towers.

Biomass is plant material from trees, grasses, or crops that can be converted to heat energy to produce electricity.

Blackwater definitions vary, but wastewater from toilets and urinals is always considered blackwater. Wastewater from kitchen sinks (perhaps differentiated by the use of a garbage disposal), showers, or bathtubs is considered blackwater under some state or local codes.

Bleed-off, or **blowdown**, is the release of a portion of the recirculating water from a cooling tower; this water carries dissolved solids that can cause mineral buildup.

The **breathing zone** is the region within an occupied space between 3 and 6 feet above the floor and more than 2 feet from walls or fixed air-conditioning equipment. (AHSRAE 62.1–2007)

A **brownfield** is real property whose use may be complicated by the presence or possible presence of a hazardous substance, pollutant, or contaminant.

A **building automation system** (**BAS**) uses computer-based monitoring to coordinate, organize, and optimize building control subsystems, including lighting, equipment scheduling, and alarm reporting.

Building density is the floor area of the building divided by the total area of the site (square feet per acre).

Building footprint is the area on a project site used by the building structure, defined by the perimeter of the building plan. Parking lots, landscapes, and other nonbuilding facilities are not included in the building footprint.

A **campus or private bus** is a bus or shuttle service that is privately operated and not available to the general public. In LEED, a campus or private bus line that falls within 1/4 mile of the project site and provides transportation service to the public can contribute to earning credits.

Carbon dioxide (**CO_2**) **levels** are an indicator of ventilation effectiveness inside buildings. CO_2 concentrations greater than 530 ppm above outdoor CO_2 conditions generally indicate inadequate ventilation. Absolute concentrations of CO_2 greater than 800 to 1,000 ppm generally indicate poor air quality for breathing.

A **carpool** is an arrangement by which 2 or more people share a vehicle for transportation.

Chain-of-custody (**COC**) is a tracking procedure for a product from the point of harvest or extraction to its end use, including all successive stages of processing, transformation, manufacturing, and distribution.

Chain-of-custody certification is awarded to companies that produce, sell, promote, or trade forest products after audits verify proper accounting of material flows and proper use of the Forest Stewardship Council name and logo. The COC certificate number is listed on invoices for nonlabeled products to document that an entity has followed FSC guidelines for product accounting.

Chemical treatment includes the use of biocidal, conditioning, dispersant, and scale-inhibiting chemicals to control biological growth, scale, and corrosion in cooling towers. Alternatives to conventional chemical treatment include ozonation, ionization, and exposure to ultraviolet light.

Chlorofluorocarbons (**CFCs**) are hydrocarbons that are used as refrigerants and cause depletion of the stratospheric ozone layer.

Churn is the movement of workstations and people within a space.

Climate change refers to any significant change in measures of climate (such as temperature, precipitation, or wind) lasting for an extended period (decades or longer). (U.S. Environmental Protection Agency, 2008)

A **coating** is applied to beautify, protect, or provide a barrier to a surface. **Flat coatings** register a gloss of less than 15 on an 85-degree meter or less than 5 on a 60-degree meter. **Nonflat coatings** register a gloss of 5 or greater on a 60-degree meter and a gloss of 15 or greater on an 85-degree meter. (SCAQMD Rule 1113)

Combined heat and power (**CHP**), or cogeneration, generates both electrical power and thermal energy from a single fuel source.

Comfort criteria are specific design conditions that take into account temperature, humidity, air speed, outdoor temperature, outdoor humidity, seasonal clothing, and expected activity. (ASHRAE 55–2004)

Commissioning (**Cx**) is the process of verifying and documenting that a building and all of its systems and assemblies are planned, designed, installed, tested, operated, and maintained to meet the owner's project requirements.

The **commissioning authority** (**CxA**) is the individual designated to organize, lead, and review the completion of commissioning process activities. The CxA facilitates communication among the owner, designer, and contractor to ensure that complex systems are installed and function in accordance with the owner's project requirements.

The **commissioning cycle** is the schedule of activities related to existing building commissioning, including the investigation and analysis, implementation, and ongoing commissioning.

The **commissioning plan** is a document that outlines the organization, schedule, allocation of resources, and documentation requirements of the commissioning process.

The **commissioning process** is a systematic quality-focused effort to ensure that building systems are designed, specified, procured, installed, and functioning in accordance with the owner's intent. The process uses planning, documentation, and verification of testing to review and oversee the activities of both designer and constructor.

The **commissioning report** documents the commissioning process, including a commissioning program overview, identification of the commissioning team, and description of the commissioning process activities.

Commissioning specification is the contract language used in the construction documents to detail the objective, scope, and implementation of the construction and acceptance phases of the commissioning process as developed in the design phase of the commissioning plan. This allows the construction contractor to ensure that these activities are considered in proposals for the construction work.

The **commissioning team** includes those people responsible for working together to carry out the commissioning process.

Completed design area is the total area of finished ceilings, floors, full-height walls and demountable partitions, interior doors, and built-in case goods in the completed project. It does not include exterior windows and doors.

Composite wood consists of wood or plant particles or fibers bonded by a synthetic resin or binder. Examples include particleboard, medium-density fiberboard (MDF), plywood, oriented-strand board (OSB), wheatboard, and strawboard.

Composting toilet system. See nonwater toilet system.

The **Comprehensive Environmental Response, Compensation, and Liability Act**, or CERCLA, is more commonly known as Superfund. Enacted in 1980, CERCLA addresses abandoned or historical waste sites and contamination by taxing the chemical and petroleum industries and providing federal authority to respond to releases of hazardous substances.

A **compressed workweek** rearranges the standard workweek (5 consecutive 8-hour days in a week), increasing the daily hours and decreasing the number of days in the work cycle. For example, instead of working 8-hour days Monday through Friday, employees work 10-hour days for 4 days per week, or 9-hour days for 9 of 10 consecutive days.

Concentration ratio is the ratio of the level of dissolved solids in the recirculating water to the level found in the entering makeup water. A higher concentration ratio results from a lower bleed-off rate; increasing the ratio above a certain point, however, leads to scaling, and water savings diminish after a certain level. This ratio is also called the cycles of concentration. Cycles refers to the number of times dissolved minerals in the water are concentrated compared with makeup water, not to water flow over the tower or to on-off cycles.

Conditioned space is the part of a building that is heated or cooled, or both, for the comfort of occupants. (ASHRAE 62.1–2007)

A **constructed wetland** is an engineered system designed to simulate natural wetland functions for water purification. In LEED, constructed wetlands are essentially treatment systems that remove contaminants from wastewater.

A **construction IAQ management plan** outlines measures to minimize contamination in a specific project building during construction and describes procedures to flush the building of contaminants prior to occupancy.

Construction and demolition debris includes waste and recyclables generated from construction and from the renovation, demolition, or deconstruction of preexisting structures. It does not include land-clearing debris, such as soil, vegetation, and rocks.

Construction, demolition, and land-clearing debris includes all of the above plus soil, vegetation, and rock from land clearing.

Contaminants are unwanted airborne elements that may reduce indoor air quality. (ASHRAE 62.1–2007)

Controls are mechanisms that allow occupants to direct power to devices (e.g., lights, heaters) or adjust devices or systems within in a range (e.g., brightness, temperature).

Conventional irrigation refers to the most common irrigation system used in the region where the building is located. A conventional irrigation system commonly uses pressure to deliver water and distributes it through sprinkler heads above the ground.

A **cooling tower** uses water to absorb heat from air-conditioning systems and regulate air temperature in a facility.

Core learning spaces are areas for educational activities where the primary functions are teaching and learning. (ANSI S12.60–2002)

Curfew hours are locally determined times when lighting restrictions are imposed. When no local or regional restrictions are in place, 10:00 p.m. is regarded as a default curfew time.

Daylighting is the controlled admission of natural light into a space, used to reduce or eliminate electric lighting.

Daylight-responsive lighting controls are photosensors used in conjunction with other switching and dimming devices to control the amount of artificial lighting in relationship to the amount and quality of natural daylight.

Densely occupied space is an area with a design occupant density of 25 people or more per 1,000 square feet (40 square feet or less per person).

Density factor (k_d) is a coefficient used in calculating the landscape coefficient. It modifies the evapotranspiration rate to reflect the water use of a plant or group of plants, particularly with reference to the density of the plant material.

Design light output is the light output of lamps at 40% of their useful life.

The **development footprint** is the area affected by development or by project site activity. Hardscape, access roads, parking lots, nonbuilding facilities, and the building itself are all included in the development footprint.

A **district energy system** is a central energy conversion plant and transmission and distribution system that provides thermal energy to a group of buildings (e.g., a central cooling plant on a university campus). Central energy systems that provide only electricity are not included.

Downstream equipment consists of all heating or cooling systems, equipment, and controls located within the project building and site associated with transporting thermal energy into heated or cooled spaces. This includes the thermal connection or interface with the district energy system, secondary distribution systems in the building, and terminal units.

Drip irrigation delivers water at low pressure through buried mains and submains. From the submains, water is distributed to the soil through a network of perforated tubes or emitters. Drip irrigation is a high-efficiency type of microirrigation.

Durable goods have a useful life of 2 years or more and are replaced infrequently or may require capital program outlays. Examples include furniture, office equipment, appliances, external power adapters, televisions, and audiovisual equipment.

The **durable goods waste stream** consists of durable goods leaving the project site that are fully depreciated and have reached the end of their useful lives for normal business operations.

Ecological restoration is the process of assisting in the recovery and management of ecological integrity and includes biodiversity, ecological processes and structures, regional and historical context, and sustainable cultural practices.

Ecologically appropriate site features are natural site elements that maintain or restore the ecological integrity of the site. Examples include native or adapted vegetation, water bodies, exposed rock, unvegetated ground, and other features that provide habitat value and are part of the historic natural landscape.

An **economizer** is a device used to make building systems more energy efficient. Examples include HVAC enthalpy controls, which are based on humidity and temperature.

An **ecosystem** is a basic unit of nature that includes a community of organisms and their nonliving environment linked by biological, chemical, and physical processes.

electrical conductivity (EC) meter measures the amount of nutrients and salt in water.

Elemental mercury is pure mercury (rather than a mercury-containing compound), the vapor of which is commonly used in fluorescent and other lamp types.

Embodied energy is the energy used during the entire life cycle of a product, including its manufacture, transportation, and disposal, as well as the inherent energy captured within the product itself.

Emissions reduction reporting is the calculating, tracking, and documenting of the greenhouse gas emissions that result directly from energy use and other operations of a building.

Emissivity is the ratio of the radiation emitted by a surface to the radiation emitted by a black body at the same temperature.

An **endangered species** is threatened with extinction because of harmful human activities or environmental factors.

An **energy audit** identifies how much energy a building uses and the purposes for which it is used, and identifies efficiency and cost-reduction opportunities. The American Society of Heating, Refrigerating and Air-Conditioning Engineers uses 3 levels of energy audits: walk-through analysis, energy survey and analysis, and detailed analysis of capital-intensive modifications.

Energy conservation measures are installations or modifications of equipment or systems intended to reduce energy use and costs.

An **energy simulation model**, or **energy model**, is a computer-generated representation of the anticipated energy consumption of a building. It permits a comparison of energy performance, given proposed energy efficiency measures, with the baseline.

An **ENERGY STAR** rating is a measure of a building's energy performance compared with that of similar buildings, as determined by the ENERGY STAR Portfolio Manager. A score of 50 represents average building performance.

Enhanced commissioning is a set of best practices that go beyond fundamental commissioning to ensure that building systems perform as intended by the owner. These practices include designating a commissioning authority prior to the construction documents phase, conducting commissioning design reviews, reviewing contractor submittals, developing a systems manual, verifying operator training, and performing a postoccupancy operations review.

Entryway systems are designed to capture dirt and other debris from occupants entering the building; they can be open floor grates or grilles set over a recessed area.

Environmental tobacco smoke (**ETS**), or secondhand smoke, consists of airborne particles emitted from the burning end of cigarettes, pipes, and cigars, and is exhaled by smokers. These particles contain about 4,000 compounds, up to 50 of which are known to cause cancer.

Erosion is a combination of processes or events by which materials of the earth's surface are loosened, dissolved, or worn away and transported by natural agents (e.g., water, wind, or gravity).

Eutrophication is the increase in chemical nutrients, such as the nitrogen and phosphorus often found in fertilizers, in an ecosystem. The added nutrients stimulate excessive plant growth, promoting algal blooms or weeds. The enhanced plant growth reduces oxygen in the land and water, reducing water quality and fish and other animal populations.

Evapotranspiration is the loss of water by evaporation from the soil and by transpiration from plants. It is expressed in millimeters per unit of time.

Evapotranspiration (**ET**) rate is the amount of water lost from a vegetated surface in units of water depth. It is expressed in millimeters per unit of time.

Exfiltration is air leakage through cracks and interstices and through the ceilings, floors, and walls.

Exhaust air is removed from a space and discharged outside the building by mechanical or natural ventilation systems.

Existing area is the total area of the building structure, core, and envelope that existed when the project area was selected. Exterior windows and doors are not included.

Existing building commissioning, or **retrocommissioning**, involves developing a building operation plan that identifies current operating requirements and needs, conducting tests to determine whether building systems are performing optimally in accordance with the plan, and making any necessary repairs or changes.

Facility alterations and additions are discussed in the Introduction of the LEED for Green Building Operations & Maintenance.

Fairtrade is a product certification system overseen by FLO International, which identifies products that meet certain environmental, labor, and development standards.

Fly ash is the solid residue derived from incineration processes. Fly ash can be used as a substitute for Portland cement in concrete.

The **Food Alliance** certifies foods from sustainable farms and ranches that produce natural products, ensure quality control and food safety, responsibly manage water and energy resources, emphasize recycling and responsible waste management, provide a safe work environment, and commit to continuous improvement of sustainable practices.

A **footcandle** (**fc**) is a measure of light falling on a given surface. One footcandle is defined as the quantity of light falling on a 1-square-foot area from a 1 candela light source at a distance of 1 foot (which equals 1 lumen per square foot). Footcandles can be measured both horizontally and vertically by a footcandle meter or light meter.

Formaldehyde is a naturally occurring VOC found in small amounts in animals and plants but is carcinogenic and an irritant to most people when present in high concentrations, causing headaches, dizziness, mental impairment, and other symptoms. When present in the air at levels above 0.1 ppm, it can cause watery eyes; burning sensations in the eyes, nose, and throat; nausea; coughing; chest tightness; wheezing; skin rashes; and asthmatic and allergic reactions.

Fuel-efficient vehicles have achieved a minimum green score of 40 according to the annual vehicle-rating guide of the American Council for an Energy Efficient Economy.

A **full cutoff luminaire** has zero candela intensity at an angle of 90 degrees above the vertical axis (nadir or straight down) and at all angles greater than 90 degrees from straight down. Additionally, the candela per 1,000 lamp lumens does not numerically exceed 100 (10%) at an angle of 80 degrees above nadir. This applies to all lateral angles around the luminaire.

Full-time equivalent (**FTE**) represents a regular building occupant who spends 40 hours per week in the project building. Part-time or overtime occupants have FTE values based on their hours per week divided by 40. Multiple shifts are included or excluded depending on the intent and requirements of the credit.

Full-time-equivalent building occupants is a measure equal to the total number of hours all building occupants spend in the building during the peak 8-hour occupancy period divided by 8 hours.

In a **fully shielded** exterior light fixture, the lower edge of the shield is at or below the lowest edge of the lamp, such that all light shines down.

Fundamental commissioning is a set of essential best practices used to ensure that building performance requirements have been identified early in the project's development and to verify that the designed systems have been installed in compliance with those requirements. These practices include designating a commissioning authority, documenting the owner's project requirements and basis of design, incorporating commissioning requirements into the construction documents, establishing a commissioning plan, verifying installation and performance of specified building systems, and completing a summary commissioning report.

Furniture, fixtures, and equipment are all items that are not base-building elements. Examples include lamps, electronics, desks, chairs, and tables.

Geothermal energy is electricity generated by harnessing hot water or steam from within the earth.

Geothermal heating systems use pipes to transfer heat from underground steam or hot water for heating, cooling, and hot water. The system retrieves heat during cool months and returns heat in summer months.

Glare is any excessively bright source of light within the visual field that creates discomfort or loss in visibility.

Graywater is defined by the Uniform Plumbing Code (UPC) in its Appendix G, Gray Water Systems for Single-Family Dwellings, as "untreated household waste water which has not come into contact with toilet waste. Greywater includes used water from bathtubs, showers, bathroom wash basins, and water from clothes-washer and laundry tubs. It must not include waste water from kitchen sinks or dishwashers." The International Plumbing Code (IPC) defines graywater in its Appendix C, Gray

Water Recycling Systems, as "waste water discharged from lavatories, bathtubs, showers, clothes washers and laundry sinks." Some states and local authorities allow kitchen sink wastewater to be included in graywater. Other differences with the UPC and IPC definitions can likely be found in state and local codes. Project teams should comply with graywater definitions as established by the authority having jurisdiction in the project area.

Green cleaning is the use of cleaning products and practices that have lower environmental impacts than conventional products and practices.

Green power is synonymous with renewable energy.

Green-e is a program established by the Center for Resource Solutions to both promote green electricity products and provide consumers with a rigorous and nationally recognized method to identify those products.

Greenfields are sites not previously developed or graded that could support open space, habitat, or agriculture.

Greenhouse gases (GHGs) absorb and emit radiation at specific wavelengths within the spectrum of thermal infrared radiation emitted by Earth's surface, clouds, and the atmosphere itself. Increased concentrations of greenhouse gases are a root cause of global climate change.

Group (shared) multioccupant spaces include conference rooms, classrooms, and other indoor spaces used as a place of congregation.

Halons are substances, used in fire-suppression systems and fire extinguishers, that deplete the stratospheric ozone layer.

Hard surface flooring includes vinyl, linoleum, laminate flooring, wood flooring, rubber flooring, wall base, and associated sundries.

Hardscape consists of the inanimate elements of the building landscaping. Examples include pavement, roadways, stone walls, concrete paths and sidewalks, and concrete, brick, and tile patios.

Heat island effect refers to the absorption of heat by hardscapes, such as dark, nonreflective pavement and buildings, and its radiation to surrounding areas. Particularly in urban areas, other sources may include vehicle exhaust, air-conditioners, and street equipment; reduced airflow from tall buildings and narrow streets exacerbates the effect.

Hertz (Hz) is the unit used to describe the frequency of vibrations (cycles) per second; 1 Hz equals 1 cycle per second.

Horizontal footcandles occur on a horizontal surface. They can be added together arithmetically when more than 1 source provides light to the same surface.

HVAC systems are equipment, distribution systems, and terminals that provide the processes of heating, ventilating, or air-conditioning. (ASHRAE 90.1–2007)

Hybrid vehicles use a gasoline engine to drive an electric generator and use the electric generator and/or storage batteries to power electric motors that drive the vehicle's wheels.

Hydro energy is electricity produced from the downhill flow of water from rivers or lakes.

Hydrochlorofluorocarbons (HCFCs) are refrigerants that cause significantly less depletion of the stratospheric ozone layer than chlorofluorocarbons.

Hydrofluorocarbons (HFCs) are refrigerants that do not deplete the stratospheric ozone layer but may have high global warming potential. HFCs are not considered environmentally benign.

Hydrology is the study of water occurrence, distribution, movement, and balances in an ecosystem.

Hydropower is electricity produced from the downhill flow of water from rivers or lakes.

Impervious surfaces have a perviousness of less than 50% and promote runoff of water instead of infiltration into the subsurface. Examples include parking lots, roads, sidewalks, and plazas.

An **incinerator** is a furnace or container for burning waste materials.

Individual occupant spaces are standard workstations where workers conduct individual tasks.

Indoor adhesive, sealant, or **sealant primer** product is an adhesive or sealant product applied on-site, inside the building's weatherproofing system.

Indoor air quality (**IAQ**) is the nature of air inside the space that affects the health and well-being of building occupants. It is considered acceptable when there are no known contaminants at harmful concentrations and a substantial majority (80% or more) of the occupants do not express dissatisfaction. (ASHRAE 62.1–2007)

Indoor carpet systems are carpet, carpet adhesive, or carpet cushion products installed on-site inside the building's weatherproofing system.

Indoor composite wood or **agrifiber is a** product installed inside the building's weatherproofing system.

Indoor paints or **coating products** are applied inside a building's weatherproofing system.

Infiltration is uncontrolled air leakage into conditioned spaces through unintentional openings in ceilings, floors, and walls from unconditioned spaces or the outdoors. (ASHRAE 62.1–2007)

Infiltration basins and trenches are devices used to encourage subsurface infiltration of runoff volumes through temporary surface storage. Basins are ponds that can store large volumes of stormwater. They need to drain within 72 hours to maintain aerobic conditions and be available for future storm events. Trenches are similar to infiltration basins but are shallower and function as a subsurface reservoir for stormwater volumes. Pretreatment to remove sediment and oil may be necessary to avoid clogging infiltration devices. Infiltration trenches are more common in areas where infiltration basins are not possible.

Infrared (or thermal) emittance is a parameter between 0 and 1 (or 0% and 100%) that indicates the ability of a material to shed infrared radiation (heat). The wavelength range for this radiant energy is roughly 5 to 40 micrometers. Most building materials (including glass) are opaque in this part of the spectrum and have an emittance of roughly 0.9. Materials such as clean, bare metals are the most important exceptions to the 0.9 rule. Thus clean, untarnished galvanized steel has low emittance, and aluminum roof coatings have intermediate emittance levels.

In situ remediation involves treatment of contaminants using technologies such as injection wells or reactive trenches. These methods employ the natural hydraulic gradient of groundwater and usually require only minimal disturbance of the site.

An **installation inspection** examines components of the building systems to determine whether they are installed properly and ready for systems performance testing.

Integrated pest management (**IPM**) is the coordinated use of knowledge about pests, the environment, and pest prevention and control methods to minimize pest infestation and damage by the most economical means while minimizing hazards to people, property, and the environment.

Interior lighting power allowance is the maximum lighting power (in watts) allowed for the interior of a building.

Interior nonstructural components reuse is determined by dividing the area of retained components by the larger of (1) the area of the prior condition or (2) the area of the completed design.

Invasive plants are nonnative to the ecosystem and likely to cause harm once introduced. These species are characteristically adaptable and aggressive, have a high reproductive capacity, and tend to overrun the ecosystems they enter. Collectively, they are among the greatest threats to biodiversity and ecosystem stability.

Laminate adhesive is used in wood or agrifiber products, such as veneered panels, composite wood products contained in engineered lumber, and door assemblies.

Lamps use electricity to produce light in any of several ways: by heating a wire for incandescence; by exciting a gas that produces ultraviolet light from a luminescent material; by generating an arc that emits visible light and some ultraviolet light; or by inducing excitation of mercury through radio frequencies. Light-emitting diodes packaged as traditional lamps also meet this definition.

Lamp life is the useful operating life of the sources of artificial light, such as bulbs.

Landfills are waste disposal sites for solid waste from human activities.

The **landscape area** is the total site area less the building footprint, paved surfaces, water bodies, and patios.

The **landscape coefficient** (K_l) is a constant used to calculate the evapotranspiration rate. It takes into account the species factor, density factor, and microclimate factor of the area.

The **leakage rate** is the speed at which an appliance loses refrigerant, measured between refrigerant charges or over 12 months, whichever is shorter. The leakage rate is expressed in terms of the percentage of the appliance's full charge that would be lost over a 12-month period if the rate stabilized (EPA Clean Air Act, Title VI, Rule 608)

A **least toxic chemical pesticide** is any pesticide product for which all active ingredients and known inert ingredients meet the least toxic Tier 3 hazard criteria under the City and County of San Francisco's hazard screening protocol. Least toxic also applies to any pesticide product, other than rodent bait, that is applied in a self-contained, enclosed bait station placed in an inaccessible location or applied in a gel that is neither visible nor accessible.

The **LEED project boundary** is the portion of the project site submitted for LEED certification. For single building developments, this is the entire project scope and is generally limited to the site boundary. For multiple building developments, the LEED project boundary may be a portion of the development as determined by the project team.

Legionella pneumophila is a waterborne bacterium that causes Legionnaire's disease. It grows in slow-moving or still warm water and can be found in plumbing, showerheads, and water storage tanks. Outbreaks of Legionella pneumonia have been attributed to evaporative condensers and cooling towers.

Life-cycle assessment is an analysis of the environmental aspects and potential impacts associated with a product, process, or service.

Life-cycle costing is an accounting methodology used to evaluate the economic performance of a product or system over its useful life. It considers operating costs, maintenance expenses, and other economic factors.

Light pollution is waste light from building sites that produces glare, is directed upward to the sky, or is directed off the site. Waste light does not increase nighttime safety, utility, or security and needlessly consumes energy.

Light trespass is obtrusive light that is unwanted because of quantitative, directional, or spectral attributes. Light trespass can cause annoyance, discomfort, distraction, or loss of visibility.

Lighting power density is the installed lighting power, per unit area.

Local zoning requirements are local government regulations imposed to promote orderly development of private lands and prevent land-use conflicts.

Low-emitting vehicles are classified as zero-emission vehicles (ZEVs) by the California Air Resources Board.

A **lumen** is a unit of luminous flux equal to the light emitted in a unit solid angle by a uniform point source of 1 candle intensity.

A **luminaire** is a complete lighting unit consisting of a lamp (or lamps) with the housing designed to distribute the light, position, and protect the lamp and connect it to the power supply.

Luminous opening refers to the part of the outer surface of a luminaire (lighting fixture) through which light is emitted (i.e., the opening where the lamps are).

Makeup water is fed into a cooling tower system to replace water lost through evaporation, drift, bleed-off, or other causes.

Management staff includes employees or contractors involved in operating and maintaining a project building and site.

Marine Stewardship Council Blue Eco-Label applies to products that meet certain principles and criteria for sustainable fishing, including sustainable harvest of the target stock, acceptable impact of the fishery on the ecosystem, effectiveness of the fishery management system (including all relevant biological, technological, economic, social, environmental, and commercial aspects), and compliance with relevant laws and standards.

Market value, presumed to be less than replacement value, is the amount that either was paid or would have been paid for a used product.

Mass transit is designed to transport large groups of persons in a single vehicle, such as a bus or train.

In LEED, a **master plan** is an overall design or development concept for the school and associated buildings and site. This concept considers future use, growth, and contraction and includes ways for managing the facility and sustainable features. The master plan is typically illustrated with narrative descriptions, building plans, and site drawings of phases and planned development.

Material safety data sheets (**MSDS**) are detailed, written instructions documenting a method to achieve uniformity of performance.

Mechanical ventilation, or **active ventilation**, is provided by mechanically powered equipment, such as motor-driven fans and blowers, but not by devices such as wind-driven turbine ventilators and mechanically operated windows. (ASHRAE 62.1–2004)

Metering controls limit the flow time of water. They are generally manual-on and automatic-off devices, most commonly installed on lavatory faucets and showers.

Microclimate factor (k_{mc}) is a constant used in calculating the landscape coefficient. It adjusts the evapotranspiration rate to reflect the climate of the immediate area.

Microirrigation involves irrigation systems with small sprinklers and microjets or drippers designed to apply small volumes of water. The sprinklers and microjets are installed within a few centimeters of the ground; drippers are laid on or below grade.

Minimum efficiency reporting value (**MERV**) is a filter rating established by the American Society of Heating, Refrigerating, and Air-Conditioning Engineers (ASHRAE 52.2–1999, Method of Testing General Ventilation Air Cleaning Devices for Removal Efficiency by Particle Size). MERV categories range from 1 (very low efficiency) to 16 (very high).

Mixed-mode ventilation combines mechanical and natural ventilation methods.

A **mixed-use** project involves a combination of residential and commercial or retail components.

The **National Pollutant Discharge Elimination System** (**NPDES**) is a permit program that controls water pollution by regulating point sources that discharge pollutants into waters of the United States. Industrial, municipal, and other facilities must obtain permits if their discharges go directly to surface waters.

Native (**or indigenous**) **plants** are adapted to a given area during a defined time period and are not invasive. In North America, the term often refers to plants growing in a region prior to the time of settlement by people of European descent.

Natural areas feature native or adapted vegetation or other ecologically appropriate features.

Natural ventilation, or **passive ventilation**, is provided by thermal, wind, or diffusion effects through doors, windows, or other intentional openings in the building; it uses the building layout, fabric, and form to achieve heat transfer and air movement.

Neighborhood is synonymous with **residential area.**

Net metering is a metering and billing arrangement that allows on-site generators to send excess electricity flows to the regional power grid. These electricity flows offset a portion of those drawn from the grid.

Net project material value includes the construction material value and the CSI Division 12 (Furniture and Furnishings) material value, the lesser of material values for mechanical and electric components, and the salvage value identified in the MR credits.

Noise reduction coefficient (**NRC**) is the arithmetic average of absorption coefficients at 250, 500, 1,000, and 2,000 Hz for a material. The NRC is often published by manufacturers in product specifications, particularly for acoustical ceiling tiles and acoustical wall panels.

Nonoccupied spaces include all rooms used by maintenance personnel that are not open for use by occupants. Examples are closets and janitorial, storage, and equipment rooms.

Nonporous sealant is a substance used as a sealant on nonporous materials. Nonporous materials, such as plastic and metal, do not have openings in which fluids may be absorbed or discharged.

Nonpotable water. See **potable water.**

Nonwater (**or composting**) **toilet systems** are dry plumbing fixtures and fittings that contain and treat human waste via microbiological processes.

A **nonwater** (**or dry**) **urinal** replaces a water flush with a trap containing a layer of buoyant liquid that floats above the urine, blocking sewer gas and odors.

Occasional furniture is located in lobbies and in conference rooms.

Occupants in a commercial building are workers who either have a permanent office or workstation in the building or typically spend a minimum of 10 hours per week in the building. In a residential building, occupants also include all persons who live in the building. In schools, occupants also include students, faculty, support staff, administrators, and maintenance employees.

Off-gassing is the emission of volatile organic compounds (VOCs) from synthetic and natural products.

Off-site renewable energy is derived from renewable energy sources and generated outside the project site perimeter; it is delivered through a private agreement with the energy-generating entity.

Off-site salvaged materials are recovered from a source different from the project site.

On-demand (or tankless) heaters heat water only when it is needed and then apply only the amount of heat required to satisfy the immediate need.

Ongoing commissioning is a continuous process that methodically identifies and corrects system problems to maintain optimal building performance; it includes regular measurement and comparative analysis of building energy data over time.

Ongoing consumables have a low cost per unit and are regularly used and replaced in the course of business. Examples include paper, toner cartridges, binders, batteries, and desk accessories.

On-site renewable energy is energy derived from renewable sources located within the project site perimeter.

On-site salvaged materials are recovered from and reused at the same building site.

On-site wastewater treatment is the transport, storage, treatment, and disposal of wastewater generated on the project site.

Open space area is usually defined by local zoning requirements. If local zoning requirements do not clearly define open space, it is defined for the purposes of LEED calculations as the property area minus the development footprint; it must be vegetated and pervious, with exceptions only as noted in the credit requirements section. Only ground areas are calculated as open space. For projects located in urban areas that earn a Development Density and Community Connectivity credit, open space also includes nonvehicular, pedestrian-oriented hardscape spaces.

Open-grid pavement is less than 50% impervious and accommodates vegetation in the open cells.

Outdoor air is the ambient air that enters a building through a ventilation system, either through natural ventilation or by infiltration. (ASHRAE 62.1–2007)

The **owner** is the person directly employed by the organization holding title to the project building and recognized by law as having rights, responsibilities, and ultimate control over the building.

Owner's project requirements is a written document that details the ideas, concepts, and criteria that are determined by the owner to be important to the success of the project.

Ozone (O_3) is a gas composed of 3 oxygen atoms. It is not usually emitted directly into the air, but at ground-level it is created by a chemical reaction between oxides of nitrogen (NOx) and volatile organic compounds (VOCs) in the presence of sunlight. Ozone has the same chemical structure whether it occurs in the atmosphere or at ground level and can have positive or negative effects, depending on its location. (U.S. Environmental Protection Agency)

Paint is a liquid, liquefiable, or mastic composition that is converted to a solid protective, decorative, or functional adherent film after application as a thin layer. These coatings are intended for application to interior or exterior surfaces of residential, commercial, institutional, or industrial buildings.

Parking footprint refers to the area of the project site occupied by the parking areas and structures.

Parking subsidies are the costs of providing occupant parking that are not recovered in parking fees.

In a **partially shielded** exterior light fixture, the lower edge of the shield is at or below the centerline of the lamp, to minimize light emitted above the horizontal plane.

Pedestrian access allows people to walk to services without being blocked by walls, freeways, or other barriers.

Percentage improvement measures the energy cost savings for the proposed building performance compared with the baseline building performance.

Permeable. See **porous pavement.**

Perviousness is the percentage of the surface area of a paving system that is open and allows moisture to soak into the ground below.

Phenol formaldehyde, which off-gasses only at high temperature, is used for exterior products, although many of these products are suitable for interior applications.

Photovoltaic (PV) energy is electricity from photovoltaic cells that convert the energy in sunlight into electricity.

A **picogram** is 1 trillionth of a gram.

Picograms per lumen-hour is a measure of the amount of mercury in a lamp per unit of light delivered over its useful life.

Plug load is synonymous with **receptacle load.**

Pollutants include emissions of carbon dioxide (CO_2), sulfur dioxide (SO_2), nitrogen oxides (NO_x), mercury (Hg), small particulates ($PM2.5$), and large particulates ($PM10$).

Porous materials have tiny openings, often microscopic, that can absorb or discharge fluids. Examples include wood, fabric, paper, corrugated paperboard, and plastic foam. (SCAQMD Rule 1168)

Porous pavement and **permeable surfaces** allow runoff to infiltrate into the ground.

Postconsumer fiber consists of paper, paperboard, and fibrous wastes that are collected from municipal solid waste streams.

Postconsumer material is recycled from consumer waste.

Postconsumer recycled content is the percentage of material in a product that was consumer waste. The recycled material was generated by household, commercial, industrial, or institutional end-users and can no longer be used for its intended purpose. It includes returns of materials from the distribution chain. Examples include construction and demolition debris, materials collected through recycling programs, discarded products (e.g., furniture, cabinetry, decking), and landscaping waste (e.g., leaves, grass clippings, tree trimmings). (ISO 14021)

Potable water meets or exceeds EPA's drinking water quality standards and is approved for human consumption by the state or local authorities having jurisdiction; it may be supplied from wells or municipal water systems.

ppm stands for parts per million.

Preconsumer recycled content, formerly known as postindustrial content, is the percentage of material in a product that is recycled from manufacturing waste. Examples include planer shavings, sawdust, bagasse, walnut shells, culls, trimmed materials, overissue publications, and obsolete inventories. Excluded are rework, regrind, or scrap materials capable of being reclaimed within the same process that generated them. (ISO 14021)

Predicted mean vote is an empirical equation for predicting the mean vote on a rating scale of thermal comfort of a large population of people exposed to a certain environment.

Preferred parking, available to particular users, includes designated spaces close to the building (aside from designated handicapped spots), designated covered spaces, discounted parking passes, and guaranteed passes in a lottery system.

Preventive maintenance is routinely scheduled equipment inspection, cleaning, and repair conducted to detect and prevent equipment failure and keep materials and systems in working order.

Previously developed sites once had buildings, roadways, parking lots, or were graded or otherwise altered by direct human activities.

A **primer** is a material applied to a substrate to improve the adhesion of subsequently applied coats.

Prior condition area is the total area of finished ceilings, floors, and full-height walls that existed when the project area was selected. It does not include exterior windows and doors.

Prior condition is the state of the project space at the time it was selected.

Process water is used for industrial processes and building systems such as cooling towers, boilers, and chillers. It can also refer to water used in operational processes, such as dishwashing, clothes washing, and ice making.

Property area is the total area within the legal property boundaries of a site; it encompasses all areas of the site, including constructed and nonconstructed areas.

Proposed building performance is the annual energy cost calculated for a proposed design, as defined in ANSI/ASHRAE/IESNA Standard 90.1–2007, Appendix G.

Protected Harvest certification standards reflect the growing requirements and environmental considerations of different crops and bioregions. Each crop- and region-specific standard addresses production, toxicity, and chain-of-custody.

Public transportation consists of bus, rail, or other transit services for the general public that operate on a regular, continual basis.

Rainforest Alliance certification is awarded to farms that protect wildlife by planting trees, control erosion, limit agrochemicals, protect native vegetation, hire local workers, and pay fair wages.

Rapidly renewable materials are agricultural products, both fiber and animal, that take 10 years or less to grow or raise and can be harvested in a sustainable fashion.

Rated power is the nameplate power on a piece of equipment. It represents the capacity of the unit and is the maximum that it will draw.

Receptacle (or plug) load is the current drawn by all equipment that is plugged into the electrical system.

Recirculated air is removed from a space and reused as supply air, delivered by mechanical or natural ventilation.

Reclaimed water is wastewater that has been treated and purified for reuse.

Recommissioning applies to buildings that were previously commissioned as part of new construction or buildings covered by existing building commissioning.

Recovered fiber includes both postconsumer fiber and waste fiber from the manufacturing process.

Recycled content is the proportion, by mass, of preconsumer or postconsumer recycled material in a product. (ISO 14021)

Recycling is the collection, reprocessing, marketing, and use of materials that were diverted or recovered from the solid waste stream.

A **recycling collection area** is located in regularly occupied space in the building for the collection of occupants' recyclables. A building may have numerous collection areas from which recyclable materials are typically removed to a central collection and storage area.

Refrigerants are the working fluids of refrigeration cycles that absorb heat from a reservoir at low temperatures and reject heat at higher temperatures.

Refurbished materials are products that could have been disposed of as solid waste. These products have completed their life cycle as consumer items and are then refurbished for reuse without substantial alteration of their form. Refurbishing includes renovating, repairing, restoring, or generally improving the appearance, performance, quality, functionality, or value of a product.

Regionally extracted materials are raw materials taken from within a 500-mile radius of the project site.

Regionally manufactured materials are assembled as finished products within a 500-mile radius of the project site. Assembly does not include on-site assembly, erection, or installation of finished components.

Regularly occupied spaces are areas where workers are seated or standing as they work inside a building. In residential applications, these areas are all spaces except bathrooms, utility areas, and closets or other storage rooms. In schools, they are areas where students, teachers, or administrators are seated or standing as they work or study inside a building.

Relative humidity is the ratio of partial density of airborne water vapor to the saturation density of water vapor at the same temperature and total pressure.

Remanufactured materials are items that are made into other products. One example is concrete that is crushed and used as subbase.

Remediation is the process of cleaning up a contaminated site by physical, chemical, or biological means. Remediation processes are typically applied to contaminated soil and groundwater.

Renewable energy comes from sources that are not depleted by use. Examples include energy from the sun, wind, and small (low-impact) hydropower, plus geothermal energy and wave and tidal systems. Ways to capture energy from the sun include photovoltaic, solar thermal, and bioenergy systems based on wood waste, agricultural crops or residue, animal and other organic waste, or landfill gas.

Renewable energy certificates (**RECs**) are tradable commodities representing proof that a unit of electricity was generated from a renewable energy resource. RECs are sold separately from electricity itself and thus allow the purchase of green power by a user of conventionally generated electricity.

Replacement value is the estimated cost of replacing a used product. This value may be equal to the cost of a similar new product or based on a new product with comparable features.

A **residential area** is land zoned primarily for housing at a density of 10 units per acre or greater. These areas may have single-family and multifamily housing and include building types such as townhomes, apartments, duplexes, condominiums, or mobile homes.

The **Resource Conservation and Recovery Act** (**RCRA**) addresses active and future facilities and was enacted in 1976 to give EPA authority to control hazardous wastes from cradle to grave, including generation, transportation, treatment, storage, and disposal. Some nonhazardous wastes are also covered under RCRA.

Retained components are portions of the finished ceilings, finished floors, full-height walls and demountable partitions, interior doors, and built-in case goods that existed in the prior condition area and remain in the completed design.

Retention ponds capture stormwater runoff and clear it of pollutants before its release. Some retention pond designs use gravity only; others use mechanical equipment, such as pipes and pumps, to facilitate transport. Some ponds are dry except during storm events; others permanently store water.

A **retrofit** is any change to an existing facility, such as the addition or removal of equipment or an adjustment, connection, or disconnection of equipment.

Return air is removed from a space and then recirculated or exhausted. (ASHRAE 62.1–2007)

Reuse returns materials to active use in the same or a related capacity as their original use, thus extending the lifetime of materials that would otherwise be discarded. Examples of construction materials that can be reused include extra insulation, drywall, and paints.

Reused area is the total area of the building structure, core, and envelope that existed in the prior condition and remains in the completed design.

Reverberation is an acoustical phenomenon that occurs when sound persists in an enclosed space because of its repeated reflection or scattering on the enclosing surfaces or objects within the space. (ANSI S12.60–2002)

Reverberation time (**RT**) is a measure of the amount of reverberation in a space and equal to the time required for the level of a steady sound to decay by 60 dB after the sound has stopped. The decay rate depends on the amount of sound absorption in a room, the room geometry, and the frequency of the sound. RT is expressed in seconds. (ANSI S12.60–2002)

Ridesharing is synonymous with **carpooling**.

Safety and comfort light levels meet local code requirements and must be adequate to provide a safe path for egress without overlighting the area.

Salvaged materials or **reused materials** are construction materials recovered from existing buildings or construction sites and reused. Common salvaged materials include structural beams and posts, flooring, doors, cabinetry, brick, and decorative items.

A **sealant** has adhesive properties and is formulated primarily to fill, seal, or waterproof gaps or joints between 2 surfaces. Sealants include sealant primers and caulks. (SCAQMD Rule 1168)

A **sealant primer** is applied to a substrate, prior to the application of a sealant, to enhance the bonding surface. (SCAQMD Rule 1168)

Seating consists of task and guest chairs used with systems furniture.

Secure bicycle storage is an internal or external space that keeps bicycles safe from theft. It may include lockers and storage rooms.

Sedimentation is the addition of soil particles to water bodies by natural and human-related activities. Sedimentation often decreases water quality and can accelerate the aging process of lakes, rivers, and streams.

Sensors are devices that undergo a measurable change in response to environmental changes and communicate this change to a control system.

Setpoints are normal operating ranges for building systems and indoor environmental quality. When the building systems are outside of their normal operating range, action is taken by the building operator or automation system.

Shielding is a nontechnical term that describes devices or techniques that are used as part of a luminaire or lamp to limit glare, light trespass, or sky glow.

Site area is synonymous with **property area.**

A **site assessment** is an evaluation of a site's aboveground and subsurface characteristics, including its structures, geology, and hydrology. Site assessments are typically used to determine whether contamination has occurred, as well as the extent and concentration of any release of pollutants. Information generated during a site assessment is used to make remedial action decisions.

Site energy is the amount of heat and electricity consumed by a building, as reflected in utility bills.

Sky glow is caused by stray light from unshielded light sources and light reflecting off surfaces that then enter the atmosphere and illuminate and reflect off dust, debris, and water vapor. Sky glow can substantially limit observation of the night sky, compromise astronomical research, and adversely affect nocturnal environments.

Soft costs are expense items that are not considered direct construction costs. Examples include architectural, engineering, financing, and legal fees.

Solar reflectance, or **albedo**, is a measure of the ability of a surface material to reflect sunlight—visible, infrared, and ultraviolet wavelengths—on a scale of 0 to 1. Solar reflectance is also called albedo. Black paint has a solar reflectance of 0; white paint (titanium dioxide) has a solar reflectance of 1.

Solar thermal systems collect or absorb sunlight via solar collectors to heat water that is then circulated to the building's hot water tank. Solar thermal systems can be used to warm swimming pools or heat water for residential and commercial use.

The **solar reflectance index** (**SRI**) is a measure of a material's ability to reject solar heat, as shown by a small temperature rise. Standard black (reflectance 0.05, emittance 0.90) is 0 and standard white (reflectance 0.80, emittance 0.90) is 100. For example, a standard black surface has a temperature rise of 90°F (50°C) in full sun, and a standard white surface has a temperature rise of 14.6°F (8.1°C). Once the maximum temperature rise of a given material has been computed, the SRI can be calculated by interpolating between the values for white and black. Materials with the highest SRI values are the coolest choices for paving. Because of the way SRI is defined, particularly hot materials can even take slightly negative values, and particularly cool materials can even exceed 100. (Lawrence Berkeley National Laboratory Cool Roofing Materials Database)

Sound absorption is the portion of sound energy striking a surface that is not returned as sound energy. (ANSI S12.60–2002)

Sound absorption coefficient describes the ability of a material to absorb sound, expressed as a fraction of incident sound. The sound absorption coefficient is frequency-specific and ranges from 0.00 to 1.00. For example, a material may have an absorption coefficient of 0.50 at 250 Hz, and 0.80 at 1,000 Hz. This indicates that the material absorbs 50% of incident sound at 250 Hz, and 80% of incident sound at 1,000 Hz. The arithmetic average of absorption coefficients at midfrequencies is the noise reduction coefficient.

Sound transmission class (**STC**) is a single-number rating for the acoustic attenuation of airborne sound passing through a partition or other building element, such as a wall, roof, or door, as measured in an acoustical testing laboratory according to accepted industry practice. A higher STC rating provides more sound attenuation through a partition. (ANSI S12.60–2002)

Source energy is the total amount of raw fuel required to operate a building; it incorporates all transmission, delivery, and production losses for a complete assessment of a building's energy use.

Source reduction reduces the amount of unnecessary material brought into a building. Examples include purchasing products with less packaging.

Species factor (k_s) is a constant used to adjust the evapotranspiration rate to reflect the biological features of a specific plant species.

GLOSSARY

The **square footage** of a building is the total area in square feet (sf) of all rooms, including corridors, elevators, stairwells, and shaft spaces.

Standard operating procedures are detailed, written instructions documenting a method to achieve uniformity of performance.

Stormwater runoff consists of water from precipitation that flows over surfaces into sewer systems or receiving water bodies. All precipitation that leaves project site boundaries on the surface is considered stormwater runoff.

A **stormwater pollution prevention plan** describes all measures to prevent stormwater contamination, control sedimentation and erosion during construction, and comply with the requirements of the Clean Water Act.

Stratified random sampling categorizes members of a population into discrete subgroups, based on characteristics that may affect their responses to a survey. For example, a survey of building occupants' commuting behavior might separate people by income level and commuting distance. To yield representative results, the survey should sample subgroups according to their proportions in the total population.

Submetering is used to determine the proportion of energy use within a building attributable to specific end uses or subsystems (e.g., the heating subsystem of an HVAC system).

Supply air is delivered by mechanical or natural ventilation to a space, composed of any combination of outdoor air, recirculated air, or transfer air. (ASHRAE 62.1–2007)

Sustainable forestry is the practice of managing forest resources to meet the long-term forest product needs of humans while maintaining the biodiversity of forested landscapes. The primary goal is to restore, enhance, and sustain a full range of forest values, including economic, social, and ecological considerations.

A **sustainable purchasing policy** gives preference to products that have little to no negative impact on the environment and society throughout their life cycle, and to the companies that supply them.

A **sustainable purchasing program** is the development, adoption, and implementation of a procurement strategy that supports an organization's sustainable purchasing policy.

Systematic sampling surveys every xth person in a population, using a constant skip interval. It relies on random sampling order or an order with no direct relationship to the variable under analysis (e.g., alphabetical order when sampling for commuting behavior).

Systems furniture includes panel-based workstations comprising modular interconnecting panels, hang-on components, and drawer and filing components or a free-standing grouping of furniture items designed to work in concert.

Systems performance testing is the process of determining the ability of commissioned systems to perform in accordance with the owner's project requirements, the basis of design, and construction documents.

Telecommuting is working by using telecommunications and computer technology from a location other than the usual or traditional place of business—for example, from home, a satellite office, or a telework center.

A **tenant** is a person or entity that pays to occupy land or space that is owned by someone else.

Tertiary treatment is the highest form of wastewater treatment and includes removal of organics, solids, and nutrients as well as biological or chemical polishing, generally to effluent limits of 10 mg/L biological oxygen demand (BOD) 5 and 10 mg/L total suspended solids (TSS).

Thermal comfort exists when occupants express satisfaction with the thermal environment.

Tipping fees are charged by a landfill for disposal of waste, typically quoted per ton.

Total phosphorus (TP) consists of organically bound phosphates, polyphosphates, and orthophosphates in stormwater, the majority of which originates from fertilizer application. Chemical precipitation is the typical removal mechanism for phosphorus.

Total suspended solids (TSS) are particles that are too small or light to be removed from stormwater via gravity settling. Suspended solid concentrations are typically removed via filtration.

Transient users are occupants who do not use a facility on a consistent, regular, daily basis. Examples include students in higher education settings, customers in retail settings, and visitors in institutional settings.

A 2-year, 24-hour design storm is a nationally accepted rate that represents the largest amount of rainfall expected over a 24-hour period during a 2-year interval. The rate is the basis for planning and designing stormwater management facilities and features.

Undercover parking is underground or under a deck, roof, or building; its hardscape surfaces are shaded.

Universal notification means notifying building occupants not less than 72 hours before a pesticide is applied in a building or on surrounding grounds under normal conditions, and within 24 hours after application of a pesticide in emergency conditions. Use of a least toxic pesticide or self-contained nonrodent bait does not require universal notification; all other pesticide applications do.

Upstream equipment consists of all heating or cooling systems, equipment, and controls that are associated with a district energy system but are not part of the project building's thermal connection or do not interface with the district energy system. It includes the central energy plant and all transmission and distribution equipment associated with transporting the thermal energy to the project building and site.

Urea formaldehyde is a combination of urea and formaldehyde that is used in some glues and may emit formaldehyde at room temperature.

USDA Organic is the U.S. Department of Agriculture's certification for products that contain at least 95% organically produced ingredients (excluding water and salt). Any remaining ingredients must consist of approved nonagricultural substances (as listed by USDA) or be nonorganically produced agricultural products that are not commercially available in organic form.

Vegetation-containing artifices are planters, gardens, or other constructs intended to host flora.

A **vendor** of certified wood is the company that supplies wood products to contractors or subcontractors for on-site installation. A vendor needs a chain-of-custody number if it is selling FSC-certified products that are not individually labeled; this includes most lumber.

Ventilation is the process of supplying air to or removing air from a space for the purpose of controlling air contaminant levels, humidity, or temperature within the space. (ASHRAE 62.1-2007).

Verification is the range of checks and tests carried out to determine whether components, subsystems, systems, and interfaces between systems operate in accordance with the contract documents.

Vertical footcandles occur on a vertical surface. They can be added together arithmetically when more than 1 source provides light to the same surface.

Visible light transmittance (VLT) (T_{vis}) is the ratio of total transmitted light to total incident light (i.e., the amount of visible spectrum, 380–780 nanometers of light passing through a glazing surface divided by the amount of light striking the glazing surface). The higher the T_{vis} value, the more incident light passes through the glazing.

GLOSSARY

Vision glazing is the portion of an exterior window between 30 and 90 inches above the floor that permits a view to the outside.

Volatile organic compounds (**VOCs**) are carbon compounds that participate in atmospheric photochemical reactions (excluding carbon monoxide, carbon dioxide, carbonic acid, metallic carbides and carbonates, and ammonium carbonate). The compounds vaporize (become a gas) at normal room temperatures.

Walking distance is the length of the walkable pathway between the building and public transportation.

Walk-off mats are placed inside building entrances to capture dirt, water, and other materials tracked inside by people and equipment.

Waste comprises all materials that flow from the building to final disposal. Examples include paper, grass trimmings, food scraps, and plastics. In LEED, waste refers to all materials that are capable of being diverted from the building's waste stream through waste reduction.

Waste disposal eliminates waste by means of burial in a landfill, combustion in an incinerator, dumping at sea, or any other way that is not recycling or reuse.

Waste diversion is a management activity that disposes of waste other than through incineration or the use of landfills. Examples include reuse and recycling.

Waste reduction includes both source reduction and waste diversion through reuse or recycling.

A **waste reduction program** encompasses source reduction, reuse, and recycling. Such a program assigns responsibility within the organization for implementation, lists the general actions that will be taken to reduce waste, and describes tracking and review procedures to monitor waste reduction and improve performance.

The **waste stream** is the overall flow of waste from the building to a landfill, incinerator, or other disposal site.

Wastewater is the spent or used water from a home, community, farm, or industry that contains dissolved or suspended matter. (Federal Remediation Technologies Roundtable)

Waterless urinals are dry plumbing fixtures that use advanced hydraulic design and a buoyant fluid to maintain sanitary conditions.

A **water meter** measures the volume of water usage. Most commercial building water meters are designed to measure cold potable water.

Wave and tidal power systems capture energy from waves and the diurnal flux of tidal power, respectively. The captured energy is commonly used for desalination, water pumping, and electricity generation.

A **weighted decibel** (**dBA**) is a sound pressure level measured with a conventional frequency weighting that roughly approximates how the human ear hears different frequency components of sounds at typical listening levels for speech. (ANSI S12.60–2002)

Wind energy is electricity generated by wind turbines.

Window-to-floor ratio (**WFR**) is the total area of the window (measured vertically from 30 inches above the finished floor to the top of the glass, multiplied by the width of the glass) divided by the floor area.

Xeriscaping is a landscaping method that makes routine irrigation unnecessary. It uses drought-adaptable and low-water plants as well as soil amendments such as compost and mulches to reduce evaporation.

This reference guide was printed on 100% postconsumer waste paper, processed chlorine free, and printed with non-toxic, soybased inks using 100% wind power. By using these materials and production processes, the U.S. Green Building Council saved the following resources:

Trees*	Solid Waste	Liquid Waste	Electricity	Greenhouse Gases	Sulfur & Nitrogen Oxides
202,745 lbs. of virgin wood, equal to 353 trees	31,795 lbs.	298,204 gallons	45,630 kWh	57,798 lbs.	91 lbs.

*one harvested tree = aprox. 575 lbs